Forging World Order

The Politics of International Organization

Forging World Order

The Politics of International Organization

Jack C. Plano
Western Michigan University

Robert E. Riggs
University of Minnesota

The Macmillan Company, New York
Collier-Macmillan Limited, London

Preface

The time is past when society can safely take slow decades and centuries to muddle through in adjustments to scientific and technological revolutions. . . . Human society with an atomic bomb in its bosom cannot lag in humane and creative adjustments to its potentially suicidal power.

DR. FRANK GRAHAM
United Nations Representative
to India and Pakistan

The time clock of technology cannot be turned back. Like it or not, mankind faces the challenge of a scientific revolution that threatens to outrun human capacity for social inventiveness. At the international level, the development of regional and global international organizations is one attempt to meet this challenge—to come to terms politically with a technologically shrinking world.

In this book our treatment of international organization is not governed by any single approach to the subject. In many sections we are unabashedly historical out of conviction that contemporary political forms and processes cannot be understood without some knowledge of their ancestry and historical evolution. We also frankly admit concern for institutions. Institutions shape outcomes by setting the limits within which power is exercised and by affecting the direction and volume of political communication. If there is a special emphasis, it is focused upon the behavior of those who participate in the political processes of international organization. We want to discover who gets what, why, and how.

Implicit in our approach is the assumption that politics is cut from the same cloth at all levels of human activity. International politics is not generically different from politics in city hall, state capitol, or house of parliament. Interest, influence, ideals, and communication determine political outcomes in all these arenas. For convenience we often speak of the behavior of states as though the state were something more than an abstraction. But this is only a manner of speaking. In international affairs as in domestic, it is human beings who communicate, perceive, evaluate, and decide.

v

This study is also underpinned by certain normative assumptions. Among them are a belief in the practical necessity of international organizations, a commitment to the democratic processes of decision-making through discussion and consensus, and a preference for political pluralism. We anticipate the day when institutions for cooperation can meet the problems of international life as meaningfully as governments now confront the problems of national societies, without sacrificing the rich diversity of varied cultures. Such an evolution can occur, however, only if national leaders and peoples cultivate what Secretary-General U Thant once called the "common interests based on our habitation of the same planet." The recognition of those common interests provides the focus for our analysis of international organization.

J. C. P.
R. E. R.

Contents

Contents

Part I

The Setting of International Organization

1 | Emerging International Institutions

Modern systems of international organization can be traced back in history to the time when man first began to live in political communities. The ancient Greek city-states attempted through the Achaean League to build a system that would discourage rivalry and conflict and encourage some measure of cooperation. A thread runs through history from these early and rudimentary efforts to preserve peace to the contemporary world of the United Nations, the North Atlantic Treaty Organization, the Organization of American States, the European Economic Community, and the Council of Europe. Despite monumental and continuing failures to eliminate war, the idealism which goes beyond the shelter of the national state has goaded mankind to "Try again!" to build upon the orderly, brotherly, and cooperative side of human nature rather than give free rein to his baser, suspicious, and destructive side. What is there about international organization that appeals to man's civilized nature—to his idealism and optimism? Why is the concept of international organization such a powerful force that it can overcome centuries of failure and innumerable conflicts? In this chapter an attempt will be made to understand contemporary international organization by analyzing the nature of the idealism that fostered it and by examining the principles and nature of early attempts at international cooperation. In the chapter that follows, the more immediate stimulus of the League of Nations and its purposeful but tragic history will be discussed.

DIVISIVE CHARACTERISTICS OF THE EARLY STATE SYSTEM

The modern state system, since its legal inception in the Peace of Westphalia in 1648, has been characterized by powerful centrifugal forces producing disunity and conflict throughout the western world. With the unifying effects of the Roman Empire and the Universal Church submerged in the parochialism of the feudal period, allegiance became particularized. The feudal system of the Middle Ages, based on the relation of vassal to

3

lord, in turn disintegrated as men fought, and were forced for reasons of security to seek a higher loyalty, that of the nation-state. The new monarchs of Europe consolidated their power through a combination of force and the ideology of national allegiance. This mythology of the national state, aided by the legal doctrine of sovereignty and the political concept of absolute monarchy, prevailed in Europe. But among the new states near-anarchy prevailed. Self-preservation was directly related to the relative power position of each state to its enemies, and all other states were actual or potential enemies.

"Machiavellian" diplomacy was everywhere practiced by princes and kings. In the new Europe each state sought to enhance its diplomatic and military positions by enriching its treasury through trade and conquest, usually at the expense of weaker states. Colonial expansion became the national imperative of the era, with each state vying to outdo others in expanding its power and influence over other lands and peoples. As trade flourished, competition for markets increased. The newly developed re-straining force of international law went largely unheeded; monarchs acted under the principle of *raison d'état* and required no other justification for their actions. Religious differences sowed other seeds of conflict, pitting Protestant against Catholic, Protestant against Protestant, and eastern Europe against western Europe. Thomas Hobbes, the seventeenth-century English philosopher, captured the spirit of the times in describing the world about him, a world of men unrestrained by political order, in which

> . . . kings, and persons of sovereign authority, because of their in-dependency, are in continual jealousies and in the state and posture of gladiators; having their weapons pointing, and their eyes fixed on one another; that is, their forts, garrisons, and guns upon the frontiers of their kingdoms; and continual spies upon their neighbors; which is a posture of war.[1]

Alexander Hamilton, writing in The Federalist papers in 1787, sought to gain support for the American union by describing the alternative to unity which still typified the world of his day:

> The nations of Europe are encircled with chains of fortified places. . . . The history of war, in that quarter of the globe, is no longer a history of nations subdued and empires overturned, but of towns taken and retaken; of battles that decide nothing; of retreats more beneficial than victories; of much effort and little acquisition. . . . Safety from external danger is the most powerful director of national conduct.[2]

[1] Thomas Hobbes, *Leviathan*, Chapter 13. See Francis W. Coker, *Readings in Political Philosophy* (New York: Macmillan, 1947), pp. 449–50.
[2] *The Federalist*, No. VIII.

The seventeenth and eighteenth centuries in Europe were, truly, years of anarchy and violence, of conquest and war. Power was the common denominator, and war was the accepted practice.

UNIFYING FACTORS

Despite the many sources of disunity and fragmentation in Europe, other emerging forces were moving peoples and nations toward closer cooperation. These centripetally directed forces were, in a sense, the inevitable reaction to the excesses of separatism and conflict. The sequence of the Renaissance and the Reformation produced the literate and cultured "European Man," with Latin as his common tongue, communicating with his contemporaries across the new political boundaries, and nurturing the ideas and ideals of western civilization. Scholars pursued the New Learning while wistfully looking back to the unity of man and spirit that had prevailed amidst the "glory that was Rome."

As the multiplicity of political units created during the feudal era were fused into larger communities, the national state, upon which modern international organization rests, began to emerge as the dominant political unit. As the number of small political entities was progressively reduced through conquest and annexation, contacts among the new states increased. The larger community of Europe began to take shape. Dynasties built on interlocking family relationships or on common interests tended to reduce the hostile competition of the new states. The Universal Church, although no longer universal in its power and influence, remained a potent force in reducing disorder and conflict.

A new awakening occurred also in the realm of economic activity as the impact of these forces moved Europe out of feudalism. As trade and commerce flourished, mankind's concern with material enrichment became a powerful motivating force moderating political rivalries. Trade frequently increases interstate conflicts, but it is a two-way street. Nations discover that it is to their advantage to secure a more orderly environment in order to promote trade contacts. Rules must be established under which the conflicts that inevitably arise through commercial intercourse can be adjusted. The early rudimentary development of international law and consular interchange first appeared in response to these needs. As trade competition among the new nations increased, it began to spill over into a race to acquire colonies in the New World. This, in turn, begot a new need for some international rules by which nations could recognize each other's titles to new lands, settle boundary disputes, and deal jointly with the common problem of piracy. Nations began to deal more directly and more frequently with such problems by entering into agreements and treaties with other states. Hence rivalries and antagonism, while continuing to grow, nevertheless tended to produce countervailing forces leading to increased cooperation. This strange but natural dichotomy continues to encourage and yet bewilder mankind today.

Near the end of the eighteenth century powerful new political forces evolved which had a most profound effect on the nature of the state system. These were the twin concepts of laissez faire and democratic nationalism, each of which dramatically recognized the new role to be played by the individual in human affairs. The Mercantilist doctrines of controlling, regulating, and directing economic activity by the state for the enhancement of the state's power gave way to the new concept of economic liberalism which replaced the state with the individual as the focus of activity. Individuals were now able to accumulate large capital reserves from profits, which could be used for investment, frequently in foreign lands. States eased or eliminated many commercial restrictions and taxes in keeping with a philosophy that called for free trade among nations as the road to national prosperity.

At the same time the philosophy of laissez faire was buttressed by a new technology which provided the means of producing goods with machines. The Industrial Revolution not only radically changed the economic methods of production but it also spectacularly increased the dependence of man upon other men. Increasing interdependence of each nation upon other nations was the inevitable by-product on the international scene. This growing relationship became particularly significant between states which supplied raw materials and those which were industrially advanced, and between trading partners where the severance of good relations might result in serious economic consequences to both.

The forces of science and invention responsible for developing the new machine technology were also helping to shrink the world through new and better devices for communication and transportation. The steamship, railroads, telegraph, and telephone made closer contacts possible, accelerated trade expansion, and, psychically, produced a new awareness in the mind of western man of his common societal relationship in a larger community of nations. Thus, in a progressive and dramatic way the old patterns of individual and national self-sufficiency began to erode and give way to new and rapidly developing systems of interdependence which, in turn, produced the rudiments of a new philosophy of internationalism among western nations.

At the same time, developments on the political level triggered forces of individualism which were destined to have far-reaching effects on the state system. The American and French revolutions, occurring near the end of the eighteenth century, were not revolutionary in the ideas and doctrines upon which they were built. The ideas were at least as old as Aristotle and can be found in the writings of political philosophers of both ancient and modern times. But their impact was revolutionary. For the first time working political systems on a national scale were built upon the principles of popular sovereignty and the importance of the individual. These principles eventually led to an era of liberal democratic nationalism.

Democracy, as a political doctrine, is predicated on the assumption that the individual is a rational creature who will willingly submit himself to a higher authority of his own choosing in order to achieve stability and order in his society. The true democrat is repelled equally by threats of anarchy and tyranny. He demands a system based on law and consent which is strong enough to ensure some degree of continuity and unity. These characteristics help to explain the impressive and salutary effect that political individualism and democratic nationalism have had on the modern state system. Closer international cooperation and codes of international law have developed in proportion to the respect accorded the individual within the states which comprise the international system. It has not been a historical accident that modern international law and institutions have been created largely at the initiative of those nations enjoying the greatest measure of freedom.

With the coming of age of democracy in the western world, new but related developments have occurred in human relations, education, individual rights, and in human aspirations. These changes have also had a profound effect upon our state system. Private international organizations of a cultural and intellectual nature came into vogue and spurred the development of mutual understanding in a new "community of peoples." Expanded areas of freedom of thought and expression freed the human spirit to speculate on new concepts of the brotherhood of mankind and on man-built institutions to implement these ideals. Early in the nineteenth century western man began to fashion a philosophy of international organization based on the common ideals of democratic freedom and intellectual liberalism. These concepts provided the foundations for the numerous, intricate, and sophisticated international institutions which were to come into being during the twentieth century—the age of international co-operation.

INTERNATIONAL ORGANIZATION AS PROCESS

With the appearance of liberal democracy in the western world the stage was set for the emergence of modern international organization. Democracy in national government fostered the growth of international organization because both involve, in essence, commitment to a *consensual process*. Just as democracy in a national political setting implies a process of public decision-making by consent of the governed, international organization implies a process of international cooperation through the consent of the states concerned.

The process of international organization is thoroughly empirical and pragmatic. It accepts the multistate system as fact and seeks only to provide more effective means to reconcile the conflicts and contradictions which characterize that system. As Dag Hammarskjold, the second Secretary-General of the United Nations, observed,

> The United Nations is not in any respect a superstate, able to act outside the framework of decisions by its member governments. It is an instrument for negotiation among, and to some extent for, governments. It is also an instrument for concerting action by governments in support of the Charter. Thus the United Nations can serve, but not substitute itself for, the efforts of its member governments. . . .[3]

In the absence of supranational government, only voluntary agreement can succeed in mitigating international conflicts, and international organization provides an institutionalized means for eliciting this agreement. It provides the principles, the machinery, and the encouragement, but the catalytic agent needed to bring about tangible results is *cooperation.* Cooperation, engendered by consent, is the key to the process of international organization. When cooperation is forthcoming, great things can be accomplished by international organs and agencies; when it is lacking, international organizations become mere "debating societies." International organization is as strong as, and no stronger than, its members want it to be.

Judged by the vast scale on which international organizations exist today, it appears that the decision-makers in most nations have accepted the premise that nations, like men, can shape and control their destinies through collective action. There can be no certainty, however, that international organization will succeed merely because the process has been accepted. Important gains in the past have, with deadly swiftness, been destroyed by a reversion to barbarism and war. And it is not only war that can weaken or destroy international organization; the slow but progressive sapping of its strength through stalemate and deadlock over numerous lesser issues can render it ineffectual and meaningless. Like national governments built upon the liberal democratic process, the greatest danger is not that of making the wrong decision but of failing to make decisions when they are desperately needed. In retrospect, the record calls for a guarded optimism about the future of the process of international organization.

[3] *New York Times Magazine,* September 15, 1957, p. 21.

THE PURPOSE OF INTERNATIONAL ORGANIZATION

The process of international organization has a number of generally accepted objectives or purposes. Unquestionably, the major purpose of international organization is the prevention of war, or, viewed affirmatively, the maintenance of peace and security. This is the *raison d'être* for the United Nations today. It corresponds to the fundamental objective of every national government—to put an end to warring among individuals within the state. In a striking if perhaps overdrawn characterization, Thomas Hobbes depicted a state of nature without government as "that condition which is called war; and such a war, as is of every man against every man . . . with the life of man solitary, poor, nasty, brutish, and short." [4] Though some critics have described Hobbes' "state of nature" as pure conjecture, societies have existed in which an offense against an individual by another individual is not regarded as a crime against society. Punishment or retribution is left to the injured person or his relatives. Such societies can become safe and civilized only when the members agree to regard an assault against an individual as a threat to the peace and well-being of the entire community. This is the purpose of lawmaking and the primary function of government.

Until the twentieth century, war was regarded in the western state system as a matter of concern only to the states so engaged. The entire body of neutrality law was erected on the supposition that other states were not interested and could remain aloof. With the growth of interdependence in economic and social matters, the concepts of national individuality and isolation slowly began to be supplemented with the idea of community. Modern war in the twentieth century swept away most of the remnants of disinterestness and aloofness. State after state found itself churned into the maelstrom of World War I, which had begun with a quarrel between Austria-Hungary and Serbia. President Woodrow Wilson recognized the significance of this change when he declared in 1916, perhaps prematurely, that the day of the neutrals is past. Formal acceptance of community responsibility was embodied in the Covenant of the League of Nations, Article 11 therein providing that "any war or threat of war, whether immediately affecting any of the Members of the League or not, is hereby declared a matter of concern to the whole League." The United Nations Charter also incorporates this principle in Article 2: "All Members shall give the United Nations every assistance in any action it takes in accordance with the present Charter. . . ."

Departure from principle in practice, however, is an all too frequent occurrence in human affairs, as later events in the history of the League of

[4] Thomas Hobbes, *op. cit.*, pp. 448–49.

Nations so calamitously emphasized. When faced with a community obligation to collectively check Italy's attack upon Ethiopia, members of the
League failed to apply effective sanctions, despite the warning by the
delegate from Haiti that "each of you may some day be somebody's
Ethiopia." In 1950, although a majority of the members were sympathetic
with the United Nations objective of checking the aggression of North
Korea, only sixteen provided military units for action. Clearly the members
of the two world organizations have never completely accepted their
community obligations, and the millennium of collective security is not yet
here. Meanwhile, the precarious pursuit of peace through the imperfect
institutions of international cooperation continues as the best hope of
avoiding a nuclear holocaust.

Maintaining peace and security in the world is not the only purpose of
international organization, although admittedly it is the most crucial. Indeed,
the list of problems with which international organization concerns itself
includes most of the difficult problems facing states in their foreign relations. They range all the way from health to economic development, from
postal rates to outer space. Each year finds the agenda of international
organs crowded with problems, new and old, created by the ever-changing
international milieu.

The purposes of international organization, then, are almost limitless. In
a more general sense, however, these manifold purposes are directed toward
three broad objectives: peace, prosperity, and order. The first of these,
peace, depends primarily upon the effectiveness of deterrents to violent
action and on the adequacy of the machinery for pacific settlement of
international disputes. The second, prosperity, may be achieved by coping
with technical problems to make greater economic activity possible, and
with political problems to make it probable. Economic areas receiving most
of the attention of international organization are economic development,
especially in the developing areas of the world, and international trade.
Finally, a major objective is to build an orderly world, a world in which
change occurs naturally and is free from violence and conflict. Generically,
this goal includes most of the efforts and programs of international organization. In a sense it is a synthesis of all three basic objectives—peace, prosperity, and order—in a common struggle against anarchy, hunger, disease,
poverty, illiteracy, extreme nationalism, discrimination, slavery, and colonialism. Viewed affirmatively, it encompasses efforts to achieve legal stability,
higher standards of living, better health, better education, improved understanding among peoples, respect for human rights and fundamental freedoms, and self-determination and political independence.

Most of the objectives of international organization are interrelated and
achievements in one area sometimes have a salutary effect in other areas.
All are related to the cause of peace in the sense that a stable peace requires

some success in reducing the tensions and frustrations associated with the outbreak of war. This is of particular consequence in the underdeveloped areas today where a serious "frustration gap" exists between the hopes and expectations of the peoples and the ability of the newly independent nations to fulfill these aspirations. Peace and security are long-range goals that must be built painstakingly on a firm foundation. They are the key to the success and even to the continued existence of international organization.

THE DEVELOPMENT OF INTERNATIONAL INSTITUTIONS

The most obvious feature of international organization is the institutional framework within which state interaction occurs. High-minded purposes and effective processes depend ultimately upon institutions through which states confer, debate, negotiate, reach agreement, and have that agreement implemented through administrative action.

Modern international institutions dating from the early nineteenth century represent a creative response to the need for a joint approach to common problems in such fields as commerce, communication, and transportation. The first examples of modern international organization were the river commissions in Europe. The Central Rhine Commission, for example, was created by an agreement between France and Germany in 1804 providing for extensive regulation of river traffic, the maintenance of navigation facilities, and the hearing and adjudication of complaints for alleged violations of the Commission's rules. The European Danube Commission was created in 1856 to regulate international traffic on the Danube River. Both river commissions still function today much the same as when they were first established, although the Danube Commission is now under Soviet control.

The development of international organization was carried a step further with the creation of international public unions in the latter half of the nineteenth century. In many cases the public unions were developed as a result of demands placed upon national governments by the members of private international associations like the International Chamber of Commerce and the International Agricultural Coordination Commission. Such demands resulted in the establishment of the International Telegraphic Union in 1865 and the Universal Postal Union in 1874. The success of these two unions paved the way for the creation of numerous international public agencies in such diverse fields as narcotic drugs, agriculture, health, weights and measures, railroads, patents and copyrights, and tariffs.

The Universal Postal Union in particular demonstrated the utility of intergovernmental cooperation to solve technical problems that arose in connection with delivering mail across national frontiers. Before its establishment, the complicated and costly nature of mail service across national boundaries threatened to disrupt the growing volume of international communication and business. A letter mailed from one country to another required special handling and the payment of postage to each country through which it was carried along the route to its destination. By creating an international public union, twenty-two governments were able to eliminate national boundary lines so far as mail routes were concerned, establish standard handling procedures, and levy uniform rates. Its success gave impetus to the development of international organizations, both public and private, to meet the burgeoning problems of a state system which was rapidly outgrowing its parochial institutions.

As cooperation among states increased during the nineteenth century, a pattern of organization and procedures developed. Each new international organization established institutional machinery somewhat unique, yet possessing certain basic characteristics in common with its contemporaries. This pattern was typified by the following essential features:

1. Membership was usually, though not always, limited to sovereign states. Unless regional in scope, such organizations typically were universal in the sense that membership was open to all qualified states without political or moral conditions.

2. The organization was created by a multilateral treaty. The treaty served as a constitution which specified the obligations of its members, created the institutional structure, and proclaimed the objectives of the organization and the means by which they would be pursued.

3. A conference or congress was usually established as the basic policy-making organ. The conference was comprised of all members of the organization and would meet infrequently, typically once every five years.

4. Decision-making was based on the principle of equalitarianism, with each member having an equal vote and decisions reached by adherence to the principle of unanimity. In time this gave way somewhat to the principle of majoritarianism, especially in voting on procedural questions.

5. A council or other decision-making organ of an executive nature was often created to implement policies between meetings of the general conference. It typically had a limited membership and was established by the conference. Its primary responsibility was to administer the broad policy decisions laid down by the general conference.

6. A secretariat was also established to carry out the policies of the conference and council and conduct the routine functions of the organization. The secretariat was headed by a secretary-general or director-general, a professional civil servant with an international reputation.

7. Some organizations, like the river commissions, exercised judicial or quasi-judicial powers. Some created special international courts to decide controversies arising out of their administrative operations.

8. Some were endowed with a legal personality enabling them to own property, to sue and be sued in specified areas, and, in some cases, to enjoy a measure of diplomatic immunity.

9. Financial support was based on contributions from member governments. The organization established a formula for contributions based on a principle such as "ability to pay," "benefits derived," "equality," or a combination of these.

10. Competence of the organization was usually limited to a functional or specialized problem area as set out in its constitution. Organizations of general competence in political, economic, and social areas were not established until the twentieth century.

11. Decision-making was carried on in two ways: (1) by drafting international treaties and submitting them to member governments for ratification; and (2) by adopting resolutions recommending action by member governments. A few possessed administrative and minor policy-making powers independent of the governments that had created them.

These basic characteristics and the procedures or *modus operandi* of early international organizations have become commonplace features of modern international institutions. Although the problems of the contemporary world are more numerous and complex, the institutional structure and methods of dealing with problems have changed little since their evolution in the nineteenth century. The major change has been in the field of international competence, with contemporary organizations operating more as political units with broad, general powers to deal with varieties of issues rather than being narrowly restricted to specific technical areas. An examination of the agenda of such organs as the General Assembly or Council of Europe would emphasize this change in the direction of national parliamentarianism.

The prolific growth of technical and administrative international agencies reflected the new world of science and technology that was reducing space and overcoming political boundaries. States offered collaboration because it was essential to carrying on business and commerce and was useful in protecting the lives, health, and other interests of their citizens. The inevitable by-product of successful technical cooperation was the growth of the belief that political cooperation might be equally productive in securing agreement among states on the more weighty questions of war and peace. Such thinking helped prepare the ground for the calling of two conferences at The Hague, Netherlands, in 1899 and 1907, the first general international conferences concerned with building a world system based on law and order. Although the first Hague Peace Conference was attended by delegates from only twenty-six nations and was largely European in complexion, the second conference moved toward universality with representatives from forty-four states, including most of the countries of Latin America. The principle of the sovereign equality of states was accepted at the conferences, with the result that the Hague system helped break the monopoly of the great powers of the Concert of Europe in handling matters of war and peace, economic and colonial rivalry. It also established precedents that contributed to the later development of international parliamentarianism. Headquarters were set up at The Hague, and international machinery to facilitate the pacific settlement of international disputes was established. An international political organization was now a possibility.

Selected Readings

EAGLETON, CLYDE. *International Government.* New York: Ronald Press, 1948.

LEONARD, L. LARRY. *International Organization.* New York: McGraw-Hill, 1951.

MANGONE, GERARD J. *A Short History of International Organization.* New York: McGraw-Hill, 1954.

POTTER, PITMAN B. *An Introduction to the Study of International Organization.* New York: Appleton-Century-Crofts, 1948.

REINSCH, PAUL S. *Public International Unions.* Boston: Ginn, 1911.

REUTER, PAUL. *International Institutions.* New York: Rinehart, 1958.

2 | *The League Experiment*

It has become fashionable to dismiss the League of Nations' two decades of effort and tribulation with a single epithet—failure. A failure they were, at least in the League's primary function of maintaining peace. But the first great experiment in general international organization cannot so easily be written off. The League's significance relates first to a historical epoch that it helped to shape. It made millions of people, including many Americans, conscious of the role of international organization in the modern world. It helped to resolve many disputes which threatened the peace, fostered technical cooperation among nations, and helped improve the economic and social conditions in some. Even its failures have been instructive to later generations, whereas its modest successes provided direct precedents for the United Nations system.

ORIGINS

Americans were living in an Age of Innocence when war was declared against the Central Powers in 1917. The other belligerents, both sides close to exhaustion, had had their idealism and fiery nationalism wrung out of them after nearly three years of savage fighting. The carnage in Europe produced, in the early years of the war, an American consensus that involvement should be avoided at all costs; then, slowly, a new consensus evolved, holding that the New World somehow had to try to save the old from extinction. If Europeans of all nationalities could live in peace under the American system of democracy, why not apply these same principles to international affairs?

Americans entered World War I fired with a holy mission to "make the world safe for democracy." American idealism was summed up in President Woodrow Wilson's peace program, submitted to Congress on January 8, 1918, in which he enunciated Fourteen Points aimed at rekindling Allied idealism and determination and weakening the enemy's resolve by promising a just peace and a new world of security and democracy. In his Fourteenth Point, Wilson declared that "a general association of nations must be formed

15

under specific covenants for the purpose of affording mutual guarantees of political independence and territorial integrity to great and small powers alike." On this point, Wilson had been significantly influenced by the proposals of various private American groups, particularly those of the League to Enforce Peace under the leadership of William Howard Taft. The program of this influential group provided (1) that a court be established to resolve legal disputes; (2) that a council be created to handle political disputes through inquiry and recommendation; (3) that the world community apply economic and military sanctions against a state which went to war before submitting its dispute for settlement; and (4) that periodic conferences be called to codify international law. Groups in Britain, France, the Netherlands, and even Germany, also sought to produce a scheme for a world organization that would help avoid another catastrophe.

Official support and discussions concerning the contemplated organization lagged only slightly behind that of private groups. Both the British and French governments appointed commissions to develop ideas concerning the establishment of the League. These rough drafts were transmitted to President Wilson in the summer of 1918; he turned them over to his close adviser, Colonel House, and requested an American draft compatible with his own views. Colonel House prepared an American draft which was revised by President Wilson personally and presented to the Versailles Peace Conference.

The chief architect of the League, unquestionably, was Woodrow Wilson. Without his support, the idea of a League of Nations would probably not have gone beyond the point of intellectual germination. While other Allied statesmen thought more cynically of how the victory won at such a terrible cost could be exploited for national gain and future security, Wilson sought to materialize his dreams of a just world based on law and democracy. Because his program appealed to millions of Europeans emerging from the trauma of war, the more cynical Allied leaders were forced by public opinion to pay at least lip service to his ideas. Wilson's ideas of a just peace were focused upon the building of a League of Nations, and Allied statesmen accepted his demands that the League be created as an integral part of the peace treaty.

Writing the Covenant

In keeping with the precedents of international decision-making, the great powers dominated the Paris Peace Conference. The Supreme War Council of the United States, Britain, France, and Italy accepted Japan into their deliberations and, through the Council of Ten, which included two representatives from each nation, managed the Peace Conference. Specific deliberations were conducted by more than fifty committees, commissions, and subcommittees, but key decisions were made by the five great powers and, on occasion, by the Big Three—Wilson, Lloyd George, and Clemenceau.

President Wilson was appointed chairman of the First Commission of the Peace Conference with responsibility to write the Covenant of the League of Nations. During the drafting debates, criticisms and reservations began to pour in from many quarters. Most significant were the rumblings of discontent emanating from the United States Senate, which President Wilson inexplicably ignored in planning and negotiating the League system. After completing a draft covenant, Wilson sailed for home determined to win over his Senate critics and repair his political bridges.

American criticisms were considered to be crucial obstacles since America's participation in the new organization was regarded as essential to its ultimate success. The more important American demands were concerned with maintaining the integrity of the Monroe Doctrine, keeping American domestic questions from League jurisdiction, ensuring veto power over decisions in both major League organs through requirement of unanimity, guaranteeing the right of withdrawal, and keeping the mandates system voluntary. When Wilson returned to the Conference, all major American criticisms and suggestions were embodied in the final draft. On April 28, 1919, the League of Nations' Covenant was incorporated into the Treaty of Versailles as its first twenty-six articles. Exchange of ratifications occurred on January 10, 1920, and all thirty-two signatories of the Treaty became original members of the League of Nations except the United States, Ecuador, and the Hedjaz, which refused to ratify.

American Defection

Why did the one nation that had provided the leadership in creating the new association of states reject the constitutional document and membership in that organization? Political analysts since 1920 have revealed a multitude of reasons. Probably no single one was decisive, but all or most contributed to a syndrome that denied American participation and started the process of enervation which culminated in the paralysis and collapse of the League system.

The primary factors involved in the decision to reject the League were political and related to the nature of the American constitutional system. Because only one third of the Senate membership plus one are needed to reject a treaty, securing the Senate's consent becomes a question of great delicacy. Often the minority party may attack the administration in power on a major treaty issue in order to produce an issue of consequence for the next election. Such was the case in 1919 when Republican opposition to the League became a carefully planned and executed political stratagem. Senator Henry Cabot Lodge, leader of the Senate Republicans, fought the treaty both politically and as part of his personal feud with Wilson. His ploy consisted of publicly accepting the idea of the League, because public opinion favored it, but of pointing out its dangers and demanding safe-guards that clearly would destroy its effectiveness. He warned that the League security system constituted an "entangling alliance," that the Monroe Doctrine would be rendered worthless, and that American mothers would be forced to send their sons to the far corners of the earth to die for causes of no concern to the United States. To safeguard American interests from these chimeras, Lodge proposed fifteen reservations to the Covenant. Such fundamental changes would have required reopening the negotiations with other treaty signatories and, if they had been accepted, would have immobil-ized the League from the start. Wilson was put into the difficult position of rejecting his own treaty at one point in the deliberations, because the reser-vations vitiated his most basic principles. While carrying the battle to the people across the nation, he suffered a stroke which took him out of the fray and ensured victory for the opposition forces.

Public opinion in the United States thereafter began to turn against the idea of joining the League. Although Warren G. Harding asserted in a campaign speech in 1920 that he, too, favored an "association of nations," this pledge was easily forgotten after he assumed the presidency as the country sought almost frantically to return to the normalcy of the prewar period. The first crippling blow against the League of Nations had been struck with the defection of the United States. The American public's passive acceptance followed by a passive opposition soon became a mood of active rejection deeply embedded in national consciousness. The Department of State, for example, dared not make public its communications with the League, and, in the Manchurian crisis of 1931, the President sent an observer who proceeded incognito to Geneva and sat mutely in the Council sessions lest American opinion be incensed. In technical areas, however, it was a different story, and the United States participated so extensively that in the late 1930's it could be said that the United States "was taking a larger share in the activities of the League than did ninety percent of its Members. . . ." [1] American defection, however, was most critical in the area of the League's attempts to establish a worldwide security system. More about this later.

League Membership

The League's initial policy of exclusivity in denying membership to the former enemy states was amended early in its history, and in time its mem-bership embraced most of the states of the world. Twenty-nine states ratified the Treaty of Versailles and, along with thirteen neutrals, became original members. New members could be admitted if they agreed to accept the obligations of the Covenant and were able to secure a two-thirds vote of

[1] Clyde Eagleton, *International Government* (New York: Ronald Press, 1948), p. 258.

the Assembly. The Covenant provided that "fully self-governing" dominions and colonies were eligible for membership, and India became a League member almost three decades before achieving independence. Sixty-three states ultimately became members of the League, although the maximum number claiming membership at any one time was fifty-eight. The increasing cooperation of the United States, the League's only major holdout, gave some credence to the League's claim to be the spokesman for the community of nations, but the withdrawal of Germany, Italy, and Japan and the expulsion of the Soviet Union in the 1930's weakened its claim to universality.

STRUCTURE AND FUNCTIONS

The League Covenant provided for the establishment of three permanent organs—the Assembly, the Council, and the Secretariat. Two semi-autonomous bodies were created outside the Covenant framework—the Permanent Court of International Justice and the International Labor Organization. They were closely affiliated with the League in terms of objectives, however, and the budgets of both were part of the League budget. The Council and Assembly also elected the judges of the world court. Of incipiently greater importance than structures were the obligations that members were required to assume toward the organization and each other. Each state, for example, undertook to "respect and preserve as against external aggression the territorial integrity and existing political independence of all Members of the League." They agreed to submit all of their disputes to arbitration, adjudication, or Council inquiry, and in no case to resort to war until three months after a settlement was offered. If any state resorted to war in violation of the Covenant, members were bound to apply diplomatic and economic sanctions and to consider the violation an act of war against the world community. Members further agreed to work together to control and reduce national armaments, and to cooperate in solving social, economic, colonial, humanitarian, and other types of common problems.

The Assembly

The Assembly of the League functioned as a diplomatic conference, with each member state permitted three delegates but a single vote. Although it resembled in many ways a legislative body of a national government, it possessed power only to solicit agreement and recommend action by League members. The first Assembly met at League headquarters in Geneva in November, 1920, and annual sessions were held each fall thereafter, along with occasional special sessions, until they were interrupted by the outbreak of war in 1939. National delegations to Assembly sessions were usually headed by premiers, ambassadors, or foreign ministers accompanied by large staffs of technical experts. Delegates were not free agents, however, as all important votes had to be cleared by their home governments and even speeches were based on instructions. The framers of the Covenant had hoped that by permitting three delegates for each member, different shades of opinion could be represented from each state, but governments kept a close rein on their delegations and demanded a unified approach to the issues considered at Geneva. The Secretary-General normally prepared the provisional agenda for the Assembly, and suggestions from members to add items were decided by the Assembly itself. Sessions began with debates on the League's extensive operations which afforded delegates an opportunity to engage in "general debate" on almost any topic of their choice. Opportunities were thus presented to members, especially the small states, to air their complaints or to present new proposals before a world forum.

The Assembly elected its President at each annual session. He was usually a well-known international personality from a small state not represented on the Council. Six vice-presidents were also elected each session who, with the President, the Chairman of the Agenda Committee, and the chairmen of the six permanent committees of the Assembly, constituted the General Committee which functioned as a steering committee for the Assembly. Most of the work of the Assembly was done in the six permanent committees with all members of the League represented on each. Debates and voting in the Assembly were mostly perfunctory since all questions first had to be considered by one of the committees and the committee vote was usually conclusive.

The scope of matters that could be considered by the Assembly was broad, indeed, since the Covenant empowered it to "deal at its meetings with any matter within the sphere of action of the League or affecting the peace of the world." Most powers were shared with the Council, but the Assembly exercised exclusive powers to admit new members, to elect its officers and determine its rules of procedure, to elect nonpermanent members of the Council, to control the League's budget, and to advise League members on the revision of treaties no longer applicable. The Assembly shared with the Council the powers to select a Secretary-General, to amend the Covenant, to elect the judges of the world court, and to deal with all substantive questions concerning disputes, aggression, social, economic, legal, and other problems brought to the attention of the League. Both major organs were authorized to elicit advisory opinions from the Court.

Although the writers of the Covenant expected the Assembly to be overshadowed by the Council, the opposite occurred during the twenty-year active history of the League. The breakdown of great power collaboration on the Council gave the Assembly, as it was subsequently to give the United Nations General Assembly, the opportunity to assert itself as the dominant organ in peace-keeping and other matters. Major issues of peace and war were aired publicly before the body representing most of the nations of the world. General debate at each session, which preceded the exploration of specific issues, attracted the high and mighty among the world's leading statesmen. Functioning as an annual general conference of nearly the entire state system, the Assembly debated major issues, promoted international cooperation, fostered a variety of social and economic programs, improved international administration, and provided some measure of protection for helpless peoples.

The Council

The architects of the League system established the Council as an executive agency to administer League policy and to function as the principal organ in handling disputes and collective security matters. The five great powers—the United States, Britain, France, Italy, and Japan—were intended to be the permanent members of the Council. The defection of the United States reduced the number of permanent members to four, but the great power club was expanded to include Germany in 1926, and Russia in 1934. The First Assembly recommended that the selection of nonpermanent members be guided by geographic, ethnic, economic, and cultural considerations to make the Council representative of the state system. The selection process, however, was marked by jealousy and intrigue as states fought for the honor of Council membership. This rivalry led to an increase of the original four nonpermanent members to six in 1922, to nine in 1926, and to eleven in 1936.

Like the Assembly, the Council was empowered by the Covenant to "deal at its meetings with any matter within the sphere of action of the League or affecting the peace of the world." In carrying out this mandate, the Council functioned as a decision-making body, an executive, a debating forum, and as a fact-finder and mediator in disputes. The liberum veto applied to all members, permanent and nonpermanent alike, except that a state could not vote on a dispute to which it was a party. Many Council powers were concurrent with those of the Assembly, but the Covenant fixed primary responsibility for some on the Council. These included determining the site of League headquarters, planning and implementing disarmament, playing the role of conciliator in disputes, taking action against aggression, and supervising the mandates system and minority treaties. The Covenant framers had accorded the Council major responsibility in these crucial areas because they expected it to function as a reconstituted Concert of Europe in maintaining peace. But the relationship between the two major organs was not one of inferior and superior, or of cabinet and parliament, or of two chambers of a bicameral legislature. They functioned only as two integral parts of the same machinery, one based on the traditional equality of states and the other reflecting the elitism of great power politics.

The Council, therefore, was intended by the Covenant framers to be a coordinate body, complementary to the Assembly rather than a rival with special jurisdiction. Yet, the prestige of the Council, the dominant role played by the great powers in world affairs, and its special responsibilities within the League framework all helped make it a potentially stronger force than the Assembly. Counterbalancing these factors were the larger membership of the Assembly and the fact that the Council usually implemented Assembly decisions, made annual reports to the Assembly, and had its size and finances controlled by the Assembly. Yet the Assembly could not ignore the reality that the League was impotent without the great powers, while the major powers on the Council could tolerate Assembly efforts to establish hegemony over the organization because they retained the veto power on both organs.

The Secretariat

One of the significant League contributions to the development of international institutions was the permanent international Secretariat. Pre-League international conferences and public unions had made some use of secretariats, but the League Secretariat played a new role. Under the leadership of the Secretary-General, it constituted the backbone of the League system, coordinating League activities, servicing League organs, providing expert advice, centralizing administration, performing housekeeping functions, and generally guiding and nudging the organization toward the achievement of its goals. Its international character was also an innovation. In the pre-League state system, the common practice had been for the state host to an international conference to provide the technical and secretarial assistance needed and, in the international bureaus and public unions, the secretariat was usually under the direction of the government of a member state. Previous secretariats had often been composed of national delegations paid by their respective governments and responsible to them. The League Secretariat, however, constituted an *international* civil service. Although the Secretariat was chosen from member states, such individuals were fully independent of their governments and responsible only to the League of Nations.

The Secretary-General, aided by a staff of Under- and Deputy-Secretary-Generals, headed the League Secretariat as its chief administrative officer. Although it was not so intended by the framers of the League Covenant, the Secretary-General functioned also in the roles of statesman and diplomat in the League's relations with member states, and as chief adviser to the Council and Assembly. The first Secretary-General, Sir Eric Drummond, a diplomat and aide to the British Foreign Secretary, was chosen by the Peace Conference for an indefinite term, and the Covenant provided that thereafter the Secretary-General would be appointed by the Council with Assembly approval. Drummond resigned in 1933 and the Assembly then fixed a ten-year term for his successor, J. L. A. Avenol, a French civil servant. Although both Drummond and Avenol regarded themselves as essentially administrators of the international staff, on many occasions both were drawn willingly or unwillingly into the political battles that raged in the Assembly and among the permanent members of the Council. The rivalry on the Council between the revisionist bloc (Germany, Italy, and Japan) and the status quo states (Britain and France) forced both Drummond and Avenol to take stands based on Covenant principles in advising the Council, and usually their positions reflected the status quo nature of the Covenant. This expanding political role of the Secretary-General of the League in response to growing rivalry among the great powers has its contemporary counterpart in the revisionist-status quo dichotomy on the Security Council of the United Nations and in the growing political role of the UN Secretary-General. Because a secretary-general must stand on the principles of his organization, and because international organizations are based logically on maintaining international stability, the Secretary-General's role in the League and in the United Nations has been frequently parallel to the interests of the status quo great powers. Like a city manager who gets caught up in factional strife on his city council, a secretary-general's detached and professional role cannot survive if he becomes—or appears to become—partisan in the heat of controversy. Thus, increasingly, in both the League and the United Nations, the Secretary-General has found himself in the role of statesman and leader while continuing to emphasize publicly the administrative and neutral character of his post.

LEAGUE INNOVATIONS

In its basic design and role, the League was both old and new. It was something old in the sense that the system was based firmly on the sovereignty of the member states; no new law could be created or obligations imposed upon a member without that member's consent. The powers of the League, as with earlier attempts to establish some degree of international order, were limited to recommendations. The Covenant, in keeping with the traditional guidelines of international law, did not seek to outlaw war but only to regulate a state's resort to this ultimate action. A special peace-keeping responsibility was accorded to the great powers, a role that had always been played by great powers in the international political system. Decisions of the organization were made on the basis of mutual agreement reflecting each state's particular interests, a decision-making system as ancient as the state system itself. Progress in technical, social, economic, and humanitarian fields was, as in the past, founded upon common treaty actions or international recommendations for national statutory enactments.

All in all, there was much in the new League of Nations system that was merely a continuation of the old traditions, customs, institutions, and decision-making procedures of the pre-League world.

But there was also much that was new, some quietly evolutionary in nature, some dramatically revolutionary in scope. The League was the first attempt to establish a permanent international organization of a general political nature with machinery functioning on a continuing basis. For the first time a community responsibility to use the collective force of the state system against an international lawbreaker was given institutional flesh and bone. Although the League could hardly be compared to a domestic political system of police action with its superior authority, independent police force, and automatic action against lawbreakers, it was, nonetheless, a step toward internationalizing the responsibility of peace-keeping. In the past, action against an aggressor had been a right of states; under the Covenant it became a duty.

The World Court

Another significant new step taken under the League system was the establishment of the first world court, the Permanent Court of International Justice. The Permanent Court of Arbitration established by the First Hague Peace Conference in 1899 was not a world court since it merely provided for panels of arbitrators from member countries from which jurists could be selected to serve as arbitrators in specific disputes. The League Council, working through its Committee of Jurists, formulated plans for an international court that went beyond the arbitration of the Hague system. The statute creating the world court took the form of a separate treaty so that states that were not members of the League could also accept its adjudicatory role. The world tribunal, which convened regularly at The Hague, possessed a broad jurisdiction in interpreting and applying international law, and contributed effectively to the settlement of international disputes. It consisted of fifteen judges selected on the basis of their competence in international law who acted independently of their own governments and reached decisions on the basis of the principles of law. Although the court had authority to render judgments in contentious cases and to hand down advisory opinions to League organs, the absence of an effective system of compulsory jurisdiction weakened its role. Much effort was expended by the League in trying to strengthen the Court's operations by the codification of international law, but these attempts were only moderately successful. Nevertheless, the fact that League members had found it desirable to establish a world court and to endow it with some authority indicated noteworthy progress in the conduct of inter-state relations.[2]

[2] For a more detailed discussion of the World Court's role, see Chapter 9.

A Mandates System

The mandates system proved to be one of the most revolutionary developments of the League. Territories and peoples seized from defeated states had always been regarded as proper spoils for the victors, but Article 22 of the Covenant embraced President Wilson's wartime demand that "the well being and development of such peoples form a sacred trust of civilization." Thus the territories and colonies surrendered by the Treaty of Versailles were made an international responsibility, and individual members of the victorious coalition were expected to provide the tutelage necessary to prepare them for self-government under League scrutiny. The Council was assigned responsibility by the Covenant to supervise the mandates system and a Permanent Mandates Commission, composed of private experts elected by the Council, was established in 1921 to advise the Council on all matters relating to the mandates.

The mandates were grouped into three classes corresponding roughly to their stage of political development. The Class A mandates which included those territories formerly part of the Turkish Empire (Palestine, Iraq, Syria, Lebanon, and Transjordan) were slated to receive full independence at an early but unspecified date. The B mandates were the former German territories in Central Africa (Cameroons, Ruanda-Urundi, Tanganyika, and Togoland) which needed a much longer period of tutelage before eventually achieving self-government. The C mandates were those which because of their small size, sparse population, or remoteness could best be administered "under the laws of the Mandatory as integral portions of its territory." Included as C mandates were South West Africa and some islands in the South Pacific area.[3] Today all of the Class A and Class B mandates are independent, most achieving their freedom under the aegis of the United Nations. The League mandates system proved to be a valuable experiment, initiating the anticolonial movement that culminated in the independence of millions of subject peoples.

Safeguarding Rights of Minorities

The protection of minority groups was another field of activity new to international organization. The responsibility for protecting minority rights was assigned to the Council by the "Minority Treaties" concluded between the Allied Powers and Czechoslovakia, Greece, Poland, Romania, and Yugoslavia. The states parties to the treaties, and to subsequent agreements of a similar nature, gave pledges guaranteeing to minorities living within their

[3] The Republic of South Africa has consistently refused to place South West Africa under United Nations trusteeship and continues to administer it as a League of Nations mandate. Three of the South Pacific mandates—the Marshalls, the Carolines, and the Marianas—are today under United States strategic trust.

boundaries certain civil rights, such as religious freedom and civil and political equality, and some social rights concerning language, education, and equal employment opportunity. Although not empowered by the Covenant, the Council accepted the duty of receiving petitions, hearing disputes, and making recommendations on controversies growing out of such guarantees. More than a dozen states entered into agreements providing for the Council to function as guarantor and arbiter of the rights established. In an action which was a forerunner to later activities in the field of human rights by the United Nations, the League Council sought to universalize minority rights in 1933 by calling upon all states to grant their own racial, religious, and linguistic minorities rights equal to those in states that had assumed a treaty obligation. In a few cases the Council also provided for recognition of the political right of self-determination of minority groups, as in the Saar where a plebiscite in 1935 determined that its people preferred union with Germany to union with France. In most cases, however, minorities were dispersed or constituted small enclaves within large states, making the principle of self-determination impossible to implement.

Social, Economic, and Technical Cooperation

The changes instituted by the League system affecting the greatest number of mankind were those in the areas of social, economic, humanitarian, and technical cooperation. Never had the world witnessed such a feverish attack upon international problems and national shortcomings as that fostered by the League through numerous committees, commissions, study groups, administrative bodies, institutes, and bureaus. Although the Covenant devoted little space (Articles 23 and 24) to encouraging cooperation of League members in nonsecurity matters, by the late 1930's most of the League's time, money, and effort were being expended in such programs. Some of the many bodies established by or brought under the aegis of the League to further cooperation among its members included:

1. Economic and Financial Organization, which carried on extensive studies, advised and submitted proposals to the Assembly and Council, sponsored economic and monetary conferences, and published the *Statistical Year-Book,* the *World Economic Survey,* and other useful publications. This organization was a forerunner of the United Nations Economic and Social Council.

2. Health Organization, which drafted conventions aimed at controlling communicable diseases and improving public health measures, fostered research in health education and infant mortality, and helped states fight serious outbreaks of plague. The World Health Organization has continued these activities as a specialized agency of the United Nations.

3. Organization for Communications and Transit, which drafted treaties and made studies in a vast number of problem areas concerned with transportation, including such matters as river and road traffic, transmission of electric power, maritime and inland navigation, and rail transport. Continued cooperation in

fostering better international communications and transit are currently carried on by the International Civil Aviation Agency, the International Telecommunications Union, and the Inter-Governmental Maritime Consultative Organization.

4. Various commissions concerned with such subjects as disarmament and military questions, mandates, intellectual cooperation, dangerous drugs, the opium traffic, slavery, and children's welfare.

5. Temporary commissions established to meet particular needs in the fields of disarmament, refugees, dispute settlement, the codification of international law, and Covenant amendment.

6. Special administrative bodies set up to care for refugees, enforce peace treaties, make international loans, and govern League protectorates.

7. International public unions brought under the centralized administration of the League and given extensive assistance by the Secretariat.

8. Registration and Secretariat publication of all treaties and agreements entered into by League members.

The League of Nations honored old traditions but was also guided by the new thinking and constructive statesmanship that typified much of its active twenty-year history. Initially, the League's objectives were closely tied to promoting the interests of the victors, which gave it a character related to their special interests and concerns. In time, many members began to regard the League as a means of reshaping the whole field of international relations to provide a sound basis for international order and well-being.

THE LEAGUE IN ACTION

The two major functions of the League, as stated in the Preamble to the Covenant, were "to achieve international peace and security" and "to promote international cooperation." The two were expected to be complementary since a secure world would encourage state cooperation in many fields, and a common attack upon the economic, social, and technical problems facing all governments would develop a sense of community that would help deter states from violence. Of the two, the security function was regarded as the more pressing.

Collective Security and Disarmament

There was little agreement on how the League should pursue its security objectives. France, for example, regarded the League's primary responsibility to be that of enforcing the provisions of the peace treaties and of guarding against a resurgence of German military power. Britain, in contrast, viewed the League as an agency to foster the peaceful settlement of disputes and protect the vital interests of the Empire. Each member, in fact, tended to define the League's peace-preserving role largely in terms of its own national interest, so that when the League was confronted with threats to the peace, it often spoke through a cacophony rather than with a single voice.

In its approach to the problem of war, the Covenant made no general statement that war is illegal. The traditional legal right of states to engage in war was circumscribed in the Covenant by provisions that made it illegal in most situations, enjoined delay in all cases, and prescribed community sanctions against the warmaker.

Arms control, but not total disarmament, was called for in the Covenant, and several major conferences for the reduction and limitation of armaments were held. Generally, the League failed to secure any meaningful arms control because of basic disagreement among the great powers: Germany demanded arms equality, France demanded security through arms superiority over Germany, and Britain called for direct and general reductions in armaments of all states. The United States created further difficulty by actively supporting a direct and universal arms reduction while refusing to join in any security guarantee system that many states regarded as a *sine qua non* to arms control. Discussions also broke down over specifics involving the composition, nature, size, and types of forces to be reduced and the means of inspection and enforcement, the very same kinds of questions that have also stymied UN disarmament efforts for over twenty years.

Another League approach to the problem of war was the peaceful settlement of international disputes. "Any war or threat of war" became under Article 11 a matter of concern to the entire League, to be taken up by the Council at the request of any member. Article 12 required disputants to submit their issues to conciliation, to arbitration, or to judicial settlement. Parties to a dispute were "in no case to resort to war until three months after the award by the arbitrators, or the judicial decision, or the report by the Council." Major emphasis was thus placed on finding common ground for the settlement of disputes rather than on the idealistic approach of trying to proscribe all wars. If the findings of the Council were not unanimous the parties were free to go to war after the three month "cooling off" period had expired. But if the Council's decision was unanimous, members of the League were obligated by the Covenant not to make war against the party that accepted it. Any disputing state which resorted to war without recourse to the settlement procedures was to be branded an international outlaw, and the sanctions provided in the Covenant were to be applied.

More than sixty disputes were considered by the League from 1920 to 1939, with thirty-five of these settled through League procedures, or the threat of direct League intervention. Twenty disputes were settled by the parties utilizing non-League settlement procedures, and eleven remained unsettled or resulted in dictated settlements by one side.[4]

In resolving thirty-five international disputes, the League used a variety

4 Quincy Wright, *A Study of War* (Chicago: University of Chicago Press, 1943), pp. 1431–32. The disputes handled by the League including pertinent data about each can be found in L. Larry Leonard, *International Organization* (New York: McGraw-Hill, 1951), Chap. 8.

of peaceful settlement procedures, some traditional, others developed by the League. Procedures used by the League in specific disputes included:

1. Commissions of Inquiry, established by the Council and consisting of states not party to the dispute. A Commission of Inquiry was used in seeking settlement of the Aaland Islands dispute between Sweden and Finland in 1921, and was used frequently thereafter. The objective of the Commission of Inquiry technique was to investigate and report the facts on which the Council could base a recommendation. In some cases the commissions became conciliation bodies when they were authorized to formulate terms of settlement and to seek agreement of the parties to the terms.

2. World Court judgments in contentious cases, and advisory opinions when requested by the Council or Assembly. In 1923, for example, Britain and France resolved their dispute over French nationality decrees in Tunis-Morocco affecting British subjects when the Court advised that the French action was international in scope rather than a matter for domestic jurisdiction. The Court's active role in settling disputes is reflected in its twenty-two year record: sixty-five cases considered, twenty-seven advisory opinions handed down, and thirty-two judgments rendered.

3. Cease-fire orders, given by the Council, or by its president when the Council was not in session. The cease-fire procedure was used successfully in the 1925 border dispute between Bulgaria and Greece. Noncompliance by one disputant with a cease-fire order could result in that state being adjudged an aggressor by the Council, with collective sanctions against it a possibility.

4. Public opinion pressures, mobilized through open sessions of the Council and the Assembly. Such pressures were used, unsuccessfully, in the 1931 Manchurian dispute between China and Japan, and with modest impact, after a long delay, in the Gran Chaco war between Bolivia and Paraguay from 1928 to 1935 in finally pressuring the disputants to accept arbitration.

5. Expulsion from the League by a vote of the Council. The drastic nature of this procedure is indicated by the fact that it was used only once, against the Soviet Union in 1939, when the Soviets rejected League appeals to desist from aggression against Finland.

6. Miscellaneous techniques, including Council conciliation; armistice, military, and boundary commissions; mediation efforts by the Secretary-General, the Council president, and the Council's *Rapporteur*.

Although the League's general record of dispute settlement was notable, in the crucial disputes involving planned acts of aggression by the great powers, it failed to measure up to its responsibilities. Each aggressive great power—Japan, Italy, Germany, and the Soviet Union—was able to achieve its immediate military objectives in spite of efforts by the League to prevent it. The League persisted in handling many cases of overt aggression as disputes because the members preferred peaceful settlement procedures to invoking sanctions.

The Manchurian Case

The League's first test in meeting aggression committed by a great power came in 1931 when Japan, claiming Chinese destruction of its railway properties, attacked Manchuria and occupied its capital of Mukden. China, charging aggression by Japan, appealed to the League under Article 11 of the Covenant. Attempts by the Council to secure a cease-fire and a Japanese withdrawal were vetoed by Japan, which requested that an on-the-spot inquiry into the facts be made before League action was undertaken.

As fighting spread in Manchuria, the Council appointed a Commission of Inquiry under Lord Lytton's direction to go to Manchuria to dig out the facts. By the time the Commission arrived in the Far East in April, 1932, the Japanese had established Manchuria as the new independent state of Manchoukuo and had begun an attack upon China proper at Shanghai. At this point, China, deeply affronted by Council procrastination, asked for transference of the dispute to the Assembly. Acting under Article 15 of the Covenant, the Assembly condemned the Japanese aggression and adopted the American-initiated Stimson Doctrine of nonrecognition of new states or governments created illegally by the use of force. A voluminous report from the Lytton Commission condemning Japan's aggressive actions in Manchuria was adopted unanimously by the Assembly but was too late to affect the outcome since the conquest was an accomplished fact. Its accuracy, however, in fixing blame and condemning aggression led to the withdrawal of Japan from the League of Nations.

The Manchurian case emphasized that situations involving overt aggression could not be successfully handled by using peaceful settlement procedures. Japan proved, and the lesson was not lost to potential European aggressors, that the cumbersome machinery and procedures of the League could be used against it to stifle effective collective action. The League suffered also from a lack of great power leadership on the Council and because the United States, the major power most concerned about Japanese aggressive tendencies, was not a member. American concern resulted in the sending of an observer to Geneva who sat quietly listening to the debates but offered nothing but moral condemnation of Japan's action. Clearly, this was not enough, nor were the League's pathetic efforts, to force a Japanese capitulation. The first major test had found the League weak and indecisive.

The Ethiopian Case

A second critical test for the League was not long in coming. In the winter of 1934, League-member Italy attacked League-member Ethiopia in violation of their mutual Covenant obligations to respect each other's political and territorial integrity and to adjust their differences peacefully. Italy, following the Japanese example, launched a diplomatic offensive in Geneva claiming Ethiopian forces had attacked first and demanding apologies and compensation. Ethiopia, not recognizing the Italian master plan to build an African empire, at first sought to negotiate, to obtain Italian agreement to arbitration, and to use the League facilities for conciliation rather than collective action. Under cover of negotiations, Mussolini mobilized his reserves for war, granting minor concessions each time it appeared that the Council would intervene. Outside of the main arena of the League a diplomatic web of intrigue developed as Britain and France, concerned more with the rising power of Nazi Germany, which had already withdrawn from the League, sought to keep Italy as a buffer to Germany. Permitting Mussolini to seize a piece of African territory seemed to the statesmen in London and Paris a small price to pay for the containment of German power. Incredibly, the United States remained aloof and President Roosevelt refused Emperor Haile Selassie's request that he call upon the parties to observe their commitment under the Kellogg-Briand Pact of 1928 not to use war as an instrument of national policy.[5]

By the autumn of 1935 Italy had completed its mobilization and on October 2, disregarding many League resolutions and Covenant provisions, launched a full-scale attack on Ethiopia. Ethiopia at once invoked Article 16 of the Covenant, holding that Italy's resort to war before fulfilling Covenant requirements must be considered an act of war against each member. All members, the Ethiopian delegate at Geneva argued, must honor their Covenant obligations by applying immediate economic sanctions against Italy, and he further called upon the Council to recommend military sanctions. Under an interpretation of the Covenant agreed upon in 1921, however, neither the Council nor the Assembly was empowered to determine that aggression had been committed; each member state was entitled to decide for itself. The levying of economic and other sanctions was likewise controlled by each state, emphasizing the veto power held by each member under the League system. Of the fifty-four League members polled, fifty indicated that Italy was the aggressor, thus obligating them to the application of economic sanctions at once and of military sanctions if recommended by the Council.

ECONOMIC SANCTIONS. For the first time in history, economic sanctions were levied against an international lawbreaker, with fifty member states participating. Numerous questions arose immediately concerning what kinds of materials should be embargoed, whether imports from Italy should be banned, what would happen to private long-term contracts, and whether an effort should be made to prevent nonmember states from violating the embargoes. A League consensus soon developed and members agreed that economic sanctions should include an arms and essential materials embargo, a ban on all loans and other kinds of financial help, a restriction

---

[5] In his refusal, President Roosevelt stated that he was sure that neither party would resort to war. This statement is regarded by historians as incredible because American intelligence had a year earlier in the summer of 1934 discovered that the Italian General Staff had completed plans for the military conquest of Ethiopia. In fact, Italian plans for an Ethiopian campaign were generally known among European diplomats, and talk of the forthcoming invasion became quite common in Rome in 1934. See, for example, Cordell Hull, *The Memoirs of Cordell Hull* (New York: Macmillan, 1948), Vol. I, p. 418.

against all imports from Italy and its possessions, and mutual support among League members to minimize their economic injury from the embargoes. By November, 1935, the economic sanctions were in effect and within a period of several months the sanctions began to have a telling effect on Italy's economy.[6]

WHY SANCTIONS FAILED. In spite of economic sanctions, the Italian armies swept into Addis Ababa and on May 5, 1936, Mussolini boasted that victory had been achieved and that Ethiopia was "Italian by right because with the sword of Rome it is civilization which triumphs over barbarism. . . ." Two months later, and eight months after sanctions had been imposed, the Assembly voted to withdraw all sanctions against Italy. Why had the economic sanctions failed? Why were they terminated after Italy had completed its conquest, thus condoning the aggression? Why had the Council not recommended military sanctions? These and similar questions were aired in Assembly debates following the withdrawal of sanctions, and the answers to them, incomplete as they may be, help to explain the difficulties of carrying out an effective collective security action against a great power within the context of the international milieu of that day.

Basic to the League's problem was the *realpolitik* objective of Britain and France to build a coalition to balance the power of Hitler's Germany. In much the same way that the East-West split has weakened the great power concert on the United Nations Security Council, the struggle in the 1930's to contain Nazi power replaced collective security as the prime concern of British and French statesmen. While sanctions were in effect, both nations continued to negotiate with Italy outside the League, preferring conciliation to applying effective sanctions. Both were instrumental in the League decision not to include oil, the lifeblood of modern armies, on the embargo list, and both ruled out naval blockade and the closing of the Suez Canal to Italy.

Other nations also contributed much to the weak-sanctions syndrome. The United States condemned Italian aggression but avoided any cooperation with the sanctions decision other than placing both belligerents off-limits for arms shipments under the Neutrality Acts. American trade, especially shipments of oil, increased sizably, with most of the increase going to the Italian African colonies which were supply bases for the military campaign. Many Latin American countries, nearly suffocating under great gluts of primary commodity surpluses, agreed in principle to sanctions but failed to apply them in practice. Four League members refused to apply

---

[6] Within two months, Italian exports had declined 43 per cent over the same month of the previous year, and imports had dropped to 47 per cent. In three months imports fell to 56 per cent of the previous year and imports of strategic items like iron ore, tin, and raw rubber had almost ceased. Thus within a short period of time economic sanctions proved effective in significantly reducing Italy's economic activity.

any kinds of sanctions, one refused to reduce imports from Italy, and seven never applied the arms embargo. The bait of stimulating national economies stagnated by the world economic depression proved to be a more powerful motivator of national actions than idealistic considerations of collective security.

Yet, ironically, the economic gains were short-lived. Italy joined the Axis powers despite British and French appeasement, the United States was eventually drawn into war against the dictators, and potential aggressors were encouraged by the League's vacillation and irresoluteness. As for the League, the imposition of sanctions by an international organization for the first time in history was a signal achievement; but the Ethiopian case illustrated that it takes more to deter aggression than covenants, organizations, institutions, procedures, and decisions. In the final analysis, effective collective security depends upon the states that make up international organizations—their people, their governments, and the policies they pursue.

The Road to Global War

The failure of the League to deter the Japanese and Italian conquests led to new aggressions. In the Spanish Civil War the League, following the non-intervention policies of Britain, France, and the United States, and ignoring the interventions of Germany, Italy, and the Soviet Union, determined that it was an internal matter and not of League concern. Germany, whose earlier violations of the Treaty of Versailles in rearming and in occupying the Rhineland had been studiously ignored by the League, began in 1938 a process of absorbing her neighbors into the Third Reich. Austria, the Czechoslovakian Sudetenland, and subsequently the whole of Czechoslovakia were gobbled up by Hitler without satiating his appetite. Japan meanwhile had begun a military campaign to conquer and annex all of China. Only in the case of the attack by the Soviet Union against Finland in the winter of 1939 did the League take action, and that in the futile form of expelling the Soviets from the League. The relative stability of the 1920's could not endure in the 1930's, as the world moved irresistably into the maelstrom of war.

Hitler's attack on Poland in September, 1939, ended the noble experiment of the League. Its major powers took up arms against Germany and its activities thereafter were limited to housekeeping duties at its Geneva headquarters. The western powers made no pretense that the war was a League action against aggression. The leaders in Paris and London obviously regarded the League and the whole concept of collective security as an irrelevancy at this point, preferring time-tested national patriotism as a rallying force for their peoples. Most League members not already involved had no stomach for general war against a great power and neutrality rather than collective action became the common policy.

An Appraisal: The League's Balance Sheet

A review of the League record might be summarized as a study in utility and futility. Conclusions about the degree of success or failure attained by the League must obviously depend upon the standard of measurement employed. If the critical test is what the Covenant framers intended, or what millions of people hoped for, or what the principles of the Covenant actually called for, the League fell far short. If, on the other hand, it is measured by what other international organizations in the past had accomplished, or what skeptics and critics predicted for it, or what the nature of the rivalry-ridden state system would permit, the League probably rates high. Any evaluation faces the danger of falling into the old pro-League–anti-League controversy that characterized the great American debate on the subject and kept it on a largely emotional level for twenty years.

A Capsule History of the League

Obviously, an appraisal of the League must recognize that its effectiveness varied in response to changes in the international environment. The peace, stability, and relative prosperity of its first decade permitted the League to make a promising start in a number of directions. Numerous international disputes were settled peacefully, the complex problem of disarmament was tackled, and the Kellogg-Briand Pact of 1928 attempted to close a gap in the League Covenant by outlawing war as an instrument of national policy. Cooperation in welfare areas was explored and foundations laid for extensive programs which flowered during the subsequent decade.

The period from 1930 to 1935 was one of challenge and uncertainty for the League. The economic depression which started with the American stock market crash in 1929 and spread across the world in a chain-reaction reduced the League's carefully cultivated channels of cooperation to a shambles. Economic nationalism and ideological rivalries spawned in the depression's wake split the status quo world into hostile camps. Japanese, Italian, and German fascism posed successive political and military challenges with which the organization and its members were either unwilling or unable to cope. A new wave of nationalism erased many of the gains of internationalism during the 1920's as League members became increasingly obsessed with their own limited conceptions of national security and with domestic problems. Government after government fought desperately to rescue its people from the brink of economic and financial collapse, social disintegration, and political revolution. As Germany rearmed, disarmament talks collapsed and the world witnessed the start of a new arms race. Economic and monetary conferences failed and the world depression deepened. The 1930–35 era was not a world of the League's making, but it was the only one available.

The world stage was now set for the League's inevitable collapse. Nine members withdrew between 1935 and 1939, some for ideological reasons, others claiming financial problems. A desperate reform movement initiated by the Assembly in 1936 sought for three years to stem the tide and refurbish the tarnished League image by updating its security provisions and by divesting the Covenant of all references to the peace treaties of World War I. The Axis Powers, bent on aggression, were not interested in returning to the League, nor were other former member states which continued to pursue independent courses. With the failure of the reform movement, the League became inoperative in the security field, and a majority of the members professed neutrality in the crises growing out of German annexations in Central Europe. When war came to Europe in September, 1939, the League remained quiescent, a posture it retained through the five years of World War II. A shell of the League organization lived on at the Geneva headquarters through the war period, only to be ignored by the architects of a new world organization who did not want their creation tainted by association with the League's failure.

An Autopsy

Just as friends of the League in its early years tended to exaggerate its novelty and its potential, critics have in retrospect emphasized its failures and undervalued its contributions. All evaluations, however, eventually return to the central question: Why did the League fail to keep the peace? Since the maintenance of peace and security was the primary objective of the League, it is only natural that its historical verdict has been delivered mainly in that area and in condemnatory terms.

In fixing blame, some observers have sought to explain the League's demise as a failure of its member states to support the principles of the Covenant. Such a rationalization fails to recognize that in the field of international organization members *are* the organization, that the League had no real existence independent of its component parts. No organization comprised of sovereign and independent entities can possibly be stronger than the will and support for common action that exists within the group. Thus, to blame the members rather than the League is a circular argument. One could as well make the point that the pre-World War I balance of power functioned well in keeping the peace but eventually failed because the states involved did not play their proper roles within the system.

Technical difficulties growing out of the League's machinery and procedures have also been blamed for its failure. It is quite true that the requirement of unanimity in both Council and Assembly on most substantive questions enabled aggressor nations to veto some countermeasures. Also, because war was not outlawed, the Covenant permitted some members to use the provisions regulating resort to war to block effective collective action. Covenant provisions dealing with disarmament were so loosely worded that no definite responsibility existed for members to reduce their arms. The sanction system was weakened in the League's early years by a Covenant interpretation permitting each member to decide for itself the question of invoking an economic embargo. Many other technical deficiencies also contributed to the League's failure, but it would be inaccurate to assign organizational weaknesses a major role in the debacle since most of the weaknesses could be, and many were, overcome by interpretation and by taking alternative pathways.

Probably the most popular explanation for League failure, in the United States at any rate, was that of American defection. Unquestionably, the American refusal to participate in a world organization sponsored by its own president induced a psychological and power vacuum which the League never fully overcame. In the security field, American policy-makers offered only moral condemnation of aggression while permitting American businessmen to continue extensive trade with the aggressors. The popular myth that American military force combined with the League against aggressors would have made the League successful overlooks the fact that American power during the 1920's and 1930's was only a potentiality awaiting the full mobilization of World War II. Contributions from the small, garrison-bound American army could hardly have influenced the outcome of any of the major military actions during the League period, and Americans were psychologically unprepared for a major effort until Pearl Harbor. American defection, then, weakened the League but was not the central reason for its ultimate collapse.

Some League critics have sought to explain its failure as resulting from its close association with the "unjust" peace treaties of World War I. The League, it is argued, was placed in the impossible position of defending the status quo of the victors against the attempts by the vanquished to undo the peace treaties imposed upon them. The League, itself, recognized this argument officially when it appointed a committee in the late 1930's to propose reforms that would free it from this incubus and, hopefully, regain the support of nations that had been alienated. Yet, the League would still have had to operate within a world based on the peace settlements even if it had in no way been associated with them. And, to the League's credit, the status quo was not tenaciously defended and justice often took precedence over the status quo, as in the case of the Saar whose people, in a League-supervised plebiscite, voted for reunion with Germany.

Finally, some critics have seen in the League's failure an example of the fundamental inability of a collective security system to keep the peace. One such group rejects the League as an impractical and idealistic concept which was foredoomed to failure because it ignored the power realities of the world. Only by fostering a balance of power through military preparedness and alliances can peace be preserved, so runs the argument, and the League diverted the status quo great powers from such a course, making disaster inevitable. Another group has also criticized the League's utopianism, but its alternative is a world government acting with substantial powers directly upon individuals. Since peace can be adequately preserved within nations by a federal government, they have argued, the world scene likewise demands a world authority with a near monopoly of power. Compelling as arguments favoring world federalism may be in theory, the world of sovereign states was hardly ready then, nor is it now, to undergo such a radical metamorphosis. Moreover, if the will to resist the aggressors had been broadly based and deeply rooted, if conditions approaching a consensus had existed, cooperation of member states could probably have done the job as expeditiously as a world federal system. Conversely, the absence of consensus under either system would have had equally deleterious results.

In conclusion, no single theory suffices to explain the League's failure. One might even conclude that bad luck had something to do with it. A combination of many factors appearing often at inopportune times made success in the security field a difficult and elusive quarry. Unquestionably, the economic nationalism engendered by the world depression created an environment uncongenial to international cooperation. And once the world had been irretrievably split between revisionist and status quo powers, the malfunctioning of the League's collective security apparatus became a matter of course. The same kind of schism has returned to enfeeble collective security in the United Nations era, as yet, however, without the same catastrophic consequences. It is to the United Nations that we now turn our attention.

Selected Readings

BURTON, M. E. *The Assembly of the League of Nations.* Chicago: University of Chicago Press, 1943.

CHURCHILL, WINSTON. *The Gathering Storm.* Boston: Houghton-Mifflin, 1948.

HULL, CORDELL. *The Memoirs of Cordell Hull.* New York: Macmillan, 1948, 2 vols.

SALTER, SIR ARTHUR. *Security: Can We Retrieve It?* New York: Macmillan, 1939.

SMITH, S. S. *The Manchurian Crisis: A Tragedy in International Relations.* New York: Columbia University Press, 1948.

WALTERS, F. P. *A History of the League of Nations.* London: Oxford University Press, 1952, Vol. I, Chaps. 1–5.

WATKINS, JAMES T., and ROBINSON, J. WILLIAM. *General International Organization: A Source Book.* Princeton: D. Van Nostrand, 1956.

3 | *Organizing the United Nations*

Like the First World War, World War II created an international climate of opinion receptive to the ideas of international cooperation. In the early war period, as the Allied powers suffered serious military reverses, the role of international organization was blurred from international consciousness. The League remained immobilized and discarded, playing no role in the global struggle it had sought to prevent. But as the Allies marshaled their power and launched a worldwide offensive, some thinking, official and unofficial, began to take shape concerning the nature of the postwar world. What kind of a world would emerge from the carnage of the most deadly war in history? How would the mistakes made by the previous generation be avoided? Could the peace be won just as the war was being won? How could talent and effort be mobilized on a massive scale to build the new world of peace?

As the day of victory approached, the major powers began to exchange ideas and discuss how they might bring them to fruition. Statements about postwar international unity began to take on meaning, to become more than propaganda weapons intended to energize Allied morale and weaken the resolve of the Axis peoples. Planning was started, negotiations undertaken, compromises reached, and preliminary agreements drawn up. Public support for the idea of postwar cooperation spurred governments to proceed with the establishment of a new organization to preserve the peace they had won at so terrible a cost. It is this road that we travel now, for the gestation period helped to mold and shape the new world organization.

THE ROAD TO SAN FRANCISCO

The United Nations Charter, which emerged from the San Francisco Conference on International Organization, was a product pieced together during the war years. The seed of the idea that a new world organization be created in the postwar era was planted by President Franklin Roosevelt and Prime Minister Winston Churchill in the Atlantic Charter of August 14, 1941. The date is significant because it was four months before the Japanese attack

38

on Pearl Harbor and the entry of the United States into the war. Churchill urged that a definite statement calling for a postwar international political organization be included in the joint statement of aspirations. Roosevelt, however, recognized that American public opinion, still basically isolationist, might react unfavorably to such a clear-cut internationalist objective. In final form the Atlantic Charter called for "fullest collaboration between all nations in the economic field" and hinted of the future "establishment of a wider and permanent system of general security." Even in this watered-down form it carried the clear implication that progress toward a world organization having security and economic responsibilities was a joint objective of the two leading democracies. On January 1, 1942, with the United States now in the war, twenty-six nations subscribed to a Declaration by United Nations which reaffirmed the principles of the Atlantic Charter. This declaration established the United Nations military alliance to which twenty-one other nations subsequently adhered, each agreeing to employ its full resources against the Axis, to cooperate with each other, and not to make a separate peace.

The vague references to international organization in these early war documents were made explicit in the Moscow Declaration on General Security signed in October, 1943, by the foreign ministers of the Big Four (Hull, Eden, Molotov, and Foo Ping-sheung). The Moscow Declaration pledged continuance of wartime cooperation "for the organization and maintenance of peace and security" and explicitly recognized "the necessity of establishing at the earliest practicable date a general international organization. . . ." It was also significant as a definite commitment by the Soviet Union to support the establishment of a world organization.

United States Planning

Almost concurrently with the outbreak of war in Europe the State Department began exploratory studies of a postwar security system. In 1941, before American entry into the war, the British government had sought to gain American participation in discussions concerning an international judicial system which might become the foundation of a general international organization. The United States expressed interest in the project, and three weeks after Pearl Harbor the State Department established an Advisory Committee on Post-War Foreign Policy. Sumner Welles, Under-Secretary of State, was made chairman of a special subcommittee on international organization to study past experience with international organization and to prepare a "Draft Constitution." These early efforts were significant in involving some of the top State Department leadership with the problems of building a world organization. In time the Department succeeded in hammering out a "Possible Plan for a General International Organization" which it submitted to President Roosevelt late in 1943.

Discussions and appraisals at the highest government levels led to still further changes and modifications and the writing of several new drafts. By the late summer of 1944 the State Department had formulated definite proposals for the new organization for discussion with the other major allied powers.

Meanwhile, private groups in the United States were also at work conditioning public opinion to the idea of international cooperation and preparing their own blueprints for peace. Business, labor, and church groups created special committees to study the problems that could be anticipated in the postwar period. Typically, such study groups concluded that a general security organization must be established and the United States must not only join but provide the leadership to ensure its success. Special unofficial study groups comprised of experts in international law and organization, such as the Commission to Study the Organization of Peace, and the Universities Committee on Post-War International Problems, drew up extensive plans for the proposed organization.

Although public opinion began to crystallize in favor of a general international organization at an early date during the war years, a significant unknown factor remained. That was the United States Congress, where American participation in the League of Nations had earlier met its demise in spite of executive action and sizable public support. The Congress tends, by the nature of its election system, to amplify the more conservative and isolationist views of the American public. The new organization would clearly need its solid support if American participation were to be meaningful. In 1943 the go-ahead signal was given by the Congress. The House of Representatives adopted the Fulbright Resolution on September 21, 1943, which put the House on record

> favoring the creation of appropriate international machinery with power adequate to establish and to maintain a just and lasting peace, among the nations of the world, and as favoring participation by the United States therein through its constitutional processes.[1]

On November 5, 1943, the Senate adopted the Connally Resolution which provided that the United States should "join with free and sovereign nations in the establishment and maintenance of international authority with power to prevent aggression and to preserve the peace of the world." The Resolution incorporated the Moscow Declaration that a general international organization be established "at the earliest practicable date" but cautioned that any treaty to effect the purposes of the Resolution "shall be made only

[1] House Concurrent Resolution 25 was authored by J. William Fulbright (D., Ark.). The Senate then drew up its own version of the Resolution. For complete text of both the Fulbright and the Connally Resolutions, see James T. Watkins and J. William Robinson, *General International Organization* (Princeton, N.J.: Van Nostrand, 1956), pp. 170, 172.

by and with the advice and consent of the Senate of the United States. . . ."

With the Congress on record as favoring American participation in a new world organization, the time had come for the major allies to move from the general to the particular. Although agreements had been reached on principles, the question remained whether they would survive the transition to specifics on such questions as membership, voting, powers, and structure. From the start the United States and the Soviet Union were recognized as the key factors in the building of the new organization, although neither had much experience in the workings of international organization machinery. The United States had refused to join the League and the Soviet Union had had a short and unhappy experience in it. Both governments knew that their nations would emerge from the war as super powers competing for leadership in the world, yet forced to cooperate with each other if another disastrous war were to be avoided.

Dumbarton Oaks Conference

Since the three major powers had been diligently working on drafts of a constitution for a general international organization, the American State Department suggested to the Russian and British governments that delegations meet to work out a single set of proposals. After negotiations, the three governments agreed to participate in the drafting of a proposed charter that would reflect their common positions. They also agreed that China should participate, although not directly with the Soviet Union, since the latter desired to preserve its position of neutrality in the Far Eastern war. The four governments met at Dumbarton Oaks, an estate in Washington, D. C., in two separate phases. Conversations were held among the American, Soviet, and British delegations from August 21 to September 28, 1944, and among the American, British, and Chinese delegations from September 29 to October 7, 1944. Although the official record of the conversations has never been made public, at the conclusion of the conference, the areas of joint agreement were published as the Dumbarton Oaks Proposals.

A surprisingly large amount of agreement emerged from the conference in an atmosphere that was cordial and cooperative. Although the allies were taking the offensive on all fronts by the summer of 1944, victory was not yet assured and all still felt the close attachment of nations whose national existence was threatened by common enemies. This wartime spirit of unity and common cause that prevailed during the years leading up to the drafting of the charter is sometimes obscured from view by the hindsight of the cold war.

The Dumbarton Oaks Proposals were intended by the four governments to constitute a basis for discussions at the forthcoming general conference on international organization. Some of the major areas covered by the Proposals and specific suggestions are herewith summarized:

Dumbarton Oaks Proposals:

Purposes: Primary function of the new Organization was to maintain international peace and security. Beyond this, it was to encourage friendly relations among nations and achieve international cooperation.

Nature: The Organization was to be based on the sovereign equality of its members. Thus it was to follow in the tradition of early international organizations and the League of Nations in its fundamental character.

Membership: All peace-loving states were to be eligible for membership. Universalism was not established as a definite goal, but it could be assumed that in time all states would become "peace-loving" and, hence, eligible for membership. New members would be admitted through action by the Security Council and the General Assembly.

Organs: Five major organs were suggested for the new organization plus such subsidiary agencies as might be found necessary. A Security Council including all great powers as permanent members and a General Assembly comprised of all members would be the two major organs. In addition there would be a Secretariat, a Court, and an Economic and Social Council.

Competence: The Security Council would have primary responsibility for maintaining peace and security. There was full agreement that all decisions in this crucial area would be reached only with the unanimity of the permanent members. Regional agencies were permitted but were not to undertake enforcement action without the authorization of the Security Council. The General Assembly would be given authority to discuss and make recommendations for solutions to international problems. The Economic and Social Council was to be empowered, under Assembly jurisdiction, to make recommendations to foster economic and social cooperation.

The Yalta Conference

Several important topics were not settled in the Dumbarton Oaks conversations. No decision was reached on whether a new court should be established to replace the existing Permanent Court of International Justice. The question of how the new world organization would deal with the mandates system and the general problem of colonialism was avoided. More important than the omissions were disagreements which arose in several areas and which were to prove too fundamental to settle at any but the highest levels. They were eventually resolved at the final wartime conference of the Big Three—Roosevelt, Churchill, and Stalin—meeting at Yalta in the Russian Crimea from February 4 to 11, 1945. The Soviets had demanded at Dumbarton Oaks a comprehensive and unlimited veto power in the Security Council; at Yalta Stalin accepted a compromise that the great power veto would not apply to decisions on procedural matters and could not be invoked by a party to a dispute. On membership, the Soviets had sought the admittance as original members of each of the sixteen Soviet republics; at Yalta this demand was reduced to additional seats for two republics, the Ukraine and Byelorussia, and was accepted by Roosevelt and Churchill. The term "peace-loving," adopted at Dumbarton Oaks as a criterion of fitness for membership, was defined at Yalta to provide original membership for any state that had declared war on the common enemy by March 1, 1945. The definition was somewhat anomalous but at least it was operational. Agreement was reached on the delayed question of mandates; a trusteeship system would be established and territories placed under it would include existing League mandates, colonial holdings taken from the enemy states, and others voluntarily placed under trusteeship. A Trusteeship Council would be established to oversee the trust system. Finally, the Big Three agreed at Yalta that the five great powers would sponsor a United Nations Conference on International Organization to meet on April 25, 1945. San Francisco was selected as the site of the Conference.

The Yalta Conference helped resolve outstanding issues among the Big Three, but the publication of the Dumbarton Oaks Proposals raised murmurings among the small powers. The views of some of the small states were carefully set forth, somewhat to the annoyance of the United States delegation, at the Inter-American Conference on Problems of Peace and War held at Mexico City in February and March, 1945. They called for universality of membership, a more powerful General Assembly, more emphasis on a world court, a special agency to promote intellectual and moral cooperation, adequate representation for Latin America on the Security Council, and the settlement of regional disputes by regional organizations, like the Inter-American system acting in harmony with the new organization. Clearly the small powers were not going to accept passively great power domination in the framing of the new Charter or in the power structure of the organization itself.

To some extent, the Dumbarton Oaks Proposals also collided with the views of informed public opinion in the United States. The wartime propaganda for a new world organization had fostered a wave of idealism bordering on utopianism among segments of the public. The Proposals, conversely, were based on the bedrock of diplomatic realism, as were, also, the compromises reached at Yalta. Consequently, many of the idealists regarded the Proposals as a step backward from the League of Nations Covenant, pointing out that the principle of national sovereignty was proclaimed more strongly than it had been in 1919, that great power domination was more solidly entrenched, and that references to law and justice were more vague. Others who had been thinking in terms of a world federal union were brought harshly back to reality.

The great powers, however, could not wait for the building of a full public consensus; to prolong the process of constructing the framework of the new organization might run the risk of destroying existing areas of agreement as the war drew to a close. Suggestions for revisions and improvements could be explored at San Francisco. In the words of Franklin D. Roosevelt, addressing the Congress upon his return from Yalta, "This time we shall not make the mistake of waiting until the end of the war to set up the machinery of peace."

United Nations Conference on International Organization (UNCIO)

The United Nations Conference on International Organization opened in San Francisco on April 25, 1945, with forty-six nations represented. Four additional delegations representing Argentina, Denmark, Byelorussia, and the Ukraine were subsequently admitted to participate in drafting the Charter. These fifty plus Poland became the original members of the United Nations. The latter did not participate in the San Francisco Conference because the United States and Britain refused to recognize the Soviet-sponsored Provisional Government, but Poland was permitted to sign the completed Charter as an original member. The controversy over Poland's participation hinted strongly of the coming ideological conflicts within the new organization.

The San Francisco Conference was an exciting, spectacular affair. It worked in the full glow of world publicity, being the largest and probably the most fully reported conference in history. In all, 2,636 correspondents were accredited to the Conference, and they daily poured forth millions of words to a not-so-breathlessly waiting world. Within the Conference, the output of documents devoured several million sheets of paper each week. Moreover, the Conference basked in the warm glow of imminent victory. On the day the Conference opened the Russians announced that they had completed the encirclement of Berlin in the last major battle of World War II. A sense of history in the making pervaded the entire Conference. Most delegates seemed imbued with a sense of grave responsibility and, like the Founding Fathers at Philadelphia, they seemed fully aware that their hurried work would affect the lives of generations in the future. Although there was less of the pioneering spirit that had pervaded the Versailles Conference a generation earlier, the League years of futility and hopelessness were all but forgotten. The world was going to make a second try.

The process of writing the United Nations Charter resembled that of a democratic constituent body drafting a constitution. The Big Five provided the leadership and initiative in most of the decision-making. The

United States delegation was particularly conspicuous in its role as god-father of the new organization. Although diplomatic practice demands that the foreign minister of the host country be chosen as the presiding officer of an international conference, in the interest of great power unity the Conference chose the foreign ministers of the four sponsoring governments as co-chairmen.[2]

Most of the detail work of the Conference was carried on in committees. An International Secretariat, headed by Alger Hiss and recruited largely from the United States, provided technical assistance to the delegations and committees. Five official languages—English, French, Russian, Spanish, and Chinese—complicated the work of the Conference which labored without the aid of the smooth-functioning multilingual translation system of today's United Nations. English and French were the working languages of the Conference, which helped to reduce some of the confusion. All speeches were interpreted into the working languages and documents were translated into all five official languages. In general, the organization and procedures of the Conference were reasonably effective in providing opportunities for discussion and debate and fair hearing for the views of all delegations.

The Conference agenda was based on the Dumbarton Oaks Proposals as modified by the Yalta Conference. The Conference rules provided for freedom of discussion, voting equality, and substantive decision-making by a two-thirds vote of those present and voting. These ground rules theoretically gave the small states an opportunity to undo the work of the great powers, but in fact no substantial change in the great power position was effected. The threat of empty great power chairs at the UN table was incentive enough for the majority to defer to the few. The small powers did sometimes obtain concessions on matters of secondary importance which, in total, added up to a significant modification of the Proposals. Bloc-politics techniques were also used at the Conference, with the twenty Latin American states and five Arab states particularly active and effective. Commonwealth states, however, did not join Britain in a voting bloc, preferring to provide leadership to the attempts to modify the great power position.

The completed charter was signed on June 26, 1945, by the delegates of fifty nations, a formality that took more than eight hours. On the same date the delegates also signed a document on Interim Arrangements that established a Preparatory Commission consisting of representatives of all member states. The Preparatory Commission met in London during November to make arrangements for the first meetings of the major organs of the new organization. It made recommendations concerning United Nations procedures, the provisional agenda for the first meeting of the General Assembly, and the transferrence of certain activities from the League of Nations.

---

[2] France was invited to become a sponsoring government but declined.

Major Decisions

Although the basic framework of the new organization will be examined in detail in subsequent chapters, the principal modifications in the Dumbarton Oaks Proposals and Yalta decisions made at San Francisco and the issues involved are herewith summarized.

VOTING IN THE SECURITY COUNCIL. The major challenge to the great power position centered around the Security Council voting formula. Australia and other middle powers led a determined fight to limit the absolute veto, but the great powers remained adamant in defense of the Yalta formula. They conceded only in a formal statement to the Conference that they would not willfully use the veto to obstruct the work of the Council. Other efforts to weaken the position of the Big Five by enlarging the size of the Council, by eliminating permanent membership of the major powers, and by defining aggression in advance were all defeated in turn.

CHARTER AMENDMENT. The small and middle powers also undertook to alter the provisions for Charter amendment which permitted the major powers to veto any proposals for change. The Big Four again successfully demurred, but granted one concession, a provision for calling a Charter review conference. By the terms of Article 109, as finally agreed upon, a Conference to propose Charter revisions could be called by a two-thirds vote of the General Assembly and any seven members of the Security Council. If not called within ten years, the question would be placed on the Assembly's agenda and a simple majority vote in that body together with a vote of any seven members of the Council would institute such a review conference. The veto, therefore, would not apply to the convening of conferences to review the Charter, but it could be invoked at the ratification stage to kill all amendments and revisions regardless of how they were proposed.

ECONOMIC AND SOCIAL AREAS. The small powers, blunted in their attempt to achieve a greater role in security matters, successfully pushed the enlarging of the social and economic powers and responsibilities of the new organization. The Economic and Social Council was recognized as a principal organ and it was given powers to call international conferences, to prepare draft conventions, and to promote higher living standards, full employment, and universal respect for human rights. The expanded social and economic role of the organization was a clear victory over Soviet disinterest and intransigence, demonstrating at an early date that substantial majorities of small powers are a force to be reckoned with when great power primary interests are not at stake.

COLONIALISM AND TRUSTEESHIP. There was general agreement at San Francisco that the mandates system should be continued in some form, although the administering powers naturally hoped to keep international restrictions to a minimum. The United States as potential administrator of the Pacific Islands mandate wanted unhampered control of the islands for security purposes. Noncolonial countries, particularly those with a recent colonial past, were strong champions of international protection for dependent peoples, not only for those in the trust territories but for all living under colonial rule. The outcome of deliberations was a distinct compromise with something for everybody. Provisions for international supervision of trust territories were strengthened but made subject to special agreements to be concluded with each administering authority. A category of "strategic trust" was created to meet the security demands of the United States by giving ultimate supervision to the Security Council rather than the General Assembly. The most vigorous anticolonialists settled for a revised British and Australian draft declaration on non-self-governing peoples, which contained no binding commitments but expressed the principle of international concern for the welfare and ultimate self-government of all dependent peoples.

REGIONALISM. Many of the delegations at San Francisco were concerned that the Charter might preclude or impair the effectiveness of existing regional arrangements or those which might be concluded in the future. The American republics sought to avoid United Nations intervention in the Western Hemisphere, which was developing its own mutual security system. Other nations expressed similar concern that the organization not be empowered to override or replace regional arrangements. As a result, Article 51 was incorporated into the Charter guaranteeing that "nothing in the present Charter shall impair the inherent right of individual or collective self-defense. . . ." All such regional agencies were expected to keep their activities "consistent with the Purposes and Principles of the United Nations" and to recognize the prior right of the Security Council to take such enforcement action as it deemed necessary. Finally, Charter provisions were adopted encouraging the use of regional arrangements "to achieve pacific settlement of local disputes. . . ."

INTERNATIONAL COURT. The question of whether the existing Permanent Court of International Justice should be continued or replaced with a new court was avoided at Dumbarton Oaks. At Yalta the Big Three agreed to call a conference in Washington prior to the San Francisco Conference to draft an amended statute for a world court. At Washington members of the United Nations military alliance created a UN Committee of Jurists which reviewed the existing Statute and drafted a proposal with minor amendments. The San Francisco Conference adopted their proposal for the Statute of the International Court of Justice. Although the World Court under the League had achieved a position of respect and remained untarnished by the political and security failures of the League, the framers reasoned that the United States and the Soviet Union could more gracefully join a new court than one they had shunned for decades. The new court, unlike the old, was integrated into the structure of the world organization, with the Charter recognizing it as a principal organ of the United Nations.

PUBLIC SUPPORT AND RATIFICATION

After signing the United Nations Charter, the fifty-one signatory states undertook its ratification through their respective constitutional processes. The process of ratification varies from state to state, although it generally involves some measure of approval by the national legislative body. Such approval may be automatic in authoritarian governments and even perfunctory in democratic states, but in some, like the United States, it may be the crucial test for a treaty. Although the great majority of treaties submitted to the United States Senate over the years have received its consent, some of the most important ones, such as the Covenant of the League of Nations and the Statute of the first World Court, have been rejected.

From the time of the Moscow Declaration in 1942, the need for Senate approval was recognized as a major hurdle to be overcome. The new organization would also need the support of the House of Representatives to make American membership meaningful, for only Congress can appropriate money; and it was believed that in the early years, at least, American contributions would provide the main financial support for the United Nations. Since public opinion was the key to obtaining congressional support, the State Department devoted much of its energies during the war years to creating a favorable image of world organization. Following the Dumbarton Oaks conversations, the detailed Proposals were made public and the State Department began a massive campaign to acquaint the public with the plans for the new organization.

Although the State Department often has been accused of overselling the United Nations through extravagant and unrealistic promises, the evidence supports the view that it proceeded cautiously, yet optimistically, to acquaint the public with the proposed organization's nature and role. The State Department's "soft sell," with its emphasis on facts and problems, proved to be the kind of realism that the public understood. Idealism, though still abundantly evident, was tempered by a new pragmatism that viewed peace as more a matter of hard work and right decisions than of international institutions *per se*. President Truman, in his speech to the final session of the San Francisco Conference, reflected this mood of qualified optimism:

> It has already been said by many that this is only a first step to a lasting peace. That is true. The important thing is that all our thinking and all our actions be based on the realization that it is in fact only a first step.[3]

[3] *Department of State Bulletin*, Vol. 13, July 1, 1945, p. 3.

Many organized groups followed the lead of the State Department in publicizing the Charter and pushing for its ratification. The Department had taken the unprecedented step of inviting representatives of nongovernmental organizations to serve as consultants to the United States delegation at San Francisco. Many of the groups involved in the campaign for ratification had been among the forty-two that participated in the framing of the Charter, including such diverse organizations as the Chamber of Commerce, Rotary International, the American Farm Bureau Federation, and the League of Women Voters. Probably the most active was the United Nations Association—formerly the League of Nations Association—whose purpose was and continues to be the mobilization of public opinion in support of international organization. The leadership of labor unions, churches, professional associations, farm and business groups—a wide variety of interests from American society—sought to develop a genuine consensus supporting the United Nations as the logical starting point for maintaining peace. Although enthusiasm occasionally outran good sense, support for the United Nations was generally hedged with reservations growing out of the nation's new political realism and sophistication.

On July 28, 1945, the Senate of the United States approved the Charter of the United Nations by a vote of 89 to 2. The lopsided vote surprised no one. Never before in American history had a treaty been studied and debated so extensively both before and after its writing. Never had the Senate participated so directly in the major steps of the treaty process or had bipartisanship operated so successfully in removing a major treaty from politics. Never before, or since, had the State Department been so successful in stimulating organized group support for a major policy objective. In a very real sense the American decision to participate in the United Nations was in accord with the democratic principle expounded in the Preamble of the Charter: "We the peoples of the United Nations . . . have resolved to combine our efforts . . . and do hereby establish an international organization to be known as the United Nations."

On August 8, 1945, President Truman ratified the Charter of the United Nations and the Statute of the International Court of Justice which was annexed to it. The United Nations came into being at 4:50 P.M. on October 24, 1945, since established as United Nations Day. At that time the Soviet Union deposited its ratification and the Secretary of State, James F. Byrnes, signed the Protocol of Deposit of Ratifications affirming that a majority of the 51 original signers (29 nations) including all five great powers had deposited ratifications with the United States. All 51 signers of the Charter ratified it by December 27, 1945. On January 10, 1946, with the opening of the first General Assembly, the United Nations began to function.

Selected Readings

CLAUDE, INIS L., JR. *Swords into Plowshares*. New York: Random House, 1964, 3rd ed., Chap. 3.

DAVIS, M., GILCHRIST, H., KIRK, G., and PADELFORD, N. "The United Nations Charter . . . Its Development at San Francisco," *International Conciliation*, No. 413, September, 1945.

GOODRICH, L. M. "From League of Nations to United Nations," *International Organization*, February, 1947, pp. 3–21.

Report to the President on the Results of the San Francisco Conference, by . . . the Secretary of State, Department of State Publication 2349, Conference Series 71, Washington: Government Printing Office, 1945.

RUSSELL, RUTH B., and MUTHER, JEANETTE E. *A History of the United Nations Charter: The Role of the United States, 1940–45*, Washington, D.C.: The Brookings Institution, 1958.

Part II

The Process of International Organization

4 | *Legal Theories and Financial Realities*

The Charter As a Constitution

The United Nations Charter, formally written and ratified as a multilateral treaty, became a *de facto* constitution with the coming into being of the United Nations organization. Like most constitution makers, the framers had sought to create a working system that would facilitate the development of an administrative substructure, allocate responsibilities, grant and circumscribe powers, demarcate jurisdictions—in short, do those jobs which are typical of a national constitution. Common to every constitution also is the enunciation, usually in hortatory language, of the principles underlying the organization. The framers fulfilled this responsibility more than adequately.

The real test of any constitution comes in the transition from principle to practice. Meeting this test is an on-going process. Words take on new meanings constantly as different people interpret them and as changing situations and fresh problems call for solutions not in keeping with older interpretations. This is the process of constitution-building; it exists because constitution makers can never fully anticipate the changes that will inevitably occur. If the framers of a constitution are imbued with sufficient wisdom, the dynamic nature of a constitution will be recognized and no attempt will be made during its framing to freeze it in the mold of its current environment. The objective will be to devise a competent guide to action instead of a detailed plan of action, a contract, so to speak, with many of the pages left blank, to be filled in as individuals and circumstances, needs and demands, problems and issues require. Such is the continuing process of constitutional interpretation, growth, and development. Although the Charter is a lengthy and verbose document, the framers, whether by intent or accident, wrote much flexibility into it, as the more than twenty-year history of the United Nations indicates.

Problems of Constitutional Development

The problems of constitutional development for an international organization like the United Nations may closely parallel those of a national constitutional system, and a comparison can be a useful enterprise if the analogy is not carried too far. The United States Constitution, for example, has developed over the years largely through the process of executive, legislative, and judicial interpretation; the Charter of the United Nations has likewise evolved mainly through interpretation by its major organs, particularly the General Assembly, the Security Council, the Secretariat, and the Court. Custom and usage, where precise mandates are lacking or are ambiguous, have been significant forces in our national development and in shaping the United Nations system as well. When either system has reached a dead end because of legalistic straitjackets, ways and means have been found to bypass or ignore the strict letter of the law. Formal amendments have been relatively insignificant in American constitutional history and for the United Nations as well, since there have been only two formal Charter amendments.[1]

In the United Nations, however, the process of constitutional development is not so clearly delineated as in most national systems. The Charter is a multilateral treaty and, consequently, is a product of international negotiations. This means that the precise meaning and application of many words and phrases in the Charter were masked by the need for agreement at the time of negotiations. Since 1945, difficulties in translations, the vagaries of power politics, conflicts of national interests, the admittance of new members, ideological rivalries, and the lack of a final judge have all contributed to the continuing problem of interpretation and development. Not that many of these factors are absent in a national constitutional system, but it is their abundance and the amount of disagreement in a diverse world that add to the problem.

NEEDED: A CONSTITUTIONAL UMPIRE. Like the United States Constitution, the Charter does not establish a definitive constitutional umpire. Who, then, shall decide questions of jurisdiction, powers, competence, and procedures? Should the International Court of Justice as "the principal judicial organ" undertake a role similar to that assumed by the United States Supreme Court in the historic case of *Marbury* v. *Madison*? Should it be the General Assembly where all members are represented and on which the Charter has bestowed the power to "discuss any questions or any matters within the scope of the present Charter or relating to the powers and functions of any organs provided for in the present Charter"? Should each major organ determine the nature and extent of its own jurisdiction and procedures? Or should

---

[1] Two amendments to the Charter were proposed by the Eighteenth General Assembly in 1963, one enlarging the Security Council from eleven to fifteen and changing its voting majority from seven to nine, the other increasing the size of the Economic and Social Council from eighteen to twenty-seven. Both amendments were ratified and took effect in 1965. The Charter amendment process provides that amendments proposed by a two-thirds vote of the General Assembly must be ratified by two thirds of the members, including all permanent members of the Security Council. Each great power thus retains a veto over all *formal* changes to the Charter.

unanimity prevail, as it has traditionally with multilateral treaties, with constitutional issues resolved only through agreement of all signatory governments?

The question of establishing a constitutional umpire was never resolved at San Francisco because it was never specifically taken up. The result has been that all of the above methods, and many others, have been used to resolve constitutional issues in the United Nations system. Decisions on constitutional questions have included interpretations made by presiding officers, by majority and extra-majority votes in major organs and other bodies, by decisions of the Secretary-General and other Secretariat officials, by advisory opinions rendered by the Court, and by decisions of member governments made outside the United Nations framework but based on interpretations of Charter provisions.

POLITICAL INTERPRETATION. Subsequent chapters will examine some of the major interpretations of the United Nations Charter in the setting and context that produced them. It should be noted here, however, that most interpretations of the Charter leading to development of the United Nations system have been made *politically* by political organs rather than *juridically* by the International Court. This anti-judicial approach of stretching the Charter pragmatically to meet problems that a strictly legal review might not sanction has been a mixed blessing. Political interpretation has enabled the organization on many occasions to free itself from its own rules and limitations and has often permitted action when a strict legal interpretation would have foreclosed or hobbled it. It has also permitted broad changes in the United Nations constitutional system to meet new challenges, as in the adoption of the Uniting for Peace system in 1950 giving the General Assembly general peace-keeping powers bestowed solely upon the Security Council by the Charter. Often, stalemates induced by bloc voting and ideological rivalries have been overcome by political interpretations that permitted flexible approaches and encouraged compromise if not consensus.

Political interpretation, however, has pricked the conscience of many conditioned to the national concept of the "rule of law," producing a kind of moral schizophrenia. Where, some Americans have asked, does pragmatism end and Machiavellianism begin? The Soviets, often on the losing side in interpretation controversies, have vehemently but unsuccessfully inveighed against political interpretation on the ground that it violates treaty obligations, a charge not without some basis in fact. Probably most objectionable in such a free-wheeling system of change is the growing uncertainty as to what the Charter really means in specific areas and what, if any, are the limits to the organization's power.

Political interpretation, based on the views of shifting majorities, does not encourage members to entrust the organization with greater authority where their own interests may be affected. Thus, liberal interpretations may broaden the United Nations theoretical competence but actually make it less competent in a practical way to deal with matters brought before it. Since the East-West struggle has been one of the main factors underlying the use of political interpretation, a moderation of the cold war may encourage the United States to take a stand more favorably inclined toward judicial interpretation of the Charter, a position psychologically and morally more satisfying to Americans.

Constitutional Principles Embodied in the Charter

The analogy between national constitutional systems and that of the United Nations can also be extended to the realm of principles. Underlying the American governmental system, for example, are basic principles that provide the philosophical underpinning and moral justification for the constitutional structure. Most of these same principles in somewhat modified form are found in the United Nations system. Among the more significant UN principles are democracy, self-determination, equalitarianism, parliamentarianism, majoritarianism, the rule of law, justice, peaceful change, separation of powers, federalism, and delegated authority.[2]

Together they constitute basic rules of international ethics which all member states are ostensibly committed to observe. These rules are a projection into the international arena of purposes and principles already accepted as having national validity. In this sense, the Charter takes a first step in the direction of an organized international community independent of the organs set up for international decision-making. Even in the most democratic of states the ideals are never perfectly realized, and certainly a great gulf exists between theory and practice in the United Nations. Nevertheless, they serve not only the purpose of building unity by fostering a consensus of idealism but, in a practical way, provide guidelines for action.

MAINTAINING PEACE AND ORDER. Foremost among the objectives set forth in the Charter is that of maintaining international peace and security. This purpose, corresponding to the national goal of achieving a peaceful, stable domestic society, is sought through the collective security arrangements provided under Chapter VII, and through the procedures for the adjustment of international disputes set forth in Chapter VI. The framers of the Charter recognized that security is a necessary corollary of peace, a relationship given added international recognition by the Munich Agreement of 1938. The framers also specified that actions undertaken by the organization to

[2] The close relationship between national constitutional principles and those embodied in the United Nations system was emphasized by Secretary-General Dag Hammarskjold in his *Introduction to the Annual Report of the Secretary-General on the Work of the Organization,* tendered to the organization in 1961. See General Assembly *Official Records* (XVI), Supplement IA.

maintain peace and security should be "in conformity with the principles of justice and international law," thus providing a moral imperative to guide United Nations decision-makers. Seemingly, they failed to recognize that situations might arise in which justice and international law might be incompatible, forcing the organization to decide which should take precedence over the other.[3]

To facilitate enforcement action against an international lawbreaker, the Charter provides that all members "refrain from giving assistance to any state against which the United Nations is taking preventive or enforcement action." Nonmember states are also expected to act in accordance with these principles so far as necessary for the maintenance of international peace and security, a radical departure from traditional international law which provides that treaties cannot obligate nonsignatory states. The framers, however, recalled that in the 1930's major aggressions were perpetrated by Japan and Germany at a time when they were not League members. Since the United Nations would possess a near monopoly of power for the foreseeable future, no difficulties in applying the new principle were foreseen in 1945.

In June, 1950, nonmember North Korea provided the United Nations collective security machinery with its first major challenge. In the many limited wars that have broken out since 1950, in Viet Nam, Kashmir, Cyprus, Malaysia, the Congo, and elsewhere, the United Nations has played a significant role in ending hostilities or in preventing escalations into major war. In some instances, the United Nations has been forced to take over the role of the domestic government in trying to preserve or restore domestic peace and order in an insurgency–counter-insurgency situation.

HUMAN RIGHTS AND FUNDAMENTAL FREEDOMS. Many nations of the world are active today guaranteeing equal rights for their citizens, a concern reflected in the United States by recent civil rights legislation. A similar objective is set forth in Charter provisions which urge "respect for human rights and for fundamental freedoms for all. . . ."

The Charter also manifests concern for developing friendly international relations based on the principles of equal rights and self-determination. The latter ideals are spelled out in the Charter's Declaration Regarding Non-Self-Governing Territories and in the provisions concerning the Trusteeship

---

[3] See, for example, Hans Kelsen, *The Law of the United Nations* (London: Stevens and Sons, 1951), pp. 365–366. Professor Kelsen comments: "Since the principles of justice are not identical with, and sometimes in opposition to, the rules of positive international law, it may be impossible to comply with the postulate to conform with both, justice and international law. . . . The—probably not intended—effect of the formula in question is that the organs of the United Nations which act under the provisions of Article I, paragraph 1, second part, may refuse to apply the rules of existing international law if they consider them to be unsatisfactory, and apply principles which they consider to be 'just.' "

system. Although not intended to encourage demands for immediate independence of all subject peoples, the Charter's proclamation of equal rights and self-determination had the effect of giving legitimacy to the political aspirations of colonial peoples.

PROVIDING A GOOD LIFE. The United Nations, like national governments, is also concerned with broad economic and social objectives. In a sense, it is dedicated to building an international "Great Society" through cooperation. The Charter places more emphasis on solving such problems than did the League Covenant, a belated recognition that maintaining a peaceful world requires more than a system of collective security and dispute settlement. The framers recognized that the causes of war are varied and deeply rooted in the social consciousness of the world's peoples. The United Nations, therefore, should be a center for harmonizing the actions of nations to attain these common ends proclaimed by the Charter through consensus and cooperation. This role has increased in scope and complexity over the years and today consumes over eighty per cent of the attention and energy of the world organization.

SOVEREIGNTY AND STATE EQUALITY. The principle of equality before the law is a basic concept underlying democratic systems of government. Its counterpart in the United Nations is found in Charter proclamations of the sovereign equality of all member states. The principles of sovereignty and equality are attributes of statehood that have been recognized by the international community for centuries, and they relate to the supreme power exercised by each state within its territorial limits and its independence of action and freedom from external control. Since all states possess sovereignty, it follows that they are all juridically equal.

Yet within the organization there are some obvious contradictions to these principles. Two of the original members of the United Nations—Byelorussia and the Ukraine—were not and never have been sovereign states. Moreover, the power of the Security Council to make decisions binding upon all UN members implies a derogation from sovereignty; and the special status of the five permanent members is a clear case of juridical inequality within the organization.

In United Nations practice, the principle of sovereign equality is often invoked by the small states to support their claims to equality with the large states. More significant, probably, has been the tendency of some large states, particularly the Soviet Union and France, to use the principle to defend their national interests from the threat of majority decision. The result is that the principle of sovereignty probably has had a greater effect in restricting the role of the United Nations than in providing a leveling influence.

RULE OF LAW. Another fundamental principle of democratic states is that of the "rule of law," which holds that all persons, including public officials, must recognize the supremacy and binding force of law. The Charter seeks also to establish a system of United Nations legitimacy by calling upon all members in Article 2 to "fulfill in good faith the obligations assumed by them. . . ." and to "give the United Nations every assistance in any action it takes. . . ."

Since means of coercion typical of domestic legal systems are not found in the Charter, the "good faith" traditionally recognized in international law as *pacta sunt servanda* (agreements are to be kept) becomes a moral imperative for the members. Some sanctions are available, however, since members which do not fulfill Charter obligations in good faith may lose the exercise of their rights and privileges (Article 5), may be expelled from the organization (Article 6), or may lose their vote in the General Assembly (Article 19). None of these enforcement measures, however, has ever been invoked, although the financial crisis of the 1960's produced a major but unsuccessful effort to apply Article 19.

DOMESTIC JURISDICTION. In some national states, federalism provides for a system of government in which power is distributed by a written constitution between a central government and regional or subdivisional governments. In a somewhat related manner, Article 2 of the Charter recognizes a dual authority when it proclaims that nothing in the Charter should be interpreted to "authorize the United Nations to intervene in matters which are essentially within the domestic jurisdiction of any state. . . ." The application of enforcement measures to maintain peace and security under Chapter VII, however, is specifically excluded from the limiting clause. The domestic jurisdiction clause resembles the Tenth Amendment of the United States Constitution in that it makes explicit a division of powers and responsibilities between two levels of political organization and provides a limitation upon the higher level to safeguard the lower from unwarranted intrusions. In effect, this Charter principle simply states that only *international* questions and problems are proper subjects for United Nations inquiry and action, and that all *national* questions remain within the complete jurisdiction of member states.

Controversy among the members within the organization has centered on the nature and intent of the domestic jurisdiction clause, with differences over whether it provides a *legal* limitation or merely proclaims a *political* principle. In practice, the latter has generally been accepted, with decisions made by United Nations organs in keeping with the political realities of the situation. Internal problems within the Republic of South Africa, for example, have been debated extensively and resolutions condemning the apartheid system and maltreatment of Africans have been adopted despite repeated invocation of the domestic jurisdiction clause. The United Nations, however, has been singularly ineffectual in trying to force South Africa to take corrective actions or to permit a UN committee to inspect conditions within the state. Some states—France and Portugal, for example—have invoked the clause in refusing to submit reports to the United Nations on conditions in their colonies, holding that their overseas possessions are part of their "metropolitan territory" and, therefore, are matters of purely local concern.

Over a period of twenty years, domestic jurisdiction has probably functioned more effectively as a psychological deterrent to UN action than as a political or legal one. The clause appears merely to reflect the normal and natural limits of a world organization operating in the milieu of sovereign states, each zealously guarding its sovereign power over what it regards as its internal affairs. Creation of a world federal government would not eliminate this problem but would probably multiply it many times.

REGIONALISM. Interstate cooperation, a halfway house in the American constitutional system between the central government and the state units, has its international counterpart in the form of regionalism. The United States Constitution refers to this middle-level organization as "interstate relations"; in its politically activist form it is known as "cooperative federalism," connoting an extensive system of teamwork among the American states to solve common problems through uniform laws, joint actions, and common agencies.

International regionalism is a recognition by participating governments that not all problems are either national or global in scope. Some international ones may be confined to a geographical area, their solutions may require action by only a limited number of states, or psychological, technical, or administrative difficulties may delimit the ability of international agencies to function beyond the region. International regionalism exists, therefore, because groups of states have found it to be the most appropriate means of solving some common problems.

Popular support for this kind of limited internationalism indicates that the individual may be better prepared psychologically to accept a regional organization which is closer, both geographically and politically, to his own government than a distant global organization. Moreover, many such organizations have infranational relationships with individuals and groups within each of the member states, which in turn has stimulated transnational participation by political parties and interest groups having a common outlook or ideology, although located in different member states. Voting by party blocs rather than by state delegations in the Council of Europe, for example, highlights this kind of transnationalism.

The framers of the United Nations Charter, although theoretically committed to universalism, recognized the political investment in regional organizations extant in 1945 and accepted the feasibility of decentralizing some international operations concerned with security, political action, and economic and social welfare. The framers compromised on the issue by providing that regional organizations would serve as adjuncts of the United Nations system subject to a measure of control and direction by it. All such arrangements and activities must also be consistent with the purposes and principles of the Charter, although no apparent means exist for enforcing this rule. Under these provisions, a host of regional organizations have been established over the past twenty years in all areas of the globe (see Table 4-1).

Collective self-defense, authorized by Article 51 of the Charter has served as a basis for the construction of numerous regional alliances in the cold war. Whether such arrangements have contributed to peace and a stable balance of power, or have seriously hampered United Nations efforts by stimulating the arms race and producing fear and insecurity, remains an unresolved issue. Their future, however, seems assured since most governments caught up in the ideological struggle have become voracious consumers of security through mutual guarantee schemes, and the process feeds on itself.

The Charter also provides that regional organizations should contribute to security by making "every effort to achieve pacific settlement of local disputes . . . before referring them to the Security Council" (Article 52). The framers recognized, wisely as it turned out, that the Security Council would be suffocated by an avalanche of disputes and situations if some intermediate agencies for handling them did not exist. Yet, the problem of distinguishing between a case that involves only regional considerations and one that concerns international peace and security persists. The Organization of American States' handling of the Cuban and Dominican cases, for example, produced angry charges from some UN members that the crises threatened world peace and should be handled by the global rather than the regional organization. Unquestionably, under the Charter the Security Council could step in and "take over" the handling of such situations at any time, but since one of the great powers is likely to be involved in the regional group's action, a veto could result. It has also been generally assumed, though not always borne out in practice, that a dispute would be less likely to escalate if handled on a regional level.

A third basic role for regional organizations involves political, economic, and social cooperation. Here, too, collaboration rather than competition has characterized the relationship between the global organization and such groups as the Colombo Plan, the Organization for Economic Cooperation and Development, the Organization of American States, and the European Economic Community. Economic regionalism, in particular, has flowered in the past twenty years as states have tried to solve their trade, balance of payments, economic development, and technical-assistance problems through comfortable arrangements with neighboring or closely interdependent states.

TABLE 4-1. Principal Regional Organizations (1966)

Region	Primarily Military	Primarily Economic	Primarily Political
West Europe and Atlantic Community	(1) NATO (2) WEU	(7) Benelux (8) ECSC (9) EEC (10) Euratom (11) EFTA (12) OECD	(19) Council of Europe (20) Nordic Council
The Americas		(13) LAFTA	(21) OAS (22) ODECA
Africa		(14) CACM (15) UDEAC (16) EACSO	(23) OAU (24) OCAM (25) Council of the Entente
Asia and Pacific	(3) ANZUS (4) SEATO (5) CENTO	(17) Colombo Plan	(26) ASPAC (27) Arab League
East Europe	(6) WTO	(18) COMECON	
Non-Geographical			(28) Commonwealth

Organization	Founded	Members	Basic Objective
(1) North Atlantic Treaty Organization	1949	15	Defense of West Europe and Atlantic Area.
(2) Western European Union	1954	7	Maintain security of West Europe.
(3) ANZUS Security Treaty Organization	1951	3	Create military defense zone in Pacific.
(4) Southeast Asia Treaty Organization	1954	8	Maintain security of Southeast Asia.
(5) Central Treaty Organization	1959	4	Maintain security of Middle East.
(6) Warsaw Treaty Organization	1955	8	Integrate East Europe defense forces.
(7) Benelux Customs Union	1948	3	Establish common market, integrate economies.
(8) European Coal and Steel Community	1953	6	Establish common market for coal, steel and iron ore.
(9) European Economic Community	1958	6	Establish common market, integrate economies.
(10) European Atomic Energy Community	1958	6	Stimulate research and development of peaceful uses of atomic energy.
(11) European Free Trade Association	1959	7	Eliminate tariffs among members.
(12) Organization for Economic Cooperation and Development	1961	21	Develop joint policies for aid and economic growth.
(13) Latin American Free Trade Association	1961	9	Encourage economic development.
(14) Central American Common Market	1960	5	Encourage economic development and integration.
(15) Central African Customs and Economic Union	1966	5	Promote economic development and integration.
(16) East African Common Services Organization	1961	3	Coordinate transport, communication, finance, commerce, social services.
(17) Colombo Plan	1951	20	Promote joint development effort.
(18) Council for Mutual Economic Assistance	1949	9	Establish planned national specialization.
(19) Council of Europe	1949	18	Foster political unity in West Europe.
(20) Nordic Council	1952	5	Consultation on common problems.
(21) Organization of American States	1948	21	Promote joint hemispheric programs.
(22) Organization of Central American States	1952	5	Consultation on continental problems.
(23) Organization of African Unity	1963	38	Encourage political unity.
(24) Common Organization of Africa and Malagasy	1965	14	Promote political, economic, social development.
(25) Council of the Entente	1959	4	Political and economic consultation.
(26) Asian and Pacific Council	1966	9	Political and economic cooperation.
(27) League of Arab States	1945	13	Foster joint defense and social policies.
(28) Commonwealth of Nations	1924	26	Consultation and economic preferences.

AN EVALUATION: REGIONALISM VS. UNIVERSALISM. Regionalism is sometimes offered as an alternative to universalism instead of as a complementary approach. Debates involving the respective advantages of each approach have usually focused on the following points:

Pro-Regionalism:

1. Regionalism is more effective than universalism because its capacities are more realistically attuned to its objectives.

2. Regionalism involves fewer states than universalism and offers greater propensities for consensus because of common traditions, similar political, economic, and social systems, and the regional nature of the problems to be solved.

3. Regionalism tends to produce greater support from the peoples of the participating states than universalism because of a closer identification of common interests.

4. Regionalism permits a more appropriate handling of administrative, technical, and functional problems than universalism because the organization's machinery is better matched with the nature and scope of its operations.

5. Regionalism is a necessary precursor to effective global cooperation because it lays the groundwork for a broader consensus.

Pro-Universalism:

1. Universalism is a more appropriate means to preserve peace than regionalism since peace is indivisible; a war anywhere in the world threatens to engulf all.

2. Universalism encourages a more effective pooling of resources to attack economic and social problems; a pooling of African regional resources, for example, would result only in a sharing of African poverty.

3. Universalism encourages a consensus of mankind based on universal principles; regionalism encourages conflict between rival blocs and economic groups.

4. Universalism recognizes that disease, hunger, illiteracy, and poverty are common to all regions of the world; a common attack carried on by a single organization, therefore, will avoid duplication and make the most effective use of available resources.

5. Universalism as embodied in the United Nations already exercises broader powers over a greater variety of subjects than any regional organization; hence, to speak of regionalism as a necessary precursor to universalism ignores contemporary facts.

Although the arguments on both sides have intrinsic merit, such debates tend to be detached from reality because the dichotomy between regionalism and universalism is largely a false one. As already noted, both types of international organization exist today, both serve useful purposes, and, both are generally complementary to each other in their purposes and operations. The world has passed the point where it could choose between them as alternative approaches; it is an obvious fact that both are here to stay for the foreseeable future because both fulfill necessary functions on their respective levels.

FINANCING THE UNITED NATIONS

The question of how extensively a multilateral organization's principles are practiced can often be answered by an analysis of the organization's budget. The short history of international organization reveals that most states have been penurious to an extreme and often grudging in providing financial support. This propensity of states to invest only the most meager resources in the work of international institutions may reflect the limited character of their commitment, the poverty of their societies, or their disagreement with some of the activities carried on by the organization. Demands by statesmen for substantial benefits from such organizations are often balanced by equal disinclinations to contribute little more than lip service to their expensive operations.

Assessment Problems

This pattern of tight-fisted prudence on international budgetary matters was well established when the United Nations began its work in 1946. Efforts were begun at once to find an equitable but adequate financing formula by a special Committee on Contributions set up to prepare a scale of assessments. Members of the committee are supposed to be experienced in financial matters and drawn from states providing a broad geographical representation. In determining assessments, the committee was originally charged by the General Assembly to utilize the criterion of ability to pay as reflected by each state's total national income, per-capita income, economic dislocation caused by the war, and foreign-exchange earnings. These factors, with the exception of dislocation caused by war, remain the basic criteria for determining assessments today, although a "floor" and a "ceiling" limitation have been added. Assessments are paid as "contributions," but they are considered binding once the General Assembly has adopted the organization's annual budget. Unlike the League of Nations, which included financing for all technical programs within its general budget, each of the thirteen specialized agencies of the United Nations has its own budget and financial system, with Assembly oversight confined to consultation and recommendations. The United Nations budget system also differs from that of the League in that budgetary questions are decided in the Assembly by a two-thirds majority rather than by the unanimity rule that often came close to paralyzing League operations.[4]

In 1946 the first scale of assessments reflected the fantastic economic

---

[4] Articles 17, 18, and 19 of the United Nations Charter establish the Assembly's general authority over budget matters.

position of the United States in a world otherwise suffering from war's aftermath. The American assessment amounted to almost 40 per cent, with the remaining 60 per cent paid by the other fifty member states. Immediate objections were raised by American leaders who argued that the United States neither had that great a capacity to pay nor did it wish to weaken the organization by a heavy dependence upon a single source of revenue. American opposition took the form of a demand that a ceiling be established prohibiting contributions of more than one third of the budget by any one state, a position that was gradually accepted over a ten-year period, with the admission of new members and the economic revival of old members easing the transition. Total American contributions to the United Nations in the 1960's approach 50 per cent despite its regular budget assessment portion of 30 per cent, reflecting a sizable American support through voluntary contributions of special UN programs. These heavy American contributions are less impressive if measured strictly in terms of ability to pay, since about twenty members contribute a greater percentage of their respective Gross National Product (GNP) than does the United States.[5]

The poorer states of the world prefer that budget assessments be based strictly on each state's national income and ability to pay. The use of national per-capita income as a factor in the assessment scale has encountered objections from states with high national incomes and small populations. In deference to this protest, the Assembly established a rule that no state should be assessed more per capita than the largest contributor. Canada is the only state to date which has had its assessment reduced under this rule.

Some members, such as the Soviet Union, have been found to talk "poor" on budget questions, refusing to accept a higher rate of assessment, while on other occasions in nonbudgetary debates they have proclaimed their great economic advancements and achievements. Much of the debate over budgetary questions, in fact, involves cold war animus as well as controversies over money, thus making it doubly difficult to solve financial issues. The Soviet Union's share of the regular budget was 6.34 per cent in 1946, but after a vigorous campaign pushed by the United States it has been increased to almost 17.5 per cent, a figure which includes the separate assessments for the Byelorussian and Ukrainian Republics. When measured as a percentage of GNP, however, the Soviet's budget payments are less impressive since over fifty members contribute a greater share of their national income. Assembly rules not only limit the maximum contribution to 33⅓ per cent (in practice, usually about 32 per cent), they also establish a "floor" of 0.04 per cent which applies to each country whose percentage would be less under the formula (see Table 4-2).

[5] Norman J. Padelford, "Financial Crisis and the Future of the United Nations," *World Politics* (July, 1963), pp. 538–39. Top contributor when payments are measured as a percentage of GNP is Nationalist China, since her assessment is based on the resources of the Chinese mainland and Formosa and GNP is that of Formosa.

TABLE 4-2. United Nations Budget: Members' Scale of Assessments

Member States	Percentages (1966–67)	Member States	Percentages (1966–67)
Afghanistan	0.05	Ivory Coast	0.04
Albania	0.04	Jamaica	0.05
Algeria	0.10	Japan	2.77
Argentina	0.92	Jordan	0.04
Australia	1.58	Kenya	0.04
Austria	0.53	Kuwait	0.06
Belgium	1.15	Laos	0.04
Bolivia	0.04	Lebanon	0.05
Brazil	0.95	Liberia	0.04
Bulgaria	0.17	Libya	0.04
Burma	0.06	Luxembourg	0.05
Burundi	0.04	Madagascar	0.04
Byelorussian SSR	0.52	Malawi	0.04
Cambodia	0.04	Malaysia	0.12
Cameroon	0.04	Mali	0.04
Canada	3.17	Maldive Islands	0.04
Central African Republic	0.04	Malta	0.04
Ceylon	0.08	Mauritania	0.04
Chad	0.04	Mexico	0.81
Chile	0.27	Mongolia	0.04
China	4.25	Morocco	0.11
Colombia	0.23	Nepal	0.04
Congo (Brazzaville)	0.04	Netherlands	1.11
Congo (Dem. Republic of)	0.05	New Zealand	0.38
Costa Rica	0.04	Nicaragua	0.04
Cuba	0.20	Niger	0.04
Cyprus	0.04	Nigeria	0.17
Czechoslovakia	1.11	Norway	0.44
Dahomey	0.04	Pakistan	0.37
Denmark	0.62	Panama	0.04
Dominican Republic	0.04	Paraguay	0.04
Ecuador	0.05	Peru	0.09
El Salvador	0.04	Philippines	0.35
Ethiopia	0.04	Poland	1.45
Finland	0.43	Portugal	0.15
France	6.09	Romania	0.35
Gabon	0.04	Rwanda	0.04
Gambia	0.04	Saudi Arabia	0.07
Ghana	0.08	Senegal	0.04
Greece	0.25	Sierra Leone	0.04
Guatemala	0.04	Singapore	0.04
Guinea	0.04	Somalia	0.04
Haiti	0.04	South Africa	0.52
Honduras	0.04	Spain	0.73
Hungary	0.56	Sudan	0.06
Iceland	0.04	Sweden	1.26
India	1.85	Syria	0.05
Iran	0.20	Thailand	0.14
Iraq	0.08	Togo	0.04
Ireland	0.16	Trinidad and Tobago	0.04
Israel	0.17	Tunisia	0.05
Italy	2.54	Turkey	0.35

TABLE 4-2.   United Nations Budget: Members' Scale of Assessments—(*Cont.*)

Member States	Percentages (1966–67)	Member States	Percentages (1966–67)
Uganda	0.04	United States	31.91
Ukrainian SSR	1.97	Upper Volta	0.04
USSR	14.92	Uruguay	0.10
United Arab Republic	0.23	Venezuela	0.50
United Kingdom	7.21	Yemen	0.04
United Republic of		Yugoslavia	0.36
Tanzania	0.04	Zambia	0.04

Nonmembers' Scale of Assessments
(for specific activities)

Nonmember States	Percentages (1966–67)	Nonmember States	Percentages (1966–67)
Federal Republic of		Republic of Korea	0.13
Germany	7.41	Republic of Viet Nam	0.08
Holy See	0.04	San Marino	0.04
Liechtenstein	0.04	Switzerland	0.88
Monaco	0.04		

Contributions

(1) To the International Court of Justice: Liechtenstein, San Marino, and Switzerland.
(2) To the international control of narcotic drugs: Germany, Korea, Liechtenstein, Monaco, San Marino, Switzerland, and Viet Nam.
(3) To the International Bureau of Declarations of Death of Missing Persons: Germany.
(4) To the Economic Commission for Asia and the Far East: Korea and Viet Nam.
(5) To the Economic Commission for Europe: Germany.
(6) To the United Nations Conference on Trade and Development: Germany, Holy See, Korea, Liechtenstein, Monaco, San Marino, Switzerland, and Viet Nam.

United Nations Operating Costs

The regular United Nations budget involving normal operating expenses for the organization has gradually increased from $19 million in 1946 to over $120 million in 1966. The overall annual costs of the United Nations system have risen from an initial $50 million to current annual costs well in excess of $500 million. Overall operations are divided into four major budget categories: (1) the regular budget; (2) the specialized agencies; (3) the special voluntary programs, mainly related to economic development; and (4) the peace-keeping operations.

In the case of the regular budget, there have been no sudden major increases nor cutbacks over the twenty-year period; it has grown at a steady pace, and its fivefold increase reflects the added costs of a more than doubled membership, new programs, and rising salary and administrative costs. The peace-keeping operations budget, conversely, added the most abrupt and dramatic increases to the overall budget, starting in 1956 with the establishment of the United Nations Emergency Force (UNEF) for the Middle East. In the period from 1956 to 1966 the costs for UNEF ran to nearly $200 million, averaging almost $20 million each year. The United Nations Operation in the Congo (ONUC), though of shorter duration, was the largest and costliest peace-keeping venture undertaken by the United Nations, with total costs of over $418 million between July, 1960, and June, 1964, when the Congo force was disbanded.

Financing for special United Nations programs through voluntary contributions has provided another significant part of the rising costs of the organization's overall operations, averaging more than double the amounts spent annually through the regular budget since 1956. Most of these expenditures for special programs have been part of the United Nations efforts to help developing nations with economic aid and technical assistance through the United Nations Development Program (UNDP). In the 1960's, special programs have constituted the largest single budget category of the four noted above, with members' annual contributions averaging more than $200 million or approximately 40 per cent of the total United Nations budget. Finally, the annual budgets of the thirteen specialized agencies have risen gradually over the years in a gentle curve almost parallel to that of the regular budget. From budgets totalling about $20 million annually during the United Nations early years, these agencies have increased their operations to an average of over $100 million each year during the 1960's. Thus, the regular budgets of the United Nations and specialized agencies have shown a slow but steady increase over the years, reflecting increasing costs and gradually expanding operations, while the peace-keeping and special program budgets have fluctuated in response to urgent needs of the organization.

Almost necessarily, the cost of most UN activities is underwritten by a relatively few countries, creating an imbalance between financial contributions and Assembly votes (see Figure 4-1). Twenty members of today's United Nations contribute almost 90 per cent of the total regular budget, whereas sixty countries constituting almost half of the membership together provide only slightly more than 3 per cent. Many of these sixty nations have difficulty meeting even this minimal financial obligation, a circumstance which testifies to the great economic gap between the rich and the poor nations.

The problem was originally even more severe for most states in the days when contributions were assessed and collected solely in the currency of the host country and a substantial dollar shortage existed in most of the world. It has been ameliorated somewhat by a growing willingness to accept non-dollar currencies in partial payment of United Nations obligations, with the portion of local currencies fluctuating in recent years between 30 and 35 per cent of the total budget. Acceptance of local currencies has been made possible by the widespread geographical dispersion of United Nations programs, so that members' currencies now are often spent in financing local

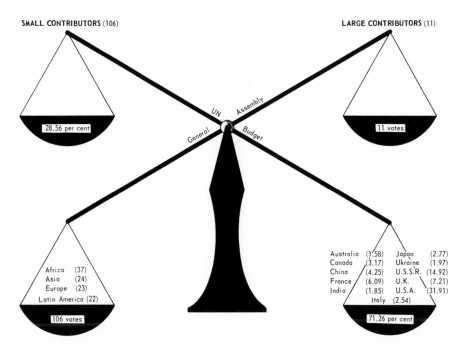

SMALL CONTRIBUTORS (106)

LARGE CONTRIBUTORS (11)

UN Assembly
General Budget

28.56 per cent

11 votes

Africa (37)
Asia (24)
Europe (23)
Latin America (22)

106 votes

Australia	(1.58)	Japan	(2.77)
Canada	(3.17)	Ukraine	(1.97)
China	(4.25)	U.S.S.R.	(14.92)
France	(6.09)	U.K.	(7.21)
India	(1.85)	U.S.A.	(31.91)
		Italy	(2.54)

71.26 per cent

FIGURE 4-1. Relationship of assessments to voting strength in the General Assembly, September, 1966.

projects. The difficulty remains, however, for undeveloped states to pay upwards of 70 per cent of their contributions in dollars, the coveted foreign exchange which they carefully hoard and prefer to expend in the purchase of machine tools and other capital goods that will help them meet development goals.

The Financial Crisis

All other budget problems of the United Nations were dwarfed by the financial crisis that paralyzed the organization in the 1960's. It involved first and foremost a political conflict over the role of the United Nations in peace-keeping operations. Only secondarily was it a crisis over the financial burdens of membership, although the deadlock materialized around the budget problem and resulted in the temporary bankruptcy of the United Nations. Financial difficulties growing out of the crisis have been moderated but still not overcome. A sizable debt is carried over from budget to budget, estimated in 1965 at $108 million, in addition to United Nations bonds outstanding amounting to well over $150 million of an authorized issue of $200 million.

The financial crisis involved not the regular budget but the special expenses incurred in the Middle East and Congo peace-keeping operations.[6] At issue were the refusals of the Soviet Union, France, and a majority of other members to pay their assessed portion of the costs for the UNEF and ONUC police forces, both costly but relatively successful ventures. The financial crisis raised the following questions about one or both of these operations:

Can security measures be undertaken only when the great powers concur in the Security Council, or are such actions also within the powers of the General Assembly?

Does the Secretary-General have the power to take action in an emergency situation which goes beyond the powers specifically delegated to him in Council or Assembly resolutions?

Can members be obligated to pay for special programs with which they disagree and vote against by the simple device of placing the program within the "regular budget"?

Can bonds issued by the United Nations to cover deficits incurred by peace-keeping operations be redeemed by regular budget assessments upon all members?

Does Article 19 of the Charter, which deprives a member of its vote in the General Assembly for incurring a two-year arrearage in contributions, apply to special peace-keeping costs?

Is the deprivation of voting privileges under Article 19 mandatory and automatic, or does it require a decision by the Assembly?

Can an advisory opinion of the International Court of Justice resolve the questions of responsibility for financing peace-keeping costs, and are individual members bound by its opinion?

Who should bear the costs of peace-keeping operations in the future?

The crisis involved, first, a basic political question over what role the United Nations should play and what specific policies should be employed to carry out this role. A consensus exists among member states that the United Nations should provide an institutional setting for parliamentary diplomacy, but when programs are proposed beyond this agreed minimum, significant political issues inevitably arise. Since France disagreed with the United Nations Middle East undertaking and both France and the Soviet Union refused to support some of the basic objectives of the United Nations Congo operation, financial issues followed in the wake of the political ones. Their refusals to pay the special peace-keeping costs in both operations were based on the constitutional position that General Assembly resolutions on peace-keeping are illegal, that the Security Council under Article

---

[6] The regular budget, although not directly involved in the financial crisis, became a matter of controversy in 1963 after the Assembly had voted the $200 million bond issue and provided for its redemption through regular budget contributions over a period of years. The Soviet Union and France refused to honor that portion of their assessments which related to bond redemption since, in their view, payments made with the borrowed funds were "illegal."

24 has exclusive jurisdiction over such matters, and that only assessments made by the Security Council under Articles 43, 48, and 50 are valid. The refusal of both nations to recognize the legality of Assembly resolutions based on the Uniting for Peace resolution of 1950 thus precipitated the organization's financial crisis.[7] According to the Soviet position, only the Security Council and not the General Assembly has the power

> to adopt decisions in all matters relating to the establishment of United Nations armed forces, the definition of their duties, their composition and strength, the direction of their operations, the structure of their command and the duration of their stay in the area of operations, and also matters of financing.[8]

The French position holds that it is the duty of the Security Council alone

> to lay down the mode of financing of the operation which it has decided upon or recommended, either in accordance with a scale to be decided upon when the expenses are divided among all the States Members, or in accordance with the system of voluntary contributions.[9]

Basic to the positions of both the Soviet Union and France is the view that the Charter, as a treaty among sovereign states, must be construed as conferring upon UN organs only those powers explicitly stated. As strict constructionists, both reject the expanded role of the General Assembly and, in particular, its decisions in the Middle East and Congo situations. Moreover, both oppose the role played by the Secretary-General in the Congo in making decisions on his own and using the Congo UN force in a manner not authorized by either the Council or the Assembly. The Secretary-General's actions were, in their view, a calculated effort to transform the office from that of an administrative officer carrying out decisions made by the Assembly and Council to that of a chief executive with powers to take the initiative and to make decisions. Since the Assembly and the Secretary-General acted beyond Charter powers in both situations, neither France nor the Soviets recognize any obligation to pay.

This constitutional position is supported by some of the numerous other members in arrears, but most of the non-Communist delinquents as well as many other UN members objected to the assessments for peace-keeping on

[7] The Uniting for Peace resolution provides that when the Security Council is unable to act in a peace and security crisis because of a veto, the General Assembly can, by a two-thirds vote, authorize members to take action against an aggressor. For a more detailed examination of the Uniting for Peace system, see Chapter 10. The Soviet Union's deficit, as of June 30, 1965, totalled $62,236,802, including assessments of $18,286,601 for UNEF, $39,223,085 for the Congo operation, and $4,727,196 for the regular budget; France owed $17,752,565 on the same date. Fourteen other nations owing about $40 million in unpaid assessments for over two years contributed to the crisis and brought the organization to the verge of bankruptcy.

[8] United Nations Document A/AC.121/2 (March 26, 1965), p. 4.

[9] United Nations Document A/AC.121/PV.7 (May 17, 1965), p. 11.

the ground that such costs should be based on a "special scale" rather than that for regular assessments. This scale should reflect "the special responsibility of the permanent members of the Security Council, the degree to which a state is involved in the situation giving rise to a peace-keeping operation, and the economic capacity of Member States, particularly of the developing countries." [10]

The Voting Impasse

The denouement of the complex financial crisis found the United States, Britain, and Canada leaders of a group which sought to force major delinquents to pay up or lose their vote in the General Assembly under Article 19. Their position was that the deprivation of voting privileges for states two years in arrears is mandatory and automatic, requiring no decision by the Assembly. This view was underscored by a 1962 advisory opinion of the International Court of Justice which held by a vote of 9 to 5 that the peace-keeping costs for UNEF and ONUC authorized by the Assembly were in fact "expenses of the Organization" within the meaning of Article 17, making all members responsible for paying them.

The implacable demand for all to pay collided head-on in the nineteenth session of the General Assembly (1964) with the immovable resistance to payment, and culminated in a virtual deadlock. To avert a showdown on the question of denying delinquents their Assembly votes, agreement was reached to avoid any formal voting and to make essential decisions solely on the basis of consensus. In this way, the United Nations, facing both financial bankruptcy and political collapse, was able to muddle through its most severe crisis intact.

Following the nineteenth session moderating forces of compromise began to take hold. The intransigent position of the United States mellowed with the recognition that no amount of pressure, whether by majority votes, a World Court advisory opinion, the threat of losing voting privileges in the Assembly, or even the imminence of a United Nations collapse, could force the financial hold-outs to pay. At a very practical level, the majority of UN members did not want to risk a confrontation that might wreck the organization. While a two-thirds majority might have reluctantly supported the United States in December, 1964, much of this support trickled away as members had second thoughts about the consequences of a showdown. Even American policy makers must have sensed the unrealism of supposing

[10] United Nations Document A/AC.121/4 (May 31, 1965), p. 17. Most of these delinquents accepted the peace-keeping roles of both the Assembly and the Secretary-General. Since the smaller nations generally favor an expanded role for the General Assembly and look to the Secretary-General to defend their interests, for them the crisis was financial rather than political in nature.

that a sovereign state could be forced to pay for UN programs of which it strongly disapproved. Carried to its logical outcome, the American position implied that a state must pay whatever sums the majority might choose to assess, for any purpose within the broad scope of the Charter, as the price of retaining voting membership. It is doubtful that even the United States was willing to pursue the principle to this logical conclusion.

American emphasis shifted from trying to force delinquents to pay to restoring United Nations solvency by voluntary contributions from the entire membership. Without conceding its position on financing and voting questions, the United States placed its new emphasis on achieving agreed procedures for financing future peace-keeping operations. The Soviet Union also moderated its position by offering to help the United Nations out of its financial difficulties by a voluntary contribution of a size and at a time to be decided solely by the Soviets. The Assembly gladly accepted the compromises of its two major financial supporters, and its twentieth session in 1965 found the Assembly returned to business as usual. The United Nations had somehow survived its biggest political-financial test.

Future Financing Problems

The search for a permanent solution to United Nations financing problems was assigned to a special Committee of 33 established by the General Assembly in 1964. Positions have changed little since the crisis. The United States and Britain continue to favor payment of peace-keeping costs by all members according to the regular assessment formula, the Soviet Union and France reject any responsibility for financing programs which they do not vote for, and most of the developing countries regard peace and security costs as "extraordinary expenses" that should be borne wholly or mainly by the great powers. The experience of the financial crisis makes clear that important members are not prepared to accept majority rule when it threatens their vital interests, and decisions cannot be forced upon them against their will. It also emphasizes that the majority of UN members are either reluctant or too poor to contribute any substantial amount to defray the cost of expensive police-force operations. What, then, is the solution to the long-range problem of financing peace-keeping and other burgeoning costs of the United Nations?

An approach used since the Assembly crisis to finance a UN police force on Cyprus won the acceptance of a unanimous vote in the Security Council. The United Nations Forces in Cyprus (UNFICYP) are financed by (1) the governments providing military contingents; (2) the government of Cyprus; and (3) voluntary contributions. Since the Soviet Union was willing to vote for the Force but not to finance it, and since the American position rejects regular assessments if other great powers refuse to contribute, the formula was the only workable compromise available. Its weakness, as noted by the Secretary-General in reviewing Cyprus operations, lies in the refusal of the great powers to provide voluntary contributions. This can only mean that the overt financial battles of 1962–64 are continuing covertly and are a source of great instability for the United Nations. The Cyprus formula can be only a temporary expedient but not a satisfactory long-range solution.

Another approach, offered by three African states and Cyprus in the midst of the financial crisis, aims at achieving a long-term solution by the creation of a permanent peace fund based on voluntary contributions. Such a fund could be used to clear up the current deficit, underwrite the costs of providing standby reserve units, and help defray at least the initial costs of future peace-keeping actions. Both France and the Soviet Union objected to the proposal on the ground that it would encourage a bypassing of the Security Council and would give the Assembly and the Secretary-General greater powers with fewer controls.

A British-sponsored approach involves voluntary contributions in the form of logistical support for national detachments by members acting individually. Under this system a number of states would finance standby reserve units of their own nationals or those of other states, equipping, training, and transporting them. All units would be subject to call by the Secretary-General upon instructions from the Council or Assembly, thus providing a quick response to an urgent need when peace is threatened. Again, those states that fear the organization will be used against them or their friends, or in such a way as to threaten their national interests, refuse to join in such arrangements.

Various approaches involving special scales of assessment for peace-keeping costs, rebates to developing countries, nonassessment for states voting against an operation, and other schemes suffer from much the same weaknesses as those discussed. These are (1) the widely held view among developing nations that peace-keeping costs are "extraordinary" expenses whose burden should be borne mainly by the developed states; (2) the absolute refusal of states that disagree with peace-keeping decisions to support them financially; and (3) the reluctance of states backing such policies to pay a disproportionately heavy part of their costs if other members refuse to pay. These dilemmas have produced a search for new, more dependable sources to finance at least a portion of the UN budget independently from its members.

NEW SOURCES. The possibilities of additional sources of income for the United Nations independent of its members are numerous, but so far no systematic exploration of them has been undertaken by the organization. Members have evinced little interest in giving the organization a substantial independent income. Scholarly friends of the United Nations, however, have engaged in extensive speculation concerning potential sources and their technical and political feasibility.[11] Although many such sources would require Charter amendment or basic changes in the United Nations structure, the principle of revenue production independent of members' contributions is well established. Each year the organization nets over $2 million from its headquarters' businesses involving stamp sales, a gift shop, investment income, and guided tours. Although this amounts to less than 3 per cent of the annual regular budget, other proposals to secure independent sources of revenue would be extensions of this principle, already accepted by all members.

Suggestions for new sources run the gamut from those which would provide minor amounts of supplemental income to those which might in themselves finance most or all UN activities. As might be expected, sources which offer the greatest potential for substantial income are also the least feasible politically. With no attempt to assess their relative merits, new sources for UN income might include the following:

1. Private contributions in the form of individual gifts, inheritances, and foundation grants; these sources could be encouraged through a joint policy of all member states making such contributions deductible expenses from national taxes.

2. Charges levied by UN agencies for services performed; for example, the World Meteorological Organization could charge a service fee for its weather data and the International Telecommunications Union could issue international radio licenses for substantial fees.

3. Tolls charged for various kinds of transportation and communications, facilitated in today's world by United Nations programs; these might include such charges as national mail commissions or the sale of UN stamps for all international mail services, tolls levied upon the ships of all nations using international waterways and canals, and air traffic using international air space.

4. Fees for international travel imposed through levies on passports and visas, by payments made to UN collectors at international boundaries, or by surcharges on national customs duties.

5. Profits earned through a UN international investment corporation, which could exploit the mineral and other forms of wealth in the seabeds of international waters and in Antarctica.

6. Charters sold to private companies or governmental agencies authorizing them to exploit the resources of the seabeds and Antarctica, with royalty rights reserved by the United Nations.

7. Fishing, whaling, and sealing rights in international waters, assigned to countries or private companies upon the payment of "conservation" fees to the United Nations.

[11] See, for example, John G. Stoessinger, "Financing the United Nations," *International Conciliation,* No. 535 (November, 1961); Arthur N. Holcombe (Chairman, Commission to Study the Organization of Peace), *Strengthening the United Nations* (New York: Harper, 1957), pp. 250–62; and John G. Stoessinger and Associates, *Financing the United Nations System* (Washington, D. C.: The Brookings Institution, 1964).

8. Rights to the use of outer space, or the operation of outer space programs by the United Nations, aimed at producing revenues through communications satellites, meteorological systems, and the future development of resources on the moon and other planets.

9. Taxes levied upon member states, collectible by their governments, and based on ability to pay judged by national income.

10. Taxes levied directly upon individuals through the cooperation of member states, based on income with a mild graduation of rates.

11. Issuance of an international currency, backed by national reserves, which could serve the dual function of financing UN programs and providing an international monetary reserve unit to ameliorate the continuing international liquidity problem.

Such sources, and the above are only a sampling of the possibilities, would reduce or eliminate the dependence of the United Nations upon national contributions. With a sizable independent source of income, peace-keeping operations and economic and social programs could be undertaken without fear of national reprisals or organizational bankruptcy. Members, however, may not regard financial independence for the organization as a virtue since it would reduce their control over the organization and its activities.

The financial crisis of the organization has made it clear that no amount of financial stability will solve the problems of ideological hostility and national particularity; in the final analysis, the problem of financing the United Nations programs is one of developing an international consensus and building a world community. Political accommodation remains a fundamental prerequisite to fiscal solvency.

Selected Readings

BRIERLY, J. L. *The Covenant and the Charter.* New York: Macmillan, 1947.

CHASE, EUGENE P. *The United Nations in Action.* New York: McGraw-Hill, 1950.

GOODRICH, LELAND M., and HAMBRO, EDVARD. *Charter of the United Nations, Commentary and Documents.* Boston: World Peace Foundation, 1949 rev. ed.

HAAS, ERNST B. "Regional Integration and National Policy," *International Conciliation,* No. 513, May, 1957.

LAWSON, RUTH C., ed. *International Regional Organizations.* New York: Praeger, 1962.

STOESSINGER, JOHN G., and ASSOCIATES. *Financing the United Nations System.* Washington, D. C.: The Brookings Institution, 1964.

TAUBENFELD, RITA F., and TAUBENFELD, HOWARD J. "Independent Revenue for the United Nations," *International Organization,* Spring, 1964, pp. 241–67.

WATKINS, JAMES T., and ROBINSON, J. WILLIAM. *General International Organization: A Source Book.* Princeton: D. Van Nostrand, 1956.

5 | Instruments of Political Decision-Making

U nited Nations operations revolve around the functions of six principal organs: the General Assembly, the Security Council, the Economic and Social Council, the Trusteeship Council, the Secretariat, and the International Court of Justice (see Figure 5-1). The organization and processes of the Assembly and three Councils will be discussed in this chapter; the Secretariat and the International Court will be presented in later chapters.

THE GENERAL ASSEMBLY

Central to the sprawling organization, resembling the Parliament at Westminster in its unifying role, the General Assembly functions as the focus for United Nations activities. "Global Parliament," "Town Meeting of the World," "Sun of the UN Solar System"—these and other catch-phrases are used to sum up, perhaps somewhat inaccurately, the General Assembly's widely diffused activities and diverse roles. Unlike the Security Council which pays homage to the elitism of great power politics, the Assembly effuses the democratic ethos of *egalitarianism, parliamentarianism,* and *majoritarianism.*

Equality of Members

The Assembly's *egalitarian* nature should be obvious to even the casual United Nations visitor: it is the only one of the six principal organs in which all member states are represented. All are represented equally, with ten delegates and one vote for each member. Efforts by some of the great powers to suggest a change to a weighted voting system have never been taken seriously by the small and middle powers. The traditional equality of all states, large and small, under international law and as participants in international conferences provides the legitimacy for retaining equal voting. The political defensiveness of the new states, some of which formed their

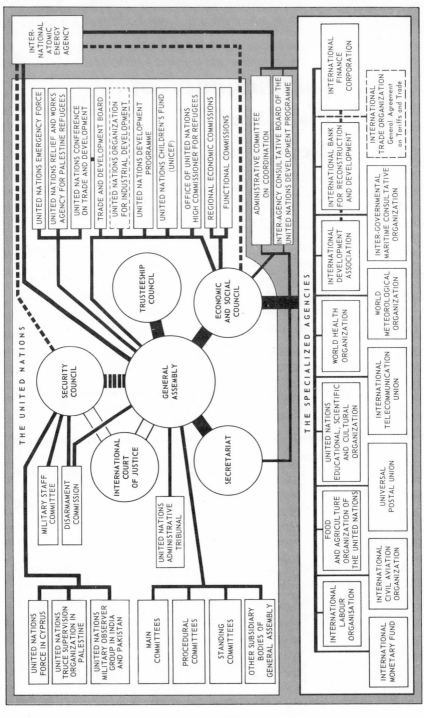

FIGURE 5-1. United Nations organizational chart, March 31, 1966. [*Source: United Nations Office of Public Information.*]

Assembly delegations at the same time they established their first governments, safeguards the principle. This equality permeates the work of the Assembly, including that carried on by its seven main committees with all members represented on each.[1]

Parliamentary Role

The parliamentary nature of the Assembly becomes evident in observing its *modus operandi*. It may be, as an astute British observer has noted, that the Assembly's operations are "a far cry from anything at Westminster." The British system's "focus" on a legislative program, its emphasis on "responsibility," its "party-whip discipline," its organized "majority and opposition," are missing or hardly discernible in the Assembly hall. Yet, the agenda is adopted, debate proceeds, votes are taken, and decisions made. To a Britisher, the processes may be puzzling but picturesque: "Like a herd of grazing cattle, that moves as it chews, head down, the Assembly gets through its day [or more often its morning] without any particular drive, yet not without a certain vaguely diffused sense of purpose." [2]

In a search for analogies, the Assembly's parliamentarian qualities may be found to resemble the continental European parliaments with their multiparty coalitions, ideological rivalries, and shifting centers of power, more closely than the orderly, compact British model. Or a watchful observer might note some similarities between the Assembly's operations and those of the American Congress. Both are more often than not caught up in clashes of parochial interests and must attempt to harmonize regional, class, creed, and racial conflicts. Both must grapple with procedural rules that often complicate rather than expedite the process of decision-making. The American federal system produces an attachment to states' rights in somewhat the same manner that the sovereign states of the world with their attachments to national interests produce a loose, untidy, somewhat anarchistic General Assembly. Yet, a parliament's main role is concerned with freedom of debate, in which issues can be discussed, decisions made, budgets approved, taxes levied, and administrative operations supervised. The General Assembly resembles all national parliaments in these significant functions. Although it does not possess a direct lawmaking authority, its competence to discuss and debate extends to *any* problem of the world or of the organization itself which a majority of members regard as proper for Assembly consideration.

---

[1] The seven standing committees of the Assembly are the First (Political and Security); the Special Political (originally an ad hoc committee which has remained numberless although now a permanent committee); Second (Economic and Financial); Third (Social, Humanitarian, and Cultural); Fourth (Trusteeship); Fifth (Administrative and Budgetary); and Sixth (Legal).

[2] H. G. Nicholas, *The United Nations As a Political Institution* (London: Oxford University Press, 1959), p. 90.

Majority Rule

The Assembly's *majoritarian* approach to decision-making is an improvement over that of the Assembly of the League which required unanimity for most actions.[3] Still, consensus, not overpowering majority votes, is the objective of Assembly politics. Consensus demands compromise, and compromises in the Assembly are sought through negotiations, pressures, demands, debates, promises, and other techniques of parliamentary diplomacy which, in art and form, closely resemble the "politics" that keeps the wheels turning in the American Congress. Numerous caucusing groups meet, plan strategy, and negotiate with other groups before significant decisions are made. The process of forging a majority resembles that of the continental parliaments where no party has a majority and policy evolves out of fleeting coalitions.

In its formative years, Assembly decision-making was largely a product of American direction and influence. The great influx of new members in the late 1950's and early 1960's has eroded but not eliminated this role, forcing the American delegation to ultimate tests of leadership in place of earlier dependence upon automatic majorities. Other great powers have also been affected by this growing independence and assertions of authority by Assembly majorities, since a veto in the Security Council no longer stops action but merely transfers the issue to the Assembly where no veto exists. Moreover, in the Assembly a voting defeat carries the stigma of condemnation by world opinion, a factor of no small consequence in a world in which great powers compete through propaganda and ideological warfare for the minds of men.

Formal Organization

Regular sessions of the General Assembly are held each year beginning on the third Tuesday in September.[4] At the beginning of each session the Assembly establishes a target date for adjournment, usually mid-December, but it is seldom met. Special sessions may be convoked if requested by the Security Council or if a majority of Assembly members agree. It is quite unique for the Assembly to confine itself to its regular autumn session, since pressing issues or dispute crises inevitably arise during the year. Emergency

---

[3] The Charter, Article 18, provides that decisions on "important questions" be made by a two-thirds majority of members present and voting. All other questions require only a simple majority. "Important questions" include those mentioned in Article 18 (peace and security recommendations, elections to the three UN councils, admission, suspension, and expulsion of members, trusteeship and budgetary questions, and those which the Assembly decides by a majority vote are to be considered "important").

[4] Through agreement of members, a regular session may begin at a later date. In American presidential election years, the opening is usually postponed until after the election to avoid the politically charged atmosphere.

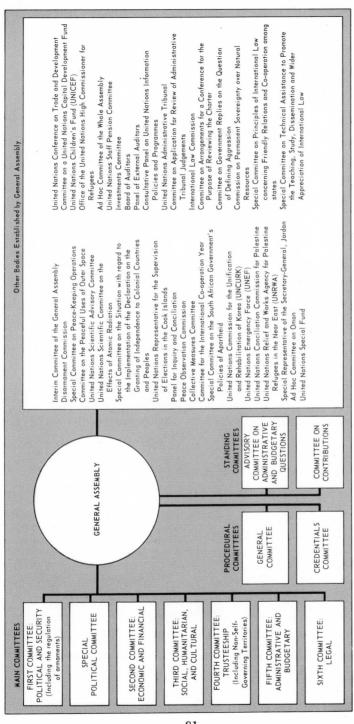

FIGURE 5-2. Structure of the General Assembly. [Source: *United Nations Office of Public Information.*]

81

special sessions may be convened within twenty-four hours under ·the Uniting for Peace resolution if a veto blocks action on a peace and security matter.

The first job facing a new Assembly each year is to elect a President and seventeen Vice-Presidents who serve for one year. It has become traditional to select as President a leading international statesman from an important small- or middle-power state. The vice-presidencies are allocated to the five great powers and to geographical areas of the world to ensure their representative character and a fair apportionment of prestige.[5] The President, the Vice-Presidents and the chairmen of the seven standing committees constitute the General Committee which functions as a steering committee for each session.

Although his formal powers are limited, the President may accomplish much through his personal influence and political adeptness. Qualities desirable to abet this role as presiding officer of the Assembly include a "refusal to be bored, a memory for faces, a capacity to slough off private and national partialities, a sense of humor coupled with a concern for the dignity of his office, a ready grasp of procedural technicalities, a proper sense of pace, and a quick feeling for the sense of the meeting." [6] Seated beside the President at all Assembly sessions is the Executive Assistant to the Secretary-General who functions as parliamentarian and adviser to the President in his role of Secretary of the General Assembly. Although the President's formal powers to control or influence the direction of debate and action resemble more closely those of the President of the United States Senate or the Speaker in the House of Commons than those of the Speaker of the House of Representatives, the very disarray of the Assembly itself demands strong yet tactful guidance. The international reputations of the Presidents, from M. Spaak of Belgium in the First Assembly to Amintore Fanfani of Italy in the Twentieth, have helped each to weather many verbal storms and to develop the office into a respectable source of Assembly power.

Proposals to Streamline the Assembly Procedures

A consensus has existed among Assembly delegations for some years that the Assembly must somehow find the means for streamlining its procedures in order to expedite the work of the organization. The rapid growth in membership has added a degree of urgency in the 1960's as the Assembly becomes further mired in procedural quicksand of its own making. Little

---

[5] In 1963, at the time when the number of Vice-Presidents was increased from thirteen to seventeen, a formula was adopted to provide for the election of seven from Asia and Africa, one from East Europe, three from Latin America, two from Western Europe and "other states" (Canada, Australia, and New Zealand), and five to the permanent members of the Security Council. These figures total eighteen because the region from which the President is elected receives one less than the formula specifies.

[6] H. G. Nicholas, *op. cit.*, p. 92.

agreement, however, has existed over the means of achieving the desired efficiency.

The Seventeenth Assembly in 1962 tried to face up to this problem by appointing an ad hoc committee to study and make recommendations on "Improvement of the methods of work of the General Assembly." The committee's report to the eighteenth session was devoted to four aspects of the problem: the organization of sessions, the conduct of debates, the work of committees, and the means of voting. Recommendations to the Assembly included:

1. Reduce time wasted during each session. The Committee computed the equivalent of 67 working days lost during the seventeenth session because meetings started late or ended early. Better scheduling of speakers and the relegation of those not prepared to speak at their appointed time to the bottom of the list were suggested. Joint statements by a number of delegations with the same viewpoint and written statements instead of oral were encouraged.

2. Expedite the Assembly's "general debate" that opens each session. Time spent on general debate has averaged over 30 plenary sessions each year during the 1960's and often speeches made by heads of government and foreign ministers during general debate are repeated by heads of delegations later in regular debate. Solutions: the Assembly President, the Secretariat, and member delegations must cooperate to "organize" general debate; presiding officers should propose a time limit on speeches; and speakers must exercise some self-restraint in their speech-making.

3. Committee work should be better organized and speeded up. Committees should start their work early in each session and should coordinate their activities through the steering committee. Related items should be grouped to reduce the proliferation of subjects on the agenda of committees. Creation of more sub-committees would help free the main committees from the detailed work of drafting resolutions.

4. Accelerate the voting process in the Assembly and main committees. An average session in the 1960's has required about 500 roll-call and show-of-hands votes. The use of electric voting equipment would provide for quicker, cheaper, and more accurate voting and would free the Assembly for other important tasks.

Many of the special committee's proposals have been implemented since 1963, including the introduction of mechanical voting equipment in 1965. Ultimately, the orderliness and dispatch with which a body like the Assembly conducts its procedural work depends upon the proficiency of the officers and committee chairmen and the willingness of heads of delegations to exercise vocal restraint in the interest of moving ahead. Critics have charged that unless greater efforts are made by all to expedite Assembly business, endless speech making and procedural wrangles may seriously restrict the Assembly's ability to act. Expansion of the General Assembly Hall in 1964 to accommodate 128 delegations presaged a membership in the near future that will place ever greater strains on the existing machinery.

Assembly Decision-Making

THE AGENDA. The decision-making process in the General Assembly generally begins with a prolonged battle over the agenda. Perhaps it might better be described as a series of skirmishes since arguments over the agenda continue intermittently throughout most of each session while debate on agreed-upon agenda items proceeds. Each agenda controversy involves a political disagreement over Assembly—and hence United Nations— powers. Efforts to keep an item off the agenda constitute the opening round, and in some cases the final one, in the opposition's bag of parliamentary maneuvers to defeat a proposal. Legal, political, financial, social, even humanitarian arguments, may be offered as justification for removing a disputed question from Assembly consideration. Most, however, are based on the constitutional position that the Charter bans such interventions as "matters which are essentially within the domestic jurisdiction of any state." Some questions, such as that of Chinese representation in the United Nations, have been fought out year after year as agenda battles. Sometimes overlooked is the fact that keeping an item off the agenda constitutes a decision by the organization just as an affirmative action is a decision. Also, keeping an item off the agenda does not prevent its proponents a hearing since agenda debates involve the pros and cons of the substantive matter as well as procedural questions.

THE COMMITTEE PROCESS. Consideration of agenda items begins in one of the seven standing committees of the Assembly. Most matters receive their most thorough airing and consideration at this stage, since the press of time permits the cumbersome Assembly to explore extensively only the most politically explosive issues. Increasingly, as in legislative bodies like the American Congress, a committee's report is accepted in Plenary with only perfunctory debate. This trend has had the effect of creating eight assemblies with a full complement of members in each, a development that has helped to keep the business of the Assembly moving forward but has also added to the general confusion of Assembly decision-making.

THE ROLE OF DEBATE. Debate in the General Assembly is another facet of its political process. At the start of each annual session the Assembly subjects itself to a time-consuming ritual known as general debate. The debate is general, since most members participate in it, but it can hardly be construed to be debate. It consists of broad and often unrelated statements by a succession of speakers concerning such matters as the state of the world, national grievances and accomplishments, and broad-gauged solutions for the world's problems. Basically, the idea is to permit each member to unburden itself in one major talk-fest so that, hopefully, the remaining portion of the session can be devoted to the organization's business.

Once the ordeal of general debate is over, the Assembly, mainly in its committees, can turn to the business of discussing specific items on its agenda. It may explore general issues or give the parties to a dispute an opportunity to air their grievances. Eventually, however, discussion is focused on proposals aimed at reaching a decision. Such decisions may or may not entail subsequent actions by the United Nations. They may involve procedural matters of the Assembly itself or of the organization; they may be concerned with substantive matters on which the Charter has empowered the Assembly to act; they may embody recommendations for some form of national action; or they may involve attempts to conciliate disputants or provide a call for collective action against an aggressor. Decision debate is usually reasonably focused and limited by the presiding officer according to the Rules of Procedure of the General Assembly.[7] Most of the discussions that take place following the period of general debate are directed toward some form of Assembly decision.

Assembly Functions

Against a backdrop of politics and diplomacy, the Assembly carries out the responsibilities assigned to it by the Charter. Assembly functions may be classified as (1) *hortatory*, (2) *quasi-legislative*, (3) *investigatory*, (4) *interpositional* and *conciliatory*, (5) *peace preservative*, (6) *budgetary*, (7) *supervisory*, (8) *elective*, and (9) *constituent*.

The Assembly has indulged in *exhortation* aimed at member states, non-members, great powers, the Security Council, other major organs—even the General Assembly itself. Sometimes referred to as "manifestoes against sin," these resolutions are the means by which the Assembly carries out the role which its supporters regard as guardian of Charter principles and the conscience of mankind, and its detractors write off as sheer hypocrisy. Through such resolutions the Assembly has called upon the permanent members of the Security Council to use the veto with restraint, the great powers to cease their war propaganda, all states to accept the maxim of peaceful coexistence, and disputants to settle their controversies peacefully according to Charter principles.

The Assembly's *quasi-legislative* function, carried on through the adoption of resolutions, declarations, and conventions, goes beyond exhortation in seeking to develop and codify international law, and to protect human rights and fundamental freedoms. In this role the Assembly most closely approximates the lawmaking activities of a national legislature. Conventions adopted by the Assembly, like the Genocide Convention that outlaws mass

---

[7] *Rules of Procedure of the General Assembly*, United Nations Publication, (New York, September, 1965). Under the rules, a majority of the Assembly may limit the time allowed each speaker and the number of times each representative may speak on a question. At any time during debate, the President may announce a list of speakers to be heard and, with the consent of the Assembly, declare the list closed. The same rules for limiting debate apply to the seven main committees.

murder of national, racial, or religious groups, become operative as law after they have been ratified by the required number of states. Many resolutions require statutory implementation by member states so that international standards apply to the conduct of individuals. Just as the Universal Declaration of Human Rights of 1948 typifies Assembly efforts at exhortation, the quasi-legislative function aims at translating these principles into law. Various covenants of human rights have been framed or are being framed by ECOSOC commissions for eventual adoption by the Assembly and ratification by member states. Where consensus and a will to act exist among members, the Assembly can truly function as a world parliament within its limited quasi-legislative role.

The *investigative* role of the Assembly complements both its quasi-legislative and dispute-settlement functions. The former is best illustrated by the work of the Assembly's International Law Commission which has conducted studies since 1948 aimed at the preparation of draft codes to develop and codify international law. Like a national legislature, significant facts must be accumulated, usually by regular or special committees and commissions before the Assembly acts. In the settlement of disputes, investigation is an essential prelude to a determination of the issues involved, the current facts, and the working out of a fair and just solution.

Assembly *interposition* and *conciliation* are special functions related to dispute settlement and are exercised similarly to those carried on by the Security Council. Assembly interposition becomes an essential action when the Security Council is unable to function because of a deadlock or a full agenda of other disputes and situations. The interposing of an Assembly presence in the Middle East in the form of the United Nations Emergency Force (UNEF) following Council vetoes illustrates this back-up role. Assembly conciliation of numerous disputes has involved the use of a variety of techniques, including good offices, mediation, commissions of inquiry and mediation, cease-fire orders, and the appointment of renowned individuals to serve as mediators.

In its *peace preservative* role, the Assembly likewise fills in the void left by Council vetoes. Since 1950, the Uniting for Peace resolution has empowered the Assembly to make appropriate recommendations for collective measures, including "in the case of a breach of the peace or act of aggression the use of armed force when necessary." Assembly actions to maintain or restore international peace and security have been undertaken in the Middle East and Hungarian crises of 1956, the Lebanon and Jordan crises of 1958, the West Irian case in 1961, and the Congo situation from 1962 to 1964.

The Assembly's *budgetary* function resembles that of a national legislature's traditional "power of the purse." All UN programs and activities of subsidiary bodies come under a measure of financial surveillance and control since all must be supported financially. Budget decisions have on occasion become the tail that has wagged the dog of substantive actions in the United Nations, as happened during the financial crisis of the 1960's.

Closely related to its budgetary function is the Assembly's *supervisory* role. It is to the Assembly that the Security Council, the Economic and Social Council, and the Trusteeship Council submit their annual and special reports on their respective operations. Although the Security Council is not a subsidiary organ in any sense, the Charter nevertheless empowers the Assembly to make recommendations to it and to call situations dangerous to peace to its attention. The Economic and Social Council and the Trusteeship Council, although designated as "principal organs," are actually subsidiary and operate "under the authority of the General Assembly . . ." (Articles 60 and 85). Decisions on economic, social, trusteeship, and related matters are, therefore, made by the Assembly on recommendations from the two councils.

The Secretariat, for its part, is primarily concerned with serving the Assembly and in turn is controlled by it. Decisions concerning the organization and work of the Secretariat, its personnel, its budget, and its total UN role are regularly made by the Assembly. Regular and annual reports on selected activities and on the work of the United Nations enable the Assembly to receive, to criticize, and to make recommendations, and, hence, to supervise the entire UN organization.

The Assembly exercises a twofold *elective* function. One phase involves the election or admission of new members into the United Nations; the other relates to the selection of the elective members of other organs. The election to membership takes place following a recommendation by the Security Council, a prerequisite affirmed by the International Court of Justice in an advisory opinion in 1950. Prospective members file an application with the Secretary-General, who transmits it to the Security Council. Most memberships have been delayed in the Security Council, sometimes for years, but once the Council makes its recommendations, Assembly action to admit has been swift.

The Assembly's elective function helps to shape the outlook and decision-making capabilities of other major UN organs. Elections are conducted jointly with the Security Council, as in the cases of selecting the judges of the International Court and the "appointment" of the Secretary-General, or by the Assembly acting alone, as in the election of the ten nonpermanent members of the Security Council, all members of the Economic and Social Council, and some members of the Trusteeship Council. Annual elections to fill the vacancies in the various organs are preceded by extensive caucusing which ordinarily, but not always, has prevented sharp wrangling over the more prestigious seats, especially those in the Security Council.

Finally, the Assembly exercises a *constituent* function in proposing formal amendments to the Charter. Such proposals must be ratified by two thirds of the member states, including all of the permanent members of the Security Council, before taking effect. Two amendments, to enlarge the Security Council and Economic and Social Council memberships respectively, were proposed in 1963 and ratified in 1965. Continuing power struggles in the world mitigate against any extensive use of the formal amending process in the future, as in the past.

THE SECURITY COUNCIL

In both the planning and writing of the United Nations Charter, the primacy of the Security Council was generally accepted. Nothing seemed more certain to the framers than the logic of its role: The United Nations' primary responsibility is to keep the peace; because keeping the peace is mainly a function of the great powers, the Security Council is the logical focus for this responsibility. For over twenty years, however, the Security Council has failed to measure up to the framers' hopes; no other organ or agency of the United Nations system has produced a greater discrepancy between prerogative and performance.

Although the logic of giving the Security Council powers equal to those of a supreme war-making organization seemed realistic in 1945, the hope that national interests of the great powers would coincide with the world community interest in peace and security has proved vain. Almost everyone, including many of the statesmen who conceived its nature and role in 1945, agrees today that the Council has not lived up to its expectations. What went wrong? Why has it failed to play its intended role? Answers to this question, of course, are found in the nature of the cold war and the basic split among the great powers over questions of ideology and territory, as well as in a host of fears and frustrations generated by twenty years of suspicions, duplicity, threats, and open warfare. Partly, too, the answer lies within the Security Council itself in its procedures and decision-making. It is the latter that will be examined here.

Council Procedures

Unlike the General Assembly with its broad jurisdiction, the Security Council is an organ of specialized responsibility. Its two main functions are to settle disputes peacefully and to meet threats to the peace with concerted action of the organization. Certain other functions were regarded by the framers as having some relationship to security, and so the Council recommends admission of new members, selects the Secretary-General and the judges of the Court jointly with the Assembly, and supervises strategic trusteeship arrangements.

The unity of the great powers is the core of the peace-keeping plan. The framers reasoned that as long as the great powers remained united in their

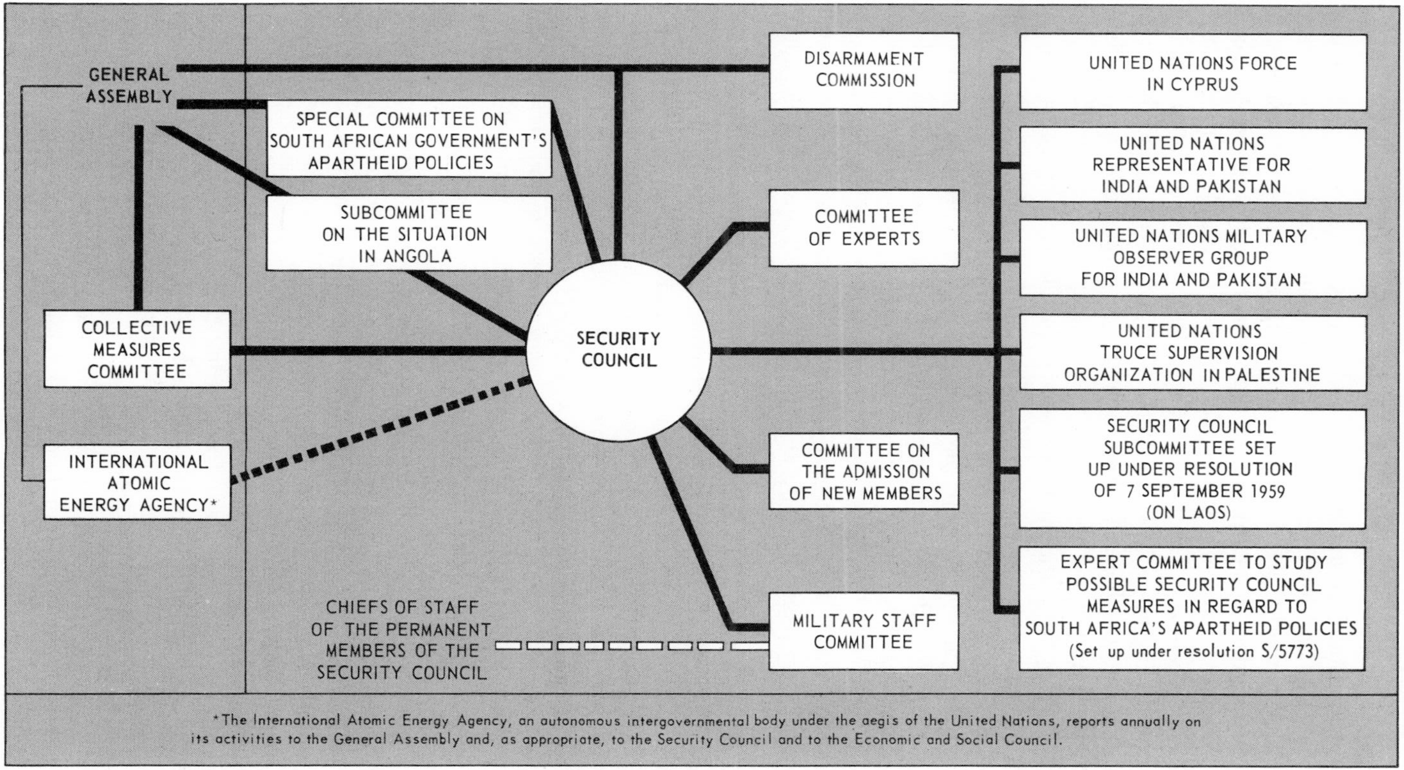
GENERAL ASSEMBLY
SPECIAL COMMITTEE ON SOUTH AFRICAN GOVERNMENT'S APARTHEID POLICIES
SUBCOMMITTEE ON THE SITUATION IN ANGOLA
COLLECTIVE MEASURES COMMITTEE
INTERNATIONAL ATOMIC ENERGY AGENCY*
SECURITY COUNCIL
DISARMAMENT COMMISSION
COMMITTEE OF EXPERTS
COMMITTEE ON THE ADMISSION OF NEW MEMBERS
MILITARY STAFF COMMITTEE
CHIEFS OF STAFF OF THE PERMANENT MEMBERS OF THE SECURITY COUNCIL
UNITED NATIONS FORCE IN CYPRUS
UNITED NATIONS REPRESENTATIVE FOR INDIA AND PAKISTAN
UNITED NATIONS MILITARY OBSERVER GROUP FOR INDIA AND PAKISTAN
UNITED NATIONS TRUCE SUPERVISION ORGANIZATION IN PALESTINE
SECURITY COUNCIL SUBCOMMITTEE SET UP UNDER RESOLUTION OF 7 SEPTEMBER 1959 (ON LAOS)
EXPERT COMMITTEE TO STUDY POSSIBLE SECURITY COUNCIL MEASURES IN REGARD TO SOUTH AFRICA'S APARTHEID POLICIES (Set up under resolution S/5773)
*The International Atomic Energy Agency, an autonomous intergovernmental body under the aegis of the United Nations, reports annually on its activities to the General Assembly and, as appropriate, to the Security Council and to the Economic and Social Council.

FIGURE 5-3. Structure of the Security Council, December 31, 1964. [*Source: United Nations Office of Public Information.*]

desire to maintain peace and security, and as long as this desire produced a
unity of purpose and fostered a unity of action, no other power or group of
powers in the world could stand against them. In some respects, the
Council is a modern reincarnation of the Concert of Europe system which
had functioned sporadically to keep the peace in Europe during most of
the nineteenth century. The Council's role was regarded by its architects
as both natural and realistic, since World War II had reaffirmed the premise
that war-making, and hence peace-keeping, is largely a great power choice.

The theories underlying the role of the Security Council served as guide-
posts in dealing with the more mundane problems of organization and
procedures for the key security organ. Five countries—China, France, the
United Kingdom, the Soviet Union, and the United States—are designated
by the Charter as *permanent* members. The ten (originally six) *non-
permanent* or *elected* members are chosen by the General Assembly for
staggered two-year terms, five elected each year. Elected members on
retirement from the Council are not immediately eligible for reelection.
This provision was inserted because under the League the elective seats on
the Council were controlled by the middle powers in most elections to
the near exclusion of the small powers. Although all members of the United
Nations other than the five permanent members are eligible for election,
the Charter, as a result of pressures from the middle powers at San Francisco,
stipulates that in the selection process due regard be "specially paid, in the
first instance to the contribution of members of the United Nations to the
maintenance of international peace and security and to the other purposes of
the organization, and also to equitable geographical distribution" (Article
23). These two considerations obviously can involve a non sequitur since
states with strategic locations, economic resources, or manpower reserves
are not evenly distributed about the globe.

From the beginning of the United Nations, the Western powers held a
majority on the Council. By virtue of a "gentlemen's agreement" in 1946, two
elective Council seats were assigned to Latin America, and one each to
Western Europe, Eastern Europe, the Middle East, and the British Commonwealth, an arrangement that normally assured the West a working majority
of nine in making Council decisions.

In the late 1950's, pressed by demands for Asian and African representation, the United States succeeded in shifting the seat allocated for Eastern
Europe to Asia. This shift proved to be only a temporary tranquilizer, however, as African, Eastern European, and Asian states clamored for greater
representation for their areas. An amendment to the Charter, proposed in
1963 and adopted in 1965 after sufficient ratifications, emerged out of these
pressures for greater representation. It provided for enlarging the Council
from eleven to fifteen by increasing the elective members from six to ten. The
new arrangement provides that the elections for the ten nonpermanent seats

will be as follows: five seats from Asia and Africa, one from Eastern Europe, two from Latin America, and two from Western European and other states. The keen competition in Assembly elections and the demands for "area representation" demonstrate that a seat at the Council table is one of the most coveted honors and crucial power positions available to members of the United Nations. The automatic voting majority that the Western powers relied upon for many years is no longer apparent in the decision-making processes of the enlarged Council.

Each Council member, permanent and elective, appoints a representative and an alternate to the Council. Unlike other United Nations organs, the Security Council is in permanent session and meets whenever a need exists. Under its rules of procedure, intervals between meetings should not exceed fourteen days. The President of the Council may convene it on his own initiative, when a member of the Council requests it, or, under circumstances prescribed in the Charter, when requested by the General Assembly or Secretary-General.

Under its rules of procedure, the Presidency of the Security Council rotates each month among its members. This provision, while safeguarding the Council from domination or abuse by a presiding officer out of sympathy with its objectives, gives the organ a discontinuity and fluidity not in keeping with its high responsibilities. The brief two-year terms of the ten non-permanent members add to the impromptu quality of the Council. Debates in the Council also lacked spontaneity and continuity since each statement must usually be studied thoroughly before it is answered, and comment on new ideas is reserved until home governments can be contacted for instructions.

Although debates are carried on in the Security Council under rules of procedure established by the Council, the Charter provides that any United Nations member may be invited to participate in any discussion if its interests are affected by the question under debate. Also, any state, whether a United Nations member or not, must be invited to participate in the discussion if it is a party to a dispute being considered by the Council. In neither case does the invited state have a vote.

When debate on a measure is completed, a vote is taken with each member of the Council having one vote. Decisions are of two types: *procedural* and *substantive*. The Charter provides that all decisions on procedural questions be made by an affirmative vote of any nine members; thus permanent and elected members have equal voting power on all procedural questions. On all other, or substantive matters, the Charter specifies that decisions shall be made "by an affirmative vote of nine members including the concurring votes of the permanent members," except that when a member of the Council is a party to a dispute it must abstain from voting. Although the words of the Charter clearly denote that substantive decisions require a "yes" vote of all five permanent members, in a practice based on numerous precedents, a permanent member's abstention from voting is not regarded as constituting a "veto" of the pending measure.[8] To kill a matter of substance before the Council, a permanent member must cast a negative vote, which constitutes a veto.[9]

Council Functions

The Security Council functions essentially as an agent for the entire membership of the United Nations, producing by its decisions and actions an institutionalized political and moral pressure. Any state, member or nonmember alike, which threatens the peace and security of the world may, if agreement can be reached on the Council, be the object of these pressures. As a rule, the Council majority has preferred a modest but sophisticated application of pressure upon the disputants rather than a blunt and forceful approach. Whenever possible, the Council has handled situations under Chapter VI of the Charter as simple disputes rather than considering collective action under Chapter VII, even when both sides have been engaged in extensive military actions.

Techniques employed by the Council vary from case to case, depending in each situation upon the political considerations involved, the degree of unity on the Council, the extent of the danger to peace, and the relationship of the dispute and the disputants to Council members, particularly the permanent members. Typical approaches used by the Council include

[8] An interesting discussion of this question occurred before the Security Council on January 20, 1948, when, in a vote on a resolution aimed at seeking a solution to the Kashmir question, the Soviet Union abstained. Other Council members charged the Soviets with using a "hidden veto" and called upon their representative to give support to the resolution, else their abstention would constitute a veto under Article 27. The British representative replied to this contention by pointing out that "by practice and precedent" an abstention is not a veto. This view was accepted by the President of the Council and continues to be the accepted interpretation of the voting procedure. Although the Soviets did not participate in the debate on the issue, later, in 1950, after the Council had taken collective action against North Korean aggression in the absence of the USSR representative, the Soviets claimed this action was invalid because it had not received the affirmative vote of all of the permanent members of the Council. Similarly, the Soviets have refused to pay for peace-keeping operations of the United Nations in the Middle East and the Congo since they had not acquiesced in some of the decisions in each case.

[9] A total of over one hundred vetoes have been cast by the Soviet Union during the twenty-year history of Security Council operations. Several additional vetoes have been used by France, Britain, and Nationalist China, but the United States has never been forced to defend its position by veto, although it has on occasion threatened to use it. The Soviet total is somewhat misleading since most of its vetoes were cast in blocking admittance to membership of American-sponsored states. The American ploy was to embarrass the Soviets and to win a propaganda victory by taking up membership applications individually and repeatedly to force numerous vetoes, a stratagem that in time gave way to a "horse-trading" arrangement by which American- and Soviet-sponsored nations were admitted simultaneously.

deliberation, investigation, recommendation, conciliation, interposition, appeal, and *enforcement.*

Deliberation usually starts with an invitation to the disputants to present their cases before the Council. The debate which follows in the Council aims not at determining which side is right but at finding some common ground for agreement. The presentations by the parties and the debate which follows are a form of catharsis which may "clear the air" and open a pathway to settlement. They may, however, serve only to educate the Council members on the difficult nature of the controversy, the great gulf that exists between the parties on key issues, or the substantial disparities in the facts presented by both sides.

Investigation often follows the opening debates since an understanding of the events leading to the controversy and a relatively dependable assessment of what constitutes the "actual facts" in the situation are necessary preconditions to Council action. Council fact-finding may take the form of further inquiries with the parties by the President of the Council or a committee appointed for that purpose. More than likely, a committee of its own members or a commission of representatives of its members will be sent to the scene of the conflict to determine the facts on the spot. Only in this way can the Council sort out the claims and counterclaims and arrive at a workable assessment of the facts involved, even though a determination of all facts with accuracy is beyond normal investigatory capabilities.

Recommendation based on the Council's facts, however acquired, may follow as a logical next step. Recommendations take the form of Council resolutions offering some substantive change in the status quo and calling upon the parties to accept it or to use it as a basis for new negotiations.

Conciliation, a time-honored diplomatic role played by third parties in disputes, is used in trying to secure the agreement of the parties to Council recommendations. The conciliation function may be applied by the entire Council, by its President, by an individual appointed to that role, by a committee or commission, or by the Secretary-General under Council mandate. Often the Council's conciliation efforts will involve an on-the-spot negotiation with high-level decision-makers of the disputing states. Every effort is made to achieve a solution whether or not it conforms to the Council's views.

Interposition is a device used by the Council to quiet a potentially explosive situation or to restore peace if fighting is in progress. Thus the Council may try to interpose some of its own members, a special commission, Secretariat officials, an observer group, or a UN police force between the forces of the disputants. Interposition may be directed at preventing the infiltration of arms, avoiding contact between opposing forces, or maintaining a cease-fire agreement. Its goal is to achieve a deterrence, not by superior force, but by virtue of its role as a disinterested party and as a symbol of world opinion. Such efforts, known as UN peace-keeping operations, have been used effectively to prevent escalations and to restore peace in Kashmir, the Congo, the Middle East, and Cyprus.

Appeal may be used by the Council or one of its agents to encourage the parties to negotiate, to refrain from aggravating a situation, to withdraw from disputed territory or to do or not do something to the end that tension between the disputants may decrease. When a dispute is placed before the Council, its initial action usually takes the form of an appeal to both parties to do nothing that might aggravate the situation. If fighting is underway, a cease-fire appeal, such as those issued by the Council in the Indonesian, Indian-Pakistani, and Cyprus disputes, may bring about a cessation of hostilities, although the Council is without authority to enforce it and, like other appeals, it depends upon the prestige of the Council and the good sense of the disputants for its success. Such exhortations by the Council have generally been successful in ending hostilities, although they have usually been buttressed by other methods used simultaneously.

Enforcement involves the imposition by the Council of sanctions against states that have engaged in "threats to the peace, breaches of the peace, and acts of aggression." Under Chapter VII of the Charter, sanctions may involve measures short of the use of armed force, including "complete or partial interruption of economic relations and of rail, sea, air, postal, telegraphic, radio, and other means of communication, and the severance of diplomatic relations." If these measures prove inadequate, the Council may order "such action by air, sea, or land forces as may be necessary to maintain or restore international peace and security." Every effort is directed toward avoiding a military showdown and the concept of using a "graduated deterrence" equal to but not beyond that necessary to restore peace guides Council actions. In a sense, when collective military actions are undertaken, the Council may have failed in its primary role, since the collective security theory assumes that most if not all lawbreaking states will desist from their aggressive acts if confronted with the threat of community action.[10]

Miscellaneous Council Functions

The Charter, while giving the Security Council primary responsibility in peace and security matters, also allocates to it certain lesser powers, most of which are shared with the Assembly. These functions are *elective, initiatory,* and *supervisory* in nature, and were designed by the framers to permit the great powers to maintain some control over significant organizational matters.

---

[10] For an extensive analysis of the Security Council's role in pacific settlement and collective security, see Chapters 9 and 10, respectively.

The election of a Secretary-General and the admission of new members both require Council initiative and consent prior to Assembly action. Admission of new members takes place after the Council recommends and the Assembly acts on membership applications. Since the veto power applies to membership questions, each new member must be acceptable to all of the great powers, a requirement that produced grave dissension on the Council for protracted periods in the 1950's. Assembly demands for universality of membership have in time pressured the great powers to modify their ideological exclusivity, although realization of universality still awaits resolution of the problems of the divided states of Germany, Korea, and Viet Nam, as well as an answer to the perennial question of Chinese representation. Solutions may await some future compromise among the permanent members of the Council like that which broke a long-standing jam of applications in 1955.

The Secretary-General is "appointed" by the Assembly following his "recommendation" by the Council, with the veto power applicable. This provision guarantees that the chief administrative official of the organization will be *persona grata,* at least when first appointed, to all of the great powers, a requirement that has produced several crises in filling the office. Although the Assembly could reject the Council's nominee, it could not then make its own selection but would have to await further Council recommendations. In every case, however, the nominees for Secretary-General from the Security Council have been readily acceptable to the Assembly.

The Council participates *concurrently* with the Assembly in the election of judges of the International Court of Justice, with five of the fifteen seats on the Court up for election every three years. A simple majority of any eight votes is required in the Council, but the two major organs must harmonize their selections since they vote separately. Unlike other actions by the Council, the elections of judges involves consideration of the qualifications of individuals, although it has been the tendency to select judges from the most important states.

The Charter provides, in another measure of control, that the Council may recommend to the Assembly that a member's rights and privileges be taken away when the Council has taken enforcement action against it. The Council, acting alone, may restore them at any time. The Council may also recommend to the Assembly that a member which has persistently violated the principles of the Charter be expelled from the organization.

Related to the Council's security role is its responsibility for supervising strategic trust territories under the trusteeship system. In this task it may call upon the Trusteeship Council if security considerations are not prejudiced to perform the normal trusteeship functions relating to political, economic, social, and educational matters in the strategic areas. Only the

American-administered Territory of the Pacific Islands (the Marshalls, the Carolines, and the Marianas) have been placed under strategic trust, and Council supervision has been minimal.

Future Role

The Security Council's future impact on the organization and the world will depend on its ability to function in peace and security matters. This role, in turn, will be conditioned by the cold war, by UN financing arrangements, by the expanding role of the Assembly, and, conceivably, by new alignments and pressures resulting from the Council's expanded membership.

That the Council is seeking to regain its position as the key organ of the United Nations is indicated by its increased activity in handling dangerous situations, such as those in the Congo, West Irian, Yemen, and Cyprus, and by its effectiveness in quickly halting the Indo-Pakistani war in 1965. Its role can be measured somewhat by the number of its annual meetings, which rose to a high of 171 in 1948, then sank to a low of five in 1959, under the influence of the cold war. In the 1960's the Council regained some of its earlier vigor, as evidenced by its frequent meetings, but it is still undergoing a readjustment to current realities. The most obvious of these is that none of the permanent members can any longer dominate decision-making in an Assembly riddled with political and ideological cross-currents and generally suspicious of great power politics. Nor can the Western powers "leave it to Dag" and the Secretariat to fill in the details of broad Assembly resolutions as they did before Hammarskjold's death in 1961.

The road to growing consensus in the Council, then, is paved not so much with an East-West rapprochement as with a collective fear of the great powers that their preferred position in the organization is slipping. It was this kind of fear that begot the original unity of the great powers at San Francisco when they jointly fought off efforts by the small and middle powers to reduce their role in the proposed organization. Whether this growing unity of the 1960's proves durable enough to survive future peace and security crises depends most on international political factors extraneous to the organization.

THE ECONOMIC AND SOCIAL COUNCIL

Although afforded the status of principal organ by the Charter, the Economic and Social Council (ECOSOC) functions under the authority of the General Assembly (see Figure 5-4). In many respects its activities resemble those of the main Assembly committees, and it has occasionally been charged with duplicating or competing with the work of the Second (Economic and Financial) and Third (Social) committees of the Assembly.

ECOSOC consists of twenty-seven members elected by a two-thirds vote in the Assembly for staggered three-year terms. Although all UN members are equally eligible for election, in practice the countries of industrial importance have been consistently elected over the years. This practice led to the expansion of the Council in 1965 from eighteen to twenty-seven in order to give the developing countries a bigger voice. A president is elected each year from one of the small or middle powers represented on the Council. Sessions are held twice annually, the first in New York in April, the second in Geneva in July. Decisions are made by a simple majority of those present and voting.

Broadly speaking, ECOSOC carries on a worldwide welfare function aimed at improving the lot of mankind. Charter references to its role, however, are so verbose and repetitive that the organization has been operating for over twenty years without a precise mandate. Countless debates have explored a diverse assortment of topics, but successes have been scattered and mostly unnoticed. Many of its operations have been carried on with little public notice, since political controversies have usually monopolized the UN spotlight.

The failure of so many of its debates to materialize into effective action programs has produced a mounting frustration among the developing nations aggravated by present rivalries and deep-rooted antagonisms of the past. Yet, despite grave discrepancies between the hopes of the framers and the accomplishments of the Council, it has carried on a vast amount of useful and potentially useful work. Later chapters on social and economic matters will explore and evaluate these programs.

ECOSOC's Functions

The Economic and Social Council's basic functions involve *deliberation, study, appraisal and recommendation, coordination,* and *quasi-legislation.* The sum of these activities, in the views of Council members, makes ECOSOC a "focus for international thinking" and a "catalyst for international action."[11]

Research and Debate

Far-reaching debates in the Council on a variety of social and economic questions typify its *deliberative* role. Recent agenda items, for example, have included discussions on housing, human rights, narcotic drug control, water resources, population problems, trade, UNICEF, industrial development, literacy, refugees, and science and technology.

Two subjects stand out in the Council's deliberations, both in frequency and in intensity. These are economic development and human rights, both

[11] See United Nations Documents E/4052, June 8, 1965, and E/4040, June 10, 1965, for a review of members' observations on the Council's role.

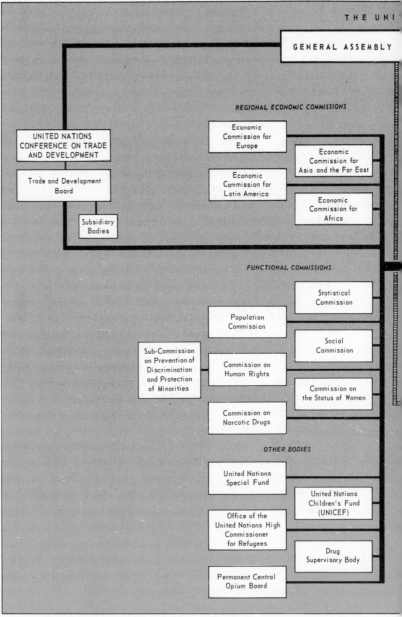

FIGURE 5-4. Main organs dealing with economic and social questions,

emotional subjects for the representatives on the Council of newly independent nations. Demands for immeasurably greater financial help from the former colonial powers, as a rightful legacy of real or imagined ex-

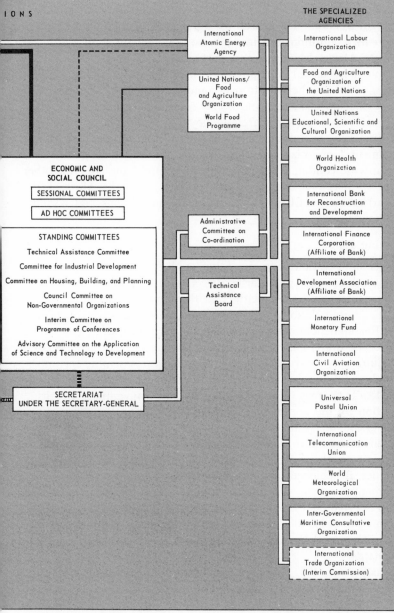

I O N S		THE SPECIALIZED AGENCIES

International Atomic Energy Agency

International Labour Organization

United Nations/ Food and Agriculture Organization

World Food Programme

Food and Agriculture Organization of the United Nations

United Nations Educational, Scientific and Cultural Organization

ECONOMIC AND SOCIAL COUNCIL

SESSIONAL COMMITTEES

AD HOC COMMITTEES

STANDING COMMITTEES

Technical Assistance Committee

Committee for Industrial Development

Committee on Housing, Building, and Planning

Council Committee on Non-Governmental Organizations

Interim Committee on Programme of Conferences

Advisory Committee on the Application of Science and Technology to Development

World Health Organization

International Bank for Reconstruction and Development

Administrative Committee on Co-ordination

International Finance Corporation (Affiliate of Bank)

International Development Association (Affiliate of Bank)

Technical Assistance Board

International Monetary Fund

International Civil Aviation Organization

Universal Postal Union

SECRETARIAT UNDER THE SECRETARY-GENERAL

International Telecommunication Union

World Meteorological Organization

Inter-Governmental Maritime Consultative Organization

International Trade Organization (Interim Commission)

December 31, 1964. [*Source: United Nations Office of Public Information.*]

ploitations of the past, keep the Western nations on the defensive. Debates on human rights are somewhat less acrimonious, but participants often fail to see the inherent illogic of governmental representatives demanding more rights for individuals in a world in which governments provide the main threats to human freedom. The search for agreement in the field of human rights is frequently consummated in common condemnations of the worst offenders: South Africa, Rhodesia, and Portugal.

Probably the most useful function performed by ECOSOC is that of making *studies* which are helping to overcome the dearth of statistical and other kinds of data on economic and social conditions in the world. Here ECOSOC operates as a super research agency and clearinghouse, directing the work of numerous committees, commissions, study groups, and private or nongovernmental organizations. The basic information so gathered is vital to attempts at coming to grips with world problems, and no other agency in history has had such a broad research mandate. Most of the studies are carried on by ECOSOC's functional commissions and regional economic commissions.[12]

Decision-Making Role

Based on its deliberations and extensive studies, ECOSOC makes *appraisals* of its findings and, by Charter directive, may make *recommendations* "with respect to any such matters to the General Assembly, to the Members of the United Nations, and to the Specialized Agencies concerned" (Article 62). Recommendations usually take the form of a draft resolution, or declaration. The drafts may embody merely a statement of general principles and require only a favorable vote in the General Assembly for implementation, such as the proclamation of the Universal Declaration of Human Rights of 1948. They may also take the form of conventions requiring affirmative action by the Assembly and subsequent ratification by a stipulated number of member states.

Drafting conventions involves the Council in what might be called its *quasi-legislative* role. It resembles the national lawmaking function in that the final product, if achieved, is a convention that binds consenting states, limits governments in their relationship to their own citizens, and makes an addition to international law. It is a much more difficult process than the mere proclaiming of principles, and very few of the many rights so blandly set forth in the Universal Declaration in 1948 are today protected by international covenants.

One such covenant, the 1952 Convention on the Political Rights of Women, serves as an example of what can be accomplished in the form of international legislation when states find ground for agreement. Such a

---

[12] The functional commissions established by ECOSOC are Human Rights, International Commodity Trade, Narcotic Drugs, Population, Prevention of Discrimination and Protection of Minorities (actually a subcommission of the Commission on Human Rights), Statistical, Status of Women, and Transport and Communications. Regional economic commissions have been set up for Africa, Asia and the Far East, Europe, and Latin America.

consensus, however, was not easily developed. Women's groups from many countries, banding together as an international pressure group, demanded and obtained from ECOSOC a Commission on the Status of Women. They followed this up by pushing the idea of feminine political equality through the Commission, ECOSOC, General Assembly, and ratification stages. The Convention guarantees women the right to vote and to hold public office equally with men in all adhering states.

Coordination Responsibilities

ECOSOC's *coordination* function relates to the activities of the thirteen specialized agencies of the United Nations. The Charter charges the Economic and Social Council with bringing these agencies into relationship with the United Nations through agreements negotiated by ECOSOC and approved by the Assembly. Integrating the activities of thirteen diverse agencies which are largely autonomous in their powers, have their own organizational machinery, adopt their own budgets, select their own secretariats, and, in some cases, antedate the United Nations organization, is no simple task. The permissive authorization given to ECOSOC has, as a result, not proved adequate to the challenge of securing effective "coordination," although various agreements have been concluded.

The growing assertion of power by the Assembly and its main committees has produced a closer working relationship between them and the specialized agencies than between the agencies and ECOSOC, but this link tends to involve more "supervision" than "coordination." More continuous coordination, however, is carried on by a committee of high secretariat officials from the United Nations Secretariat and the secretariats of the specialized agencies, functioning as an international administrative cabinet.

Future Role

The Economic and Social Council has recognized its own inadequate impact on United Nations policies and in recent years has reconsidered its position in the organization. Changes in ECOSOC's operations suggested by its members to achieve better results include:

> a shift from 'reviewing past activities to examining future programmes'; concentration at each session on a 'limited number of broad issues [defined well in advance] which could form the subject of consideration in depth'; reduction of reports to a 'coherent, assimilable and readily understandable whole'; monthly meetings when necessary . . . [and] reorganization of the committee structure. . . .[13]

This concern coupled with the increased activity of the new twenty-seven-member Council bode well for its future role.

[13] "Issues Before the 20th General Assembly," *International Conciliation,* No. 554 (September, 1965), pp. 188–89.

THE TRUSTEESHIP COUNCIL

Although the Charter designates the Trusteeship Council a principal organ of the United Nations, it is, like ECOSOC, subordinate to the General Assembly. Its function, to supervise nonstrategic trust territories for the Assembly and strategic trusts for the Security Council, involves only recommendation powers (see Figure 5-5).

Membership Criteria

Membership on the Trusteeship Council is accorded to three types of members: (1) states which administer trust territories are automatic members; (2) permanent members of the Security Council which do not administer trust territories are automatic members; and (3) enough additional states are elected to strike an equilibrium between trust administering and nonadministering states.[14] Unlike the League of Nations Mandates Commission, which was composed of colonial "experts" elected as individuals, the Trusteeship Council members are representatives of states. This arrangement has produced not only a more vigorous Council, but a more politically effective one as well.

Trusteeship Functions

In carrying out its responsibilities, the Trusteeship Council exercises powers involving *deliberation, recommendation, supervision, petition,* and *visiting missions.* The first two functions are similar to those of ECOSOC: the Council may *deliberate* on any matter within its jurisdiction through studies and debates, and may recommend action to the General Assembly based on its evaluation. Recommendations, however, relate to contemporary problems of specific trust territories or their administration and, unlike those of ECOSOC, do not usually take the form of proclamations or law.

Supervision of Trust Administration

The Council's *supervisory* role involves overseeing the governance of trust territories by administering states. An elaborate questionnaire drawn up by the Council has served for twenty years as a basic supervisory tool. Ques-

[14] By 1965, only one elective member remained on the Council. This member, together with the nonadministering permanent members of the Security Council, China, France, and the Soviet Union, balanced the four remaining administering states, the United States, the United Kingdom, Australia, and New Zealand. The Trusteeship Council now consists of the five great powers, Australia, New Zealand, and one elective member. The territories originally brought under the system were Cameroons (Britain); Cameroons (France); Nauru (Australia-Britain-New Zealand); New Guinea (Australia); Ruanda-Urundi (Belgium); Somaliland (Italy); Tanganyika (Britain); Territory of the Pacific Islands (United States); Togoland (Britain); Togoland (France); and Western Samoa (New Zealand).

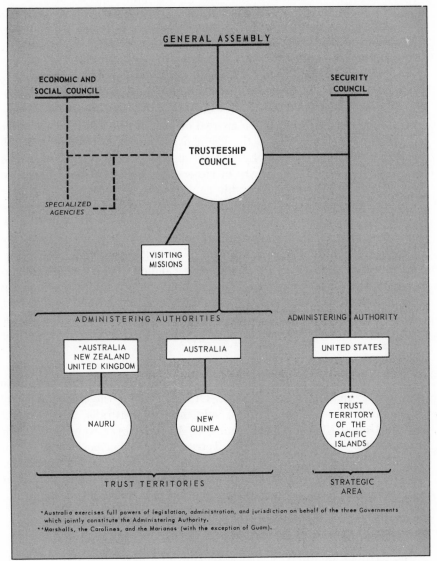

FIGURE 5-5. Structure of the International Trusteeship System, January 1, 1965. [*Source: United Nations Office of Public Information.*]

tionnaire replies and other reports from administering states are subjected to rigorous written and oral cross-examinations and evaluations, forcing each trust-holding state to defend its actions or lack of them. Out of these confrontations emerges the Council's annual report to the Assembly, permitting, this time by the Assembly, another inquiry, another debate, and another evaluation of how well administering states are living up to their mandated responsibilities. Little wonder that most trust states impatiently pushed their trust territories toward independence and self-government!

Normal supervisory tools are supplemented by two additional techniques that permit the peoples of trust territories to *petition* the United Nations for a redress of their grievances, and that provide on-the-spot investigations by *visiting missions* of the Trusteeship Council. Numerous petitions, sometimes several hundred in a single year, air real or imagined abuses. Such petitions may be submitted directly to the Council by delegations representing the people of a trust territory or by written appeals, with no approval needed from the administering authority in either case. Some petitions have been debated extensively in the Assembly as well as in the Council.

Each visiting mission is composed of four individuals, two chosen by administering and two by nonadministering states on the Council. Missions check general social and economic conditions, the extent to which the people are being prepared for self-government, and seek answers to specific questions raised in debates in the Trusteeship Council and Assembly. Mission members solicit the views of a cross-section of the population, including labor leaders, tribal chiefs, local administrative officials, and private individuals. Reports by visiting missions indicate the extent to which the administering authority of the trust territory is achieving Charter objectives.

Council Successes

The Trusteeship Council is one of those rare human institutions threatened with extinction by its successes. Of the eleven trusteeship agreements concluded by the United Nations, only those of Australia, New Zealand, and the United Kingdom over Nauru, of Australia over New Guinea, and of the United States over the Trust Territory of the Pacific Islands remain. The other trust territories of the Cameroons, Ruanda-Urundi, Somaliland, Tanganyika, British Togoland, French Togoland, and Western Samoa are now independent states and all but the last are members of the United Nations.

South West African Case

One territory, South West Africa, remains in a hazy legal status, a center of controversy since 1946. This former German colony was mandated to the Union of South Africa by the League of Nations. In 1946 South Africa refused to place it under the new trusteeship system and took action to incorporate the territory into the Union proper. In 1950, the International Court of Justice ruled in an advisory opinion that although South Africa was not obliged to place the territory under the trusteeship system, its obligations as a Mandatory power continued, including the submission of reports and petitions to the Trusteeship Council.

In the mid-1960's, demands for UN sanctions, a new contentious case before the World Court, numerous condemnatory resolutions, and threats of military intervention by some African states stress the growing impatience of member states with South Africa's intransigence.[15] It has become obvious that the Republic of South Africa will not respond to pressures engendered by debates, proclamations, and resolutions. Effective sanctions, however, would be well nigh impossible without the close cooperation of the United Kingdom and the United States, both of which are reluctant to agree to stringent sanctions because their investments and trade with South Africa are substantial.

Selected Readings

ALKER, HAYWARD R., JR. "Dimensions of Conflict in the General Assembly," *American Political Science Review,* 58, September, 1964, pp. 642–57.

KEOHANE, ROBERT OWEN. "Political Influence in the General Assembly," *International Conciliation,* No. 557, March, 1966.

KHAN, MUHAMMAD ZAFRULLA. "The President of the General Assembly of the United Nations," *International Organization,* Spring, 1964, pp. 231–40.

NICHOLAS, H. G. *The United Nations as a Political Institution.* London: Oxford University Press, 1962, 2nd ed.

RIGGS, ROBERT E. *Politics in the United Nations.* Urbana: University of Illinois Press, 1958.

VANDENBOSCH, AMRY, and HOGAN, WILLARD N. *Toward World Order.* New York: McGraw-Hill, 1963, Chap. 5.

[15] The case was brought to the International Court by Ethiopia and Liberia in 1960. After six years of procrastination, the Court on July 18, 1966, dismissed the case on the basis of a legal technicality—namely, that Ethiopia and Liberia had no right to bring the suit as individual members of the League of Nations. The deciding vote in the 8–7 decision was cast by Court President Sir Percy Spender of Australia who held that only the League Council could legally bring such an action. The Court's ruling touched off a storm of protest from African nations and a call for direct action against South Africa by the thirty-eight-nation Organization of African Unity.

6 | *The Political Process— Participants*

Politics, defined as a social relationship involving power, authority, or influence, may exist without formal organization. Within an organization, however, politics may be identified mainly with the interaction of those who participate in making the organization's decisions. A political participant, by definition, is anyone who influences or tries to influence the decision-making process. In international organization influence may be exerted by representatives of states, spokesmen for nongovernmental interests, secretariat officials and even by agents of other international organizations. The effectiveness of political participation is enhanced by formal membership rights, but the fact of participation is tested by the intent and capacity to exert influence, not by the legal relation of membership.

MEMBERSHIP AND ORGANIZATIONAL GOALS

The question of membership is nevertheless of central importance because the chief participants in international organizations are the official representatives of member states. Member states interpret the objectives of the organization, determine its policies, and provide the means for carrying out its programs. Most international organizations are subject to other influences stemming from the institutional structure of the organization itself and from nonstate interests. But, by and large, member states determine what can and will be done. This means that familiarity with the membership and policies governing admission of new members is essential to an understanding of the political processes of an international organization.

The relationship between membership and organizational objectives is reciprocal. Members, through their participation in the political process, give operational meaning to the objectives of the organization. But objectives, in turn, influence the membership pattern of the organization. If military security is the goal, for example, membership will be limited to states perceiving a common threat to their security. Under present conditions, one would not expect to find the United States and the Soviet Union as partners in a mutual defense organization. Yet little more than two decades ago those two countries were joined in a military coalition known as the wartime United Nations, united by their perception of a common threat in Nazi Germany. The rising might of China as a genuine great power in the east permits speculation that another twenty years hence could well find ·defensive organizations with membership alignments startlingly different from the present.

The connection between goals and membership is equally obvious in other types of international organizations. If cooperation within a given geographical region is the objective, membership is generally open to states located within the region. Since, for example, the Arab League seeks to foster Arab unity and cooperation, membership is limited to states with predominantly Arab populations. Particular goals of technical cooperation may also affect membership as evidenced by the World Meteorological Organization in which membership is constitutionally open only to states "having a meteorological service." Examples abound that illustrate the point that the principles of selectivity affecting membership in international organizations spring from the objectives of the organizations as perceived by their members.

By the same token, where objectives of international organization have been universal in scope, membership eligibility has tended toward universality. This is notably true of special-purpose organizations designed to facilitate cooperation in an important if narrow substantive area, such as promotion of world health, agricultural production, or cooperation in communications and transit across national boundaries. To the extent that such activities have been of interest to states generally, membership has typically been thrown open to all states without political or moral conditions, subject, however, to approval by a specified majority of member states. Before 1955, when UN membership was controlled like that of an exclusive private club, comparative membership charts showed that many of the single-purpose, specialized agencies tended to be universal in membership, encouraging the participation of nearly all countries interested in cooperation. Countries that remain unrepresented in most of the specialized agencies have generally done so as a matter of choice and not as a result of exclusiveness on the part of the organizations. The principal exceptions have been the Communist "halves" of China, Viet Nam, Korea, and Germany.

The purposes and principles set forth in the League Covenant and the UN Charter are manifestly broad enough to be shared almost universally, but both constitutions embrace selectivity in the sense that they set forth criteria that can be used to exclude some applicants. Both organizations, especially in their earlier years, practiced selectivity in fact. In each case, however, the passing of years brought liberalized attitudes and both ultimately opened their doors to most political entities that could be called self-governing states. The triumph of the universalist approach appeared to

spring from a growing recognition that the broad objectives of world organization could best be achieved if the membership were general. In the
days before quasi-universality had become the rule in the United Nations,
Secretary-General Trygve Lie voiced a sentiment that even then was shared
by many governments:

> The United Nations is the one organization in existence that belongs to
> the whole world and I believe every reasonable step should be taken to
> enable the whole world to belong to the Organization. There are all kinds
> of governments and all kinds of economic and social systems. The United
> Nations is the place where they should meet to negotiate, and, when
> necessary, to mediate and to conciliate.[1]

Except for the partitioned victims of cold war controversy, that sentiment
dominates United Nations admission policies today, just as it came to
dominate the attitudes of League members toward admission.

THE LEAGUE EXPERIENCE

The League principle of selectivity was set forth in Article 1 of the Covenant, which made membership open to "Any fully self-governing State,
Dominion or Colony." Admission was conditioned, however, upon "effective
guarantees" of the applicant's willingness to fulfill its international obligations and to accept any currently enforced prescriptions of the League as
to armaments. The admission process required an affirmative act on both
sides, amounting in form to the creation of a contractual relationship. The
prospective member agreed to assume certain obligations under the Covenant, in consideration of which the Assembly by a two-thirds vote granted
the privilege of membership. The Assembly action, however, was based
upon its own independent determination that the applicant had the will and
the capacity to accept the responsibilities of membership. A direct challenge
to the principle of selectivity was met and defeated in the first session of
the Assembly when members voted down 29 to 5 an Argentine proposal

> That all sovereign States recognised by the community of nations be
> admitted to join the League of Nations in such a manner that if they do not
> become Members of the League this can only be the result of a voluntary
> decision on their part.[2]

The Assembly majority wished neither to solicit a formal snub from the
United States, nor to give up the Assembly's privilege of deciding when, if

---

[1] *Annual Report of the Secretary-General on the Work of the Organization, 1949–1950,*
Official Records of the General Assembly, 5th Sess., Supp. No. 1, United Nations Document A/1287, p. xiii.

[2] Aleksander W. Rudzinski, "Admission of New Members: The United Nations and
the League of Nations," *International Conciliation,* No. 480 (April, 1952), p. 148.

ever, a defeated Germany or a Bolshevist Russia should be permitted to join the organization.

Nevertheless, the League Assembly took a pragmatic rather than an ideological approach in its appraisal of the qualifications of prospective members, and no applicant objectively capable of maintaining an independent existence as a sovereign state was ever rejected. Good judgment was evident in those few instances when rejection of an applicant was felt necessary. Events quickly proved the wisdom of the first Assembly in denying the applications of Armenia, Azerbaijan, Georgia, and the Ukraine whose independence of Russian domination was at best temporary. On the other hand, the admission of the Baltic states of Latvia, Lithuania, and Estonia was denied in 1920, but granted the following year when their independence from Russia seemed assured. In a rather difficult case, the application of Liechtenstein was rejected in 1920 on the ground that this state did not "appear to be in a position to carry out all the international obligations imposed by the Covenant." After 1921 no application for membership was disapproved for any reason, convincing evidence of a determination to apply the principle of selectivity as leniently as possible.

The tendency toward leniency in the application of Covenant standards for admission was buttressed by the concept of the League as fulfilling a reform function. In Assembly discussions accompanying the admission of the ex-enemy states of Bulgaria and Hungary, the feeling was expressed that the international engagements of the two states, particularly those stemming from the peace treaties, would become more binding by reason of their admission to the League. The same broad-mindedness and optimism were shown in 1923 toward Ethiopia, one of the last great strongholds of the slave trade. Instead of rejecting the Ethiopian application outright, or demanding immediate abolition of slave trading as the price of admission, the Assembly asked only for a declaration of future intention to adhere to international conventions affecting the slave trade. The application was then approved in the hope that once Ethiopia became a member, its standard of behavior would be raised. Extracting verbal guarantees of good behavior from applicants was by that time a general practice. Albania, Estonia, Finland, Latvia, and Lithuania had all been required to sign a pledge to respect the rights of minorities within their borders as a condition of entry into the League. The League thus moved toward universality on the theory that membership would make "bad men good and good men better," as well as providing a broader base for carrying on cooperative projects within the League framework.

The tendency of the League to maintain the form of selectivity while pursuing the substance of universality is strikingly evident in the judicious combination of two separate paths to League membership—application and invitation. The common route was application upon the initiative of the prospective member. For each applicant a fact-finding subcommittee of the Assembly was appointed to investigate the pertinent facts and submit a report in accordance with guidelines laid down by a standard questionnaire. Representatives of each applicant state were invited to meet with the committee and present any information or arguments in behalf of its application. Following this careful, impartial investigation, the subcommittees, after 1921, always found that the applicant was qualified or at least could be found to qualify upon the verbal acceptance of specific obligations.

Admission by invitation was reserved for states that, upon inquiry, were found willing to join but reluctant to apply and submit to routine investigation. Thus the application and investigation procedure was bypassed in order to solicit the membership of Mexico (1931), Turkey (1932), the Soviet Union (1934), and Egypt (1937). This procedure found a precedent dating from 1919 when thirteen neutral countries had accepted an invitation to have their names listed with the signatories of the Versailles Treaty as original members of the League. The precedent was not followed, however, until the 1930's when the honeymoon period of the League was definitely over and it appeared as an attempt to bolster the declining power and prestige of the League. In any event by virtue of original membership, application, and invitation, the League numbered within its ranks at one time or another some sixty-three political entities. The peak membership of sixty was reached in 1934 upon the admission of Soviet Russia and Ecuador and before the required two-year waiting period had elapsed to make official the withdrawals of Germany and Japan.

The reference to withdrawals from membership adds a final somber tone to the tale of League membership. Ultimately the drive for universality was not thwarted by exclusiveness from within—as a group the League members recognized that the goals of the organization were consonant with, and could never be fully achieved without, universal membership. Instead, the impetus for disassociation from the League came from individual governments that ceased to share some of the vital goals of the League as interpreted by the majority, or that found the halting progress toward the achievement of shared goals outweighed by the burdens of membership. To the original forty-two acceding states named in the Annex to the Covenant, twenty-one members were added before the outbreak of World War II. But during the same period eighteen states withdrew, including Germany (1933), Japan (1933), and Italy (1937), three of the great powers. The Soviet Union signified its dissociation from the objectives of the League by attacking Finland in 1939, in obvious violation of the Covenant, and was expelled.

The ultimate downfall of the League sprang from the growing inconsistency between the organization's primary goal of maintaining peace and the increasingly insistent demands of powerful members for change. The gap between organizational objectives and national objectives was symbolized by the exit from the League of Germany, Japan, Italy, and Russia. A meaningful political dialogue could no longer be carried on within the organization among members having such irreconcilable interests. The fields of common interest that still remained were overshadowed by sharply divergent national attitudes toward maintenance of the status quo as the price of peace.

The numerous withdrawals from League membership, as well as the non-membership of the United States, point to another kind of membership problem not related to any basic divergence between national objectives and the objectives of the League as an institution. It was simply the conviction of some governments that League membership was not worth the effort of involvement and the shouldering of consequent responsibilities. The United States never joined, for reasons detailed and repeated almost *ad nauseam* by historians, but most of the reasons can be covered by the broad assertion that American policy makers did not regard membership in the League to be important enough to offset the sacrifices that would be entailed. Most of the withdrawals from the League membership came in the middle and late 1930's when the fortunes of the League were clearly in decline. Yet, as early as 1925, Costa Rica resigned because it could not "afford" to pay its $5000 annual assessment. Many Latin American states were perennially in arrears in their budgetary assessments, and some were generally absent from League meetings. Brazil and Spain withdrew from membership in 1926 for no better reason than the refusal of the Assembly to grant them status as permanent members of the Council. Under coaxing, Spain experienced a change of heart before the two-year waiting period had elapsed, but Brazil chose to resign its membership permanently. Other withdrawals occurred in the middle 1930's as the League more and more took on the aspect of a sinking ship. Thus the League failed to achieve and maintain universality not only because of serious disagreements in the pursuit of common objectives, but also because some states did not consider the rewards of participation to be great enough.

MEMBERSHIP IN THE UNITED NATIONS

The concept of general international organization as a "congregation of the just" was more pronounced in the framing of the UN Charter than in the drafting of the League Covenant. At the San Francisco Conference several Latin American countries, like Argentina in the early days of the League, took a position that membership should be universal from the outset. Needless to say, this position was quickly squelched by representatives of governments whose past and continuing involvement in world war had taught them to distinguish between international lawbreakers and lawkeepers, between war-making and peace-loving states. Only the lawkeeping peace-lovers were to have part in the organization. States that had not already proved their allegiance to law and the love of peace by declaring war on the Axis powers in time to meet the March 1, 1945, deadline would be admitted to full fellowship with the righteous only after careful scrutiny by the righteous. Nor would mere lip service to the ideals turn the trick. Universality was recognized as an ideal to aim for, but membership was to be limited to those who had proved themselves fit by deeds, not words.

The distillation of this sentiment appears as Article 4, paragraph 1, of the United Nations Charter:

> Membership in the United Nations is open to all other peace-loving states which accept the obligations contained in the present Charter and, in the judgment of the Organization, are able and willing to carry out these obligations.

A cynic, viewing the record of the parlous contest over admission of new members, might conclude that the United Nations had spent the first ten years trying to decipher the meaning of Article 4, paragraph 1, and finally concluded that it didn't mean a thing, as membership for all but partitioned states has become virtually automatic. A somewhat more charitable view is suggested by Hadwen and Kaufmann:

> In the early days of the United Nations applications for membership appear to have been closely studied. Latterly a country has been considered eligible for UN membership if it declares itself willing to assume the obligations prescribed in Article 4 of the Charter. The membership of the United Nations is now so varied that almost any applicant can compare its position in some respects with at least one existing member. There is a natural political reluctance to cast the first stone against a new applicant.[3]

The earlier, more restrictive view of membership is readily explicable in terms of the wartime setting of the San Francisco Conference: The restrictions were drawn with the Axis enemy expressly in mind. The passion, the insult and the injury of a most frightful war gave substance to the concept of a world divided into good and bad nations. Cooperation with governments that had sought the destruction of the wartime United Nations and whose destruction the grand alliance was then seeking, appeared almost unthinkable. From that vantage point in history, how could any state that subscribed to the ideology and tactics of the fascist powers be integrated into an orderly international community? How could such states be brought into the new international organization without disruptive effects? These rhetorical questions have an odd, archaic ring today; but they were basic to the attitude which shaped the membership provisions of the charter.

[3] John G. Hadwen, and Johan Kaufmann, *How United Nations Decisions Are Made* (Leyden: A. W. Sythoff, 1962), p. 128.

The Soviet Union clung more tenaciously than others to the principle that wartime conduct was an important determinant of eligibility for membership, but other political considerations crept in immediately. Although Afghanistan, Iceland, Sweden, and Thailand were admitted in 1946, the Soviet Union vetoed the applications of Jordan, Ireland, and Portugal. Doubt was expressed as to Jordan's independence, but Portugal and Ireland were kept out simply because of their wartime relations with fascist countries and their lack of diplomatic relations (in 1946) with the USSR. The latter objections created a restriction upon membership well beyond the intent of Charter Article 4.

On the other hand, two Soviet protégés—Albania and Mongolia—failed to win the endorsement of seven members of the Security Council. Although objective reasons could be given for the failure of Albania and Mongolia to qualify, their rejection foreshadowed the formation of new cold war alignments which were shortly to dwarf the significance of wartime alliances. At this early stage, however, the incipient East-West split did not prevent the United States from bargaining for the simultaneous admission of all five rejected applicants. This was the original membership "package deal," the first of many such unsuccessful attempts during the first ten years to enlarge the United Nations. Ironically, the Soviet Union refused to recede from its position that membership be based on the individual merits of each applicant.

By 1947 cold war lines had hardened, revealing the incongruity of the tactical positions assumed respectively by the United States and the Soviet Union on the question of membership. Outvoted at every turn in the Assembly and the Security Council, the Soviet Union had no hope of securing approval of its protégés by arguing their individual qualifications. Political leverage, not argument, was needed. The most promising possibility was to tie the admission of the Communist satellites to the admission of other states which commanded majority support in the Security Council and the General Assembly. Accordingly, the Soviet Union switched tactics and became a package dealer, using its veto to bar individual applicants.

By contrast, the United States occupied a position of strength which dictated the consideration of each application on its individual merits. Supported by a safe and generally overwhelming numerical majority in the Assembly and Security Council, the United States and its allies had no pressing motives for seeking a change in the composition of the organization and certainly none for accepting a Soviet package including new Communist memberships. Happily for the West, the membership provisions of the Charter were readily adaptable to the kind of conflict which now ensued. Even the Soviet Union had to admit that most of the vetoed applicants met the requirements outlined in the Charter, and a plausible case could be made that the Soviet satellites did not. The persistent veto of qualified applicants thus appeared as blackmail, an unconscionable attempt to foist an illegal and immoral package deal upon the organization. This made good propaganda for the West, and the opportunities for moralizing on the improper conduct of the Soviet Union were seldom missed. The ultimate resolution of the admissions controversy was to have a far-reaching effect on UN political processes, but in the meantime the controversy itself had become a major political issue.

While the cold war raged at its height, the ranks of the pro-Western majority held firm and the propaganda was effective. To some extent the United Nations assumed the appearance of an anti-Soviet coalition from which the exclusion of additional Communist members, even at the cost of excluding a great many more non-Communist states, seemed justified. Supporters of enlarged membership grew more concerned and more vocal with each passing Assembly session, but their ire was vented largely on the Soviet Union. The fourth Assembly even went to the length of requesting the International Court of Justice to determine whether the General Assembly could legally grant membership without a Security Council recommendation. The Court of course said no.

This state of affairs could not continue forever. If the Western position conformed more closely to the letter of the Charter, the Soviet position was closer to its logic—a logic which demanded that membership in the organization be consonant with the universalism of its objectives. If the United Nations were regarded as an anti-Soviet coalition or an association of like-minded states, with correspondingly limited goals, the application of Article 4 to justify the exclusion of the Soviet satellites made at least as much sense as the original intent to exclude Germany, Italy, Japan, and Spain. But if the real objects were "to practice tolerance and live together in peace with one another as good neighbors," to bring about settlement of disputes "by peaceful means," to "achieve international cooperation" in solving a wide range of economic and social problems, and "to be a center for harmonizing the actions of nations in the attainment of these [and other] common ends," the purposes of the organization could be achieved only by reaching toward truly universal membership. Viewed in this light the willingness of a state to assume membership, with all of its practical consequences for international cooperation, might well be regarded as evidence of peace-lovingness and acceptance of Charter obligations.

With the relaxation of cold war tensions which followed the Korean Armistice and the death of Joseph Stalin, new attitudes toward the membership issue developed. The perceptible loosening of the Western coalition, portents of corresponding fissures in Eastern Europe, and the growing assertiveness of African and Asian countries threw the question of admissions into new perspective. Freed from the total fixation upon cold war imperatives, the United Nations could be viewed more in its aspect as a world organization. As a result the propaganda appeal of the United States position weakened dramatically. Some members even began to wonder whether the United States, rather than the Soviet Union, was the real enemy of universality. Fortunately for the United States, the decline of McCarthyism and its attendant phenomena provided the necessary domestic maneuvering room when the need for change became expedient.

The expedient day arrived in 1955, perhaps hastened by "the spirit of Camp David" and the euphoria of the 1955 Geneva summit meeting, and the United States assented to a deal involving the admission of sixteen new members, including several Communist applicants. The agreement almost fell through when China vetoed the application of Mongolia, and refused to budge from this position, but ultimately a peculiar compromise was reached by which the Soviet Union accepted the continued exclusion of Japan as compensation for the continued exclusion of Mongolia. This was the great divide. In 1946 four new members had been admitted, five others were admitted between 1947 and 1950 and membership remained stabilized at sixty for the next five years. After the Great Compromise of 1955, however, the dikes were down to an onrushing stream of applications. Delays imposed upon the admission of Japan and Mongolia demonstrated that great power politics had not been entirely banished from admission procedures, but the multiplying newly created sovereignties of the world had only to cry out, "Open Sesame." With a few notable exceptions, membership in the organization has now become available for the asking. In numerical terms, the magnitude of the transformation wrought in the composition of the organization is indicated in Table 6-1.

Aside from the peculiar problem of China, the principal exceptions to the new universality are Switzerland, Germany, Viet Nam, and Korea. Switzerland, the former seat of the League and the present site of United Nations European headquarters, has remained aloof out of conviction that membership is incompatible with Swiss neutrality. The governments of both halves of Viet Nam and of Korea have applied for membership, but their political status has precluded great power agreement on their admission. Germany—East or West—would undoubtedly accept membership if it could be attained upon suitable conditions, and East Germany formally applied in 1965. Suitable conditions are not likely to materialize, however, in the absence of agreement among the major powers and among the peoples themselves on the question of whether Germany constitutes one state or two, and by what government (or governments) Germany should be represented in the United Nations. It is unlikely, in the present state of affairs, that West Germany would accept membership in a United Nations that also accorded separate membership to East Germany. On the other hand, the prospects for agreement upon unification in the near future seem slim. For the foreseeable future, the nonmembership of such states will

TABLE 6-1.　UN Membership and Geographic Region

Admission Date	Western Europe	Eastern Europe	Asia	Africa	Latin America	Other	Total Membership	Number of Admissions
Original Members	8	6	9	4	20	4	51	
1946	10	6	11	4	20	4	55	4
1947	10	6	13	4	20	4	57	2
1948	10	6	14	4	20	4	58	1
1949	10	6	15	4	20	4	59	1
1950	10	6	16	4	20	4	60	1
1955	16	10	21	5	20	4	76	16
1956	16	10	22	8	20	4	80	4
1957	16	10	23	9	20	4	82	2
1958	16	10	22	10	20	4	82	1 *
1960	17	10	22	26	20	4	99	17
1961	17	10	24	29	20	4	104	4 *
1962	17	10	24	33	22	4	110	6
1963	17	10	25	35	22	4	113	3
1964	18	10	25	36	22	4	115	3 *
1965	18	10	26	37	22	4	117	3 *
1966	18	10	27	39	24	4	122	4 *

* Membership totals do not correspond with the number of admissions in 1958, 1961, and 1964–1966, for the following reasons: (1) Syria and Egypt gave up their separate memberships in 1958 when the United Arab Republic was formed, but regained them in 1961 when Syria decided to resume its sovereign, independent status. (2) The union of Tanganyika and Zanzibar to form the Republic of Tanzania in 1964 had the same effect on UN membership as the 1958 UAR merger. (3) Indonesia withdrew from the United Nations in 1965 and resumed participation without formal readmission in 1966.

stand as a symbol of the kinds of political, economic, and social problems that political partition does not solve. In the meantime, West Germany maintains an observer at UN headquarters, has purchased $10 million in UN bonds, and holds membership in many specialized agencies.

The impact of an expanding membership upon the political processes of the United Nations was not fully appreciated when the Great Compromise was reached in 1955. Certainly, few would have dared to predict a membership approaching 120—an increase of one hundred per cent—within one decade. The transformation has been nonetheless significant. At the technical level, increased membership has posed a challenge to the adequacy of the UN's physical facilities. In 1964, UN conference facilities were expanded to provide for a membership of 128. The mechanical process of reaching an organizational decision has been lengthened merely by the fact that more people speak, and more people must be brought into negotiations. The increased consumption of valuable time in roll-call voting, directly proportional to the number of delegates called to respond, constituted a growing problem until 1965 when a push-button electrical voting system was installed. The range of represented interests has been broadened, and the decisions reflect in both form and substance the interests and ideological biases of the new United Nations majority. The interests of the underdeveloped, the anticolonial, the neutralist are better served because they are represented by more voices and more votes. These changes mirror the changing face of international politics. One can only speculate upon the fate of the United Nations as a world organization had the membership been forever frozen in the image of the 1950 world scene.

The expansion of UN membership also invites comparison with the League of Nations. At the end of twenty years the League had become merely a caretaker operation, discredited and devitalized, with eighteen withdrawals and one expulsion testifying to its vanished prestige and influence. By contrast, the United Nations has a twenty-year record of constantly increasing membership. It has extended no formal invitations to reluctant states and made no pretense of impartial investigation of each candidate's qualifications. Qualified applicants have been left waiting at the gate for years with not even an opportunity to speak a word for themselves. Yet nearly every new state, and most of the older ones, have beaten a path to the UN, ultimately to be rewarded by admission. And accomplishments have been substantial enough to command the continued adherence of every member. Even Indonesia, which withdrew early in 1965 in protest against the election of the Republic of Malaysia to a nonpermanent seat on the Security Council, returned to the fold the following year. Although delegates of the Soviet Union, South Africa, France, and others have occasionally walked away from a UN meeting they have ultimately returned. The rewards of participation have been sufficient to keep the membership substantially intact and expanding.

Chinese Representation

The continued exclusion of Communist China has been the most controversial exception to the rule of universality. The question is technically not one of membership. China was a Charter member of the organization and has been continuously represented in the meetings of the United Nations from the beginning. The question of "admitting" China, therefore, does not come before any of the UN organs. The principal forum for the controversy is the General Assembly where each session the matter appears as a challenge to credentials, that is, which government shall represent China? This frame of reference is perfectly logical because both governments pretend to speak for the whole of China, embracing the mainland and Taiwan. Such an approach begs the real issue, however, since neither government exercises control over the whole area each claims to represent. In practical terms each speaks for different territory and peoples. Whichever way the credentials question is decided, a sovereign entity is bound to go unrepresented in the United Nations. A decision on credentials would have the practical effect of granting membership in the organization to one and denying membership to the other, at least as far as Assembly participation is concerned. At the present time the National Government represents China in all organs of the United Nations where such representation is appropriate. Other organs might follow the lead of the Assembly if it were to endorse the Peking regime, although China could conceivably be represented by different governments in the Assembly and the Security Council since each body is the judge of the credentials of its members.

The obvious way out of the impasse would be to recognize Peking as the representative of China and to admit Taiwan as a new member of the United Nations, a prescription commonly called the doctrine of the "two Chinas." This solution would conform to the facts of sovereignty as it is now exercised and also serve the principle of universality. As is often the case, the obvious solution is not the most practical, since neither of the two governments principally involved is likely to accept it. If the Nationalist Government were to be ousted from the Chinese seat on the basis of credentials, including the loss of its permanent membership in the Security Council, the government of Taiwan would have little enthusiasm for reentering the club as a junior member. Whatever may come with the passing of Chiang Kai-shek's rule in Taiwan, his investment in the fiction of the National Government of China is too great to permit participation in an organization which effectively denies the fiction.

Similar considerations affect the position of Peking. Communist recognition that Taiwan is no longer a part of China might not entail as great a loss of face as Nationalist acceptance of the fact that China is not a part of Taiwan. Yet Peking has shown no signs that its opposition to a two-China deal is any less adamant than that of the National Government. Members of the United Nations in gradually increasing numbers appear more anxious to have Communist China's participation than Peking is to participate. The Chinese Communists have given no indication of a willingness to make concessions for the sake of United Nations representation, and certainly none so great as to admit the right of Taiwan to separate membership. Unless Taiwan and Peking both undergo a drastic change of heart, an eventuality which seems highly unlikely, the United Nations will not be big enough for both of them in the foreseeable future.

Given the necessity for a choice between the two, the proverbial unbiased stranger might find something anomalous in the decision of the Assembly year after year to seat representatives of ten million people on Taiwan in preference to representatives of a government controlling 700 million Chinese on the mainland. For those more familiar with the historical antecedents of the controversy, the anomaly may not be wholly removed but the explanation is fairly obvious. The continued exclusion of Communist China is due to the remarkable influence of the United States, Peking's own persistently truculent conduct, and the transformation of a credentials question into a problem of qualification for membership in the organization.

If Peking had been willing to bridle its contempt for the traditional niceties of international intercourse and restrain its readiness to resort to violence as an instrument of policy, its representatives might now be seated in the United Nations. The initial manhandling of foreign nationals and property by the Chinese Communists following their ascent to power in 1949 raised doubts about their capacity for responsible international behavior and contributed to American reluctance to extend diplomatic recognition. The outbreak of the Korean War and subsequent Chinese intervention not only hardened the American position on diplomatic recognition but also gave substance to the argument that Communist China did not meet the Charter requirements for membership in the United Nations. The argument was technically irrelevant to the issue of representation, but it had practical weight because most members were willing to see the issue for what it was—a problem of membership.

The implications drawn from these early events by the United States reflected adversely upon Peking's love of peace and willingness to carry out the obligations of membership. The subsequent conduct of the Chinese People's Republic did little to improve the image. The termination of the Korean War provided occasion for Communist China to step up subversive activity in Southeast Asia and increase pressure upon the offshore islands of Quemoy and Matsu. When the memory of these crises dimmed, China dealt its supporters a slap in the face by attacking India. As if deeds were not proof enough of aggressive tendencies, Chinese leaders openly sneered at Soviet preachments of peaceful coexistence and vociferously proclaimed the inevitability of violence as a means of extending their system to the whole world. The United Nations itself came under verbal assault as "a vile place for a few powers to share the spoils." [4] It is such conduct that has given needed and timely support to American efforts in the Assembly to save China's seat for Taiwan.

An examination of voting in the Assembly on the Chinese representation issue, 1950–65, shows a fairly steady accretion of support for Peking. The trend seemed quite clear during the decade 1951–60 when the issue was being avoided by a vote to postpone consideration during the session. The percentage favoring postponement moved from 61.7 per cent in 1951 to a peak of 73.3 per cent in 1954, followed by a progressive decrease each year to a low of 42.4 per cent in 1960. However, the Assembly voted in 1961 to treat the question of Chinese representation as an "important" matter requiring a two-thirds vote, and since that time the question has been posed directly as a proposal to substitute Peking delegates in place of those from Taiwan. The question was similarly framed in 1950. Significantly, 55 per cent

[4] Radio Peking, quoted in *Minneapolis Tribune*, Jan. 7, 1965, p. 3.

of the membership opposed the displacement of Nationalist China in 1950, and 51.8 per cent were opposed in 1963. In 1965, however, the shift of France and a number of French-oriented African countries to the side of admitting Red China led to an even split in the voting, 47 to 47 with 20 abstentions. In 1966 Nationalist China regained some of the lost ground. So long as the issue requires a two-thirds majority, Peking's seating in the General Assembly is unlikely to occur. But the two-thirds requirement could be revoked by the vote of a simple majority.

TABLE 6-2.   General Assembly Voting on the Representation of China
1950–1966

Year	Total Membership	Members Favoring Nationalist China		Members Favoring Communist China	Members Abstaining	Members Not Voting
1950	60	33	(55.0%)	16	10	1
1951	60	37	(61.7%)	11	4	8
1952	60	42	(70.0%)	7	11	0
1953	60	44	(73.3%)	10	2	4
1954	60	43	(71.7%)	11	6	0
1955	60	42	(70.0%)	12	6	0
1956	79	47	(59.5%)	24	8	0
1957	82	47	(57.3%)	27	7	1
1958	81	44	(54.3%)	28	9	0
1959	82	44	(53.7%)	29	9	0
1960	99	42	(42.4%)	34	22	1
1961	104	48	(46.2%)	36	20	0
1962	110	56	(50.9%)	42	12	0
1963	111	57	(51.4%)	41	12	1
1964				(No Vote Taken)		
1965	117	47	(40.2%)	47	20	0
1966	121	57	(47.1%)	46	17	1

Note: From 1951 through 1960 the motion was to postpone further consideration of the issue. In 1950, and since 1961, the motion has been to seat Red China in the General Assembly in place of Nationalist China.

Viewed in a long-range perspective, the seating of Communist China appears inevitable as a consequence of the same forces that brought the United States to the Great Compromise of 1955. There is reason to believe that a majority of United Nations members, including some which have in the past abstained or voted out of deference to the United States, believe that the objectives of the United Nations can be achieved more effectively with Communist China inside the organization. This conclusion follows logically from the rationale of the 1955 Compromise which influences the present attitude of the organization toward admission of new members. The Compromise implied that cold war interpretations of peace-lovingness and willingness to fulfill Charter obligations were to be abandoned, just as World War II concepts had similarly been abandoned, in favor of less restrictive interpretations. In 1946 the objectives of the United Nations were operationally defined to exclude participation by fascist states; later they were redefined to preclude admission of additional Communist states; since 1955 they have been redefined to exclude essentially no state that is willing to accept the Charter and open itself to the kinds of diplomatic contact and interchange that are inescapable concomitants of active membership.

The position of the United States (and of the *voting* majority) is thus anachronistic. This apparent anachronism in American policy persists for a variety of reasons. Domestic public opinion has been carefully cultivated over the years by several administrations to reject categorically Communist China's participation in the United Nations. This position, reflected in numerous polls and elections, has become hard and rigid to the point that any compromise would be regarded by the mass public as appeasement pure and simple. Also, American relations with Taiwan, carefully cultivated since 1949, would be seriously jeopardized at the slightest hint of any "deal." A reversal in American policy would raise questions among staunch allies about American steadfastness and convey the image of abandoning friends under pressure. In addition, the millions of Chinese in Southeast Asia would probably react to such a switch with a transfer of mass support to Peking. These factors, together with the troublesome role that the Peking regime could be counted on to play as a participant in the UN political processes, explain American reluctance to proffer a new compromise. American policy makers are not ready to eat humble pie now or in the foreseeable future.

PARTICIPATION BY NONMEMBERS AND NON-SELF-GOVERNING TERRITORIES

Membership is extremely important, but political participation in international organizations is not limited strictly to member states either in law or in practice. In many instances, participation by nonmembers has been actively solicited and received. Despite rejection of the League Covenant by the United States Senate, communications were regularly dispatched from League headquarters to the United States government, and League overtures were ultimately rewarded with wide American participation in League meetings. After the early years of aloofness, American delegates were found at most League-sponsored conferences on nonpolitical questions, and the United States made substantial contributions to the League budget for these activities. United States delegates took an active part in League disarmament conferences, and in 1931 an American diplomat sat as a nonvoting participant in League Council discussions at one stage of the Manchurian dispute. For practical purposes, the United States consulate at Geneva served as a permanent if not altogether official mission to the League of Nations. Nor was the United States the only nonmember participant. Even Brazil, which quit the League in 1926, continued to cooperate in many economic and social programs under League auspices.

A similar pattern of nonmember participation has characterized the

United Nations. "Permanent Observers" at the General Assembly are currently maintained by the Federal Republic of Germany, Monaco, the Republic of Viet Nam, the Republic of Korea, and Switzerland. Before ·their admission to the United Nations, such countries as Austria, Finland, Italy, and Japan were also represented by observers at the United Nations. It goes without saying that the observers consult as well as observe, and their governments have contributed financial support to technical assistance, refugee relief, the UN Children's Fund, and other economic and social programs. Although observers have no vote, and no formal voice in the Assembly, the views of their governments are in fact represented. Other UN organs are also open to observers. At a recent session of ECOSOC, UN records listed thirty-eight "observers from UN member states not members of the Council" in addition to observers from West Germany, Switzerland, and the Vatican.

The nonmember observer system is an extralegal expansion of political participation since the United Nations Charter makes no provision for it. The Charter, however, does have constitutional provision for participation by nonmember states in the peaceful settlement of disputes. In this limited area, nonmembers are granted some of the privileges of members, contingent upon acceptance of equivalent obligations.

In contrast to the League and United Nations, a number of the specialized agencies permit participation by non-self-governing entities.[5] The constitution of the Universal Postal Union goes so far as to provide full voting membership for specified non-self-governing territories—the practical effect of which is to enhance the voting power of the metropolitan country. Most of the named dependencies have since become independent, however. Several other organizations, including the FAO, IMCO, ITU, and WHO, have a category of associate membership which offers a voice but no vote to dependent territories.

PRIVATE INTEREST GROUPS

The range of political participants is not exhausted by a discussion of member states, nonmember states and non-self-governing territories. The twentieth century has seen a very significant meshing of activity by private interest groups ("non-governmental organizations" or "NGO's" is the UN expression) with the processes of intergovernmental organizations. Although

---

[5] League membership was open, on condition, to any "fully self-governing State, Dominion or Colony" (Article 1, par. 2). Canada, Australia, South Africa, New Zealand, and India were named as original members of the League although their self-governing status was at least ambiguous in 1920. Membership in the United Nations is open only to "states" (Articles 3, 4), but Byelorussia and the Ukraine, obvious nonstates by any objective standard, were included as original members by virtue of Franklin D. Roosevelt's compromise with Joseph Stalin at Yalta.

much of the contact is informal in nature, a surprising amount of interest-group consultation now takes place through constitutionally established forms. The International Labor Organization is far and away the most daring innovator, allowing full participation with voting rights to representatives of private interests. The ILO tripartite representational system permits each member state to send four delegates to the General Conference—two representing the government, one representing employer interests, and one delegate chosen in consultation with national labor organizations. This balanced combination of public and private interest dates from the formation of the ILO in 1919 and is still unique; but consultation without right of participation in debate and voting is becoming increasingly common in other bodies.

The UN Economic and Social Council, under Article 71 of the Charter, is authorized to "make suitable arrangements for consultation with nongovernmental organizations" and currently has such "arrangements" with more than 300 national and international organizations "concerned with matters within its competence." In 1964 ten of that number were included in category A, reserved for organizations with a "basic interest" in most Council activities.[6] An additional 131 were category B organizations—those with special competence but concerned only with a few Council activities; and 214 were listed on the "Register," a third class of organizations not qualified for the first two but still able to make a "significant contribution." Placement in any of the three categories requires affirmative action by ECOSOC. All are entitled to send observers to public meetings of ECOSOC and its commissions and to consult with the secretariat on matters of mutual concern. Category A and B groups have the right to submit written statements on pending issues for circulation to members of the Council, a privilege that organizations on the Register may exercise only upon the invitation of the Secretary-General. Class A groups have the further privilege of presenting their views orally at special hearings of the Council, as well as proposing items for the provisional agenda of the Council and its commissions.

Other intergovernmental organizations have a variety of provisions for consultation with private groups. The World Bank charter calls for the creation of an Advisory Council of not less than seven members representing banking, commercial, industrial, labor, and agricultural interests. The

[6] These included two business organizations (International Chamber of Commerce and the International Organization of Employers), three labor groups (International Confederation of Free Trade Unions, International Federation of Christian Trade Unions, and the World Federation of Trade Unions), one agricultural organization (International Federation of Agricultural Producers), the International Cooperative Alliance, and three noneconomic organizations (Inter-Parliamentary Union, World Federation of United Nations Associations and the World Veterans Federation). *Yearbook of the United Nations, 1964,* p. 377.

Food and Agriculture Organization is authorized to consult with national and international bodies concerned with nutrition, food, and agriculture. The International Telecommunications Union has an International Consultative Committee on which recognized private operating agencies in the communications field may participate. The organizations of the European Community—ECSC, EEC, and Euratom—are also served by legally constituted advisory bodies on which private interests are represented—and on certain issues the advisory body must be consulted before final decisions are taken by the governmental agencies of the community.

The arrangements cited above illustrate the extent to which private interest groups have been institutionally integrated with the decision-making structure of international organizations, at least in an advisory capacity. Probably even more significant are informal contacts with interest groups, not unlike those which are familiar to the student of national governmental processes. This is particularly true of the European Economic Community where the existence of supranational institutions has led to the formation of new international associations specifically for the purpose of influencing Community decisions. Most intergovernmental organizations, in fact, have a variety of contacts with private groups. UNESCO, for example, not only has developed a vast clientele of private groups but actually relies on them for the administration of certain UNESCO programs. Additional contacts are fostered by the national UNESCO commissions formed in most member countries.

Just as intergovernmental organizations have dealings with a large number of private associations, private groups may be concerned with the activities of many intergovernmental organizations. A good example is the International Air Transport Association to which nearly all important world airline companies belong. The Association has consultative status with ECOSOC, holds representation on the ITU Consultative Committee, and cooperates closely with the Universal Postal Union and the World Meteorological Organization, all of which engage in activities directly affecting world air transport. As one might suspect, the Association has especially intimate relationships with the International Civil Aviation Organization. Not only does the IATA cooperate with the ICAO in the formulation of standards, it can sometimes go even further by encouraging uniform arrangements on matters such as airline rates on which governmental representatives to ICAO may be unable to agree.

Generalizations about the role of private interest groups are risky because of the wide variation from one intergovernmental organization to another and the paucity of reliable data. Nevertheless, a few tentative comments will be ventured. Nongovernmental organizations are active at many points in the political process. This includes participation in formal consultative arrangements as well as informal contact with members of secretariats, technical committees, governing boards and executive committees, and national delegations to international conferences. The influence of interest groups on international organization may also be exerted indirectly through contact with national governments.

Observation further suggests, but without the confirmation of carefully marshaled comparative data, that the influence of nongovernmental organizations is greatest when directed toward economic, social, cultural, and humanitarian issues and least when concerned with the more "political" issues of peace, security, and national prestige. It is no accident that of the four collegiate organs of the United Nations, only the Economic and Social Council gives constitutional consultative status to private groups. This undoubtedly bespeaks a feeling that nongovernmental organizations have an interest in economic or social issues that is specific, direct, and immediate, while their interest in political questions is indirect, diffuse, and shared with people generally. It may also represent a carry-over from national affairs where governmental officials often lend an attentive ear to interest groups concerned with domestic problems but, even in democratic pluralistic societies, appear to regard public opinion in foreign affairs as an object to be manipulated rather than heeded, except within very broad limits.

Private group activity is also more evident in areas where an international agency has the capacity to affect directly the particular interests of the group. This may account for the relatively insignificant influence of private groups upon the General Assembly of the United Nations. The Assembly can make recommendations and pleas, but it has little power to take authoritative action affecting the interests of private groups. The typical Assembly resolution is couched in such general terms that it can have only the most tenuous relationship to the concrete interest of any particular nongovernmental organizations. Representatives of private organizations in fact make contact with Assembly delegations but their influence appears to be minimal. One highly unusual exception was the Assembly decision in 1947 to partition Palestine. The pressure of pro-Zionist groups upon Assembly delegations and their home governments was insistent, sustained, and in some instances very effective. Exceptions aside, what has been said of the Assembly applies to the Economic and Social Council and with even greater force to the Security Council.

Quite a different picture emerges in the European Community of Six where international institutions have the power to regulate, reward, and punish the conduct of private groups and individuals. As a result, pressure group activity has increased with the expanding scope and effectiveness of Community operations. New international associations of private groups have been formed in order to obtain better representation of interests. For somewhat analogous reasons, UNESCO is also a focus of effective private group activity. A major function of UNESCO is to encourage educational, scientific, and cultural interchange among persons of different nationality. When an international organization is in a position to hand out favors such as fellowships and scholarships, contracts for writing and publication, and subsidies to support private international societies fostering such interchange, there is obvious incentive for private groups to attempt to influence the allocation of the rewards. Similarly, the direct and immediate concern of the International Air Transport Association with the activities of ICAO invites close collaboration between public and private international organizations.

The influence of nongovernmental organizations should not be overestimated. Intergovernmental organizations are still run largely by governments, not by private organizations. Nevertheless, the attention of private groups is being increasingly directed toward international organization. As public international organizations develop the capacity to affect the fortunes of nongovernmental groups, they will engage the interest of groups and inevitably become a focus of pressure group activity.

THE SECRETARIAT OFFICIAL AS POLITICAL PARTICIPANT

The political functions of international secretariats are discussed in a subsequent chapter, but a description of participants in the political process would be incomplete without a brief reference to the international civil servant. In any political system the line between the making and the execution of decisions—between policy and administration—is hard to draw. The policy decisions of "legislative" bodies take on color and character from the subsequent "administrative" decisions which give them effect. Furthermore, administrative officials are often participants in the political process in an even more primary sense, and this is true of international secretariats as well as national administrations. Albert Thomas, the almost legendary first Director-General of the ILO, played the role of vigorous policy executive or "chancellor," and national delegates not infrequently heeded his counsel. Eric Drummond, often cited as the archetype of the apolitical British civil servant, knew how to keep his peace in public but wielded substantial influence upon the course of League events by his skill and pertinacity in quiet, private negotiations with governmental representatives. Although differing in many ways, the first three UN Secretaries-General— Trygve Lie, Dag Hammarskjold, and U Thant—have all felt a responsibility to bring the weight of their office and their uniquely international point of view to bear on issues confronting the United Nations. Secretaries-general of international organizations, by whatever title they are called, have been and are now participants in the political processes of their respective organizations with a kind and extent of influence exceeding that of many delegates holding credentials from member states.

In terms of power and influence wielded, much depends upon the incumbent himself. For example, a Secretary-General who has a broad view of the role of the organization, who interprets the Constitution liberally, who knows how to make effective political use of his personal powers of persuasion can exert substantial influence on the decision-making processes. His successor, on the other hand, may view the organization, its Constitution, and his own office in narrow administrative terms and, hence, be largely an unsophisticated observer of the dynamics of decision-making. The former, like Albert Thomas of the ILO, leave a lasting imprint on their organization because they have helped to determine its goals, direction, competence, and policies.

The influence of the secretariat upon the political process is not restricted to the activities of the chief administrative officer. Others farther down in the hierarchy participate as well. Experience, expertise, and neutrality may qualify secretariat officials for the role of counselor or informal adviser to delegates whose respect and friendship they have earned. Ties of friendship, mutual trust, and mutual interest permit an international civil servant to approach delegates with proposals for action, not only in areas directly affecting the conduct of administration but in matters relating to the larger areas of substantive concern to the organization.

In some functional organizations, much of the political initiative is regularly left to the secretariat. Indeed, one cannot overlook the immense policy implications of budget preparation—a task regularly left to secretariats. Recognition of its importance is implicit in the practice, recently developed by the United States and other major contributors of funds, of "concerting their views more effectively on budget and program issues and bringing them to the attention of the secretariats of UN agencies in time to influence budget proposals." [7] Perhaps the point is somewhat overdrawn by one scholar who speaks of "secretariat officials in agencies which are to a large degree the property of their staffs and special constituencies, and in which governments are practically confined to the tasks of paying the bills and exercising sporadic and ineffectual policy control." [8] Nevertheless, the statement underscores the point that in international organization, as in national government, neat divisions of persons into "legislative" and "administrative" roles are not realistic. If administrators are capable of influencing the making of institutional decisions they also may be participants in the political process.

[7] Richard N. Gardner, *In Pursuit of World Order: US Foreign Policy and International Organizations* (New York: Praeger, 1964), p. 38.

[8] Inis L. Claude, Jr., *Swords into Plowshares,* 3rd rev. ed. (New York: Random House, 1964), p. 362.

INTERNATIONAL ORGANIZATIONS AS PARTICIPANTS

The discussion of participation in the political processes of international organization surely has turned full circle when international organizations themselves must be considered as participants in the decision-making processes of other international organizations. Yet, such is the case. Representatives of the European Common Market even now represent the Six in some aspects of GATT tariff negotiations and, when the customs union is fully established, will be the principal negotiating agent. The GATT secretariat, in turn, maintains contact with the European supranational authorities in Brussels. In the United Nations Development Program, the participating intergovernmental organizations jockey vigorously to influence the allocation of available funds. At a lower level, coordination of technical assistance is facilitated by interagency committees of secretariat officials. The field would by no means be exhausted to mention such relationships as the regular interchange between ECOSOC and the specialized agencies, collaboration between the Economic and Social Council of the Organization of American States and the UN regional Economic Commission for Latin America, and the regular liaison maintained between Euratom and the International Atomic Energy Agency. Such phenomena illustrate an often ignored political fact—that international organizations are more than mere channels for national diplomatic activity. An international organization with permanent institutions is itself a political entity capable of participating in the political processes of the international system.

Selected Readings

BOCK, EDWIN A. *Representation of Non-Governmental-Organizations at the United Nations.* Chicago: Public Administration Clearing House, 1955.

BOWETT, D. W. *The Law of International Institutions.* New York: Praeger, 1963.

CLAUDE, INIS L., JR. *Swords into Plowshares.* New York: Random House, 1964, 3rd ed., Chap. 5.

RUDZINSKI, ALEKSANDER W. "Admission of New Members: The United Nations and the League of Nations," *International Conciliation,* No. 480, April, 1952.

STEIN, ERIC. *Some Implications of Expanding United Nations Membership.* New York: Carnegie Endowment for International Peace, 1956.

WALTERS, F. P. *A History of the League of Nations.* New York: Oxford University Press, 1952, Chaps. 6, 27, 30, 33, 46, 48, 64.

7 | *The Political Process— Interaction*

National interest and power may ultimately determine who gets what in the international arena, but perceptions of interest and use of power are modified by the institutions through which power is exercised. The trend of our times is toward more and more complex structuring of state interaction through the proliferation of international organizations. This in turn has required adaptation by the participants to the requirements of interaction within the framework of new institutions. It has required the modification of old forms of national representation and the development of new techniques of exerting influence at the international level. To the student of international politics the most significant questions that can be asked about international organization relate to the kinds of adaptations it requires of member states, the ways in which participation modifies national perceptions of interest, and the extent to which participation affects the exercise of national power. These are questions to which definitive answers have not been found—and perhaps never will be—but they should be asked. This chapter will present information and concepts that may be helpful in framing tentative answers to these important questions.

NATIONAL ORGANIZATION FOR UN PARTICIPATION

U. S. participation in international organizations works like a funnel. At one end, experts in government agencies recommend policies for the United States to adopt in the United Nations on a wide variety of topics. At the other end, U. S. spokesmen in international forums are expected to state these policies with clarity and authority. This presents the government with a formidable task of coordination.[1]

What Bloomfield said of United States participation applies in greater or lesser degree to other members of international organizations. The need to formulate national policies on a wide range of issues for discussion at international meetings places an added strain on a nation's foreign policy

[1] Lincoln P. Bloomfield, *The United Nations and U. S. Foreign Policy* (Boston: Little Brown & Company, 1960), p. 263.

machinery. Many countries feel compelled to formulate policy on specific issues that never would have concerned them except for their participation in an international organization. Even for issues that would have meant national involvement in any event, policies must be framed with a view to the kinds of action the international organization might be expected to take and the singular kinds of diplomatic negotiation that take place there. When a country is required to state its position in a great number of international meetings, on diverse subjects and at diverse places, in addition to maintaining the traditional range of interstate contacts through normal diplomatic channels, "a formidable task of coordination" is indeed created. Most countries are not as highly organized in the realm of foreign policy operations or as deeply concerned with the outcome of such a bewildering variety of international issues as is the United States. But all must make some adaptation of their foreign policy machinery and process to the requirements of international organization.

The organizational response of the United States to its growing involvement with the new conference type of diplomacy is impressive. A major subdivision of the Department of State—the Bureau of International Organization Affairs—is concerned exclusively with United States participation in international organizations.[2] Other functional and geographic bureaus of the department normally employ full-time advisers for UN affairs who serve as key points of contact for coordinating their work with that of the Bureau of International Organization Affairs. This only suggests the scope of the organizational response, since primary responsibility for relations with regional and military organizations are lodged elsewhere in the Department of State and in the Defense Department. Indeed, international conferences can and do involve participation by officials in every major department of government. The significance of UN activities is underscored by the status of the chief United States representative to the United Nations, as a member of the President's cabinet since 1953.

The far-ranging activities of the United Nations and related international organizations produce a constant flow of UN-oriented information within the national policy-making system. Almost any major foreign policy problem confronting the United States can have a "United Nations" aspect, even when UN action is not a feasible alternative. The subdivision of the State Department most directly concerned with a foreign policy question must maintain liaison with the Bureau of International Organization Affairs not only to make sure that the problem is considered in terms of a possible UN solution, when appropriate, but also to consider a possible UN reaction to other courses of conduct.

---

[2] The evolution of the unit is suggested by the changing titles assigned during the course of its existence—Office of Special Political Affairs, Bureau of United Nations Affairs, and now Bureau of International Organization Affairs.

If an issue is to come before the United Nations, upon the initiative of either the United States or some other member, the Bureau has responsibility for clarifying the possible policy alternatives and preparing position papers to guide the actions of American representatives in the United Nations. This, again, is not a self-contained operation. Although the International Organization Bureau may have primary responsibility for preparing the policy position, it will approach the task through the creation of a small working group—a temporary interoffice committee including representation from geographic and other interested bureaus—to do the groundwork and make the initial policy recommendations. Preparation of UN positions on economic and social issues may also require coordination with the policies of other executive departments through the operation of an interdepartmental coordination committee. Not all questions slated to come before an international organization are given equal attention, but elaborate policy preparation is often necessary if US spokesmen at international meetings are to speak with the voice of unity, coherence, and authority.

Missions and Delegations

Another development in the administration of foreign policy that has accompanied the amazing growth of twentieth century international organization is the permanent mission. The League of Nations pioneered this development, and the United Nations has made it almost universal. Most members now maintain missions to the United Nations in New York on a year-round basis. Many states also have permanent representation at the UN European Office in Geneva and at the headquarters of other international organizations, generally in the form of small permanent missions, or liaison officers attached to local diplomatic missions or consulates.

The permanent mission to international organization is related generically to the traditional diplomatic mission, but there are differences in activity and in orientation arising from the multilateral character of its relationships with representatives of other countries. The mission is not accredited to a single foreign government but to an organization in which many governments are represented. In any national capital multilateral contacts occur among diplomats from the various national embassies in the capital. But this is incidental to the primary mission of representation to the host government and not the fundamental object. The UN diplomat, on the other hand, deals constantly with many national viewpoints and policies and often operates through procedures that are more congenial to national parliaments than to chanceries and foreign offices.

The permanent mission has attained its most characteristic development at the United Nations in New York. Members of the Security Council find the maintenance of a permanent mission indispensable to the discharge of their responsibilities on a body that is "so organized as to be able to function continuously." All members of the organization must have representatives in New York three or four months a year, and sometimes longer, to attend sessions of the General Assembly. Others are engaged at different times in the formal meetings of other major organs of the United Nations and the very numerous subsidiary UN commissions, committees, and subcommittees.

If participation in regular meetings were the principal activity of missions to the United Nations, their permanence could probably not be justified by nonmembers of the Security Council. Such meetings are important for their symbolic aspects as well as for their utilitarian functions, but a great deal more of the work of the missions is carried on outside the meeting chambers and between the sessions of UN bodies. As one participant in the process stated in 1961,

> Preparations for forthcoming meetings, preliminary negotiations, and the task of becoming acquainted with representatives of 99 countries take time. A considerable amount of work is done on items and issues which may never formally come before any UN body. Continuous working relations must be maintained with the Secretary-General and key members of his staff, an especially important factor 1) in the area of economic and social issues, where UN agencies and Secretariat personnel have considerable responsibility for carrying out decisions taken by UN meetings, and 2) in aspects of the political field where the United Nations has been given organizational or constitutional responsibilties, exemplified by the United Nations Emergency Force, the United Nations Truce Supervision Organization, and the United Nations Operation in the Congo.[3]

The continuing need to prepare, to maintain contacts, to negotiate and to exchange information accounts for the burgeoning of the permanent mission.

Each country has a chief of mission as its permanent representative at the United Nations, usually a person holding the diplomatic rank of ambassador. Below the chief the size of the UN mission varies with the interests and resources of the state. In June, 1966, the permanent missions ranged in size from the one-man mission of Iceland (plus supporting clerical staff) to the Soviet delegation with fifty-seven persons of diplomatic rank listed in the UN Bluebook. The United States mission consisted of forty-two officials and a total permanent staff of more than one hundred.

When the General Assembly is in session most permanent missions are substantially augmented by the appointment of Assembly delegations and supporting staff, including both clerical and professional personnel. Each state is entitled by the Charter to five representatives and five alternates, with no constitutional limitation on the clerical or advisory staff, which usually consists of permanent mission personnel as well as officials from

[3] See Richard F. Pedersen, "National Representation in the United Nations," *International Organization*, Vol. 15, No. 2 (Spring, 1961), p. 257.

foreign offices, diplomatic posts, or other agencies of government. It is customary for the permanent representative to be one of the delegates, but he is often outranked on the delegation, at least for part of the session, by the foreign minister or other influential political representative of his country. Some states send a full delegation of professional diplomats, while others include prominent persons from other ministries of government. Many, including the United States, send one or more members of parliament and prominent persons from private life. Women regularly have a part in the staffing of both missions and delegations. The United States delegation to regular sessions of the General Assembly has always included at least one woman as delegate or alternate as well as two members of Congress chosen in alternate years from the Senate and the House.

The role of the UN delegate is fixed by the milieu in which he functions, and the term "parliamentary diplomacy," coined by Dean Rusk, is an apt way of phrasing what goes on there. The emphasis must be placed on "diplomacy" rather than "parliamentary," however, because the delegate comes as a representative of his government to negotiate agreements rather than as a representative of his constituency to enact laws. Nevertheless, the UN delegate has much in common with his parliamentary counterpart. He engages in a constant round of discussion with colleagues and participates in a species of formal parliamentary action. He gathers information of relevance to policy issues and performs a variety of public relations functions. He must carefully plan his public utterances with an eye to the impact on opinion at home, abroad, and in the UN chambers. His immediate task is to seek out areas of common interest with other delegates and embody that interest in resolutions that can command a voting majority.

The basic difference beween a UN diplomat and a national legislator springs from the relationship of the UN representative to his government. Everything is done, or should be done, not only with a view to the interest of his country but in conformity with his government's instructions. This does not rule out all freedom of action because instructions on a given topic may be vague, or nonexistent, and the delegate himself may be able to influence the content of his instructions by the opinions and information he channels to the home office. There are, indeed, vast differences in the quality of instructions from one delegation to another. Some governments turn out lengthy and detailed instructions severely circumscribing the delegate's freedom of action, while other governments on some issues "appear to instruct their delegation in terms of the position of other governments, i.e. 'Vote more or less like —' or 'If — votes "no" you can abstain'." [4] Some governments may provide no instructions at all on a given issue, leaving the delegate to apply only a general policy to the situation, if in fact his govern-

[4] John G. Hadwen and Johan Kaufmann, *How United Nations Decisions Are Made* (Leyden: A. W. Sythoff, 1962), rev. ed., p. 34.

ment has a policy. The representative of a government which gives sparing instructions will ultimately answer for his actions, but in the short run his maneuverability is greatly enhanced.

Regardless even of the differences in instructions, no government can fully anticipate all of the twists and turns of UN parliamentary diplomacy. All delegations have a large measure of discretion as to tactics, and all have considerable, if unmeasurable, influence upon policies. The need for quick decision on an unanticipated turn of events may require action on the spot by the delegation. If the decision is of sufficient importance instructions will be obtained from home, but the very urgency of a situation that evokes a request for additional instructions provides opportunity for the delegation to influence policy. An experienced member of the United States permanent mission to the United Nations has thoughtfully analyzed delegation influence upon policy.

> The influence of a delegation on policy may be exerted from the time when an issue first arises, but it is strongest after actual consideration of an issue has begun. If a delegation reports, on the basis of its negotiations, that an objective cannot be achieved without modification, or if it recommends that the diplomatic cost of achieving the objective would be too high to justify pursuing it, its judgments necessarily carry considerable weight, as it is the only authority in a position at that moment to evaluate most of the available facts. Missions and foreign offices naturally seek to anticipate such a situation in preparing their policy positions, and missions to the United Nations customarily advise their foreign offices on the feasibility or desirability of varying courses in advance. However, anticipation is not fact, and when anticipated difficulties actually arise, the influence of the negotiators is much greater than beforehand. As a source of information on the attitudes of other governments and delegations, as an agency of the government professionally concerned with effective use of the United Nations in foreign policy, and as a tactically minded unit which may be able to predict whether certain lines of policy may or may not be successfully carried out, a delegation is likely to exert substantial influence on policy formulation throughout the consideration of any individual issue.[5]

When the last word is in, nevertheless, the delegations to international meetings have a responsiveness to their governments that is unmatched by any ordinary relationship of a national legislator to his constituency or even, in democratic societies at least, to his political party.

THE INSTITUTIONAL FRAMEWORK OF INTERACTION

The aggregate of national interest and national power supply the dynamics of the political process in international organization, but the institutional

[5] Pedersen, *op. cit.*, p. 259.

setting conditions the outcome. One obvious limitation imposed by the setting is the subject-matter competence of the organization. Narrow-purpose organizations like the specialized agencies are limited by their charters to a specific subject area, be it the promotion of world health, the supplying of development funds, or the regulation of maritime transport. Regional organizations, by reason of membership as well as constitutional prescription, are limited to matters of particular concern to states of the region. The League and the United Nations, by their nature as general international organizations, have been much less restrictive in scope. Both have extended their legal purview to virtually everything under the sun except matters of "domestic jurisdiction." As indicated in an earlier chapter, even this limitation has had little deterrent effect upon members of the United Nations who were determined to have an issue considered there. The issue of jurisdiction has ultimately always boiled down to who has the votes to put an item on the agenda. Consequently, the one practical limitation upon the subject-matter competence of the United Nations is the interest of its members in not having an issue discussed.

A second institutional characteristic affecting political outcomes is procedure governing debate, deliberation, and voting. If decision-making procedures accurately mirror the actual distribution of national power among members of the organization at any given time, the effect of procedure is minimal. But procedure almost necessarily reflects a distorted image of other power relationships. This is true for at least three reasons. Power in international relations is indispensable to action—but it is not readily defined or measured. In its most meaningful sense, power is always relative to the achievement of a particular objective, and this very relativity adds to the ambiguity of the concept. It is possible, for example, that one or a few "powerful" states may have the nuclear megatonnage literally to blow up the world and yet not have the power, singly or in combination, to obtain agreement upon a charter for international organization having a voting arrangement that reflects the differences in military potential. Some forms of power are so specialized and so absolute that, as Walter Millis suggests, it is "as impossible to change the power of a multimegaton thermonuclear bomb into usable political or social values as it would be to change a $1,000 bill in a country drugstore on a Sunday." [6] Even a studied attempt to devise voting procedures corresponding precisely to distributions of national power could deal only in approximations. A second difficulty is the fact that some power relationships change, while procedures remain relatively static. What may be a close relationship between power and formal influence one year may be far out of balance at a later period. Finally, statesmen who draw up constitutions for international organizations are not

[6] Walter Millis, "The Uselessness of Military Power," in Robert A. Goldwin, ed. *America Armed* (Chicago: Rand McNally & Co., 1963), p. 28.

rigorously "political men," altogether governed by cold calculations of national power; they are also influenced by ideals. The ideal of a harmoniously functioning world community, or the ideal of respect for the sovereign equality of even small states, may weigh in favor of creating institutions where not quite all of the lion's share of formal decision-making authority is given to the lions.

A third important effect of institutions upon the substance of international decision-making is the opening of new channels of communication and sources of information. This has implications for both power and interest. Participation in international organizations may broaden the interests of governments, giving them objectives where they had none before. Other interests may change in the light of new information and understanding. Hopefully, under the impact of intensive multilateral interchange of views and aspirations, national interests will be broadened to harmonize with the concept of an international community interest. This is not an inevitable result of participation in international organizations; quite the contrary, discussions may sharpen policy differences and arouse new antagonisms. In either event, however, the concept of national interest is modified as the result of the new forms of interchange. Likewise, channels of communication via international organizations can result in new alignments of states with very significant effects upon power relationships. Small states with common interests, for example, may find strength in the unity of common cause pursued through the political processes of international organizations. In a world in which information variables are so crucial to national policy-making, the new communication network created by international organization cannot fail to have its impact.

Voting in the International Arena

More detailed consideration must now be given to voting procedures as a means by which institutional structures affect political outcomes. The advent of voting as a means of arriving at decisions in the international arena was closely tied to the rise and growth of international organization. The international conferences of an earlier period were primarily negotiating bodies without "action" responsibilities. Their function was to negotiate agreements that could be embodied in treaty form for ratification by the respective national governments. Voting implies a process of deciding, and all the important deciding—as well as the implementation of decisions—was the prerogative of governments individually. The time-hallowed principles of national sovereignty and equality seemed to demand nothing less than the complete dispersal of decision-making authority among national units.

With the development of international organizations having permanent secretariats, organizational budgets, and "constitutional" subject-matter competencies, a new dimension was added to inter-state relations. The organizations themselves became entities with legal, and one might add political, personalities. Budgetary funds, though raised through national contributions, were then disbursed by the organization, and secretariats did the bidding of the collectivity—not of the individual national units. A growing number of decisions of international organizations became operative immediately by reason of institutional action without necessity for referral to the treaty-ratification processes of individual members. Voting, a time-honored practice in domestic politics, appeared as the logical means by which the new organizations should formally arrive at decisions.

The shift of real, if limited, decision-making power to international organizations understandably placed a strain upon the principles of state sovereignty and equality. Both principles can be made meaningful and reasonable if considered strictly as juridical concepts. In any other context, however, state equality is a fiction, and the material base of state sovereignty—construed in terms of practical independence and freedom of action—is being constantly eroded by technological advances. If maintenance of the legal fictions was relatively harmless in any earlier day, their inconsistency with the operating requirements of organized international cooperation has today become more than a theoretical problem. The principle of equality presupposes that each state should have an equal voice in the decisions of international organization. Yet states have neither equality of interest in the substance of organizational decisions, nor equality of power and responsibility for their implementation. The divorce of the power to decide from interest in and responsibility for the outcome of decisions can have pernicious consequences.

The problem is compounded by the implication necessarily arising from the principle of sovereignty that no state can be bound without its consent and, hence, that decisions should be taken only by a unanimous vote. Such a requirement strikes at the capacity of the organization to produce decisions at all. In part, the difficulty is one of efficiency—the wheels of the organization will turn more slowly or not at all if unanimity must be reached on every matter. In part, also, the problem is interrelated with the questions of interest, power, and responsibility. Decisions may be of such a nature that their effectiveness depends upon the concurrence of all, or of certain states, and no meaningful decision can be taken without that concurrence. In many instances, however, action might profitably be launched without the concurrence of states having little practical interest in or responsibility for the matter.

The present functioning of international organizations displays varying kinds of compromise between principle and practicality. Equality of voting rights continues to be the general rule, although its impact has been blunted in several ways and it has been abandoned by a few organizations in favor of a distribution of voting power more accurately registering the actual distribution of interest, power, and responsibility. This is true of organizations whose primary function is the handling of money—the International Bank, the International Monetary Fund, the International Finance Corporation, and the International Development Association—where voting power is governed by contributions.[7] In a literal sense, he who pays the piper calls the tune. Commodity councils, such as the Wheat and Sugar Councils, allot votes according to volume of imports and exports of the commodity. Still another form of unequal or weighted voting is exemplified by the Rhine River Commission where in the early nineteenth century the principle of interest triumphed over sovereign equality, resulting in the apportionment of voting power, for certain purposes, in a proportion roughly equivalent to river frontage. Inspection of the foregoing examples suggests that weighted voting is most common where the weighting principle can be tied to a single measurable criterion directly related to the primary function of the organization. An exception to this generalization is the European Economic Community which provides for national representation in its Parliamentary Assembly, and voting on specified issues in its Council, on the basis of arbitrary formulas related to no readily measurable criteria.[8]

When weighted voting is not feasible, organizations often recognize differences among states by the creation of special executive or deliberative bodies of limited membership on which representation can be granted according to some rough approximation of interest, power, and responsibility. Thus the "Big Five" are permanent members of the Security Council, twelve of twenty-four governmental seats on the ILO Governing Board are allotted to states of "chief industrial importance"; states of "chief importance in air transport" are given preference in the election of the ICAO Council; extent of interest in shipping and maritime trade determines eligibility for the IMCO Council. The Trusteeship Council membership, as another example, includes states administering trust territories, the permanent members of the Security Council, and elective members.

In the constitutions and the day-to-day practice of international organizations, the rule of unanimity in voting has suffered a more far-reaching eclipse than has equality. During the past century one bastion after another has fallen to the onward sweep of majoritarianism in international voting procedures—first in the more technical international public unions and later in political conferences. Unanimity still governs some organizations of limited membership, including the NATO Council, the Arab League Council,

---

[7] In 1966 the World Bank had more than one hundred members, but the United States exercised more than twenty-five per cent of the voting power, and six leading contributors held a majority of the votes.

[8] Seats in the Assembly are allotted as follows: France, Germany, and Italy, 36 each; Belgium and the Netherlands, 14 each; Luxembourg, 6.

COMECON, and the Council of the OECD, among others, but most international organizations conduct business by concurrence of a simple or qualified majority. Even in the Security Council, which retains the principle of unanimity for permanent members, decisions are made by a form of qualified majority. In the other policy-making organs of the United Nations decisions require only a simple majority of members voting on the issue, with the single exception of the General Assembly requirement of a two-thirds majority on "important" measures.

In view of the great diversity of attitudes and values among nations, one may query why they have submitted to majority voting in so many matters of international concern. The answer lies partly in the demand of a technologically shrunken world for international cooperation in larger and larger doses, not only to mitigate conflict but also to meliorate confusion. If a certain amount of majoritarianism is the price to pay for effective cooperation, states will perforce pay it. At the same time, one must recognize that the spread of majority voting in international organizations does not necessarily mean the triumph of "majority rule" in international affairs. To pass a resolution by majority vote is one thing; to take action that is practically effective and legally binding upon all members is quite another.

A careful examination of the law and practice of international organizations reveals that majorities have much more authority to recommend than to command, and that the latter is largely limited to matters on which a high degree of consensus exists or which do not seriously impinge upon the vital interests of states. Members of the Universal Postal Union can alter certain postal regulations by a two-thirds majority vote; but one finds substantial consensus on the general objectives to be promoted by the UPU. Likewise, a high degree of consensus upon the objects of union has permitted a gradual increase in the number and importance of binding decisions that may legally be taken by organs of the European Community without unanimous concurrence of member states. Most international organizations can adopt binding recommendations with respect to operations of their secretariats, the filling of electoral offices, the expenditure of budgeted funds, and other housekeeping activities. While such internal "lawmaking" power is important, it does not ordinarily affect the vital interests of states.

Except for power over internal operations, one looks almost in vain for authority to make binding decisions in any of the four major policy-making organs of the United Nations. The General Assembly, the Economic and Social Council, and the Trusteeship Council are clearly limited to nonbinding recommendations. The Security Council, in Chapter VII of the Charter, is empowered to make "decisions" that members have agreed, by ratification of the Charter, "to accept and carry out," but only with respect to enforcement measures directed toward a "threat to the peace, breach of the peace, or act of aggression." The failure of the Security Council to reach accord upon the "special agreement or agreements" contemplated in Article 43 has nullified the power of the Security Council to make binding decisions for the use of military force, and until the 1966 Rhodesian crisis the Security Council had never ordered members to take any of the "measures not involving the use of armed force" contemplated in Article 41 of the Charter.[9] Practically speaking, the Security Council, like the General Assembly, has been limited to exhortation rather than command. If more substance is to be added to the form of majority rule than now prevails, states must look to the creation of the greater consensus that will constrain majorities to act responsibly and elicit general confidence that majorities will so act.

Voting in the Great Assemblies: League and United Nations

The League Assembly and the UN General Assembly, with their equal voting rights for nations large and small, illustrate the tenacity of the sovereign equality ideal. The rule of "one state, one vote" was quite incongruous with the distribution of power among potential members of the League of Nations in 1919. It was, however, consonant with the precedent of the Hague Conferences, the legal doctrine of sovereign equality, and the demands of the small states to be so recognized and represented. Moreover, the great powers at the Versailles Conference regarded equal voting in the Assembly as no threat to their positions of influence in the organization. They contemplated that the Assembly would meet every three or four years, while the main business of the League was conducted through the Council. In any event the great powers could exercise the influence begotten of great power and, as a last resort, prevent hasty Assembly action by exercise of the veto which the rule of unanimity in voting accorded to each member, large or small.

When the United Nations Charter was drawn the same pressures for equality of voting rights in the General Assembly were present. They were buttressed by the experience of a League Assembly that had met annually —much oftener than anticipated—but had behaved on the whole responsibly and had in fact been amenable to great power influence. Although the great powers, as well as the lesser ones, lost the protection of the veto when the unanimity rule was abandoned for a qualified majoritarianism, the powers of the General Assembly were limited to recommendation only. At the San Francisco Conference the possibility of weighted voting in the General Assembly was considered but discarded as impractical and unnecessary.

In contrast to the vitality of sovereign equality, the rule of unanimity has declined markedly in international organization. The League Covenant contained important exceptions to the unanimity principle. The appoint-

---

[9] In June, 1950, the Security Council "recommended" that UN members furnish assistance necessary to repel the attack upon South Korea.

ment of a Secretary-General, increases in the size of the Council, and all procedural matters could be decided by a simple majority. Admission of new members required a two-thirds majority, and an Assembly report on a dispute referred from the Council could be adopted by the concurrence of all members of the Council and a majority of other members. The effects of the unanimity rule were mitigated in other ways by a volume of custom and precedent stopping short of actual Covenant amendment. Absences and abstentions were ignored in determining the outcome of a vote, and the category of procedural questions was broadened greatly. In addition, much Assembly business came to be transacted by the use of the informal recommendation approved by a simple majority. The Covenant specified that decisions required unanimity but was silent on recommendations.

The lessons of the League were not lost. The statesmen at San Francisco specified certain "important" questions that should require a two-thirds majority of members present and voting, with provision for the Assembly by a simple majority vote to designate other questions or categories of questions as "important" enough to require a two-thirds majority.[10] All other questions were left to be decided by a simple majority. The General Assembly subsequently adopted the League practice of including abstentions as well as absences among those not· "present and voting." Given a large number of abstentions, this means that even an important measure can be adopted by considerably fewer than a majority of the members.

In the two decades and more that have elapsed since the framing of the Charter, serious thought has been given to proposed changes in Assembly voting rights. The sources of dissatisfaction with equality of voting right, primarily among the larger powers, are various. The expansion of the United Nations to include many small, newly independent states has multiplied the voting disparity of small states over large. The limited diplomatic experience, as well as the small size and resources, of many new members raises doubts about the wisdom of their participation on terms of equality. Moreover, the partial transfer of responsibility for the maintenance of peace and security from the Security Council to the Assembly, which may now be in the process of reversal, has made the stakes of General Assembly action greater. The concern about Assembly voting procedures may also be a tacit admission by the great powers that their informal influence has not been a wholly effective means of guiding Assembly action.

Probably more fundamental than these reasons, although related to them,

10 The enumeration in Charter Article 18 includes "recommendations with respect to the maintenance of international peace and security, the election of the nonpermanent members of the Security Council, the election of the members of the Economic and Social Council, the election of members of the Trusteeship Council . . . ; the admission of new Members to the United Nations, the suspension of the rights and privileges of membership, the expulsion of Members, questions relating to the operation of the trusteeship system and budgetary questions."

is the fact that the General Assembly has not behaved as responsibly as the Assembly of the League. Too often, groups of states have lost sight of the ultimate function of the organization as a means of facilitating agreement and pursuing programs of common action. Instead, members have looked for proximate victory in a display of voting power, running roughshod over the rights and interests of the minority. The United States on many occasions has successfully forged voting majorities for resolutions that were totally unacceptable to states in the minority whose cooperation was essential to achieving the purposes of the resolutions. The reluctant minority in such instances has generally included the Soviet bloc, and the adoption of the resolutions has brought some minor cold war victories. From the standpoint of national interest, using the United Nations to generate propaganda and to exert political pressure on the Soviet Union, and occasionally on other countries, may have been justifiable. Certainly it was so regarded by American policy makers. But it did not enhance the reputation or the capacity of the General Assembly for responsible behavior, for promoting genuine agreement, and for speaking bold words only when it had a reasonable prospect of undertaking bold deeds.

In recent years, for reasons related to the changing composition of the Assembly, the United States has posed less often as the ringleader of a voting majority determined to have its way, no matter how futile the gesture or how unrelenting the opposition. This role has been assumed by anticolonial majorities and economically underdeveloped majorities. One may justify and rationalize the conduct of these and other intermittently overbearing groups in the Assembly, but the implications for the "one state, one vote" principle still remain. If majorities, consisting largely of small states with limited material power and often limited diplomatic experience, can use the power conferred by UN voting procedures to "coerce" one or more of the great powers, policy makers of the larger powers will understandably remain disenchanted with the principle of equal voting rights. Such disenchantment will scarcely lead to adoption of any scheme for weighted voting because of the inherent difficulty of devising any particular plan that will not work to the relative disadvantage of at least enough states to block Charter amendment. It is all too obvious, as Goodrich noted several years ago, that "the formulas proposed have generally been complicated and have raised more problems than they resolve." [11] Readjustment may be

---

[11] Leland M. Goodrich, *The United Nations* (New York: Crowell, 1959), p. 128. Harlan Cleveland, Assistant Secretary of State for International Organization Affairs, reported in 1963 that a computer study of the effect of weighted voting in the General Assembly demonstrated such a change was not desirable for the United States. The State Department Report concluded: "We have therefore considered fifteen possible voting arrangements. . . . When applied against a sampling of 178 roll-call votes on a varied range of issues beginning in 1954, when there were sixty UN members, and ending in 1961, when there were 104 members, none of the weighted arrangements pro-

sought, however, through such an expedient as the creation of a screening committee dominated by the great powers for important issues in the Assembly and, quite possibly, through reemphasis upon the role of the Security Council in matters of peace and security.

Voting in the Security Council

When the League Covenant added organizational flesh and bone to the Concert idea, the traditional rule of unanimity in Council voting was modified by certain important exceptions. Under Article 15, the Council was authorized to recommend measures for pacific settlement of a dispute without the concurring vote of the parties. The Covenant further provided that "matters of procedure . . . including the appointment of committees to investigate particular matters" should be decided by a majority vote of members represented at the meeting. This provision was in fact interpreted broadly. The Council also learned to ignore abstentions as well as absences in determining the existence of the required unanimity, despite the seemingly contrary import of Article 5 which called for "agreement of all the Members of the League represented at the meeting."

By institutionalizing the special position of the great powers in Security Council voting procedures the Charter moved a good deal farther from both equality and unanimity than the Covenant had dared. The voting arrangements represented a compromise between the new spirit of majoritarianism and the persisting realities of power elitism. A carefully contrived voting formula agreed upon at Yalta fixed the required majority at seven affirmative votes, the seven to include all five of the permanent members on nonprocedural issues. (In 1965, Charter amendment increased the size of the Council from eleven to fifteen, and the required majority from seven to nine.) An exception for cases of pacific settlement was again included in the form of a requirement that a party to a dispute abstain from voting in its own case. The retreat to a qualified majority wiped out the veto of the small powers on the Council, and as noted in an earlier chapter, many of the smaller states at the San Francisco Conference bitterly resisted retention of the veto by the five permanent members. On this point, however, the major powers were united, adamant, and unambiguous: Without the great power veto there would be no Charter. Faced with this alternative the opponents of the veto yielded and the Yalta formula was adopted.

The Security Council veto is an eloquent testimony to the reluctance of

---

duced general results as favorable to US interests as the one-state-one-vote principle. This is because the overall success of US policies in the UN has in very large measure depended upon the support of the smaller states and it is these smaller states whose voting power is heavily reduced under any weighted voting system." See *Weighted Voting*, Study, United States Department of State, June 2, 1963.

the great powers to relinquish or circumscribe their right of independent national decisions upon matters affecting their vital interests. This attitude was implicit in Secretary of State Cordell Hull's assurances to a group of Senators in a briefing preceding the San Francisco Conference that "our Government would not remain there a day without retaining its veto power." [12] The issue, indeed, involved more than mere concern for great power prerogative. Without the concurrence of all major powers, the United Nations could conceivably find itself in the position of starting enforcement action that it could not finish for lack of cooperation from an essential collaborator. Worse yet, a decision to use force in the name of the United Nations over the objection of a state controlling large military forces could be the means of turning localized conflict into a major war. The veto was intended to avoid such situations and, above all, to preclude the initiation of enforcement action by the organization directly against one of the major powers. In the words of one of the architects of the Charter, "This would be the equivalent of a world war, and a decision to embark upon such a war would necessarily have to be made by each of the other major nations for itself and not by any international organization." [13]

The experience of more than two decades has not invalidated the basic assumptions underlying the veto as they relate to enforcement action, but it suggests that the framers of the Charter gave the veto unnecessarily broad scope. By the end of 1965 the Soviet Union had cast 103 vetoes, and France, Britain, or China had participated in a half dozen others. Of the total number, forty-five were used by the Soviet Union and one by China to prevent approval of membership applications. One can hardly contemplate the ten-year deadlock over admission of new members and the continual rejection of proposals for the pacific settlement of disputes without wondering whether the right to cast a veto in such instances really contributes to world peace and security.

On the other hand, events have not conclusively demonstrated that the veto has done more harm than good. The persistent vetoing of membership applications has been exasperating, but only the Republic of Korea and South Viet Nam still remain outside the organization on that account. When a positive contribution to peace and security by international organization has been objectively feasible, and the Security Council could not act, the General Assembly or the Secretary-General has often managed to step into the breach. This was true in Korea, the Suez crisis, and in the Congo, to name only the more striking examples of UN action without great power agreement. The Security Council voting formula has served to delay and to

---

[12] Cordell Hull, *The Memoirs of Cordell Hull* (New York: Macmillan, 1948), Vol. 2, p. 1664.

[13] Leo Pasvolsky, "The United Nations in Action," *Edmund J. James Lectures on Government* (Urbana: University of Illinois Press, 1951), pp. 80–81.

annoy but generally not to cripple the organization in its peace-keeping functions.

Many vetoes have been almost frivolous or inconsequential in their practical effects. In 1963 the Security Council was unable to utter official condemnation of the murder of two Israelis in an incident along the Israeli-Syrian border; in 1949 the Council was unable to tender official congratulations to the Netherlands and Indonesia upon the successful conclusion of their negotiations for Indonesian independence. In 1954 a Soviet dissent prevented the referral of the Guatemalan complaint to the Organization of American States, but the matter was effectively removed from Security Council consideration nevertheless.

It cannot be denied that action on a number of very important questions has been forestalled by the veto, without any compensatory follow-up action by the Assembly or the Secretary-General. But in most such instances the action prevented would have been impossible in any event without the cooperation of the great powers concerned. One may deplore the Soviet veto of various proposals for disarmament and the control of atomic energy, but the stumbling block was Soviet disagreement—not the peculiarities of Security Council voting procedure. With or without a formal veto, disarmament and atomic energy control are not possible without Soviet cooperation. The veto killed a Security Council resolution calling for an end to the Berlin blockade in 1948, but no one seriously contends that only the Security Council voting formula stood between the United Nations and an early termination of the blockade. The one practical effect of the veto was to prevent the Council from adopting a resolution that had no prospect of being heeded. Similarly, one can harbor an honest doubt that India would have honored a Security Council resolution urging cease-fire and withdrawal of its troops from Goa, even if such a resolution could have been adopted without the concurring vote of the Soviet Union. The Security Council should not be criticized too strongly for the existence of a procedure that prevents the Council from undermining its own authority by issuing orders that can be disregarded with impunity.

Furthermore, one can plausibly contend that the veto has had utility for the organization as a whole by enabling the Soviet Union to remain within the United Nations as an active participant. If during the years of Western dominance in the Assembly the Soviet Union had been forced to accept the will of the Western coalition in the Security Council, it might have withdrawn from the organization. The few occasions on which delegates of Britain, France, and China have cast the veto indicate that they too value the protection of the unanimity rule. Although the United States has not yet sought refuge in the veto, no responsible government spokesman has advocated elimination of the veto rule—modification, yes, but elimination, no.

The severity of the voting formula has in fact been mitigated in Security

Council practice. In accordance with League of Nations precedent, abstention of a permanent member has not been counted as a veto, even though the Charter expressly states that nonprocedural decisions must include "the concurring votes of the permanent members." Security Council action in the Korean crisis of June, 1950, while the Soviet delegate was temporarily absent, set a further precedent—subsequently contested by the USSR—that the absence of a permanent member does not constitute a veto either. By practice and general acquiescence, the Security Council has also established broad categories of questions that are regarded as procedural and hence not subject to the veto.

Even the "double veto," early regarded with much apprehension by the smaller powers as a means of extending the range of questions that can be vetoed indefinitely, has been used sparingly. The Charter does not specify how the Security Council, in the event of disagreement, shall decide whether a question is procedural or nonprocedural. At San Francisco the great powers agreed that the issue would be decided as a nonprocedural question and therefore subject to veto. This meant that a permanent member could gain the right to veto any matter at all, regardless of whether it was sensibly a question of procedure or not, simply by voting against the preliminary motion to declare it procedural. In practice, the double veto was successfully utilized three times by the Soviet Union in the early years of the organization. When China attempted to use the double veto in 1950 to deny a hearing to Chinese Communist spokesmen, however, the maneuver was thwarted by a ruling from the chair that the question was procedural. Since China was unable to muster seven affirmative votes, the President's ruling stood. The device of a ruling from the chair was used again in 1959 to circumvent the attempted Soviet veto of a resolution creating an investigating commission for Laos. The Soviet Union acquiesced in the presidential ruling of 1950 but objected loudly in 1959. The paucity of precedents leaves the legal picture unclear, but also suggests that the double veto has not been attempted often enough to be a serious problem.

The Flow of Information

Voting procedures are important because they set the institutional bounds within which decisions must be reached. Even more important, however, is the flow of information among the participants which precedes the voting. The kind of information available to the decision-makers, interacting with their values, determines the kinds of decisions that will be reached. Viewed as a link in an international communication network, the United Nations is a source of and a channel for information bearing upon national decision-making processes. At the same time the United Nations is itself a decision-making system that receives and utilizes information relevant to its own processes. One cannot fully appreciate the relationship of the organization to its members without considering both dimensions of this multidirectional communication process.

A constant stream of information originating with other UN delegations, the Secretariat, and journalistic accounts of UN activities pours into the foreign offices of member states. The United Nations also stimulates a heavier flow of information directly between foreign offices of countries mutually concerned with an issue that has been thrown into an international forum. The approach of a General Assembly session, for example, is always the signal for increased intergovernmental consultations both at New York and in national capitals. Members with a particular interest in the disposition of an issue will seek through pre-session discussions to obtain the widest measure of support for their positions and proposals. On other issues they may consult simply to obtain the information necessary to appraise their own policies intelligently in the light of positions held by others.

Whatever the scope of pre-session consultations, the beginning of an Assembly session brings a new phase in the processes of communication, negotiation, consultation, and compromise. At this point the character of the United Nations as a generator of information affecting national policy merges with its character as a system which receives and circulates information relevant to its own decision processes. National governments now become sources of information flowing into the UN system. Obviously this change in character is analytical rather than sequential—the information flow is in fact a reciprocal process in which feedback in all directions is virtually continuous.

At the Assembly, various channels of communication are available for continuing the dialogue. Debate in committee and plenary sessions has importance for symbolic reasons but is less significant as a vehicle for reaching agreement. A public address may serve to dramatize and occasionally to clarify positions, but reconciliation of differences requires a kind of negotiation and bargaining that flourishes in a more private setting. This can take place in quiet person-to-person exchange in halls and corridors, or even in the Assembly chamber. It can occur in clubs, bars, ballrooms, restaurants, and lounges. Issues can be hammered out among groups, large or small, in delegation offices or vacant rooms in the UN headquarters building. The spoken word is supplemented by the written note hastily scribbled and passed during the heat of debate, or the more carefully prepared statement sent out from delegation offices. Such less formally structured channels of communication are the effective means by which the Assembly's business is transacted and the alignments formed that make up the Assembly's shifting majorities.

Caucusing Groups

The extralegal patterns of communication that facilitate the process of decision-making are not altogether without formal structure. The private, ad hoc interchange between delegates drawn temporarily together by their common interest in an issue is a persisting and inevitable part of the political process. But other forms of interchange occur on a more routinized basis. These range in scope from the regular luncheon engagements of two friendly delegates whose governments consistently have common interests to the organized voting blocs or caucusing groups meeting at regular weekly or bi-weekly intervals, with time and place prearranged, established routines for the conduct of discussions and secretarial assistance drawn from one or more of the delegation staffs.

The activity of blocs has increasingly claimed the attention of governments, the press, and students of international organization. In the present discussion the expression *caucusing group* will be used in preference to *voting bloc* because the latter expression conveys an impression of group voting solidarity which is misleading save for the Soviet bloc. Even the monolithic front of the Soviet bloc has cracked in recent years under the pressure of Albanian defection and rumblings of independent action in Romania and elsewhere. Although a similar phenomenon of interdelegation coalition-formation characterizes most international conferences in some degree, attention here will be focused upon the General Assembly where the system has flowered in a rather specific and concrete form.

A caucusing group has been described as "any group of member states in the Assembly which has some degree of formal organization, holds fairly regular meetings, and is concerned with substantive issues and related procedural matters before the sessions of the General Assembly." [14] At the end of 1966 there were at least nine distinguishable caucusing groups in the Assembly, in addition to several incipient subgroupings and other more ephemeral combinations. They included the Asian-African group, the Arab group, and African group, the Benelux group, the Commonwealth group, the Latin American group, the Scandinavian group, the Soviet bloc, and the group of Western European and "other states." The "others" in the Western European group are Canada, Australia, and New Zealand. The membership of each group as of 1966 is shown in Figure 7-1. Examination of the figure reveals great overlapping of membership among the various groups. A few members of the Assembly, including, at this writing, China, Israel, South

14 Thomas Hovet, Jr., *Bloc Politics in the United Nations* (Cambridge: Harvard University Press, 1960), p. 31. Hovet defines a *bloc* as "a group of states which meets regularly in caucus and the members of which are bound in their votes in the General Assembly by the caucus decision." By this definition the only true bloc is the Soviet bloc, and even its solidarity has weakened with the defection of Albania and the loosening of intrabloc ties.

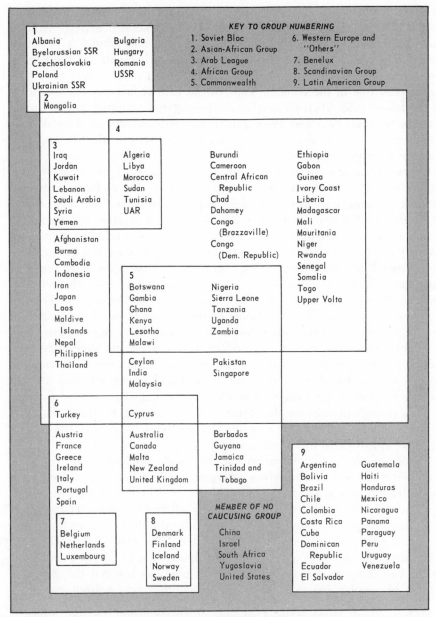

FIGURE 7-1. Caucusing Groups in the United Nations.

Africa, the United States, and Yugoslavia, do not belong to any caucusing group.

The Arab, Benelux, Commonwealth, Latin American, Scandinavian,

Western European, and Soviet caucusing groups have existed, at least in incipient form, from the founding of the United Nations. As new members have been added to the United Nations, their membership has been enlarged. The Asian-African group dates from the early months of the Korean war when delegates from twelve Asian and African states jointly affected a mediatorial role in the conflict. The African caucus first became operative in the fall of 1958 when six newly emergent states, admitted to the United Nations between 1955 and 1958, joined the small handful of older African members in an avowed attempt "to produce an African identity and personality in international affairs." [15]

Caucusing among regional and other groups received its initial impetus from electoral contests in the General Assembly. By seeking agreement beforehand, groups of members might hope to obtain an "equitable share" of elective positions on the Security Council and other bodies with a rotating membership. Secret balloting in Assembly elections precludes analysis of voting patterns, but observers agree that decisions of caucusing groups have been crucial in determining the outcome of elections. One early result of the caucusing was a series of "gentlemen's agreements" allocating elective seats on the Security Council, the Economic and Social Council, the Trusteeship Council, the International Court of Justice, the General Committee of the Assembly and certain other Assembly committees among various "geographical distribution groups." [16] Most of these agreements have since been embodied in Assembly resolutions. Although the geographical distribution groups are not based altogether on geographical contiguity, and are not entirely coterminous in composition with caucusing groups, the relationship is close enough to enhance the status of the caucusing groups as informal decision-making bodies. This amounts to a partial delegation of the Assembly electoral function to the caucusing groups.

States brought into combination initially for the purpose of getting office soon began to concern themselves with policy. If group action was effective in elections, why not also in dealing with issues? The Soviet bloc, of course, demonstrated impressive unity on virtually all matters from its inception. For other groups, caucusing sessions early proved to be convenient channels for exchange of information on policy matters. The step from exchange of information to complete agreement upon issues is a broad one, and none of the caucusing groups except the Soviet bloc has bridged the gap as a matter of regular practice. Even the monolithic Soviet front has been

[15] Ghana, "Draft Memorandum, Conference of African States," undated, quoted in Hovet, *ibid.*, p. 94.

[16] On the enlarged Security Council, five of the ten nonpermanent seats go to Africa and Asia, one to Eastern Europe, two to Latin America and two to Western Europe and "other" states. Of the twenty-seven seats on ECOSOC the distribution is Asia and Africa twelve, Eastern Europe three, Latin America five, and Western Europe and other states seven.

broken by an occasional abstention and on rare occasions an opposition vote. Given the atomistic structure of international society, ultimate authority to make policy decisions resides with individual governments, and no government can be forced to comply with the decision of a United Nations caucusing group. Nevertheless the fruits of group collaboration have proved enticing, and analyses of Assembly voting patterns have shown a fair degree of group solidarity, particularly among the Soviet, Arab, Scandinavian, and Benelux groups. For these four groups the "solidarity" voting, to use Hovet's term,[17] has invariably been over eighty per cent and often in excess of ninety per cent of all roll-call votes in an Assembly session. Voting agreement among the states concerned has tended to increase after the formation of a caucusing group with its organization and procedure for regular consultation, as compared with voting solidarity among the same states before the organization of the caucus.

A study of roll-call votes cast in the Assembly from 1946 through 1958, shows that the degree of identical and solidarity voting within caucusing groups has varied widely, however (see Table 7-1).[18] Caucusing groups are beset with centrifugal tendencies which increase with the size of the group.

TABLE 7-1. Voting Agreement of Caucusing Groups on Roll Call Votes in the General Assembly, 1946–1958

Group	Identical Voting %	Solidarity Voting %
Soviet	95.97	99.81
Benelux	77.7	94.6
Scandinavian	68.4	92.7
Arab	62.5	90.2
African *	45.5	91.0
Asian-African *	33.4	76.4
Latin American	29.2	64.2
Commonwealth	13.1	41.6

* Figures for Africa are based only on three sessions, 1956–1958. Figures for Asian-African group cover the period 1950–1958.

Source: Thomas Hovet, Jr., *Bloc Politics in the United Nations* (Cambridge: Harvard University Press, 1960), pp. 50, 51, 62, 67, 71, 74, 77, 87, 95.

[17] Hovet, *op. cit.*, p. 50n. A solidarity vote is one in which no member of a group votes against any of the others in the group, although one or more may abstain. This is to be distinguished from an "identical" vote in which all members vote alike, whether yes, no, or abstention.

[18] See note 17 for explanation of *solidarity* vote. A more recent study of two Assembly sessions, the fifteenth (1960) and the eighteenth (1963), utilizes a different technique for computing agreement scores and finds somewhat greater agreement among regional groups. The roll-call voting record of each state is paired with that of every other state in the group and the frequency of voting agreement between each pair is computed by a system in which complete agreement is 100, complete disagreement 0, and abstention paired with either a *yes* or *no* vote is 50. The author of the study produces the following table of agreement scores for six regional groups. The *mean* is the average score for all pairs of states within the group; the *low* is the lowest score occurring for any pair of

It is no coincidence that the four groups in Table 7-1 with the highest solidarity scores are also the four smallest caucusing groups. The differences of outlook that divide Commonwealth states make intra-group voting conflict the rule rather than the exception, even though the group members continue to value the caucus for its consultative and exchange-of-information function. The Asian-African group is so large and encompasses such a wide range of interests that it is likely to be split, in some small way at least, by nearly every issue that divides the Assembly. The splintering effect is also characteristic of the African and Latin American groups, although neither is so large in membership. Overlapping group membership also tends to inhibit group solidarity, while strengthening intergroup ties.

The inescapable fact is that cohesiveness varies from issue to issue. While the Asian-African group may have high cohesion on issues of self-determination or economic development, it may be badly split on cold war issues or on particular political disputes. The East-West division of the world cuts across the North-South demarcation lines—the lines that divide the industrialized, developed countries from the agrarian, underdeveloped lands. The complexities of world politics, springing from intricate patterns of national interest and power, cannot be neatly contained in the United Nations by the device of the caucusing group. Some national interests may run essentially along caucusing group lines; others cut through the caucus alignments; still others tend to unite two or more groups in common cause. Caucusing group solidarity can be an important determinant of national policy in the United Nations, rooted as such groups are in the expediency of Assembly

---

states on all of the roll-call votes used; the *high* is the highest score for any pair of states within the group.

Group	15th Session Mean	15th Session Low	15th Session High	18th Session Mean	18th Session Low	18th Session High
Eastern Europe	99.4	98.8	100.0	98.9	95.8	100.0
Latin America	83.7	68.4	95.4	91.1	78.9	100.0
Western Europe	79.2	57.8	98.4	83.5	60.9	98.6
Africa	78.9	55.1	97.9	88.1	68.8	100.0
Asia	77.6	52.6	96.2	82.4	55.0	97.6
Africa-Asia	76.5	48.1	98.1	85.2	54.1	100.0

See Robert Owen Keohane, "Political Influence in the General Assembly," *International Conciliation*, No. 557 (March, 1966), pp. 10–11.

Keohane's figures, as compared with Hovet's in Table 7-1, could reflect greater group cohesion after 1958 and perhaps a shift in the kinds of issues considered by the Assembly. Primarily, however, the difference is in the method used. By Hovet's method, nineteen Latin American states might vote yes on a series of roll-call votes, but, if the twentieth state voted no, the group score for both identical and solidarity voting would be 0. Using Keohane's method, the low would be 0, but the high would be 100, and the mean would be 90 (based on 190 possible pairings for each vote, 171 pairings registering agreement and 19 registering disagreement). Keohane comments that, on the whole, "the regional groups maintained greater cohesion than the mean for the Assembly," but "the differential was not strikingly large." *Ibid.*, p. 11.

politics and the bedrock of group interests extending well beyond the confines of the United Nations. But in the present state of international society, group solidarity cannot be the prime national interest; and Assembly decisions will continue to cut across group lines.[19]

Although opinions may differ, the growth of caucusing groups in the Assembly can be regarded as both natural and beneficial to the organization as a whole. It has been natural in the sense that men with common interests in a competitive situation will attempt to increase their competitive advantage by pooling energies for the attainment of the common ends. It has proved beneficial in a variety of ways. The caucusing group provides additional effective channels of communication among members of the Assembly. It facilitates compromise among members of the group and helps to clarify their positions. Often it saves Assembly time by permitting speaking assignments on particular issues to be filled by one or a few delegates from a group in place of the many who might otherwise speak. Caucusing can also save the time and energy of delegates by multilateralizing negotiations at the informal level, eliminating in some instances the necessity for an extensive series of bilateral negotiations.

The system unquestionably has its less desirable side. The group caucus can create power relationships within the Assembly at variance with the actual distribution of national power, and result in the adoption of a resolution which has "no practical significance because only countries which could implement it have voted against it." [20] It can, and sometimes does, lead to the bargaining of votes and logrolling on a grander scale than would be otherwise possible. It can, and occasionally has, added an element of rigidity to the Assembly negotiating process. If rigid group lines were substantially to impair the fluidity of ad hoc coalition-formation around specific issue-oriented centers of common interest, the effect would indeed be unfortunate. Despite the undesirable aspects of the system, however, the existence of caucusing groups is probably justified by their useful if not indispensable function of building consensus at a secondary level.

---

[19] The trans-caucusing group nature of Assembly voting behavior is amply attested by roll-call voting studies. Clusters of states with high voting agreement scores bear some relationship to existing caucusing groups but show enough important divergences to demonstrate that the influence of the caucusing group is by no means determinative of a state's voting behavior in the Assembly. See Leroy N. Rieselbach, "Quantitative Techniques for Studying Voting Behavior in the U.N. General Assembly," *International Organization*, Vol. 14, No. 2 (Spring, 1960), pp. 291–306; and Arend Lijphart, "The Analysis of Bloc Voting in the General Assembly," *American Political Science Review*, Vol. 57, No. 41 (December, 1963), pp. 902–17. A much more extensive analysis of Assembly voting patterns and their implications for world politics is found in Hayward R. Alker and Bruce M. Russett, *World Politics in the General Assembly* (New Haven: Yale University Press, 1965).

[20] A. Loveday, *Reflections on Administration* (Oxford: Clarendon Press, 1956), p. xiv.

Who Gets What?

Action by the General Assembly, like most other international conferences, is symbolized by the adoption of a resolution. Each resolution is a statement of "who gets what" with respect to a given issue, and each represents the acquiescence of a required majority of members in a particular allocation of values. Nearly all such actions are the products of extensive negotiation and compromise. When the political process works at its best, the final product is the expression of a common interest among states that have the will and the ability to do whatever its implementation requires.

Pressure and Influence

Sometimes the multifaceted consultation process fails to carve out the requisite area of common interest. In that event, all proposed resolutions may be rejected or else reduced to meaningless platitudes. Before accepting this unhappy outcome, however, a determined delegation may resort to pressure tactics—that is, to methods going beyond a factual exposition of the merits of the case. Bonds of friendship, of military security, of cultural homogeneity, of economic dependency may be invoked. Pressure may consist not so much in what is said, as in how it is said. When reluctant delegates are repeatedly buttonholed in New York and their governments subjected to insistent appeals at home, the pressure begins to be noticed. In this context an appeal for "good relations," carries an unmistakable hint that relations may be strained by failure to cast an appropriate vote. For a large country merely to express a strong opinion in conversations with a small power dependent upon it may constitute pressure. If no more is said, the small country is left to weigh the uncertain consequences of taking a position that is displeasing to its more powerful patron and benefactor. Such subtle interchanges constitute pressure at a low level and are a common occurrence in the Assembly.

The crasser forms of threat or promise are also utilized, but they are generally too costly to invoke very often. Threats arouse resentment and bribes do not build mutual esteem and respect over the long run. Most Assembly decisions are simply not important enough to justify the threat to alter levels of foreign aid or to take other forms of retaliatory action. Only on very important issues do the stakes of Assembly action appear to justify strong bilateral pressures.

Another form of pressure is the generalized threat of noncooperation with Assembly programs or obstruction of the organization's work. The prospect of noncooperation by the United States, for example, has thus far deterred the Assembly's economically underdeveloped majority from approving large-scale UN programs of development aid. Soviet action in the 1964–65 financial crisis represents the other tactic. The Russian threat to disrupt the organization by withdrawal was a formidable weapon in fighting off the American attempt to take away its vote in the Assembly.

Although pressure tactics are used by most states from time to time, the larger states obviously are in a better position to apply pressure. In this way the influence of national power may be translated into votes in the Assembly, and to a varying extent, realities made to triumph over the artificial distribution of formal voting power.

The small powers, nevertheless, are much more important in the General Assembly political process than their size and resources would warrant. They have votes that must be won if the Assembly is to adopt a resolution, and they have their own methods of influence. The very fact of great power rivalry enables some small countries to resist the pressure of one power by threatening to seek aid and support from another. The doctrine of nonalignment also serves to strengthen the bargaining position of some countries in regard to the great powers. Nonalignment is a prestige symbol in UN circles, and a public commitment to nonalignment serves notice to the great powers that a high price must be paid for any concession that would impair that nonaligned status. Small powers may also hope to influence the political process affirmatively by active participation in UN politics. They can present draft resolutions that structure the parliamentary situation by defining issues and setting the framework for debates. They can exercise whatever powers of persuasion their representatives may possess. They can appeal to group and ideological ties and exert the pressures of persistence. They can also trade their votes. As in domestic legislatures, votes are marketable commodities and support on one issue can sometimes be bought by a commitment to give support on another.

Within this milieu, some small states are unquestionably more influential than others. One variable is the skill of a state's diplomatic representatives. A change in personalities often works a change in the relative influence of particular delegations because some persons are more persuasive than others, more facile at compromise, more adept at fostering helpful contacts. The influence of a state is also affected by the resources it is willing and able to devote to its UN representation. A mission with the staff and facilities to research the issues and maintain contact with other delegations often becomes an influential source of information and advice to others. Officeholding can also enhance the influence of a state, at least temporarily, through increments of prestige, access to information, control over procedure, or the right to participate in the deliberations of select bodies. Membership on the Security Council almost invariably augments the influence of the incumbent.

Prestige is another important ingredient of influence, although the ingredients of prestige are not always clear. Prestige is often related to positions on political issues with which the government is identified. Norway, Sweden, Canada, and Ireland, for example, are well regarded because they are thought to be liberals on colonial questions, moderates on the cold war, and without an ax to grind. Yugoslavia has also held influence because of its unique position as a Communist country that is not subservient to the Soviet Union. The nature of a country's domestic regime may also affect its prestige. Brazil's prestige among many countries of Africa, Asia, and Latin America was substantially impaired by the 1964 coup d'état which replaced the constitutional leftist regime with a military government more closely aligned with the United States. Portugal and South Africa have essentially no prestige in the Assembly, because of apartheid and their colonial policies. Israel, which might otherwise be expected to wield some influence as a relatively well-developed, well-represented, and well-governed Asian state, finds its position stalemated by the implacable hostility of thirteen articulate Arab enemies.

The Structure of Winning Coalitions

The patterns of political influence within the United Nations were never clear-cut or simple, and they have become more complex with the passing of years. The United States continues to be the most influential member of the organization, although American influence has suffered a decline in recent years. The Soviet allegation of an American "mechanical majority" in the General Assembly during the first decade was very nearly an expression of the truth in its practical effects, if not in its more insidious implications. The cold war dominated UN politics just as it permeated the whole field of international politics. Backed by a responsive majority of friends and allies, the United States delegation time and again utilized the Assembly as an instrument in the cold war, while the Soviet bloc languished in a perpetual and unrepentant minority status.

Just as the cold war set the pattern for UN activities of the early years, great changes in international relationships which became pronounced in the mid-1950's could not fail to have their impact upon the world forum. The partial detente in the cold war, the loosening of coalition structures on both sides, the renaissance of Western Europe and the growth of a neutralist third force in the world brought changes to the United Nations— changes in both the structure of influence and the nature of the issues having priority. Even before the drastic enlargement of UN membership, and the consequent multiplication of non-Western votes, the new international forces had begun to reshape the activities of the Assembly. Issues of colonialism and self-determination, and demands from the economically underdeveloped lands, had been moving toward a position of increasing prominence in Assembly deliberations from the early 1950's. This trend was accentuated by the mass influx of new members, most of which were virulently anticolonial and unabashedly mendicant. While these issues were growing in importance, representatives of many Western nations began to have second thoughts about the utility of maintaining the United Nations as an anti-Soviet coalition.

In this altered situation the diminution of Western influence was virtually inevitable. The United States still retains the ability to muster a majority on most issues where the East-West confrontation is clearly the dominant question. Victory may require greater energy, however, and the majorities are less overwhelming than in the years of the mechanical majority. Moreover, the cold war has dominated relatively fewer and fewer UN issues, thus reducing the area in which United States influence in the past has been most effective. As the problems and demands of Asia, Africa, and kindred states crowd the agenda of UN organs, the influence of countries from these regions is enhanced by their direct interest in the issues as well as their expanded voting power. The new complexion of the United Nations has also permitted the Soviet bloc to escape from its former role as an isolated, perpetual minority. On colonial questions the Communist delegates can vote with the anticolonial majority; on economic matters their fortunes may be cast variously with the industrial contributing states or in moral support of the underdeveloped recipient states, depending upon the precise nature of the issues.

Significantly, both the United States and the Soviet Union vote in the minority oftener than most UN members. A tabulation of majority agreement scores for seventy-nine resolutions adopted by roll-call votes during the ninth, fourteenth, and seventeenth Assemblies shows that the United States voted *against the majority* more often than ninety-three of the 110 members included in the tabulation, and only four members voted against the majority more often than the Soviet Union.[21] Superpower disagreement with the majority is not quite as chronic as might be implied from such figures: the United States voted with the majority on seventy-one per cent of the resolutions, and the Soviet Union was in agreement fifty-eight per cent of the time. Nevertheless, the fact is clear that the two members which by all estimates are the most influential in the organization do not vote in the majority as often as most other states do.

There are several explanations of this paradox. First, the interests of the great powers on a wide range of issues are more sharply defined than those of most small countries; hence the United States and the Soviet Union have less flexibility in adapting their policies to those of a UN majority. Second, the superpowers often counteract one another when pulling hard on opposite sides of an issue. Third, on many issues they do not choose to exert their influence strongly because important interests are not directly engaged or

---

[21] Catherine Senf Manno, "Majority Decisions and Minority Responses in the UN General Assembly," *Journal of Conflict Resolution* (March, 1966), p. 8.

because their power cannot be converted at reasonable cost into readily usable increments of influence in the Assembly. Fourth, frequent voting with a majority is not so much a question of influence as of interests and positions on issues. The small states, which wield most of the votes, apparently have more in common with one another than they do with the great powers. Given the present complexion of the Assembly, a country which votes anticolonial, underdeveloped, and moderately pro-western will generally be in the majority. A number of Asian, African, and Latin American countries head the majority agreement list because their views on issues happen to coincide best with the views of the differing majorities which coalesce around the major types of issues before the United Nations.

Some notion of the shifting coalitions that form UN majorities may be obtained from an examination of Table 7-2, based on roll-call votes in the 1965 Assembly. The six issues in the Table are chosen for illustrative purposes only and are not to be considered as a reliable sampling of all issues on which a roll-call vote was recorded. The resolutions or motions adopted may be briefly summarized as follows:

1. Anticolonialism. This resolution urged the Special Committee of Twenty Four (on colonialism) to set deadlines for accession to independence of each territory; requested all governments to withhold assistance of any kind from Portugal and South Africa until they renounce their policies of colonial domination and racial discrimination; urged colonial powers to dismantle military bases in colonial territories; and asked the Special Committee to keep the Security Council apprised of developments that might threaten peace and security.

2. Convention on Elimination of Racial Discrimination. The Convention itself was approved 104 to zero with one abstention. The roll-call vote included in Table 7-2 was taken on a section dealing with reservations to ratification by member states. By this provision, a reservation was declared incompatible with the Convention and hence unacceptable if two thirds of the states parties objected to it. The object of this provision was to prevent countries from ratifying with reservations that condoned the practice of discrimination. The practical effect could be to deter some countries from ratifying at all.

3. Korea. This was essentially a repeat of earlier years, reaffirming UN objectives in Korea, urging unification under a democratic government, and continuing the mandate of the United Nations Commission for the Unification and Rehabilitation of Korea (UNCURK).

4. Pacific Settlement. Britain, the United States, and others had urged the establishment of a special committee to study the broad question of peaceful settlement, with particular attention to improved UN procedures. The vote was on a motion by Ghana to defer consideration of the question to the following year.

TABLE 7-2. Roll-Call Voting Alignments on Six Issues in the Twentieth General Assembly, 1965.

Issue	Vote (Yes-No-Abstain)	Prevailing Coalition	Opposing Coalition	Abstaining	Position of United States	Position of USSR
Anti-colonialism	74-6-27	32 Africa 18 Asia 11 Lat. Am. 11 Soviet 2 W. Europe	4 W. Europe 1 South Africa 1 United States	3 Asia 10 Lat. Am. 14 W. Europe	No	Yes
Convention on Racial Discrimination	62-18-27	32 Africa 16 Asia 3 Lat. Am. 10 Soviet 1 Cyprus	13 Lat. Am. 4 W. Europe 1 United States	8 Asia 3 Lat. Am. 15 W. Europe 1 Congo (Dem. Repub.)	No	Yes
Korea	61-13-34	14 Africa 10 Asia 18 Lat. Am. 18 W. Europe 1 United States	2 Africa 10 Soviet 1 Cuba	18 Africa 13 Asia 1 Finland 1 Jamaica 1 Yugoslavia	Yes	No
Pacific Settlement	48-27-8	28 Africa 9 Asia 10 Soviet 1 Cuba	5 Asia 5 Lat. Am. 16 W. Europe 1 United States	3 Asia 2 Lat. Am. 2 W. Europe 1 Nigeria	No	Yes
Financing UNEF	44-14-45	8 Africa 11 Asia 9 Lat. Am. 16 W. Europe	10 Soviet 4 Lat. Am.	22 Africa 10 Asia 8 Lat. Am. 3 W. Europe 1 United States 1 Yugoslavia	Abstain	No
Tibet	43-26-22	4 Africa 8 Asia 18 Lat. Am. 13 W. Europe	9 Africa 5 Asia 11 Soviet 1 Cuba	6 Africa 8 Asia 2 Lat. Am. 6 W. Europe	Yes	No

Key to regional designations:

1. Africa: African states
2. Asia: Asian states, except Mongolia
3. Lat. Am.: Latin American states
4. Soviet: Soviet bloc (including Mongolia), and Yugoslavia
5. W. Europe: Western European states, and Australia, Canada, New Zealand

5. *Financing UNEF.* The cost of the Emergency Force, estimated at $15 million for 1966, was to be financed by assessing the less developed countries a total of $800,000, the balance of $14,200,000 to be assessed against the developed countries. Within these classifications (developed, and less developed), expenses were to be borne in proportion to the regular UN scale of assessments.

6. *Tibet.* The Assembly renewed its call for Communst China (not specifically named) to stop depriving the Tibetan people of fundamental rights and freedoms, and appealed to all states to do their best to further the purposes of the resolution.

The issues are arranged in Table 7-2 in order of the size of the affirmative majority. Significantly, the first is a clear-cut colonial issue, and the second —although a technical detail of ratification—is related to racial discrimination which is an important aspect of the colonialism syndrome. The prevailing coalition on the first issue—Africa, Asia, the Soviet bloc, and part of Latin America—is typical of colonial questions. The only negative votes were from colonial countries. A sizable bloc of abstainers—more than on many anticolonial resolutions—suggests that this resolution was extreme in demanding target dates for independence (even for small scraps of territory) and the wholesale dismantling of military installations without regard to their contribution to peace and security. On the Racial Discrimination Convention, the blurring of the substantive issue in the technical question of reservations drew a substantial number of Latin American states into the opposition along with the United States, France, Belgium, Spain, and Australia. Most of Western Europe, several Asian countries, and a few Latin American countries abstained. The hard core of the prevailing majority was again most of Africa, the Arabs, a few other Asians, the Soviet bloc, and a sprinkling of Latin Americans.

The Korean question, in which the United States still continues to take a strong interest, has a long history of UN action favorable to the Western position. In 1965 a winning coalition was forged with the fairly solid support of Western Europe and Latin America, joined by moderately pro-Western countries of Africa and Asia. The only opposition was the Soviet bloc, supported by Algeria, Cuba, and Congo (Brazzaville). The hard-core nonaligned countries—most Arabs and many other Asians and Africans—simply abstained. This vote is to be contrasted with the Tibetan issue, where the outcome was closer. Indeed, the Tibetan resolution could not have been adopted if a two-thirds majority had been required. The prevailing majority was built around the West European–Latin American coalition, with some accretions from the Westward-leaning (or anti-Peking) countries of Asia and Africa. A number of Western European countries abstained, however, and a few Latin American states were either absent or abstaining. The Soviet bloc was again the core of the opposition, but it picked up support from most of the Arabs and a few other Africans and Asians, as well as from Cuba and Yugoslavia.

The remaining two issues present a somewhat more confused picture. The prevailing majority in support of the motion to defer discussion of improved pacific settlement procedures was composed of the Soviet bloc and the most militantly anticolonial countries of Africa and Asia. The proposal to review UN pacific settlement procedures was a British initiative, and the move to brush it aside was regarded by UN observers as a protest at Britain's failure to take stronger action against Rhodesia's unilateral declaration of independence. The opponents of the motion to defer were Western Europe and the United States, abetted by a few Latin Americans and Asians. Fourteen Latin American states did not participate in the vote at all.

The prevailing coalition on UNEF financing was drawn from several geographical groups and was composed largely of the more moderate elements of each group. Although abstentions (including the United States) outnumbered affirmative votes, the only outright opposition came from the Soviet bloc and Cuba, joined by three other Latin American states. This unusual alignment suggests that the issue transcended regional lines, anticolonial biases, and East-West divisions. A substantial majority was dissatisfied with this particular financing scheme but could not agree on any other. The ball had to be carried by the political moderates who were willing to support a viable, if uninspired, compromise.

Politics of Peace-Keeping Finance

The subject of peace-keeping finance, which reached crisis proportions in 1964 and 1965, provides a revealing study in changing issues, alignments, and pressures within the Assembly. From 1960 through 1963, the United States utilized a judicious mixture of persuasion, pressure, and compromise to secure majority votes on resolutions embodying the assessment principle for financing the Congo peace-keeping operation. In the crisis, however, the United States suffered political defeat in a showdown that never came to a vote.[22]

The crisis was created by the refusal of the Soviet Union, France, and a number of other states to pay their assessments for the UN force in the Congo, and the adamant insistence of the United States that Article 19 of the Charter should be applied to take away their voting rights in the Assembly. The application of Article 19 was the immediate issue in 1964; but there were other important issues as well, including collective respon-

---

[22] See Chapter 5, *supra,* for a fuller analysis of the substantive issues. Two good accounts of the financial crisis, which complement each other in their coverage, are Keohane, *op. cit.,* pp. 42–64; and, John G. Stoessinger, *The United Nations and the Superpowers* (New York: Random House, 1965), pp. 90–113.

sibility for peace-keeping, the legality of the assessments, the financial solvency of the UN itself, the integrity of the Assembly in sticking by its resolutions, the political advisability of forcing a great power to pay for UN projects that contravened its national interests, and the risk that pressing the issue might force Soviet withdrawal and consequent disruption of the organization. To a great extent, the action of the Assembly depended on how the issues were perceived and which issue, at any given moment, seemed the crucial one.

France and the Soviet Union early raised legal objections to assessments for the Congo force, but a majority was persuaded to see the issue initially as one of collective responsibility for peace-keeping and of finding a practical way to defray the cost of UN operations in the Congo. The Secretary-General estimated the cost for 1960 (July through December) at $66,625,000, while 1961 expenses were expected to exceed $100 million—considerably more than the total regular budget. Hammarskjold himself came out strongly for the assessment principle, on grounds both of financial necessity and the need for collective responsibility in financing the force. The position was in harmony with the UNEF precedent and was heartily supported by the United States. The vote in favor of a resolution embodying the assessment principle was a scant 46 to 17 with 24 abstentions, however, hardly a ringing endorsement. The Soviet Union, which voted in the negative, denied the constitutional authority of the Assembly to make a decision on a matter that was essentially the province of the Security Council. Substantively, the Soviets had urged that the main burden be placed on "the chief culprits—the Belgian colonizers," the remainder to be made up by voluntary contributions.

Subsequent resolutions on financing commanded somewhat more support, but at the cost of special concessions to the poorer countries and accepting the principle that ONUC costs were not regular UN expenses, even though raised by assessment. The initial financing measure, adopted in December, 1960, had applied the regular assessment scale but recommended that voluntary contributions be used to reduce up to fifty per cent the assessment of states with the least capacity to pay. It also stated flatly that the costs were "expenses of the Organization" within the meaning of Article 17 which, presumably, meant that the sanctions of Article 19 would be applicable. A second resolution was adopted in April, 1961, with 54 in favor, 15 opposed, and 23 abstaining. The margin was larger than before, but the resolution was slightly different. The reference to "expenses of the Organization" was retained, but there was no specific reference to Article 17. In addition, the reduction in the assessments of the poorer countries was put on a more substantial basis. In December, 1961, a third resolution with similar financial arrangements was approved by the significantly larger margin of 67 in favor, 13 opposed, and 16 abstaining. This probably reflected greater satisfaction with the functioning of the Congo force, which had taken firm steps against Katanga during the intervening months. It also reflected a change in the wording of the resolution. Earlier resolutions had tacitly recognized that peace-keeping expenses were of a special nature, by granting rebates to the poorer countries. In December, 1961, this was made explicit by the statement that ONUC expenses were "essentially different in nature" from the regular expenses of the United Nations.

At the same time, under American prodding, the Assembly moved directly to confront the legal issue raised by the defaulters. Having omitted reference to Article 17 in the December, 1961, financing resolution, the Assembly asked the International Court of Justice to render an advisory opinion stating whether expenditures authorized for ONUC and UNEF were "expenses of the organization" within the meaning of Article 17. When the Court rendered an opinion in the affirmative, the Assembly in December, 1962, mustered its greatest show of unanimity on the financial issue by voting 76 to 17 with 8 abstentions to "accept" the opinion.

This action did not, in fact, constitute widespread acceptance of the decision's logical consequences for the application of Article 19. Six of the seventy-six had opposed a reference to Article 17 in the 1960 resolution, and three others had recently expressed a preference merely to "take note of" rather than to "accept" the advisory opinion. In voting for the resolution, Afghanistan explicitly stated that its vote for the resolution did not signify acceptance of financial assessments. India, likewise, explained its affirmative vote as a gesture of respect for the opinion of the Court, while expressly denying that the vote had any relevance for the application of Article 19. A number of states, like India, appeared to distinguish between a legal principle which they were willing to uphold and political action which they might be unwilling to undertake. Another special factor was the attitude of the Secretary-General. By making a personal plea to uphold the authority of the Court, he lent his own prestige to the issue and facilitated a shift in focus from politics to law. This, combined with a very real concern for the financial stability of the organization, contributed to the large majority in support of the resolution.

By the fall of 1964, the Soviet Union and several other states were two years behind in total UN contributions, the amount specified for the application of Article 19. France would be similarly in default by January 1, 1965. With the United States insisting on a showdown, political issues began to take precedence over legal principle.

As the protagonists approached the confrontation, the Soviet Union and France were firm in their resistance to the assessment, although leaving the door slightly ajar on the question of financing future UN forces. The United States maintained that past assessments were not negotiable, but was also ready to discuss new arrangements for the future, including its own proposal for a standing finance committee dominated by the large contributors. Reportedly, if not officially, the United States was even willing to consider a procedure by which permanent members of the Security Council could be exempted from paying for peace-keeping operations to which they objected. Positions on future expenses thus left room for maneuver. But for past assessments the issue was clearly joined—the United States demanding that Article 19 be applied and the major defaulters absolutely refusing to admit their obligation to pay.

On this issue the great power positions were all-important. Their interests and prestige were more directly engaged than those of most small powers; and the stakes were high enough to warrant strong pressures. Although the small powers had a general interest in the outcome, there was no special interest around which to rally the voting strength which collectively they possessed. The anticolonial or economic biases which provided a guide on so many issues were largely irrelevant here, as were regional and caucusing group ties. The small powers felt their impotence in the circumstances and looked to the great powers for clues to appropriate behavior.

In such a setting, the United States committed what can only be regarded as grievous strategic and tactical blunders. Strategically, the United States overestimated its own resolve and possibly miscalculated the willingness of an Assembly majority to go to the political brink against the Soviet Union and France. In capacity for bilateral arm-twisting, the United States defers to no one in the United Nations. But in this particular situation, the United States had no threat strong enough to counter the Soviet threat to leave the United Nations if deprived of its vote in the Assembly. Arguments about legal principle, constitutional integrity, Assembly prestige, and even financial insolvency all paled before the much more compelling specter of an organization shattered by Soviet withdrawal. The United States had staked a good deal of prestige on the issue, but was apparently not willing to stake its own future membership and participation. Given the presumably lower value placed by the Soviet Union upon the United Nations, and the greater humiliation of disenfranchisement, the Soviet threat was quite credible and more formidable than any threat the United States could bring to bear.

Tactically, the United States took positions that allowed for no retreat without loss of face—and then retreated. In the first place, the controversy was focused on the application of Article 19, the point at which United States support was probably weakest. The United States further insisted that the issue be joined on the opening day of the session. As one American official stated, "November 10 is the opening of the General Assembly, and November 10 presents the inevitable and inescapable issue of Article 19 unless requisite payments are made before that opening." [23] Having assumed

[23] *Official Records of the General Assembly*, 19th Sess., 1964–65, Annexes, Agenda item 21, p. 16.

this position, the United States then acquiesced in a postponement of the opening day from November 10 to December 1. During the interim the United States agreed not to raise Article 19 until after the lengthy general debate, on condition that no vote would be taken until that time. The "opening day" confrontation had first been postponed, then abandoned. Despite all the brave American words, the Soviet Union was permitted to participate beyond the opening day without a challenge to its vote.

While the Assembly sat, United States representatives entered into negotiations with the Soviet Union on the question of past assessments—a question that had previously been treated by the United States as not negotiable. At the end of the general debate the "no-vote" agreement was extended to other business of the Assembly—a clear indication that the United States was now unwilling to precipitate the crisis. When Albania, bent on mischief, demanded a resumption of normal voting procedure, the United States beat another tactical retreat by permitting the Assembly to take a "procedural" vote overruling the Albanian demand. The United States had earlier looked on while the Soviet Union cast its vote in a special "consultation" to fill a hotly contested seat on the Security Council. The United States had said the defaulters should not vote without challenge; they were nevertheless permitted to vote. These concessions, though each was slight in itself, suggested that the United States position was not as impervious to modification as earlier statements had indicated.

Whether or not the United States could have obtained a two-thirds majority on December 1 is not clear. What is clear is that the United States did not make good its threat to demand a confrontation, and thereafter its support for a strict application of Article 19 declined markedly. If the United States was willing to compromise, why should others risk the confrontation at all? An Afro-Asian proposal that the "question of the applicability of Article 19 should not be raised" at the session was never put to a formal vote, but in practice it was adopted. Many states, which at first had perceived the crisis primarily in financial or legal terms, came to perceive the vital controversy as one of institutional survival. A firm stand and credible threats had strengthened the Soviet bargaining position, while susceptibility to compromise reduced the impact of American pressures and brought a dwindling of support for applying Article 19.

In August, 1965, the United States formally gave up the fight. Ambassador Arthur J. Goldberg announced that "the United States regretfully accepted the simple and inescapable fact of life that a majority of the 114 member states was unready to apply Article 19." [24] This was an obviously correct summation of the temper of the Assembly, but the Goldberg statement also revealed that the United States was subject to sober thoughts about the principle of collective responsibility with its corollary of compulsory assess-

[24] Quoted in Stoessinger, *op. cit.*, pp. 108–109.

ment. The day might come when the United States would choose not to support a peace-keeping operation, or some other UN program. Concession on the principle of compulsory assessment today could work to American advantage tomorrow. Concession was an acknowledgment not only of political defeat but of a basic shift in the United States perception of the issues.

THE CONSEQUENCES OF UN ACTION

If UN action is symbolized by the adoption of a resolution, what are the practical consequences of such "action"? Will the resolution be enforced— or will its effectiveness be confined to verbal realms? There is no single, simple answer to these questions because UN resolutions are not all alike and much depends upon the circumstances of the case.

The consequences of UN action may perhaps be better understood if it is considered in terms of the forces that give weight to the decisions of national governments. When a state acts in domestic affairs, it invokes the sanction of law backed by a legal monopoly of the legitimate use of force. As a practical matter, governments of most states expect to use physical coercion only in the case of the occasional deviant lawbreaker. Nevertheless, the state's legal monopoly of force, though exercised sparingly, serves to maintain the level of order and respect for law that is essential to a smoothly functioning polity.

If the polity is in fact to function smoothly, however, the threat of physical coercion must remain in the background and its use be the exception rather than the rule. A government that must habitually resort to violence to obtain compliance with its rules is unstable at best. In a well-ordered state the daily homespun of obedience to law is woven of threads of habit, of legitimacy, of underlying consensus upon the goals of the state, and of rational recognition that general obedience to law is in the general interest. The viability of a state, and of the government of a state, rests heavily upon its capacity to command widespread acquiescence in and obedience to political rules without the necessity of physical coercion.

In addition to the protective and regulatory functions of government, which require widespread obedience to law, national governments also perform service functions. These are dependent not so much upon obedience of the citizenry as upon the availability of material resources and administrative apparatus for application of the resources to the task at hand. All national governments have the power to raise money by various forms of compulsory levy, and all have some type of administrative machinery. Given a satisfactory level of obedience to law, the effectiveness of government action is closely correlated with the availability of taxable resources and the efficiency of public administration. The states of Western Europe, North America, and the Soviet Union, for example, have highly effective governments not only because of widespread habitual obedience to law, consensus, and rational acceptance of rule, but also because their resources are relatively great and their administrative machinery relatively efficient. Such states are to be contrasted with a country like the Congo which enjoys neither widespread habitual obedience to law nor administrative efficiency, and whose governmental revenues are small. Indeed, even the Congo government's monopoly of the legitimate use of physical force has been challenged by dissident groups.

The material and moral underpinnings of UN action may be fruitfully compared with the sanctions of state action in terms of four categories suggested above: (1) The authority of law backed by physical force, (2) customary obedience, (3) financial resources and (4) administrative efficiency. As discussed in an earlier section, international organizations have very little authority to make decisions that are legally binding upon members in their relationships with one another. Resolutions of international organizations that bear directly upon state conduct seldom have the sanction of law and must remain largely hortatory in character. Paradoxically, the Charter of the United Nations appears to repose in the United Nations a legal monopoly of physical coercion in international affairs, with the exception of the right of self-defense. The self-defense loophole is vast, however, and in practical terms the United Nations neither has a monopoly of such force nor makes any grandiose claim to it. At best, the United Nations can serve as a catalytic agent or as a focal point for mobilizing international force to counteract deviant behavior.

Likewise, the force of customary obedience to the recommendations of international organizations has generally been weak, although it varies greatly from one organization to another. At one end of the scale, the regulations of the Universal Postal Union are observed with a regularity that would do credit to national administrations. All of the elements of customary obedience are there—habit, legitimacy, broad consensus as to goals, and recognition of a common interest in international postal regulation. As one moves away from purely technical activities to subject areas that have a higher and higher "political" content, the element of customary obedience declines markedly. States have not yet developed habits of indiscriminate compliance, for example, with General Assembly recommendations. Nor do they recognize the right of the Assembly to make recommendations which ought to be honored by compliance. The Charter itself has achieved a certain legitimacy—nearly all members pay lip service to its ideals, purposes, and principles. But the process of concretizing the ideals through specific action of UN organs has not yet been legitimated. Furthermore, there is no underlying consensus among the membership upon the operational goals of the organization, as contrasted with the verbal consensus upon abstract ideals. Thus, "obedience" or compliance is left to rest upon rational acceptance of the necessity for and the coincidence of national interests in particular UN policies and programs. The action of a UN majority may sometimes create "moral" force or political pressure which affects a member's concept of its interest in compliance, but this is a far cry from the forces that underpin rules promulgated by national governments.

International organization also stands in a different position from national governments in its ability to command financial and other material resources. Although standards of financial support in the form of budgetary assessments have been developed and are customarily adhered to, international organizations are still ultimately dependent upon the material resources that individual states are willing to supply, not upon what majorities are moved to demand. This should not suggest that the sums raised by contribution are inconsequential. The regular United Nations budget has exceeded the $120 million mark for a year's operations, while contributions to all activities within the United Nations system have gone beyond a half billion dollars a year. Nevertheless, the United Nations receives its monetary sustenance by sufferance, not by right. The sale of publications and postage stamps does not yet constitute an important source of independent income.

The fourth category—that of administrative efficiency—will be discussed in greater detail in the next chapter. At this point we may say that the secretariats of international organizations have generally proved equal to the administrative tasks imposed upon them. International organizations have scored their most signal successes when actions recommended by policy organs have been of the type that could be implemented through the agency of international civil servants. At its best, international administration has compared favorably with the best national administrations. At almost all times the standard of international public service has been higher than that of many national governments. As a witness to this relative excellence, many of the emerging countries of the world look to the United Nations Secretariat for technical assistance in public administration. The comparison of national and international administrative efficiency is further sharpened by reference to the Congo crisis in which a complete collapse of public services in the Congo during those troubled years was prevented only by the introduction of technicians and public administrators on a massive scale under UN auspices.

Bearing in mind the rather limited basis of power of international organizations, as set forth in the four categories delineated above, we may briefly summarize the consequences of UN action. Where UN resolutions have initiated programs involving administrative action, and members have found their interests sufficiently involved to contribute the necessary funds and personnel, the consequences of UN operations have been substantial.

The United Nations has registered solid accomplishment in areas ranging from research studies to technical assistance and from para-military operations in Egypt and the Congo to outright combat in Korea. On the other hand, where resolutions have called upon member states to undertake or to forego a certain course of action, the record is very checkered. In many instances members comply because they are in sympathy with the resolution. Occasionally states are moved to compliance, or a show of compliance, by the "moral force" of the resolution—which is a function of the value placed by states upon having their policies in line with those of voting majorities in international organizations, for whatever reason. In numerous other instances UN recommendations are flatly ignored by governments that perceive no self-interested basis—however broadly or narrowly construed—for compliance. No given UN majority could persuade the Soviet Union to withdraw its troops from Hungary in November, 1956. And no amount of repeated urging has yet induced the Republic of South Africa to abandon its apartheid policies. In the absence of consensus, legitimacy, compelling habits of obedience, rules having the force of law and physical sanctions to support the rules, the United Nations must rely upon a convergence of interests. Without that convergence, UN resolutions will be limited to their verbal effects.

Selected Readings

ALGER, CHADWICK F. "Non-resolution Consequences of the United Nations and Their Effects on International Conflict," *Journal of Conflict Resolution*, Vol. 5, 1961, pp. 128–45.

ALKER, HAYWARD R., and RUSSETT, BRUCE M. *World Politics in the General Assembly*. New Haven: Yale University Press, 1965.

BAILEY, SYDNEY D. *The General Assembly of the United Nations*. New York: Praeger, 1964, rev. ed.

BLOOMFIELD, LINCOLN P. *The United Nations and U. S. Foreign Policy*. Boston: Little Brown and Company, 1960.

CLAUDE, INIS L., JR. *Swords into Plowshares*. New York: Random House, 1964, 3rd ed., Chaps. 7, 8.

HADWEN, JOHN G., and KAUFMANN, JOHAN. *How United Nations Decisions Are Made*. Leyden: A. W. Sythoff, 1962, rev. ed.

HIGGINS, ROSALYN. *The Administration of United Kingdom Foreign Policy Through the United Nations*. Syracuse, N.Y.: The Maxwell School of Syracuse University, 1966.

HOVET, THOMAS, JR. *Bloc Politics in the United Nations*. Cambridge: Harvard University Press, 1960.

JIMENEZ DE ARECHAGA, EDUARDO. *Voting and the Handling of Disputes in the Security Council*. New York: Carnegie Endowment for International Peace, 1950.

Koo, Wellington, Jr. *Voting Procedures in International Political Organizations.* New York: Columbia University Press, 1947.

Riches, Cromwell A. *Majority Rule in International Organization.* Baltimore: Johns Hopkins, 1940.

————, *The Unanimity Rule and the League of Nations.* Baltimore: Johns Hopkins, 1933.

Riggs, Robert E. *Politics in the United Nations: A Study of United States Influence in the General Assembly.* Urbana: University of Illinois Press, 1958.

8 | The Politics of International Administration

I n a very real sense, modern international organization was born with the creation of the permanent international secretariat. Without a permanent secretariat the institutions of multilateral action become little more than a discontinuous series of conferences, incapable of administering truly international tasks. With a permanent secretariat, international organization has the capacity to operate programs of technical assistance, administer peace-keeping missions, and carry on a host of informational, regulatory, and service functions. It also gains the capacity, at least incipiently, to exert an independent influence on the course of international events.

THE INTERNATIONAL CIVIL SERVICE

The genuinely international civil service—one that is broadly international in composition as well as function—dates only from the establishment of the League of Nations and the International Labor Organization at the close of World War I. The need for a permanent administrative staff had been recognized much earlier by the international public administrative unions, and the permanent bureaus or secretariats of such technical organizations as the Universal Postal Union performed tasks that were international in scope. But these bureaus were not international in composition. Characteristically, the personnel were citizens of the state that played permanent host to the headquarters of the organization and were often national officials given leave from their normal assignments to serve the international organization for a period of time. This practice of placing national civil servants on temporary duty as staff of an international organization is often called "secondment," a British expression. The International Institute of Agriculture set a precedent when its charter of 1905 provided explicitly that staff members were to seek and receive instructions only from their superiors within the institute, and not from any national government.

The League covenant made no express provision for the internationaliza-

171

tion of the staff. It simply stated that "The Secretariat shall comprise a Secretary-General and such secretaries and staff as may be required." At an early stage in planning for the organization of the League secretariat, Sir Maurice Hankey suggested that the work be performed under the supervision of the Secretary-General by nine national secretaries, drawn from the nine members of the Council, each assisted by his own national staff. To Sir Eric Drummond, first Secretary-General of the League, goes the credit for insisting upon the "creation of a secretariat international alike in its structure, its spirit, and its personnel." The decision to establish a multinational civil service recruited individually rather than as contingents of national representatives now appears in perspective as "one of the most important events in the history of international politics."[1] The Secretariat of the International Labor Organization, under the leadership of Albert Thomas, adopted a similar concept of an international civil service.

Codifying the experience of the League and ILO, the UN Charter expressly provided for a secretariat that was to be unitary in structure, recruited individually on a broad geographical basis, and responsible in official conduct only to the Organization. Other intergovernmental organizations, which have proliferated greatly since World War II, have also looked to these standards and have applied them to an ever-growing international public service. At their peak the staff of the League and ILO numbered scarcely more than a thousand. Today the United Nations system has more than 20,000 regular civilian employees.

Problems of Diversity

In many ways an international secretariat faces the same kinds of problems that bureaucracies face everywhere—problems of internal decision-making, communication, lines of authority and responsibility, recruitment and retention of competent personnel, and so on. But compared with national civil services, especially in the more highly developed states, an international secretariat must adjust to markedly difficult environmental conditions and special problems related to its own internal functioning.

Internally, the most obvious problem is that of integrating within a single administrative machine the diverse attitudes, tongues, backgrounds, and abilities of personnel recruited from the four corners of the earth. The difficulty is compounded by the relative newness of international institutions and hence the absence of well-established standards and procedures within which the differences can be submerged. Norms and administrative techniques appropriate to the tasks of international organization are being gradually developed, however, and time and experience may be expected to supply the precedent that can perform the stabilizing function of estab-

[1] F. P. Walters, *A History of the League of Nations* (New York: Oxford University Press, 1952), p. 76.

lished tradition. Nevertheless, problems associated with continued recruitment of diverse human material are likely to remain.

Still more intractable are the special environmental conditions affecting international secretariats. A national civil service, at least in the developed countries, functions within a relatively homogeneous political culture.[2] There is broad consensus upon the basic functions of national government, the means by which political decisions are reached, and the limits of legitimate governmental authority. In the absence of a shared political culture in the world community, the secretariat lacks both the guidelines that would make its own choice of actions easier and the legitimacy that would make its functions acceptable to its clientele. Absence of guidelines may also give the secretariat greater freedom of action, but this can be a risky kind of freedom as Dag Hammarskjold found in his conduct of the Congo operation. In any governmental system the conduct of administration requires a certain amount of bargaining and negotiation with the clientele to be served or regulated. In the international field the lack of shared political values and orientations greatly widens the range of issues that must be negotiated. Norms for specific activities, such as the enforcement of standards in technical assistance programs, can be built up through practice. But the process is complicated by the need to adapt them to differing national contexts.

Sources of Political Support

The international secretariat also lacks the formal links with the centers of governmental power that characterize national civil services. At the apex of the national administration is a president or prime minister who controls the administration and effectively ties it to sources of political power in the polity. In the United States the President draws power from his constitutional prerogatives, his control of the administrative establishment, his electoral mandate, and his relationship with his political party and other influential groups within the society. The administrative departments work under his direction and he in turn defends and supports them. An analogous situation prevails in countries with the parliamentary system of government, with the further advantage of having a chief executive who speaks for a dominant political party or coalition in the national legislature. In addition the taproots of administrative agencies often reach down into a solid foundation of interest group support among the clientele they serve—another important connection with the sources of political power.

At what points, one may ask, does the international secretariat tap into

[2] Some problems of the international civil service here represented as unique may in fact be pertinent to governmental administration in newer and less developed countries where diversity of language, a heterogeneous political culture, and the absence of well-developed administrative tradition also exist to a substantial degree. See, for example, the discussion of Fred W. Riggs, "International Relations As a Prismatic Society," *World Politics*, Vol. 14 (October, 1961), pp. 144–81.

streams of influence within the political system of which it is a part? The staff of some international organizations, such as UNESCO, the International Civil Aviation Organization and the World Bank, have in fact established good relationships with private groups which can exert influence upon governments within the special field of their competence. To an even greater degree this appears true of the European community organs, whose regulatory and service functions directly affect large numbers of individuals and groups within the community, and thereby tend to create mutual relationships of demand and support. Such contacts are analogous to the agency-clientele relationship which helps sustain departments of national administrations, but in range and intensity of support the accretion of strength to the international secretariat can hardly be comparable.

The international civil servant can and does from time to time lobby with the national delegates just as national government administrators establish their lines of communication with national legislators. But the efficacy of this relationship, while not to be dismissed as a source of support to the international secretariat, is nevertheless diminished by the delegate's dependence upon instructions from his government. It is also weakened by the international civil servant's prime duty to avoid compromising himself or his organization in maintaining the attributes of neutrality, impartiality, and independence of national governments.

In comparison with a president or prime minister, the typical secretary-general or director-general of an international secretariat has very limited political prerogatives, no constituency, no electoral mandate and scarcely anything resembling leadership of a dominant political party or coalition in the policy-making body of the organization. The job, of course, is as big as he can make it; and such individuals as Albert Thomas in the ILO or Eugene R. Black and George D. Woods in the World Bank, have carved out a respectable sphere of support and influence for themselves and their office. The Commission of the European Community organizations also possesses important decision-making authority, within the constitutional framework of the organization. But even there, dependence upon member governments is the dominant theme. And when one turns to the United Nations, the scarcity of reliable political support for the Secretary-General is an all too apparent fact of life.

The Administrative Process

An international secretariat, like other bureaucracies,[3] must satisfy the requirements of hierarchy, rational distribution of tasks, and technical spe-

[3] The term bureacracy as used here refers simply to the "system of authority, men, offices, and methods" that any large-scale organization uses to carry out its programs. See John M. Pfiffner and Robert V. Presthus, *Public Administration*, 4th ed. (New York: Ronald Press, 1960), p. 40.

cialization. The form in which the United Nations Secretariat has presently come to terms with these requirements is indicated by the organization chart in Figure 8-1.

An estimate of the relative amount of administrative energy generated by the various organizational units may be gleaned from Table 8-1 which lists the number of persons employed in each of the major administrative units. The vast majority of UN personnel are engaged in economic and social affairs or in the supplying of administrative services. Relatively few are involved in political or dependent area functions of the organization.

Authority and Responsibility

The distribution of tasks and responsibilities, with corresponding lines of authority, is not quite as rational or as neat as might appear from a quick appraisal of the organization chart. This is noticeably true of the economic and social field in which a number of programs are quite independent of the Department of Economic and Social Affairs and, for that matter, of the Secretary-General as well. For various reasons of practicality and politics, not the least of these being the necessity to rely upon not wholly identical groups of voluntary financial contributors, the General Assembly has created a number of operating programs for which the Secretary-General has little or no administrative responsibility. These include the work of the United Nations Development Program (combining the Expanded Program of Technical Assistance and UN Special Fund), the United Nations Children's Fund, the UN High Commissioner for Refugees, and the UN Relief and Works Agency for Palestine Refugees in the Near East. Each of these programs has a director who is responsible to his own governing body and independent of control by the Secretary-General. With the exception of UNRWA, however, the personnel of the "independent agencies" are governed by the Staff Rules and Regulations applicable to all Secretariat personnel and participate in the Pension Fund of the United Nations. Furthermore, appointments to the staff of the Development Program are made by the UN Director of Personnel, acting, however, for the director of the program rather than for the UN Secretary-General. Appointments to the staff of the International Court of Justice are also beyond the control of the Secretary-General. The Court makes its own appointments.

Another anomaly arises from the special position of the staff serving the four regional economic commissions of ECOSOC (see Figure 8-1). In both theory and practice such personnel are a part of the regular UN Secretariat, appointed through regular channels and answerable ultimately to the Secretary-General. Geographic distance tends to breed a certain independence, however, and geography in this case conspires with divided lines of authority to create occasional divergences of outlook and interest between headquarters and regional secretariats. The regional staff operates under

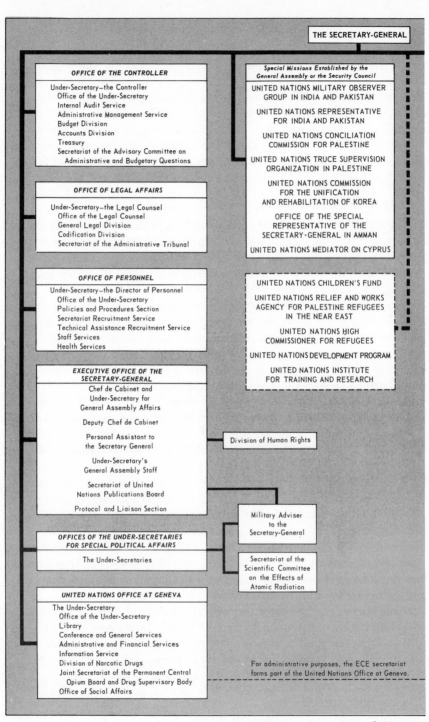

THE SECRETARY-GENERAL

OFFICE OF THE CONTROLLER

Under-Secretary—the Controller
Office of the Under-Secretary
Internal Audit Service
Administrative Management Service
Budget Division
Accounts Division
Treasury
Secretariat of the Advisory Committee on
Administrative and Budgetary Questions

OFFICE OF LEGAL AFFAIRS

Under-Secretary—the Legal Counsel
Office of the Legal Counsel
General Legal Division
Codification Division
Secretariat of the Administrative Tribunal

OFFICE OF PERSONNEL

Under-Secretary—the Director of Personnel
Office of the Under-Secretary
Policies and Procedures Section
Secretariat Recruitment Service
Technical Assistance Recruitment Service
Staff Services
Health Services

**EXECUTIVE OFFICE OF THE
SECRETARY-GENERAL**

Chef de Cabinet and
Under-Secretary for
General Assembly Affairs

Deputy Chef de Cabinet

Personal Assistant to
the Secretary General

Under-Secretary's
General Assembly Staff

Secretariat of United
Nations Publications Board

Protocol and Liaison Section

**OFFICES OF THE UNDER-SECRETARIES
FOR SPECIAL POLITICAL AFFAIRS**

The Under-Secretaries

UNITED NATIONS OFFICE AT GENEVA

The Under-Secretary
Office of the Under-Secretary
Library
Conference and General Services
Administrative and Financial Services
Information Service
Division of Narcotic Drugs
Joint Secretariat of the Permanent Central
Opium Board and Drug Supervisory Body
Office of Social Affairs

*Special Missions Established by the
General Assembly or the Security Council*

UNITED NATIONS MILITARY OBSERVER
GROUP IN INDIA AND PAKISTAN

UNITED NATIONS REPRESENTATIVE
FOR INDIA AND PAKISTAN

UNITED NATIONS CONCILIATION
COMMISSION FOR PALESTINE

UNITED NATIONS TRUCE SUPERVISION
ORGANIZATION IN PALESTINE

UNITED NATIONS COMMISSION
FOR THE UNIFICATION
AND REHABILITATION OF KOREA

OFFICE OF THE SPECIAL
REPRESENTATIVE OF THE
SECRETARY-GENERAL IN AMMAN

UNITED NATIONS MEDIATOR ON CYPRUS

UNITED NATIONS CHILDREN'S FUND

UNITED NATIONS RELIEF AND WORKS
AGENCY FOR PALESTINE REFUGEES
IN THE NEAR EAST

UNITED NATIONS HIGH
COMMISSIONER FOR REFUGEES

UNITED NATIONS DEVELOPMENT PROGRAM

UNITED NATIONS INSTITUTE
FOR TRAINING AND RESEARCH

Division of Human Rights

Military Adviser
to the
Secretary-General

Secretariat of the
Scientific Committee
on the Effects of
Atomic Radiation

For administrative purposes, the ECE secretariat
forms part of the United Nations Office at Geneva.

FIGURE 8-1.   United Nations

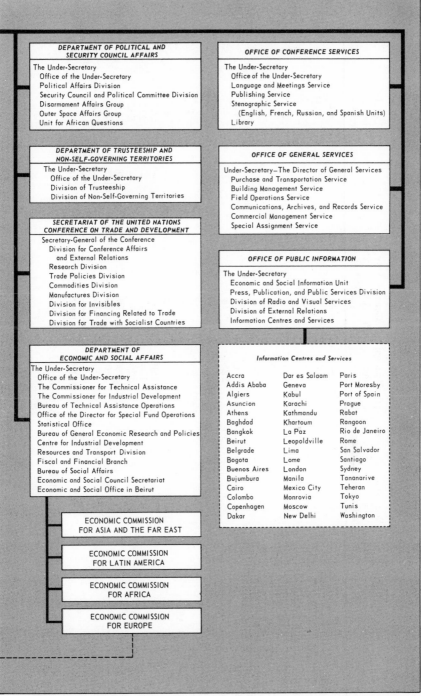

**DEPARTMENT OF POLITICAL AND
SECURITY COUNCIL AFFAIRS**

The Under-Secretary
  Office of the Under-Secretary
  Political Affairs Division
  Security Council and Political Committee Division
  Disarmament Affairs Group
  Outer Space Affairs Group
  Unit for African Questions

**DEPARTMENT OF TRUSTEESHIP AND
NON-SELF-GOVERNING TERRITORIES**

The Under-Secretary
  Office of the Under-Secretary
  Division of Trusteeship
  Division of Non-Self-Governing Territories

**SECRETARIAT OF THE UNITED NATIONS
CONFERENCE ON TRADE AND DEVELOPMENT**

Secretary-General of the Conference
  Division for Conference Affairs
    and External Relations
  Research Division
  Trade Policies Division
  Commodities Division
  Manufactures Division
  Division for Invisibles
  Division for Financing Related to Trade
  Division for Trade with Socialist Countries

**DEPARTMENT OF
ECONOMIC AND SOCIAL AFFAIRS**

The Under-Secretary
  Office of the Under-Secretary
  The Commissioner for Technical Assistance
  The Commissioner for Industrial Development
  Bureau of Technical Assistance Operations
  Office of the Director for Special Fund Operations
  Statistical Office
  Bureau of General Economic Research and Policies
  Centre for Industrial Development
  Resources and Transport Division
  Fiscal and Financial Branch
  Bureau of Social Affairs
  Economic and Social Council Secretariat
  Economic and Social Office in Beirut

ECONOMIC COMMISSION
FOR ASIA AND THE FAR EAST

ECONOMIC COMMISSION
FOR LATIN AMERICA

ECONOMIC COMMISSION
FOR AFRICA

ECONOMIC COMMISSION
FOR EUROPE

OFFICE OF CONFERENCE SERVICES

The Under-Secretary
  Office of the Under-Secretary
  Language and Meetings Service
  Publishing Service
  Stenographic Service
    (English, French, Russian, and Spanish Units)
  Library

OFFICE OF GENERAL SERVICES

Under-Secretary—The Director of General Services
  Purchase and Transportation Service
  Building Management Service
  Field Operations Service
  Communications, Archives, and Records Service
  Commercial Management Service
  Special Assignment Service

OFFICE OF PUBLIC INFORMATION

The Under-Secretary
  Economic and Social Information Unit
  Press, Publication, and Public Services Division
  Division of Radio and Visual Services
  Division of External Relations
  Information Centres and Services

Information Centres and Services

Accra	Dar es Salaam	Paris
Addis Ababa	Geneva	Port Moresby
Algiers	Kabul	Port of Spain
Asuncion	Karachi	Prague
Athens	Kathmandu	Rabat
Baghdad	Khartoum	Rangoon
Bangkok	La Paz	Rio de Janeiro
Beirut	Leopoldville	Rome
Belgrade	Lima	San Salvador
Bogota	Lome	Santiago
Buenos Aires	London	Sydney
Bujumbura	Manila	Tananarive
Cairo	Mexico City	Teheran
Colombo	Monrovia	Tokyo
Copenhagen	Moscow	Tunis
Dakar	New Delhi	Washington

Secretariat, June, 1965.

Table 8-1. United Nations Secretariat, 1966

	Sec.-Gen. and Under-Secs.	Directors and Principal Officers	Other Professional Level Staff	General Service Principal Level	General Service Other Levels	Manual Workers	Local Level Positions	Total
Controller	1	9	80	25	81	—	—	196
Legal Affairs	1	5	29	5	24	—	—	64
Personnel	1	7	41	13	79	—	—	141
Int. Staff and Pension Brd. and U.N. Pension Comm.	—	1	4	3	12	—	—	20
Executive Office	2	5	16	4	22	—	—	49
Division of Human Rights	—	2	33	—	21	—	—	56
Office of Under-Secs. for Special Pol. Affairs	2	2	6	2	10	—	—	22
Geneva Office	1	13	225	18	471	75	—	803
Political and Security Affairs	1	9	51	3	27	—	—	91
Trusteeship and Non-Self-Governing Terr.	1	3	29	3	17	—	14	67
Economic and Social Affairs	4	42	424	41	332	—	—	843
ECE	1	8	87	2	100	—	—	198
ECAFE	1	9	120	—	—	—	205	335
ECLA	1	9	124	—	—	—	235	369
ECA	1	7	133	—	—	—	242	383
Conference Services	1	15	499	79	486	28	—	1108
General Services	1	8	60	48	483	175	—	775
Public Information	1	13	155	16	106	—	230	521
Total	21	167	2116	262	2271	278	926	6041

Source: *General Assembly Official Records*, 20th Session, Supplement No. 5, pp. 70–84.

the general direction of the Secretary-General; but its primary function is to serve the regional economic commission, which is a body composed of specified member states having an economic interest in the region. Thus the Director of the Economic Commission for Latin America (or Europe, or Africa, or Asia and the Far East) has lines of responsibility running to the Secretary-General in New York and through him to the General Assembly. But the Director is also responsible directly and primarily to the commission, and through the commission to ECOSOC and the General Assembly. One should not exaggerate the degree of internal friction that is generated. Headquarters and regional staffs are obviously interested in pursuing the same ultimate objectives. Nevertheless, one of the primary issues of organizational policy within the UN Secretariat has been the optimum degree of centralization and decentralization of Secretariat functions.

Top Management

Politics merges with and dominates administrative considerations in the structure and recruitment of top management within the UN Secretariat. The Secretary-Generalship, of course, is a completely political appointment. Although personal qualifications are obviously important, the field is narrowly limited by the requirement of political acceptability. The UN Charter states simply that "The Secretary-General shall be appointed by the General Assembly upon the recommendation of the Security Council" (Article 97). Since the Security Council recommendation is clearly a nonprocedural matter, however, the recommendation is subject to all the hazards of cold war politics. In practice, whenever the Security Council has been able to agree on a candidate, the General Assembly (where only a simple majority is required) has hastened to add its formal approval. At an informal level, the five permanent members have followed the practice of conferring privately among themselves to seek agreement before presenting a candidate to the full Security Council. Agreement has not always been possible, however. In 1950, when Trygve Lie's first five-year term was about to expire, the Soviet Union vetoed Lester Pearson of Canada and Paul-Henri Spaak of Belgium, and the United States then threatened to veto any candidate other than Lie. An absolute impasse was reached, and the Secretariat was prevented from going without a leader only by the questionable expedient of extending Lie's term an additional three years by General Assembly resolution.

Given all the political considerations that surround the appointment, it is no surprise that all three Secretaries-General have come from small countries uncommitted in the cold war and not strongly identified with any controversial political position. By tacit agreement, no national of one of the five permanent members will be appointed; and for obvious reasons, no national of a state militarily aligned with either the United States or the

Soviet Union could win Security Council approval. (Lie's appointment antedated the cold war and the entry of Norway into the North Atlantic Alliance.) A citizen of South Africa, Portugal, Israel, or of any Arab state would also have difficulty surviving the nominating process because of their governments' strong identification with particular political controversies. Swedish nationality still carried eligibility in 1953 when Lie resigned, and Dag Hammarskjold was chosen. Hammarskjold's performance in office earned his reappointment for a second five-year term in 1958. When Hammarskjold's second term was cut short by his death in an airplane crash over Northern Rhodesia in September, 1961, the neutralist countries of Asia and Africa seemed to be the most eligible to supply a candidate. U Thant of Burma was temporarily installed as Acting Secretary-General in November and in the following year was given an appointment in his own right.[4]

Political considerations also govern other aspects of top echelon recruitment and organization. Although purely administrative issues have sometimes arisen, a Committee of Experts reporting to the General Assembly in 1961 was only being realistic when it acknowledged that "the problem of the organization at the top level" was not "solely, or even primarily, a matter of administrative organization."[5] The initial distribution of top level posts was determined by an informal agreement among the permanent members of the Security Council to have a national of each of them appointed as an Assistant Secretary-General. The Soviet Union was specifically awarded the top post in the political department and has held it ever since, except for a few years in the mid-1950's. That arrangement set a precedent for "politicization" of top level appointments which other members have not been reluctant to follow. As a result, competition among member states for undersecretary and principal director posts has been keen, despite general recognition that the rules of independence, neutrality, and impartiality apply at high as well as low levels of the secretariat.

Another unanticipated consequence of the initial apportionment of top posts among the permanent members of the Security Council has been the downgrading of the political affairs department. As long as a Soviet national was in charge of political affairs, that department could not be expected

---

[4] Aside from the kind of political acceptability discussed here, an individual's chances for nomination are apparently enhanced by prior exposure to UN politics. All three of the incumbents had served as members of their respective national delegations to the United Nations prior to their appointment as Secretary-General. Perhaps, as Donald C. Blaisdell suggests, the candidate, "like aspirants for party nominations for the United States presidency, . . . should be known but not too well known. Although Lie, Hammarskjold, and Thant had all been members of the Norwegian, Swedish, and Burmese delegations respectively, none had taken a prominent part in United Nations conference or General Assembly debates." Donald C. Blaisdell, *International Organization* (New York: Ronald Press, 1966), p. 108.

[5] *Report of the Committtee of Experts on the Review of the Activities and Organization of the Secretariat*, United Nations Document A/4776, June 14, 1961, p. 5.

to administer with enthusiasm the tasks imposed upon the Secretariat by an anti-Soviet coalition in the General Assembly. In practice, therefore, the office of the Assistant Secretary (now Under-Secretary) for Political and Security Council Affairs has frequently been bypassed in favor of action through the Executive Office of the Secretary-General. This has not been done because of insubordination of the Soviet department head. The various incumbents have scrupulously carried out orders even when the Soviet Union has opposed UN action as contrary to the Charter. Rather, the shift has taken place to provide security of information and undivided purpose in dealing with delicate problems. The heavy burden of political activity in the Secretary-General's office has led to an increase in his staff and the creation of two under-secretaryships for "Special Political Affairs."

This developing pattern of informal organization within the top echelons of the Secretariat could scarcely avoid Soviet disapproval, and it was made even less palatable by the fact that the closest confidants of Lie and Hammarskjold were either Americans or nationals of other Western states. At no time was the preeminence of Western-oriented personnel in key Secretariat positions more obvious than during the early phases of the Congo crisis when the Secretary-General's chief advisers were Andrew Cordier, Hammarskjold's executive assistant; Ralph Bunche, an under-secretary for special political affairs; and Heinz Wieschhoff, an African specialist in the Secretariat. All three were United States citizens. All were international civil servants of integrity and ability, but as one observer noted, "it would not be difficult to imagine Washington's reaction if three Russians had been appointed instead." [6]

It was against such a background of frustration within the Secretariat and setbacks to Soviet policies in the Congo that Khrushchev in 1960 offered his "Troika" proposal for a three-man Secretary-Generalship. The informal system of representation had failed; now formal provision should be made within the Secretariat to represent the three major camps—Communist, capitalist, and neutralist—at the very highest level, each vested with a veto power over Secretariat decisions. The Western states, the Afro-Asians, and indeed the vast majority of UN members stood with Hammarskjold against the Soviet attempt to cripple the office. But U Thant, in accordance with a compromise reached by the United States and the Soviet Union in the negotiations leading to his appointment, designated eight top Secretariat officials as "principal advisers" to be consulted individually as the occasion should demand. The original eight were nationals of the United States, the Soviet Union, France, India, Czechoslovakia, Nigeria, the United Arab Republic, and Brazil. Experience since that time indicates that the designation of "principal advisers" has not inhibited the growth of significant

[6] Richard I. Miller, *Dag Hammarskjold and Crisis Diplomacy* (New York: Oceana, 1961), p. 293.

informal consultative relationships between the Secretary-General and selected members of his staff, whether or not included among the eight. The eight were not intended to serve, and have not served, as a cabinet or collective advisory body.

Recruiting the International Public Servant

International secretariats, like national bureaucracies, face the generic problem of finding the right man for the right job. The search for talent at the international level is complicated, however, by the need for linguistic skills and geographical acceptability in addition to technical competence. Prospective recruits may also be deterred by the problems of transplanting their families to an alien environment. In the United Nations these special difficulties, fortunately, do not extend to "general service" and "manual worker" categories including lower level administrators, clerks, secretaries, machine operators, technicians, messengers, chauffeurs, mechanics, and custodial personnel, among others. Such positions are filled by local recruitment without regard to geographical distribution and are mostly nationals of the host country.

Recruitment contacts for professional and administrative positions in the United Nations are made through universities, professional associations, and other private agencies, as well as through governments. Candidates are evaluated primarily on the basis of references, past record and experience, and a personal interview, although written examinations are occasionally used. Most of the interviews for UN employment are conducted in the field by UN personnel assigned to regional or other field offices. The utilization of governments for making recruitment contacts enhances the possibility of political pressure upon recruiting authorities but, within the United Nations at least, governments have usually resisted the temptation to insist that particular individuals be hired regardless of qualifications. A number of governments informally screen their nationals before UN employment (the United States does so by formal arrangement with the organization), and an unfavorable report will ordinarily prevent the hiring.

Although individuals are recruited on the basis of merit, the recruitment process is politicized by the requirement of geographical distribution. The Charter attaches "importance" to the recruitment of staff "on as wide a geographical basis as possible," but makes it clearly secondary to "the necessity of securing the highest standards of efficiency, competence and integrity." In practice the Secretary-General has tried to place efficiency first, with substantial support for this position from the United States and countries of Western Europe which have always been heavily represented in the Secretariat. Areas less well represented, especially the countries of Eastern Europe and newer states of Asia and Africa, have fought for the principle of equitable geographical distribution as though it were the paramount consideration. Their rationale is that efficiency in the broader sense is not possible unless all national viewpoints are adequately represented in the Secretariat.

A compromise reached in 1962, based on the assumption that approximately 1,500 positions will be subject to geographical distribution, established three main criteria for the allotment of these Secretariat posts: (1) Each member is entitled to a minimum of one to five posts; (2) one hundred posts are reserved for distribution on the basis of population factors not adequately reflected in the other two criteria; and (3) the remaining posts are allotted on the basis of budgetary contributions. Conscientious efforts by the Secretariat have brought all regional areas except Eastern Europe within or close to the mathematically desirable range (see Table 8-2). Although a

TABLE 8-2. Desirable Ranges and Distribution of
UN Staff Subject to Geographical Distribution
31 August 1965

Region	Desirable Ranges	Number of Staff
Africa	90–199	124
Asia and the Far East	235–233	236
Europe, Eastern	292–233	167
Europe, Western	316–276	343
Latin America	98–149	159
Middle East	36– 74	67
North America and the Caribbean	456–315	352
Subtotal	1,525–1,475	1,448
Nonmember States		43
Total		1,491

Source: *Personnel Questions, Composition of the Secretariat,* Report of the Secretary-General, United Nations Document A/6077, October 27, 1965, p. 3.

broadly recruited international secretariat has manifest political and functional advantages, the pressure to conform to a fairly rigid distribution pattern greatly complicates the task of recruiting the best qualified people.

Intimately related to the geographical composition of the Secretariat is the problem of career versus fixed-term appointments. The need to recruit large numbers of people rapidly led initially to the filling of most UN positions by temporary appointments. As late as 1948 only twenty-four per cent of UN employees were permanent staff. By the mid-1960's the proportion of permanent staff fluctuated around seventy-five per cent, however. Even supporters of a career system admit that fixed-term appointments are appropriate for posts of higher direction where rotation is desirable, for needed specialists who are not willing to make a career of UN service, and for posts that are temporary because of the nature of the work.

Others would go much farther than this, arguing that the secondment of national officials to international organization on temporary appointment promotes mutual understanding between national and international public services. The Soviet Union, a strong proponent of the latter viewpoint, will not permit its citizens to accept permanent UN appointments. The new states of Africa and Asia also favor short-term service because they cannot afford to give up scarce administrative talent on a permanent basis, and a brief period with the United Nations Secretariat can provide useful training for officials from the national service. From the standpoint of the United Nations, however, the short-termer may spend more time learning than producing, he may not feel whole-hearted loyalty to the organization, and the position he occupies might be more appropriately filled by promotion from within the ranks. Both the General Assembly and the Secretary-General have indicated approval of the three-to-one ratio of career to fixed-term appointments as a viable compromise between the two points of view.

Quite apart from circumstances that are relatively unique to the international scene, high-quality personnel cannot be recruited and held without an attractive salary scale. The League ideal was to maintain a level of remuneration equal to the best of national civil services. Although neither the League nor the United Nations has had the resources to achieve the ideal, the pay and perquisites presently compare favorably with most public pay scales. The rates of pay in 1966 for executive and professional categories are shown in Table 8-3. The Secretary-General's salary in 1966 was $46,200, plus an expense allowance of $22,500. His under-secretaries received $30,-000. In addition, there are allowances for dependents, education of children, and cost-of-living adjustments.

The take-home pay of every employee is reduced by a staff wage assessment levied to reimburse employees whose salaries are subject to national income taxation. Most members of the United Nations have ratified the Convention on Privileges and Immunities of the United Nations, which exempts Secretariat salaries from such taxes. The United States Senate balked at ratification, however, because of the exemption of American employees from income taxation and military service.[7] As a result, a portion of the United States' UN contribution is returned each year in the form of what is, in effect, a tax upon the salaries of all UN employees.[8]

[7] With these two major exceptions, the International Organizations Immunities Act of December 29, 1945, Public Law 291, 79th Cong., 1st Sess., had already accorded UN personnel essentially the same privileges and immunities as contained in the convention.

[8] Each employee subject to such taxation of course pays his own tax, but he is reimbursed from the wage assessment fund.

TABLE 8-3. Salary Scales [a]

Directors, Principal Officers and Professional Category

(In US dollars)

Effective 1 January 1966

Level	I	II	III	IV	V	VI	VII	VIII	IX	X	XI	XII	XIII
					Step								
					Directors and Principal Officers								
Director	24,050 (17,430)	24,700 (17,820)	25,350 (18,210)	26,000 (18,600)									
Principal Officer	20,000 (14,800)	20,650 (15,222.50)	21,300 (15,645)	21,950 (16,067.50)	22,600 (16,490)	23,250 (16,912.50)	23,900 (17,335)						
					Professional Category								
Senior Officer	17,400 (13,110)	17,900 (13,435)	18,400 (13,760)	18,900 (14,085)	19,400 (14,410)	19,900 (14,735)	20,400 (15,060)	20,900 (15,385)	21,400 (15,710)	21,900 (16,035)			
First Officer	13,900 (10,730)	14,330 (11,031)	14,760 (11,332)	15,190 (11,633)	15,620 (11,934)	16,050 (12,232.50)	16,480 (12,512)	16,910 (12,791.50)	17,340 (13,071)	17,770 (13,350.50)	18,200 (13,630)	18,630 (13,909.50)	
Second Officer	11,270 (8,889)	11,630 (9,141)	11,990 (9,393)	12,350 (9,645)	12,710 (9,897)	13,070 (10,149)	13,430 (10,401)	13,790 (10,653)	14,150 (10,905)	14,510 (11,157)	14,870 (11,409)	15,230 (11,661)	15,590 (11,913)
Associate Officer	9,050 (7,287.50)	9,360 (7,520)	9,670 (7,752.50)	9,980 (7,985)	10,290 (8,203)	10,600 (8,420)	10,910 (8,637)	11,220 (8,854)	11,530 (9,071)	11,840 (9,288)	12,150 (9,505)		
Assistant Officer	6,920 (5,690)	7,200 (5,900)	7,480 (6,110)	7,760 (6,320)	8,040 (6,530)	8,320 (6,740)	8,600 (6,950)	8,880 (7,160)	9,160 (7,370)	9,440 (7,580)			

[a] The net equivalent of each salary step, after application of the Staff Assessment Plan, has been added to the table for the information of the staff.
Source: UN Staff Rules.

Loyalty

A call to the international civil service demands that national loyalties be transcended by a primary loyalty to the international organization and the world community it represents. The question often raised is whether international officials can and do make this transition in fact. The Swiss scholar, William Rappard, speaking as a delegate to the League Assembly in 1930, was not too hopeful. He observed that "truly international officials are possible but very difficult to find. You have to transform into devoted servants of the international community men who are naturally attached to their native soil, and this is almost a miracle." A much less equivocal conclusion was later voiced by an outstanding group of League officials, reflecting on twenty years of experience with the world organization: "Experience shows," they said, "that a spirit of international loyalty among public servants can be maintained in practice." In recent years the issue has been still more sharply joined. To Nikita Khrushchev, the fact was clear that "there are no neutral men." To this Dag Hammarskjold uttered a stout denial, saying in effect, "I am a neutral man."

One must conclude from the experience of both the League and the United Nations that international officials can put international interests, as they conceive them, above the interest of any single state or group of states. The key elements of this international loyalty, aptly stated in the Staff Regulations, are integrity, independence, and impartiality. Integrity, although a matter of personal ethics, provides the essential basis for impartiality in dealing with member governments. Hammarskjold specifically related this quality to his own capacity for neutral action:

> I am not neutral as regards the Charter . . . . I am not neutral as regards facts . . . . But what I do claim is that even a man who is in that sense not neutral can very well undertake and carry through neutral actions, because that is an act of integrity.[9]

Hammarskjold believed that this kind of integrity and devotion to the international ideal permitted an international civil servant to be impartial in his dealings with member states and with problems affecting their interests. Many others who have served with international secretariats or who have observed them in action would agree.

Independence of national control is a condition that involves the behavior of member governments as well as that of secretariat officials. The UN Charter states that the Secretary-General and his staff "shall not seek or receive instructions from any government or from any other authority external to the Organization." Member states, on their part, undertake "to

[9] Quoted in Sydney D. Bailey, rev. ed. *The Secretariat of the United Nations* (New York: Praeger, 1964), p. 28.

respect the exclusively international character of the responsibilities of the Secretary-General and the staff and not to seek to influence them in the discharge of their responsibilities." Member states and secretariat officials have typically, if not exclusively, conformed to the spirit of these injunctions. During the League days the governments of Nazi Germany and Fascist Italy attempted, with partial success, to control their nationals on the Secretariat. In the main, however, the League Secretariat held firm. The UN record has been better still. No member state has openly assumed the right to instruct its nationals on the Secretariat or encouraged them to insubordination.

Nevertheless Khrushchev had a point. All international civil servants do not measure up to ideal standards of integrity, impartiality, and independence. All secretariat officials do not put the organization first. Soviet nationals on the UN Secretariat are punctilious in following orders, but they are bypassed in the discussion of certain questions because information entrusted to them is not likely to remain entirely confidential. Nor is the Soviet Union the only state that maintains close relationships with its nationals on the Secretariat. The official on fixed-term appointment, in fact, has every reason to maintain the best of relations with his colleagues in the national service from which he is only temporarily disjoined.

Moreover, even a man who is perfectly honest, impartial, and independent in dealing with things as he sees them has difficulty transcending his cultural bias. Dag Hammarskjold was the epitome of the international civil servant. But he was a Westerner, and his ultimate values were drawn from the Western cultural heritage. In the sense of which Khrushchev spoke, Hammarskjold was not and could not be ideologically neutral. Andrew Cordier, another official of great integrity, made a crucial judgment about closing the Leopoldville airport and radio station which significantly affected the balance of political power within the Congo. He did it in the service of an international ideal. Yet one feels almost certain that a Russian in the same position, even one of equal integrity and impartiality, would not have made the same decision.

From the Soviet point of view it was perfectly reasonable to urge the creation of a three-man Secretary-Generalship. Since no man could be "neutral," the remedy was to establish equal representation for the major viewpoints in international affairs. The Troika proposal was rejected not because it was illogical but because the majority of UN members supported Dag Hammarskjold personally and, perhaps more important, were not ready to barter away the capacity for executive action in exchange for greater representativeness in the office of the Secretary-General.

It is ironic that the only state outside the Soviet bloc to make a major issue of Secretariat loyalty has been the United States. The United States mounted a concerted campaign in 1952 and 1953 to root out American nationals on the Secretariat who were regarded as disloyal to their country. This attack on the Secretariat was, temporarily at least, more disrupting than Khrushchev's Troika blast and did not even have the virtue of logical consistency. Since the accusation, apparently, was Communist sympathies on the part of a small number of American employees of the Secretariat, the United States was in the position of saying that certain attitudes might be legitimately held by some Secretariat officials (Russians, for example) but not by others.

The United States' position was consistent, however, with the current mood of domestic politics and was a product of a general movement within the country to expose and ostracize anyone who was, or had been, or had ever been closely associated with, a Communist sympathizer. As an incident of this far-flung inquiry, a Special Federal Grand Jury in New York and the Internal Sub-Committee of the Senate Judiciary Committee turned up a number of UN officials who either admitted past membership in the Communist party, or when questioned about it, invoked the Fifth Amendment. From the public, the press, and the Congress came a massive verbal assault upon the United Nations for its harboring of "disloyal" American employees. When the executive branch added its demand for their dismissal, the pressure became unbearable. Secretary-General Lie ultimately dismissed eighteen officials, including twelve whose offense was taking refuge in the Fifth Amendment. Lie did so after being assured by an ad hoc committee of three international lawyers that the act of invoking a national constitutional privilege against self-incrimination was presumptive evidence of improper conduct in an international official.[10]

Lie shortly relinquished the reins of administration to Dag Hammarskjold, whose firmness and skillful diplomatic action, combined with a decline in the severity of the American Communist hunt, ultimately repaired most of the damage. The United Nations Administrative Tribunal subsequently heard appeals of the permanent members of the Secretariat who had been dismissed by Lie, and they were awarded compensation. The International Court of Justice upheld the decision of the Administrative Tribunal. This outcome contributed substantially to maintaining the independence of the Secretariat—an independence that could scarcely exist if member states exercised a right to determine at any time which of their nationals ought to remain in the employ of the Secretariat.

The Tasks of International Administration

The most characteristic activity of an international secretariat, developed to a fine art in the United Nations, is the servicing of international conferences. It is a rare working day at UN headquarters when at least one

---

[10] The jurists added the further dictum that a country playing permanent host to an international organization was entitled to protect itself against the risk of subversive activity by secretariat officials.

UN committee is not in session, and often several are in progress at once. Each meeting must be provided with the necessary interpreting, a technique refined by the UN Secretariat to a system in which the words of each speaker can be simultaneously interpreted into each of the five official languages—English, French, Russian, Spanish, and Chinese. Each meeting also produces documents that must be printed in the working languages— English and French—and sometimes in the other official languages. For these purposes the United Nations maintains a staff of more than 500 interpreters and translators, in addition to the army of clerks who man the typewriters and run the duplicating machines.

The work of the Secretariat also extends to the substantive problems with which the conferences deal. For a wide range of issues, from social welfare services to disarmament and the pacific settlement of disputes, the Secretariat is assigned duties of information collection, research, and reporting. Secretariat specialists in economic development, international law, or the politics of given geographical areas must be prepared to advise the Secretary-General and, on occasion, representatives of member governments. Secretariats may also assume responsibility for substantive field operations. The UN Secretariat now offers technical assistance in such diverse fields as human rights, social welfare services, and public administration, financed both by its regular budget and through the United Nations Development Program. Operating responsibilities in the political area have included the administrative direction and logistical underpinning of UN peace-keeping forces in Egypt, the Congo, Cyprus, and New Guinea, and the servicing of somewhat smaller observational, investigative, and mediatory operations in Greece, the Middle East, Kashmir, and elsewhere.

Obviously, the Secretariat must perform its own internal housekeeping tasks—staffing, financial administration, property maintenance, supply procurement, and the like. The United Nations also conducts its own postal administration, including the issuance of postage stamps, and engages in large-scale publishing activities. The Office of Public Information, with branch information centers in more than forty countries, employs a professional and clerical staff of over 500 in its efforts to supply information and maintain good public relations.

The Budgetary Process

The Secretariat can function effectively only if it has the necessary financial support. For this it must rely upon contributions from member states. The Secretary-General is responsible for the initial preparation of the annual budget of the organization, but his estimates are based on the amounts required to carry out programs already authorized by the policy-making bodies. If the Assembly wills an act but not the means to perform it, great frustration within the Secretariat can readily develop.

The regular budgetary process begins, as in most governmental organizations, with the preparation of a budget request by the Secretary-General on the basis of departmental estimates reconciled and trimmed to fit the overall program by the Budget Division of the Controller's Office. Following League of Nations precedent, the General Assembly has established a financial watchdog committee called the Advisory Committee on Administrative and Budgetary Questions, which carefully examines the budget prior to its formal consideration by the Assembly. The Secretary-General appears before the Committee to defend and explain his requests. The Advisory Committee is composed of individuals appointed for three-year terms to serve in a private technical capacity, but they are also officials of member governments and are likely to represent their governments in subsequent consideration of the budget by the General Assembly. The Advisory Committee appears to conceive its role as one of challenging estimates and recommending reductions, although the increase in the regular annual UN budget from under $20 million in 1946 to more than $120 million in 1966 indicates that the Advisory Committee and the Assembly have not been impervious to pleas for increased appropriations.

When the hearings are concluded, the Advisory Committee submits its report to the Assembly where, in the course of the session, members of the Assembly's Fifth (Administrative and Budgetary) Committee again debate the budget among themselves and with the Secretary-General. In the committee the debate becomes more political and substantive, but not more friendly to the Secretariat. Some governments see in the budget debate an opportunity to attack not only the budget estimates but also any underlying substantive policies with which they happen to disagree, even though the substantive issues have presumably been discussed and settled elsewhere. As a rule, the Fifth Committee discussion ends in acceptance of the Advisory Committee's recommendations—a logical conclusion considering that the members of the Advisory Committee, however "personal" their capacity, are drawn from countries representing a wide geographical sampling and a preponderance of influence in the organization. The General Assembly then approves the recommendations of the Fifth Committee.[11]

The budget debate is a painful annual ritual that the Secretariat must undergo as the price of maintaining its existence as a dynamic creative influence in the international arena. Of this drawn-out, repetitious process a United States Senate subcommittee once observed, "Rarely have so many important people taken so much time to spend so little in the way of public funds."[12] The process undoubtedly keeps the Secretary-General and his staff mindful of their dependence upon the good opinion of the member

[11] For a more detailed discussion of the budget process, see J. David Singer, *Financing International Organization* (The Hague: Martinus Nijhoff, 1961).

[12] U. S. Senate Committee on Foreign Relations, Subcommittee on the U.N. Charter, *Budgetary and Financial Problems of the United Nations,* Staff Study No. 6, Washington: Government Printing Office, 1954, p. 9.

governments and of the need for careful budgeting. Perhaps also it has a cathartic effect upon member governments, easing somewhat the financial pain and enabling them to assure their own appropriating bodies that United Nations funds are being managed carefully. In any event, the budget process lays bare the political matrix within which administrative action occurs and reflects the contending interests that must be reconciled before effective administrative action is possible.

THE SECRETARIAT IN THE POLITICAL PROCESS

Our examination of secretariat structure and process has shown how pervasively the administrative process is affected by its political milieu. Secretariats, in turn, respond with significant inputs of influence into the policy processes of their respective organizations and of the larger international political system. The discussion that follows will analyze the influence that secretariats exert through the exercise of initiative and political leadership in the administration of programs, participation in the decisions of policy-making organs, and the practice of diplomacy.

Policy Through Administration

Administration begins where the commands of policy-making bodies end. Commands vary in their degree of specificity, however, and they necessarily leave room for administrative discretion in application to particular cases. In this sense, administration is simply policy making at a relatively high level of specificity. But sometimes commands are stated so broadly that important decisions of substance must be made by the administrators, and the administrators literally become the organization's policy makers. The Congo crisis illustrates how far this implicit delegation of legislative authority can go in international organization. Faced with deadlock in the Security Council and crises too fast-moving for the ponderous machinery of the Assembly, the Secretary-General and his associates had to make crucial decisions about the disposition and use of UN forces which substantially altered the course of events in the Congo. Even without fundamental disagreement within the deliberative organs, a secretariat may be elevated to an important policy-making role. In the fall of 1956 Dag Hammarskjold was given wide latitude in the establishment and operation of UNEF, and subsequently in clearing the Suez Canal. Delegation of broad authority in these instances was due less to deadlock than to general confidence in the ability of the Secretary-General, lack of time to hammer out more specific instructions, and the inherent inability of the General Assembly to provide detailed guidance to administrators in a crisis situation.

Administration may also become entwined with larger policy decisions in less direct and dramatic ways. Research studies and reports of Secretariat officials have become the basis for subsequent proposals by member states for action by the General Assembly. A League historian estimates that the monumental *Nutrition Report* issued in 1937 by a special committee of the League Assembly had far-reaching effects upon the attitudes of governmental officials and private groups in many countries by calling attention to the abysmally low levels of nutrition in most parts of the world.[13] Nearly every existing international organization can point to reports drawn by expert secretariat personnel which were the basis for subsequent action in fields as diverse as public administration, labor standards, eradication of disease, water resource development, or peace-keeping operations.

Successful performance of assigned duties by the secretariat can lead to demands for more of the same. UNEF had to be built almost from the ground up when the Suez crisis arose; but the UNEF precedent made a peace-keeping force the logical UN response to chaos in the Congo and the threatened civil war in Cyprus. Successful experiments in the administration of technical assistance by international organizations have brought demands for increased assistance. On the other hand, ineffective performance by a secretariat may lead to the modification or abandonment of programs.

Participation in the Decisions of Deliberative Bodies

The preceding section has suggested ways in which a secretariat may affect organizational policy by acquiring broad substantive discretion or through feedback to governing bodies of the organization. Secretariat officials also participate directly in the decision-making processes of the governing bodies themselves. Among existing international organizations, probably no secretariat enjoys greater influence upon organization policy than the staff of the World Bank, which not only frames the program for discussion by its Executive Directors and Governing Board but generally secures approval for what the Bank President and his staff recommend. The UNESCO Secretariat also fixes the agenda and prepares a program for action by its governing body, although the UNESCO General Conference is often disposed to alter the program. The European Common Market represents yet a different relationship. By constitutional fiat, policy-making authority is divided between the Council of Ministers, which speaks for governments, and the Commission, which heads the administrative establishment. Some types of decisions are made by the Commission alone, some by the Council alone, and others of considerable importance by the concurrent action of both.

All these organizations are to be contrasted with the United Nations in which most agenda items are proposed by member states and simply compiled by the Secretariat in the preliminary agenda. Although the UN Secretary-General may also suggest items for the consideration of the deliberative

[13] Walters, *op. cit.*, pp. 754–55.

organs, he does not submit a legislative program. The Secretary-General does, of course, prepare the budget for the United Nations, and this is one of the more significant and hotly contested legislative matters to come before the Assembly each year. He may also have important discretion in deciding whether, and in what form, matters carried over from a preceding session shall appear on the current agenda.

These differences in the role of international secretariats reflect differing degrees of consensus among a working majority upon the goals and functions of the organization. The World Bank handles a relatively narrow range of issues on which its dominant members are in broad agreement. The United Nations, on the other hand, deals with a wide range of questions including many which intrude upon sensitive political ground. Consensus is obviously much easier to reach in the former instance. Numbers and homogeneity of membership also affect consensus. Other things equal, consensus should come easier to six Western European states than to 122 members of the United Nations.

Whether or not an international secretariat exercises a substantial role in initiating program proposals, other avenues of participation in the decision-making process are open. Chief administrators frequently are authorized to take part in formal discussion and debate. All of the policy-making organs of the United Nations have some provision for hearing the Secretary-General. In addition, staff members conduct their own lobbying operations with varying degrees of directness outside the debating chambers. Nor is the initiative necessarily left with the Secretariat. Individual civil servants are often consulted because of their expertise in a particular subject area, and the Secretary-General will most certainly be consulted if members are seriously considering the proposal of new functions or responsibilities for the Secretariat. On some questions the Secretary-General may be drawn into informal negotiating processes because he represents a relatively neutral and impartial viewpoint on an issue, or because he can serve as a useful channel of communication among the various parties. At a tactical and procedural level, secretariat officials are storehouses of advice and information on such matters relevant to policy as the conduct of meetings, drafting of resolutions, and the tactics of effective advocacy.

The Practice of Diplomacy

A third way in which international officials may hope to influence organizational policy and the larger international system is through the practice of quiet diplomacy. Diplomacy, in this context, should be clearly distinguished from "conference diplomacy" or "parliamentary diplomacy." The latter terms are generally applied to the process by which representatives of governments, acting through international organizations and conferences, attempt to reach decisions by means of deliberative and voting procedures adapted from domestic legislatures. Put more concisely, conference diplomacy is a process of reaching international decisions through public discussion and voting. Quiet diplomacy, on the other hand, is a process of seeking agreement through private discussion and consensus.[14] In the practice of international organizations the two processes are often intertwined, but they are analytically, and to some extent operationally, separate. Hammarskjold recognized this distinction when he observed in 1958,

> The legislative process in the United Nations is not a substitute for diplomacy. It serves its purpose only when it helps diplomacy to arrive at agreements between the national states concerned. It is diplomacy, not speeches and votes, that continues to have the last word in the process of peace-making.[15]

Quiet negotiations are constantly conducted by secretariat officials on many subjects with which their organizations are concerned. For analytical purposes, these contacts may be grouped within general categories—(1) diplomacy in the conduct of organizational programs; (2) diplomacy in support of organizational decisions; and, (3) diplomacy in mediating controversies among states.

In the conduct of UN programs, a striking example of effective diplomacy on a related series of important issues emerged from the Suez crisis of 1956. In pursuance of Assembly resolutions the Secretary-General had to negotiate with member states the terms on which UNEF contingents would be made available, assembled in Italy, transported to Egypt, and supplied all the while. Even more delicate was the process of reaching agreement with Egypt on the terms under which the forces would be permitted to function on Egyptian territory, including their composition, deployment, lines of communication and supply, and their status with respect to Egyptian jurisdiction. The action also involved the Secretary-General and his aides in negotiating the withdrawal of British, French, and Israeli troops from their positions in Egypt. When order was restored, Hammarskjold was assigned the task of arranging the clearance of the Suez Canal which had been blocked with sunken vessels at the order of President Nasser when seizure of the Canal seemed imminent. The Suez episode, which lasted over a period of many months, must be regarded as a triumph of quiet diplomacy conducted by the UN Secretary-General.

The Suez crisis is only a spectacular example of diplomatic processes

---

[14] Conference diplomacy, by definition, is always multilateral. Quiet diplomacy may be either bilateral (between two parties) or multilateral (among more than two parties). Howard H. Lentner uses these distinctions in "The Diplomacy of the United Nations Secretary-General," *Western Political Quarterly* (September, 1965), pp. 531–50.

[15] Dag Hammarskjold, "The Element of Privacy in Peace-Making," text of address delivered at Ohio University, Athens, Ohio, *United Nations Review* (March, 1958), pp. 10–12.

that are used regularly in carrying out the programs of international organizations. Every technical assistance project is the product of extensive and detailed negotiations among governments and the responsible international organizations. When the World Bank or the International Development Association lends money for a development project, or the International Monetary Fund grants credits to ease a country's balance of payments, the deal is first worked out by careful negotiation between representatives of the international organization and the country concerned. Programs for refugee relief often require diplomatic negotiations among representatives of one or more international organizations, the host country, the countries supporting the refugee relief program, and private organizations that cooperate in the relief activities. Whenever the policy-making body of an international organization authorizes its secretariat to engage in an operating program, it thereby authorizes the secretariat to enter into diplomatic contact with the governments and other agencies whose cooperation is required.

Diplomatic activity is also undertaken by secretariats in support of organizational decisions not involving operating programs. Many resolutions adopted by the deliberative bodies of the United Nations and other international organizations do not establish programs for the secretariat to carry out but rather make recommendations for action by member governments. Secretariats often use their persuasive powers to gain support and compliance with such decisions. In the UN financial crisis, the UN Secretary-General has been tireless in his negotiations with governments—particularly the big financial contributors—to encourage them to support UN resolutions calling for subscriptions to UN bonds, contributions to a UN rescue fund, and other financial measures. Frequently, the UN Secretary-General is given a mandate by the Assembly or Security Council to enter into negotiations with particular countries to obtain their compliance with resolutions. The Security Council mandate for the Secretary-General to deal with the government of South Africa in an attempt to obtain compliance with resolutions on race relations illustrates one such endeavor that proved fruitless. In almost equally unpromising circumstances the Secretary-General in 1955 successfully implemented a mandate from the Assembly to negotiate the release of eleven American airmen held captive by China from the Korean war. In both of these cases, interestingly enough, the governments concerned did not recognize the authority of the UN organs to adopt resolutions on the subject, but they did recognize the Secretary-General's authority to negotiate for the organization.

Perhaps the most characteristic form of diplomatic activity by secretariat officials, at least in the United Nations, is the mediation of controversy between states. The role of mediator, conciliator, and consensus-builder often appears in the quiet negotiations that occur behind the scenes of conference diplomacy. Many a compromise between governments, later embodied in a resolution, has been forged with the help of a timely suggestion or the mediatory services of a secretariat official. The expertise, impartiality, and continuity of secretariats become especially important in negotiations that continue over a long period of time. At the nuclear test ban negotiations in Geneva, for example, the American, British, and Russian negotiators were usually aided by UN Secretariat disarmament experts who more than once smoothed a path to agreement.

The UN Secretary-General and his staff are also frequently involved in the mediation of particular disputes among countries. Involvement in such instances can come through a mandate from the Assembly or Security Council, or at the request of one or more parties to the dispute. It may even come at the initiative of the Secretary-General himself. As an example of the first, when the Security Council created a UN force for Cyprus in 1964, it also requested the Secretary-General to appoint a mediator to attempt a reconciliation of the Greek and Turkish communities on the island. U Thant's constant efforts to play the role of mediator and pacifier in the Viet Nam conflict illustrates a kind of intervention by the Secretary-General on his own initiative. Obviously, the prospects for settlement are likely to be better when one or all parties to a dispute request the services of the Secretary-General. Such was the case in 1958 when Thailand and Cambodia, in preference to utilizing one of the UN forums, asked the Secretary-General to designate a representative to help them find a solution to a dispute. The work of the representative Johan Beck-Friis of Sweden was eminently successful. This happy result, obviously, does not always follow. In October, 1956, the Secretary-General's office was the scene of negotiations at the request or acquiescence of all concerned. What appeared to be a promising start toward agreement on principles to govern the status of the Suez Canal was suddenly obliterated by the Israeli, British, and French resort to armed force.

Political Leadership: Cultivating Support

Political leadership and initiative cut across all avenues of secretariat influence—administration, policymaking and diplomacy. As here conceived, it combines two important functions—(1) cultivating support and (2) taking independent initiative. The task of cultivating support is not essentially different from that of national administrators, although the international setting makes it more difficult. The Secretary-General must get support wherever he can, and this includes cultivation of the governments that are his legislators, private interest groups, and the general public. Governments are also "clients" of the Secretariat—that is, the direct recipients and beneficiaries of most of its services. The cultivation of their support thus begins with the attempt to serve them well. The successful political leader also counts the cost before taking action or assuming a public stance that will antagonize influential members. Trygve Lie's decision to discharge American Secretariat employees was intimately related to his need for political support. The action appeared necessary to mollify his most influential "legislator-client." Hammarskjold's cultivation of the Afro-Asian members paid off handsomely when he came under attack from the Soviet Union for his conduct of the Congo operation.

The support of private groups can be helpful to the work of international secretariats and is sought with varying degrees of concern by nearly all. The staff of the ICAO has drawn substantial strength from its close working relationship with the International Air Transport Association, a nongovernmental organization of world airline companies. The staff of the World Bank has cultivated and won the confidence of the world banking community by maintaining good liaison, the appointment of respected financiers to key positions, and the adoption of sound banking practices. This confidence has been an element of no little importance in establishing the Bank secretariat's strong position. The Secretariat of the ITU has both formal and informal arrangements for consulting with public and private telecommunications services throughout the world. The United Nations, through its Office of Public Information, maintains liaison with numerous national and international organizations having an interest in its work. The favors that the OPI is able to dispense do not often extend beyond the issuance of passes to the UN premises, tickets to UN meetings, and information on the activities of the organization. But support must be cultivated whenever and however possible. The UN Department of Economic and Social Affairs also does its best to serve the more than three hundred international nongovernmental organizations that are granted consultative status with the Economic and Social Council.

Nor is the general public neglected. Literally millions of persons have passed through the revolving doors at the visitors entrance to the UN Headquarters to receive the polite ministrations of its busy information clerks and smartly uniformed tour guides, and to witness its public meetings. A constant stream of news releases and other information emanates from New York, Geneva, and UN information centers throughout the world. Publications range from documentary reports of proceedings and Secretariat research to slick brochures lauding the accomplishments of the United Nations and its related agencies.

Other agencies carry on an active public relations program in their own behalf. The UNICEF greeting card and Halloween "trick or treat" collections have a broader purpose than that of raising funds. By involving thousands of persons with UNICEF activities they build public support for its programs. The United States Committee for UNICEF, aided by state and local branches, has for years conducted a vigorous campaign to detect anti-UNICEF propaganda and counteract it by distribution of pro-UNICEF leaflets, writing letters to editors, supplying information to local news media, and eliciting the support of other interested private groups. Throughout the world, private United Nations Associations serve as unofficial public relations organizations for the United Nations and its related agencies, often using information prepared by national or international headquarters in consultation with the UN Office of Public Information.

Political Leadership: Initiative

The Secretary-General's ultimate objective in creating support is to influence the affairs of the organization and the larger political community through the exercise of independent initiative. The development of political leadership in the office of the UN Secretary-General has been subject to widespread comment and will be the focus of our discussion here. The potentiality of the Secretary-Generalship for providing bold leadership "of international thought and action" was early recognized by the first incumbent. "I had no calculated plan for developing the political powers of the office of Secretary-General," Trygve Lie later recalled, "but I was determined that the Secretary-General should be a force for peace." [16] His successors likewise have considered themselves as international spokesmen, dedicated to building the influence of the office and the organization. Hammarskjold was self-consciously acting in this capacity when he offered his celebrated defense of the United Nations as a "dynamic instrument of governments" rather than mere "static conference machinery." [17]

Political initiative is exercised by the UN Secretary-General in a number of ways. Taking public positions on issues is one common method. The Secretary-General's *Introduction* to his *Annual Report on the Work of the Organization* has become a kind of "State of the World" message in which important developments of the year are recounted, prospects for the future assayed, the Secretary-General's views set forth, and recommendations offered for the promotion of UN objectives. The Secretary-General also makes his views known through numerous public addresses each year in a variety of forums, through releases and statements to the press, and in private conversations with governmental representatives. He also frequently exercises his right to speak on issues in the meetings of UN deliberative bodies.

Such personal involvement with issues can carry certain hazards, especially if UN members are sharply divided. Trygve Lie incurred the displeasure of one or more of the great powers on several occasions. His outspoken support of UN military intervention in Korea won him undying Soviet

[16] Trygve Lie, *In the Cause of Peace* (New York: Macmillan, 1954), p. 42.

[17] *Introduction to the Annual Report of the Secretary-General on the Work of the Organization, 16 June 1960 to 15 June 1961,* Official Records of the General Assembly, Sixteenth Sess., Supplement No. 1A, United Nations Document A/4800/Add.1, pp. 1–8.

enmity and eventually cost him his job. Nevertheless, Lie's successors have not hesitated to exercise the same kind of political initiative, and Dag Hammarskjold ultimately found himself defending UN actions in the Congo against Soviet attack which, had he lived, might well have cut short his tenure in office.

Lie, Hammarskjold, and Thant have all insisted on the right of the Secretary-General to take a stand on international issues. Hammarskjold rationalized his own penchant for verbal intervention in terms of the Secretary-General's unique role as spokesman for the organization:

> The Secretary-General may interpret his constitutionally objective position in such a way as to refuse to take a stand in emerging conflicts, in order thus to preserve the neutrality of the office. He may, however, also accord himself the right to take a stand in these conflicts to the extent that such a stand can be firmly based on the Charter and its principles, and thus express what may be called the independent judgment of the Organization.[18]

Lie had earlier expressed much the same sentiment:

> The Secretary-General is not to be "neutral" above all else . . . . Rather, the duty of the Secretary-General is to uphold the principles of the Charter and the decisions of the Organization as objectively as he can.[19]

U Thant has defended the Secretary-General's prerogative but confined his advocacy to safer issues or safer positions and thus avoided creating antagonisms among the large powers or substantial numbers of small ones.

The Secretary-General's opinion on issues carries considerable weight if the Secretariat has special expertise or interest in the issue concerned. In matters of Secretariat structure, finance, and powers, the Secretary-General obviously has both special knowledge of the problems involved and a particular interest in their solution. The Secretary-General engages actively in support of his budget proposal each year, and his opinions—although not governing—are given careful attention. In an entirely different situation, Dag Hammarskjold's public defense of the Secretary-Generalship against the challenge of the Soviet "Troika" proposal in 1960 was a crucial element in determining the outcome. If he had shown a willingness to compromise, the powers of his office might have been altered substantially.

The Secretary-General also speaks with the authority of special interest and expertise regarding programs the Secretariat administers. This is as true of economic and social programs as it is of peace-keeping operations in the Congo, Suez, Cyprus, and elsewhere. In such instances, the Secretary-General and his agents are closer to the facts of the issue than the representatives of most governments, and his arguments weigh accordingly.

[18] Address in Copenhagen, May 2, 1959, reprinted in *United Nations Review*, Vol. 5 (June, 1959), p. 25.

[19] Trygve Lie, *op. cit.*, pp. 342–43.

Similar conditions obtain where the Secretary-General is engaged in mediatorial activities, either in person or through an appointed mediator.

Besides participating in debate, the Secretary-General may exercise political initiative by making "legislative" proposals to the policy-making bodies of the organization. Secretariats in some international organizations regularly prepare a legislative program for action by their policy-making organs. In the United Nations, the right to propose agenda items has been used but sparingly by Secretary-Generals. Trygve Lie used this device in 1950 to present his proposal for a "Twenty-Year Program for Peace." The program was received by the General Assembly without enthusiasm, and little practical result came of it. Lie's successors have not emulated his example in taking such flamboyant legislative initiatives.

The paucity of agenda items formally inscribed at the request of the Secretary-General is not an accurate indicator of his activity in initiating proposals for legislative action. On the contrary, UN Secretary-Generals have initiated proposals leading to UN resolutions within the framework of issues already under consideration by one of the deliberative organs. Plans approved by the General Assembly for the establishment of UNEF and the subsequent clearing of the Suez Canal, for example, were largely a product of UN Secretariat initiative on a matter already on the Assembly agenda. Hammarskjold was successful in securing approval because the plans were offered in the context of a recognized need for action and in consultation with the governments whose support was essential. On matters running the full gamut of UN activities—peace and security, dependent territories, economic and social affairs, law and administration—a request by the Assembly for study and report has been treated by the Secretariat as a vehicle to produce proposals for action by subsequent meetings of policy-making organs. Secretariat initiatives may occur in the still quieter form of suggestions given to governmental delegates who seek Secretariat advice, or who, on somewhat different terms, are willing to front for a Secretariat proposal. By such means, ranging from the direct proposal of an agenda item to the quiet planting of an idea with a receptive delegation, the Secretariat maintains a continuing initiative in the legislative processes of the organization.

In addition to leadership in public discussion and in the UN legislative process, the Secretary-General has developed a capacity to initiate action directly affecting the course of events outside the organization. This stems in part from the increasingly "broad diplomatic and operational functions" delegated by the policy-making organs.[20] The phenomenon of executive growth through delegation is illustrated by the Suez crisis of 1956 and the Congo crisis of 1960, in which the Secretary-General was given—or acquired by default—broad discretion in the implementation of general objectives.

[20] Bailey, *op. cit.,* p. 41.

Article 98 of the Charter requires the Secretary-General to perform "such other functions as are entrusted to him" by the other major organs, and Hammarskjold interpreted this as a mandate to do whatever he found necessary to implement the broad directives given him by the General Assembly and the Security Council.

Hammarskjold succeeded, where Lie had tried and largely failed, in carrying the theory and practice of executive power yet a step further. Neither man believed the political functions of the office were limited to those expressly conferred by a policy-making body. Political philosopher that he was, Hammarskjold clearly distinguished between the specific responsibilities conferred upon him by the policy-making organs and the more general responsibilities and prerogatives inherent in the office of Secretary-General. When deadlock in the Security Council prevented enlargement of the United Nations Observer Group in Lebanon in the summer of 1958, he enlarged it on his own initiative, explaining to the Security Council that under the Charter he "should be expected to act without any guidance from the Assembly or the Security Council' should this appear to him necessary towards helping to fill any vacuum that may appear in the systems which the Charter and traditional diplomacy provide for the safeguarding of peace and security." [21]

U Thant circumspectly continued the practice of taking political initiatives on his own responsibility. The UN temporary executive authority in West New Guinea (1962), the observer mission in Yemen (1963), and the UN plebiscite in North Borneo and Sarawak (1963) were initiated by U Thant on his own responsibility, although each action was subsequently approved by the General Assembly or Security Council. At the height of the 1962 Cuban missile crisis Thant's appeal for a voluntary suspension of Soviet arms shipments to Cuba and of American quarantine measures provided a formula which helped avert a direct confrontation at sea. Since 1964 the Secretary-General has attempted, albeit unsuccessfully, to assume a mediating role in the Viet Nam conflict.

The Basis of Secretariat Influence

The fact is well established that secretariats have extensive involvement in the political processes of international organization. If effective participation implies a capacity to influence the process, what are the sources of secretariat influence? Some of these "elements of power" have been suggested in the foregoing discussion and will be briefly summarized here.

1. Constitutional prerogatives. The charter of an organization gives the secretary-general certain rights, powers, and duties. The UN Charter, for example, contains a somewhat more copious grant of authority to the

[21] Official Records of the Security Council, 13th Year, 837th meeting, July 22, 1958, p. 4.

Secretary-General than did the League Covenant. The constitutional prerogatives of the Commission of the European Economic Community are still greater. Legal rights are a source of positive influence.

2. *An administrative organization.* The secretariat is a working organization often embracing hundreds, and, in the case of the United Nations, thousands of individuals. It is an organization which can perform or withhold service. Its operating programs affect the welfare of many people. The organization may even include armed forces which, within limits, do the bidding of the secretary-general. Such an organization is a source of power.

3. *Information.* Many states rely upon the secretariat to provide reliable information and even advice on a wide variety of topics. This "information power" may result from technical expertise of secretariat personnel, continuity of service and depth of experience, or access to sources of information that for various reasons are not directly available to governments.

4. *Neutrality.* However difficult the achievement of absolute neutrality in international affairs, one source of secretariat strength is the position it occupies as the spokesman for the whole community. A reputation for neutrality enhances the value of secretariat officials as observers and mediators, and thus enhances their influence. A reputation for neutrality, impartiality, and integrity contributes to the influence of a secretary-general and his associates as a trusted repository of confidential information and a virtually indispensable channel of communication.

5. *Support of clientele and public opinion.* Secretariats may achieve influence through the support of the groups or states they serve. The secretariat may also derive strength from popular support within member states and from the prestige of the secretary-general's office. Private groups on occasion provide funds, facilities, and advice to aid the secretariat. They may also lobby with member governments in support of secretariat programs.

All international secretariats draw upon these sources of influence, but not all in equal measure. Some of the variation is attributable to differences in constitutional grants of authority. Another variant is the personality and ability of the incumbent secretary-general. Albert Thomas, first Director-General of the ILO, was a promoter of causes, a reflection of his background as "a politician, a trade unionist, a social campaigner and reformer." [22] On the other hand, Sir Eric Drummond brought to the League the self-effacing anonymity of the British civil servant who, while leaving the stage to others, exerted his influence through management, counsel, and negotiation "behind the scenes." Trygve Lie by contrast, delegated administration to deputies and emphasized the political function of the UN Secretary-General both as a public figure and a quiet negotiator. Hammarskjold appeared in many

[22] Georges Langrod, *The International Civil Service* (Leyden: A. W. Sythoff, 1963), p. 311.

ways to combine the best aspects of both the Lie and Drummond types—concern for administrative detail, mastery of quiet diplomacy, and zealous advocacy of secretariat initiative. Although U Thant has done much to preserve the political functions bequeathed to him by Lie and Hammarskjold, his has been a less dynamic approach. To the present time, the highwater mark of the UN Secretary-General's prestige and influence was probably reached sometime during the last year and a half of Hammarskjold's life.

But personality does not explain all of the variation in the political performance of secretariats, even after constitutional variables have been accounted for. As Sir Eric Drummond once commented, "It is quite, quite certain that Albert Thomas in my job would have been forced to resign. They wouldn't have stood for it. He would have tried—and failed. The 'Chancellor' wouldn't have been successful." [23] The limits of the possible are set not alone by constitutional strictures and personal capacities but also by the tasks of the organization and by its political environment. We have already considered how consensus among member states is one key to secretariat influence, and how a narrow range of technical functions is more conducive to this kind of consensus. If performance of the organizational task also generates its own financial resources, as with the World Bank, the secretariat's dependence upon member states is further reduced. Innumerable variables in the political environment of the organization may bear on the secretariat's freedom of political action. Past experience of the League created a frame of mind conducive to the acceptance of a greater political role for the Secretary-General of the United Nations. Patterns of power distribution among members of the organization can affect a secretary-general's freedom of action. Crisis may create opportunity for a chief administrator to take initiative; deadlock in the policy-making organs may make it necessary. Relevant also are the political values of the states that are dominant in the organization. Systematic comparative surveys of secretariat influence are yet to be made, and these are but a few of the possible variables. General observation suggests, however, that twentieth-century conditions are conducive to an expansion, however halting, of both the administrative and political functions of international civil servants.

Selected Readings

BAILEY, SYDNEY D. *The Secretariat of the United Nations.* New York: Praeger, 1964, rev. ed.

FOOTE, WILDER, ed. *Dag Hammarskjold: Servant of Peace.* New York: Harper and Row, 1962.

[23] Quoted in Stephen M. Schwebel, *The Secretary-General of the United Nations* (Cambridge: Harvard University Press, 1952), p. 3.

The International Secretariat of the Future. London: Royal Institute of International Affairs, 1944.

LANGROD, GEORGES. *The International Civil Service*. Leyden: A. W. Sythoff, 1963.

LASH, JOSEPH P. *Dag Hammarskjold: Custodian of the Brushfire Peace*. Garden City, N.Y.: Doubleday, 1961.

LIE, TRYGVE. *In the Cause of Peace*. New York: Macmillan, 1954.

LOVEDAY, A. *Reflections on International Administration*. Oxford: Clarendon Press, 1956.

PHELAN, E. J. *Yes and Albert Thomas*. New York: Columbia University Press, 1949.

RANSHOFEN-WERTHEIMER, EGON F. *The International Secretariat: A Great Experiment in International Administration*. Washington: Carnegie Endowment for International Peace, 1945.

SCHWEBEL, STEPHEN M. *The Secretary-General of the United Nations*. Cambridge: Harvard University Press, 1952.

SCOTT, F. R. "The World's Civil Service," *International Conciliation*, No. 496, 1954.

WINCHMORE, CHARLES. "The Secretariat: Retrospect and Prospect," *International Organization*, Summer, 1965, pp 622–39.

Part III

The Search for Security and Stability

9 | *The Resolution of International Conflict*

Political settlement of disputes as a means of maintaining international peace plays a significant role today as it has since the beginning of the modern state system. Some such techniques antedate the western state system, and their origins are lost in the haze of antiquity. *Political* approaches to dispute settlement are supplemented by the *legal* methods of arbitration and judicial settlement. Together they comprise the tools of pacific settlement upon which the state system depends in its attempts to prevent the use of force to resolve differences.

Traditional settlement methods employed for several centuries, usually by third states, have been supplemented in the contemporary world by a variety of new adaptations exercised mainly by organs and agencies of the United Nations. The problem of achieving agreement between disputants, however, remains difficult, the real issues often clouded, and the key to a settlement elusive. Many disputes remain unsettled, though the parties may be temporarily pacified, to erode slowly away over the years or, perhaps, to reappear intermittently, often in more virulent form with each new outbreak.

The dispute between India and Pakistan over Kashmir exemplifies the latter; for twenty years it has defied the United Nations and the state system's best efforts to achieve agreement. For this reason, and because the dispute has provided a laboratory for testing and evaluating the use of a great variety of political settlement techniques and tools, the Kashmir dispute will be referred to extensively in this chapter to illustrate the problems, frustrations, and occasional successes of dispute settlement in the United Nations era.

CAUSES FOR DISPUTES

Like individuals, nations have almost unlimited numbers and kinds of grievances against each other. Since there are over 130 countries in the state system, and each state's actions may affect many others, the resulting multiplicity of interactions inescapably produces frictions and misunderstandings.

207

Most of them are of minor consequence and are settled simply and unnoticed through routine diplomacy.

Some actions of states, however, may violate international norms or present a challenge to other states' national interests. Even if they do neither, they may appear that way in the subjectively oriented perceptions of political leaders and people of other states. Such actions are vigorously protested by the injured state through diplomatic channels, and demands are made that the wrong be righted in some appropriate way. If satisfaction is not obtained, the disagreement may escalate into an open dispute, other parties may be drawn in, and the matter becomes a concern to the entire state community. At this point, typically, the dispute is more difficult to settle because it involves matters of national honor and prestige.

The causes of disputes are as varied as the interactions and relationships that characterize the workings of the state system. Any matter, given impetus by frustration, national honor, suspicion, or plans of conquest, can become a major international dispute. Most disputes during the era of the United Nations have involved matters of real substance rather than ruffled national egos, but the latter are always present in disputes. Although various classifications are possible, a number of post-1945 disputes will be examined under five major headings: [1] A. *Territorial and Boundary Questions;* B. *Cold War Questions;* C. *Independence Questions;* D. *Domestic Questions;* and, E. *Intervention Questions.*

A. Territorial and Boundary Questions

Territorial and boundary disputes involve claims and counterclaims to jurisdiction over territory, and controversies over fixing boundary lines between states. Territorial and boundary questions are dangerous to peace because they arouse mass emotions in defense of what the peoples of both disputing states regard as sacred national territory. The principle of self-determination, ideally a key to settlement, is often rejected by the party with weaker support from the indigenous people of the disputed area.

KASHMIR. The difficult and explosive nature of territorial disputes emerges out of the Indian-Pakistani dispute over Kashmir. Two limited wars—one in 1947–48, the other in 1965—and twenty years of unsuccessful attempts to settle the dispute illustrate the depths of national attachments to that piece

---

[1] A more specific and detailed classification of disputes that have come before the United Nations during its first twenty years is provided by *International Conciliation* in its "Issues Before the 20th General Assembly." No. 554 (September, 1965), p. 13. Categories of disputes recognized therein included: "(1) A dispute between neighboring states, generally involving charges of aggression; (2) an attack by a more powerful state on a weaker one; (3) foreign troops stationed in another country; (4) treaty violations; (5) enforcement of a decision of the International Court; (6) the claim of one state to the territory of another; (7) violation of human rights by the majority or by a ruling minority; (8) dissension within a country; (9) emergence of a dependent territory into independence."

of territory. The dispute started when the Hindu Prince of Kashmir, a feudal Princely State under British paramountcy, joined the new state of India after his predominantly Muslim subjects rose in rebellion. In response to his appeal, the Indian army occupied two thirds of the state.

The Kashmir case, although a territorial dispute, is embittered by a thousand-year history of suspicion, hatred, and conflict between the two communities, Hindu and Muslim. The United Nations in its efforts to settle the dispute has tried to cut through the maze of issues by focusing on a solution by self-determination of the Kashmir people through a UN-supervised statewide plebiscite. Although both parties agreed to the plebiscite solution, the Indian government has refused to permit its implementation, holding that legally Kashmir is Indian territory, and preferring the *fait accompli* of Indian occupation of the state to a free vote in which the people would likely vote for union with Pakistan. Pakistani frustrations have led its government in the 1960's to reach border agreements and other understandings concerning Kashmir with Communist China in a desperate effort to keep the dispute alive. The failure of the United Nations to resolve the issues over a twenty-year period can be explained by the conflict of national honor and prestige, the irreconcilability of legal and moral positions, the intensity of the national interests involved and the United Nations fixation on a solution by plebiscite to the exclusion of other possibilities.

WEST IRIAN (WEST NEW GUINEA). This territory remained in dispute from 1949, when the Netherlands granted independence to Indonesia but retained control over West Irian, until 1962 when a UN cease-fire agreement was accepted by the two countries. By that agreement the Dutch relinquished control over the territory to a United Nations Temporary Executive Authority (UNTEA). Under an agreement subsequently worked out in the General Assembly and by the Secretary-General, Indonesia took over full administrative authority from UNTEA in 1963. Indonesia agreed that a plebiscite would be held "before the end of 1969" to determine whether the 700,000 inhabitants wish to remain with Indonesia or establish an independent state.

SINO-INDIAN DISPUTE. In 1962, Communist China launched an attack against Indian border positions from Ladakh in Kashmir to the Northeast Frontier Agency area. The dispute concerns the boundary line between the two countries. India claims the old McMahon line established by the British during the Empire period, but Communist Chinese leaders have declared it an "illegal remnant of imperialism." Although large-scale fighting ended early in 1963, numerous border incidents and the confrontation of two huge military forces have continued to threaten the peace. The boundary dispute is a rare example of a major controversy that has not been placed under United Nations jurisdiction and of one in which a party is not a member of the United Nations.

B. Cold War Questions

Disputes involving East-West power confrontations have been the most dangerous to world peace during the United Nations era. Fertile ground for such disputes existed already in the immediate post-World War II world with the emergence of a bipolar power structure, the existence of numerous political and power vacuums, ideological rivalry, disagreements over peace treaties, the forging of military alliances, and a new arms race. The United Nations has been hamstrung in resolving many cold war disputes since the Charter framers never intended the organization to operate in a milieu of great power confrontations.

IRAN. In 1946, Iran, prodded by the United States and Britain, brought the first dispute to the Security Council to pressure the Soviet Union to withdraw its troops from northern Iran as provided by a wartime agreement. Within five months, the Soviets and Iran reported to the Council that negotiations for the withdrawal were progressing satisfactorily. The subsequent removal of Soviet troops from Iranian territory raised the hope that the permanent members were receptive to subtle pressures from the Council, a hope shattered by later events.

BERLIN BLOCKADE. In 1948, the Soviet Union imposed restrictions on transportation and communications between the Western occupation zones and the Four-Power administered city of Berlin. The Soviets defended the action as retaliation to a Western-initiated currency reform in the American, British, and French occupation zones, but it was also an obvious attempt to strangle Berlin's lifeline to the West and make it dependent upon Soviet resources. The Berlin airlift kept supplies moving into the beleaguered city while the Security Council discussed the question at length. Significantly, agreement to lift the blockade was encouraged in 1949 through "corridor diplomacy" consisting of informal talks at United Nations headquarters between the chief American and Soviet delegates.

KOREA. Korea, divided by American and Soviet occupation forces at the close of World War II, posed the serious problem of how to reunify the people of a single country split by political, ideological, and power factors. The problem of creating a single national government was placed before the United Nations in 1947 by the United States with the recommendation, opposed by the Soviet Union, that free elections supervised by the United Nations be held to establish a Korean National government. The dispute became a collective security problem in 1950 when North Korean forces launched an attack against the Republic of Korea. Three years of fighting ended with a stalemate and an armistice with each side retaining their positions north and south of the thirty-eighth parallel. The dispute concerning reunification continues since neither the United Nations nor any other agency has been able to find the key to a solution acceptable to both sides.

C. Independence Questions

Numerous disputes of the United Nations period have emerged from the anticolonial struggles of peoples in Asia, Africa, and the Middle East. In the building of sixty new nations it was inconceivable that the transition from colonial dependence to sovereignty and independence should not produce some conflict in its wake. What is surprising is that the liquidation of the imperial system involving a billion people could be largely peaceful and dispute-free. Of the disputes that occurred, some related to struggles between the mother country and the revolutionaries, while others have been concerned with the relationship of the new nations to their neighbors and with liquidation of post-independence problems involving economic and military rights retained by the former governors.

INDONESIA. Hostilities broke out in 1946 between Indonesian rebels, armed by surrendering Japanese units, and the forces of the Netherlands returning to reimpose the prewar colonial rule. Early attempts to bring the dispute before the Security Council met protests from the Netherlands that the situation was a matter within its domestic jurisdiction, a ploy used by colonial powers frequently but seldom successfully in keeping colonial disputes removed from UN jurisdiction. In time, the Netherlands accepted a United Nations Committee of Good Offices, a UN cease-fire order was agreed to by both sides, and, under pressures from the United Nations and some of its members, the Netherlands granted independence to Indonesia in 1949. The following year, Indonesia became a member of the United Nations.

PALESTINE. In the transition of Palestine from a League of Nations mandate to the independent states of Israel and Jordan, the main controversy involved not the relations between the people of the territory and the Mandatory Power, Britain, but the historic rivalry between the Jews and Arabs. The Jewish population, swelled by an influx of refugees from Europe, demanded the establishment of a new Jewish state at the site of their ancient homeland. Arabs in Palestine and in the neighboring Arab states opposed the Jewish plan, and extensive fighting broke out in 1947. The General Assembly, seeking to resolve the impasse, recommended a plan for the political partition of Palestine into Jewish and Arab states with an economic union of the two. Through the combined efforts of the General Assembly, the Security Council, a fact-finding Special Committee on Palestine, a conciliating United Nations Palestine Commission, and two United Nations Mediators (the first was Count Folke Bernadotte of Sweden who was assassinated by Jewish terrorists in September, 1948; he was replaced by Dr. Ralph J. Bunche of the UN Secretariat) an armistice agreement was put into effect in July, 1949. The new state of Israel was admitted to the United Nations in the same year. After twenty years there still remains a reservoir of unsettled issues. No peace treaty has been signed and the Arab states remain technically at war with Israel, refusing to recognize her right to existence. Arab-Israeli borders are the perpetual scene of armed incidents, and the United Nations continues to care for almost one million Arab refugees who fled from Israel during the hostilities.

PORTUGUESE TERRITORIES IN AFRICA. Portugal's African territories of Angola, Mozambique, and Portuguese Guinea are the major remnants of the colonial empires that kept much of the globe for centuries under the domination of European powers. Guerrilla warfare conducted by national movements in the three territories for over six years during the 1960's has done little to break Portugal's hold on them. Efforts by the Organization of African Unity and the United Nations to mediate the situations have been rejected by Portugal whose government considers the territories to be "provinces not colonies."

United Nations pressures on Portugal to resolve the dispute by granting independence to the peoples of the three territories were initiated in 1960 with the General Assembly's Declaration on the Granting of Independence to Colonial Countries and Peoples. In 1963 the Security Council, on request of thirty-two African states, declared that Portugal should cease all acts of repression, grant a general political amnesty, and recognize the right of self-determination of the peoples of Angola, Mozambique, and Guinea. Since 1963 the African bloc has stepped up its activities to generate international pressures and, increasingly, has demanded collective UN sanctions against Portugal.

D. Domestic Questions

The Charter in Article 2 restrains the United Nations from intervening in "matters which are essentially within the domestic jurisdiction" of states and does not require members to submit such matters to settlement. Nevertheless, a significant number of disputes since 1946 have involved questions in which the entire situation developed within the boundaries of a single state. As already noted in Chapter 4, disputes concerning domestic questions have produced studies, debates, and condemnatory resolutions, but little action on the part of the United Nations. Regional organizations like the Organization of African Unity have likewise threatened and cajoled, but actual interventions have been rare and undertaken by states acting individually.

SOUTH AFRICA. The issue of South African discrimination against minorities was first placed before the General Assembly by India in 1946. India charged South Africa with governmental discrimination against its Indian minority population in violation of the Capetown Agreements of 1927 and 1932, which guaranteed equality of treatment for one another's resident nationals. In the first year of United Nations operations the Assembly also adopted a resolution urging the Union of South Africa to place the South West African mandate under the trusteeship system. In the 1950's and 1960's, South Africa's internal social policy of *apartheid* (separate development of the races) has come under increasing condemnation by UN organs and commissions. In the three cases—treatment of Indian nationals, South West Africa's status, and the apartheid system—South Africa has rejected almost one hundred resolutions of the General Assembly, refused admittance to the state for UN investigatory commissions, and insisted that all three are domestic matters wholly within the jurisdiction of South Africa. Attempts by the Commonwealth of Nations to force a liberalization of her social policies resulted in South Africa's withdrawal from the Commonwealth. Pressures from the Organization of African Unity in the mid-1960's have likewise failed to obtain a response from the South African government.

SPAIN. In 1946, the Security Council and the Assembly both debated the question of Spain's internal political regime. Although the Franco government did not constitute an immediate threat to international peace, it engaged in internal repressions of freedom and had come to power with the support of Nazi Germany and Fascist Italy. The Assembly rejected the position that a state's governmental system is strictly a matter of domestic jurisdiction and declared that the Spanish regime was a *potential* threat to peace. Spain was debarred from membership in the United Nations and the specialized agencies and a withdrawal of ambassadors from Madrid was called for. A proposal to topple the Franco regime by more forthright action failed to raise the two-thirds vote necessary. In 1950, the Assembly revoked its recommendations concerning the specialized agencies and diplomatic representation, and in 1955 Spain was admitted to the United Nations. The Spanish case illustrates the general reluctance of United Nations members to use the organization to interfere in the domestic matters of states other than by condemnatory resolutions, since the leaders of many are fearful that their states may some day be the object of international displeasure.

THE CONGO. Just one week after Belgium granted independence to the Congo in June, 1960, an army mutiny touched off widespread violence, disorder, and pillaging, directed mainly against Europeans. The rich mining province of Katanga thereupon announced its secession from the Congo, putting the new state in danger of disintegration. Goaded by Secretary-General Dag Hammarskjold, the Security Council established the United Nations Operation in the Congo (ONUC), initially composed of troops furnished by six African states and two European neutrals. The United Nations "presence" was aimed at preventing the disintegration of the state through secession, restoring domestic peace, rebuilding the Congo's shattered economy, and generally establishing conditions essential to stability and order.[2] ONUC grew into a 20,000-man, 29-nation force aided by the largest civilian team ever put into the field by the United Nations carrying out a countrywide technical assistance program. After numerous Council and Assembly sessions, extensive military operations, the martyr's death of Secretary-General Hammarskjold while pushing negotiations for unity of the state, and the expenditure of over $418 million (precipitating a financial crisis in the organization), the United Nations was successful in restoring a measure of political stability and economic viability to the new state. The ONUC force was withdrawn and disbanded in June, 1964, but the civilian technical assistance program continued. Although the United Nations operation involved internal matters, the domestic jurisdiction question did not arise because UN help had been requested by the Congo government.

E. Intervention Questions

Some of the most serious disputes of the United Nations era have involved interventions by neighboring states or great powers in domestic political struggles, revolutions, and civil wars. The dangers of such interventions stem from the likelihood of counterinterventions by third states and escalation into a major war. Dangers of counterintervention rise proportionally to the extent that the intervening state is involved in ideological and power struggles already extant in the world. Each intervening state legitimatizes its actions by being "invited in" by the contesting regimes or communal groups.

GREECE. In 1946, Greek Communists and other left-wing elements commenced a guerrilla war to overthrow the reconstituted monarchy. The rebels were supplied with arms by Albania, Bulgaria, and Yugoslavia, and used the latter country for a base of preparations for attacks and as a haven when pursued by government forces. The Greek government requested the Security Council to investigate the situation as a threat to peace, and in 1947 a Commission of Investigation composed of representatives of all members of the Council was established. The majority of the Commission reported that Yugoslavia, Albania, and Bulgaria were intervening in Greek affairs and that this constituted a "threat to peace within the meaning of the Charter." A minority report by the Soviet Union and Poland rejected

[2] Secretary-General Dag Hammarskjold adopted a Plan of National Reconciliation to reintegrate secessionist Katanga province in the Federal Republic of the Congo and to restore domestic order. The main elements of the Hammarskjold Plan were (1) A federal constitution for the Congo; (2) an agreed formula for dividing revenues and foreign exchange between the central and provincial governments; (3) a standard currency; (4) integration of all forces into a national army and police structure; (5) a general political amnesty; and (6) a reconstitution of the central government to provide representation for all political and provincial groups. By 1964, these objectives had been substantially achieved by the United Nations.

both the facts and conclusions presented by the majority. The split on the Council brought the General Assembly into the dispute, a transfer of jurisdiction that was to become a typical occurrence in later years. The Assembly urged the four countries involved to settle their dispute peacefully and established a Special Committee on the Balkans to implement UN resolutions and mediate the dispute. United Nations pressures, the Soviet-Yugoslav split, and extensive bilateral economic and military aid from the United States to the Greek government under the newly proclaimed Truman Doctrine led Yugoslavia to close her borders to the Greek rebels. Communist efforts to establish an ideological and power hegemony over the Balkans were halted at the Greek borders and the first serious post-World War II intervention was thwarted by international and counterinsurgency actions.

HUNGARY. In 1956, an internal revolution in Hungary overthrew the Communist regime. Against a backdrop of bloody massacres of former Communist officials and the new regime's withdrawal from the Warsaw Pact, the Soviet Union intervened with massive force to crush the Hungarian freedom fighters. Efforts by the Security Council to take action were vetoed by the Soviet Union on the grounds that the situation was a domestic question and that the Soviet forces had been invited into the state by Hungary's legitimate government. Transferred to the General Assembly under the Uniting for Peace system, that body by resolution called upon the Soviet Union to cease its aggression and to withdraw its troops. The Assembly ordered the Secretary-General to investigate the situation with on-the-spot observers, to submit a fact-finding report, and to suggest means by which the aggression could be brought to an end. Fear of touching off a general war restrained the Assembly from taking enforcement action against the Soviet intervention. Over the years numerous condemnations, diplomatic sanctions, and economic and political reprisals have failed to weaken Communist control over Hungary, and in the 1960's a policy of *rapprochement* between the organization and the regime has somewhat cleared the air. The Hungarian case reaffirms the rationale of the framers of the UN Charter in 1945 that the organization was never intended to be used as a police force against a great power.

VIET NAM. Like Hungary, the Viet Nam situation involves an intervention by a great power to prevent the loss of a state and its people to its ideological and power rivals. American military efforts involving over 400,000 troops by early 1967 are sanctioned by the invitation of the government of the Republic of Viet Nam. The rebel Viet Cong group and its political arm, the National Liberation Front, are supported by military aid from North Viet Nam. Efforts to mediate the situation have been attempted unsuccessfully by a Commonwealth Mission, by representatives of neutralist countries and African states, and by numerous governments acting independently. United Nations efforts have been confined to several abortive mediation efforts by the Secretary-General and the President of the General Assembly, and, in February, 1966, a Security Council debate initiated by the United States. Future escalations by both sides may force the Council or the Assembly to press for negotiations and a return to the principles of the Geneva Agreements of 1954. Since three of the parties involved—the two Viet Nams and Communist China—are not members of the United Nations, the usefulness of UN organs as negotiating forums is limited.

Multiple Causes for Disputes

The foregoing represent only a small sampling of the sixty-seven "disputes," "situations," "questions," and "complaints" relating to peace and security placed on the agenda of the United Nations during its first twenty years. Moreover, additional disputes have been handled by regional organizations or bilaterally. The difficulty of classifying international phenomena becomes obvious from our brief perusal of these disputes: Few have resulted from a single cause. The Kashmir case, for example, involved questions of human rights and self-determination for the people of Kashmir as well as a struggle between India and Pakistan for possession of the state. Korea was both an example of intervention and a cold war conflict. The Congo case was probably the most complex of all the disputes handled by the United Nations, involving cold war rivalry, intervention, human rights, and independence issues. As a rule, multiple causation factors tend to increase the difficulty of the search for a solution.

DISPUTE ISSUES

Complexity of causation is matched by the complexity of issues that typify most disputes. In many cases the Council or Assembly does not seek to resolve a single dispute but, in effect, a bewildering maze of them. For analytical purposes, the issues that characterize most disputes may be divided, somewhat less than neatly, into four categories: *general issues, factual issues, legal issues,* and *political issues.*

General Issues

Controversy over the basic nature of a dispute is a characteristic problem of pacific settlement. In some cases one of the parties may deny that a dispute exists or that there are any grounds for disagreement. Parties may accept a variety of pacific settlement approaches offered by the United Nations or by third parties, or may even achieve a solution without ever agreeing on what exactly is in dispute. The Kashmir case offers an example of this kind of problem. India has argued for almost twenty years that the dispute is limited to issues concerning Kashmir. Pakistan maintains that the Kashmir question is only one set of issues falling under the broader classification of "India's failure to accept and her attempts to undo partition." Pakistan's charges include those of genocide against Muslims in India, the military conquest of Junagadh and Hyderabad, the refusal of India to turn over to Pakistan her share of military supplies and cash balances when both were granted independence, and other related issues.[3] Only in a legal settlement by arbitration or adjudication, where the parties submit precise questions in advance for determination by a tribunal or court, is there a need for agreement on the nature of the dispute before settlement is possible.

Factual Issues

Disputants often disagree vehemently over incidents and events leading up to a conflict, what each party has done or not done, and the current state of affairs in the disputed area. When, for example, two parties to a dispute present their respective cases before the Security Council or General Assembly, the UN organ has before it two different versions of the facts. Before it can make recommendations on terms of settlement, it must have some knowledge of objective facts. It may attempt to obtain these "actual" facts through cross-examination of the representatives of the parties and through testimony and documents submitted by third parties. Failing to secure enough evidence on which to base its terms of settlement, the UN organ may establish a commission of inquiry to go to the scene of the dispute to observe the existing facts. Or the United Nations may try to get the parties to reach agreement without making determinations of facts, since the main objective in pacific settlement is not to dispense justice but to secure the agreement of the disputants to a formula of settlement. Usually, though not always, knowledge of the facts aids a mediating body in achieving a settlement.

Legal Issues

Legal issues arise from a dispute about the principles of law applicable to a given set of facts. Such disputes may be susceptible to arbitral or judicial solution. Questions of law are closely intertwined with questions of fact which, as noted above, are often difficult to determine, and questions of both law and fact may be placed before a competent tribunal. In some cases law and justice may not be complementary; but, if governments sincerely want to settle a dispute, no more expeditious means of resolving key issues exists than to place them before a court or tribunal.

Political Issues

Political issues are the most intractable because they are created by conflicts of *national interest*. Facts can be found, and law can be construed, but when interests clash, settlement cannot occur unless the parties reduce

[3] United Nations Document S/646, January 15, 1948.

their demands. When multiple political issues confuse and aggravate a dispute, a mediating third party may sometimes cut through the maze by putting its influence behind a "single-package" or short-cut solution. International organizations have also been able to mobilize pressures for compromise, enable the parties to "let off steam," or keep the disputants talking until the perspective of time can reveal that some interests are less vital than others. All too often, however, states will not permit their interests to be eroded—not by proposals for "just" solutions, by the pressures of the world community, or by the threat of war with the opposing party. States are guided by the aphorism that "primary interests are not negotiable," and primary interests are so broadly defined in the contemporary era that the settlement of political issues is difficult indeed.

DISPUTE SETTLEMENT

Regardless of the nature or causes of a dispute, an urgency exists in the international community to get it settled before positions become solidified, national honor and prestige increase the difficulties, or inflamed passions result in war. The threat of war is always present in every dispute, and the history of the state system records numerous examples of resort to this *ultima ratio* by disputants. But the threatening and disruptive nature of disputes has produced a countervailing force—pressures and techniques employed by third states, by regional organizations, and in the contemporary world, by the United Nations. The outbreak of a serious dispute produces an almost immediate reaction from the world community, with moderating and pacifying forces brought to bear upon the disputants to restrain their actions. Some techniques are traditional, others are recently developed variations of the older approaches to settlement.

Traditional Settlement Tools

Diplomacy is the oldest and most viable technique for settling disputes. The machinery of diplomacy operates within international norms governed by custom, tradition, international law, and specific agreements between the disputants. Compromise is the ingredient essential to successful negotiations, and no dispute can be settled without a willingness on the part of both disputants to agree to some "give" in their efforts to "take" or achieve a solution in keeping with their national interests. Compromise becomes elusive, however, when either party tries to avoid displays of irresoluteness, a "soft" approach, or appeasement. It then becomes necessary for a third party to enter the dispute to explore procedures or terms for reaching a settlement.

Good offices are tendered by a third state to the disputants to provide an atmosphere that will facilitate their use of diplomacy. The negotiator usually meets with the parties separately to urge resumption of negotiations. Technically, the third state remains aloof from the issues of the dispute. Good offices are particularly useful when bilateral negotiations between the parties break down and neither side takes the initiative to renew them, fearful that such action would be an indication of weakness.

Mediation is a natural follow-up to the tendering of good offices. The mediator seeks to break the diplomatic stalemate by aiding in the discussion of substantive issues and by suggesting new procedures for settlement. A mediator may meet with the parties either separately or jointly, but must maintain an air of impartiality throughout.

Conciliation results when a mediating state proposes terms of settlement or rules that ought to govern a settlement. Conciliation implies an active role by the intervening state, meeting with the parties either separately or jointly. Efforts to conciliate the contending parties involve a continuing search for a formula that will resolve the major issues without doing violence to the primary national interests of either, and will leave the national honor of both intact. Traditionally, an offer of good offices, mediation, or conciliation was regarded as a friendly act by the parties, but in today's ideologically divided world such offers may be ignored or rejected by the disputants as an unwarranted interference. This has enhanced the United Nations role since preserving peace by mitigating disputes is an obligatory function for the world organization under the Charter.

Arbitration and adjudication are legal procedures by which arbitrators or judges resolve a dispute by applying international law to the facts in the case and rendering a judgment or award. Once the parties accept either procedure, a settlement of the legal issues of the dispute is a foregone conclusion since the parties agree to abide by the decision of the tribunal or court. The difficulty, however, is in getting parties to agree to arbitration or judicial settlement. When vital interests, matters of honor, or the interests of third states are involved, arbitration and adjudication are unlikely to be acceptable to the parties. Further exploration of these tools of settlement will follow in the latter part of this chapter.

SETTLEMENT BY REGIONAL ORGANIZATIONS

In drafting the United Nations Charter, the framers realized that the United Nations would be physically incapable of handling every dispute that might arise. In Article 33, they provided that parties to a dispute should first seek a solution by traditional means of settlement or by "resort to regional agencies or arrangements . . . ." No precise dividing line, however, was laid down to determine when a dispute should be handled by a regional organization and when the United Nations should assume jurisdiction. The result has been that political circumstances rather than abstract

Charter principles have prevailed in matters of dispute jurisdiction, with regional organizations generally able to function more independently of the United Nations than the Charter framers had intended.[4]

Most political regional organizations make provision for settling disputes among their members. Military alliances, like NATO, SEATO, and the Warsaw Pact, however, are primarily concerned with "external threats," although in practice the alliance machinery is also used in attempts to resolve disputes among the signatories. Economic regional organizations, like the Common Market and the Free Trade Association, limit dispute settlement to economic issues that arise over the terms of union. Most issues of jurisdiction between the United Nations and regional organizations have involved the most active political regional group, the Organization of American States (OAS).

The Inter-American Peace System

The basic documents under which the OAS operates—the Rio Pact of 1947 and the Pact of Bogota of 1948—give the OAS authority to suppress conflict and settle disputes among members. Both are products of the twentieth century efforts of the United States to multilateralize the Monroe Doctrine and to keep Europe out of American disputes.

THE PACT OF BOGOTA. The Ninth International Conference of American States in 1948 established the Organization of American States and laid down, in the Pact of Bogota, the basic principles of the Inter-American peace system. Each American state is obliged by that agreement to settle all of its disputes with other American states by peaceful means. No particular method of settlement is required, but a number of procedures are available and disputants must try as many as necessary to reach agreement. Techniques specified by the Pact include the traditional procedures of good offices, mediation, inquiry, conciliation, arbitration, and adjudication. The last of these makes use of the International Court of Justice for justiciable questions when both parties agree to a judicial settlement or when both have accepted compulsory jurisdiction of the Court.

When traditional methods of settlement fail, the organization itself may step in to effect a settlement. Acting for the OAS in such circumstances could be any of three organs so empowered: (1) the Organ of Consultation composed of the foreign ministers of all American states; (2) the Council, consisting of ambassadors from all American states, meeting in Washington, D. C.; and (3) the five-member Inter-American Peace Committee, utilized by but technically not a part of the OAS. Of the three, the Organ of Consultation wields the greatest powers, with authorization not only to employ

---

[4] For a discussion of the regionalist challenge to UN supremacy, see Inis L. Claude, Jr., "The OAS, the UN, and the United States," *International Conciliation*, No. 547 (March, 1964), pp. 16–20.

pacific settlement tools but to apply diplomatic, economic, and military sanctions when deemed necessary. The Council, however, may act provisionally for the Organ of Consultation since the latter is called only for the most urgent crises.

The elaborate machinery of the Inter-American Peace System aims at settling *all* American disputes by action of American states, thereby excluding the United Nations in its peace-keeping role from the hemisphere. The United Nations, consequently, has been limited largely to debates over jurisdiction and to some review of OAS actions in exercise of its Charter right to be kept "fully informed" of regional activities affecting peace and security. Situations dangerous to peace in Guatemala, Cuba, and the Dominican Republic have produced acrimonious jurisdiction controversies between the global and regional organizations, but the United Nations has been restricted to a minimal role in each.

Guatemala. In 1954, the Guatemalan government headed by Jacobo Arbenz Guzman appealed to the Security Council to halt aggressive attacks launched against it from Nicaragua and Honduras by a rebel band with the support of the United States. The American government regarded the Arbenz regime, although duly elected, Communist oriented and a threat to the hemisphere. In the Security Council, American efforts to refer the Guatemalan complaint to the OAS were vetoed by the Soviet Union on the grounds that the dispute involved an act of aggression against a legitimate government and that the OAS was dominated by the United States. The veto, however, could not prevent the OAS from assuming jurisdiction. While the debate in the Council over the question of jurisdiction continued, the Arbenz regime was ousted and the new rebel government under Colonel Carlos Castillo Armas informed the Council that the case was closed. Actions undertaken by the Inter-American Peace Committee and a projected meeting of the foreign ministers of the OAS were cancelled since the outcome was acceptable to the regional group. The Guatemalan case shows clearly that the Security Council can do little to prevent regional action when a great power prefers that the matter be handled locally.

Cuba. In 1960, Cuba appealed to the Security Council, charging the United States with "intervention" and "conspiracy to commit aggression." The case involved American collusion with a group of Cuban expatriates whose attempt to topple the Castro government culminated in the abortive 1961 Bay of Pigs invasion. The United States regarded Cuba as a Communist base from which subversion and revolution would be exported to other countries of Latin America. As in the Guatemalan case, the United States argued that Cuba's complaint involved a regional issue and that the Organization of American States had assumed jurisdiction with a meeting of the Council of the OAS and a scheduled Meeting of Consultation of Ministers of Foreign Affairs. The Security Council, American delegates argued, should not assume jurisdiction of the case until and unless the OAS failed to settle the dispute. The Council, without renouncing its jurisdiction or Cuba's right to appeal to it, turned the case over to the OAS.

The Castro government next appealed to the General Assembly and succeeded in getting its case inscribed on its agenda in the autumn of 1960. The United States, recognizing its weaker voting position in the Assembly, did not contest jurisdiction but won a parliamentary battle by postponing consideration of the case. While the First Committee of the Assembly deliberated on the matter, the American-sponsored but ill-fated invasion of Cuba occurred. American denials followed by admissions of complicity led ultimately to the adoption by the Assembly's First Committee of a Mexican draft resolution critical of American actions and devoid of any reference to OAS jurisdiction. Although the Mexican proposal failed to secure the necessary two-thirds vote in the General Assembly, its support by six Latin American states was a defeat for the American principle of OAS jurisdiction of hemispheric disputes. The Cuban case illustrates that the primacy of regional jurisdiction over regional disputes, easily maintained in the Security Council, can be challenged in an Assembly mindful of its worldwide role.

Within the OAS, however, American influence prevailed. At the Punta del Este conference in 1962 the Castro government was ostracized from the OAS, marking the first application of the expulsion sanction provided by the OAS Constitution. In 1964, Cuba's efforts to "export" its revolution to Venezuela led to a decisive vote in the OAS to reduce trade with Cuba and break diplomatic relations with the Castro regime. All OAS members except Mexico have complied with this decision. These actions indicate that Latin American states are placed under much greater pressures to follow American leadership in the OAS than in the United Nations.

Dominican Republic. The political realities which guided American policy makers in their attempts to restrict the Cuban case to OAS jurisdiction were soon reinforced. On April 14, 1965, a popular revolt occurred in the Dominican Republic aimed at overthrowing the ruling military junta and restoring "constitutional government." President Lyndon Johnson, mindful of the difficulty of expunging Communism from Cuba once it had become entrenched, ordered American troops into the country in the first American military intervention in Latin America since 1926. Their announced mission was to protect American lives, but several days later the President declared that their assignment was "to prevent another Cuba" in the Western Hemisphere.[5] On May 6, the Council of the Organization of American States resolved to set up an Inter-American Peace Force to take over the American role of maintaining order.[6] On May 1, three days after the initial American

[5] *New York Times*, May 16, 1965.
[6] The decision was reached by a bare two-thirds majority, 14 to 5. Uruguay, Mexico, Chile, Peru, and Ecuador voted against the resolution, and Venezuela abstained.

action, the Soviet Union placed the Dominican question on the Security Council's agenda and called for "an urgent meeting to consider the question of the armed intervention of the United States in the internal affairs of the Dominican Republic." The Council issued a cease-fire order and requested the Secretary-General to report on the situation. Both factions accepted the Council's call for a truce on May 21. In subsequent debates in the Council, the question of jurisdiction—Security Council or OAS—became a central issue once again. The rival positions taken before the Council on the question of jurisdiction are summarized in the following paragraphs.[7]

For UN Jurisdiction: The claim that the Dominican question should be left to the OAS is an attempt to dodge responsibility. Article 39 of the Charter makes the Council duty-bound to consider the matter. Article 52 provides that all actions of regional organizations must be consistent with the purposes and principles of the United Nations. The Security Council, and no other organ, is entrusted by the members of the United Nations with primary responsibility for maintaining international peace and security. Article 53 categorically prohibits the application of coercive measures by regional organizations without Council authorization. Nowhere does the Charter provide that armed aggression can be inflicted by one country against another on the pretext that it is in the same hemisphere or part of the same regional organization. (*Nikolai Fedorenko, USSR*)

For OAS Jurisdiction: The principles of communism are incompatible with the principles of the Inter-American system. Revolution within a hemispheric country is a matter of concern to the OAS when its purpose is to establish a communist dictatorship. Article 33 of the Charter calls for the solution of problems by peaceful means, by regional organizations. Since the Dominican question is a regional problem, the OAS should deal with it. Article 52 also makes it clear that regional organizations should make every effort to settle local disputes before referring them to the Council. The OAS action is not an enforcement action but a peace-keeping operation similar to the United Nations actions in Cyprus, the Congo, and the Middle East. United Nations efforts in the Dominican Republic would merely duplicate the work of the OAS and would give contending factions an opportunity to play off one international institution and its representatives against another. (*Adlai E. Stevenson, United States*)

As in the Guatemalan case, the OAS retained primary jurisdiction over the Dominican question. Following the truce agreement a temporary government was installed in power by the OAS and an uneasy peace settled over the country, broken by numerous incidents. On June 1, 1966, the election of

[7] UN Monthly Chronicle, UN Office of Public Information, Vol. II, Nos. 5, 6, and 7, May, June, and July, 1965.

Joaquin Balaguer as President put the Dominican Republic back on the road to constitutional government and was followed by the withdrawal of OAS contingents. A national reconciliation between the political extremes appears unlikely, however, and the OAS may face a responsibility of future interventions to maintain order.

Fundamentally, the Dominican case and other issues concerning OAS-UN jurisdiction represent but another aspect of the cold war. The Soviet Union's position is based on its demand that no jurisdiction or action concerning a dispute anywhere in the world should be out of reach of its veto power. The Guatemalan, Cuban, and Dominican cases cast the Soviets in the strange role of supporting the principle of broad United Nations competence while the United States was placed in the equally unfamiliar role of limiting the world organization's powers. The jurisdictional disputes also reveal that the Charter's scheme for encouraging regional agencies to deal with local disputes within a framework of UN controls has created rather than solved problems. It remains unlikely that the United Nations will be able to assert its authority over regional operations that involve great powers.

United Nations Settlement Procedures

When a dispute is submitted to the Security Council or General Assembly, both the organization and its members assume certain legal and moral obligations aimed at achieving a peaceful settlement. General obligations are set forth in the "Purposes and Principles" of Chapter I of the UN Charter, and specific responsibilities are detailed in Chapters VI and VII dealing with pacific settlement and collective security respectively. Despite a wide range of obligational designs for settling disputes, however, in no case can the organization impose a final settlement upon the parties. Both Council and Assembly have almost unlimited powers of recommendation but neither can insist that the disputants accept either specific settlement procedures or substantive terms of settlement.

Any dispute or situation likely to endanger peace and security may be referred to the Council or Assembly (1) by any member of the United Nations; (2) by any nonmember state which accepts the obligations of the Charter; or (3) by the Secretary-General. As a rule, disputes are first submitted to the Council unless that body has a full agenda, but in no case may the Assembly make any recommendations while the Council has jurisdiction. Once the United Nations has assumed jurisdiction of a dispute or situation it may employ a varied assortment of pacific settlement tools, some traditional and some innovated by the League or the United Nations. Its flexibility is great since the Charter in no way limits UN organs in prescribing techniques of settlement or terms of settlement.

Appeals to Refrain from Aggravating a Situation

The initial action following the submission of a dispute to the United Nations typically takes the form of an appeal from the Security Council or from its President to the disputing governments. Such appeals call upon the parties to refrain from taking any action that might aggravate the dispute, to take all measures within their power to improve it, and to inform and consult with the Council immediately upon any material change in the situation. Similar appeals, usually in the form of identical telegrams to the two governments, may be dispatched periodically throughout the course of a dispute whenever a danger exists that relations between the parties may take a turn for the worse.

The purpose of such appeals is to throw both parties on the defensive so that neither will be able to take advantage of a hiatus before the Council takes action. Their effectiveness depends upon the prestige of the United Nations with the parties, the degree of bellicosity between the parties, and the significance of the subject of the dispute to the national interests of both governments. Generally, Council appeals to refrain from aggravating a situation have had a direct effect in minimizing conflicts between the disputants at least temporarily.

Cease-Fire Orders

When fighting erupts in a dispute, an international organization like the United Nations is confronted with its most serious challenge. In theory, hostilities between disputants call for the levying of sanctions under Chapter VII of the Charter dealing with breaches of the peace. In fact, however, there is a general reluctance in an organization made up of "outsiders" not directly involved in a dispute to use coercion. Efforts of the United Nations follow the role of peacemaker rather than policeman in the use of diplomatic, political, and legal approaches short of the application of force. The first objective of the organization must be to stop the fighting so that other conciliatory efforts may bear fruit.

The League of Nations set a precedent in 1925 when its Council stopped the fighting between Greece and Bulgaria by issuing a cease-fire order to the belligerents. Although the Charter makes no mention of the power to issue cease-fire orders, it is implied from the Council's authority under Article 40 to "call upon the parties concerned to comply with such provisional measures as it deems necessary or desirable." Though called cease-fire *orders*, they are in fact nothing more than *recommendations*. They do, however, carry behind them the prestige of the Security Council, since the "orders" are issued either by the Council itself or by a commission or other agent acting for the Council. Their permissive nature can be seen from the form in which they are usually proclaimed:

THE UNITED NATIONS SECURITY COUNCIL resolves that . . . . The Governments of _____ and _____ agree that their respective High Commands will issue separately and simultaneously a cease-fire order to apply to all forces under their control as of the earliest practicable date or dates to be mutually agreed upon.

In many cases both belligerents are willing to obey the "order" since both may wish to stop fighting but are fearful of taking steps to institute a truce which might be interpreted as a sign of weakness. Cease-fire orders issued by the Security Council or its agents have been instrumental in stopping the fighting between Indonesians and the Dutch, the Jews and Arabs, the Cypriot Greeks and Turks, and, on two occasions, the Indians and Pakistanis. In the Israeli-Arab, Indo-Pakistani, and Greek-Turkish disputes, the successful use of cease-fire orders to achieve an armistice represents the high point of United Nations efforts in each case, since no final political settlements have been achieved. Stopping a wanton slaughter and preventing a serious escalation of the fighting, however, are in themselves major achievements.

Discussion

The Council or Assembly, before making any kind of recommendation, invites the representatives of the parties to present their cases in written documents and orally. In this way the United Nations tenders its good offices to the disputants by providing a forum in which both can freely air their grievances and, conceivably, reach an understanding that will permit a subsequent settlement through bilateral diplomacy.

The theory that discussions by the parties, before the Council or Assembly, produce agreement is often vitiated by UN experiences. Both parties in such exchanges may be more interested in scoring debating points before the bar of world opinion than in honestly seeking common ground for agreement. Often the parties confine their discussions to the sterile fields of making charges and countercharges of aggression, to disagreements over the origin of the dispute, and to controversies over exactly what is in dispute. Contrary to theory, also, these exchanges may widen the gulf between the parties, make their positions more unalterable, and, on balance, worsen rather than repair relations between them. This problem is illustrated by a Council member's comment in the Kashmir case—a dispute which holds the record in the United Nations for time consumed, efforts expended, and techniques of settlement attempted without securing a settlement—as the Council braced itself for another "tortuous round of speeches" from the parties: [8]

I frankly doubt the utility of threshing out again in the Security Council the manifold and complex issues which are at stake in this case. Tentative

[8] Security Council, Official Records, S/VP. 232, Third Year, January 23, 1948, p. 171. The comment came from the delegate from Norway.

suggestions swiftly become unalterable opinions when they are expressed in this Council, and arguments advanced in the heat of discussion have a tendency to become vested with the habiliments of national prestige.

Discussions may also produce useful results. The Council or Assembly members are made aware of the positions of the parties, some of the facts involved, and possibly fruitful areas in which to seek compromise. The parties, themselves, are able to "blow off steam" in a relatively innocuous way that epitomizes the United Nations role: Better to talk than to fight! Bitter exchanges between the parties may at least alert the Council or Assembly to the gravity of the dispute.

Consultation and Quiet Diplomacy

Consultations between the representatives of the parties and the President of the Security Council, the President of the General Assembly or the Secretary-General are another means by which the organization tenders its good offices. Consultations are used particularly to break an impasse between the parties stemming from the presentation of their cases before the full Council or Assembly. Either body may recommend that its presiding officer or some other UN official "consult" with the representatives of the parties. Consultations consist of official yet informal, closed-door chats over dinner or in some other relaxed atmosphere. The nonpublic nature and informality of the negotiations between the parties encourages a vital flexibility essential to all successful diplomacy. The representatives of the parties can, under these conditions, refrain from embellishing their statements with emotional appeals for public support.

In addition to consultative meetings sponsored by UN officials, the UN Headquarters itself provides a good-offices atmosphere receptive to "quiet diplomacy" among members and between members and Secretariat officials. Representatives of the parties intermingle with diplomats of other delegations informally in the delegates' lounge and elsewhere in the Headquarters' buildings. Secretary-General Dag Hammarskjold popularized quiet diplomacy with his frequent and relaxed discussions with representatives of disputing states in a "behind-the-scenes" diplomacy. Often his efforts led to final settlements reached outside the United Nations framework, as in the Iranian, Trieste, and Suez controversies.

Quiet diplomacy is a blend of private and public procedures which together comprise a new and distinctive approach. Its increasing use and effectiveness result from the practice of UN members of maintaining permanent missions at the Headquarters to attend the growing numbers of sessions of major organs and to deal with other organizational business. Significant negotiations are also carried on behind the scenes among the members of the various voting blocs and caucusing groups. As a result, informal negotiations go on endlessly at Headquarters involving hundreds of delegates in conversations related to significant issues. Many agreements reached publicly in the Council or Assembly fostering the settlement of disputes have been preceded by "corridor negotiations," caucuses, or simply by consultative spadework carried on over scotch and soda.

UN Mediation and Conciliation

The transition from good offices to mediation and conciliation occurs when the Council or Assembly recommends *procedures* or *terms* of settlement to the parties in the form of resolutions. Such efforts are a recognition that bilateral diplomacy has not proved fruitful and that the polarized positions of the parties must be moderated by institutional pressures.

Recommendations for settlement *procedures* may include those for renewed bilateral negotiations on a higher level of officialdom, consultation, inquiry and mediation by a UN Commission, appointment of a United Nations Representative or Mediator, referral to a regional agency, arbitration, or adjudication. *Terms* of settlement may take the form of recommendations for a solution by self-determination through the holding of a plebiscite, a new demarcation of boundary lines, partition of a disputed territory, internationalization of a controversial area under UN administration, or other formulas that relate to the heart of the dispute. Conciliatory efforts must include an acceptable *quid pro quo* for both sides to be successful.

As a rule, UN organs are more successful in securing the acquiescence of the parties to try new settlement tools than in gaining their support for a particular "solution." Political techniques are, of course, more acceptable to the parties than arbitration or adjudication since legal approaches produce definite settlements. In offering terms of settlement, there is a danger that once the Council or Assembly decides on a "just" solution the United Nations may lose its flexibility. In the Kashmir case, for example, the Council has doggedly refused to alter its decision that the dispute between India and Pakistan be settled by a plebiscite in the state despite almost twenty years of Indian intransigence. The Kashmir case also illustrates that getting the agreement of the parties to a solution may not produce the results anticipated in the agreement. Both India and Pakistan agreed to a plebiscite for Kashmir in 1949, but India has refused to permit the implementation of that agreement. After a half century of Indian demands that the British recognize the right of the Indian people to self-determination, India could not openly and arbitrarily reject the principle's application to the people of Kashmir. Yet, because a plebiscite contravened her national interest, India has steadfastly prevented its realization.

Commissions of Inquiry and Mediation

Handling a dispute at the United Nations Headquarters poses two serious limitations: (1) The difficulty of getting an objective overview of the dispute on which to base settlement recommendations, and (2) the frustration of trying to obtain the agreement of representatives unable to depart from the instructions of their home governments. The first problem relates to the need for some understanding of the conditions that produced the dispute and a knowledge of contemporary facts so that recommendations will be realistic. This need can be met by the appointment of a fact-finding commission by the Council or Assembly to conduct an on-the-spot investigation.

The second, also a characteristic problem of pacific settlement, results in negotiation and mediation carried on by long distance communications. It has become fashionable to poke fun at the "robot" function of Soviet diplomats, but, in fact, on major issues every nation demands that its representatives keep in close contact with the Foreign Office, and any departure from instructions must be approved. The appointment of a commission enables the Council or Assembly to carry the mediation directly to the scene of the dispute and there deal personally with high-level decision-makers of both governments.

Typically, the two functions—fact-finding and mediation—are combined in a single commission of inquiry and mediation. Like the League of Nations, the United Nations has established a commission of inquiry and mediation in the most important disputes to come under its jurisdiction.

Commissions have varied in size from three to eleven, those concerned mainly with fact-finding being larger than those having mainly conciliation or truce responsibilities. The selection of commission members has been based on Security Council membership, geographical factors, representation for the parties, and relationships to the parties of the dispute. Individual members, however, represent their governments rather than serving as technical experts.

Commissions of inquiry and mediation engage in activities similar to those described by the United Nations Commission for India and Pakistan (UNCIP) in one of its many reports to the Security Council: [9]

> On different occasions during the past year it [the Commission] engaged in separate negotiations; it requested the two Governments to submit their own proposals. It submitted to both parties on its own initiative compromise formulas. On numerous occasions it sent delegations to confer with both Governments. It entrusted its Sub-committees with specialized tasks. The Commission also invited both Governments to joint meetings of military representatives as well as of representatives of cabinet rank. Finally, it suggested arbitration . . . .

The impact of UN commissions in dispute settlement has varied, but the effectiveness of localized inquiry and mediation has proved itself in the

[9] UN Document S/1430, December 5, 1949. UNCIP secured the agreement of India and Pakistan to demilitarize Kashmir and to permit the determination of its future status by a plebiscite. This decision remains today as the United Nations key to achieving a settlement of the Kashmir case.

Indonesian, Kashmir, and Palestine cases. When commissions have failed to secure agreement, they have still performed a useful function by keeping in regular contact with the disputants, by observing changes in the situation or in the parties, and by providing a moderating influence through a United Nations "presence."

Mediator or Representative

A single individual may, in some disputes, provide more flexibility in the search for agreement than the Security Council, General Assembly, or a commission. As already noted, the Presidents of the Council and Assembly and the Secretary-General have functioned effectively in this role at United Nations Headquarters. The appointment of a UN Mediator or Representative carries this useful approach to the site of the dispute, to the capital cities of the parties, or to a neutral meeting place.

In the Palestine case, the General Assembly appointed Count Folke Bernadotte to break the deadlock between Arabs and Jews over the partition plan and secure an armistice in the bloody communal war. Following Bernadotte's assassination by extremist elements, his chief aide, Dr. Ralph Bunche of the UN Secretariat, took over as acting Mediator and ultimately achieved a truce. In the Kashmir case, the Security Council appointed Sir Owen Dixon of Australia as United Nations Representative after the United Nations Commission for India and Pakistan failed to secure the agreement of the parties and was torn with internal dissent over the proper approach to settlement. Sir Owen's successor, Dr. Frank Graham of the United States, pressed the parties relentlessly for several years to agree to the demilitarization of Kashmir as a necessary preliminary to the holding of a UN-supervised plebiscite. In the end, he, too, failed to overcome Indian intransigence rooted in a fear that a fair plebiscite would result in the loss of Kashmir.

The appointment of Dag Hammarskjold as Secretary-General in 1953 signaled a reduced emphasis on the use of specially appointed UN Mediators and Representatives. The "Leave it to Dag" approach adopted by the Council and Assembly, abetted by Hammarskjold's own broad interpretation of the powers of his office and his responsibilities therein, led to an increasing role for the Secretary-General as representative and mediator. While this change may keep UN settlement efforts congruous within the organization, it may also stifle the kind of flexibility that statesmen of the world not associated with the organization could provide.

In the Cyprus case, Secretary-General U Thant demonstrated that a combination of a Special Representative of the Secretary-General working closely with a UN Mediator appointed by the Security Council may combine the best of both approaches. For example, upon the death of UN Mediator Sakari Tumioja in Cyprus in 1964, the Secretary-General's Special Representative in Cyprus, Galo Plaza, was appointed UN Mediator, providing a continuity in the approach to settlement.

Preventive Diplomacy

The only creative innovation the United Nations has added to the peace-keeping techniques of international organization is "preventive diplomacy." This approach aims at preventing extensions or escalations of the cold war from arising out of local disputes or power vacuums. Former Secretary-General Dag Hammarskjold, who fathered and nurtured the new concept, described its role in moderating cold war situations: [10]

> Preventive action in such cases must, in the first place, aim at filling the vacuum so that it will not provoke action from any of the major parties, the initiative from which might be taken for preventive purposes but might in turn lead to a counter action from the other sides. The ways in which a vacuum can be filled by the United Nations so as to forestall such initiatives differ from case to case, but they have this in common: Temporarily, and pending the filling of the vacuum by normal means, the United Nations enters the picture on the basis of its non-commitment to any power bloc, so as to provide to the extent possible a guarantee in relation to all parties against initiatives from others. . . .

Preventive diplomacy is complementary to peaceful settlement in that both seek to ease tensions in a dispute, both need the consent of the state or states involved, and both have the objective of achieving a stabilization of the situation. The distinguishing characteristics of preventive diplomacy are found in the new peace-keeping role played by the mass of uncommitted nations in the General Assembly and in the fundamental objective of restricting the area of cold war conflict rather than preventing the disputants themselves from going to war. The main thrust of preventive diplomacy is to prevent the intervention of rival power blocs into areas of dispute that are nominally outside of their respective spheres.

Approaches used by the United Nations in applying preventive diplomacy to dangerous situations fall generally into four categories: (1) Observer groups that supervise cease-fires, demilitarized zones, and truce lines; (2) UN forces interposed between belligerents; (3) UN forces used to quell internal conflict and maintain domestic order; and (4) UN forces used to prevent or curtail armed conflict between communal groups.

The use of an observer group or a United Nations "presence" to supervise a peace arrangement provided the background of experience for the organization's more extensive role as a "third force." Such UN groups have operated effectively in the Balkans (1946–54), in Indonesia (1947–49), in Palestine (1947–   ), in Kashmir (1948–   ), in Lebanon (1958), in West Irian (1962–63), and in Yemen (1963–64).

The essence of preventive diplomacy is found in the last three categories

[10] *Introduction to the Annual Report of the Secretary-General on the Work of the Organization, 16 June 1959 to 15 June 1960,* General Assembly, Official Records, Fifteenth Sess., Supp. No. 1A, p. 4.

wherein United Nations police forces have engaged in more direct peace-keeping operations. Three situations—the Middle East in 1956, the Congo in 1960, and Cyprus in 1964—are examples of the evolution of this new approach to cope with situations unforeseen by the Charter framers. The first two in particular involved the danger of cold war confrontations and provided Secretary-General Dag Hammarskjold with the opportunities to develop his concept of preventive diplomacy. Secretary-General U Thant reiterated the basic principles developed by his predecessor in noting the appropriate application of the peace-keeping approach through the UN Cyprus Force: [11]

> This is not collective action against aggression undertaken under Chapter VII of the Charter . . . . It is, in brief, an attempt on the international level to prepare the ground for the permanent, freely agreed solution of a desperate and dangerous situation by restoring peace and normality. The nature of this operation is far nearer to a preventive and protective police action; it is not a repressive military action.

Though situations and UN responses differ, all peace-keeping operations have some common characteristics: (1) Consent of the host government must be secured to the composition and stationing of the UN Force on its territory; (2) the UN Force must be under the control of the Council or Assembly and its role must be limited to self-defense; (3) the UN Force or Organization must not interfere in the domestic affairs of the host state unless requested; (4) the UN Force must be composed of voluntary contingents from states having a neutral interest in the outcome of the case.

The United Nations' successful experiences with peace-keeping operations have led eight governments to make standby arrangements for future crisis use. The eight—Canada, Denmark, Finland, Iran, Italy, the Netherlands, Norway, and Sweden—have earmarked special troop units as contingents for UN Forces. A closer liaison among contributing states to achieve some standardization and military balance is being undertaken.

Preventive diplomacy employing peace-keeping operations seems to be well established as a distinctive UN settlement tool in both theory and practice. Generally, the United States and the Western bloc have supported its use and the Soviet bloc has gone along in tacit agreement, though refusing to contribute financially to the upkeep of peace-keeping forces. Although the approach has reduced the role of the great powers in dispute settlement, their willingness reflects the overriding objective of avoiding a military showdown in a nuclear world.

Dispute Settlement—Legal Approaches

ARBITRATION. Arbitration differs substantially from the political approaches already examined. In the words of J. B. Moore, an eminent international

---

[11] United Nations Press Release SG/SM/76, May 26, 1964. The Secretary-General made the statement in an address before the Canadian Parliament.

jurist, "Mediation is an advisory, arbitration a judicial function. Mediation recommends, arbitration decides." Characteristic features of the arbitration process include (1) the selection of arbitrators by the parties; (2) the submission of a precise question for decision; (3) the agreement of the parties to accept a decision or award as binding; and, (4) the application of international law to the facts to reach a decision.

During the nineteenth century almost 300 arbitration treaties were concluded and arbitration was used to settle over 200 disputes. The use of arbitration in the twentieth century was spurred by controversies growing out of World War I, but it has dwindled during the United Nations era. In a few disputes handled by the United Nations, arbitration has been recommended to the parties, but one or both have rejected it. An insight into the reasons for the demise of arbitration as a settlement tool may be found in an analysis of the Security Council's failure to secure India's agreement to its use to break a stalemate over the demilitarization of Kashmir.

India's objections dealt with technical points. The Council sought to secure arbitration of political rather than legal questions; it specified equity (justice) rather than international law as the basis for reaching a decision; it proposed a single individual as Arbitrator (U.S. Fleet Admiral Chester W. Nimitz), instead of permitting the parties to select a panel; it provided that the Arbitrator determine the questions to be decided rather than getting the prior consent of the parties through an agreement (*compromis*). The Indian government found these proposed procedures "novel" and "without precedent."

Underlying the technical objections was a more significant factor: Arbitration would lead to the demilitarization of Kashmir and the holding of the UN plebiscite, actions that would be likely to vitiate one of India's most vital interests, her control of Kashmir. This kind of fear is endemic in the contemporary world, rendering arbitration useless for settlement of the more significant disputes. In questions involving vital interests or national honor, a state prefers to entrust settlement to political approaches. Its use in the contemporary world is consequently limited to settling small claims under provisions of bipartite compulsory arbitration treaties.

JUDICIAL SETTLEMENT: THE INTERNATIONAL COURT OF JUSTICE. Although several early attempts were made to establish regional courts to hear and decide international legal disputes, an effective international court did not make an appearance until the Permanent Court of International Justice was established by the League. With the dissolution of the League system in 1946, the new International Court of Justice was set up as its successor.

In most respects the Statute for the new Court duplicates the old, with the major exceptions that the International Court of Justice is designated a major organ of the United Nations and all UN members are automatically parties to the Statute of the Court. States not members of the United Nations, however, may accede to the Statute under conditions laid down by the General Assembly and upon recommendation by the Security Council. Four states have joined the Court under these provisions: Switzerland (1947), Liechtenstein (1950), Japan (1954), and San Marino (1954). The Court sits in permanent session at The Hague in the Netherlands, although there have been lengthy periods when the judges, for lack of cases, have spent their time engaged in legal research.

Selection of Judges. Fifteen judges comprise the Court. When a state party to a case is not represented by a national on the Court, an additional judge (or two, if neither party is represented) of appropriate nationality is appointed for that case. Candidates for election to the Court are nominated from "national groups" and special "national groups" to provide "representation of the main forms of civilization and of the principal legal system of the world. . . ." [12] Judges are elected from the nomination lists by the General Assembly and the Security Council, voting separately, with a majority vote needed in each. They serve nine-year terms, five elected every three years, and are eligible for reelection. No state may be represented by more than one judge on the Court. Judges are nominated and elected as individuals on the basis of their legal backgrounds and qualifications.

Jurisdiction of the Court. The competence of the Court extends to cases brought by states that are parties to a dispute and accept the Court's jurisdiction. Advisory opinions may be rendered on questions of international law at the request of major organs of the United Nations, subsidiary bodies granted this privilege by the General Assembly, and of disputing states if both accept the jurisdiction of the Court. Although the Court will not hear cases brought by individuals, a state may represent the interests of some of its citizens in a case.

The main jurisdictional controversy of the Court concerns the question of compulsory jurisdiction. Article 36 of the Statute, the so-called optional clause, provides that states may agree in advance to accept compulsory jurisdiction of the Court in all cases involving certain issues. [13] Almost one half of the more than one hundred states that are parties to the Statute have accepted the optional clause, but some states, such as the Soviet Union, Yugoslavia, and Cuba, have never ratified it.

---

[12] *Statute* of the ICJ, Article 9. The "national groups" were established by the Permanent Court of Arbitration established by the Hague Peace Conferences of 1899 and 1907 to give proper representation to the state system of that day in setting up panels of available arbitrators. The special "national groups" are comprised of states not currently signatories to the Permanent Court of Arbitration, paticularly the new nations of Asia and Africa, appointed under the same conditions as those specified for the Permanent Court of Arbitration.

[13] Article 36 specifies that compulsory jurisdiction will apply in all legal disputes concerning "(a) The interpretation of a treaty; (b) any question of international law; (c) the existence of any fact which, if established, would constitute a breach of an international obligation; (d) the nature or extent of the reparation to be made for the breach of an international obligation." These categories embrace most of the legal questions that arise in disputes.

Most states that have ratified the optional clause, however, have attached reservations excluding the application of compulsory jurisdiction from certain kinds of cases and providing for termination of the commitment on notification or at the end of a specified period of time.[14] The American commitment, for example, became a farce when the United States Senate in the process of giving its consent added to the normal exclusion of matters "essentially within the domestic jurisdiction of the United States of America" the enfeebling Connally Amendment, "as determined by the United States of America." Since the Connally Amendment leaves the United States the sole judge of what is a domestic question, compulsory jurisdiction is rendered null and void as a practical matter. Other states followed the American lead, and only a general abandonment of reservations by many nations would have a real impact on the Court's docket of cases. Under the principle of reciprocity, a state's reservations also excuse any other state involved in a legal dispute with the reserving state. If American domestic courts operated on this basis, it is doubtful that any defendants would accept any court's jurisdiction in civil cases. Despite these reservations, however, over six hundred international treaties include clauses conferring jurisdiction upon the Court to decide issues concerning their interpretation and application.

Decisions. The Court's decisions are made by majority vote and cannot be appealed, although under unusual circumstances involving new evidence a losing party may apply to the Court for a revision of judgment. Nine of the regular judges constitute a quorum. Each decision applies only to the parties in that case and does not restrict other states or constitute a general precedent. In reaching decisions, the Court applies treaties, custom, legal principles, and authority in that order.[15] When both parties agree, a case may be decided *ex aequo et bono* (on the basis of "equity" or justice), rather than by law, with the Court exercising its own judgment to reach a fair decision. Compared to the thirty-two judgments and twenty-seven advisory opinions rendered by the Permanent Court of International Justice, by

[14] See Julius Stone, "The International Court and World Crisis," *International Conciliation,* No. 536 (January, 1962), p. 22. According to Stone, categories of reservations most frequently invoked by states accepting the optional clause include "(1) Past disputes . . . (2) Disputes for which treaties in force provide other means of settlement . . . (3) Disputes concerning questions which by international law fall solely or essentially within a state's domestic jurisdiction. (4) Disputes involving members of a special grouping such as the Commonwealth of Nations. (5) Disputes as to questions of territorial status. (6) Disputes arising out of particular named treaties. (7) Time limits. . . ."

[15] Article 38 of the Statute stipulates that the Court in deciding disputes should apply "(a) international conventions, whether general or particular, establishing rules expressly recognized by the contesting states; (b) international custom, as evidence of a general practice accepted as law; (c) the general principles of law recognized by civilized nations; (d) subject to the provisions of Article 59 [the decision binds only the parties], judicial decisions and the teachings of the most highly qualified publicists of the various nations, as subsidiary means for the determination of rules of law."

July, 1966, forty-nine cases were submitted and twenty-nine judgments rendered by the Court and it had issued thirteen advisory opinions.

Although both courts have played a significant role in settling disputes, their main contributions to dispute settlement procedures have developed out of their advisory opinions. These opinions have generally favored an expanded competence over disputes for international organs, a recognition of international organization as a legal personality capable of taking claims action against states, a broad interpretation of the international character of secretariat personnel and their independence from national control, and an expansive view of the financial powers of international organizations. Although advisory opinions are not binding upon international institutions, those of the two international courts have been applied by the League and United Nations organs to resolve internal organizational and procedural questions. Individual member states, however, have not always been willing to accept the Court's opinions in organizational matters, as reflected in the rejection by the Soviet Union and France of the Court's opinion holding them responsible for financing peace-keeping costs.

DEVELOPMENT OF INTERNATIONAL LAW. International law has been a subject of considerable controversy during the era of the United Nations. It has been glorified by publicists, condemned by "realists," and ignored by diplomats and statesmen in crucial disputes. Unquestionably, the legal approach to the settlement of disputes must be built on a comprehensive body of rules and principles which provides norms binding on all members of the international community. It is widely believed today that international law in this broad sense does not exist, that the law is primitive and full of gaps. Others charge that its Western origins have alienated the support of Communist-bloc states and the new nations of the non-Western world. Communist states, for example, demand a "progressive" development of law since "former international law . . . is a colonial law," not relevant in today's world.

The work of the United Nations in clarifying and codifying international law belies these charges. The General Assembly, held responsible by the Charter for the codification of international law, tackled this problem by establishing the International Law Commission in 1947. The Commission consists of twenty-one members, elected for five-year terms, who represent the "chief forms of civilization and the basic legal systems." Twenty years of continuous effort have produced numerous draft conventions on a wide variety of legal topics including in recent years Conventions on Diplomatic Relations (1961), on Consular Relations (1963), and, currently, a Convention on the Law of Treaties. Several of its drafts have been approved by the General Assembly and have come into force after ratification by member states, but the Commission's work must also be judged by its extensive identification and clarification of existing rules in force by custom or treaty that have contributed to the process of judicial settlement.

The slow but progressive work of the International Law Commission in building a comprehensive body of rules was supplemented in 1963 when the Assembly established a Special Committee on the principles of international law concerning friendly relations and cooperation among states. The Special Committee, established by demand of Asian, African, and Communist states, is undertaking a study of how to "modernize" and "universalize" international law.[16] It is not surprising that topics debated by the Special Committee—such as guerrilla war, the fomenting of civil strife, defining wars of aggression—produced acrimonious debate between the protagonists of a "new" international law and the defenders of the "old" law. Until this gap can be bridged, international law will probably remain only a competent guide to *normal* state relations. A universal ethical and ideological consensus may not be a prerequisite for the growth of international law, but without it law will not be an effective tool for resolving conflict situations.

Strengthening the Legal Approach. Many disputes regarded as strictly political in nature may involve significant legal issues which if resolved by arbitration or adjudication could contribute to a settlement. However, one or both parties frequently refuse to recognize the existence of "legal issues," with the result that the legal methods of settlement are seldom applied. Increasingly, commentators are asking, What's wrong with the legal approach? Why do the parties in most disputes avoid legal settlement? As already noted, the parties may believe that a vital national interest is at stake and prefer to limit settlement techniques to political approaches. In other cases, a state may regard the entire legal approach prejudiced against its interests, from the development of international law to the rendering of judgments. A wider use of the legal approach may depend upon fundamental changes that convince the leaders of many of the nations of the world that justice would prevail if they submitted their conflicts to a legal settlement.

The United Nations has already made some progress in trying to evolve a world law out of a code of principles developed within a limited Western state system. Pressures to speed up this cumbersome process are applied by those jurists who recognize that if law is not accepted as objective and just, the remainder of the process becomes merely ornamental. But more

---

[16] The Special Committee began its project with an examination of four principles: (1) Refraining from the threat or use of force; (2) peaceful settlement of international disputes; (3) nonintervention in the domestic jurisdiction of another state; and (4) the sovereign equality of states. Study of three additional principles—the duty of states to cooperate, equal rights and self-determination, and the duty to fulfill Charter obligations —is scheduled for future sessions of the Special Committee.

changes are obviously needed. Many critics are concerned about the predominantly Western composition of the International Court. Asian, African, and Soviet-bloc states must be allotted a larger share of the tribunal's seats to overcome the widespread belief that the court is partisan and politically motivated. An American repeal of the Connally Amendment might have a psychological impact that could result in a mass elimination of the strangling reservations placed upon compulsory jurisdiction. Innovations in the form of regional courts from which appeals could be taken to the International Court might encourage legal settlements. Adoption of the rule of *stare decisis* so that precedents would govern future decisions might add a measure of logic and consistency to such a global system. Adjusting the legal approach to settlement of disputes to the contemporary world provides a difficult if not impossible challenge, but the transition must be attempted if a lawful society is the goal.

CONCLUSIONS ON DISPUTE SETTLEMENT

During the first twenty years of the United Nations era, sixty-seven cases involving disputes or situations relating to peace and security have been placed before the United Nations. The record shows that most of these cases have been resolved by the direct or indirect efforts of the United Nations. Those which have most persistently avoided settlement have involved bitter communal feuds over territorial jurisdiction: Kashmir, Israel, and Cyprus. Even here, however, the United Nations has produced cease-fires and truce agreements. Only the passage of time may erode the hatred of one community for the other to permit reasonable settlements, or the growing power of one party may force the other to accept its bitter pill. If the latter should occur, it must be remembered that United Nations efforts are not directed at rendering justice to all, but have as their primary objective the maintenance of peace and security in the world.

Of the disputes brought before the United Nations, forty-five have concerned problems arising out of World War II and the transition of almost half the world from colonialism to independence and statehood. Neither of these is likely to be a major causal factor for future disputes, although the decolonization of Portuguese territories in southern Africa will undoubtedly cause some trouble. Controversies over neocolonialism, racism, minorities, and territorial grievances will apparently hold the center of the stage. Cold war disputes between the Soviet and Western blocs may continue to decrease, but those between the United States and the Asian Communist states may more than fill this gap. Increasingly, preventive diplomacy and peacekeeping operations may have to be applied to fill Asian power vacuums to avoid a showdown escalation between the United States and Communist China.

The United Nations over the first twenty years of its history has demonstrated an amazing versatility and vitality buttressed by a will to innnovate. Ultimately, peaceful settlement techniques that foster negotiations between the parties have proved most successful. Peace-keeping has become an essential auxiliary of peaceful settlement, operating as a holding operation to gain time for diplomatic negotiations. Often, a mere United Nations "presence" has served to moderate the parties and influence the course of events.

Contrary to popular misconceptions, the Charter framers at San Francisco in 1945 never contemplated that the United Nations would or could abolish differences of interest that arise among nations. What the founders did believe was that the United Nations would help keep international disputes within peaceful bounds, a task that would be much more difficult without a United Nations. They rejected the notion of irreconcilable conflicts among nations that must be settled on the field of battle. Instead they proclaimed the principle that all conflicts, no matter how fundamental, could and must be settled by pacific means. The twenty-year record of the United Nations in the field of dispute settlement illustrates that the Charter framers were not utopian visionaries.

Selected Readings

BLOOMFIELD, LINCOLN P. "Law, Politics and International Disputes," *International Conciliation*, No. 516, January, 1958.

CLAUDE, INIS L., JR. "The OAS, the UN, and the United States," *International Conciliation*, No. 547, March, 1964.

CURTIS, GERALD L. "The United Nations Observation Group in Lebanon," *International Organization*, 18, Autumn, 1964, pp. 738–65.

GARDNER, RICHARD N. "Needed: A Stand-by UN Force," *New York Times Magazine*, April 26, 1964.

GLAHN, GERHARD VON. *Law Among Nations*. New York: Macmillan, 1965.

JACOBSON, HAROLD K. "ONUC's Civilian Operations: State-Preserving and State Building," *World Politics*, 17, October, 1964, pp. 75–107.

LISSITZYN, OLIVER J. "International Law in a Divided World," *International Conciliation*, No. 542, March, 1963.

STONE, JULIUS. "The International Court and World Crisis," *International Conciliation*, No. 536, January, 1962.

10 | *The Quest for Global Peace*

ALLIANCES AND THE BALANCE OF POWER

The concept of military alliance is virtually as old as the institution of war between political communities. The Book of Genesis gives accounts of alliances and wars among rival groups of kings in the days of Abraham. Thucydides' History of the Peloponnesian Wars is the story of alliances and counteralliances among contending groups of Greek city-states, and of attempts by Sparta and Athens to establish a more universal system of security by conquest. The advent of the modern state system in Western Europe nearly two millennia later found statesmen still attempting to construct an international security system based on shifting alliances and alignments. A similar prescription for security prevailed at the beginning of the present century, as the world was being rapidly transformed by the on-going industrial revolution. Indeed, one may argue that from the days of Abraham to the assassination of Archduke Francis Ferdinand at Sarajevo, the techniques and character of interpolity security arrangements changed very little—only enough to fit the change in contracting entities.

If interpolity security arrangements changed very little from Abraham to the Archduke, the character of war changed very drastically and was destined in the next half century to undergo even more profound transformation. While the world shrank, man's capacity for destruction expanded; and as the ferocity of war increased, the prospect of its localization seemed to decrease. Before the twentieth century, European wars had often been globalized by the extension of military conflict to the dependencies of the contending powers. But the global wars of that earlier era were more like a series of tenuously connected local wars; and, perhaps even more significantly, they lacked the total commitment of spirit and resources that characterizes modern warfare. Traditionally, war was often a viable instrument of foreign policy. Wars could not only be fought: they could also be won. By the twentieth century, however, major war was becoming an increasingly self-defeating exercise in which the costs were great even to the victor.

The mechanism bequeathed to the twentieth century for the prevention

240

of war and the control of force in international relations is commonly known as the "balance of power." This expression can be as ambiguous as its use is unavoidable. In the literature of international relations "balance of power" is used variously to denote a situation, a policy, or a system.[1] As a situation it may refer to a supposed "equilibrium" in the distribution of power among states, or to any specified distribution of power. As a policy, it has multiple meanings. It may refer to the action of a state in the role of the balancer throwing its weight to the weaker side of an international confrontation in order to deter potential aggressors. It may mean the efforts of any state or coalition to achieve a condition of "equilibrium," as first one side and then the other seeks to redress a real or apparent imbalance. Or a "balance-of-power policy" may simply be a euphemism for an international struggle for power.

As a system, and this is perhaps the most useful of its meanings, balance of power quite generally denotes a set of international relationships in which order is preserved by confronting power with power so that no state becomes powerful enough to dominate the system. Ideally, war will be forestalled by confronting potential aggressors with a combination of opposing states too strong to tackle. If war should nevertheless occur, the system should continue to operate so that no state emerges from the conflict with overweening power. The system functions without central coordination and without much regard to any common ideals, except the obvious concern to prevent undue concentration of power in others. Combinations to deter prospective war-makers are brought together by the actions of governments whose individual national interests are threatened by a common danger, or whose immediate interests can otherwise be furthered by common action. Such combinations are generally limited in objective, temporary in duration, and shifting in composition. Typically, the balance system is called into play when a state or group of states seeks to alter an existing power relationship. The action of the "revisionist" or "imperialist" states produces a reaction from the "status quo" powers, which band together to preserve their interests. The balance of power thus moves into operation and the outcome may be deterrence through strength, accommodation through bargaining, or war through failure of the system.

The outbreak of World War I convinced all doubters that the balance-of-power system had weaknesses as a peace-keeping mechanism. A system in which coalescence of states depended upon the coincidence of particular national interests, rather than recognition of general interest in keeping the peace, did not always confront aggressors with overwhelming opposition. Apparently, also, all statesmen were not as rational in calculating the odds as the proper working of the system would presume, and even rational judg-

[1] See Inis L. Claude, Jr., *Power and International Relations* (New York: Random House, 1962), Chaps. 2, 3.

ments were subject to serious miscalculation. The size of the stakes sometimes outweighed the risks—as in Napoleon's dream of European hegemony; or contrarily, the very narrowness of the immediate issue could blind the powers to the intensity of its possible repercussions and lead governments unwittingly to topple the first domino—as at the outbreak of World War I. In the years preceding 1914, moreover, the system had developed a rigidity of alignments that robbed it of the fluidity that theory—and apparently practice—required for the effective operation of the balance-of-power mechanism.

THE ADVENT OF COLLECTIVE SECURITY

To point out the weaknesses of the balance of power was one thing, but to find a workable substitute for it was quite another. The need for a universal security system seemed appallingly apparent, but such systems existed only in the minds of a long line of political dreamers dating back to Dante and beyond. Historically, disparate political communities had been brought within a single integrated security system by conquest and political federation and, at a lower level of integration, by the omnipresent (and discredited) military alliance. Alexander the Great proved that conquest on a grand scale was possible in the ancient world, and Rome demonstrated that a relatively stable system of peace and security could be built to last for long periods of time upon a foundation of conquest. The colonial empires of Britain, France, Spain, and other European countries are more recent examples of the extension of an integrated security system by conquest. Varying combinations of conquest and political federation are to be found in the unification processes of modern Germany, Italy, and the United States. Except for Rome, however, none of these systems approached universality even in a relative sense, and all were of dubious value as patterns for action in 1919 because they were established by the elimination of the separate sovereignties of the constituent communities. Conquest was obviously out of the question—a totally unacceptable, self-defeating, and basically irrelevant model. Political federation, likewise, was utterly unfeasible given the diversity of values, political behavior, economic status, and forms of social organization characterizing the world's many political communities.

Nineteenth- and early twentieth-century precedents in international cooperation left sovereignty unscathed but fell far short of the ideal model for an integrated security system in other respects. The Concert of Europe—that loose-knit system of great power consultation spawned by the Napoleonic Wars and continued sporadically to the eve of World War I—was more a state of mind than an organization. It was neither well integrated nor universal and only indifferently effective; and it was little more than an appendage to the balance-of-power system. When the Serbian crisis arose in the summer of 1914 the Concert technique of great power consultation was not even called into play. In addition to the Concert, there was the legacy of the Hague Conferences and the considerable experience of organized international cooperation in economic and social fields. Although suggestive of organizational forms and procedures, the international conference and the public administrative union were not security systems. The hard fact remained that nothing in history constituted a working precedent for what the men of Versailles had to do if they were to create an effective, integrated, universal system of security within a community of sovereign states.

It is no historical accident that both of the monumental twentieth century organizations for the maintenance of peace and security—the League of Nations and the United Nations—were born of wartime travail. War speeds the processes of change by disrupting old behavior patterns and motivating men to accept innovation aimed at mitigating the problems so cruelly emphasized by the war. During the years of the Great War a number of schemes for the collective enforcement of peace received wide currency among the public, particularly in Britain and the United States. Active proponents of an enforced peace came from business, government, and academic life, and the idea gained substantial public support. Buttressed by this widespread sentiment, the leaders of the victorious Allies meeting at Versailles in 1919, with Woodrow Wilson in the forefront, were prepared to innovate. They took the ideal of a universal, integrated security system, hitherto the domain of dreamers, and fused it with nineteenth century international organization, using in the process much of their own ingenuity to forge the essential compromises between ideals and realities. The result was the world's first significant approach to a collective security system among otherwise independent entities.

The Nature of Collective Security

Since World War I, the expression *collective security* has passed into common parlance and, in the process, has lost much of its capacity to convey a specialized meaning. *Collective security* is now applied indiscriminately to almost any arrangement among two or more countries that involves the possibility of joint military action. It has become the virtue word by which alliances are made to sound respectable. Although the word *alliance* is being rehabilitated from the disrepute into which it fell as a result of the presumed role of military alliances in precipitating the First World War, collective security is still a more potent symbol of the use of military power for good, rather than evil, purposes. Hence such arrangements as NATO, SEATO, and CENTO are commonly characterized as collective security arrangements, regardless of their basic character as military alliances directed against an external threat. Collective security has thus become almost a synonym for a "good" or a "defensive" alliance, as contrasted with a bad (someone else's) alliance which may be used for "aggressive" purposes.

Despite the debasement of the term collective security as it has passed into common currency, it remains an expression capable of transmitting a specialized meaning and will be so used in this study. Briefly characterized, collective security is a set of relationships among a group of states in which all are agreed to provide mutual protection against international threats from any source, including threats arising from within the group. A collective security arrangement is distinguished from an alliance by its inward orientation: While an alliance is geared solely to an external threat, a collective security system is concerned with the potential threat to members of the system posed by other members of the system. Although collective security is usually conceived on a universal scale, and those who delight in the formulation of rules for the functioning of such systems usually have the world as their model, a collective security arrangement including any group of three or more entities is at least theoretically possible. Indeed, an arrangement like the Rio Pact may have elements of both collective security and an old-fashioned alliance. To the extent that the Pact is directed toward defense against external aggression it is an alliance; to the extent that it is concerned with international violence within the hemisphere it becomes truly a collective security organization.

The three essential elements of an effective collective security system are *consensus, commitment,* and *organization.* At the very minimum level of *consensus,* members of the system must agree that peace as such is goal of national policy and that conflict involving any member of the group is the concern of all. Without basic consensus upon the indivisibility of peace and security, the system is permeated by a selectivity that is incompatible with the principle of all-for-one and one-for-all. "Selective security" is substituted for collective security. The *commitment* to collective security, has both a positive and a negative aspect. Members of the group are bound affirmatively to combine their force to meet any threat to the security of the community. On the negative side, they are committed to refrain from unilateral use of military force to achieve purely national objectives. Ideally, the commitments should be so binding and so widely embraced that any attempts "to change the *status quo* by violence are unlawful and doomed to frustration through opposition in overwhelming force." [2] Without the commitment, consensus remains a meaningless abstraction. But commitment, too, courts failure in time of crisis if there is no *organization* to make it effective. Every commitment is a general commitment until a specific crisis arises. If, at this point, each member of the group is free to decide how and when its commitment shall be honored, the possibility of selective enforcement becomes all too imminent. Collective security requires a central decision-making

[2] Andrew Martin, *Collective Security* (Paris: UNESCO, 1952), p. 7.

organ empowered to decide how and when action shall be taken on behalf of the community against any threat of aggression.

Considered as a whole, the logical requirements of an *effective* collective security system approximate world government in the most important area of international relations. If the state gives up the right to use armed force in the pursuit of national policy, the right to choose its friends and enemies —or to remain neutral—in the event of armed conflict, and the right to deploy its own armed forces, why shrink from something called world government? What more vital inroads upon sovereignty could a world federation make? To pose the question is to suggest a most important reason why the world has not yet seen a thorough-going collective security system and probably will not be ready for one until it is also ready for world government. As Loewenstein observed, "To all intents and purposes a state's right of disposal of its military potential is the most sensitive segment of national sovereignty, and that part which traditionally is impervious to foreign decision or control." [3] Collective security would tread upon this sensitive area demanding that control be shared—even dominated—by international organization. Collective security demands too much: the men who make national policy are not yet ready to accept such broad restrictions upon national sovereignty and upon their freedom of action.

This perverse conclusion does not mean that collective security remains entirely without practical impact upon world affairs—quite the contrary. The concept of collective security has affected the thinking of practical politicians as well as theoreticians, dreamers, and crusading zealots. It has shaped evolving international institutions, and it has modified the course of world events in some degree. The complete consensus, the unalterable commitment, the effective central organization have not materialized; but there have been partial consensus, partial commitment, and partially effective institutions. Some things in life are susceptible to treatment in absolutes: The high jumper either clears the bar or he misses, and the candidate for office either wins the election or he loses—there is no practicable middle ground. But many types of social phenomena are highly relativistic—there are degrees of good government, there is a wide continuum separating war from peace. If collective security may be regarded in relative terms, the world of the past half century has had a degree of collective security, or at least an approach to collective security.

The League and Global Security

The disparity between the bark and the bite of collective security is well illustrated in a comparison of principle with practice in the history of the League of Nations. Article 10 of the Covenant, regarded by President Wilson as the heart of the Covenant, declares unequivocally that "The Mem-

[3] Karl Loewenstein, "Sovereignty and International Co-operation," *American Journal of International Law* (April, 1954), p. 235.

bers of the League undertake to respect and preserve as against external aggression the territorial integrity and existing political independence of all Members of the League." All things considered, this was a very loud bark. But Manchuria, Ethiopia, and ultimately a host of other members fell victim to violence without a shot being fired in their defense in the name of the League and, indeed, without any state being obligated by the Covenant to fire such a shot. The Covenant had no military teeth with which to bite, in vindication of its grand pretensions as protector of the independence and territorial integrity of its members.

A reading of the Covenant brings a distinct impression that the drafters of the Covenant intended the League to be an effective instrument of collective security, even though their legal commitments stopped considerably short of the goal. Nowhere is there a more concise statement of the essence of collective security than in Article 11, which declared, "Any war or threat of war, whether immediately affecting any of the Members of the League or not, is hereby declared a matter of concern to the whole League, and the League shall take any action that may be wise and effectual to safeguard the peace of nations." Obviously this sweeping assertion of purpose and principle did not bind any member state to any specific future course of action, but it had the ring of real intent "to safeguard the peace of nations."

The same determination to enforce the peace is apparent in Article 16, by which members bound themselves to mount economic and financial sanctions against Covenant-breakers. True, the Covenant had gaps which left room in certain circumstances for aggressive war, as, for example, war against a party to a dispute which had refused to comply with recommendations unanimously endorsed by the Council, or war against any party if the Council was divided. But as far as it went, Article 16 represented a sweeping advance commitment by all League members to the use of nonmilitary sanctions. The sanctions were automatic in the sense that the legal obligation was fixed at the moment any State resorted to war "in disregard of its covenants under Articles 12, 13 or 15," although the Covenant fixed no specific method by which the fact of a resort to war in disregard of covenants could be authoritatively determined. The obligation extended to "the severance of all trade or financial relations, the prohibition of all intercourse between their nationals and the nationals of the Covenant-breaking State, and the prevention of all financial, commercial or personal intercourse between the nationals of the Covenant-breaking State and the nationals of any other State, whether a Member of the League or not." Although military sanctions against Covenant-breakers were neither automatic nor legally required of member states, Article 16 nevertheless charged the Council "in such case to recommend to the several Governments concerned what effective military, naval or air force the Members of the League shall severally contribute to the armed forces to be used to protect the covenants of the League." Article 17 authorized application of the same sanctions to nonmember states that made war upon a League member under similarly unjustifiable circumstances. The Covenant clearly gave the impression of strength not weakness, firmness not vacillation, action not hesitation.

However, the League failed to live up to the Covenant's brave words. At the theoretical level, the force of the collective security commitment was weakened by Assembly resolutions adopted in 1921 emphasizing the right of each state to determine for itself how and when to apply economic sanctions under Article 16. Paradoxically, succeeding years witnessed efforts to strengthen the Covenant by forging firmer commitments of mutual assistance and wholly outlawing aggressive war. When the practical test of capabilities and intentions arose, however, no sanctions at all were used to meet Japanese aggression in Manchuria, and the League's economic sanctions were used against Italy only half-heartedly in the Ethiopian crisis.[4]

THE UNITED NATIONS AND COLLECTIVE SECURITY

Those who framed the United Nations Charter were not willing to concede the inadequacy of collective security as a system for the control of power and preservation of international peace. The failure of the League was viewed as a failure of will and of institutions—not inadequacy of concept. With the United States and the Soviet Union participating from the outset—and the lesson of a second world war that had been even more devastating than the first—there might be hope for a resurgence of will to enforce the peace. Given the hoped-for determination to make global security a reality, the institutional inadequacies could be cured by providing a more workable organization—one with more teeth in it and fewer loopholes for aggressors to wiggle through.

Collective Security in the Charter

The new security organization did in fact profit from the experience of the interwar years. Instead of outlawing aggressive war only under certain circumstances, the Charter took a leaf from the 1928 Pact of Paris and committed all Members to "refrain in their international relations from the threat or use of force against the territorial integrity or political independence of any state, or in any other manner inconsistent with the Purposes of the United Nations." The overall impact of the Charter was to limit the legitimate use of force in international relations to (1) self-defense, individual or collective (Article 51); (2) action, joint or several, against "enemy" states of World War II (Article 107); (3) joint action by the Big Five on behalf of the Organization, pending the availability of troops under Article 43

---

[4] See Chapter 2, *supra*, for a discussion of League peace-keeping efforts.

(Article 106); and, (4) any other use of force, but only such as might be authorized by the Security Council. The Charter apparently did not ban revolutions and civil wars which, strictly speaking, are not concerned with the use of force in "international relations." The Security Council can of course take cognizance of civil disturbances if they become a threat to international peace and security.

In realistic terms, Charter restrictions are unlikely to provide either a legal or a practical obstacle to a country really bent on military action, even with the requirement of Article 51 that all defensive action be immediately reported to the Security Council and remain subject to the right of the Council to undertake any peace-keeping action it deems necessary. After all, governments on both sides of the 38th parallel pled self-defense in the Korean War, as did Hitler when he attacked Poland in 1939. But at least the framers tried, and on the surface most of the so-called gaps in the League Covenant were absent from the new Charter.

Even more important was the attempt to put sharper teeth into the Charter. Gone was the automatic economic sanction, which the League by interpretation had made dependent upon a series of individual national decisions that the time was ripe for the sanctions to be applied. In its place, the Security Council was given the right to decide when and what kind of nonmilitary sanctions should be required, and all members were obligated "to accept and carry out the decisions of the Security Council" in accordance with the Charter. The military sanction was designed to be a still greater improvement upon the Covenant. Where the League Council could only recommend action to member states, the Security Council was to have ear-marked troops, supplied by prior agreement with members and awaiting only the Council's call to action. Once the special agreements were concluded, the right of members to withhold military support from Security Council action (at least within the limits set by the special agreements) was at an end. With the forces thus placed at its disposal, the Security Council was free to "take such action by air, sea, or land forces" as might be "necessary to maintain or restore international peace and security." This was indeed strong medicine: The Security Council was to take action on its own initiative, without waiting for each member state to decide for itself.

In one important respect the Charter provided less collective security than the Covenant. Nonmilitary sanctions under the Covenant were theoretically available against any country, large or small, without the possibility of veto by the party concerned. A report on a dispute by the League Council did not require the concurrence of the parties to the dispute, and the economic sanction was supposed to operate without further action by the Council if a member violated its covenants. Under the Charter, however, all enforcement action having a legally binding character requires a prior decision by the Security Council—where all nonprocedural matters are subject to the veto. The special position of the permanent members of the Security Council was a conscious compromise with the principle of collective security as well as a concession to common sense. It was tacit recognition that the world, with its unequal distribution of power and conflicting national interests, was not ready for an undiluted dose of collective security.

Critics had constantly pointed out that the theory of collective security treated all wars as incipient world wars, with the practical danger that collective security would in fact turn localized wars into world war if powerful forces were ranged on both sides. The United Nations was rigged to prevent such an unhappy eventuality. Worldwide conflagration was unlikely to result from UN intervention in a fight if the great powers were all on the side of the United Nations. The chances of an escalated conflict would be almost nil, while the prospect of quickly squelching the outburst of violence would be very good indeed. The scope of the global security operation would be restricted, but within the area of feasible operations the United Nations could act effectively and with a minimum of risk.

The Nonimplementation of Article 43

On paper, the UN Charter seemed to provide all the requisites of an integrated collective security system, within the area not proscribed by the veto. The Charter registered a broad consensus upon the desirability of peace and the indivisibility of security. Members were legally committed to accept and carry out decisions of the Security Council, and the Council was empowered to make decisions (not just recommendations) concerning the use of both military and nonmilitary sanctions. Here then was consensus, commitment, and central decision-making machinery merged in a coherent collective security system.

Or was it? With respect to nonmilitary sanctions it probably was, subject of course to the limitations of the veto. Under Chapter VII of the Charter, dealing with threats to the peace, the Security Council has but to command members to take economic or diplomatic sanctions against an offending state and all members are legally bound to obey. Until recently this Security Council prerogative to call for mandatory nonmilitary sanctions was no threat to national freedom of action because it was never used. In April, 1966, however, the Security Council determined that the situation resulting from Rhodesia's unilateral declaration of independence was a threat to the peace and authorized Britain to use force if necessary to stop tankers carrying oil destined for Rhodesia. In December, the Council ordered a mandatory embargo of arms and oil and a boycott of Rhodesia's main exports. This historic precedent could point the way to wider use of the mandatory nonmilitary sanctions, particularly against white minority regimes in Africa. UN members may defy such Security Council decisions in practice, but they can do so only by disregard of a legal obligation incurred with ratification of the Charter.

In the case of military sanctions, however, the legal bridges leading back to national freedom of action were not so neatly burned by ratification of the Charter. The right of the Security Council to take military action upon its own initiative was predicated upon the subsequent contracting of "special agreements" with members of the organization, as provided in Article 43 of the Charter. Article 43 merits quotation in full not only because it represents the missing keystone in the arch of the UN collective security system but also because it illustrates how the statesmen at San Francisco, like their predecessors at Versailles, shrank from that final commitment of armed force to the cause of collective security. They chose to postpone until a later day the surrender of the right to dispose freely of their military forces.

> 1. All Members of the United Nations, in order to contribute to the maintenance of international peace and security, undertake to make available to the Security Council, on its call and in accordance with a special agreement or agreements, armed forces, assistance, and facilities, including rights of passage, necessary for the purpose of maintaining international peace and security.
>
> 2. Such agreement or agreements shall govern the numbers and types of forces, their degree of readiness and general location, and the nature of the facilities and assistance to be provided.
>
> 3. The agreement or agreements shall be negotiated as soon as possible on the initiative of the Security Council. They shall be concluded between the Security Council and Members or between the Security Council and groups of Members and shall be subject to ratification by the signatory states in accordance with their respective constitutional processes.

The last sentence of paragraph three is particularly significant—the agreements were to be subject to ratification in accordance with the respective constitutional processes of member states. A moral commitment had been made, but acceptance of the Charter added little to the legal obligation of member states to support UN enforcement action with their armed might.

From the perspective of the postwar failure to implement Article 43, one might be tempted to belittle the vaunted military teeth of the Charter as mere window dressing cleverly designed to give the appearance of collective security without demanding the limitation upon national sovereignty which alone could give it substance. Machiavellianism of such a high order, however, does not fit well with most accounts of the San Francisco Conference. Motivations at the Conference were a strange mixture of idealism and conflicting national interests, a yearning for the fruits of international cooperation and a jealous concern for sovereign rights and prerogatives. The Charter was necessarily a compromise, but its collective security provisions were not a sham, with Article 43 a carefully planted joker. Postponement of the ultimate commitment was a manifestation of the extreme sensitivity of the issue, joined with the concern that the completion of a Charter should not be unduly delayed by the difficult search for agreement in detail. This was but one of a number of hard questions left to be resolved later because the constitution makers had more urgent immediate objectives.

Provision of troops for UN use was in fact treated as a matter of the highest priority. One of the first acts of the Security Council after its organization in 1946 was to instruct its Military Staff Committee to develop principles on which Article 43 agreements could be negotiated. After months of deliberation the Committee submitted a report that revealed a modest area of agreement, mostly on principles already set forth in the Charter, and a substantial area of disagreement on the crucial issues running largely but not exclusively along cold war lines. In general the United States wanted a relatively large, free-wheeling force of land, sea, and air units, stationed wherever the Security Council in special agreements with individual members might decide, in instant readiness to fight anywhere and to stay until the Security Council recommended withdrawal. In the American scheme, contributions from each of the five permanent members were to be "comparable," in accordance with the size and character of the armed forces of each country, but not necessarily "equal" in contribution of tanks, planes, ships, men, and every other specific category of armaments.

The Soviet Union, on the other hand, wanted a relatively smaller force, equality of contributions by the permanent members, and a clear definition of the conditions under which the force might be used. For example, the Soviet Union insisted that no UN military bases, as such, should be established; that all contingents should remain within their respective national territories until called into action; and that all UN units should be required to withdraw to their own territory within ninety days after the completion of any military action. Britain, France, and China, despite minor differences of viewpoint, sided generally with the United States with one critical exception—the size of the proposed force. Their proposals also envisaged relatively small contingents, only slightly larger than the Soviet plan.

In the perspective of two decades it is not at all clear which of the opposing positions was the more reasonable (or unreasonable) under the circumstances. The American plan would doubtless have meant a more effective military arm of the collective security system, assuming that effectiveness is equated with capacity to wield a mighty sword. A large force is more formidable than a small one, and its readiness would be increased by stationing contingents at strategically located UN bases throughout the world. The Soviet principle of equality of contribution could easily result in either a very small force, or an unbalanced force, or both. China, for instance, was long on military manpower but short on everything else. Would individual contributions of tanks, aircraft, and naval vessels be limited to whatever

China could spare? And, since neither the Chinese nor the Soviet navy possessed battleships or aircraft carriers, was the UN force to dispose only of lesser naval craft? Ironically, supporters of a United Nations force today would be more than happy to start with a force of the size that the Soviet Union apparently would have approved in 1947; but at the time the Soviet proposals appeared in American eyes as an intransigent mockery of the grand vision of an effective collective security system.

In retrospect the Soviet position appears to partake somewhat less of mocking intransigence than of realism. If the force was not to be used against a major power, why was a large one needed? Or was it the American intention to use the force even against a permanent member? The Soviet Union surely could not have been reassured by the following remarks of the British representative, made during the course of Article 43 discussions in response to a Belgian complaint about the lack of machinery to deal with a breach of the peace by a permanent member:

> Any one of the permanent members . . . by exercising its vote could arrest the movement of the United Nations forces. There is, unfortunately, no way out of that. The only answer—and it is admittedly only a partial answer—is provided by Article 51 . . . . If any one of the permanent members guilty of a breach of the peace or an act of aggression were to call a halt to the United Nations force, the remainder of the United Nations would be entitled under that Article to take action against that Member. Their forces, already made available to the Security Council, could legitimately be jointly employed to that end for so long as the Security Council failed to take the measures necessary to maintain international peace and security. Thus, the plan which we aim at formulating will, we may hope, go as far as it is possible towards organizing against an aggressor the forces of the rest of the United Nations.[5]

Size was not the only basic objection. If contributions were "comparable" rather than "equal," the more mobile parts of the force—the kind most likely to be used in emergencies—would come from the West which was strong in air and naval contingents. Large numbers of foreign troops stationed in UN bases throughout the world could become a means of exerting political pressure on the host country, or neighboring countries, while troops at the unrestricted command of the Security Council might remain in a theater of action for political purposes long after the fighting was over—or so the Soviet Union argued. From its minority position, the Soviet Union could ill afford to risk the establishment of a large UN striking force not carefully hedged with legal and practical restrictions upon its future use.

The result of these unreconciled differences was a continuing deadlock in the Military Staff Committee—a deadlock that has continued from 1947 to

[5] Official Records of the Security Council, 2d Year, No. 45 (June 10, 1947), pp. 994–95.

the present. Without agreement on guidelines for the force, no special agreements under Article 43 could be negotiated. The broad Charter commitment to collective security was never translated into a specific commitment to supply men and material. Despite the intent of the Charter, members retain the practical right to remain militarily neutral in the event of conflict and to decide for themselves, according to the circumstances of each case, how their military forces shall be used.

Korea and Collective Security

The UN Charter envisioned only a limited system of collective security, one which relied heavily upon the Big Five for its coercive power but which excluded the five (and their friends) from the sanctions of the system. The nonimplementation of Article 43 further weakened collective security by eliminating the legal commitment to supply armed forces to the Security Council. Henceforward, if there were to be collective action at all, it would be collective action on a voluntary, ad hoc basis. Given the broad divergence of views among permanent members of the Security Council, at least two of the three ingredients of an effective collective security system were obviously lacking by mid-1947—the binding commitment and the viable central decision-making organ. In absolute terms the absence of these two elements meant that there was no collective security system at all. But relatively speaking, the United Nations still represented an incipient collective security system, although rendered much less effective by its obvious deficiencies. If the system did not work to curb aggression or to quell the outbreak of violence all or most of the time, perhaps conditions might occasionally be right to bring collective force to bear through the medium of the organization.

In June, 1950, conditions were right. A UN observational group already in South Korea was able to provide immediate and relatively unbiased confirmation that an armed attack by North Korean troops had in fact taken place. The absence of the Soviet delegate in protest against the continued seating of Nationalist China made the Security Council, for once, a viable decision-making organ in time of crisis. In Japan and Okinawa the United States had troops that could be quickly moved to the scene of the fighting. Although the Council could only *recommend* military action, the voluntary commitment of forces by the United States and subsequently by fifteen other members of the United Nations made collective action possible.

Faced with these unanticipated developments, the Soviet delegate abruptly terminated his boycott in August and snuffed out the Security Council's capacity to act in the Korean crisis. In accordance with a precedent well established by this time, the issue was removed from the deadlocked Security Council to the General Assembly. The Assembly had only the power to recommend, and its large size created an unwieldiness ill-suited to giving strategic direction to a large and complex military operation. It could make general policy recommendations, however, and with vigorous United States leadership it was able to act with some dispatch on crucial issues in the early months of the conflict. Ultimately, Chinese intervention and rising concern lest the Korean War touch off a third world war brought stalemate and blighted hopes for a unified Korea, but at least the independence and territorial integrity of the Republic of Korea had been preserved by UN action.

Paradoxically, the Korean conflict did not bring a renascence of the United Nations as a vehicle for mobilizing collective military force against aggression. This is due in part to the ambiguous forms in which conflict has occurred in the post-Korea period. Civil wars, revolutions, guerrilla warfare, clandestine infiltration and subversion, with foreign intervention in the guise of assistance to contending domestic factions, are the common forms of violence that have ruptured the peace of the world. This new dimension of conflict brings into question the very appropriateness of a collective military response, as well as immeasurably increasing the already difficult task of singling out an aggressor. Given the nature of such conflicts, collective military action under UN auspices might serve only to widen the scope of the conflict without reaching any of the underlying problems. And if enforcement action is decided upon, should it be directed against one or more of the domestic factions actually engaged in hostilities, or should a military blow be struck against the foreign sponsor or abettor? The possibility that the Korean experience may have encouraged the use of more covert forms of aggression in place of overt military invasion does little to enhance the usefulness of collective military sanctions in meeting the kinds of threats that do exist.

Quite apart from the increasing difficulty of fitting traditional collective security concepts to the facts of modern conflict, the Korean experience threw into sharp relief some of the basic defects of the United Nations as an instrument for launching collective military sanctions. If Korea proved that collective sanctions of a sort could be organized under cover of the United Nations, it created little confidence that such an operation could or would be repeated in the future. The central decision-making apparatus of the United Nations was shown to be unsuited to decisive action in times of crisis. Although the Security Council rose to the emergency in June and July of 1950, the very singularity of the circumstances highlighted the basic debility of the organ. Only the absence of the Soviet delegate made action possible, and his return reduced the Security Council to its accustomed paralysis in the face of East-West conflict. There is little reason to believe that the Soviet delegate will again be absent in time of crisis as long as the Soviet Union remains a member of the organization.

Although the Assembly attempted to fill the breach, it was too large and unwieldy and too divided in counsel to be an effective organ of collective security, a condition which the Uniting for Peace resolution did nothing to remedy. If this was true with a body of sixty members, it is *a fortiori* true today with a doubled membership embracing an ever larger number of countries which are neutralist in cold war matters but, in some instances at least, ever ready to resort to national and international violence in pursuit of their own ends.

The record of the United Nations bears witness to the unwillingness or inability of the Assembly to become again an instrument of military enforcement action. When China subjugated Tibet by force, the United Nations was filled with cries of anguish and sympathy but no serious consideration of military intervention. Nor was there evidence that the Assembly was regarded as an appropriate agency to rally military support for India in its brief border war with China. When India wiped out Portugal's centuries-old protectorate in Goa by military action, there was no thought of Assembly censure, not to speak of sanctions, against India. Nonmilitary sanctions, of course, have been recommended in the cases of Rhodesia and South Africa; and conceivably, the Assembly might lend moral support even to military action against white minority regimes in Africa if the more militant anti-colonists should resort to armed force. But enforcement action by an Assembly-sponsored military force appears extremely unlikely, even in the service of anticolonialism.

Besides showing the weakness of the central decision-making organs, Korea also revealed the riskiness of dependence upon the voluntary commitment of forces in time of crisis. Just twenty-two countries offered military forces, and only sixteen of the offers proved to be of usable size and quality. Most of the other non-Communist members offered moral support but were either unable or unwilling to contribute to the military effort. Of the UN forces actually committed at the time of peak strength, 50.32 per cent of the ground forces, 85.89 per cent of the naval forces, and 93.38 per cent of the air force was furnished by the United States. In view of the Republic of Korea contributions of 40.10 per cent, 7.45 per cent, and 5.65 per cent, respectively, the military contributions of the remaining members of the United Nations were obviously small.[6]

The military operation in Korea was under the direction of a Unified Command, a euphemism generally understood to mean United States command. General Douglas MacArthur, until his removal by President Truman, was military commander in the field, and his main line of responsibility ran

[6] United States Department of State, *United States Participation in the United Nations,* Report of the President to the Congress for the Year 1951, Publication 4583 (Washington, D.C.: U.S. Government Printing Office, 1952), p. 288. Important contributions of supporting assistance—medical supplies, hospital units, and transportation facilities—were made by other UN members, including Denmark, India, Norway, and Sweden.

to the United States government, not to the United Nations. The Unified Command reported to the United Nations, but only what Americans saw fit to report.

The United Nations undoubtedly provided an extremely valuable political cover for United States operations in Korea, giving the action a United Nations character rather than an exclusively national character. But this is a questionable kind of collective security when the military response to aggression is so heavily dependent upon the leadership, men, and materiel of a single great power. Militarily speaking, the one important commitment was the United States commitment, made under the pressure of crisis circumstances after an assessment of the national interests involved; and it might have been made in the absence of the United Nations. This is not the kind of long-range, indiscriminate commitment to collective action that effective collective security demands.

If, from the point of view of the United States, the burden of military action was unequally shared among the members of the organization, some members began to suspect that the military action was serving far from universally shared objectives. The United States, in some respects, appeared to be using the United Nations as an instrument of its foreign policy to further its cold war objectives, despite the contrary view held by many that United States action in Korea under the United Nations flag had greatly strengthened the organization. Since collective security could readily be used as a moral and political cloak for the United States in its power struggle with world Communism, Communist states rejected and neutralist members increasingly grew disenchanted with the whole idea.

If the Korean episode of collective security fell far short of the ideal system contemplated by the Charter, in one respect it exceeded the carefully delimited bounds of the Charter: The military arm of the organization was turned against the interests of a permanent member of the Security Council, with all the explosive potential for a third world war that the veto had been designed to prevent. Korea did not lead to a direct military confrontation of the giants and to world war, but at times the thread on which the Damoclean sword hung suspended seemed perilously slender to many UN members. Although the powers exercised the restraint necessary to keep the war limited, a guarantee of limitation was certainly not inherent in the situation. With the development of tactical atomic weapons, this kind of action presents UN members with an even more dangerous gamble and raises the question "whether the Korean pattern of limited military action for limited objectives is likely to be repeated." [7]

Korea also demonstrated another basic flaw in the functioning of the Charter system of collective security: the absence of consensus on the kind

[7] Leland M. Goodrich, in William R. Frye, *A United Nations Peace Force* (New York: Oceana Publications, 1957), p. 194.

of world that was supposed to be made secure. Enforcement of peace in a national political system is feasible because of general agreement upon political goals and the existence of machinery for the peaceful settlement of most disputes as they arise. Collective security, by attempting to outlaw violent change, assumes that available methods of peaceful change and pacific settlement are adequate to resolve international differences and satisfy legitimate national aspirations. The unreality of this assumption is well illustrated by the Korean War where the only settlement possible was an agreement to exchange prisoners and to stop fighting along a line roughly corresponding to the *status quo ante*. A divided Korea was perpetuated and the underlying problems that precipitated the crisis in the first place remained unresolved. By its failure to break the military stalemate, the United Nations never gained the capacity to enforce a settlement on terms of its own choosing. By taking sides at all, it lost the capacity to serve as a neutral forum for pacific settlement of the basic dispute. Within the United Nations itself opinion was so divided that the members could scarcely agree upon the roster of participants in a proposed political conference on Korea. Without greater agreement upon the kind of world to be made secure, the nations were not ready for collective security.

Uniting for Peace

Another legacy of the Korean conflict is the Uniting for Peace resolution adopted by the Assembly on November 3, 1950. On its face it appeared to represent a resurgence of the collective security idea, but the atrophy of the organizational structure established by the resolution is one of the most convincing evidences of the practical demise of collective security. At the time of the resolution's adoption, the full significance of the Korean crisis had not yet unfolded. The format of the resolution was hammered out in Assembly committees during the months of September and October when the United Nations army in Korea was pushing rapidly northward in pursuit of complete and final victory. The first trickle of Chinese troops out of Manchuria was not detected until late October, and a complaint of Chinese intervention was lodged with the Security Council on November 6, three days after the plenary session of the Assembly put its seal of approval upon the Uniting for Peace program. The resolution was the child not of adversity but of collective action triumphant—at least prospectively triumphant. The United States masterminded the plan from inception to adoption with the avowed intent of making the United Nations a more efficient instrument to deal with future Koreas in which the cold war might turn hot. The United Nations system had worked reasonably well this time (or so it appeared) but only because of fortuitous circumstances that might not occur again. Next time the Assembly should be prepared to act quickly from the outset, whatever the circumstances. Despite bitter opposition from the Soviet bloc of five, the resolution was adopted by the overwhelming majority of 52 to 5 with 2 abstentions (Argentina and India). This optimistic initiative took place before military reverses and the growth of a new neutralism in the world had placed the Korean War in a perspective less flattering to the idea of collective military intervention.

In substance the resolution formally affirmed the responsibility of the General Assembly to deal with international violence when the Security Council was unable to act, and asserted the right to make "appropriate recommendations to Members for collective measures, including in the case of a breach of the peace or act of aggression the use of armed force when necessary." [8] In addition to this bold statement of Assembly prerogatives in the field of peace and security, the major provisions of the resolution were as follows:

1. Establishment of a procedure for calling the General Assembly into "emergency special session" upon twenty-four hours notice by a vote of any seven members of the Security Council or upon request of a majority of the members of the Assembly. The procedure is available when the Security Council, through lack of unanimity among the permanent members, is unable to act in the face of a threat to international peace or an act of aggression.

2. Creation of a fourteen-member "Peace Observation Commission," including representatives of the five permanent members of the Security Council, to be available for immediate assignment as observers in any area where international tensions may threaten peace and security.

3. Creation of a fourteen-member "Collective Measures Committee" to study and report on methods of strengthening international peace and security.

4. A recommendation that member states survey their resources to determine what support they might give to Assembly programs for the maintenance of peace and security, and that members train, organize, and equip contingents of their national armed forces for prompt availability as UN units. The Secretary-General was authorized to create by appointment a panel of military experts to give technical advice to states upon their request.

Of the four major provisions just cited, only the first has current significance. The last three have fallen into complete desuetude. The Peace Observation Commission functioned only once, as an observer group along Greece's northern frontiers replacing the former UN Special Committee on the Balkans. It was discontinued in August, 1954, at the suggestion of Greece. In May, 1954, Thailand also asked for POC observers to patrol its border with Laos and Cambodia, but the request was vetoed in the Security Council and Thailand subsequently decided not to raise the matter in the

[8] General Assembly Resolution 377 (V), November 3, 1950.

Assembly. The membership of the POC has been regularly renewed at two-year intervals but it stands only as a useless appendix to the organization, a victim of Soviet opposition and sober second thoughts. The Collective Measures Committee, in a series of reports to the Assembly in 1951, 1952, and 1954, prepared an impressive catalog of political, economic, and military sanctions together with suggestions for their use in particular situations. In 1954 the committee was directed to remain ready to pursue further studies as requested by the Assembly, but no further studies were ever called for.

The plea for members to earmark troops for UN service proved no more fruitful. Of sixty governments receiving a questionnaire relating to the survey of national resources and the earmarking of troops, only 43 replied. A few replies were negative, even hostile, but the majority expressed sympathy for the project without making specific commitments. In this they had the example of the United States which likewise failed to earmark contingents. The only relatively unconditional offers to earmark national units were from Thailand, Greece, Norway, and Denmark for a total of 6,000 men, and an offer of two destroyer escorts from Uruguay. The old problem of collective security—advance commitment versus national freedom of action—was again in evidence, and freedom of action again came out on top.

The demise of the Peace Observation Commission, the Collective Measures Committee, and the troop earmarking program accurately reflected the decline of enthusiasm for the United Nations as a mechanism of collective security, under the aegis of either the Security Council or the General Assembly. The emergency special session has survived as a useful device for facilitating Assembly consideration of disputes and threatening situations but not with a view to instituting military action against any of the parties concerned. The procedure was invoked in the Suez and Hungarian crises of 1956, the Middle Eastern crisis of 1958, and in 1960 to deal with problems of the Congo. In none of these instances was serious consideration given to the recruitment of a UN fighting force, although UN forces with substantially different functions were created to deal with both the Suez and the Congo situations. Far from representing a resurgence of collective security, the deployment of UN forces in Egypt and the Congo embodied an entirely different security role for the United Nations. The procedural reform of the Uniting for Peace resolution lived on, but in the service of other techniques of global security.

NONMILITARY SANCTIONS

Collective security was never intended to rest solely upon military force. Provisions for economic and diplomatic sanctions were written into the League Covenant, and a partial embargo of trade with Italy was actually imposed during the Italo-Ethiopian War. The UN Charter also provides for nonmilitary sanctions, most pointedly in Article 41, which authorizes the Security Council to enforce its decisions by "measures not involving the use of armed force." Such measures may include "complete or partial interruption of economic relations and of rail, sea, air, postal, telegraphic, radio, and other means of communication, and the severance of diplomatic relations." Moral condemnation is not specifically cited as a form of sanction, but this is another penalty short of military action that the United Nations may impose upon states that fail to heed its recommendations or decisions. Nearly all of these sanctions have been utilized by the United Nations at one time or another since 1946, but none of them has been strikingly successful in accomplishing UN objectives.

Moral condemnation, although frequently invoked, has been virtually useless in getting states to comply with UN directives. This is perhaps because condemnatory resolutions are usually reserved for states that have already flouted an earlier, more mildly-worded recommendation. A state that has once shown its determination to resist UN pressures is not likely to be restrained by more words—even words of condemnation. In fact, the most noticeable short-run effect of moral condemnation has been to harden the position of the recalcitrant state and worsen its relations with the United Nations. Condemnation did not deter the Soviet Union from carrying out its repression of the Hungarian revolt in 1956, nor did censure cause Hungary, Bulgaria, and Romania to desist from their persecution of political and religious leaders in 1949 and 1950. Condemnation of Chinese intervention in the Korean War left Peking totally unrepentant. And piles of condemnatory resolutions have not yet induced South Africa to abandon its discriminatory racial policies.

Diplomatic and economic sanctions have scarcely been more effective, although one must note that the Security Council never used its power to declare *mandatory* sanctions until 1966. With but one exception, to be discussed below, all UN-sponsored nonmilitary sanctions have been based on *recommendations,* which members are legally free to accept or reject. In 1946 the Assembly recommended withdrawal of ambassadors and ministers from Spain, and the barring of Spain from membership in UN agencies, in the hope of toppling the fascist Franco regime. Franco was totally unmoved, the diplomatic ban was revoked in 1950, and Spain was admitted to the United Nations in 1955. A nondiscriminatory embargo on shipment of arms to Israel and the Arab states, recommended by the Security Council, was rather widely observed until 1955, but the Soviet-Egyptian arms deal of that year and American aid to Israel and members of the Baghdad Pact set off a new arms race in the Middle East. An Assembly-sponsored embargo on arms and war materials bound for Albania and Bulgaria in 1949, aimed at cutting aid to Greek rebels, was wholly ineffectual. The main suppliers of arms were communist countries that refused to recognize the embargo.

Likewise, an Assembly ban on shipment of strategic goods to China in 1951 was ignored by many countries and had no dampening effect on China's will to resist the United Nations in Korea.

South Africa and Rhodesia have been objects of the most recent UN attempts to impose nonmilitary sanctions. In 1962, by a resolution since reiterated, the General Assembly recommended severance of economic and diplomatic relations as a means of forcing South Africa to abandon its apartheid policies. The general economic and diplomatic ban was not complied with by the United States, Britain, and other important trading partners of South Africa; but an embargo on arms and war materials—recommended by the Assembly and subsequently endorsed by the Security Council in 1963—has been widely observed. Since 1963 the Security Council has been under pressure from the anti-colonialist states to endorse the general economic embargo and, indeed, to make nonmilitary sanctions obligatory under Chapter VII of the Charter. The United States and Britain, at the end of 1966, were still holding out against such action.

Rhodesia's unilateral declaration of independence from Britain in 1965 provided the occasion for the historic first invocation of *mandatory* nonmilitary sanctions by the United Nations. In November, 1965, the Security Council recommended an arms and oil embargo against Rhodesia, together with other economic and diplomatic measures. When this proved ineffectual in forcing Rhodesia to retract its declaration of independence, the Security Council acted under Chapter VII of the Charter in April, 1966, to authorize Britain to use force if necessary to stop oil tankers on the high seas from proceeding with their Rhodesia-bound cargoes. In December, 1966, after the breakdown of negotiations between Rhodesia and Britain, the Security Council ordered a mandatory embargo of arms, oil, and motor vehicles and parts, and a mandatory boycott of major Rhodesian exports. African demands for Britain to police the embargo by force were rejected. At the year's end, Rhodesia still clung to its unilateral independence with white minority rule.

The Nonsanctions Force

Collective security as envisioned by the Charter never became a reality, but the problem of uncontrolled international violence still remains. Fortunately, the men who run the policy machinery of international organizations have been pragmatic rather than dogmatic in their attempts to relate the organization to problems of world peace and security. If the nonimplementation of Article 43 made the original Charter plan unworkable, and voluntary enforcement action in the Korean style also had serious drawbacks, other approaches to the problem of uncontrolled violence in international affairs might be explored. In the course of this continuing exploration the United Nations has developed the concept of the peace-supervising force, which in its as yet unexhausted variety of forms constitutes one of the United Nations' most creative contributions to international peace and security.

The nonfighting, nonsanctions, peace-supervising force is basically different from the sanctions force in schemes for collective security. The sanctions force is designed to coerce a government to change its policies in some respect; the peace-supervising force, as it has developed in practice, functions only as long as the host government agrees to its continued presence. The sanctions force relies upon its capacity to intimidate or to triumph in a contest of arms; the peace-supervising force, mainly by the fact of its presence, maintains an order previously agreed upon. Technically, the peace-supervising force is also coercive in the sense that it is designed to induce observation of some agreement; but the inducement is intended to be "more moral than physical."

In some respects the nonsanctions force is more akin to the machinery of peaceful settlement than to enforcement action under the Charter. It serves to separate combatants who are willing to be separated, to bring order and stability to an area by reason of their presence, and to perform nonfighting police functions. Hopefully, the return of peace and stability will permit a negotiated settlement of the political differences that necessitated UN intervention in the first place. And yet the purpose of the force is not to settle disputes. Although the peace-supervising force may help create conditions conducive to settlement of the underlying problems, it is more concerned with curbing disorder and quelling or preventing the spread of violence than with settling disputes *per se*. In the case of the UN Security Force in New Guinea, the basic political issue between the Dutch and the Indonesians was resolved before the force appeared on the scene; the task of the force was simply to maintain civil order and perform routine police functions pending the transfer of control to Indonesia. The United Nations Emergency Force in the Middle East (UNEF) presents a striking contrast but comes no closer to casting the peace force in the role of judge or mediator. After more than a decade of activity along the Israeli-Egyptian border, UNEF still provides the indispensable buffer that separates the spark from the tinder; but political settlement is nowhere in sight.

This perhaps illustrates the difficulty of classifying current UN peace-keeping activities in the traditional categories of sanctions or pacific settlement. The Charter neatly separates its prescriptions for the pacific settlement of disputes (Chapter VI) from enforcement action (Chapter VII), but in the world of men and nations the peace-keeping function may involve a great variety of specific means that cannot readily be compartmentalized. Even in national political systems where the central government has a legal monopoly of coercive force and rests upon a solid foundation of consensus, the negotiatory aspects of the law cannot always be readily separated from the enforcement aspects—a fact to which any practitioner of criminal law in the United States can testify. The preceding chapter has discussed the role of nonsanctions forces in connection with the process of pacific settlement; here they will be considered in the context of global security arrangements as the latest expression of the organization's evolving military arm.

Antecedents of UNEF

The establishment of the United Nations Emergency Force (UNEF) in Egypt and the Gaza Strip was a signal triumph of innovation, ingenuity, administrative skill, and international cooperation that will long stand as a tribute to the United Nations. There should be no denigration of that superb effort to suggest that the concept of an international nonfighting, peace-supervisory force was not entirely without historical precedent.[9] Under the aegis of League of Nations, the Saar plebiscite of 1935 was supervised by a 3,300 man force consisting largely of British troops supplemented by small contingents from Italy, the Netherlands, and Sweden. The force arrived on the scene in December, 1934, and left two months later, its mission accomplished without incident. The contrast with UNEF, which still patrols the Gaza Strip, is obvious; but it was an international force. The "Leticia" dispute between Colombia and Peru (1932–34) also led to the creation of a League-sponsored nonfighting force—international in name if not altogether in substance. The League Council deputized the troops of Colombia to act for the League and keep order in the disputed territory during an interim period of League administration of Leticia, pending transfer of control to the Colombian government. Such remote activities were of scant worth to the General Assembly and the Secretary-General as guides to the task at hand in November, 1956—but they were historical precedents for an international force in the service of a general international organization.[10]

Of more immediate value as working precedent was the United Nations' own experience with nonfighting "presences" in tension areas. In Greece, Kashmir, and Palestine groups of armed military observers patrolling sensi-

[9] Lester B. Pearson, then Foreign Minister of Canada and more recently Prime Minister, has called the force "an improvised experiment" with "neither precedent nor organization available to the Assembly" in establishing it. See Pearson, "Force for U.N.," *Foreign Affairs*, Vol. 35 (April, 1957), p. 400. Gabriella E. Rosner also maintains that for practical purposes, UNEF was unprecedented, and her arguments merit careful consideration. See her *The United Nations Emergency Force* (New York: Columbia University Press, 1963), pp. 207–22.

[10] The League had earlier contemplated an international police force to maintain order in the city of Vilna while a plebiscite was held to resolve a dispute between Poland and Lithuania. Before the troops could be assembled and transported to Vilna, however, the plebiscite idea was discarded in the face of Lithuanian reluctance to accept a plebiscite verdict and Soviet threats to intervene if troops of League members were stationed so near to Russian boundaries.

tive borderlands under a UN mandate had been organized by the United Nations as part of its general peace-keeping function. The observation team along the northern frontiers of Greece numbered about twenty observers, plus auxiliary personnel. The Kashmir truce team, functioning continuously since 1949, has been somewhat larger. The United Nations Truce Supervision Organization, established in 1948 to police a temporary truce between Israel and her Arab neighbors, was also destined to become a permanent peace-keeping fixture. In 1949, before the conclusion of armistice agreements, UNTSO supplied 682 military personnel to police the Arab-Israeli truce. After 1949 UNTSO was gradually reduced to an observer group of between forty and fifty in number. In 1949 the General Assembly also authorized the Secretary-General to establish a permanent 300-man UN Field Service to put the servicing of field missions on a more systematic basis.

The UNEF operation reaped the benefit of this body of organizational precedent. Frye reports that in the early planning stages the UN Field Service "was invaluable in untangling knots, providing experience and know-how, and supplying communications for the troops." [11] Moreover, the cadre for UNEF was drawn directly from the UN Truce Supervision Organization. For a military commander, the Secretary-General turned to Major-General E. L. M. Burns, a Canadian, stationed in Jerusalem as chief of staff of UNTSO. When the storm broke, he and his staff were dispatched to the Neapolitan airport of Capodichino to take charge of the troop contingents arriving to become part of UNEF.

The idea of a UN peace-supervising force in fact antedated the Suez crisis by several years. Spurred by the outbreak of violence in Indonesia, Kashmir, and Palestine, Secretary-General Trygve Lie in 1948 proposed the creation of a substantial UN Guard force. In the introduction to his annual report for 1947–48 he announced that the Secretariat had already undertaken a study of

> proposals for the creation of a small United Nations Guard Force which could be recruited by the Secretary-General and placed at the disposal of the Security Council and the General Assembly. Such a force would not be used as a substitute for forces contemplated in Articles 42 and 43. It would not be a striking force, but purely a guard force. It could be used for guard duty with United Nations missions, in the conduct of plebiscites under the supervision of the United Nations, and in the administration of truce terms. It could be used as a constabulary under the Security Council or the Trusteeship Council in cities like Jerusalem and Trieste during the establishment of international regimes. It might also be called upon by the Security Council under Article 40 of the Charter, which provides for provisional measures to prevent the aggravation of a situation threatening the peace.[12]

[11] Frye, *op. cit.*, p. 25.

[12] *Annual Report of the Secretary-General on the Work of the Organization, 1 July 1947 to 30 June 1948,* Official Records of the General Assembly, 3rd Sess., Supp. No. 1, United Nations Document A/565, pp. xvii–xviii.

The suggested size of the UN force was "from one to five thousand men."

A few months later, spurred to action by the assassination of Count Folke Bernadotte, UN Mediator in Palestine, Lie formally requested the third Assembly (1948) to consider the establishment of a UN Guard "several thousand strong." He also urged the immediate creation of an 800-man force to perform guard duties "entirely non-military" in character and acting "only with the consent, express or implied, of the territorial sovereign." [13] Inoffensive as the latter proposal might appear, reaction from the Soviet Union was hostile, and the other great powers were decidedly unenthusiastic. The plan was shelved and in its place the General Assembly created the previously mentioned 300-man "Field Service" to systematize the servicing of UN field missions, guard premises at headquarters and abroad, and maintain order at UN meetings. At the same time the Assembly established a "Panel of Field Observers," to consist of persons available for any observation, truce, or plebiscite functions that the Security Council or General Assembly might authorize. The value of the Field Service has already been noted; the Panel of Field Observers has never been used.

UNEF

The United Nations Emergency Force was, nevertheless, a striking innovation, all the more so because the force passed from idea to reality during a few short, crisis-ridden days. The October 30, 1956, Israeli invasion of Egypt, followed shortly by Anglo-French bombing of Egyptian airports and the seizure of the Suez Canal Zone, had brought stunned, angry protests from around the world and created the most believable threat of world war since Korea. Soviet threats, and rumors of Communist "volunteer" armies preparing for service in the Middle East, added a note of deepest urgency to the crisis.

The British and French veto of a Security Council resolution calling for cease-fire and troop withdrawal led to the convocation of the first "Special Emergency Session" of the Assembly under the procedure outlined in the Uniting for Peace resolution. The Assembly voiced its own plea for cease-fire and troop withdrawal and, in the early hours of Sunday morning, November 4, authorized the Secretary-General to prepare a plan for an emergency international force. Although Hammarskjold was given a forty-eight-hour deadline, his preliminary report was ready in twelve hours. Sunday night (early Monday morning) the Assembly approved the establishment of a UN Command, named General Burns to head the command, and authorized the recruitment of a staff of officers from countries other than the great powers. A second Hammarskjold report was ready within the forty-eight-hour limit, and the Assembly placed its stamp of approval on the plan November 7. General Burns and his staff had already flown to

[13] United Nations Document A/656, p. 10.

Capodichino to receive the first units of the emergency force, which arrived November 10; and just five days later, the delay arising from the difficulty of securing Egyptian consent to the entry of the force, the first contingent —a group of forty-five Danes—landed at Abu Suweir airfield ten miles west of Ismailia. The speed with which the organization and its members mounted such a constructive response to the crisis is all the more remarkable in view of the equally shattering events then transpiring simultaneously in Hungary.

The force, at its peak numbering about 6,000 men from ten countries, was intended to be temporary. In fact a cease-fire had been obtained on November 6, even before the Hammarskjold plan for UNEF was formally endorsed by the Assembly; and the withdrawal of the last Israeli soldiers was completed by March, 1957. But more than a decade later a "temporary" force of some 4,000 men from seven countries still patrols the Egyptian side of the dusty borderline with Israel.[14] The UNEF mandate to assist in the creation of peaceful conditions in the area has required continued functioning of the force as a border watch.

Not only is the first UN experiment with a peace-supervising force still with us, but the precedents it established have had important consequences for subsequent versions of the force. Particularly careful attention must therefore be given to the political guidelines that emerged from that experience. Hammarskjold's plan for the establishment of UNEF, approved by the General Assembly in its resolutions of November 5 and November 7, 1956, laid down a number of basic principles to govern the organization and functioning of the force.[15] Among the more important were the following: (1) Exclusion of great powers from participation in the force; (2) vesting of political control of UNEF in the Secretary-General, assisted by a military Advisory Committee composed principally (but not exclusively) of representatives of participating states, and subject to the overall approval and direction of the Assembly; (3) limitation of UNEF to nonfighting functions, i.e., those which could be performed with the consent or acquiescence of all governments concerned; (4) maintenance of the political neutrality of the force, with its functions so defined as to restore the political balance existing before the fighting broke out; (5) insistence upon the right of the organization to determine the composition and function of the force, subject to the consent of the host country to the stationing of UN troops within its territory; (6) assessment of the cost of salaries and equipment to the participating country, with all other expenses of the force financed outside the normal UN budget by a special levy on all members.

---

[14] Of twenty-four governmental offers to participate, ten were ultimately accepted, from Brazil, Canada, Colombia, Denmark, Finland, India, Indonesia, Norway, Sweden, and Yugoslavia. Troops contributed by Colombia, Finland, and Indonesia have since been withdrawn.

[15] United Nations Documents A/3289 and A/3302.

Some of these principles were modified in practice and subsequently reformulated by Hammarskjold in a report to the General Assembly summarizing the first two years' experience with UNEF.[16] The reconciliation of UN prerogatives with host state sovereignty, as contemplated in item 5 above, posed particularly thorny problems and in fact delayed UNEF's entry into Egypt by several days. Assuming that initial agreement might be reached, what was to protect either UNEF or the Egyptian government from subsequent unilateral arbitrary action by the other in case of conflict in their interpretations of the proper function of the force? This potentially complicated issue was resolved by the simple expedient of a mutual declaration that each would be guided by "good faith" in the interpretation of the purposes of the Force. Based on the UNEF experience the Secretary-General also concluded that any subsequent status-of-forces agreement with a host country must accord full freedom of movement to the peace force within the area of its operations and all necessary facilities for access and communications. As for the national composition of the force, the views of Egypt were given great weight, without recognizing an absolute Egyptian right to veto participation of any given national contingents. In practice, the Secretary-General excluded units from any member that might be considered as having a special interest in the situation.

The 1958 Hammarskjold report on UNEF drew additional conclusions of relevance to the functioning of future UN peace-keeping forces. Some of the more salient observations may be summarized as follows: (1) The peace force should be established only by authorization of the General Assembly or Security Council, and remain directly responsible to the parent body, but be administratively integrated with the UN Secretariat under instructions from the Secretary-General. (2) The Advisory Committee should advise only, and not control, the Secretary-General in the exercise of his responsibilities. (3) The force should not be a party to internal conflicts or be deployed in situations essentially internal in nature, or be used to "enforce any specific political solution or pending problems or to influence the political balance decisive to such a solution." (4) Although the rule of "no combat activity" was sound, the force should have the right of self-defense; it might return fire, but could not take the initiative. (5) Troop-supplying states should pay costs that would be incurred if the military units remained in national service; all other costs should be borne by all members in accordance with the normal UN scale of contributions.

The General Assembly withheld approval of the Secretary-General's 1958 report, largely because its sentiment was against any kind of action that would tend to commit the organization, even morally, to the recruitment of peace-keeping forces in the future. Nevertheless, that report, together with

[16] United Nations Document A/3943.

the principles originally proposed in November, 1956, has provided political guidelines for peace-keeping forces subsequently established in the Congo, West New Guinea, and Cyprus, even though each has obviously been a unique operation. In one important area—the financing of peace-keeping forces through assessments upon all members—the principles have been vociferously challenged and are undoubtedly in the process of substantial modification. But in most respects, the principles evolved from UNEF have provided the basic pattern for subsequent UN peace-supervising forces.

ONUC

The imprint of UNEF is clearly to be seen in the United Nations Operation in the Congo, generally referred to by the French acronym ONUC.[17] The great powers were excluded from participation in the force; political control was in the hands of the Secretary-General, assisted by an Advisory Committee, and subject to the Security Council and General Assembly; the participating states were selected in consultation with the Congolese government; the force entered the Congo with the consent of that government— although there were times when it was difficult to determine what government was entitled to give consent to UN actions; and the financing followed the UNEF model with a special assessment based generally upon the regular budgetary schedule to provide the UN share of the expense. ONUC also attempted to maintain its role as a nonfighting force, although the terrific demands of maintaining civil order, self-defense, and threading a tenuous path between contending domestic factions sometimes made this goal impossible.

Political neutrality with respect to outside powers was maintained to a surprising degree, despite strong pressures from some African states (including contributors to the force) and from the Soviet Union. Domestically, however, the actions of the force tended to support the Central Government at Leopoldville against the secessionist state of Katanga, and at one crucial juncture to favor President Joseph Kasavubu and Colonel Joseph Mobutu in their internal conflict with Premier Patrice Lumumba. Although this result scarcely comported with Hammarskjold's observations in 1958 that UN peace-keeping personnel could not be "permitted in any sense to be a party to internal conflicts" and that their "role must be limited to external aspects of the political situation," the circumstances were extenuating. The domestic situation was so confused that ONUC could scarcely do anything that did not appear to favor one domestic group over another. UN officials

[17] ONUC is here used with reference to the UN military force in the Congo, although technically it applies to the extensive civilian operation as well.

Both the United States and the Soviet Union supported the Security Council resolution to establish ONUC in July, 1960, while Britain, France, and China abstained. The Soviet bloc, Britain, and France were among the nineteen abstaining in 1956 when the General Assembly established UNEF.

in the Congo were under orders to remain absolutely neutral in domestic conflicts but such a position, however "irreproachable in theory," was "impossible to apply in practice without drawing the criticisms of all factions, internal and foreign." [18]

Quite apart from principle, certain other similarities with the UNEF operation were apparent. Just as General Burns and his UNTSO staff had been called from Palestine to command the Suez peace force, the initial command of ONUC was thrust upon Major-General Carl Carlsson Von Horn, Burns' successor as UNTSO chief of staff. The same haste—or one might say dispatch—in throwing the military organization together was also evident. Within forty-eight hours of the Security Council's July 14, 1960, resolution authorizing the force, the first Tunisian troops disembarked in the Congo, unhampered by the diplomatic resistance that had characterized UN negotiations with Egypt in 1956; and by the end of July more than 11,000 troops from eight countries were on duty with ONUC. Once more United States airlift facilities for the transport of men and material, especially in the early stages when rapid build-up was required, proved crucial—a fact that led two informed commentators to observe how disconcerting it is "even to speculate on how the UN would go about establishing a military mission without the aid of the United States Air Force." [19]

To suggest important similarities between the UNEF and ONUC should not becloud the uniqueness of each force and, indeed, the special difficulties of the UN action in the Congo. Ruth Russell captured the essence of the situation when she observed, "The whole Congo episode has been so much confusion worse confounded that any effort to analyze it inevitably distorts the picture by imposing a certain artificial order upon the chaotic reality." [20] ONUC was much larger than UNEF, numbering 20,000 men at its peak strength with troops contributed by twenty-nine countries over the whole period of action. But the task confronting the UN was larger still. Although formal withdrawal of Belgian troops was accomplished by early September, 1960, a number of Belgian military "advisers" remained, as did other foreign "mercenaries." The initial ONUC mandate from the Security Council was to oversee the withdrawal of Belgian troops and to assist the Congolese authorities in maintaining law and order. The mandate was subsequently extended to include the withdrawal of all Belgian forces, mercenaries, and other foreign military personnel. Even more broadly, the force was authorized to take "all appropriate measures to prevent the occurrence of civil war in the Congo, including arrangements for cease-fires, the halting

---

[18] Ruth B. Russell, *United Nations Experience with Military Forces: Political and Legal Aspects* (Washington, D.C.: The Brookings Institution, 1964), p. 102.

[19] Edward H. Bowman and James E. Fanning, "Logistics—Experience and Requirements," in Lincoln P. Bloomfield, ed., *International Military Forces* (Boston: Little, Brown and Company, 1964), p. 147.

[20] Russell, *op. cit.*, p. 86.

of all military operations, the prevention of clashes, and the use of force, if necessary, in the last resort." [21] This was no small order for ONUC's small band in an area more than four times as large as France, with its already inadequate system of transportation and communication disrupted by widespread domestic disorder.

Belgian military intervention, followed by more than a threat of Soviet intervention, accompanied by continuing attempts at political intervention by other African states, thoroughly internationalized the crisis. At the United Nations wide cleavages in both the Security Council and the General Assembly forced the Secretary-General to make policy decisions without the firm guidance and support that could have eased the terrible responsibility, if not the technical difficulty, of his task. The Soviet Union, which initially supported the establishment of ONUC when the principal threat to international stability was Belgian military intervention, subsequently became disenchanted and even hostile. Moreover, ONUC was subject to short-notice troop withdrawals by governments which disagreed with the trend of events that UN action in the Congo appeared to be taking at various times.

Nor should it be forgotten that the military operation was accompanied by a massive injection of technical assistance personnel, more than 1,100 by the end of 1962, without whose presence a complete breakdown of public administration and essential technical services was almost a certainty. The civilian personnel were recruited through the UN specialized agencies as well as the United Nations itself, and the entire effort was coordinated by a UN Secretariat official of under-secretary rank.

Although civilian aid still continues on a reduced scale, the ONUC military force encountered well-publicized financial difficulties and was forced to withdraw in mid-1964. Whatever its shortcomings under extremely trying circumstances, it had notable accomplishments to its credit —the Belgian troops, mercenaries, and foreign military advisers were gone; the secession of Katanga and other areas of the Congo had been prevented; and, a modicum of law and order had been established and maintained. The threat of intervention by foreign governments was substantially reduced and the Congo, for the time at least, had been insulated from the worst effects of cold war rivalry, including a possible East-West military confrontation. The continuing contribution of ONUC to law and order in the Congo was made distressingly evident by the outbreak of internal strife in the fall of 1964 upon the heels of the withdrawing UN troops—internal strife which, ironically, led the central government to enlist the services of foreign mercenaries on its own behalf.

[21] Security Council Resolution, February 21, 1961, United Nations Document S/4741. This was, in effect, a mandate to thwart the secession of Katanga which relied upon an army of "mercenaries" and foreign military personnel.

UN Forces in West New Guinea and Cyprus

The establishment of UN peace-supervising forces in West New Guinea and in Cyprus further illustrates the combination of uniqueness and conformity to a common pattern that has thus far marked this kind of venture in global security. With slight deviations, they have followed the UNEF precedent in matters of force composition, freedom of movement, political control by the Secretary-General under authorization from the Assembly or Security Council, consent of the territorial sovereign, attempted political neutrality, and limitation of the force to nonfighting functions. Both forces, however, were deployed in situations "essentially internal in nature," although the international ramifications were also clear and urgent. The financing of both operations also followed a different pattern from UNEF and ONUC, influenced no doubt by the growing impasse over the financing of peace-keeping forces by mandatory assessment according to the regular UN budgetary scale. The Netherlands and Indonesia—the two parties most intimately involved in the West New Guinea dispute—agreed to share all UN expenses equally; and the force in Cyprus has been financed entirely by voluntary contributions, largely from the states of the Atlantic community, without any attempt to relate the expense to the regular assessment formula.

The United Nations Security Force in West New Guinea (UNSF), unlike the other three forces, came into being as the result of prior political settlement between the major disputants. After years of dogged resistance to Indonesian claims to West Irian, both in and out of the United Nations, the Dutch finally succumbed in August, 1962, to a combination of Indonesian diplomatic and military threats, the fear of Communist gains in the event of hostilities, threats of Soviet intervention, entreaties from the Secretary-General, diplomatic pressure from the United States, and mounting domestic demands to get rid of the burden. The August, 1962, agreement committed the Netherlands to turn over the administration of the territory to a UN Temporary Executive Authority (UNTEA), thus creating in effect a temporary UN-administered trusteeship. At any time after May 1, 1963, the UN administrator was authorized to transfer governmental authority to Indonesia, subject to the right of the native Papuans to determine their own political fate by a plebiscite before the end of 1969. Within this framework the Security Force was required only to maintain the authority of the UNTEA and supplement existing Papuan police in the maintenance of law and order.

The arrangement was approved by the Assembly without opposition, and by early December a force of 1,596 persons was serving under UN colors. This included 1,485 Pakistanis engaged in routine guard and police functions, and an air contingent for supply and liaison activities, composed of ninety-nine Americans and twelve Canadians. The presence of the Americans violated the principle of great power exclusion, but the political settlement had drained the situation of its cold war potential and the use of United States airmen was acceptable to all parties as a concession to convenience. When the force was withdrawn at the termination of UN administration, it had the distinction of being, thus far, the only peace-supervising force to leave the scene of action with its mission fully accomplished—and this because the dispute was resolved before the force was ever called into being.

The United Nations Force in Cyprus (UNFICYP) is the most recent in the series of UN peace-supervising forces. It was created to cope with conflict between Greek and Turkish communities in Cyprus which threatened to engulf the entire island in a tide of violence and bring armed intervention by Greece and Turkey. The Cypriot constitution, framed in 1959 as a compromise acceptable to Greece, Turkey, Britain and Cypriot leaders, had brought independence to Cyprus but not internal peace. Majority rule —which would have meant rule by leaders of the Greek Cypriots constituting eighty per cent of the island's 600,000 population—was modified by placing a legislative veto in the hands of the Turkish minority. In the absence of good faith, good will, or rational behavior, the constitution was scarcely workable. And without the consent of the Turkish minority and of the British, Greek, and Turkish governments, it could not legally be amended.

Predictably, the machinery of government stalled, the Greek Cypriot majority set about to amend the constitution unilaterally, and domestic violence ensued. Bloodshed and the formation of rival terrorist groups on Cyprus brought Greece and Turkey to swords' points once more, with Britain in the middle as mediator, peace-maker, and policeman. An offer to form a joint peace-making force composed of British, Turkish, and Greek units under British command was accepted by Cyprus late in 1963, but it proved unable to quell the violence. The Cypriot government, in preference to an augmented three-power force, leaned strongly toward replacing it with UN-supervised units. These developments led the United Kingdom to ask the Security Council to deal with the problem.

The Security Council's authorizing resolution displayed the marks of past experience in setting the frame of reference for UNFICYP. The force was to be of a size and composition determined by the Secretary-General in consultation with the governments of Cyprus, Greece, Turkey, and the United Kingdom. Its commander was to be appointed by and report to the Secretary-General. The peace-force objectives were specified only in the general terms of preserving international peace and security, preventing a recurrence of fighting in Cyprus, and contributing as necessary to the maintenance of law and order. The costs were to be met by countries contributing contingents, by Cyprus, and by voluntary contributions. The initial mandate was limited to a three-month period, beginning March 4, 1964.

As it was put together during the first three-month period, the force consisted of approximately 7,000 troops from Canada, Ireland, Finland, Denmark, Austria, Sweden, and the United Kingdom. The inclusion of British troops violated the general rule excluding participation by the permanent members of the Security Council, but the British offer proved acceptable to all parties, and was not specifically prohibited by the Security Council resolution. In addition to the military units, 173 civilian police were contributed by Austria, Australia, New Zealand, Denmark, and Sweden. As in the past the Secretary-General relied upon previous UN operations to supply his top command. General P. S. Gyani of India, commander of UNEF until his resignation in January, 1964, to become the Secretary-General's special representative in Cyprus, was named commander of UNFICYP. The UN costs of the force, which leveled off at about $7 million a quarter, have been met by voluntary contributions from seventeen countries, in addition to Cyprus, Greece, Turkey, and the United Kingdom. Eleven of the twenty-one contributors, and those accounting for the bulk of the contributions, are members of NATO.

UNFICYP stands as another example of the "temporary" peace force which is becoming a permanent part of the international scenery. Like ONUC, UNFICYP was initially created pursuant to a resolution of the Security Council. Unlike ONUC, it has thus far managed to retain the confidence of all permanent members of the Security Council, thus avoiding the need for subsequent recourse to the General Assembly. Because of its manifest contribution to peace and order, and the equally manifest elusiveness of a general settlement of the Cyprus problem, UNFICYP has continued to exist by repeated extensions of its mandate.

The UN Peace Force: Retrospect and Prospect

In retrospect, the peace-supervising force marks a return to the Charter assumption that the military arm of the organization should not be used to coerce a great power. Even more, it is a tacit admission that the United Nations is ill suited to organizing military sanctions against any country, large or small. The framers of the Charter foresaw the dangers of making the organization a potential catalyst for general war between the giants, and they devised the Security Council veto to preclude such a UN role. What they could scarcely foresee was the extent to which the pervasiveness of East-West rivalry would give to nearly every armed conflict, or threat of conflict, the potentiality of great power involvement on opposite sides. In practical terms, the use of any kind of military sanctions under UN auspices now appears either too dangerous or politically unfeasible, or both.

The United Nations is still capable of a constructive role in matters of global security, however, when the two superpowers see a common interest in the termination of hostilities and maintenance of order. As new centers of power develop in mainland China and Western Europe, world peace may become less exclusively the ward of the United States and the Soviet Union; but heretofore, the mutual acquiescence of the two superpowers has permitted violence to be curbed in such diverse places as Indonesia, Palestine, Kashmir, Cyprus, and the Sinai peninsula without resort to international military sanctions. That UN peace efforts in such areas have been facilitated by outside diplomatic and economic pressure upon the participants, and occasional threats of unilateral military intervention, merely underscores the fact that UN sanctions forces, while politically unfeasible in any event, are practically unnecessary when Soviet and American interests converge. In such a setting the peace force becomes a highly useful instrument for performing local police functions while a settlement is being effectuated or, in the more usual case, providing a modicum of restraint and separating combatants in a necessarily volatile situation where the parties have accepted peace without settlement.

The peace-supervising force has thus been politically feasible and highly useful when the two superpowers have acquiesced and the consent of all parties immediately concerned could be obtained.[22] The financial feasibility of such forces remains yet another problem. Considering the apparent contribution of UNEF and ONUC to peace and stability, their combined cost was relatively small—some $15 to $20 million a year for the former and approximately $100 million a year for the latter. But the unwillingness of some members to pay the costs of peace-keeping nevertheless brought the United Nations to the verge of bankruptcy. The financial impact of the Congo crisis was temporarily cushioned by the issuance of UN bonds up to an authorized amount of $200 million. By the end of 1965, $155 million had been subscribed, half by the United States on a matching basis. But ONUC had to be disbanded and withdrawn from the Congo in 1964 because of the financial drain upon the organization, not because its usefulness had been outlived.

The financial crisis, with all its grim portent for the continued viability of the United Nations, was in truth a symptom of an even more fundamental political problem—the control of UN peace-keeping operations. Both France and the Soviet Union maintained that the sole control of UN forces, whether of the sanctions or the peace-supervisory variety, should remain with the Security Council where each of the five permanent members held the veto. This contention provided the legal basis for their refusal to pay for operations authorized by the Assembly. But it also registered their

---

[22] The United States voted in favor of all four peace forces heretofore created; the Soviet Union abstained on the Assembly vote to create UNEF and voted in favor of the others.

objection to the deployment of UN forces without their consent, and to the principle that a state can be forced, on pain of deprivation of its Assembly vote, to pay for any UN security function that a majority of the Assembly decides to make chargeable to the organization as a whole. The issue of control, symbolized by the embroilment over finances, lies at the heart of the problem. This is underscored by the fact that the total arrearage, though large in comparison with UN resources, is small in terms of national outlays for security. Without the underlying legal and political issues, the United States could pick up the entire deficit with no noticeable financial strain.

The experiences of Cyprus and New Guinea illustrate that financial needs can be met, however precariously, if there are no complicating political factors. When the General Assembly approved the UN Security Force in West New Guinea in September, 1962, it also approved a prior agreement between Indonesia and the Netherlands to share equally all expenses of the force. The creation of the UN Cyprus force, likewise, was made dependent upon voluntary contributions by interested members, and the United States and its allies have found no political barriers to paying virtually the full cost. Admittedly, contributions to UNFICYP have been grudging to the point of threatening its existence, but the force has thus far managed to hang on. These experiences indicate that neither the Assembly nor the Security Council need be financially precluded from establishing further peace-supervising forces if the advocates of action are willing to pay for it themselves, without attempting to unload part of the burden on other states which oppose, or, at best, merely tolerate the operation.[23]

What, then, is the future of the UN peace-supervising force? Schemes for putting the peace force on a more stable, permanent basis have understandably followed in the wake of UN experience. Indeed, in the spring of 1963 the Scandinavian countries of Norway, Denmark, and Sweden jointly announced a decision to make available on a standby basis a 3,000 man force for service in nonfighting UN missions upon the call of Assembly or Security Council. Secretary-General U Thant was quick to make grateful acknowledgement of the offer and urge other countries to "consider following the lead of the Scandinavian countries in this matter."[24] Several other members have since indicated a readiness to create standby units for use under carefully specified conditions.

Such developments clearly augur a future for the UN peace-supervising force. But without substantial—and at present unforeseeable—changes in the political environment of the United Nations, the force will remain on an ad hoc basis with continuity provided chiefly by the accumulated experience of the Secretariat and of the participating countries. An increased

[23] For a fuller discussion of UN financing, see Chapter 4.
[24] *United Nations Review* (July, 1963), p. 56.

readiness may perhaps arise from the availability of standby units. Such units must still await the call of the Assembly or Security Council, however, and this in turn will probably await the agreement—or at least the acquiescence—of the United States and the Soviet Union. Hence the forces are likely to be used only where noncontroversial police functions are required or where both superpowers recognize, at least initially, that the unchecked spread of violence might involve a threat to their own peace and security. For reasons of practical efficiency, if not of faith in the impartiality and neutrality of the Secretariat, administrative control of peace-supervising forces will probably remain with the Secretary-General subject to the general authority of the Assembly or Security Council. Because of the past unhappy experience of ONUC and UNEF, the peace-supervising force of the immediate future will have to rely upon voluntary contribution rather than compulsory assessment. If such arrangements leave each state the maximum of freedom of action, this is perhaps in keeping with political conditions in a world where collective security failed to materialize at the global level because it did not or could not make sufficient allowance for national freedom of action.

GLOBAL SECURITY AND INTERNATIONAL ORGANIZATION

In the fall of 1961, the United States submitted to the General Assembly a plan for "General and Complete Disarmament." An integral part of the plan was a proposal to build a "United Nations peace force" strong enough, ultimately, to "deter or suppress any threat or use of force in violation of the purposes and principles of the United Nations." In the final stage of disarmament the force would be so strong that "no state would have the military power to challenge" it.[25] The scope of the proposal was breathtaking, to say the least, if it could be taken seriously. It went much farther along the road toward an integrated universal security system than the men of Versailles—or of San Francisco—had dreamed of. The proposal in fact created a noticeable ripple on the UN diplomatic pond, but the reaction was in no sense commensurate with the drastic alteration of the conditions of international life the proposal contemplated. The explanation of this anomaly is perhaps twofold. Lip service to collective security in its various forms is a long and honorable tradition in the United Nations, and no sensible person really expected this sally into the world of tomorrow to bring more practical results than its predecessors. The whole episode illustrates the grand paradox of global security today. Men cherish the ultimate ideal of an orderly, peaceful world made secure by force wielded in the common interest; but their actions and their operational ideals almost negate the very notion of a common interest.

[25] *Department of State Bulletin*, Vol. 45 (October 16, 1961), pp. 653–54.

Stanley Hoffman aptly characterized the UN security effort when, at the time of the Suez crisis, he compared it to the mythological Sisyphus, forever condemned to roll a stone uphill and never permitted to reach the top.[26] But perhaps the plight of world organization is not so eternally void of hope as that of Sisyphus. No one can feel very confident about ever getting to the top, but occasionally the stone rollers reach a plateau that marks a real gain over previous efforts to promote world peace and security. The establishment of the League of Nations was such an advance, for all its inability to stave off aggression and a catastrophic world war. If interpolity security arrangements changed very little from the days of Abraham to the assassination of the Austrian Archduke at Sarajevo, the creation of the League of Nations interjected a new and lasting element into the international system. The League symbolized widespread acceptance of the principle of common interest in the maintenance of peace and security, and it was an institutional embodiment of the principle. Even World War II could not wipe out this notable advance; the United Nations carried on where the League left off.

It is easy to overemphasize the impact of the League and the United Nations. If twentieth century international organization marks a plateau in the ascent toward world peace and security, it is still very far from the top. In fact, both the League and the United Nations have had to exist in a world where national armaments, alliances, and some form of the balance of power are the chief reliance of states in their quest for security. The polarization of military power and the advent of nuclear weapons with rocket delivery systems have worked far greater modifications in the balance-of-power system than has the advent of international organization.

Indeed, the most highly touted feature of world organization—collective security—has heretofore proved unworkable and substantial doubts even of its desirability remain unallayed. Honest critics have yet to be satisfied that doctrinaire versions of collective security hold no danger of turning localized wars into general wars; of inviting "universal intervention in other people's local affairs and in matters of which an understanding is quite wanting"; and of creating a collective force which, if it were strong enough to do its job properly, might itself constitute a threat to world peace and security.

Nevertheless, if doctrinaire collective security has little relevance for present problems, the same pessimistic appraisal is not applicable to the whole gamut of global security techniques. The present global balance of power, if it is to preserve peace and provide security, is desperately in need of the services the United Nations can provide as a means of communication, mediation, and judicious intervention in time of crisis. The United Nations can play a crucial role in helping to reduce in number and severity

[26] Stanley Hoffman, "Sisyphus and the Avalanche: The United Nations, Egypt and Hungary," *International Organization* (Summer, 1957), pp. 446–69.

the possible points of East-West tension which could result in a collision of irreconcilable interests. Giving a reverse twist to collective security, which calls for universal involvement in every international conflict, the United Nations can serve to insulate other peoples' conflicts from the worst effects of cold war rivalry.[27] By contributing to stability in localized areas, peace-supervising forces have indirectly promoted the stability of the global balance-of-power system. In the perspective of history, the peace-supervising force may well mark the approach to a new plateau in man's ascent to world peace and security.

Selected Readings

BLOOMFIELD, LINCOLN P. *International Military Forces.* Boston: Little, Brown and Company, 1964.

BOWETT, D. W. *United Nations Forces: A Legal Study.* New York: Praeger, 1964.

BOYD, JAMES M. "Cyprus: Episode in Peacekeeping," *International Organization,* Winter, 1966, pp. 1–17.

CLAUDE, INIS L., JR. *Power and International Relations.* New York: Random House, 1962.

FINKELSTEIN, MARINA S., and FINKELSTEIN, LAWRENCE S., eds. *Collective Security.* San Francisco: Chandler Publishing Co., 1966.

FRYE, WILLIAM R. *A United Nations Peace Force.* New York: Oceana Publications, 1957.

GOODRICH, LELAND M. *Korea: A Study of U. S. Policy in the United Nations.* New York: Council on Foreign Relations, 1956.

GOODRICH, LELAND M., and SIMONS, ANNE P. *The United Nations and the Maintenance of International Peace and Security.* Washington, D.C.: The Brookings Institution, 1955.

LEFEVER, ERNEST W. *Crisis in the Congo: A United Nations Force in Action.* Washington, D.C.: The Brookings Institution, 1965.

ROSNER, GABRIELLA E. *The United Nations Emergency Force.* New York: Columbia University Press, 1963.

ROYAL INSTITUTE OF INTERNATIONAL AFFAIRS. *International Sanctions.* London: Oxford University Press, 1938.

RUSSELL, RUTH B. *United Nations Experience with Military Forces: Political and Legal Aspects.* Washington, D.C.: The Brookings Institution, 1964.

WAINHOUSE, DAVID W. *International Peace Observation: A History and Forecast.* Baltimore: The Johns Hopkins Press, 1966.

[27] Dag Hammarskjold called this function "preventive diplomacy." See Chapter 9 for a discussion of preventive diplomacy in the context of pacific settlement.

11 | *Alliances for Regional Security*

As our discussion of global security has indicated, the age of international organization has not yet devised an effective substitute for the military alliance. The post-1945 alliance system, however, is significantly different from its earlier counterparts. Peacetime alliances of the past were little more than agreements among two or a few countries for joint military action in the event of armed attack by specified third parties. In contrast, alliances today are often broadly multilateral in membership and widely ramified in scope. Agreement for concerted action in the event of attack is supplemented by joint preparation in advance of attack. This in turn makes defense budgets and arms levels in one state the concern of all. The general economic health of alliance partners becomes a matter of joint interest and perhaps the object of "mutual aid" to assure their continued contribution to the common defense. Alliance solidarity becomes a factor in the handling of intergroup disputes, and the danger of alienating a member of the military coalition must often be weighed in the formulation of other aspects of foreign policy.

Alliances—especially the multilateral variety—have also become highly organized, with regular meetings of the parties, operating budgets, and supporting secretariat staff. Some are integrally related to a more comprehensive regional organization. The Organization of American States, the Arab League, and the Organization of African Unity have alliance features, but they also deal with a broad range of economic, social, and political problems. The North Atlantic Alliance gave rise to a military organization independent of any multifunctional regional structure, but NATO collaboration has encouraged proponents of the Atlantic Community idea to press for the establishment of parallel institutions for cooperation in nonmilitary fields. Other regional military pacts have also fostered economic and social cooperation.

In this chapter our attention will be directed to a number of multilateral alliances which are, or function within the framework of, regional organizations. The term *regional* is adopted in deference to common usage and to the United Nations Charter, which makes specific provision in Chapter

VIII for regional security arrangements. One should recognize, however, that national interest rather than geography is the basis of membership. Most regional organizations have a particular geographic region as their focus of interest or membership, but not necessarily. The concept of a North Atlantic region had to be stretched considerably to cover all the territory from Alaska to Turkey; and the Commonwealth, sometimes grouped with regional organizations, has members on all habitable continents. The Arab League forms a contiguous if not very compact area of the Middle East and North Africa, but the criterion for membership is status as an independent Arab state rather than geographical location. The Southeast Asia Treaty Organization includes the United States, Britain, and France among its members, although they are all located thousands of miles from Southeast Asia. The regional designation is apt, however, because all of the members have a recognized interest in the defense of the treaty area which is limited to South and Southeast Asia and the Southwest Pacific. These facts suggest that geographical connections may give rise to interest, but interest transcends geographical considerations in the formation of alliances.

REGIONAL ARRANGEMENTS AND THE UN SYSTEM

The United Nations Charter places primary responsibility for international peace and security upon the shoulders of the world organization, with regional organizations playing a secondary role. Relevant Charter provisions focus on three central issues—peaceful settlement, self-defense, and enforcement action.[1] Regional associations are expressly encouraged to take the initiative in settling local disputes, subject to the authority of the Security Council to concern itself if necessary. The right of individual states or regional groupings to make an unfettered military response to armed attack is also clearly established by recognition of "the inherent right of individual or collective self-defense." The provision for collective self-defense was written with the developing Inter-American security system in mind and at the insistence of the American states. Nevertheless, the primacy of the United Nations is preserved. All action taken in self-defense must be immediately reported to the Security Council, the Council retains full authority to take any concurrent action it finds necessary, and the right of unrestricted self-defense terminates when the Security Council has taken "measures necessary to maintain international peace and security." In the field of enforcement action, as distinguished from self-defense, the Security Council's predominance is even more forcefully established. With the exception of measures against the enemy states of World War II, the Charter states categorically that "no enforcement action shall be taken under

[1] Enforcement action is essentially synonymous with the use of sanctions, whether diplomatic, economic and financial, or military.

regional arrangements or by regional agencies without the authorization of the Security Council."

The relationship between the United Nations and regional security arrangements as set forth in the Charter may thus be summarized: (1) Settlement of disputes through regional agencies is encouraged, but subject to the authority of the Security Council to intervene as it sees fit. (2) Regional action in self-defense against armed attack is authorized, but not to the exclusion of concurrent UN action and only until the Security Council takes measures necessary to restore peace and security. (3) With the exception of self-defense and measures against the ex-enemy states, regional agencies are not to undertake enforcement action without prior authorization of the Security Council.[2]

The Charter plan for a world security system did not work out. Because of bitter East-West rivalries the Security Council never acquired its military punch, and members utilized Article 51 to justify expansion of collective self-defense arrangements all out of proportion to the puny enforcement arm of the general system. The United States led the retreat to regional security and regional autonomy. From the Pact of Rio de Janeiro (1947) to NATO (1949) to ANZUS (1951) to SEATO (1954) to CENTO (1955) and numerous bilateral military pacts, the United States has become the hub of the most complex and extensive system of alliances the world has ever known. Other states have followed suit in a more modest way with such arrangements as the Western European Union, the Arab League, and the Warsaw Pact, as well as a host of bilateral alliances. There is a question of how much security the regional and bilateral arrangements have provided, but their establishment has brought about a drastic change in the security system envisioned at San Francisco.

In contrast to the collective self-defense provisions of Article 51, which have been stretched beyond recognition, the Security Council's control over enforcement action under Article 53 has been almost completely devitalized. The leader of the assault upon Article 53 has been the Organization of American States, which has not only authorized sanctions without the provocation of armed attack but has brashly asserted its legal right to do so. When economic and diplomatic sanctions were laid against the Trujillo regime and Castro's Cuba, the United States assured the Security Council, with little historical accuracy, that nonmilitary sanctions were not "enforcement action" within the meaning of Article 53. When the OAS Council authorized the use of armed force if necessary during the Cuban missile

---

[2] If there is any doubt on this point, the reader should consider the "supremacy clause" contained in Article 103: "In the event of a conflict between the obligations of the Members of the United Nations under the present Charter and their obligations under any other international agreement, their obligations under the present Charter shall prevail."

crisis of October, 1962, the United States did not even try to reconcile OAS action with Article 53 but rested its case on the general grounds of OAS autonomy within the hemisphere. OAS retroactive endorsement of United States military intervention in the 1965 Dominican revolt drove another nail into the coffin of Article 53. In defending this action before the Security Council, Ambassador Adlai Stevenson argued that the Dominican force was not an "enforcement action" but a "peace-keeping operation" like UNEF and ONUC.

This development is rooted in practical reality, if not in legal principle, and the right of "regional autonomy" has been exercised elsewhere. The Organization of African Unity did not obtain Security Council authorization to initiate its program of economic and political warfare upon South Africa and Portugal's colonial regime. The Arab League has never been deterred by concern for Article 53 from taking diplomatic and economic sanctions against Israel. Soviet suppression of the Hungarian revolt in 1956 without serious hindrance by either the United States or the United Nations was another manifestation of the same reality—namely, that order will be enforced in a region by and on behalf of those having the power to enforce it. Even in 1945, the Charter prescription for centralized supervision of security functions was incongruent with the existing distribution of power and developing conflicts of national interest. Regionalism has since proved better able to accommodate the divergent interests and capabilities.

THE WESTERN ALLIANCE SYSTEM: NATO

The decision of France in 1966 to withdraw from the military organization of the North Atlantic Alliance could be a development of far reaching significance. France continues to value the commitments of mutual aid in event of attack and the arrangements for high-level political consultation, as evidenced by its desire to remain a party to the treaty and participate in meetings of the NATO Council. But President DeGaulle's action signifies his belief that a peacetime military organization of the Atlantic powers no longer serves the interest of European and world security.

The possible consequences of French dissociation from NATO are many. It could lead to the atrophy and dissolution of the whole NATO military structure. This is unlikely, however, given the premium which the United States, Germany, and some other members of the alliance continue to place upon it. The crisis undoubtedly will lead to a reexamination of the internal workings of NATO, but one cannot predict at this point whether any reorganization will be fundamental or simply the minimal adaptation to the requirements of operating without France and French facilities. It almost certainly will lead to a reappraisal of NATO objectives and the relationships of NATO powers to one another and to the world. Whether this will bring more genuine sharing of burdens and responsibilities for decision-making, or fresh and imaginative approaches to detente with the Soviet Union, also remains to be seen.

The withdrawal of France has placed a great question mark over NATO. But this should not obscure the fact that NATO is still the kingpin of the Western alliance system and by far the most impressive of regional alliances.

Origin and Purpose

NATO, at its inception, represented a collective response to the threat of Soviet military aggression in Europe. In 1947 Britain and France had signed the fifty-year Dunkirk treaty of alliance and mutual assistance, directed against the revival of German aggression. The irrelevance of this commitment to the immediate security needs of Western Europe became distressingly obvious when the democratic Czech regime fell before a Soviet-backed coup in February, 1948. In the lengthening shadow of Red dominance in Eastern Europe, Britain and France met in Brussels with representatives of the three Benelux countries to create a wider treaty of mutual assistance aimed at "resisting any policy of aggression." The Brussels Treaty, signed in March, 1948, also envisaged the strengthening of economic, social, and cultural ties. This evidence of European cooperation, coupled with growing American perception of a Soviet threat, sparked a transatlantic dialogue on problems of Atlantic security which culminated in the signing of the North Atlantic Treaty on April 4, 1949, by the United States, Canada, the five Brussels powers, Denmark, Iceland, Italy, Norway, and Portugal. The twelve were joined by Greece and Turkey in 1952, thus extending the Atlantic Community into Asia, and the Federal Republic of Germany was added in 1955.

The essential object of the alliance is to give Western Europe the benefit of the American deterrent against Soviet military attack, and to provide mutual support in case an attack should nevertheless occur either in Europe or North America. No one has yet demonstrated that the Soviet Union ever contemplated a direct military attack upon Europe or North America, but this does not belie the apprehension which then existed and still exists to some extent. Although reference is made to encouraging economic collaboration and promoting friendly relations generally, the principal treaty commitments relate to military security. All members agree (1) to "develop their individual and collective capacity to resist armed attack," (2) to "consult" whenever the security of any of them is threatened, and (3) to "assist" any member subjected to armed attack in Europe or North America. The commitment to give assistance in the event of armed attack is limited by two important qualifications. The protective blanket does not extend to possessions of the treaty members outside of Europe, North America, and the North Atlantic area as defined in the treaty (which technically excludes

Hawaii, among other areas); and each party is bound only to take "such action as it deems necessary," which after all is not a legal obligation to do very much. Obviously the extent of the real commitment is determined by the continuance of a common interest and the technical arrangements that may be developed for the joint use of force.

Structure

Aside from the revolutionary decision of the United States to accept permanent entanglement with the destiny of Europe, the most impressive thing about the North Atlantic Alliance is the complex organizational super-structure that has sprouted from the treaty base. The original treaty, of fourteen short articles and a brief preamble, provided only for a "council . . . so organized as to be able to meet promptly at any time," a "defense committee," and such other "subsidiary bodies as may be necessary." Today the "subsidiary bodies" include a civilian secretariat staff in excess of 900, a separate military advisory and command structure, an extensive network of council committees and numerous special operating agencies. The chart of NATO organization appearing in Figure 11-1 undoubtedly hides some of the complexity of the structure, but it may give an idea of the relationship of the various organs to one another.

The North Atlantic Council is the political heart of the system, con-stituting both its legislative and executive arm. The Council makes alliance policy and is also responsible for its execution. There is no treaty provision for voting, other than a requirement of unanimity for the admission of new members, and decisions are reached by discussion and consensus. On matters such as the budget, election of a Secretary-General, admission of new members, or major policy questions affecting the whole alliance, consensus means unanimity. In other instances it may simply mean that unconvinced members are willing to let the others cooperate in policy matters of interest to them. In its stress upon consensus, NATO is even more sovereignty-oriented than the United Nations, which provides for some form of majority rule in all of its organs. One might assume that the relatively greater homogeneity within the NATO community would favor the exten-sion of majoritarianism, but member states have generally not been willing to give up their individual veto in matters vitally affecting their security.

The routine work of the Council is conducted by permanent representa-tives of ambassadorial rank maintained at NATO headquarters in Paris, meeting at least weekly. The more important issues tend to be reserved for the ministerial meetings of the Council, usually held in December and May, at which foreign ministers or finance or defense ministers, or all of them, may be in attendance. Heads of state may also meet in NATO Council session, but so far this has occurred only once, in December, 1957. In the interest of frank and free discussion, the Council deliberates in private and

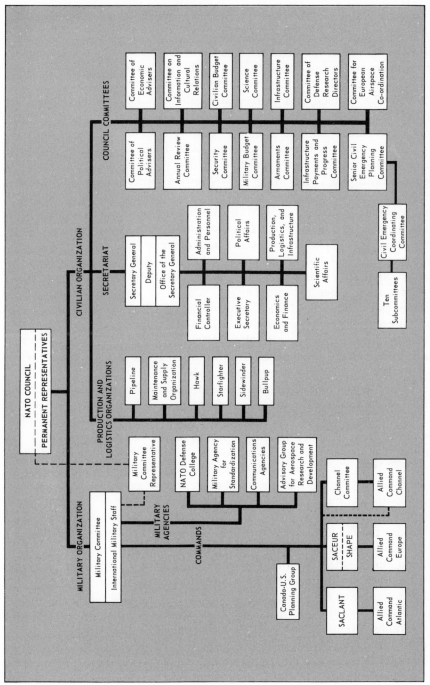

FIGURE 11-1. NATO organization chart. Liaison and coordination for certain operational matters.

its proceedings are never published, except for an official communiqué issued at the end of a conference. The Council is assisted by a large number of standing committees consisting of NATO government officials who are usually expert in the technical work of the committees.

Under the Council is a secretariat headed by a Secretary-General appointed for an indefinite period. The 1949 treaty said nothing about a permanent secretariat, and none was created until 1952. The work of the secretariat is now organized in seven major divisions, as indicated in Figure 11-1. The secretariat serves meetings of the Council and its committees and performs the usual study and reporting functions on political and economic matters of concern to the alliance. Like any public organization concerned with survival, it has an information service and press section to look out for public relations. It is also careful to maintain political liaison with national NATO delegations and with other international organizations, both governmental and nongovernmental. Since 1956 the Secretary-General has presided at working sessions of the Council and has been specifically empowered to offer his good offices in case of disputes among NATO powers (an outgrowth of the Cyprus dispute). Close contact with governmental points of view is probably facilitated by the practice of seconding national officials to serve with the NATO secretariat for terms of two or three years. At the professional and executive level, the majority of secretariat officials are short-term appointees seconded from national service.

The military command structure is kept separate from the civilian organization of the secretariat and Council committees. Integration of civilian and military policy within NATO, to the extent that it occurs, takes place primarily at the Council level. At the top of the military hierarchy is the Military Committee, a chiefs-of-staff counterpart to the Council, but officially responsible to the Council. Meetings at the chiefs-of-staff level occur at least twice a year, and in the interim permanent representatives carry on the day-to-day business of military planning at their Washington headquarters.[3]

Before the defection of France, the Military Committee's executive arm was a three-member Standing Group, composed of Britain, France, and the United States, with offices, appropriately enough, in the Pentagon. Two-way communication with the NATO Council was provided by a Standing Group Representative to the Council. The Standing Group also supervised a number of special military agencies, which are discussed briefly in the following paragraphs. French withdrawal from the military organization, and consequently from the Standing Group, provided the occasion for a rethinking of its role. A number of the smaller members of NATO had at times voiced dissatisfaction with the elitist composition of the Group, and its working

---

[3] Iceland, which has no army, is permitted civilian representation on the Military Committee.

relationships with the larger Military Committee left something to be desired. As a result, the Standing Group was abolished and its functions transferred to the Military Committee. The Standing Group Representative to the NATO Council became the Military Committee Representative.

Under the Military Committee are the three military commands (Allied Command Europe, Allied Command Atlantic, and Allied Command Channel) and the Canada-US Regional Planning Group which is responsible for North American defense.[4] Of the four, only the European command has military forces assigned in time of peace although forces for the other commands are earmarked. In 1962 the United States made a show of assigning five earmarked Polaris submarines to the Atlantic command, but the transfer was only on paper—the subs remained under the control of the Commander of the United States Atlantic Fleet, to whom they were assigned in his capacity as SACLANT. Even the forces "assigned" to the European headquarters (SHAPE) remain under the residual control of national general staffs, who, as France and others have demonstrated, may withdraw them at will. SHAPE acquires full command of the assigned units only when war breaks out; in the meantime it must secure national government consent to the deployment of troops. "In effect," as one commentator asserts, "the NATO Command is not an instrument of command but an instrument of high-level coordination and persuasion."[5] Nevertheless, SHAPE has functioned as an effective joint command and military planning operation, exercising day-to-day control over as many as twenty-four divisions from seven countries.

In addition to these major structures of civilian and military cooperation, a number of "specialized agencies" have been created to administer operating programs in production and supply and to perform certain functions of continuing coordination. On the civilian side, subsidiary to the NATO Council, are the Central Europe Operating Agency (to manage the fuel pipelines); the NATO Maintenance and Supply Organization (to provide a common system for supply of spare parts); and the Hawk, Sidewinder,

---

[4] The Commanders are referred to, respectively, as Supreme Allied Commander, Europe (SACEUR); Supreme Allied Commander, Atlantic (SACLANT); and the Channel Committee. The European command headquarters (SHAPE, for Supreme Headquarters Allied Powers, Europe) serves Allied Command Europe (ACE). Commenting on the "proliferation of organizations with undecipherable abbreviations," Timothy W. Stanley observed with tongue in cheek that one "can hardly be blamed if he perpetrates such whimsical horrors as

> ELLA needs AGARD ENCAse
> her SHAPE makes men
> forget ERFA ACE."

NATO in Transition (New York: Praeger, for the Council on Foreign Relations, 1965), p. 387n.

[5] Philip E. Jacob and Alexine L. Atherton, *The Dynamics of International Organization* (Homewood, Ill.: The Dorsey Press, 1965), p. 142.

Bullpup, and Starfighter Production Organizations (to coordinate European production of F-104G Starfighter aircraft and the three varieties of missiles). Agencies established on the military side of the organization chart, under the supervision of the Standing Group, include the NATO Defense College in Rome which enrolls between fifty and sixty senior officers and civilian officials in each of its two terms a year; a Military Agency for Standardization (of military procedure and material); a number of communications agencies; and an Advisory Group for Aerospace, Research and Development.

Decision-Making

The complexity of the structure virtually ensures that patterns of influence and decision-making within the organization likewise will be complex. One must, first of all, come to grips with the fact of United States predominance, based primarily on economic and military might. The economic renascence of Europe and the apparent subsidence of the Soviet threat, have decreased the relative dependence of Europe upon the United States and hence their susceptibility to American leadership. But American predominance especially in military strength remains a continuing reality. American predominance is echoed in press accounts of NATO deliberations and indeed is imbedded in the institutional practice of the organization. It is no accident that the Military Committee, the Canadian-US Planning Group, and the Atlantic Command (and formerly the Standing Group) have headquarters in the United States, or that SACLANT and SACEUR have always been Americans.

Predominance, however, is a far cry from domination, as is amply illustrated by the European rebuff to the Multilateral Nuclear Force so strongly advocated by the United States. The absence of majority voting, as well as the whole concept of a peacetime partnership among democratic, independent states, assures that the approach to decision-making in the organization shall be consensual. Attempts by the United States to dictate from its strength would kill the spirit of cooperation on which the partnership must feed and alienate the European political support on which the United States has come to depend in its dealings with other parts of the world. The position of the United States as the most powerful member of the coalition may be an important factor for other members to consider; but they remain free agents nevertheless. French President DeGaulle's decision to require the removal of NATO installations from France shows how far freedom of action within NATO can go.

The need for consensus among such self-consciously sovereign partners poses a real challenge to the institutions for political decision-making. As one careful observer has noted, NATO's organization reflects "the inevitable immobilism of 13- to 15-member participation in all activities" and makes frustration "the almost universal experience" of anyone who really tries

"to get something done quickly within the NATO environment." [6] The difficulty of engineering consensus has enhanced the role of secretariat officials
and technical experts in the decision-making process. The Secretary-General
presides at sessions of the Council and in 1956 was formally commissioned
to use his good offices in intra-NATO disputes. This was, in a sense, official
recognition and formal institutionalization of a role already assumed by the
Secretary-General as a participant in the policy-making process. The value
of the secretariat both as an intermediary in the search for negotiated solutions and as a spokesman for collective interest had already been demonstrated. The NATO Council has also regularly utilized the expedient of
shunting difficult problems to committees or to technical experts in the
hope of reaching a compromise solution in an atmosphere somewhat freer
of political considerations. Although the Council cannot delegate its power
of decision, the fact of agreement at a technical level, or the existence of
a proposal bearing the experts' stamp of approval, may create pressures for
acceptance by the Council, especially if the alternative is continued immobilism in the face of crisis.

Another problem arises from the separation of military planning from
political decision-making of a broader character. Theoretically, the NATO
Council, a civilian body, stands at the apex of both the civil and military
branches of the NATO hierarchy. But, practically speaking, the formulation
of military policy takes place almost entirely within military channels,
and "the military and civil channels meet only at the highest level, where
it is hard to effect modifications." [7] Within the military hierarchy, SHAPE
has been the dominant center of military planning. SHAPE has had the advantage of being closer to operating problems than the Military Committee
or the Standing Group, and it has been unhampered by the need to
reconcile the views of fifteen governments (Military Committee) or even
three governments (Standing Group) before taking a position. SHAPE
has thus tended to supplant or bypass the Military Committee and the
Standing Group in giving military advice to the Council, and under General
Lauris Norstad (1956–63) SHAPE in fact "attained a high degree of independence from national views." [8] At the top level, the NATO Council lacks
the kind of unity and forcefulness that enables a government to exercise
firm control over its military arm, and as a result political and military
problems tend to be approached in isolation from one another in the crucial
exploratory stages of planning. As Buchan noted in 1963,

> The NATO Council in Paris has little authority over the military planning
> of either the Standing Group and the Military Committee in Washington

[6] Stanley, *op. cit.*, p. 376. The two smallest members, Iceland and Luxembourg, often
do not participate in deliberations unless they are directly concerned.
[7] Alastair Buchan, *NATO in the 1960's* (New York: Praeger, 1963), p. 125.
[8] Stanley, *op. cit.*, p. 387.

or of their most dynamic subordinate command, Supreme Headquarters Europe. The Council is consulted, it is informed, it is advised by the military authorities as occasion serves, but it does not wield a real authority over the work of the international military institutions of the Alliance that is in any way comparable to that which national cabinets wield over national military planning.[9]

All this does not imply any usurpation of authority by the NATO military staffs, or cast any doubt upon their ability and integrity. It does mean, however, that NATO is substantially denied the integration of political, economic, and military planning which coalition defense in a nuclear age seems to demand.

Appraisal

In many ways the accomplishments of the North Atlantic Alliance have been impressive. In 1949, NATO was "essentially a traditional guaranty pact, simply committing its members to come to each other's assistance and calling for minimal peacetime collaboration." It has since evolved into "an integrated military-political organization, exacting unprecedented peace-time contributions and commitments." [10] Elaborate consultative arrangements keep NATO members in constant consultation on NATO problems.[11] In military matters SHAPE has become a dynamic instrument of collective planning and a viable joint military command giving effective direction to several hundred thousand troops of differing nationalities. In practice, the national contingents have not been mixed below the divisional level, but they have trained in joint maneuvers and engaged in a fairly widespread exchange of officers. Supporting the joint command in Europe is an infrastructure program which includes some 220 all-weather airfields, 5,600 miles of fuel pipelines, and 27,000 miles of communications and signals networks as well as numerous naval facilities, radar warning installations, missile sites, and related projects. The infrastructure facilities represent a truly integrated aspect of the NATO program, used jointly by NATO members and administered by the NATO command.[12] In addition to these there are such NATO agencies as the Hawk and Sidewinder production organizations, the common maintenance supply service, and the NATO Defense College. Another notable feature of NATO is the

---

[9] Buchan, *op. cit.*, p. 115.

[10] Robert E. Osgood, *NATO: The Entangling Alliance* (Chicago: University of Chicago Press, 1962), p. 23.

[11] In addition to official consultations an unofficial NATO Parliamentarians' Conference has met annually since 1955.

[12] The pipeline is an exception. It is managed on the "civilian" side by a Central Europe Operating Agency (CEOA), responsible to the Central Europe Pipeline Office (CEPO) and the Central Europe Pipeline Policy Committee (CEPPC) which in turn are subsidiary to the NATO Council.

Annual Review inaugurated in 1952 (put on a three-year basis in 1962), which provides a basis for determining burden sharing within the organization through the exchange of detailed information on national military and economic programs. The contribution that all this had made to the security of the North Atlantic area remains largely speculative since no one can count the battles which, on account of the NATO deterrent, were not fought. But the organization and its works constitute a notable achievement in international cooperation.

Our appraisal of NATO would be one-sided if no further reference were made to the very real problems besetting the alliance. There is a widespread recognition that the NATO partners are drifting apart, that military considerations are not adequately meshed with the politics and economics of the Atlantic community, that the organization lacks clear-cut purpose and sense of direction. DeGaulle's attempt to retain the benefits of the defense commitment while unloading the burdens of participation in an integrated defense effort is the most striking symptom of the ailment.

The reasons for this condition are manifold. In part, NATO is a victim of success. European economic recovery and the rebuilding of European defenses, combined with an apparent change in Soviet tactics, have substantially reduced the fear of a Soviet attack in Europe. The threat and the feeling of mutual dependence no longer have the urgency they had in 1949. In such an environment, disunity thrives.

As we have already noted, NATO also has organizational difficulties. The problem is not so much the proliferation of committees and agencies as it is the lack of integration, particularly as between military and civilian planning. A single integrated hierarchy would go a long way toward mitigating the difficulties that arise from failure to unite political, economic, and military aspects of policy at an early enough stage in planning to provide an optimum blend. Many supporters of the Atlantic Community idea suggest that the problem is not merely one of better integration within NATO but one of broadening the NATO base to include wider cooperation in political, economic, and cultural affairs. There is room for debate whether NATO should attempt to do more than it is doing at present, or simply attempt to do its job better; but in either event, structural revisions are being urged from many quarters.

The structural shortcomings of NATO are related to a much more deepseated malaise: lack of agreement upon the basic guide posts for the Alliance, whether expressed in terms of military strategy or larger political considerations. There is no accepted military doctrine that would justify the goal of thirty ready divisions in Europe, as opposed to twenty-two or twenty-five or thirty-five. There is no agreed principle governing the relative importance of conventional and nuclear forces, or the tactical and strategic uses of nuclear weapons, or even the appropriate force contributions of individual states, assuming a given overall level of forces. In a broader perspective, there is no doctrine that clearly sets forth the relationship between the defense of the Atlantic area and the defense of other parts of the world to which individual members are committed. And, since military strategy is linked with problems of economic and political cooperation, the lack of consensus in these areas inhibits the constructive evolution of a viable NATO defense posture.

The control of nuclear weapons has been a persistent source of irritation within the alliance. Despite all the talk about an equal partnership, the United States has thus far been unwilling to share control of nuclear weapons with its allies on terms acceptable to them.[13] President DeGaulle has reacted to the American nuclear monopoly by building an independent French nuclear deterrent. Germany has been perhaps the most active proponent of shared control within NATO, in part at least because of the Western European Union treaty obligations not to produce chemical, biological, or nuclear weapons. A NATO nuclear force would provide Germany a legitimate voice, if only a shared one, in the control of nuclear weapons. The United States proposal for a multilateral force (MLF), consisting of international ("mixed-manned") crews on vessels armed with Polaris missiles, was enthusiastically supported by Germany, despite the fact that the last finger on the safety catch was still American. Objections to the expense, feasibility, and reality of shared control—especially from France—killed the idea, and no acceptable substitute has yet been produced. But the problem still remains.

The lack of common direction finally comes to rest upon one fundamental reality that all international organizations must face—the insistence of each state upon the right to pursue its own self-interest. This lies at the root of both the military and political problems nagging at NATO. The NATO command cannot be sure of troops once assigned, because members are free to withdraw their units at any time. From 1959 through 1965, France gradually dissociated itself from the integrated NATO command by withdrawing the French Mediterranean fleet from NATO operational control, removing naval officers from staff posts in NATO naval commands, barring American-controlled NATO nuclear warheads from French soil, and deciding to use a smaller caliber of ammunition for light weapons than the one agreed upon by NATO. In 1966 President DeGaulle took the ultimate step of requiring that all integrated NATO facilities, including SHAPE, be removed from French soil or be placed under French control; and the last

---

[13] In December, 1966, the NATO Council created a Nuclear Defense Affairs Committee (open to all NATO members) with a smaller, expert planning subgroup of seven members (U.S., U.K., W. Germany, Italy, and three rotating seats). The object was to give NATO allies a voice in the deployment and control of American nuclear weapons, and in crises that might involve the decision to use such weapons, without an actual transfer of nuclear hardware or elimination of the United States' veto on decisions. The precise role of these bodies remains for future definition.

of French divisions in Germany were withdrawn from the European Command. Although DeGaulle's actions may seem to many to be unenlightened, they are no more self-interested than the United States' insistence upon maintaining a nuclear deterrent free from effective outside control, or the unwillingness of other NATO members to spend as much for defense, proportionately, as the United States does.

Divergent national interests also give rise to problems of a more general character affecting the solidarity of the alliance. The primacy of national interest has led many Europeans to speculate whether, in the age of the balance of terror, the United States would risk nuclear destruction of its own cities by responding to a Soviet attack upon Europe. Conversely, some have shuddered at the thought that the United States might use its nuclear weapons prematurely or unwisely. Unity has more than once been sapped by clashing policies toward self-determination of particular groups of colonial peoples. The Suez crisis, which placed the United States squarely against Britain and France on a matter vital to the interests of both of the latter, administered a blow from which the alliance has never fully recovered. The heavy American commitment in Viet Nam raises misgivings among some alliance partners concerning both the diversion of resources and the general policy issue involved. NATO will probably continue to exist in some form as long as there is recognition of a mutual, external threat. But, like the UN system of security, it must continually come to terms with national freedom of action.

WESTERN EUROPEAN UNION

As a means of joint defense, the 1948 Brussels Pact between Britain, France, and the Benelux powers became unnecessary with the creation of NATO. In 1951 the Brussels organization formally handed over its defense responsibilities to NATO and retired to the background as a forum for discussion. In 1954, however, the organization was refurbished and given a new lease on life as a means of controlling German rearmament. France had just rejected the European Defense Community, thus killing the prospect of German remilitarization within the framework of a European army, and an alternative had to be found. The pressure was great because of American demands that NATO requirements for ground troops in central Europe be met with German divisions. The outcome was the Western European Union, which was in effect the Brussels Pact extended to include Germany and Italy and given arms control functions. WEU thus became the vehicle for facilitating controlled German rearmament, and Germany was admitted to NATO the following year.

As the WEU now stands, its members are still committed to give one another "all the military and other aid and assistance in their power" in the event of armed attack upon one of them in Europe. This is noticeably stronger than the NATO pledge for each state to take "such action as it deems necessary, including the use of armed force." Operational responsibilities for defense have all been assumed by NATO, however, and activities in the social and cultural fields were relinquished to the Council of Europe in 1960. The remaining functions of WEU relate to the control of armaments and armed force levels, and the discussion of defense problems. Even in the area of arms control, little of practical consequence has been accomplished because the emphasis has been upon increasing the levels of armaments and armed forces rather than limiting and controlling them. Nevertheless the organization has extensive powers of inspection to ascertain compliance with agreed arms levels and to enforce the ban on German production of atomic, biological, and chemical weapons. The organization also considers itself competent to discuss problems of European security, to give advice, and to encourage members to undertake larger defense responsibilities.

The organization of WEU consists of a Council that meets in London and an Assembly that meets in Strasbourg. Representation on the Council is normally an ex officio function of WEU ambassadors to London, and the Assembly is composed of the members of parliament who represent the WEU powers in the Consultative Assembly of the Council of Europe. The Assembly is served by a small WEU secretariat in Paris. Two subsidiary agencies of the Council—the Agency for Control of Armaments and the Standing Armaments Committee—are also located in Paris.

The Council is the formal decision-making body and decisions must be unanimous unless otherwise specified. Some important questions relating to arms control are taken by a two-thirds or simple majority. The Assembly may only discuss and recommend, but the members of national parliaments who comprise its membership have not hesitated to speak out on many policy matters, generally in support of a European rather than a national viewpoint. Speaking and voting as individuals, and responsible only in a general way to the national parliaments that appoint them, they have felt free to urge their personal views upon the Council. The Assembly has assumed the right to review Council reports and has secured the cooperation of Council members in meeting regularly with the Assembly to respond to written and oral questions in the manner of the interpolation procedure utilized by European parliaments.

In 1954, WEU achieved importance as a means of securing French consent to German rearmament. At the present time its significance lies primarily in providing a framework for political consultation between Britain and the Six of the European Community. The Assembly also has importance as the only parliamentary structure among official European intergovernmental organizations having the right to discuss defense activities. It has in fact offered constructive recommendations for concerted policies on such matters as the maintenance of better balanced and integrated conventional forces, more equitable sharing of costs of troop maintenance and supply, standardization of arms, and common control of nuclear weapons. The Arms Control Agency has potential significance, particularly in view of the fact that it may present to the Council questions that can be decided by a simple majority. But France's rejection of its treaty obligation to submit the level of its nuclear weapons stocks to a majority decision of the Council casts doubt on the viability of the whole arms control system. Suggestions have been made that WEU be revitalized as a genuine European defense organization within the NATO framework, or even that WEU be made an independent nuclear power. The major powers have not taken kindly to these suggestions.

SECURITY IN THE AMERICAS

Organization for security in the Americas is a response to the threat of external aggression; but even more, it is a response to intrahemispheric security needs and the search for an alternative to unilateral intervention. The renunciation of unilateral intervention by the United States in the early 1930's was a "Good Neighborly" gesture that paved the way for periodic consultation of foreign ministers and a genuinely cooperative security policy as World War II approached. Early declarations of common purpose spoke of unity against external aggression, but near the end of the war the commitment was broadened to include aggression launched from within the hemisphere as well. In 1947 the obligations of mutual aid and consultation were placed on a treaty basis by the Inter-American Treaty of Reciprocal Assistance (Rio Pact).

Other institutions of regional cooperation had also been developing over the years, beginning with the first Inter-American Conference in 1889–90. An outgrowth of the first conference was a permanent Commercial Bureau of the American Republics, subsequently renamed the Pan American Union. The threads of Inter-American cooperation were drawn together in the Charter of the Organization of American States, drafted at Bogota in 1948. In that document the Inter-American Conference of nineteenth century origin was designated as the "supreme organ" of the OAS; the periodic meeting of foreign ministers was formally designated as an Organ of Consultation to deal with "problems of an urgent nature"; the Pan American Union was incorporated as the secretariat of the new structure; and the Rio Pact security obligations were reiterated. A Council of permanent representatives in Washington was established to provide continuing supervision of the organization between conferences.[14]

[14] In 1948 the OAS embraced every independent state in the hemisphere except Canada—a total of twenty-one republics. In the mid-1960's the admission of Jamaica and of Trinidad and Tobago was under consideration.

In its security objectives the Inter-American system differs somewhat from the North Atlantic Alliance. NATO has always been directed specifically against the Soviet threat. The Rio Pact, while intended to bring the Latin American Republics within the protective military umbrella of the United States, was not drafted to meet a pressing threat from any particular outside source and is directed against potential foes generally. A still more fundamental difference is the element of collective security in the Rio Pact, that is, the concern with aggression by one member state against another. In practice the collective security provisions of the Pact have affected inter-American relations far more than provision for mutual defense against external aggression.

The Rio Pact and the OAS Charter also go farther than the North Atlantic Treaty in their specific concern with "aggression which is not an armed attack" or, indeed, "any other fact or situation that might endanger the peace of America." In objective, the system stands poised to meet any threat of aggression, direct or indirect, arising from within or outside the hemisphere.

The actual commitments, as one might suspect, are more limited than the objectives. In case of armed attack, each state is bound to "assist in meeting the attack" but is left free to "determine the immediate measures which it may individually take" until a meeting of the organization decides upon collective measures. For acts of aggression other than armed attacks, parties are bound only to consult. However—and this is a vital distinction from the NATO commitment—a two-thirds vote of members may authorize collective sanctions ranging from the recall of chiefs of diplomatic missions to the use of armed force. A safety valve is provided by a proviso that no state can be required to use armed force without its consent; but even with this loophole the Rio Pact is the strongest legal obligation the United States has assumed for the defense of other states. Theoretically, the United States could be obligated against its will to break off diplomatic relations or sever all economic ties with an aggressor.

The structure for implementing the mutual defense provisions of the Rio Pact and the OAS Charter is relatively simple. When an emergency arises, the Treaty calls for consultations by ministers of foreign affairs or any other body that might in the future be agreed upon. The OAS Charter designates ministers of foreign affairs as the Organ of Consultation, but the OAS Council may serve provisionally as the Organ of Consultation if quick action is needed pending a meeting of the ministers.

The only permanent military apparatus is the Inter-American Defense Board, a body created in 1942 to coordinate planning for hemispheric defense. The Board was given continuing status by the OAS Charter, although its fundamental character remained unchanged. The predominant role of the United States is institutionalized by regulations which provide that the chairman, the director of the staff, and the secretary shall always be members of the armed forces of the host country (the Board meets in Washington). The Board's authority is very limited. It can deal only with defense against threats from outside the hemisphere, thus avoiding the delicate problem of planning for the defense of one Latin American state against attack by another. Its recommendations are not binding on any state, and it has no authority to organize armed forces or establish a unified command. Mutual assistance in military equipment takes place outside the organization, through bilateral pacts concluded by the United States with most Latin American countries. In 1962, the occasion of its twentieth anniversary, the Board established an Inter-American Defense College. If the United States proposal for a permanent OAS peace-keeping force were to be adopted the Defense Board might well acquire more significant advisory functions.

The predominance of the United States, already observed in NATO, is still more pronounced in the Inter-American system. In matters relating to hemispheric defense, the United States position remains essentially unchallenged because no other country has the resources to meet a serious threat. In intrahemispheric problems, with which the system has been primarily concerned, the United States is still influential but cannot ignore the views of Latin American states. The expulsion of Cuba in 1962 and the creation of the OAS force for the Dominican Republic were carried by the bare minimum requirement of fourteen votes; and the United States has not yet been able to enlist sufficient support for the establishment of a permanent peace-keeping force. Pressure has its limits and if it is indiscriminately applied it might destroy the measure of voluntary cooperation essential to the long-run effectiveness of the whole Inter-American system.

As a regional security arrangement, the OAS has taken a militant verbal stand against international Communism, but otherwise has been of only marginal significance in dealing with extrahemispheric threats. It has made notable efforts, however, to deal with problems arising within the hemisphere. In numerous instances the OAS has helped to stem armed conflict between American states and provided machinery for pacific settlement. As earlier noted, the OAS has also experimented in the use of sanctions against wrongdoers within the hemisphere. The first instance occurred in 1960 when the foreign ministers of the OAS voted to apply diplomatic and partial economic sanctions against the Dominican Republic in retaliation for acts of indirect aggression against Venezuela. In January, 1962, the foreign ministers expelled the Castro government from the organization and voted to impose limited economic sanctions upon Cuba. In July, 1964, the economic sanctions were extended and members were ordered to break diplomatic relations with Cuba—a measure with which all but Mexico complied. At the height of the Cuban missile crisis in October, 1962, the

OAS Council went to the full extent of authorizing the use of armed force if necessary in support of the United States naval blockade of Cuba to enforce the removal of Soviet missiles.

In the wake of the April, 1965, Dominican revolt, the OAS Council made an epoch-shattering decision to establish the first Inter-American peace force. Unfortunately for the prestige and autonomy of the organization, the decision came as the tail to the kite of massive unilateral intervention by the United States with more than 20,000 troops, in obvious violation of the OAS Charter. The decision permitted United States marines to wear the OAS armband and brought 2,500 Latin American soldiers, mostly from Brazil, to share the peace-keeping chore with them. This gave the military holding operation a façade of multilateralism and made the diplomatic position of the United States more tenable, although much of Latin America and the world remained unconvinced that the United States actions had been justified either by the threat to American lives and property or the fear of Communist infiltration of the Dominican revolutionary movement.

Within the organization there remained great uneasiness over the implied endorsement of military interventionism, a policy traditionally anathema to all of Latin America. The decision to create the force had in fact been approved by a bare two-thirds majority, under heavy pressure from the United States, and only by counting the vote of the Dominican representative—a rather singular circumstance since the nonexistence of a viable government in the Dominican Republic was the ostensible reason for creating the force at all. The deep-seated Latin American aversion to sanctioning the principle of intervention, whether unilateral or collective, has thus far thwarted United States proposals to establish a permanent OAS force.

Despite a record of solid accomplishment in the field of peace and security, the Inter-American system faces trying times ahead. It has demonstrated a capacity to cope with overt military aggression, but indirect aggression and political subversion are a different matter. Genuine popular revolts are not always readily distinguishable from Communist-abetted indirect aggression. Unrest in any given country can have elements of both. The United States, as evidenced by its military intervention in the Dominican revolt, is deeply committed to prevent the rise of new Communist regimes—such as the one established in Cuba—under the guise of social revolution. Many Latin American governments, especially those making progress toward democracy, are deeply concerned lest United States (or even collective OAS) intervention be utilized to suppress a genuine social revolution. This is a dilemma that cannot be resolved easily, but it is one which the Inter-American security system will be increasingly required to face.

The Asian Component: SEATO and CENTO

The Southeast Asia Treaty Organization (SEATO) and the Central Treaty Organization (CENTO) are creatures of the cold war, owing their existence primarily to the United States drive to extend its policy of military containment of Communism to the Middle East and to South and Southeast Asia. SEATO was formed in the fall of 1954 after the French defeat in Indochina and the ensuing partition of Viet Nam. An invitation to join was extended to all non-Communist countries of South and Southeast Asia, but Pakistan, Thailand, and the Philippines were the only Asian states to join. For the others the prospect of military assistance and a joint guarantee of their security by the United States and its allies was not a sufficient inducement to abandon their neutralist stance. The SEATO guarantee was expressly extended to the territory comprising Laos, Cambodia, and South Viet Nam, despite their nonmembership. The three Asian members were joined by Australia, New Zealand, the United States, Britain, and France.[15]

The object of the association was to strengthen the capacity of the Asian members to resist aggression, facilitate joint planning for defense, and to provide collective legitimization for a United States military guarantee of the area. The treaty is specifically concerned with "subversive activities directed from without" as well as with armed attack. In neither case are the commitments very specific, however. In the event of armed attack within the Treaty area, defined to include the general region of Southeast Asia, the Southwest Pacific, and the territories of all Asian parties, each member agrees to "meet the common danger in accordance with its constitutional processes," while a threat other than by armed attack requires the parties only to "consult immediately." The United States commitment is further attenuated by the written understanding that its pledge to act in the face of armed attack applies only to Communist aggression. The treaty also contains a generalized commitment to economic cooperation, in recognition of the close connection between economic and military capabilities.

The principal organ of SEATO is a Council of permanent representatives meeting at Bangkok throughout the year, supplemented by an annual meet-

[15] In 1951 the United States entered into a tripartite security pact with Australia and New Zealand aimed at securing the latter two nations against future Japanese aggression and obtaining their consent to the 1951 Treaty of Peace with Japan. ANZUS, as the arrangement is called, has a permanent Council, a consultative organ of foreign ministers meeting annually, and a committee of military representatives which meets as needed. Decisions of the organs are made by unanimity. Although military planning is the chief function of the organization, the Council has also concerned itself with cooperation in the peaceful uses of atomic energy.

ing of foreign ministers. A permanent secretariat of less than one hundred serves the organization at Bangkok. Among the Council's subsidiary organs are a Committee of Security Experts, which gathers information on the nature and extent of Communist penetration; an economic committee; and a committee concerned with cultural and educational affairs. Decisions of the Council are by unanimous consent.

Any candid appraisal of SEATO accomplishments must be pessimistic. In the nonmilitary sphere, SEATO has fostered a small but growing amount of educational exchange and has induced low-budget economic cooperation in such activities as vocational training and agricultural research. In the security sphere, SEATO's military planners have produced plans for joint military operations; the Committee of Security Experts has uncovered useful information on Communist subversive tactics; and military exercises involving two or more SEATO members have been held from time to time. Although these activities may have intrinsic merit, any substantial connection between SEATO operations and the general security of the area has yet to be demonstrated.

The most significant relationships among the SEATO powers are still on a bilateral basis. These relationships include the military and economic aid which the United States has handed out lavishly in parts of Southeast Asia and Pakistan over the years. SEATO itself has no troops, no infrastructure, no military command. When Communist indirect aggression in Laos reached a crisis in 1961 and 1962, the SEATO Council was unable to agree upon any affirmative action to honor its commitment to that beleaguered country. As a fitting denouement, the SEATO protective umbrella was officially withdrawn from Laos with the agreement of all concerned. Cambodia also announced an intent not to avail itself of SEATO protection. In Viet Nam, a second major test, individual members of SEATO have joined the United States in giving military assistance to the Saigon regime, but SEATO has been unable to agree on collective action. At the ministerial meeting held in London in the spring of 1965, France ostentatiously refused to endorse the escalation of American military support to South Viet Nam, and Pakistan tendered its approval only with significant reservations. Both countries subsequently became more openly critical. These developments suggest that SEATO may have some usefulness as a medium of communication, but it is sadly lacking as an action body, a guarantor of security, or even as a means of legitimizing United States military intervention in the area.

The United States' determination to complete a circle of anti-Communist alliances around the Soviet Union and China led to the creation of CENTO in 1955, hard on the heels of the newly formed SEATO. The organization was to constitute a geographic link between NATO in the west and SEATO in the east, and provide a channel for injecting American military influence into the Middle East. Originally called the Baghdad Pact, because of its origin in a treaty between Turkey and Iraq, signed at Baghdad, the roster of members was complete with the accession of Britain, Pakistan, and Iran. The United States remained outside the organization, but became associated as a paying sponsor and an influential if nonvoting participant in its deliberations. Other Arab states of the Middle East had been sounded out for membership, but only Iraq was willing to overlook its heritage of Western exploitation, forsake neutralism, and join an anti-Communist security organization. Iraq's participation in the arrangement was both a symbol and a source of division within the Arab world, but that irritant was only temporary.

In 1958 the violent overthrow of the pro-Western Iraqi government brought Iraq's formal withdrawal from the pact the following year. Shorn of its only Arab member, the organization moved its headquarters from Baghdad to Ankara and changed its name to the Central Treaty Organization. Faced with the impending Iraqi withdrawal, the United States formalized its status as an associate (but not a member) of the organization early in 1959 by signing bilateral "agreements of cooperation" with Turkey, Pakistan, and Iran.

The commitments of the CENTO pact are the vaguest and loosest of any of the alliances we have yet considered. The parties simply agree to "cooperate for their security and defense." The 1959 executive agreements concluded by the United States with the three Middle Eastern countries are somewhat more specific, if not exactly ironclad. The agreements commit the United States to take such action against direct or indirect aggression "as may be mutually agreed upon" and to furnish each of the governments "such military and economic assistance as may be mutually agreed upon." The only commitment of the Middle Eastern signatories is to utilize the assistance in a manner consistent with agreed objectives.

Organizationally the original Baghdad Pact provided only for a Permanent Council. The structure has since been elaborated to include Economic, Liaison, Countersubversion, and Military Committees, in addition to a civilian secretariat, a Combined Military Planning Staff, and a number of subsidiary bodies. The Council meetings, which operate by consensus, have been utilized as a center for discussion of political questions extending well beyond the immediate concerns of CENTO. With the United States and Britain providing financial assistance, CENTO's economic activities have included the construction of a highway linking Turkey with Pakistan and a railway from Turkey to Iran, the modernization of port facilities, and the development of telecommunications. Technical assistance in agriculture, crop marketing programs, and the promotion of tourism have been other CENTO projects. Military activities have embraced basic planning for defense, joint military maneuvers, and other training programs.

Any evaluation of CENTO as a regional security arrangement must be tentative. CENTO undoubtedly functions as a useful channel of communication among its members and the United States, but it has not developed the consultative links with NATO and SEATO that were originally hoped for. Its economic activities have also been obviously constructive, if overshadowed by the much greater sums for economic and military assistance passing from the United States to Turkey, Pakistan, and Iran through bilateral channels. Whether its military and decision-making apparatus will add significantly to the security of the region in time of crisis is an open question, because no crisis has yet presented itself. The withdrawal of Iraq was a serious blow, reflecting adversely upon the prestige of the organization rather than upon its capacity to act. In the absence of a CENTO force and joint Military Command, one may reasonably suppose that individual calculations of national interest rather than CENTO ties will govern the response of each nation should a crisis arise. If joint action should be thus indicated, CENTO may provide a useful framework within which to undertake it.

COMMUNIST COALITION: THE WARSAW TREATY ORGANIZATION

The systematic buildup of anti-Soviet military coalitions was bound to evoke a Communist countermove, and the entry of West Germany into NATO was the last straw. On May 14, 1955, a pact was signed at Warsaw uniting the Soviet Union and its East European satellites (all of the Communist states except Yugoslavia) in a common defense organization. Originally intended as a counterpart to NATO which the Soviets could offer to abandon in exchange for the dismantling of NATO, the Warsaw Treaty Organization has become an enduring part of the East European political landscape. Its active membership now includes the Soviet Union, Bulgaria, Czechoslovakia, East Germany, Hungary, Poland, and Romania. China, once associated as a permanent observer, has ceased to participate; and Albania, an original member, has not attended meetings since 1962 because of its rift with the Soviet Union.

The formal commitments of the treaty are much the same as those encountered in the Western alliances—to consult when threatened with armed attack and to give whatever aid each considers necessary if an armed attack actually occurs. The treaty calls for the establishment of a Unified Command and a Political Consultative Committee, the latter being the institutional equivalent of the Council in Western defense organizations, with jurisdiction extending to "all important international questions" involving the "common interests" of members. Shortly after the treaty was signed, the Soviet Union announced the creation of a joint command headed by a Soviet commander-in-chief with headquarters situated in Moscow. A truly international unified command, as the treaty appeared to require, has never been established. The Political Consultative Committee and its secretariat were functioning by early 1956.

The geographical propinquity and political relationship of Warsaw Pact members preclude the organization from being simply another SEATO. But in terms of institutions, joint planning, and unified command of joint forces, it is far from being another NATO. The Political Consultative Committee was originally scheduled to meet at least twice yearly, but the lapse of a year or even two between meetings is the rule. This is not the kind of institutional arrangement within which genuine, continuing consultations flourish. An eminent authority suggests that the Soviet Union may be reluctant "to push the development of the WTO too far lest it become a genuine consultative organ," leading perhaps to demands for greater sharing of control and information.[16] The military aspects of the organization also remain essentially static, with no troops assigned to WTO or any real integration of national contingents.

Although the military potential of the Warsaw Pact has not been highly developed, its political significance remains. In recent years the substance of independence has been gradually returning to the East European states. During this time the Warsaw Pact has represented "the single most important formal commitment" binding these states to the USSR.[17] One of the most frequently cited charges against Imre Nagy in 1956 was that he violated the unity of the bloc by his unilateral attempt to take Hungary out of the WTO. In addition, the Pact provides a rationale for stationing Soviet troops in satellite territory, with their attendant political influence. The Pact also appears to place a legal limitation upon the exercise of sovereignty by bloc members, through its restriction upon the contracting of alliances or agreements that are "incompatible" with the Warsaw Pact. The organization further serves as a forum for the ritualistic expression of unanimous support for Soviet foreign policy initiatives. Given the East European community of interest fashioned around Soviet domination, the Warsaw Pact should continue to have political significance for some time to come.

DEFENSE OF THE ARAB WORLD

The Arab League embraces a group of largely underdeveloped countries sharing a common language, religion, and culture, but divided by separatist traditions and conflicting aspirations of rival nationalist leaders. Within the League, collective defense is but one aspect of regional collaboration on a

[16] Zbigniew K. Brzezinski, *The Soviet Bloc: Unity and Conflict*, rev. ed. (New York: Praeger, 1961), p. 447.
[17] *Ibid.*, p. 171.

broader front, which aims at policy coordination in virtually all matters of common interest. The original signatories of the pact creating the Arab League in March, 1945, were Egypt (now the United Arab Republic), Iraq, Lebanon, Saudi Arabia, Syria, Transjordan (now Jordan), and Yemen. They have since been joined by Libya (1953), Sudan (1956), Morocco (1958), Tunisia (1958), Kuwait (1961), and Algeria (1962).

Security arrangements give the usual mutual guarantees against external aggression but, like the inter-American security system, provide for protection again one another as well. If aggression occurs, the 1945 Pact of the League of Arab States requires the convocation of the League Council, which may decide by a unanimous vote what common measures are to be taken. (If the aggressor is a member, its vote is not counted in determining unanimity.) A supplementary Treaty of Joint Defense and Economic Cooperation (April 13, 1950) contains a more sweeping promise by each state to take whatever measures are necessary, including armed force, to repel armed aggression against any of them. The later pact also calls for consultations "whenever there are reasonable grounds for the belief that the territorial integrity, independence, or security" of any of them is threatened. Each state remains the judge of its own contribution, except when the Council decides otherwise. Since the Council must function by unanimity in such matters, no member can be legally bound to act against its will.

Arab League organs with security functions include the Council as the top policy-making body, a Political Committee, a Joint Defense Council of foreign ministers and defense ministers, and a Permanent Military Commission. The function of the Permanent Commission is to assist the Joint Defense Council in preparing detailed plans for defense, the coordination of military policies, and the eventual unification of national armed forces. The Political Committee, composed of foreign ministers of the members or their diplomatic representatives in Cairo, draws up recommendations for the League Council and has tended to become the practical center of decision-making on most issues. Its recommendations are ordinarily approved without serious debate. The League Headquarters and permanent secretariat are located in Cairo.

In security matters, the Arab League has proved to be long on talk and short on action—with one notable exception. When Kuwait achieved independence in 1961, the threat of invasion from Iraq, which claimed Kuwait as part of its own territory, led the Sultan of Kuwait to call for help from Britain under a treaty of military assistance. Kuwait also sought support from the Arab League. Galvanized to action by the return of British troops to Kuwait the League responded by sending a 3,300 man peace force drawn from Saudi Arabia, the UAR, the Sudan, Jordan, and Tunisia, under a Saudi Arabian commander. The bulk of the troops were from Saudi Arabia and the UAR. The British withdrew from Kuwait before the end of the year and the Arab League force remained until February, 1963.

In Arab disputes with outsiders, the League has usually managed to maintain a vociferously vocal united front. This kind of unity at the verbal level has enhanced Arab influence at the United Nations where talk is of the essence. But in crisis situations, the League has been unable to back its words with deeds. In the war that followed Israel's declaration of independence in 1948, the Arab Liberation Army proved a complete fiasco as a unified military operation. Political rivalries, self-centered nationalism, and inadequate machinery for coordination stifled the joint military effort, despite a substantial common interest in crushing Israel. When Israel, Britain, and France launched a direct armed attack upon Egypt in 1956, the League shouted loudly in the United Nations and elsewhere but lifted no finger to provide joint military assistance in support of the UAR. The success of the Kuwait peace force brought increased interest in Arab collective defense mechanisms, and in 1964 the League established an Arab joint military command and appointed a single commander-in-chief. No troops have as yet been assigned to the joint commander, however, and there is no assurance that the recent efforts to achieve coordinated military action will be more effective than the earlier ones. One should not, of course, underestimate the political value of the kind of unity that exists among Arab states; but until tighter bonds of community have been forged among them, the military commitments of the League are likely to remain ephemeral.

REGIONAL SECURITY FOR AFRICA

The establishment of the Organization of African Unity (OAU) in 1963 marked the confluence of the African intellectual's dream of Pan-African unity with the politician's more mundane concerns for accelerated economic growth, the eradication of colonialism from Africa, and increased African influence in the world. The strength of the drive for African unity was substantially weakened, however, by national particularisms and rivalries for leadership. As a result, the OAU Charter reflected the desire for the fruits of cooperation on a broad front but shrank from any very specific, binding commitments. The organization now embraces every independent state of Africa except South Africa and Rhodesia.

Of all regional organizations we have thus far examined, the OAU has the least specific security commitments. Defense of sovereignty, territorial integrity and independence is listed as one of the five purposes of the organization; and "cooperation for defence and Security" is one of the six fields in which members agree to "coordinate and harmonise their general policies." Beyond this, the Charter authorizes the Assembly of the Organization to establish a Defense Commission as one of several "Specialized Commissions" designed to promote the harmonization of policies at a more technical level. The Charter does not specify that an attack on one is an attack on all, and no state is legally obligated to come to the aid of any other if an attack occurs. Presumably the Assembly, consisting of Heads of State meeting annually, or the Council of Ministers (Foreign Ministers or other ministers) meeting semiannually or oftener, might respond to aggression with specific recommendations for joint action. But nothing in the Charter suggests that member states are bound to comply with such recommendations. The Charter utters "unreserved condemnation" of "political assassination as well as of subversive activities," and pledges its members to observe this and other enumerated standards of conduct toward one another.

If the organization has done little to implement the rather vague Charter provisions for collective self-defense, its deep concern for the eradication of colonialism from Africa has had a most important bearing on the peace and security of the continent. From the outset, the Organization has fostered a policy of aggression, both direct and indirect, against the governments of Rhodesia, South Africa, and of territories still under colonial rule. At the Addis Ababa meeting which drafted the OAU Charter, the African Heads of State unanimously approved a program of action to speed the independence of African peoples still subject to foreign domination. The catalog of approved techniques ranged from severance of diplomatic and economic relations to the creation of liberation armies and volunteer corps to wage war against other African governments regarded as alien and oppressive. The immediate fruit of this resolution was a Decolonization Committee, sometimes known as the Committee of Nine, established to coordinate aid to African liberation movements. Its principal responsibility thus far has been the administration of funds contributed by member states for the support of "freedom fighters" in Angola, Mozambique, and South Africa. When the Ian Smith regime unilaterally declared the independence of Rhodesia in November, 1965, the OAU voted to use armed force if necessary to unseat his white minority government. By 1967 the force had not materialized.

DEFENSE OF THE COMMONWEALTH

The Commonwealth of Nations consists of twenty-six independent states, formerly part of the British empire, which continue to accept the British monarch as their titular sovereign or, in the case of the republics, as the titular "head of the Commonwealth." [18] The Commonwealth is neither regional in any geographic sense nor, strictly speaking, a security organization. Yet it is an arrangement for organized consultation on defense topics as well as other matters, and as such merits comment here.

The chief function of the Commonwealth is consultation, and the most august organ of consultation is the Conference of Prime Ministers which meets whenever there is an issue of general concern. Numerous other meetings of Commonwealth representatives, particularly on economic subjects, have been common since 1945. Consultation on many subjects also takes place through High Commissioners (the Commonwealth family's equivalent of ambassadors), finance and other ministers, military leaders, civil servants, and others, often by informal exchange with "opposite numbers" in other Commonwealth countries. As one British authority has observed, the purpose of such consultation is "to facilitate cooperation, should the members wish it, on any particular point, but there is no duty to agree or to concert policies." [19] If there is any obligation resting upon Commonwealth members, it is the obligation to inform and consult other members on matters of common concern. Yet, so flexible are the rules of association that a member may choose not to consult if national interest should so dictate. British secrecy in undertaking the invasion of Egypt in 1956 raised outcries within the Commonwealth but it is now recognized as being in harmony with the accepted principle that national interest takes priority over the obligation to consult.

There exists no Commonwealth charter or general treaty of mutual assistance committing members to come to one another's aid. Over the decades, the British fleet has given protection to other Commonwealth countries while the latter have supplied bases and manpower, most notably in the two world wars. This is still an element in Commonwealth relations, although the overseas members have grown much more dependent on their own resources and upon American aid. Britain has bilateral defense agreements with a number of Commonwealth countries, and an exchange of military information occurs as a part of the general Commonwealth consultative process. Nevertheless, there is no planning for concerted military action by the Commonwealth as a whole. Interests are diverse, and Commonwealth conferences normally avoid the discussion of issues on which vital interests clash. They have further developed the practice of "elective discussion" by which a particular topic will be considered only by countries

[18] Independent members of the Commonwealth at the end of 1966 included the United Kingdom, Canada, Australia, New Zealand, India, Pakistan, Ceylon, Ghana, Nigeria, Cyprus, Sierra Leone, Jamaica, Trinidad and Tobago, Uganda, Kenya, Malaysia, Tanzania, Malawi, Malta, Zambia, Gambia, Singapore, Lesotho (Basutoland), Botswana (Bechuanaland), Guyana (British Guiana), and Barbados.

[19] Graeme C. Moodie, *The Government of Great Britain,* 2d ed. (New York: Thomas Y. Crowell Company, 1964), p. 183.

with a specific interest in it. In security matters, this permits neutralist Commonwealth countries gracefully to absent themselves from discussions of defense topics that concern the others. The Commonwealth, with its heterogeneous composition and extremely permissive relationships, is not equipped to be an action organ in the field of defense; it is, however, a communications channel of continuing significance.

A BALANCE SHEET OF REGIONAL SECURITY

The rise of the regional security arrangement illustrates the truism that consensus on vital interests is easier to reach among a relatively small homogeneous group of states than among a large, heterogeneous group like the United Nations. On the other hand, the growth of regionalism points to the development of larger communities of interest than those which characterized the world before the two world wars when bilateralism was the rule. Although no one would suggest that the present patterns of regional security organization are immutable, the tenacity and expansion of regional security arrangements in the past two decades suggests that they are more than a transitory phenomenon.

In structure, regional security systems show a basic similarity. Typically, each has a policy-making Council or Assembly (or both) in which member states are represented with equal voice. Decision by unanimous consent is the rule, although some organizations utilize a two-thirds or even a simple majority for some types of questions. Councils are generally supplemented by specialized committees, and all are serviced by a permanent secretariat. Each regional security organization has a body for military planning, sometimes operating in connection with a joint military command. Typically, also, regional security organizations promote collaboration in economic and other nonmilitary fields, or are related to a broader regional organization that does so.

Treaty commitments of regional alliances also tend to follow common patterns. All commitments to resist aggression are applicable to a particular geographical area. The area is ordinarily defined in terms of the territories of member states, although NATO excludes territories outside of Europe, Turkey, and the "North Atlantic area"; the Rio Pact draws a protective envelope around the Americas extending from the North Pole to the South Pole; and SEATO excludes the homelands of its three most powerful members, while specifically including the territory of certain nonmembers.

In case of a threat of armed attack, advance commitments are generally limited to consultation. Consultation could lead to collective sanctions, but the power and procedures of consultative bodies are such that no state can be required to participate in sanctions without its consent, except in the OAS. Essentially the same kinds of commitments exist with respect to subversion and indirect aggression, to the extent that these contingencies are provided for. The Rio Pact, SEATO Pact, and OAU Charter are explicit in their concern for indirect aggression or subversion, while NATO and the Arab League deal with the matter in more general terms. If a direct military attack occurs within the treaty area, members of regional organizations are generally pledged to the use of armed force if necessary. NATO, the Inter-American System, SEATO, the Warsaw Pact, and the Arab League are very specific in calling for an armed response to armed attack; CENTO treaties and the OAU Charter are very vague. But in every case each state is left juridically free to determine for itself the extent of its individual contribution, until collective action is agreed upon, a condition that may greatly attenuate the commitment. As for collective action, all regional systems except the OAS and the OAU require the consent of all parties to decisions calling for sanctions, and even they cannot bind nonconsenting states to use armed force. OAU resolutions are only recommendatory, and the OAS Charter specifically provides that no member may be required to use armed force without its consent.

If regional security systems show similarities in structure and commitments, they show great contrasts in activity. On this score NATO stands in a class by itself. Where others merely talk of defense or carry on a few joint maneuvers, NATO has acted to create a working international command, a collective military force, an impressive infrastructure, and an extensive system of defense-related consultation. The OAS, while furnishing little protection against external aggression, has evolved an active system for dealing with regional conflicts, including the use of diplomatic and economic sanctions and, in one instance, a regional peace force. The Arab League stands in a different class as the one regional organization whose commitment to resist direct armed attack has been tested, and found virtually worthless. The others have not experienced direct aggression. The OAU is also unique in concentrating its collective efforts upon subverting nonmember regimes rather than providing for the defense of its own members.

In addition to their concern with armed attack, threats and subversion, and related economic and cultural collaboration, regional defense arrangements perform certain other functions. Perhaps most important, they serve as channels of communication among the membership. The impact of multilateral interchange is often significantly different from a series of bilateral conversations, and a joint sharing of views in a conference setting may sometimes be the only feasible way of coordinating policies. In systems revolving around a single dominant power, the regional organization may give collective legitimization to the influence exerted in the area by the major power. Paradoxically, the organization may also place a collective restraint upon the actions of the strong, as the price of legitimization. For example, although Europe is highly dependent upon the military capabilities of the United States, the members of NATO also have a voice, however small, in the defense policies of the United States. On the other hand, the infrequent meetings of the Warsaw Pact's political committee may be an attempt by the Soviet Union to obtain the benefits of legitimization without paying the price.

The final, most difficult assessment of regional security arrangements concerns their impact on world peace and security. To the extent that they have successfully handled disputes and outbreaks of violence within their respective regional areas, the contribution to peace and security can scarcely be doubted. In other respects, however, the evaluation is not so clear-cut. On the positive side, some of the regional pacts have had a deterrent function. The specific deterrent effect is hard to judge because no one can determine with certainty whether or not aggression was intended and would have taken place in the absence of regional alliance systems. Nevertheless, one can assert with confidence that NATO increased the probability of an American response to attack upon Europe and to that extent served as a deterrent to Soviet designs upon the area. Other regional arrangements may also have helped to deter the more overt forms of armed aggression. One can also argue that regional security organizations contribute to the conditions of peace in another way by promoting, at least incidentally, cooperation in economic and other spheres of action.

On the other hand, alliances contribute to the growth of international tension as counteralliances are formed and rival groups engage in competitive arms races. Most of the alliance partners of the United States have been the recipients of military assistance designed to raise the level of their national armaments and military preparedness. No potential enemy state thus threatened can afford to let the challenge go unanswered. Obviously, no one can measure the tension that has resulted from the encirclement of the Soviet Union and China by a ring of Western military alliances, or compare it with the degree of tension that might have existed had both sides relied solely on national armaments and bilateral security pacts. But Western alliances have been the target of Soviet propaganda blasts so often as to raise a presumption that they are regarded as threats and sources of tension in themselves. Turning to the broader societal framework of security, the argument that regional alliances have promoted economic and social cooperation can be answered with an equally plausible counterargument. By fostering excessive concern for military solutions to essentially social problems, regional defense organizations may be contributing to the diversion of attention and resources from the real roots of insecurity, which lie in demands for political recognition, economic betterment, and social change.

Such an evaluation is inconclusive because, in one situation or another, regional security arrangements have had all of the postulated effects: they sometimes deter, they sometimes breed tension, they sometimes promote economic and social cooperation, and they sometimes absorb attention and resources that ought to be devoted to eradicating more basic causes of national and international insecurity. In another perspective, however, regional alliances are at most only a secondary cause of anything. For the most part they reflect rather than create the international situation around them. Realistically, deterrence rests largely upon national power and primarily that of the United States and the Soviet Union. The deterrent capability is essentially independent of regional organization and could be shared by one state with others under a variety of arrangements. Tensions, likewise, result from rivalries and basic clashes of interest that are largely independent of international organization. As for the misplaced emphasis on military solutions at the expense of more constructive approaches to security, this too is more the product of national hostilities and anxieties than of the alliances through which such attitudes are expressed.

In the abstract, a universal system of security in which all acquiesced would be preferable to anything now existing; but the collapse of the UN security system demonstrates that this ideal is unattainable now. A disarmed world living at peace with justice may be an ultimate goal; but the real world with all its weapons, violence, and injustice is the only one we have. Given these unpleasant facts, the regional approach to security may well be preferable to unilateralism or bilateralism, indicating as it does the growth of larger communities of interest. The fact that regionalism tends to include elements of nonmilitary cooperation is a further plus factor. The attempt to promote consensus within the framework of world institutions should obviously not be abandoned, but this by no means precludes an approach to peace through broader consensus and functioning institutions at the regional level.

Selected Readings

BRZEZINSKI, ZBIGNIEW K. *The Soviet Bloc: Unity and Conflict,* rev. ed. New York: Praeger, 1961.

BOUTROS-GHALI, BOUTROS. "The Addis Ababa Charter," *International Conciliation,* No. 546, January, 1964.

BUCHAN, ALASTAIR. *NATO in the 1960's: The Implications of Interdependence,* rev. ed. New York: Praeger, 1963.

CLAUDE, INIS L., JR. "The OAS, the UN, and the United States," *International Conciliation,* No. 547, March, 1964.

DREIER, JOHN C. *The Organization of American States and the Hemisphere Crisis.* New York: Harper & Row, for the Council on Foreign Relations, 1962.

FENWICK, CHARLES G. *The Organization of American States: The Inter-American Regional System,* 2nd ed. Washington, D.C.: Kaufman Printing Co., 1963.

KISSINGER, HENRY A. *The Troubled Partnership: A Reappraisal of the Atlantic Alliance.* New York: McGraw-Hill, for the Council on Foreign Relations, 1965.

LAWSON, RUTH C., ed. *International Regional Organizations.* New York: Praeger, 1962.

MACDONALD, ROBERT W. *The League of Arab States: A Study in the Dynamics of Regional Organization.* Princeton, N.J.: Princeton University Press, 1965.

NATO, Facts about the North Atlantic Treaty Organizations. Paris: NATO Information Service, 1965.

PADELFORD, NORMAN J. "The Organization of African Unity," *International Organization,* Summer, 1964, pp. 521–42.

ROBERTSON, A. H. *The Council of Europe,* 2nd ed. New York: Praeger, 1961.

STANLEY, TIMOTHY W. *NATO in Transition.* New York: Praeger, for the Council on Foreign Relations, 1965.

12 | *Strategies for Disarmament*

Regional security pacts and global security systems offer pathways to peace, but both may ultimately lead to the use of force. Disarmament offers an approach to security that eliminates the need for balancing power with power or energizing the world community into action against a lawbreaker; peace is simply a consequence of a world without weapons.

Disarmament as an approach to peace and security assumes that armaments increase not only the destructiveness but also the likelihood of war. It is advocated not simply as a means of making wars less ferocious but of making them less frequent. Apparently, neither imbalance nor relative equality in the distribution of arms among rivals is a touchstone of international stability. When one power has, or believes it has, a preponderance of power, the temptation to commit aggression may become irresistible, as it did for Adolf Hitler. But a relatively equal distribution of arms may stimulate an arms race among anxious rivals, creating the mutually reinforced tension, distrust, and buildup of armaments that characterized the period that led to World War I. Once an arms race is under way, it becomes self-propelling, feeding on its own fears, hatreds, and misguided assumptions about military might and intentions. Armaments become their own rationale, their own justification, their own ultimate morality. Durable peace is hard to find in a world where weapons abound and can be easily put into use.

THE DISARMAMENT LABYRINTH

The objective, then, of disarmament is to build a peaceful world by ridding it of weapons of war. The solution is so simple, so obvious, so preferable to its alternative that it might appear to an impartial observer, if one could be found, that only a dedicated warmonger or a potential aggressor could conceivably resist its logic. Yet the historical record of disarmament through agreement reveals appallingly few and mostly short-lived examples. Why the failure to achieve this almost universally acclaimed objective?

What follows is an analysis of some of the major problems that help to explain the disarmament impasse.

The Security Question

The difficulty of securing disarmament can perhaps be understood best if it is related to the question of why nations arm in the first place. If an arms race causes war, what then causes the arms race? Obviously, the building of weapons of war is related to the objectives of the state. Nations arm for security, to protect the existence of the state, but they also arm to pursue political ends. For centuries, arms have offered the opportunity and provided the means for states to carry out national policies. So long as leaders regard military capacity as essential to the fulfillment of their state's vital interests, the abandonment of that capability through international agreement is unlikely.

The "Vested Interests"

Disarmament in today's world must take account of the armaments that nations already possess. How does a nation communicate pacific intent to a rival when it has the military capability in instant readiness to destroy the rival completely? How can the arms race be reversed in a world in which $130 billion is spent each year for military purposes, over 20 million men are in armed forces, and another 35 million people are engaged in military production? There may well be too many vested interests in the world of armaments and military services to challenge the status quo successfully.

The economic consequences of disarmament are viewed ambivalently in some states. Total disarmament would permit states to devote the huge savings to economic betterment. (The annual savings for the United States and the Soviet Union together would amount to almost $100 billion.) However, many observers fear that there would be a loss of jobs and profits or a dislocation of their nation's economy. Communists expound the doctrine that capitalism depends on the artificial stimulus provided by arms production and war. Although little evidence exists to substantiate that charge, many Americans have reacted adversely to the closing of defense plants and arsenals in economy moves. The military-industrial complex functions as a powerful force in both the Soviet Union and the United States against any disarmament proposal that threatens a loss of status or income. A successful disarmament plan, therefore, must take economic consequences into full account.

The Threat of Deception

The technological revolution that has dramatically changed the mode of warfare has also increased the difficulty of disarmament. Arms reduction in a world of conventional weapons might mean that one side could achieve an initial advantage through deception. Though not likely to be decisive, a violation could give the attacking state a significant edge. With the advent of thermonuclear, chemical, and biological weapons, however, treachery in a disarmament agreement could be decisive. Moreover, the ability to deceive has increased; it is far easier to hide a few intercontinental rockets and their thermonuclear warheads than to conceal several divisions of troops or a fleet of battleships. Fear of deception has led the United States to insist that an effective system of inspection be operational *before* any disarmament measures are implemented.

Ideological Rivalry

A world of conflicting values cannot provide the best milieu for reaching agreement on disarmament. When one side in an ideological struggle becomes convinced that the other is bent on conquest or destruction, any proposal for a reduction in arms is regarded as a devious inducement for a nation to weaken itself, providing the enemy an opportunity to attack. Any disarmament agreement must depend upon some minimal amount of good faith and a belief that the other side will live up to its terms. But a deep gulf between ideological enemies makes trust a rare commodity.

In more than twenty years of disarmament negotiations between the Soviet Union and the United States, ideological hostility has led to a "deaf man's dialogue." Both sides favor the reduction of arms and propose various schemes to accomplish it, but neither seriously considers the other's proposals because it fears a trap. Each side believes that if the other were sincerely interested in disarmament, it would cease its diversionary tactics and accept the other's logical and responsible plan. The will to survive, however, may in time force a moderation in the two ideological camps and build enough understanding to permit a start toward mutual arms reduction.

The Need for Full Participation

A meaningful disarmament agreement requires the participation of all the great powers. If one or several states with sizable military strength were not included, the delicate balance of power provided by a carefully worked out schedule of arms reductions would be constantly in danger of being upset. It is difficult to get all major powers to support disarmament because one or several may prefer an independent policy or may regard the existing power distribution in the world as favorable to their national interests. France between the wars, for example, was interested in maintaining arms superiority over Germany, not in a general disarmament. Both Communist China and France have refused to participate in current disarmament negotiations. It is doubtful that the United States or the Soviet Union would ever agree to reduce their nuclear weapons or subject them to control without the participation of all nuclear powers. An antiproliferation treaty that would limit some states but not those refusing to sign it is also a highly dubious prospect.

The Propaganda Barrier

The appeal of disarmament to millions of human beings has made it a prime subject for psychological warfare. Diplomats confident that the other side will reject their proposals are free to advance radical schemes designed to make their country appear *avant garde* in its search for peace. The simpler the proposal and its approach to the problem, the more likely it will receive the approbation of an observing world.

The majority of states, neutralist in their orientation toward the cold war struggle, regard their foreign policy mission to be chiefly one of achieving great power rapprochement and disarmament. This desire has resulted in obvious efforts by both sides to appeal in their proposals to the great mass of nonaligned states rather than to the negotiators sitting across the table. Sweeping Soviet proposals for general and complete disarmament, with control machinery to be established *later*, have been matched by American plans providing for a maximum of elaborate international inspection and enforcement but deemphasizing the problems of overseas bases and German rearmament which are central to Soviet security considerations.

Pressures for great power agreement on disarmament emanate regularly from the majority of states in the General Assembly, challenging both sides to find new platitudes to accept principles while tabling concrete proposals "for further study." Each side must preserve its image—that of a peace-loving, humanitarian, but horrendously powerful nation that would gladly lay down its arms and contribute the savings to economic development but for the intransigence and uncompromising hostility of the other side. It is noteworthy that the most significant agreement in the arms control field during the past twenty years—the Partial Nuclear Test-Ban Treaty of 1963 —was reached through closed negotiations among American, British, and Soviet diplomats.

The Speed of Change

An increasingly significant factor working against consensus is the realization that much scientific research and development for peaceful purposes can be related to weaponry; hence, no disarmament agreement can really stop progress in military technology. The development of a decisive new weapon which could upset the agreed balance of arms is a potential danger both sides would have to assume in any arms control or disarmament agreement. No inspection or control system could offer full protection against such an eventuality. In an age of intensive exploration of the atom and of new ventures in outer space, any disarmament agreement could be rendered obsolete within a short period of time unless it provided for periodic updating. It may be that the day has already passed when disarmament through agreement was rationally practicable.

Over the years, disarmament negotiators have faced a basic dilemma: As scientific knowledge grows and technology changes with revolutionary speed, disarmament agreements become increasingly dependent upon trust; but trust is vitiated by the fear of new, secret weapons spawned by advancing technology. The very forces that call for an end to the arms race to save the human race from destruction are those which appear to make agreement to disarm too dangerous for national security interests. Somehow, science and technology must be released from their subservience to the gods of war and converted into allies of disarmament and peace.

The Problem of Timing

There is a pervasive tendency for both sides in an arms race to delay and procrastinate with the belief that the future will offer a more propitious time for entering into a disarmament agreement. That right moment never seems to occur. Instead, new weapons, military confrontations and other crises, and the burgeoning growth of military capabilities on both sides increase the need for disarmament but decrease its likelihood.

The Western-Soviet arms race since 1945 is a case in point. When the military rivalry commenced, both sides had just finished fighting a major war and one had suffered the mass destruction of its cities and calamitously high civilian and military casualties. The other side had a monopoly of nuclear weapons which it offered to sacrifice in return for a world security system. Both were faced with major problems of recovery from the war. In retrospect, those first few years following World War II appear to have been an ideal time for disarmament; yet negotiations failed dismally. Since then, the cold war has developed, alliance systems and overseas bases have been established, new weapons of mass destruction have been perfected, both sides have become peripherally or directly involved in local wars, and there has been a proliferation of nuclear weapons. The grounds for insecurity and fear are no longer hypothetical or based on a future potentiality; mass extermination is now a proximate danger. Yet, each nation continues to manufacture "overkill" capacity in a vain effort to achieve a uniliteral position of strength that would give it a preferred position in disarmament negotiations.

The conventional wisdom on military and defense matters dies slowly. Both sides, it appears, still follow the old maxim that national security is a function of spending money, manufacturing weapons, and fielding armies. In the pre-atomic age, such efforts may have increased a nation's security when they outstripped those of an opponent; today, with both sides already in possession of military capabilities far in excess of those needed to destroy each other, the dangers of war from overheating the arms race or as a result of human aberration or mechanical error may in fact *decrease* a nation's security. Conditions may once again be ripe for disarmament, but neither of the major opponents shows any signs of recognizing or acting on this timeliness. The psychology of the arms race produces a relentless "falling behind, catching up, going ahead" channel of thought that repeats itself endlessly. A disarmament agreement may finally be obtained when both sides simultaneously break the arms-race psychosis and decide that the opportune time has arrived.

The "Ratio" Problem

During negotiations, the future power relationship among the parties becomes a matter of grave concern. Each nation seeks a minimum goal of maintaining parity and a maximum advantage of arms superiority from a prospective agreement. Because power and security are never absolute but always relative, each proposal must be carefully weighed to determine its potential impact on all the parties. The result is an unending series of calculations by military tacticians who prefer to err on the conservative side, in keeping with their general distaste for disarmament as a security objective. The problem of balancing different categories of forces (strategic vs. tactical, air vs. naval, nuclear vs. conventional) provides an additional complication.

Although general and complete disarmament or a system of enforcement by a global police force might overcome the fear of disadvantage, the difficulty of phasing out arms through stages remains. At each stage, no party can be left relatively weaker than at an earlier point, and each strives to compare more favorably with its power rivals. Since it is impossible to achieve complete parity, each state must be led to believe that it will be advantaged by successive stages of disarmament. The difficulty in successfully pulling off this sleight-of-hand maneuver is evidenced by the twenty-year disagreement between the United States and the Soviet Union over the numbers and types of forces to be disarmed at each stage and the ratio of forces that would remain. Despite the difficulty of determining ratios, the problem remains central to disarmament and must be faced.

Technical Problems

From the earliest postwar discussions of the Baruch Plan in 1946, most of the hundreds of disarmament discussions have concerned "inspection and control." American proposals for twenty years have consistently offered to exchange a dependence on armaments for an international system that could safeguard security through enforcement. The Soviet Union has accepted the general proposition that inspection and control are necessary, but the details of implementing those vague terms have resulted in little more than an exchange of recriminations.

An effective inspection system to verify disarmament accords must resolve such issues as (1) the extent of access to each country's territory; (2) the frequency of on-the-spot surveillance; (3) the timing—a resolution of whether inspection arrangements should go into effect before or after the disarmament measures they will verify; (4) the nature of aerial and ground reconnaissance to guard against the possibility of a surprise attack; (5) a means of detecting weapons in outer space; (6) the determination of what constitutes a weapon or potential weapon; (7) the selection of areas to be included in a progressive territorial demilitarization; and (8) the composition, powers, and number of inspection teams.

The technical questions concerning the detection of violations lead to a second and equally difficult set of issues that involve the political and military consequences of a violation once it has been detected. To what extent, for example, will world opinion contribute to enforcement and sanctions? What role should the injured state or states play if they detect an evasion? What kind of international authority should be set up and what should be the nature of its sanctions? Should the injured state be entitled to undertake "restorative measures" following a detected violation to restore the military balance that would have existed without a disarmament agreement? What role should the United Nations and regional organizations undertake in the enforcement of sanctions? No disarmament agreement is possible in the contemporary world until a consensus can provide answers to these questions.

Sovereignty and Nationalism

The search for answers to the technical questions leads to the heart of the disarmament dilemma. The controversy over inspection and control is only symptomatic of the basic contradiction between international needs and national prerogatives that has stymied most disarmament efforts. Two forces which emerged early in the history of the modern state system—state sovereignty and nationalism—constitute the major legal and emotional barriers to the idea of inspection and control by "foreign" elements. A disarmament agreement, by its very nature, would limit the sovereign power of a state to exercise full control over the area most vital to its security. The ardent nationalist resents the access, free movement, and "snooping" within his state that must accompany an enforcement system.

An effective disarmament arrangement in the contemporary world must be based on some form of international government. For example, in formulating the Acheson-Lilienthal proposals that became the basis for the Baruch Plan, Dean Acheson insisted that inspection would not be adequate if the production of fissionable materials remained under national control, and enforcement would be insufficient unless a veto-free international body could punish a violator. The question of the feasibility of disarmament essentially boils down to the question, Is the world ready for a measure of world government? Although it may be a logical necessity for sheer survival, there is as yet no consensual support in any country, including the United States, for such a drastic curtailment of national prerogatives. The sovereign state system may be obsolete when it is objectively evaluated within the context of intercontinental missiles and thermonuclear weapons systems, but in the minds of human beings nationalism and sovereignty still offer the best approach to security. A successful disarmament system, then, requires first and foremost a basic change of attitude among the populations of the great power states. The true nature of the arms race today concerns whether or not attitudes will change rapidly enough to enable mankind to survive or whether war by plan or accident will provide the final catastrophe for the state system.

A SURVEY OF DISARMAMENT EFFORTS

Historically, disarmament efforts have been aimed at securing an arms reduction, a "freeze" in the level of armaments, limiting weapons to an agreed ratio, a prohibition of specified types of arms, or a local demilitarization. It was not until 1960 that the goal of "general and complete disarmament" was proclaimed by a unanimous vote of the United Nations General Assembly. Schemes envisioning universal peace written by Jean Jacques Rousseau, Immanuel Kant, William Penn, and other visionaries had postulated the ideal of a completely disarmed world prior to the nineteeth century, but their utopian schemes had had little impact except in intellectual circles.

Although Russian, British, French, and Italian statesmen made practical proposals for arms reduction during the nineteenth century, the only successful agreement reached during that period was the Rush-Bagot Treaty of 1817 by which the United States and Britain agreed to demilitarize the Great Lakes in perpetuity. That agreement remains to this day the most successful disarmament understanding ever negotiated. The first international conference with disarmament as its major objective was called by Czar Nicholas of Russia at The Hague in 1899. Although no agreement could be reached on the main topic of the limitation of armaments and war budgets, the First Hague Conference did adopt declarations proscribing the use of certain weapons in order that war could be made more humane.[1]

[1] Few countries in attendance dragged their feet more on disarmament questions than the United States. The chief American delegate, Captain (later Admiral) Alfred Mahan, received instructions that arms limitation "could not profitably be discussed" because of the inferior position of American arms to those of leading European powers. Rather than agree to a naval limitation, he openly stated that the United States planned to increase the size of its Pacific fleet to strengthen its role in the competition for Asian markets. On the question of banning dumdum bullets and asphyxiating gas as barbaric weapons, Captain Mahan joined with the British delegate to vote against outlawing the former and cast the lone negative vote on the latter. A lively account of the personalities and issues involved in the two Hague Peace Conferences can be found in Barbara W. Tuchman, *The Proud Tower* (New York: Macmillan, 1962), pp. 229–88.

Two innocuous resolutions calling upon the twenty-six states represented at the Conference to consider the limitation of their war budgets "for the increase of the material and moral welfare of mankind" were adopted unanimously. At the Second Hague Conference in 1907, the delegates accepted the fact that the arms race had made disarmament impracticable and so pursued other avenues to avoid war. A brief discussion, another meaningless resolution, and the subject was laid to rest. Ironically, some delegates expressed the opinion that the question of disarmament should be reopened at another conference in 1915.

Disarmament Efforts During the League Era

The Covenant of the League of Nations followed the prescription advocated by Woodrow Wilson in one of his Fourteen Points. It provided that armaments, as a recognized cause of war, should be "reduced to the lowest point consistent with national safety" but retained in sufficient numbers to provide for "the enforcement by common action of international obligations." This close relationship between disarmament and collective security as two phases of a single approach to peace and security was accepted as an essential unity by the Covenant framers. More specifically, three approaches to arms limitation were employed within the framework of the postwar peace settlements. First, through League efforts and treaty provisions, the Rhineland, Danzig, the Aaland Islands, and certain other territories were completely demilitarized. Second, the Versailles Treaty imposed extensive limitations upon Germany's military forces and provided for inspection and control by Allied authorities. Third, the League encouraged and sponsored disarmament studies and conferences aimed at implementing Covenant provisions for a reduction in armaments.

The first postwar effort to limit arms, however, took place outside of the League framework. In 1921, the Washington Naval Conference—called by the United States and attended by representatives of Britain, France, Italy, and Japan—set the pace for arms limitation negotiations. A treaty signed the following year limited the size of warships, restricted the construction of battleships and aircraft carriers for ten years, limited new construction thereafter by a ratio agreement (United States, 5; Britain, 5; Japan, 3; France, 1.67; and Italy, 1.67), and imposed limitations on naval bases in the Pacific. Subsequently, some of the parties violated the spirit and others the letter of the agreement. Britain and the United States engaged in a "cruiser race," Japan devised ingenious variations of the prohibited vessels to nullify the intent of the treaty, and France refused to implement any limitations in the absence of a general European security arrangement. The record of violations and subterfuge that followed the Washington Naval Arms Limitation Treaty and the countermeasures undertaken in response to evasions call attention to the difficulty of implementing a disarmament agreement without international inspection and enforcement machinery.

The League was even less successful in its efforts to promote a general reduction in armaments. Several commissions appointed by the Council to study and recommend disarmament plans failed to find a formula acceptable to the great powers. Each major state had its particular approach to the subject, and its own conception of how security could be safeguarded; the only area of mutuality was a common suspicion of the others' intentions. The only encouragement to the League's efforts during the 1920's came with the signing of the Locarno Treaty of 1925 which sought to normalize relations between France and Germany by a collective guarantee against aggression in the frontier areas between the two nations. The spirit of Locarno fostered a hope that general disarmament would soon prove feasible and a Preparatory Commission established in 1925 was assigned the task of preparing the ground for a major international disarmament conference. After five years of sporadic effort, the Commission prepared a Draft Convention in 1930 that reflected mostly the inability of its members to reach accord on limiting their armed forces. The main provisions of the Draft called for the reduction of military budgets, some reductions in naval armaments, and the establishment of a Permanent Disarmament Commission. The deepening economic depression, however, served notice that although states could not agree on disarmament, the coming struggle to preserve fiscal solvency might force them to curtail arms production.

The long-heralded World Disarmament Conference was finally convened at Geneva in 1932 with sixty-one states represented. Disregarding the Draft Convention, each of the major nations in turn offered its scheme to a skeptical group of delegates. The French plan envisaged a comprehensive security system that included qualified disarmament, an international control system, compulsory arbitration, and an international police force under League jurisdiction to guarantee security. Britain offered a plan that would outlaw the use of "offensive" weapons through a reinforced League security system, provide for disarmament by stages over a five-year period, and outlaw weapons of mass destruction. Germany demanded equality with France in any disarmament program. The United States proposed a uniform reduction in forces so that each nation would retain the same arms ratio with all others that it had before the agreement. The American plan was regarded by most Conference delegates as an oversimplified scheme that would encourage aggression and penalize defensive armies.

The flicker of hope that an acceptable formula might be discovered through conference debate was extinguished when Adolf Hitler was appointed Chancellor in 1933 and withdrew Germany from the Conference and the League. The Conference finally adjourned in 1934 in complete failure, although the basic conflict between German demands for arms equality and the French insistence on arms superiority over Germany had immobilized the Conference almost from the start. The Conference, however, was not a total loss. Agreement on broad principles, though never formalized, indicated a general revulsion against the use of chemical and bacteriological weapons, a consensus that arms should be reduced and military budgets curtailed, and a general acceptance that an international authority should be established to supervise any disarmament agreement that could be reached. Debates at the Conference and in the League Assembly over a period of twenty years helped to prepare the world for the next round in the disarmament cycle under the United Nations.

The United Nations and Disarmament

The effort to secure disarmament during the United Nations era differs from that of the League period in several significant aspects. For one thing, the pressures to reach agreement have been more persistent and have grown out of a sense of grave urgency. The atom bomb that was dropped on Hiroshima, although it followed the writing of the Charter by several months, alerted the world to the new potentiality for a calamity far beyond the destructiveness of World War II. The ensuing period after 1946 of cold war with full-scale rearmament, the framing of the NATO and Warsaw pacts, intermittent crises, and the development of intercontinental missiles with thermonuclear warheads—all occurring within a setting of frenetic ideological hostility—forged a link in many minds between disarmament and sheer survival. Over fifty new nations, whose people had ignored the arms race and the threat of war in quiet colonial subservience during the 1930's, now joined in a rising chorus of those awakened to the danger of global war. The United Nations has provided them a ready forum to air their demands for great power retrenchment in the arms race.

CHARTER PROVISIONS FOR DISARMAMENT. Disarmament was not assigned a prominent role by the framers in pursuing the primary goal of peace and security. The failure to stress disarmament perhaps can be ascribed mainly to the ignorance of the framers about the nuclear device that American scientists were secretly preparing to test at the very time the Charter was written. Added to this, the frustrations of the League period and the emphasis on the use of an international army to maintain peace and security through community force influenced the framers against setting forth extravagant, lofty goals that might be unrealizable.

Unlike the League Covenant that had called for an outright *reduction* in arms, the Charter merely proclaims the objective of arms *regulation*. Regulation implies the need for a strategically balanced ceiling on armaments so that the collective security machinery of the United Nations can function in a world not obsessed with the fear of an imminent and massive attack. The close relationship between the two objectives—disarmament and collective security—led the framers to assign responsibility for both functions to the Security Council aided by the Military Staff Committee (Articles 26 and 46, respectively). Giving the same bodies the responsibility of formulating plans for disarmament *and* for the use of military forces offered no contradiction for the framers, who considered progress in each area essential to the maintenance of peace and security. Moreover, disarmament was to *follow*, not precede, the full implementation of a global security system. The innovation of the atomic bomb, however, invalidated the otherwise logical plan of the framers by destroying the potential for strategically balancing the forces of the great powers.

United Nations Disarmament Negotiations—A Twenty Year Survey

PHASE I: THE ATOMIC IMPASSE. Initial efforts in the disarmament field were undertaken by the United Nations Atomic Energy Commission established by the first General Assembly resolution in January, 1946.[2] In recognition that the unlocked secret of atomic energy possessed great potentialities for peaceful purposes as well as grave dangers for all of mankind, the Assembly rather than the Security Council was chosen by the great powers to create and empower the Commission. The Assembly resolution called for the Commission to develop "with the utmost dispatch" a plan to provide for (1) the exchange of scientific knowledge for peaceful purposes; (2) the control of atomic energy to limit its use to peaceful purposes; (3) the elimination of atomic and other weapons of mass destruction; and (4) the establishment of an inspection and enforcement system to safeguard against evasions.[3]

The United States, with a monopoly of atomic weapons, offered a plan at the first meeting of the Atomic Energy Commission that would eventually provide for a sharing of its atomic secrets under an international control system. The proposal was based on recommendations made in the Acheson-Lilienthal Report and was presented by elder statesman Bernard Baruch. In its fundamentals, the Baruch Plan provided for a transition to peaceful atomic control by stages, each dependent on the successful implementation of the preceding stage before further progress would be attempted. The plan called for the creation of an International Atomic Development Authority which would operate an elaborate inspection and control system under Security Council direction unhampered by the veto power. All atomic weapons would be destroyed once the control system became operational and the manufacture of new bombs would be outlawed. The Authority would then exercise exclusive ownership of atomic raw materials, control

[2] Membership on the Atomic Energy Commission consisted of all members of the Security Council plus Canada. The latter was included because it had participated jointly with the United States and Britain in the development of the first atomic bomb.

[3] Department of State Bulletin, XIII (1945), p. 782. The Soviet Union backed the Commission's objectives and called for an early agreement on all points.

all atomic activities, encourage their beneficial use for all nations, hold a monopoly on research and development in the field of atomic explosives, and license national atomic research for peaceful purposes. In sum, the plan would establish a world federal government restricted to the field of atomic energy, where its powers would be virtually supreme. The broad framework of this initial American position has remained substantially unchanged in the more than twenty years of negotiations that have followed the presentation of the Baruch Plan.

The Soviet Union emphatically rejected the American proposal in favor of the immediate outlawing of all atomic weapons followed by the establishment of a minimum system of control. In the Soviet view, each state should accept responsibility for the peaceful development of atomic power and for policing the prohibition against atomic weapons within its borders, subject to periodic oversight by an international authority. Enforcement action would be undertaken by the Security Council against violators, but only with the agreement of all permanent members. Thus the first confrontation between the United States and the Soviet Union produced basic disagreements over the timing (which comes first, complete disarmament or an inspection and control system?), peaceful development (by national or international authority?), inspection (what powers should the international authority possess and how frequently should it conduct inspections?), and control (should the veto power apply to action against violators?). The gulf between the major parties over the details of controlling atomic energy has been altered little since that initial encounter.

New Efforts with an Old Approach. The Soviets, placed on the defensive by the Baruch Plan and outnumbered on the Atomic Energy Commission, took the offensive in the latter part of the General Assembly's first session in 1946 with a proposal for general and complete disarmament, including conventional and atomic weapons. The proposal apparently was an effort to overcome the propaganda advantage gained by the United States in offering to relinquish its monopoly and contribute its know-how to the peaceful development of atomic power for mankind. Moreover, the special treatment accorded atomic disarmament overlooked the fact that the new weapon, although more of a qualitative than quantitative change in armaments, figured prominently in the assessments of the major power rivals as a weapon that could decisively affect the power ratio in conventional arms. The Soviet Union obviously preferred to discuss the broad, innocuous subject of general disarmament while carrying on a crash program to develop an atomic bomb to offset the American advantage.

The conflict between the American approach favoring separate discussions for the control of mass destruction and conventional weapons and the Russian call for a combined discussion of all disarmament topics resulted in a compromise in the Assembly providing for "separate but parallel" discussions. A resolution entitled "Principles Governing the General Regulation and Reduction of Armaments," adopted unanimously in late 1946, expressed agreement that conventional armaments should be reduced, atomic weapons prohibited, and an international control system intermeshed with the collective security machinery of the Security Council. Although agreement on principles had been reached, agreement to take specific, detailed action to implement principles proved to be an infinitely more difficult task. The Security Council followed the Assembly's directive by establishing a Commission for Conventional Armaments in 1947, but that body at once became deadlocked over the same issues that had precluded agreement on atomic disarmament. Phase I of the disarmament dialogue ended in 1952 with neither Commission able to claim any tangible progress toward disarmament.

PHASE II: A UNIFIED APPROACH. Three events had a notable impact on disarmament negotiations during the early 1950's. These were (1) the explosion of a Soviet atomic device in 1949; (2) the Communist victory in the Chinese civil war in 1949; and (3) the outbreak of the Korean conflict in 1950. The first, by ending the American atomic monopoly, made the Baruch Plan obsolete. The second resulted in a boycott by the Soviet Union of all disarmament talks attended by the Chinese Nationalists. The third demonstrated that atomic weapons might never be used in a limited war, thus conferring an advantage upon the side which possessed a superiority in conventional arms. As a result of these new factors, the United States dropped its opposition to a unified approach and called for an integration of atomic and conventional discussions.

By a resolution adopted in the General Assembly in 1952, the objectives and the work of the two Commissions were assigned to a single Disarmament Commission and were aimed at "the regulation, limitation, and balanced reduction of all armed forces and all armaments" and "the elimination of all major weapons adaptable to mass destruction." The new Disarmament Commission functioned under the Security Council with the latter's eleven members plus Canada represented on it. Its efforts to prepare a draft treaty to achieve the reduction and control of *all* armaments foundered on the same rocks of disagreement over timing, inspection, and control that had stymied its predecessors. The Soviet bloc reiterated its 1946 position that placed priority on the signing of a general disarmament treaty, while the Western states continued to focus their efforts on the need for an effective disclosure, verification, and control system. *Plus ça change, plus c'est la meme chose!*

PHASE III: THE FIVE-POWER DISCUSSIONS. By mid-1953, both the United States and the Soviet Union had successfully tested thermonuclear devices, a Korean armistice had been signed, and new leaders had assumed power in the Soviet Union following the death of Stalin. The changing international milieu gave some promise that a solution to the disarmament problem might be found. Again, the General Assembly initiated the new phase by urging a breakthrough with a new, "realistic" approach—negotiations by a Disarmament Commission subcommittee consisting of the United States, the Soviet Union, Britain, France, and Canada. By limiting discussions to the five "principally involved" powers, the Assembly sought to curtail the temptation to use disarmament talks for propaganda purposes. The Soviets at first demanded a more balanced membership on the subcommittee with the addition of Communist China, Czechoslovakia, and India. Russian demands for parity in membership on the negotiating body and for the participation of Communist China continued to be major grievances for some years thereafter. The creation of the Ten-Member Disarmament Commission in 1959 achieved the first goal and the growing Sino-Soviet split in the 1960's softened Russian demands for the second.

Following the creation of the five-member negotiating body, President Dwight Eisenhower presented a dramatically new Atoms for Peace proposal to the General Assembly in an additional move to break the disarmament deadlock. The President called for the establishment of an international atomic energy agency to promote the peaceful international application of the new power. States in the atomic club were urged to reduce their national stockpiles of fissionable materials by making contributions to the international agency for research and power development. The International Atomic Energy Agency (IAEA) was subsequently established by the United Nations in 1957 with headquarters in Vienna and with the cooperation of all the atomic powers. The Soviets, while supporting the development of IAEA, rejected the idea that the Atoms for Peace program was in any way related to the issues of disarmament.

After winning the post-Stalin internal power struggle, Nikita Khrushchev launched a "peaceful coexistence" offensive in 1955. Because Soviet leaders had failed to prevent West Germany from joining NATO, they offered concessions on disarmament in exchange for agreement on a new proposal to freeze arms at their 1954 levels—an obvious ploy aimed at preventing German rearmament. For the first time in nine years of negotiations, the Soviet Union accepted the Western position that an inspection system must be established *before* the prohibition of atomic weapons became effective. This new position on the question of timing reflected the growing unease of Soviet as well as American leaders over the danger of a surprise thermonuclear attack by a party which surreptitiously retained possession of such weapons. The deadlock, however, continued in other areas.

A new approach was offered by President Eisenhower at the Geneva summit conference in the summer of 1955 to reduce the existing threat of surprise attack and break the stalemate in negotiations. He proposed an "open skies" plan by which the two major nuclear powers would permit unrestricted aerial reconnaissance of each other's territory. A mutual exchange of blueprints of military establishments and a continuing inspection by on-the-site observers were included in the final proposal. Although the Soviets met some of the American demands for security, in the end they rejected the open skies approach on the ground that its primary purpose was "espionage."

In 1957, in a major effort to achieve agreement, the Disarmament Commission subcommittee of five met in London for seventy-one negotiating sessions. The Western powers and the Soviet Union reformulated all phases of their disarmament proposals in an attempt to reach a comprehensive agreement for the entire field. Primary emphasis in the talks, however, was focused on five critical issues: (1) conventional force levels; (2) inspection against surprise attack; (3) control of outer space; (4) prohibition of nuclear weapons; and (5) the cessation of nuclear weapons testing.

Although there was some measure of agreement on each of the major issues, in proceeding from the general to the specific the area of agreement quickly withered and then disappeared. On force levels, for example, there was agreement only on a first-stage reduction to 2,500,000-man military establishments for the United States and the Soviet Union and 750,000-man establishments for Britain and France. The United States refused to agree to reductions beyond this point until there had been "progress toward the the solution of political issues." Discussion on aerial inspection against surprise attack reached a stalemate when neither side would agree to permit aerial inspection of its vital areas. On the main question of banning nuclear weapons, both sides reverted to their original positions, taken over a decade earlier. The Soviets called for a treaty prohibiting all nuclear weapons as a first step, and the United States remained adamantly opposed to such a ban in the absence of an effective inspection and control system.

From 1957 to 1959, negotiations on general disarmament were first subordinated to and then replaced by a debate over the proper forum for disarmament talks. The orbiting of the first "sputnik" earth satellite in 1957 bolstered Soviet confidence and hardened their position in favor of a broader forum for expounding their views on disarmament questions. Although the Assembly increased the size of the Disarmament Commission from eleven to twenty-five and added two additional Soviet-bloc states, the Soviets rejected the new approach and refused to participate in its work. Still, two hopeful moves occurred during the boycott in 1958. In the first, the Soviet Union announced a unilateral cessation of nuclear testing, although it retained the right to "act freely" if other powers continued to test. Since the Soviets had just completed a long series of tests and the United States was about to begin one, prospects for observing the voluntary ban were not good. World pressures, however, led the United States to adhere to it. In the second, a Conference of Experts composed of scientists from the leading nuclear powers convened at Geneva in the summer of 1958 to try to reach agreement on the technical problems involved in a ban on all nuclear testing.

PHASE IV: THREE PLUS EIGHTY-TWO PLUS TEN EQUALS ZERO. The Soviet boycott of the Disarmament Commission ended suddenly in the fall of 1958 with the creation of two new disarmament bodies. The first, which offered the Soviets the forum they had long sought, was an eighty-two-nation United Nations Disarmament Commission created by the General Assembly.[4] The mammoth new "negotiating forum," with all members of the world organization represented, was not expected to produce direct results, but many nations supported it as a means of marshaling world pressures to force concessions from the great powers. In 1960, the United States called the Disarmament Commission into session to pressure the East European states to resume negotiations after they had staged a walkout at Geneva. It was not subsequently called into session until 1965 when the Soviet Union requested a meeting of the then 114-nation Disarmament Commission to overcome once again a hiatus in great power negotiations. The huge Disarmament Commission, true to its critics' forecasts, failed to resolve any issues in the arms control dialogue, but its sessions proved useful in securing a resumption of great power negotiations and in exploring approaches not ordinarily considered by the great powers, such as the inclusion of Communist China in disarmament talks and the calling of a World Disarmament Conference.

The second new disarmament group consisted of a Three-Power Conference—Britain, the United States, and the Soviet Union—which met in Geneva in October, 1958, to draft a treaty to ban nuclear testing. It was called after Eastern and Western scientists at the Geneva Conference of Experts reached a unanimous conclusion that "a workable and effective control system to detect violations of an agreement on the world-wide suspension of nuclear weapons tests" is technically feasible. The new body, while not officially under UN jurisdiction, was serviced by UN personnel and met at the European regional headquarters of the United Nations.

The test-ban negotiations were the culmination of an almost world-wide, often boisterous "ban the bomb" campaign during the 1950's coupled with repeated resolutions in the General Assembly demanding that the nuclear powers halt their nuclear test explosions. Scientists from many countries had expressed grave concern over the high level of radioactive pollution stemming from Western and Soviet thermonuclear tests. As a result of the world outcry, the emphasis in disarmament talks shifted from what increasingly appeared to be the utopian goal of total disarmament to the partial but more immediate test-ban measure. The Soviet Union, however, noting

---

[4] General Assembly Resolution 1252 D (XIII), November 4, 1958.

that France continued to carry out nuclear tests while Britain and the United States negotiated on the test-ban treaty, referred to the Western position as "an artificial division of labor."

The main issues developed over the years that stood in the way of agreement to permanently outlaw testing were (1) timing, with Britain and the United States demanding that a thoroughly effective control system be established *before* outlawing tests; (2) the number of control posts, with the two Western nations insisting on a minimum of twenty-one located on Soviet soil and the Soviets proposing a maximum of fifteen; (3) the frequency of inspections, which the Soviets wanted to limit to three annually against the Western demand for a minimum of twelve and a maximum of twenty; (4) the composition of the Control Commission, posing the question of whether its membership should be based on East-West parity or reflect equality for all nuclear powers; and (5) the chief executive of the Control Commission, with the Soviet call for a tripartite Administrative Council, each of its three members having the veto power, opposed to the Western demand for a single administrator. Soviet insistence on the "troika" principle—similar to their demand for a three-man presidium to replace the Secretary-General—evoked a totally negative response from the other nuclear powers whenever it was suggested. When the Soviets broke the three-year moratorium and began a series of massive test-bomb explosions in September, 1961, the Three-Power Conference was hurriedly adjourned. The American reaction was a series of underground and atmospheric tests that brought world condemnation of the two leading nuclear powers to a crescendo.

Meanwhile, agreement was reached in 1959 to establish a new Ten-Nation Committee to try again to achieve a consensus on general and complete disarmament. The decision to create the Committee constituted a recognition by the great powers that the eighty-two nation Disarmament Commission was too unwieldy for useful negotiations and too uncertain as a propaganda medium. The new forum accepted the perennial Soviet demand for "parity" between Eastern and Western members by including five Soviet-bloc states (Bulgaria, Czechoslovakia, Poland, Romania, and the USSR) and five Western-bloc states (Britain, Canada, France, Italy, and the United States). The Committee, like the Three-Power Conference on writing a nuclear test-ban treaty, was technically not under United Nations jurisdiction but was serviced by UN personnel and met at the UN Geneva headquarters in the old League of Nations building. A new Soviet proposal for general and complete disarmament which had been presented to the General Assembly by Premier Nikita Khrushchev served as the initial focus for Committee discussions.

When the ten nations began their deliberations in March, 1960, they were little closer to reaching agreement on general disarmament than when discussions had begun almost fifteen years earlier. The Western position, developed mainly by the United States but also reflecting Anglo-French proposals, placed major emphasis on controlling nuclear weapons. Included were proposals for halting production of fissionable materials for weapons, the banning of nuclear tests, a prohibition against transferring nuclear weapons to nonnuclear nations, international control of outer space, the eventual destruction of ballistic missiles, and the gradual elimination of all nuclear weapons following the establishment of international inspection and control machinery. The far-ranging Soviet position called for a nonaggression pact between NATO and the Warsaw Pact states, a universal renunciation of the use of atomic weapons, a freezing of military budgets, the withdrawal of all troops from foreign bases, an end to war propaganda, atom-free zones in Central Europe, Africa, the Far East, and the Pacific, and the establishment of ground control posts to prevent surprise attack.[5] Both sides placed an unusually high degree of emphasis on the role of a United Nations international police force operating under the Security Council to preserve peace and security in a disarming world.

Despite a modicum of agreement on general principles, the two sides engaged mainly in a propaganda battle during their 1960 confrontations. Their failure to come to grips with specific issues led Senator Hubert Humphrey to conclude: "The essence of the Soviet plan was lots of talk about disarmament, little control, and no study. The essence of the Western plan was lots of study, a bit of control, and an uncertain and indefinite amount of disarmament." [6]

While discussions were underway, an American U-2 observation plane was shot down over the Soviet Union. The impact of this incident upon the abortive Paris "summit" conference between Khrushchev and Eisenhower resulted in a shockwave of bitterness and name calling that spilled over to the Geneva conference. The East European group charged the West with bad faith and departed in a huff, resulting in another hiatus of nine months in general disarmament talks. Phase IV of the disarmament dialogue ended in 1960 with the possibility of tangible agreement further removed than at any time since 1946.

PHASE V: A NEW EXPERIENCE. The dangers to world peace that resulted from the Berlin crisis of 1961 and the pressures of world opinion mobilized in the General Assembly drove the United States and the Soviet Union to discuss the resumption of disarmament negotiations. A series of bilateral talks in the summer of 1961 resulted in a Joint Statement of Agreed Principles for Disarmament Negotiations (McCloy-Zorin Agreement). The joint statement set forth a series of general principles on which substantial

[5] *United Nations Review,* Vol. VIII, No. 11 (November, 1961), p. 10.

[6] *Congressional Record,* Vol. 106, No. 117, 86th Congress, 2nd Sess., June 24, 1960, p. 2.

agreement had been reached in the past,[7] including (1) balanced disarmament by stages; (2) establishment of pacific settlement procedures; (3) maintenance of peace by United Nations forces; (4) inspection access unrestricted by veto; and (5) control by an international disarmament organization. The statement concluded with a call for all states participating in disarmament talks "to achieve and implement the widest possible agreement at the earliest possible date."

The creation of a new negotiating body by the Sixteenth Assembly in 1961 marked the recognition of the growing stake in disarmament for the nonaligned nations and of their voting power in the Assembly. The new Eighteen-Nation Disarmament Committee (ENDC) was established by adding eight countries (Brazil, Burma, Ethiopia, India, Mexico, Nigeria, Sweden, and the United Arab Republic) to the membership of the defunct Ten-Nation Committee. The McCloy-Zorin Agreement served as the initial agenda for the resumption of discussions on general disarmament by the new committee. From the start, the ENDC was weakened by the refusal of France to participate on the ground that serious disarmament negotiations should be limited to the four nuclear powers. Near the end of 1961, three-power talks were also resumed on the subject of a test-ban treaty, spurred on by the Soviet tests which had included the detonation of a "monster bomb" of more than 50 megatons (50 million tons of TNT equivalent). As negotiations in both committees dragged on, each enveloped in deadlocks over specific issues in the fields of inspection and control, it became evident that past failures were again repeating themselves. The Soviet insistence on the troika principle for the administration of the inspection and control system with a veto for each representative—East, West, and Nonaligned— impeded progress in other areas as well.

In 1962, the United States and the Soviet Union presented separate proposals to the ENDC for general and complete disarmament which remained the basic positions of the two sides in 1966. The proposals incorporate a greater degree of consensus, based on the McCloy-Zorin Agreement, than had existed at any time in the past; yet beneath the veneer of agreement each offers radically different prescriptions for specific steps.

Both plans call for (1) complete nuclear and conventional disarmament implemented in three stages; (2) the establishment of an International Disarmament Organization (IDO) to enforce controls through inspection and verification; and (3) the establishment of effective peace-keeping machinery. The main differences in the two drafts concern the question of timing as applied to the extent of disarmament within each stage and the point of transition from one stage to the next, and differences over inspection, control, and peace-keeping arrangements.

[7] For the complete statement, see Donald C. Blaisdell, *International Organization* (New York: Ronald Press, 1966), Appendix D.

TABLE 12-1. Disarmament Proposals (as of 1966) USSR-USA

Topics	Stage 1	Stage 2	Stage 3
Duration			
USSR	18 months	24 months	12 months
USA	36 months	36 months	"as promptly as possible"
Nuclear Weapons			
USSR	Cease testing and outlaw transfers of weapons.	Eliminate all weapons of mass destruction.	Eliminate all weapons of mass destruction.
USA	Cease testing under international control and outlaw transfers of weapons.	Reduce nuclear weapons to minimum levels.	
Delivery Systems			
USSR	Eliminate all delivery systems (except small number of homebased ICBM's).		Eliminate all delivery systems.
USA	Reduce delivery systems by 30 per cent.	Reduce delivery systems by additional 50 per cent.	Eliminate all delivery systems.
Outer Space			
USSR	Prohibit all military uses of space.		
USA	Refrain from orbiting nuclear weapons and limit production, stockpiling and boosters for space vehicles.		
Conventional Arms			
USSR	Reduce by 30 per cent.	Reduce by an additional 35 per cent.	Eliminate except as required for internal peace-keeping.
USA	Reduce by 30 per cent.	Reduce by an additional 50 per cent.	Eliminate except as required for internal peace-keeping.
Military Manpower			
USSR	Reduce American and Soviet armies to 1.9 million men each.	Reduce both armies to 1 million men.	Reduce to number necessary to maintain domestic order and provide contingents for UN police force.
USA	Reduce Soviet and American armies to 2.1 million men each.	Reduce both armies by 50 per cent.	

333

TABLE 12-1, cont'd.

Topics	Stage 1	Stage 2	Stage 3
Military Budgets			
USSR	Reduce military budgets proportionately to arms and manpower reductions.		Limit military expenditures to maintaining international and national police forces.
USA	Submit reports on military budgets and seek agreement on verifiable reductions.		
Military Bases			
USSR	Eliminate foreign bases and withdraw all troops.		Eliminate foreign bases and withdraw all troops.
USA		Eliminate specific foreign bases through agreement.	
Transitional Measures			
USSR	Prohibit joint, and require advance notice of national, military movements and maneuvers; exchange military missions; establish communication systems.		
USA	Give advance notice of major military movements; exchange military missions; establish observation posts and communications systems.		
Inspection and Peace-Keeping			
USSR	Establish IDO to supervise destruction of arms. IDO to function under Security Council.	IDO supervision of arms destruction.	Place national militia contingents under Security Council direction; command of troop units vested in body composed of "three principal groups of states" and each must agree to peace-keeping actions.
USA	Establish IDO to inspect and control destroyed and remaining arms. IDO to function under Security Council.	IDO inspection and control over disarmament steps and remaining arms.	UN Peace Force to function under Security Council; veto power not applicable to peace-keeping actions.

334

The main innovation in both the American and Soviet proposals was the creation of an IDO that would have "unrestricted access without veto to all places as necessary for the purposes of effective verification." Both plans call for the IDO to function within the framework of the United Nations, which would have the full responsibility for safeguarding peace and security. The Soviet version, however, would accept the Security Council as presently constructed, whereas the American draft calls for "strengthening the structures, authority, and operation of the United Nations so as to improve its capability to maintain international peace and security." This can only mean that the application of the veto power in the Security Council to the maintenance of peace in a disarmed world is unacceptable to the United States.

Another crucial gap between the parties relates to the decision-making structure of IDO. The Soviets have retained their troika demand for a presidium and staff that would give equal representation to the East, West, and Nonaligned groups of states. The Anglo-American position calls for a single Administrator to manage IDO under the direction of its Control Council. Until these disparate views over timing, the veto, and the administrative structure of IDO can be harmonized, no amount of progress in other disarmament areas will achieve the fundamental consensus needed for a final agreement. The American and Soviet positions on all three issues remain strikingly similar in basic content to those which they took initially in 1946.

Areas other than the negotiations on general and complete disarmament fared surprisingly well during Phase V. In his annual report in 1964, Secretary-General U Thant was able to declare that "more significant progress in achieving some measures of disarmament has taken place since the summer of 1963 than in all the years since the founding of the United Nations." [8] The developments that the Secretary-General referred to included (1) a partial nuclear test-ban treaty; (2) the establishment of a direct communications link between Washington and Moscow; (3) a General Assembly resolution to ban nuclear and other weapons of mass destruction from outer space; (4) unilateral reductions in the military budgets of the United States and the Soviet Union; and (5) voluntary cutbacks in the production of fissionable material for military purposes by the Soviet Union, the United States, and Britain. Although the cutbacks in defense spending proved to be short-lived because of the expanding crisis in Viet Nam, the others have been observed. After twenty years of largely sterile negotiations, these four advances, along with the Antarctic Treaty of 1959, remain the only tangible evidence that disarmament is a feasible objective.

[8] "Introduction to the Annual Report of the Secretary-General on the Work of the Organization," *UN Monthly Chronicle,* Vol. 1, No. 7 (December, 1964), p. 44.

A TWENTY-YEAR BALANCE SHEET

Unlike the sporadic efforts of the League of Nations, disarmament negotiations have been conducted within and outside the United Nations almost continuously for over twenty years. The nature of the new weapons of mass destruction has given a persisting sense of urgency to the search for consensus.

In retrospect, how meaningful were these profuse efforts to achieve a disarmament agreement? What hope do they offer for the future control of arms and armies? Have the major powers moved closer to agreement or has there instead been a retrogression that has widened the initial divergence over the Baruch Plan? To what extent have the negotiators seriously sought agreement and how often have they used the discussions as a propaganda sounding board? What should be the future role of the United Nations?

Questions like these lack precise answers. Disarmament talks go on within a political framework in which the participants in the dialogue mask their words so that their precise meaning is often obscure. From the start, negotiations have been surrounded by an air of unreality, with neither side believing that the other is negotiating in good faith. Yet, in spite of all the drawbacks, agreements have been reached in several limited areas. These successful negotiations will be examined first, followed by an analysis of potentially useful approaches to partial or complete disarmament that have received some attention in the past and may provide the key to a future agreement.

Antarctic Demilitarization

The first disarmament agreement to emerge during the cold-war period provided for the demilitarization of the Antarctic continent. Twelve governments with interests in the region (including the United States and the USSR) agreed in the Antarctic Treaty of 1959 that

1. The use of the region for military activities of any kind is forbidden;
2. Each signatory has the right to inspect the installations of the others to ensure that no treaty violation has occurred;
3. Territorial claims on the continent remain unrecognized and no new claims may be made;
4. No nuclear explosions or dumping of radioactive wastes is permitted;
5. Disputes under the terms of the Treaty will be settled peacefully; and
6. Signatories agree to cooperate in scientific investigations in the region.

The Antarctic Treaty provides a model for the potential demilitarization of other regions in the world. No known violations have occurred and the right of national inspection has been fully acknowledged. Although no joint arrangements exist for governing the area, Antarctica is at least partially "internationalized" by the voluntary system.

Guided by the example of the Antarctic Treaty, an American and a Soviet scientist proposed a similar plan in 1964 for the demilitarization of the Arctic.[9] The two advanced their scheme as a potential first step in a zonal disarmament that could incorporate additional zones after each successful demilitarization. The Antarctic, however, may prove to be a unique example for demilitarization purposes. Unlike the Arctic with its proximity to a major military confrontation, the Antarctic is far removed from the power centers of the world.

Partial Nuclear Test-Ban Treaty

The Moscow Treaty of 1963 capped years of frustration, propaganda exchanges, and fruitless negotiations. Each state adhering to the treaty agrees

> to prohibit, to prevent, and not to carry out any nuclear test explosion, or any other nuclear explosion, at any place under its jurisdiction or control . . . in the atmosphere; beyond its limits, including outer space; or underwater, including territorial waters or high seas.

Because of the seismological problem in detecting underground nuclear tests and distinguishing them from natural earth tremors, subsurface tests are not prohibited by the agreement. The Soviet Union and the United States have each carried out numerous underground tests since the treaty took effect in October, 1963.

Although there was a clear implication that the "partial" nature of the test ban would be made complete as soon as technology had advanced to the point of ensuring the detection of all such tests, negotiations have lagged behind scientific advancements. Moreover, the treaty is a partial one in another equally significant respect: although over one hundred nations had subscribed to the treaty by 1966, two atomic powers—France and Communist China—have refused to sign it and each has conducted atmospheric tests since 1963. Both reject all suggestions that they voluntarily comply with the treaty's provisions.

Why, after years of failure to secure agreement on limiting nuclear weapons, did a consensus suddenly evolve? The obvious answer is that conditions had ripened so that the three parties that negotiated the treaty—Britain, the United States, and the Soviet Union—regarded it as fully complementary to their respective national interests. Each country had exploded bombs of immense power and had perfected sophisticated devices for use as both strategic and tactical weapons. The bombs had reached such a magnitude

---

[9] See Alexander Rich and Aleksandr P. Vinogradov, "Arctic Disarmament," *Bulletin of the Atomic Scientists* (November, 1964), pp. 22–23. Their plan was the first specific disarmament proposal jointly authored by scientists of the two countries.

of power that it had become too dangerous and nonsensical to test more powerful ones. Levels of radioactive fallout engendered by the Soviet and American tests in the early 1960's reached proportions that might offer a potential danger to future generations through gene mutations. Moreover, it had become increasingly difficult to ignore the rising clamor of world opinion demanding a cessation to all testing.

Although the test-ban treaty is an encouraging forward step, it is doubtful that similar conditions of surfeit, danger, and popular agitation could have an equal impact on the search for agreement in the field of general and complete disarmament. Yet, other partial disarmament or control measures may be instituted when another convergence of great power interests occurs. The treaty represents an acknowledgment by the three major nuclear states that the dangers of an uncontrolled arms race may outweigh the fear that the other side may not honor the agreement. It represents a substantial compromise in the American position against entering into any disarmament agreement without the safeguards of inspection, verification, and control. It has not in fact, however, seriously restricted either side's military efforts in the arms race.

Washington-Moscow "Hot Line"

The 1962 Cuban missile crisis dramatized the need in the nuclear age for some means of direct and rapid communication between the leaders of the Soviet Union and the United States. To reduce the possibilities of a great power clash through miscalculation, accident, or failure of communication, the United States in 1963 proposed that each side give advance notice of major military movements, that ground observation posts be established at key transportation centers, that aerial observation be permitted by both sides, and that a teletype communications link be established between Washington and Moscow. The Soviet representative initially dismissed all proposals as potential sources of espionage, but later announced that his government would accept the teletype cable as a step that "might have certain positive benefits." The two governments signed an agreement and the "hot line" was installed between the two capitals.[10]

Although the communications link was hailed by some observers as a major innovation to reduce the threat of accidental war, others expressed amazement that no such precautionary arrangement had existed between the two governments during the years of major crises. At the height of the Cuban missile crisis, for example, President Kennedy had to fall back on commercial facilities to communicate with the Kremlin. The main danger of war through misunderstanding occurs during a crisis when each side's

[10] Memorandum of Understanding, June 20, 1963, Conference of the Eighteen-Nation Disarmament Committee, Document ENDC/97. In 1966, French and Russian leaders agreed to establish a similar communications link between Paris and Moscow.

preparations *against* a surprise attack may appear to the other to be a preparation *for* an attack. Between crises, other situations may develop that the hot line may help to explain or moderate. For example, radar distorted by meteors or other natural phenomena could lead one side to believe that an attack is underway or, through human or mechanical error, a major city may be destroyed. If, for example, a large American or Russian city were suddenly atomized, would the leaders of that state undertake an immediate full-scale retaliatory attack or would they first communicate with the other? The former action could lead to the complete destruction of both countries with hundreds of millions of casualties; the latter might conceivably prevent an all-out nuclear exchange, but the problem of "compensation" for a destroyed city would remain. No past experience in warfare can give satisfactory answers to the new dangers of the atomic age. The communications link is merely an improvisation to reduce the threat of irrational responses; only a complete nuclear disarmament with adequate safeguards could eliminate the threat of nuclear war.

Peaceful Uses of Outer Space

The launching of the first earth satellite in 1957 added the problem of preventing military exploitation of outer space to the complex of disarmament issues. The General Assembly took an initial action the following year when it established a special Committee on the Peaceful Uses of Outer Space to draft a set of principles governing national conduct in the new environment. After early failures and a long deadlock over legal issues, the United States and the Soviet Union reached agreement within the Committee in 1963. The General Assembly thereupon unanimously adopted the Committee's draft in the form of a Declaration of Legal Principles Governing the Activities of States in the Exploration and Use of Outer Space.[11]

The Assembly action was a first step toward developing a code of space law. Although the code was only a declaration of principles, the major space powers endorsed it and in a subsequent resolution declared that they would continue work on the Committee to draft an international space agreement.

Major principles to guide states in using and exploring space were enunciated in the Declaration. Outer space and celestial bodies were "internationalized," international law was made applicable, states were made internationally responsible for their activities in outer space, and the responsibility to render emergency assistance to astronauts and their vehicles and to return them safely to their country of origin was proclaimed. The resolution also endorsed the exchange of scientific information on space programs and the establishment of a world "weather watch" under the sponsorship of the World Meteorological Organization.

[11] General Assembly Resolution 1962 (XVIII), December 13, 1963.

In addition to the Declaration of Principles, the General Assembly adopted six resolutions from 1958 to 1963 relating to outer space. A composite of these proclamations affirms several additional guidelines for space activity:

1. The exploration and use of space should be "only for the betterment of mankind."

2. All states should benefit from space activities regardless of their scientific or economic development.

3. The United Nations should serve as a center for coordinating space activities and for the exchange of information.

4. International cooperation in space activities will foster closer relations between nations and peoples.

Space cooperation between the United States and the Soviet Union got off to a good start with bilateral agreements in 1962 and 1964. These provided for a coordinated weather satellite program and for joint satellite communications tests. Subsequent activities by both countries related to potential military use of space dramatized the need for agreement on a space treaty.[12] In December, 1966, a consensus was finally achieved and a draft treaty was approved by the General Assembly without a dissenting vote. When ratified, it will bar weapons from outer space and guarantee free access for all nations to the moon and other celestial bodies.

General and Complete Disarmament

The unrelenting failure to secure a general disarmament agreement during twenty years of strenuous negotiations beclouds the principles and specifics on which the East and West have achieved some measure of consensus. The gap between the contestants, though still a fundamental one unlikely to be bridged by a sudden breakthrough, may not be quite so broad as popular imagination would have it. At least substantial areas of agreement have been hammered out in various forums within and outside the framework of the United Nations. By 1966, these included the following:

---

[12] For an analysis of military possibilities in space, see George C. Sponsler, "The Military Role in Space," *Bulletin of the Atomic Scientists* (June, 1964), pp. 31–34. In August, 1965, President Johnson announced an American program to develop a Manned Orbiting Laboratory (MOL) to test the feasibility of using manned spaceships to inspect and destroy enemy satellites and to serve as command posts to direct military operations on earth. In May, 1966, the President called for early adoption of a treaty prohibiting any nation from claiming sovereignty over the moon or other celestial bodies or stationing weapons of mass destruction on them. The Soviets in a letter to Secretary-General U Thant the following month agreed that a space treaty "would ensure conditions for a peaceful exploration and use of the moon. . . ." (*New York Times,* June 5, 1965, p. 1E.) Although the Soviets have exhibited a rocket designed to put nuclear weapons in orbit around the earth, neither they nor the United States have directly violated the principles expressed in the Assembly resolution on outer space. Both, however, have defied the spirit of that agreement by their military research and development space programs.

1. All states will disarm by general treaty.

2. Disarmament will proceed by stages, with a "balanced" level of armaments at each stage.

3. Disarmament steps do not require the fulfillment of political pre-conditions.

4. Conventional armaments and military manpower will be reduced to the amounts and numbers needed for keeping internal order.

5. All nuclear weapons and their delivery systems will be eliminated.

6. Production and testing of nuclear weapons will be banned.

7. Fissionable materials will be used only for peaceful purposes for the benefit of all mankind.

8. A United Nations Peace Force will be established before disarmament is completed.

9. An inspection system to provide verification will be set up, including aerial reconnaissance.

10. Disarmament will be enforced by an international control organ operating under Security Council jurisdiction.

11. Financial savings accruing from reduced arms budgets will be used to foster economic development in the developing countries.

Within each category of agreement, substantial issues remain on questions of timing, force levels, the nature of the inspection system, the composition of the control body, and the decision-making process within the total enforcement system. Political preconditions, though formally ruled out as necessary precursors to disarmament steps, obviously exist in fact. No agreement is likely to be reached until the problems of a divided Germany and the Viet Nam war have been resolved. Nor will the Soviet Union and the United States agree to disarm without the participation of Communist China and France, neither of which has shared in the minimal consensus noted above. These gaps nullify the concurrence on principles and keep general disarmament talks in a never-never land where negotiations go on incessantly but real communication and understanding are, indeed, rare commodities.

STRATEGIES TO BREAK THE DEADLOCK

When Columbus undertook his epic voyage, some scientists had thought for some years that the earth was round; yet the fear among mariners that the earth might after all prove to be flat postponed the discovery of the New World. Similarly, nations which recognize that a major war would be too catastrophic to contemplate are yet fearful to venture onto the uncharted seas of general disarmament. Is there a strategy that might prove useful in breaking the deadlock by overcoming the uncertainties about the viability and effects of a disarmament agreement? What additional partial disarmament measures might contribute to building a better base for general disarmament? A small sampling from the profusion of approaches offered by statesmen and scholars to overcome the dilemma or afford a partial remedy will be examined in the following pages.

The Direct Approach

The problem of developing a useful approach to disarmament starts with the question of whether the major effort should be placed on reducing arms or on developing security. Those who advocate a "direct" approach regard the arms race itself as the main source of fear and insecurity. The solution they offer is simple: "The way to disarm is to disarm." These words have reverberated through the chambers of the League and of the United Nations on many occasions. As arms are reduced, so holds the theory, the familiar cycle that produces the upward spiral in the arms race (increased arms produce greater fear and insecurity which, in turn, produce greater expenditures on arms, and so on) will be reversed. Reduced international tensions will follow in the wake of disarmament, encouraging the further elimination of arms. The Soviet Union and India have been the most vocal proponents of the direct approach during the United Nations era; the United States and Britain which supported the direct approach during the League period have changed since 1946 to the indirect approach.

The Indirect Approach

Those who advocate an indirect approach regard armaments as a reflection of the deep insecurities of the state system. Disarmament, therefore, should be recognized for what it is—a fundamentally *political* problem that involves the totality of relations among those nations caught up in the arms race. Disarmament becomes the secondary, not the immediate, objective. Major political conflicts must first be ameliorated, an effective collective security system established, and carefully planned inspection, verification, and sanctions arrangements made operational. Disarmament cannot be feasible, therefore, until there is a convergence of national policies on these issues. For the United States, this might mean that preconditions for disarmament would include resolution of the German, Vietnamese, and Korean questions, an operational United Nations police force without a Security Council veto, and an inspection and control system meeting American standards for safeguarding against violations.

When the Soviet Union on several occasions offered package proposals for full and complete disarmament within a brief period of years, there was little wonder that the West with its indirect orientation to disarmament did not take the offers seriously. On the other hand, American preoccupation with political details may have convinced the Soviets that Western avowals of willingness to disarm are merely perfidious cold war strategies. Whatever the interpretations by each of the other side's motives, twenty years of deadlock provide substantial reason to believe that general disarmament is not plausible unless the two opposing approaches can be reconciled or unless one side proves willing to change its tactics.

Unilateral Disarmament

Some disarmament advocates offer the radically novel strategy of one-sided initiative to secure an arms reduction breakthrough. Once such an action has started the disarming process, mutual reciprocation would theoretically give it the motive power necessary to accelerate its momentum. Underlying unilateral disarmament theories is an assumption that the reduction of arms is really a matter of common interest, but inertia, tension, mistrust, fear, and habit make it at least appear to be beyond realization.

Several religious groups advocate a complete unilateral disarmament. If the other side uses the opportunity to impose its control, a Gandhian passive resistance would be employed against the conqueror. Utopian schemes of this nature, while no one can be certain they would fail, are impracticable because neither side in the arms race would place its national security or way of life in the hands of its opponent.

Several disarmament theoreticians have worked out unilateral schemes that depend upon reciprocal initiatives and responses rather than an abject surrender of retaliatory power by one side.[13] One of the most widely discussed of these—Charles Osgood's proposed policy of Graduated Reciprocation in Tension-reduction (GRIT)—calls for a deliberate "peace offensive" by the United States with "deeds rather than words" to induce correlative acts by the other side. Specifically, Osgood's program would be launched with "unilateral initiatives" in two types of activities—one, a gradual arms reduction to reduce the physical threats of conflict and, two, a withdrawal from a geographical area in which Western and Soviet power is in direct confrontation. Osgood's goal is to reverse the tensions-arms-race spiral sufficiently to create an atmosphere in which a full-blown solution to the problem of disarmament could be worked out. To succeed, he cautions that American unilateral acts must (1) be perceived by an opponent as reducing the threats to his security; (2) be a clear invitation to reciprocation; (3) be carried out even though no guarantee of reciprocation exists; (4) be planned in sequences and continued even when no reciprocation occurs; and (5) be announced in advance and widely publicized. Unilateral initiatives are not posited as a substitute for bilateral negotiations but only as a "psychological primer" to reverse the trend of the arms race by demonstrating good intentions. If the other side fails in due time to reciprocate or tries to take advantage of the unilateral reductions or withdrawals, the plan calls for a return to a hard-line policy to halt such encroachments.

[13] See, for example, Amitai Etzioni, *The Hard Way to Peace* (New York: Collier Books, 1962); and Charles Osgood, *An Alternative to War or Surrender* (Urbana: University of Illinois Press, 1962).

Although a partial unilateral disarmament would be unlikely to threaten the security of a state that has the power to destroy its opponent many times over, it lacks mass appeal because it violates the injunction not to encourage a potential aggressor through signs of weakness. Would the Soviet Union accept an opportunity to reverse the arms race by reciprocating American initiatives and vice versa, or would each pass them off as "Trojan horse" tactics? The nature and history of the contemporary arms race present some evidence that unilateral initiatives by either side might produce useful responses. Neither participant has strained its capabilities to the utmost in developing its arsenal, preferring some semblance of balance to an all-out drive for a massive superiority. Moreover, periods of reduced tension during the cold war have produced reductions in arms on both sides. None, however, has had a lasting impact. New crises have had a tendency to boost arms production in both countries to more than counterbalance previous cuts. Although unilateral disarmament schemes may be rational enough in their inherent logic, they must function in a highly irrational arms race environment. Only if they were adequately tested could their value be proved or disproved, a test which neither side shows any inclination to initiate.

Disengagement and Denuclearization

Although the idea of setting up a demilitarized zone or region to separate two potentially hostile armies is not a new one, the approach at first attracted only minor attention in the field of disarmament diplomacy. In 1957, however, the Communist side indicated an interest through a proposal made by Adam Rapacki, Foreign Minister of Poland. The Rapacki Plan called for the denuclearization of Central Europe (Czechoslovakia, Poland, East and West Germany) followed by a "disengagement" of Soviet and Western forces through a staged withdrawal from the region. The interest aroused by the Rapacki Plan produced a virtual avalanche of disengagement proposals from the East and the West.[14]

The object of disengagement is to reduce tension and avoid incidents between two major armies within a specific geographical area in order to avoid a major clash. The proximate confrontation of Western and Soviet forces in the heart of Europe makes the demilitarization of Germany the crucial issue in most disengagement schemes. All the schemes have foundered because neither West Germany nor other NATO members have been willing to consider the question of German neutralization. Western advocates of disengagement have argued that it would release several Warsaw Pact members from Soviet control, would facilitate settlement of

---

[14] For a review of these early proposals, see Eugene Hinterhoff, *Disengagement* (London: Stevens and Sons, 1959). In a two-year period, sixty plans were offered by Western scholars and statesmen and about twenty proposals came from the Warsaw Pact countries.

the German problem, and would constitute a valuable experiment in controlled disarmament. Western statesmen and military leaders have objected mainly on the ground that it would place NATO in a militarily weak position by the withdrawal of West Germany and by severely reducing NATO's system of defense in depth. Denuclearization of the region, moreover, would be disadvantageous to the West because of Soviet superiority in conventional weapons.

In the 1960's, numerous proposals have been presented in the General Assembly to reduce the threat of nuclear war in various regions of the world. A resolution adopted by the Assembly in 1961 requested all countries to "consider and respect the continent of Africa as a denuclearized zone." In 1963, the Soviet Union unsuccessfully advanced a proposal to denuclearize the Mediterranean, an area in which only the United States maintains nuclear armaments with its Polaris submarine fleet. The Assembly adopted a resolution in the same year to "initiate studies" on barring nuclear weapons from all of Latin America.

Most of the opposition to banning nuclear weapons from geographical areas of the world has come from the United States government which believes that such measures, if not accompanied by progress toward general and complete disarmament, increase rather than diminish the threat of aggression. In 1965, however, the White House Committee on Arms Control and Disarmament recommended to the President that the United States encourage the development of nuclear-free zones in Latin America, Africa, and the Middle East. The Committee suggested that for an initial venture, the United States should sign a treaty with the Soviet Union to establish a northern demilitarized zone (Bering Strait and equal areas of Alaska and Siberia) under a United Nations inspection system.

Demilitarization and disengagement proposals have aroused interest and debate but have failed to evoke the support of the major powers directly involved. The main obstacle has been the difficulty of defining a zone or region for neutralization that would not strategically disadvantage either side. Ten years of debate indicate that such proposals are unlikely to prove acceptable unless they are part of a broader political or general disarmament agreement or, as in the Antarctica Treaty of 1959, they apply to regions considered to be of little strategic importance.

Halting Nuclear Proliferation

The American postwar monopoly of atomic weapons ended in 1949 when the Soviet Union exploded its first atomic device. Three years later, Britain exploded a fission bomb, followed by France in 1960, and Communist China in 1964. With the "nuclear club" now containing the world's five major powers, the negotiation of a nonproliferation treaty was given a priority rating on the 1966 agenda of the Eighteen-Nation Disarmament Commission.

France, however, has boycotted the Commission from the start, and Communist China has never been asked—or indicated a willingness—to participate. At least ten nations having the scientific and technological capacity to join the club are now standing by, debating whether or not to expend the effort and the money necessary for membership. Perhaps as many as ten additional countries have or will soon have that capability.

What happens if the number of nuclear states expands to fifteen or to twenty-five? Would the threat of a major war be greater or would nuclear proliferation reduce the danger of conflict? Does a state like India need a nuclear capability for its defense against a threatening nuclear-armed neighbor or will guarantees from a friendly great power suffice? How could a nonproliferation treaty prevent a state from "going nuclear"? Much controversy exists among experts and statesmen on the answers to these and related questions concerned with the spread of nuclear weapons.

The debate over the proliferation of nuclear weapons has tended to polarize. One group regards nuclear diffusion as an obvious danger that will increase the possibility of nuclear war, probably more than proportionally to the addition of each new state. The second group views the dissemination of nuclear weapons as inevitable and probably not too serious. At any rate, this group is concerned that too much thought and effort are being placed on prevention of diffusion (which many regard as a hopeless undertaking) with little or no consideration given to the problem of how to manage a multinuclear world.[15]

Senator Robert F. Kennedy in a 1965 Senate speech warned that "the need to halt the spread of nuclear weapons must be a central priority of American policy. Of all our major interests, this now deserves and demands the greatest additional effort. . . ." Probably the foremost reason for the sense of urgency is the belief that the diffusion of nuclear weapons immeasurably increases the danger of nuclear war. E. L. M. Burns, for example, notes that

> While there are only two players, each possessing a thorough knowledge of the awesome power of which they and their opponent dispose and each capable through experience and much hard thinking of predicting the other's reactions, it is possible to believe that surprises and hasty or irrational decisions will be avoided. But what if additional players enter the game,

[15] For a discussion of the debate over the danger or lack of it in nuclear proliferation, see Jeremy J. Stone, "On Proliferation: Where's the Danger?," *Bulletin of the Atomic Scientists*, Vol. XXI, No. 9 (November, 1965), pp. 15–18. The view that proliferation constitutes a great danger is set forth by William C. Foster, "New Directions in Arms Control and Disarmament," *Foreign Affairs*, Vol. 43, No. 4 (July, 1965), pp. 587–601; and by E. L. M. Burns, "Can the Spread of Nuclear Weapons Be Stopped?", *International Organization*, Vol. XIX, No. 4 (Autumn, 1965), pp. 851–69. A contrary outlook is set forth by David B. Bobrow, "Realism About Nuclear Spread," *Bulletin of the Atomic Scientists*, Vol. XXI, No. 10 (December, 1965), pp. 20–22.

each with independent power to initiate nuclear warfare? If, to use a mathematical analogy, there were more independent variables in the equation? It is clear that this will introduce the possibility of unforeseen reactions and combinations of circumstances, of risks that are not calculable.[16]

The process of expanding the nuclear club tends to be self-propelling. Each new entry strengthens the political and strategic motivations for another or several states to expend the effort. If, for example, Israel explodes an atomic test bomb, the United Arab Republic would unquestionably embark on a crash program to catch up. If India gets atomic weapons, why not Pakistan? It is difficult to foresee where the drive to achieve nuclear capability will end. The proliferation thus encouraged will make great power disarmament infinitely more difficult and could encourage an intensification of American and Soviet developmental and stockpiling efforts. As the nuclear club expands, atomic weapons may be increasingly accepted as the normal means for waging war, and the probability that they will be used mounts with each additional finger on the trigger. States that get caught up in the nuclear race will also find it far more difficult to meet other priorities, such as finding the means for financing economic development. The result may be a growing internal instability and revolution-proneness in states with marginal capabilities that could encourage rash or even irrational actions by their leaders. Worst of all, a "catalytic war" could be touched off by a small power which surreptitiously used an atomic bomb to destroy a major Russian or American city.

From another point of view, however, preoccupation with preventing nuclear diffusion may weaken the ability of the contemporary nuclear powers to cope with the problem when it occurs. No one has yet been able to develop a satisfactory plan to prevent the spread of nuclear weapons or to posit the means by which the agreement of all existing or potential members of the club can be secured. Moreover, a case can be made that a widespread nuclearization may, just as it has produced a "balance of terror" among the great powers, make war increasingly unattractive. Local nuclear power balances might then complement their global counterparts and usher in a new era of total peace. Means of coping with a multinuclear world may evolve as the diffusion of weapons occurs. For example, one nation, such as the United States, might extend its deterrence system to include retaliatory strikes against any state that violated the injunction not to use weapons of mass destruction. Or a system of "compensatory diffusion" might enable a state threatened by another's nuclear capability to purchase nuclear weapons for its defense, thus restoring a local balance.

The problems of a nuclear-diffused world may have to be faced in the

---

[16] E. L. M. Burns, *op. cit.,* p. 855. Lieutenant General Burns is former Chief of Staff of the UN Truce Supervision Organization (UNTSO) and Commander of the UNEF in the Middle East and has served as Canada's representative on the ENDC since 1962.

future, but contemporary efforts are directed at trying to avoid them through international agreement. Although the wide dissemination of nuclear weapons has been a matter of concern since 1945, the drive to conclude a nonproliferation treaty started with the Irish Resolution (General Assembly Resolution 1665, XVI, December 4, 1961). The Resolution called upon all states to conclude a treaty to prevent nuclear states from "relinquishing control of nuclear weapons and from transmitting information necessary to their manufacture" and to obligate nonnuclear countries "not to manufacture or otherwise acquire control of such weapons."

Although any antiproliferation treaty would have to include at least these two types of pledges, some states have seen the need for a broader agreement. In 1965, for example, India presented a proposal to the 117-nation Disarmament Commission for "an integrated solution of the problems of proliferation." The scheme called for

1. An undertaking by the nuclear Powers not to transfer nuclear weapons or nuclear weapons technology to others;

2. An undertaking not to use nuclear weapons against countries which do not possess them;

3. An undertaking through the United Nations to safeguard the security of countries which may be threatened by Powers having a nuclear weapons capability or embarking on a nuclear weapons capability;

4. Tangible progress towards disarmament, including a comprehensive test ban treaty, a complete freeze on the production of nuclear weapons and means of delivery as well as a substantial reduction in the existing stocks; and,

5. An undertaking by non-nuclear Powers not to acquire or manufacture nuclear weapons.[17]

The Disarmament Commission, recognizing that its 117-nation membership was not conducive to negotiating a treaty, recommended that the ENDC reconvene and give priority to writing a treaty to prevent nuclear proliferation, as well as extending the scope of the test-ban treaty to include underground tests. The ENDC began deliberations on an American draft treaty in August, 1965, patterned on the simple approach of the Irish Resolution. The American plan would involve a pledge by nuclear and nonnuclear states "not to take any other action which would cause an increase in the total number of States and other organizations having independent power to use nuclear weapons . . . and not to assist . . . or to receive assistance in the manufacture of nuclear weapons. . . ."

The main issue that has developed between the American and Soviet delegations at Geneva concerns the proposed system for multilateral control of American nuclear weapons within NATO. More precisely, the Soviet Union had held for over a decade that it would never agree to any treaty that permits West Germany to have a voice in determining when nuclear

[17] United Nations Document DC/PV.75, May 4, 1965, pp. 16–17.

weapons will be used. In 1965, the Soviets reaffirmed this position by objecting to the American view that a NATO multilateral arrangement would not violate the American draft proposal nor constitute nuclear proliferation:

> The establishment of multilateral nuclear forces of NATO in any form would mean that nuclear weapons would be spread and that West German militarists would gain access to them, and this is a serious threat to the cause of peace in Europe and throughout the world.[18]

American negotiators are caught in a dilemma; they apparently want to conclude an antiproliferation treaty, but they do not want to reject the demands of the Federal Republic of Germany for assurance that nuclear weapons, strategic as well as tactical, will be available for the nation's defense. If American nuclear weapons are not made available through some multilateral arrangement, a resulting lack of faith in the American "nuclear umbrella" for the defense of the nation could lead a future German government to undertake their manufacture and deployment.

The idea underlying proposals for a NATO Multilateral Force (MLF) or Atlantic Nuclear Force (ANF) is to satisfy an apparent German demand for a credible nuclear deterrent through a multilateral weapons system that avoids *national* proliferation. The Soviets, however, regard the multilateral plans as proliferation and want all such schemes fully proscribed by the treaty. American policy makers are sensitive to German demands because that nation's contribution of twelve divisions provides the bulk of conventional forces for NATO and, with the withdrawal of French forces from the organization, German participation is indispensable. The question of nuclear weapons for Germany is likely to remain the central issue in future deliberations on a nonproliferation treaty.

Although the problem of nuclear diffusion may not be resolved by the signing of a treaty, other related fields of arms control may prove to be of direct value as components in the effort to halt the spread. If, for example, a test-ban treaty prohibiting *all* nuclear tests received the same broad support accorded to the partial agreement of 1963, many potential members of the nuclear club might be dissuaded from making the effort. Other correlative developments might include agreements to establish nuclear-free zones or continents and great power agreements not to transfer or sell aircraft or missile delivery systems. Many of the nations capable of producing atomic weapons—India, Japan, Sweden, and Italy, for example—are vigorously nonnuclear and are unlikely to undertake their development for political, psychological, or prestige reasons. Once a middle power nation develops the bomb, however, the floodgates may open wide, with all the consequences that may entail.

[18] United Nations Document DC/PV.72, April 26, 1965.

Epilogue: The Case for Total Disarmament

Arms control schemes and tangible progress achieved through partial disarmament measures are unquestionably useful elements in the battles waged to bring the arms race under a semblance of control. Measures like a comprehensive test-ban treaty, an antiproliferation agreement, and regional demilitarizations would comprise significant steps in their own right as well as reducing tension and encouraging additional steps. Only *total* disarmament, however, holds any real promise that the human race will survive the threat to its very existence.

That contemporary weapons of mass destruction offer the dismal prospect of human extinction can no longer be doubted. At the Hiroshima kill-ratio of approximately four deaths per ton of explosive power, the estimated 32 billion tons of TNT equivalent in the combined nuclear arsenals of the United States and the Soviet Union have the capability to destroy 128 billion people—forty times the population of the earth. When the deadly effects of radioactive fallout and of chemical and biological weapons of mass destruction are added to this estimate, only the most imperturbable optimist can talk about a meaningful aftermath to nuclear warfare.

Yet, as the survey of disarmament diplomacy since 1946 indicates, the propensity to move toward agreement on general and complete disarmament does not increase proportionally to the growing dangers. In fact, since 1962 negotiators have been diverted from their earlier detailed discussions of general disarmament to the consideration of first-step, partial measures. Even though the successful conclusion of the test-ban negotiations has been hailed by many as a significant forward step, the partial nuclear test-ban treaty may have proved to be a fruitful area for agreement solely because it does not present a real threat to the continuation of the arms race. Little time has been available in discussions for examining the potentials of schemes advanced by scholars and diplomats to break the deadlock in general disarmament. The constant reiteration of old positions by both sides has enabled each to gain a fluent understanding of what the other will not accept, but little effort has gone into a search for consensus other than on basic principles. As a useful procedural step, the establishment of separate negotiating bodies to consider partial disarmament measures would permit more specialization in the search for agreement and would free the ENDC to focus on the overall problems of general and complete disarmament.

What is the basic reason for the failure of the major powers to make any really tangible progress toward total disarmament over a period of twenty years? Is it a mistrust born of ideological hostility? If mistrust were the main ingredient of the stalemate, an enforcement system not dependent upon mutual trust could probably be hammered out. Is it conflict over political issues, such as the reunification of Germany, that stands in the way? If so, such issues might respond to increased efforts at negotiation. Can it be that each government believes that the arms race is favorable to its national interest in pursuing cold war goals? Perhaps because Communism has shown little strength at the ballot box, the Soviet strategy of "wars of national liberation" to achieve the "historically inevitable" victory of Communism demands a nuclear stand-off with the West and abundant supplies of conventional weapons for revolution-prone societies. From the American viewpoint, the arms race stimulates the domestic economy and weakens the Soviet Union by forcing it to devote a large portion of its best talent and industrial capacity to producing weapons, thus reducing its capability to provide a good life for its citizens and to offer more foreign aid to the developing states. Each side, it appears, may believe that the continuation of the arms race is advantageous to the achievement of its objectives, or at least that status quo is less risky than the unknown risks of a disarmed world. The seemingly unbridgeable gulf between them, therefore, may be more a function of national political strategy than of the commonly accepted explanations of mistrust and failure to agree on the specific details of phasing, inspection, and control. If so, the difficulty of resolving the manufactured stand-off may be greater than that of disposing of the deadlock over issues that have been making headlines for many years. Only if the cold war were brought to an end and conflicting national interests harmonized could a disarmament agreement become an achievable objective.

Whatever the reasons for the stand-off, the major powers must sooner or later (or, perhaps, *too* late?) recognize that a general disarmament agreement, even an imperfect one, is in the national interest of all. But even if every great power sincerely wanted total disarmament, the problem would remain of finding a formula that could provide a breakthrough, a so-called alternative to "overkill." The literature of disarmament offers numerous plans which in their theoretical innocence try to come to grips with the harsh realities of the nuclear threat. Stephen James and Morton Deutsch, for example, offer a scheme for the exchange of thousands of "peace hostages" to insure against a surprise attack.[19] J. David Singer suggests a plan by which the United States and the Soviet Union would progressively transfer their national military units to the United Nations until the UN force reached a strength greater than either of them singly.[20] Quincy Wright finds the solution to the arms race in the development of a "universal law for mankind." Grenville Clark and Louis B. Sohn offer a model of world government, complete disarmament, and a preoccupation with the economic

---

[19] See, for example, Quincy Wright, W. M. Evan, and Morton Deutsch, eds., *Preventing World War III: Some Proposals* (New York: Simon and Schuster, 1962).

[20] J. David Singer, *Deterrence, Arms Control, and Disarmament* (Columbus: Ohio State University Press, 1962).

development of poor societies. Kenneth Boulding calls for a five-stage development toward world order, with *tacit contract* the first, and *world government* the final stage.[21] These plans are only a small sampling of the rich variety of schemes offered to avert the threat of world catastrophe. Any one of the proposed models would probably be preferable to the contemporary danger, but the basic problem remains—how do we get from here to there?

In a more practical vein, how can the deadlock within the ENDC over general disarmament steps be resolved or how, at least, can some measure of progress be encouraged? If a disarmament agreement can be reached, the evolution of world law and world institutions may follow as necessary components to maintain the peace. The most comprehensive proposals set forth by an official body in the United States were presented to the President in 1965 by the special White House Committee on Arms Control and Disarmament. A summary of the main recommendations, some of which go beyond official American policy and may, therefore, offer suggestions for future initiatives in the field of disarmament diplomacy, are offered here for thoughtful consideration. The committee recommended:

1. The conclusion of a nonproliferation treaty with an agreement pledging nuclear powers (a) not to attack nonnuclear states and (b) to defend nonnuclear states if thus attacked;

2. A comprehensive nuclear test-ban treaty;

3. A U.S.-U.K.-USSR treaty to cease production of weapons-grade fissionable material;

4. An agreement to open all atomic energy plants to inspection by the IAEA.

5. The development of nuclear-free zones in Latin America, Africa, and the Near East, and a U.S.-USSR treaty to demilitarize the Bering Strait and areas of Alaska and Siberia under UN inspection;

6. A moratorium on the deployment of antiballistic missile systems, and a freeze on the number of strategic delivery vehicles and their progressive reduction;

7. UN supervision of the transfer and sale of all arms;

8. The development of an effective security system to protect the less developed nations;

9. The conclusion of a nonaggression pact between NATO and the Warsaw Pact organizations;

10. The admittance of the People's Republic of China into a genuine disarmament dialogue;

11. The establishment of a UN peace force and a UN observation corps;

12. A repeal of the Connally Amendment to strengthen the International Court.

[21] For an examination of these and various other proposals, see Richard A. Falk and Saul H. Mendlovitz, eds., *The Strategy of World Order—Toward a Theory of War Prevention,* Vol. 1 (New York: World Law Fund, 1966).

CONCLUSIONS

The problem of controlling armaments is fundamentally a problem of abolishing war and providing for security through world law and order. This can only mean that any general disarmament agreement must operate within the peace-keeping framework of the United Nations. The two major nuclear powers have shown some proclivity in the mid-1960's to return to the framers' concept of collective security to keep the peace in a disarmed world. Perhaps no disarmament scheme put forth officially or in a scholarly treatise offers a more practical approach to ending the stand-off than a United Nations security system functioning as its architects had envisioned.

But other, more immediate tasks confront the world organization. The most imperative of these, perhaps, is to develop a peace-keeping approach to end the limited war in Viet Nam that has poisoned the air for the great powers at a time when genuine consensus on several partial disarmament measures appeared to be evolving. High on the UN priority list also rests the problem of securing the agreement of France, Communist China, and Cuba to the partial nuclear test-ban treaty, and of gaining the participation of the first two in disarmament discussions. The objective of bringing all the nations of the world together in a World Disarmament Conference to be held "not later than 1967" was endorsed by the General Assembly in 1965 as a means of encouraging the participation of Peking and Paris.[22] When the World Disarmament Conference meets, a meaningful dialogue can be carried on only if every major nation of the world is represented.

Disarmament is not a problem that can be isolated from the development of an international legal, political, economic, and social system. The progressive evolution of a world community depends upon concurrent programs in these fields to moderate conflict and tension with a spirit of unity that could conceivably render armaments obsolete. The transformation of international relations from that of a system exuding power, tension, fear, and conflict to one of cooperation, understanding, and common action may be an impossible undertaking. If so, general disarmament may prove to be an ever-elusive quarry.

[22] General Assembly Resolution 2030 (XX), November 29, 1965. The plan for a World Disarmament Conference under UN auspices for member and nonmember nations alike was first proposed at the Conference of Non-Aligned Countries held in Cairo in 1964. The Resolution was adopted in the General Assembly by a vote of 112–0, with France abstaining and Nationalist China refusing to participate.

Selected Readings

BARKER, CHARLES A., ed. *Problems of World Disarmament*. Boston: Houghton-Mifflin, 1963.

BLOOMFIELD, LINCOLN P., ed. *Outer Space*. Englewood Cliffs, N.J.: Prentice-Hall, 1962.

BOLTON, ROGER E., ed. *Defense and Disarmament*. Englewood Cliffs, N.J.: Prentice-Hall, 1966.

BURNS, E. L. M. "Can the Spread of Nuclear Weapons be Stopped?", *International Organization*, Vol. XIX, No. 4, Autumn, 1965, pp. 851–69.

BURTON, JOHN W. *Peace Theory*. New York: Alfred A. Knopf, 1962.

FALK, RICHARD A., and MENDLOVITZ, SAUL H., eds. *The Strategy of World Order*, Vols. 1–4. New York: World Law Fund, 1966.

FISHER, WALTER R., and BURNS, RICHARD DEAN, eds. *Armament and Disarmament: The Continuing Dispute*. Belmont, California: Wadsworth, 1964.

HENKIN, LOUIS, ed. *Arms Control*. Englewood Cliffs, N.J.: Prentice-Hall, 1961.

HERZOG, ARTHUR. *The War-Peace Establishment*. New York: Harper and Row, 1963.

JACOBSON, HAROLD KARAN, and STEIN, ERIC. *Diplomats, Scientists and Polticians: The United States and the Nuclear Test Ban Negotiations*. Ann Arbor: University of Michigan Press, 1966.

KINTNER, WILLIAM R. "A Reappraisal of the Proposed Nonproliferation Treaty," *Orbis*, Vol. X, No. 1, Spring, 1966, pp. 138–51.

LEFEVER, ERNEST W., ed. *Arms and Arms Control*. New York: Praeger, 1962.

NOGEE, JOSEPH. "The Diplomacy of Disarmament," *International Conciliation*, No. 526, January, 1960, pp. 235–303.

SPANIER, JOHN W., and NOGEE, JOSEPH L. *The Politics of Disarmament*. New York: Praeger, 1962.

VAN SLYCK, PHILIP. *Peace: The Control of National Power*. Boston: Beacon Press, 1963.

WASKOW, ARTHUR I. *Keeping the World Disarmed*. Santa Barbara: Center for the Study of Democratic Institutions, 1965.

13 | *The Revolution of Self-Determination*

During the past half century the international system has been transformed by the disintegration of colonial empires. Since 1945 the number of independent states has doubled, and the process has a distance yet to run before the last remnants of empire have been accounted for. In this vast revolution of self-determination, international organization has had a growing involvement. Where the League of Nations was content to exercise minimal supervision over the administration of a few ex-enemy territories, the United Nations has become an active instrument for promoting self-government and independence for colonial peoples everywhere. The expanding role of international organization has been largely a function of the changing environment, but the organization has interacted with its environment to reinforce the developing anticolonial mood and to ease some of the pain of adjustment. In no other problem area has international organization had a more significant impact upon the international politics of this century.

MANDATES UNDER THE LEAGUE

The League Mandate system originated in a political compromise at Versailles. It was not the product of disinterested humanitarianism or a design carefully prepared in advance. The Allies were faced with the practical problem of disposing of territory taken from Turkey and Germany, and the Mandate system was the best compromise available. Independence, annexation, or restoration of the colonies to their former masters would have been the most obvious possibilities, but all of these were effectively ruled out by serious objections from one or more influential allies. Restoration, understandably, was not viewed with enthusiasm from any quarter at Versailles. Independence did not satisfy the security demands of some of the Allies, and there was general agreement that most of the territories outside of Europe were not ready for it.

Annexation had many advocates, and claims to conquered territory were openly advanced by France, Belgium, Japan, the Union of South Africa,

Australia, and New Zealand. But annexation also met with objections. President Wilson had included a disclaimer of territorial aggrandizement in his Fourteen Points, and he had succeeded in obtaining from the Allies a pre-Armistice paper commitment to "no annexations." This pledge meant that any demands for annexation had to be put forward in the awkward form of an exception to the general principle. Annexationists were also faced with the formidable opposition of Woodrow Wilson who was determined that the war he had fought for principle should not now appear as a contest for pelf. Britain, which might have been expected to side with the annexationists on the basis of its imperial tradition and secret wartime agreements with France for the partition of Turkish dominions in the Middle East, assumed a position of neutrality. This reflected strong "no annexation" demands from elements within the Labor and Liberal Parties and official concern about public commitments of political support given to the Arabs during the course of the war.

Such a situation called for inventiveness, and the resulting compromise had a touch of political genius. Britain and the annexationists were awarded control of all the territory in question, but the control was to be exercised under a "mandate" from the League of Nations. In their administration of the mandated areas they were to be accountable to the League and subject to its supervision.

The mandate provisions of the Covenant did not represent a clear-cut victory for either the idealists or the annexationists. Article 22 of the Covenant declared to the world that the "well-being and development" of peoples in the conquered territories was "a sacred trust of civilization" to be undertaken by the advanced nations "as Mandatories on behalf of the League." This doctrine had an obvious affinity with the somewhat older and still more patronizing notion of the "White Man's Burden," but the recognition of an international trust for conquered territory undoubtedly represented a step forward from the days of the old imperialism. The statement of principle was also significant for what it omitted. Except for the Arab portion of the Ottoman Empire, the Covenant made no reference to independence or even self-government as an ultimate objective for the trust territories. Nor is there even the breath of a suggestion that other areas under colonial rule were in any sense a trust.

The impact of compromise is also evident in the classification of conquered territories into three groups, subsequently known as A, B, and C mandates, on the basis of their political development, geographical location, economic conditions, and "other similar circumstances." [1] The relative

---

[1] *Covenant* provisions for mandates are found in Article 22. Mandates and Mandatories were as follows: Class A—Palestine (Britain), Syria and Lebanon (France), and Iraq (Britain); Class B—Tanganyika (Britain), Togoland (Britain), Togoland (France), Ruanda Urundi (Belgium), Cameroons (Britain), Cameroons (France); Class C—Western Samoa (New Zealand), Nauru (Britain, Australia, New Zealand), New Guinea (Australia), and the North Pacific Islands (Japan).

political sophistication of the Arabs, and the British wartime commitments to them, made the Turkish dominions candidates for the Class A mandate. As such their status as independent nations could be "provisionally recognised subject to the rendering of administrative advice and assistance by a Mandatory until such time as they are able to stand alone." The tutelage stage for these countries was subsequently extended longer than the indigenous peoples desired, but Iraq gained independence in 1932 and the other mandated areas of the Middle East achieved full statehood in the wake of World War II without undergoing a period of United Nations trusteeship.

At the other extreme were the Class C mandates, which were to be "administered under the laws of the mandatory as integral portions of its territory." South West Africa and the German Pacific islands were placed in this category, ostensibly because of "the sparseness of their population, or their small size, or their remoteness from the centres of civilisation, or their geographical contiguity to the territory of the Mandatory." To a large extent these rationalizations were grounded in fact, and a good case could be made that they could best be governed in administrative union with the Mandatory. The overriding fact remains, however, that Class C status was the maximum amount of internationalization that the annexationists in Australia, New Zealand, and South Africa would gracefully accept.

The remaining German territories in Africa were placed in Class B. They were not to be administratively annexed but were nevertheless to be governed as colonies without explicit provision for ultimate independence or self-government. Inhabitants of all classes of mandates were guaranteed freedom of conscience and religion, and protection against abuses such as the slave trade and traffic in arms and liquor. An open door to the trade and commerce of all nations was supposed to be maintained in Class A and B mandates.

The means of enforcing Covenant obligations were minimal. The only machinery provided by Article 22 was a "permanent Commission . . . to receive and examine the annual reports of the Mandatories and to advise the Council on all matters relating to the observance of the mandates." The Permanent Mandates Commission, as it was called, consisted of nine (subsequently ten) individuals appointed by the Council to serve as private experts. The council made a practice of appointing a majority from nonmandatory states, but, with one or two exceptions, the members were all from states that had colonial possessions. The members of the Commission were generally persons of high ability who took seriously their responsibility to provide international supervision and, if possible, upgrade standards of colonial administration. At the same time, their backgrounds enabled them to understand and appreciate the problems faced by the mandatory countries.

Even if the Commission had been hostile, which it was not, it had no real power to affect the policies of the mandatory states other than the power of persuasion, exhortation, and publicity. Its principal tools of supervision were the right to receive annual reports on the mandated territories and to make recommendations to the Council. The Commission developed comprehensive questionnaires to facilitate uniform and complete reporting, and a representative of the mandatory participated in all Commission discussions of its mandate. The Commission did not assume authority to visit the territories or make any other on-the-spot inquiries to check the accuracy of reports. Written petitions were entertained, but petitions from indigenous inhabitants had to be routed through the mandatory and all other petitions were sent to the mandatory for comments. Petitions that were repetitious of previous petitions, anonymous, or outside the terms of the mandate were unacceptable, and most petitions were never forwarded by the Commission to the Council because they were regarded as too trivial or unacceptable. The majority of petitions received came from the Class A mandates.

The Permanent Mandates Commission functioned under the Council and made its recommendations to the Council rather than directly to the mandatory. The Council seldom acted on mandates without the advice of the experts on the Commission and it usually accepted their advice. Nevertheless, the Council was a political body not prone to giving needless offense to the mandatories and, in any event, it had no more power than the Commission to take effective enforcement action against a mandatory which failed to honor its "sacred trust." The Assembly, without any special authorization in the Covenant, also developed the practice of making recommendations each year on some aspect of mandate administration. Like the Commission and the Council, the Assembly was limited to exhortation and the sanction of publicity.

The Mandates system was a product of conflicting interests and forces which came to a focus at the Versailles Conference. Given this environment, its record of accomplishment was bound to be spotty. Probably its most outstanding achievement lay in establishing the principle of international accountability for the administration of colonial territories. The trust idea antedated the League, but League structures provided a rallying point for the supporters of trusteeship while giving permanence and specific content to the idea. It is doubtful that prevailing attitudes and expectations regarding the treatment of dependent peoples could have been altered so rapidly in the past half century without the conditioning effect of the League Mandate system.

Some impact was also made upon the quality of administration of the conquered territories, through the force of publicity, quiet persuasion, and the mandatories' own sense of international accountability. Mandatory administrators were often willing to listen to suggestions from experts on the Commission whose competence and previous experience in colonial administration qualified them to give realistic advice. Commission recommendations were sometimes widely adopted as policy by the mandatories. The mandatories, for example, generally refrained from mass naturalization of mandate peoples and did not enlist them for general military service—two practices specifically disapproved by the Commission. The mandate system fell short of the more idealistic hopes and expectations, but there is wide agreement that the League's methods of friendly persuasion helped to fix the welfare of indigenous peoples as the standard of administration.

THE TRUSTEESHIP PRINCIPLE

The United Nations trusteeship system was also the product of political compromise rather than the effervescence of disinterested humanitarianism. In contrast with Versailles, however, the issue at San Francisco, was not narrowly confined to the question of conquered territories. Much to the dismay of several colonial powers, questions were raised about the applicability of trusteeship to the whole colonial system. Although no one seriously objected to continuing the mandates in some form, Britain, France, Belgium, the Netherlands, and South Africa were adamantly opposed to the involuntary extension of the system to other territories. The more conservative view was epitomized by Winston Churchill's wartime observation that he had not "become the King's First Minister in order to preside over the liquidation of the British Empire."

The United States, also a colonial power, was in an ambivalent position. At one stage in wartime planning, the State Department had tentatively proposed that international trusteeship be applied to all dependent territories in order to assure "the welfare of the inhabitants and the general interest of other peoples. . . ."[2] As the war progressed, this idealistic anti-colonialism was countered by a growing security interest in the Japanese-mandated Pacific islands of special concern to the Departments of War and Navy. The clash of views continued to the eve of the San Francisco Conference and disabled the United States delegation from playing the role that Wilson had played at Versailles—that of an unstinting champion of self-determination.

There were other forces at work which compensated for America's lack of the Wilsonian zeal. Not the least of these was the twenty-five year precedent of the League Mandate system. Much of what had to be fought for at Versailles was conceded at San Francisco. Of great importance also were the events of World War II, which drastically weakened the colonial powers, loosened their hold on colonies in Asia and the Pacific, and gave impetus to native nationalist movements. In contrast to Versailles, moreover, the anti-

[2] *Postwar Foreign Policy Preparation, 1939–1945*, Department of State Publ. 3580 (Washington, D.C.: 1949), p. 481.

colonial interest had new and vigorous spokesmen at the San Francisco Conference. Egypt, Syria, Iraq, India, and other former dependencies which had achieved legal or de facto statehood now loudly trumpeted the cause of their fellow nationalists still under colonial domination. The Soviet Union, which had not been represented at Versailles, was another supporter of the anticolonialist cause.

Above all, there was at San Francisco a pressing apprehension that the just treatment of colonial peoples and their evolution toward self-government was somehow connected with the maintenance of international peace and security. In the League Covenant the "well-being and development" of colonial peoples provided the rationale for League action. In the UN Charter, by contrast, the first objective of the trusteeship system is "to further international peace and security." The necessary connection between war and colonialism is not entirely self-evident, but available causative hypotheses include the Marxian theory of imperialist rivalry, animosity between subject peoples and their colonial masters, and the supposed unwholesome social conditions fostered by the colonial relationship.[3] Once the connection is assumed, on whatever ground, trusteeship is justified as a war-preventative measure. This rationale was evident in the discussions at San Francisco and in the completed Charter.

The forces supporting wider involvement for international organization were able to achieve a modest increase in its power and responsibilities. A strengthened trusteeship system replaced the mandate system and a declaration regarding non-self-governing territories committed members to submit economic and social information on all of their colonies. A somewhat greater departure from the League Covenant were the announced goals of the system which included ultimate "self-government or independence" for trust territories and "self-government" for all other dependencies. Although the consequences of this shift in avowed objectives and the extension of UN concern to all colonies may not have been fully anticipated in 1945, they constituted the opening wedge for what has since become a broadside attack in the United Nations upon the old colonialism in all its manifestations.

The Nature of the Trusteeship System

The trusteeship system was not intended to bring revolutionary change. If independence or self-government was the goal, its achievement was not anticipated in the immediate future. The Trusteeship Council, as successor to the Permanent Mandates Commission, was constituted of governmental representatives instead of private experts, and the administering powers were given parity of membership with representatives of nonadministering

---

[3] For a discussion of the theory of trusteeship as an approach to peace, see Inis L. Claude, Jr., *Swords into Plowshares*, 3rd ed. (New York: Random House, 1964), pp. 318–22.

countries.[4] This assured the administering powers that if they remained united they could not be outvoted on the Trusteeship Council. Furthermore, each trust territory was to be brought within the system by a separate agreement drawn up by the administering member and approved by the Assembly. Although the Assembly would have the right to amend or reject the proposed agreement, the administering authority had the practical option of not submitting to trusteeship at all. Under these circumstances the Assembly could not be too demanding in its consideration of trusteeship agreements.

The Trusteeship Council, however, was given improved means of inquiry into the conduct of trust administration. The practice of the annual report, based on a comprehensive questionnaire, was borrowed from the Permanent Mandates Commission. To this was added by explicit Charter provision the right to "accept petitions and examine them in consultation with the administering authority." As interpreted, this enabled complainants to petition the Trusteeship Council directly either orally or in writing, without relying on the willingness of the administering power to forward petitions. A third and still more potent tool provided by the Charter was the right to send visiting missions to trust territories to gain first-hand knowledge of conditions.

If the organization had practical means for informed criticism of the administering states, it still possessed no legal powers of coercion. Criticism from the Assembly might have practical weight but its recommendations regarding trusteeship, as in other matters, could have no binding effect. The administering powers thus matched their effective control of the territories and legal immunity from UN recommendations against the organization's capacity to publicize, criticize, and mobilize the weight of diplomatic opinion.

Although such a balance of forces appeared to favor national control over international supervision, the United States obtained an additional safeguard against unwanted interference with its administration of the Pacific Islands trusteeship. The meddling of a General Assembly majority might be annoying and inconvenient, whatever the legal force of its resolutions. To obviate this possibility, the Charter provisions for trusteeship were drawn to include the concept of a "strategic area." If an administering authority, in the trusteeship agreement, chose to designate all or part of a trust territory as a "strategic area," all matters relating to the area became the province of the Security Council rather than the General Assembly. There the United States would be protected by its veto from any adverse recommendation.[5]

[4] The Charter formula gives membership to all administering powers, all permanent members of the Security Council, and as many other members elected for three-year terms by the Assembly as are needed to balance the Council equally between administering and nonadministering powers. United Nations Charter, Article 86.

[5] The terms of the trusteeship agreement approved by the Security Council also permit the United States to give economic preference to its own nationals and to close any part of the territory to UN supervision if "security reasons" require.

The Functioning of Trusteeship

By 1947 all of the Class A mandates had received, or were shortly to receive independence, and all of the Class B and C mandates had been placed under trusteeship except South West Africa.[6] By the Charter, trusteeship was made specifically applicable to territories held under mandate and to territories that might be "detached from enemy states as a result of the Second World War," but the invitation was also open to any state that might voluntarily wish to place any of its own colonies under trusteeship. No state accepted the latter invitation, although Italian Somaliland, which had been detached from Italy during the war, was given a period of trusteeship under Italian administration. The legal evolution of territories placed under mandate and trusteeship is shown in Table 13-1.

The trusteeship system has clearly functioned in a manner conducive to the rapid achievement of independence or self-government. Of eleven territories placed under trusteeship, eight have come to full independence or have been united, on the basis of a UN-approved plebiscite, with an adjoining independent country. Of the three remaining, Nauru is a small Pacific Island of 5,000 population which will remain under trusteeship until the phosphate deposits which constitute its economic base are exhausted, presumably by the end of the century. Plans are being made for the mass transfer of Nauruans to another island when the phosphate is used up. New Guinea, as wild and primitive a territory as any in the world, is at least two or three decades away from any meaningful act of self-determination, despite demands in the Assembly for a shorter route to independence. In the Pacific Islands trusteeship, the inhabitants have been making rapid progress toward self-government, particularly since 1960, and the trusteeship could possibly be terminated by the end of the present decade. A form of self-government short of actual independence is anticipated, since American military interests seem to preclude a complete withdrawal. In effect, the Trusteeship system has nearly worked itself out of business.

One may raise a serious question of how much the Trusteeship system, as such, has contributed to the development and hastened the independence of the trust territories. It is much easier to recount the activities of the United Nations than to measure their effects. Criticism in the Trusteeship Council and the General Assembly has undoubtedly spurred the administering authorities to put the best possible face on their conduct of territorial affairs. The effect on substance as contrasted to appearances is open to more doubt, but occasionally administering authorities have responded to recommendations with a clear-cut modification of policy, such as the United States' decision to introduce English as the language of instruction in the ele-

[6] South West Africa was never placed under trusteeship. See the discussion in Chapter 5.

Territory	Class of Mandate	Mandate Administered by	Trusteeship Administered by	Present Status
Palestine	A	United Kingdom		Independent: Jordan (1946), Israel (1948)
Syria and Lebanon	A	France		Independent: Syria (1946), Lebanon (1946)
Iraq	A	United Kingdom		Independent (1932)
Tanganyika	B	United Kingdom	United Kingdom	Independent (1961)
Togoland	B	United Kingdom	United Kingdom	Merged with Ghana (1957)
Togoland	B	France	France	Independent (Togo, 1960)
Ruanda Urundi	B	Belgium	Belgium	Independent: Rwanda (1962), Burundi (1962)
Cameroons	B	United Kingdom	United Kingdom	Part merged with Nigeria, part with Cameroon (1961)
Cameroons	B	France	France	Independent (Cameroon, 1960)
Nauru	C	Australia, New Zealand, United Kingdom	Australia, New Zealand, United Kingdom	Trusteeship
New Guinea	C	Australia	Australia	Trusteeship
North Pacific Islands	C	Japan	United States	Strategic Trusteeship
South West Africa	C	Union of South Africa	—	Mandate *
Western Samoa	C	New Zealand	New Zealand	Independent (1962)
Somaliland	—	—	Italy	Independent (Somalia, 1960)

363

* In 1966 the General Assembly by resolution declared the South West African mandate to be terminated, but implementation awaited the report of a special committee in 1967.

mentary schools of the Pacific Islands in 1961 and to move the territorial headquarters from Guam to Saipan in 1962. Usually the response has been more diffuse and indirect, so that specific advances in territorial administration are difficult to relate in a causal way to particular recommendations or criticisms.

Petitions and visiting missions have made possible more detailed scrutiny of trust administration, and thereby increased the pressure on administering authorities to justify their policies. At its height of activity the Trusteeship Council received several hundred written petitions annually and considered as many as 250 in a session, besides granting an occasional hearing to an oral petitioner. By utilizing a Standing Committee on Petitions to do the preliminary screening and make recommendations, and debating only the most important petitions, the Trusteeship Council has managed to keep this time-consuming process within bounds. Aside from the informational function, the petitioning procedure has made administering authorities more alert to the legitimate grievances of the local populace and sometimes resulted in direct relief to the complainant. In one instance, two inhabitants of the Pacific Islands found that an oral petition to the Trusteeship Council accomplished what three years of direct negotiations with the United States had failed to achieve—a settlement of their claim against the United States for property taken without just compensation.

Visiting missions have also served the dual function of providing information for the Trusteeship Council and serving as an outlet for native views and grievances. Missions composed of two persons nominated by the administering states and two by the nonadministering states, plus supporting staff, have visited trust territories every three years. Their reports appear to receive serious attention from administering authorities and have in some instances foreshadowed policy change. Australia, for example, took steps to give the New Guinea territorial legislature an elective majority, in accordance with recommendations of a 1962 visiting mission. New Zealand's revision of its regime for Western Samoa in 1947 also had a direct relationship to findings of the Trusteeship Council's first visiting mission to that area.

In several territories the UN supervisory function has been made concrete through the sending of plebiscite teams and election observers during the final stages of preparation for self-government. This has also had the effect of helping to legitimate the regimes ultimately established. UN-supervised plebiscites in British Togoland and British Cameroons gave international sanction to the union of the former with Ghana and the partition of British Cameroons between Nigeria and the emerging Republic of Cameroon. A similar plebiscite in Western Samoa paved the way for the adoption of a new constitution and the achievement of independence in 1962. In French Togoland, Rwanda, and Burundi, the presence of UN observers at pre-independence elections enhanced the international acceptability of the native regimes thereby established.

Evaluation of Trusteeship

Considered as a whole, trusteeship has probably helped to raise standards of administration in the trust territories and hastened the coming of independence. This has resulted in part from its contribution to the general climate of opinion and in part from specific suggestions and criticisms that have strengthened progressive elements within the administering authorities and kept them mindful of their obligations to the peoples of the trust territories. Trusteeship has fostered some increase in readiness for self-government and has unquestionably encouraged more articulate native demands for national independence. Assuming, as one must, that the forces of change were already inherent in the colonial relationship, the trusteeship system has provided a more orderly and peaceful process by which the change could occur. In none of the trust territories has the transition to independence been marked by such violence as that which accompanied termination of colonial status in Algeria, Indonesia, and Viet Nam.

This brief summary of developments in the trusteeship field should not obscure the fact that trusteeship has been but one aspect of a much wider movement for decolonization. Several African and Asian dependencies of France and Britain became independent before the first trust territories achieved that status in 1960.[7] While eight trust territories were gaining statehood from 1960 to 1962, eighteen other former colonies which had never experienced trusteeship were undergoing the same transformation. The Trusteeship system no doubt has contributed to the creation of a climate of opinion congenial to decolonization, but the system itself has been swept along with the general trend of events.

The trusteeship system has never achieved the scope that its more ardent supporters at San Francisco had hoped for. Except for Somaliland, it did not expand territorially beyond the League mandates. The possibility that other non-self-governing territories might be placed under trusteeship appears never to have been seriously considered by any colonial power. For several months during 1962–63, the United Nations itself administered a "trusteeship" for West New Guinea, but this temporary arrangement fell entirely outside the trusteeship system. It was simply a political and administrative device to facilitate the agreed transfer of territory from the Netherlands to Indonesia in settlement of a long-standing dispute. In meeting the larger problem of colonialism, the United Nations has consistently turned to other means than trusteeship.

NON-SELF-GOVERNING TERRITORIES

In the "Declaration Regarding Non-Self-Governing Territories," contained in Chapter XI of the Charter, the colonial powers acknowledged a

---

[7] British Togoland achieved "self-government" in 1957 through merger with Ghana.

"sacred trust" to promote the well-being and self-government of all their dependencies. They were not willing to accept independence as a goal for their colonies or to accept any degree of international supervision, but they agreed to submit data "of a technical nature relating to economic, social, and educational conditions in the territories" for "information purposes." There was general accord at San Francisco that the Declaration embodied only moral commitments, dependent upon the good faith of the colonial powers for their fulfillment and involving no UN right to intervene in what was regarded by the colonial powers as a matter of domestic jurisdiction.

Today the picture is drastically altered. Independence has become not merely a goal but an accomplished fact for the vast majority of the colonial peoples of 1945. Within the United Nations the original Charter assumption "that each colonial power should at its own discretion and in an unhurried way lead its dependent peoples to well-being and self-government" has given way to the proposition that colonialism is "an intolerable and illegitimate abuse to be done away with as speedily as possible by the international community." [8] This revolutionary change in ideology has been accompanied by an organizational assault upon the whole structure of colonialism. The cumulative effects of relatively minor accretions of authority in the early years paved the way for bolder action in the 1960's, which has now erased any essential distinction between trust territories and other non-self-governing areas. The transformation reflects changing reality in the world environment and has altered the relations of power within the organization, but it is also a basic amendment of the Charter without the niceties of ratification.

The Committee on Information

The first step toward establishing UN responsibility for all dependent territories was innocuous enough—the creation of an ad hoc committee of the General Assembly to examine the information transmitted by the administering members and make recommendations to the Assembly.[9] Some of the administering members maintained legal reservations about the competence of the General Assembly to examine the information and make recommendations on the subject, either by itself or through a committee. But this did not deter the majority of the Assembly from continuing the special committee until 1963, at first on a year-to-year basis and later by three-year extensions of its mandate.

The Committee on Information from Non-Self-Governing Territories, as it came to be known, represented an attempt by the anticolonial majority in the Assembly to create a quasi-trusteeship system for all dependent terri-

---

[8] Rupert Emerson, "Colonialism, Political Development, and the UN," *International Organization*, Vol. 19 (Summer, 1965), p. 486.

[9] Eight countries—Australia, Belgium, Denmark, France, the Netherlands, New Zealand, the United Kingdom, and the United States—enumerated seventy-four territories on which they would transmit information as specified in Article 73(e) of the Charter.

tories. The Committee aped the Trusteeship Council in its composition, having an equal number of administering and nonadministering members.[10] It had no provision for permanent representation of the Big Five, however, and the Soviet Union and China generally did not hold membership on it. Like the Trusteeship Council, the Committee also prepared a questionnaire to guide members in reporting.

Without the benefit of a solid constitutional foundation, and possessing a built-in moderation arising from its composition, the Committee on Information was not an aggressive instrument of anticolonialism. The tendency to moderation was reinforced by its ground rules, established by the Assembly in the early years of the United Nations when the organization was not completely dominated by the anticolonial forces. By its original terms of reference the Committee was debarred from examining "political" information despite the fact that some countries voluntarily submitted it. Even on economic and social matters, the Committee could not make recommendations applicable to individual territories, but only recommendations of general application. The Committee was also denied the right to accept petitions or to send out visiting missions to the territories.

Because of these limitations on the Committee on Information, the initiative for continued encroachment upon the prerogatives of the administering powers remained largely with the General Assembly and its Fourth Committee. A very early step in this direction was the request that governments voluntarily include political information in their annual reports. Later, as the attainment of self-government by various territories became an issue, the Assembly began to demand that administering authorities submit sufficient information on constitutional changes in the territories to enable the Assembly to determine whether self-government had in fact been attained. The Assembly's right to make such a determination was a much more crucial issue than its demand for information, and the colonial powers vehemently rejected the notion. The result was something of a standoff, since the anticolonialist forces had the votes to control the Assembly but the administering members were in a position to cease the transmission of information whenever they chose.

The admission of Spain and Portugal in 1955 raised the related question of who decides when and if new members must begin to transmit informa-

---

[10] From 1954 to 1963 the administering states did not quite have parity in committee meetings. Belgium boycotted the meetings from 1954 to 1961 when it ceased to be a member. Portugal, which formally was made a member in 1961, never participated.

From 1947 to 1954 the Committee had sixteen members. As colonies achieved self-governing status, Denmark withdrew in 1954, Belgium in 1961, and the Netherlands in 1962. In 1961 Spain and Portugal were added to its membership as administering members. In 1963, before it was abolished, the membership consisted of Australia, France, New Zealand, Portugal, Spain, the United Kingdom, and the United States as administering members; and Ecuador, Honduras, Liberia, Mexico, Pakistan, the Philippines, and Upper Volta as nonadministering members.

tion on any of their dependencies. The question was far from academic, since both Spain and Portugal solemnly assured the United Nations that they had no non-self-governing territories. The UN wheels turned slowly in dealing with this anomalous situation, but by 1960 the Assembly flatly assumed the right to decide the question and informed Portugal and Spain of their obligation to transmit information. Spain capitulated to the pressure, but Portugal, intransigent to the last, has continued to insist that its far-flung pieces of empire are all equal and integral parts of a single self-governing state.

In 1961 the rising tide of anticolonialism produced a significant change in the working rules of the Committee on Information. The Committee was given authority to discuss political subjects and to make recommendations specifically directed toward the problems of territories located in the same area or region. The practical effect of these changes was not great because of the Committee's disbandment in 1963. The Assembly's action was significant, however, as a portent of things to come.

SELF-DETERMINATION AND POLITICAL CRISIS

While the Assembly busied itself with the project of turning all non-self-governing territories into quasi-trusteeships, the United Nations was also faced with a series of political crises arising from a colonial matrix. During the early years of the organization the alignment of colonial and anti-colonial forces was not clearly drawn and the issues were sometimes perceived as having a complexity inconsistent with the taking of doctrinaire positions. The question of Palestine came before the United Nations in 1947 at the initiative of a harassed mandatory power that could no longer bear alone the impossible burden of reconciling Arab and Jewish claims to the Holy Land. The issue was not whether self-determination should be granted but how and by whom it should be exercised. In the Dutch-Indonesian conflict, mediated by the Security Council from 1947 to 1949, the issue of self-determination was inherently sharper than in Palestine, but the security issue was uppermost and the actions of the Security Council were usually taken in that context. Assembly debates on the former Italian colonies of Libya, Eritrea, and Somaliland, which took place from 1949 to 1951, were also relatively free from the kind of anticolonial recrimination that has since come to characterize all UN debates on colonial questions. The decision to give almost immediate independence to Libya may well have contributed to the growing colonial problem, however, by giving encouragement to nationalist forces in neighboring North African territories. The case is also notable as the one instance in which, by virtue of the Treaty of Peace with Italy, the Assembly's decision was legally binding upon the countries that would have to implement it.

Self-determination for the French North African possessions of Tunisia and Morocco provided the issue which brought the contest between colonial and anticolonial positions in the United Nations sharply into focus. Much talk about threats to peace and violations of human rights did not obscure the fact that self-determination was the real issue. There was a difference, however, between the United Nations of the 1950's and the organization of a decade later: anticolonialism was emergent but not yet ascendant. In 1951 six Arab sponsors of Morocco's cause could not even persuade the Assembly to discuss the question. In 1952 the Security Council refused to place the Tunisian question on its agenda, and the following year it resisted entreaties to discuss Morocco. When the Assembly agreed to discuss the questions in 1952, it acted with great forbearance. In the case of Morocco, a two-thirds majority could not be found even in favor of "self-government." Admonition to develop "free political institutions" was the strongest wording the anticolonialists could obtain. The Assembly's consideration of these questions from 1952–55 undoubtedly increased the diplomatic pressure upon France and gave heart to North African nationalists, but, in retrospect, Assembly recommendations on the subject seem almost quaintly courteous.

The debates on Cyprus and West Irian (West New Guinea) further illustrate the restraint imposed on the Assembly by the balance of political forces. Five times, from 1954 through 1958, Greece proposed that the status of Cyprus be discussed by the Assembly. In 1954 there was a brief discussion without parliamentary action, and the following year the item was not even included on the agenda. In 1956 the Assembly was able to agree on a weak resolution expressing its desire for a peaceful, democratic, and just solution and a hope for continued negotiations. In 1957 a stronger anti-British and anticolonial draft was approved in committee, but Greece could not obtain the required two-thirds majority in the plenary meeting of the Assembly. In 1958 the Assembly once more settled for an expression of confidence that a peaceful, just, and democratic solution would be reached. The Cyprus dispute was a very delicate and complex issue, involving as it did a three-cornered hassle among NATO partners, the aspiration of the Cypriots to self-determination, and the overriding interest of the United States in keeping a NATO family quarrel under wraps. But one feels assured that the Assembly of today would not restrict itself to such polite comments on an issue of self-determination. The Dutch-Indonesian dispute over West Irian confirms the impression that moderation was a product of the Assembly balance of forces, not anything inherent in the issue. In four tries, 1954–57, Indonesia failed to get a two-thirds majority for a resolution supporting its position against the Dutch "colonialists." The best the Assembly could do, in 1955, was to express its hope that negotiations then under way would be fruitful.

The question of Algerian independence provides a chronological bridge from the period of anticolonialism emergent to anticolonialism ascendant, and mirrors accurately the change that was taking place. The Assembly considered the Algerian question during every session from 1955 through 1961. In 1955 no action at all was taken; in 1956 the Assembly hoped that a peaceful, democratic, and just solution in conformity with the Charter would be found. The next year the Assembly went so far as to urge negotiations, but in 1958 and 1959 a two-thirds majority was not available for any recommendation at all. This stalemate reflected the unwillingness of the anticolonialist bloc to support a weak statement and their inability to obtain a strong one. In 1960, however, with the admission to UN membership of seventeen former colonies, the inhibitions of the earlier period vanished. The right of the Algerian people to "self-determination" was vigorously asserted, despite France's bitter objections to discussing the item at all. And in 1961 the Assembly called upon both parties to implement the right of the Algerian people to "self-determination and independence." One cannot say with confidence that the Assembly had any more influence upon the French decision to grant Algeria independence in 1962 than upon the granting of independence to Morocco and Tunisia in 1956. But the temper of the Assembly was plainly different.

THE ALL-OUT ASSAULT ON COLONIALISM

By 1960 the anticolonial revolution was rapidly approaching its zenith. Four decades of mandate and trusteeship had established the principle of international accountability for the administration of a select group of territories, with independence as the ultimate goal. Fifteen years of gradually expanding activity under the Declaration Regarding Non-Self-Governing Territories had gone far to establsh the principle of international accountability for the well-being and self-government of all colonial peoples. Repeated recourse to the United Nations in alleged crisis situations had established at least a prima facie connection between colonialism and the periodic outbreak of violence. Within the world community, the day of colonialism was rapidly passing. Eighteen territories which had achieved full independence since 1945 were already members of the United Nations, and seventeen more were waiting to be admitted at the opening of the Fifteenth Assembly in 1960. Most other dependencies of any substantial size were moving rapidly toward independence with the consent and cooperation of their colonial overseers.

An Anticolonial Manifesto

Amid these signs of a revolution well on its way to completion, the General Assembly in 1960 took a step of unusual symbolic importance. For years the anticolonial forces had argued the principle of self-determination in support of their attack upon the old colonial order. Now with domination of the Assembly assured, they turned the organization into an instrument for the complete legitimization of their cause. By resolution of the General Assembly they transformed principle into right and explicitly denied the legitimacy of the old order. In the historic "Declaration on the Granting of Independence to Colonial Countries and Peoples," the collective voice of the world community solemnly asserted that the subjection of peoples to alien domination is a denial of fundamental human rights, contrary to the UN Charter and an impediment to world peace; and that all peoples have a right not only to self-determination but to immediate and complete independence.[11] The fathers of the League Mandate system must have turned in their graves, but their successors in the Assembly adopted the resolution 90 to zero with 9 abstentions. This was indeed an ideological triumph. The old order had not merely been challenged and defeated in the field—most of its adherents had been won over to the principles of the new. In a message delivered to the parliament of the Union of South Africa early in 1960, British Prime Minister Harold Macmillan warned:

> In different places it may take different forms, but it is happening everywhere. The wind of change is blowing through the continent. Whether we like it or not, this growth of national consciousness is a political fact. We must all accept it as a fact. Our national policies must take account of it.[12]

How briskly the "wind of change" was blowing! No country cast a vote against the Declaration, and the abstainers consisted of eight colonial powers (Australia, Belgium, France, Portugal, Spain, South Africa, the United Kingdom, and the United States), and Rafael Trujillo's Dominican Republic.[13]

As long as the anticolonial revolution was not complete, the principles of the Declaration were bound to have disruptive effects if taken at face value

[11] General Assembly Resolution 1514 (XV), December 14, 1960. The Declaration provided that (1) alien domination is contrary to the Charter, (2) all peoples have a right to self-determination, (3) inadequacy of political, economic, social, or educational preparedness is no excuse for delaying independence, (4) all repressive measures against dependent peoples should cease, so that they can exercise freely their right to complete independence, (5) all powers of government should be immediately transferred to remaining dependent peoples, (6) disruption of national unity or territorial integrity of a country is contrary to the Charter.

[12] Quoted in David W. Wainhouse, *Remnants of Empire: The United Nations and the end of Colonialism* (New York: Harper and Row, 1964), p. 28.

[13] Edward T. Rowe, in "The Emerging Anti-Colonial Consensus in the United Nations," *The Journal of Conflict Resolution*, Vol. 8 (September, 1964), pp. 209–30, traces the growth of anticolonial sentiment as expressed in roll-call votes on colonial questions during the first sixteen sessions of the Assembly, 1946–61. Taking two sessions as a unit, Rowe's statistics show a steady rise in the percentage of anticolonial votes and a persistent decline in colonial votes from biennium to biennium. The trend is explained in part by the admission of new members and in part by a growing anticolonial consensus among the older ones.

as a guide to action. The principle was carried to its logical conclusion when India, upon invading Portuguese Goa in December, 1961, referred to its conduct as an "embodiment of the principles" in the Declaration and a "new dictum of international law." For one not accustomed to anticolonialist doublethink, it might seem anomalous to suppose that an Assembly resolution, which is legally binding on no one, can create international law which overrides express Charter prohibitions upon the use of force. But the basic issue, as the Indian representative admitted to the Security Council, was moral, not legal. Portugal's centuries-old occupation of Goa constituted permanent aggression, and India was justified in "getting rid of the last vestiges of colonialism. . . . Charter or no Charter, Council or no Council." [14] Like the American Declaration of Independence, the Declaration of 1960 was an appeal to a higher law—a higher law that African nations may well invoke should they choose to eliminate from Africa the "permanent aggression" of Portugal or the Republic of South Africa.

The Committee on Decolonization

Within the United Nations, the Declaration presaged a more vigorous assault upon the last bastions of colonialism. In 1961, as we have noted, the Assembly reviewed the functioning of the Committee on Information and expanded its terms of reference. The Fourth Committee also set a precedent by granting, for the first time, a hearing to petitioners from two non-self-governing territories.

Of considerably more importance in the long run was the creation of a seventeen-member "Special Committee on the Situation with Regard to the Implementation of the Declaration on the Granting of Independence to Colonial Countries and Peoples." Known, for obvious reasons, as the Committee of Seventeen, it was assigned to study the Declaration and make appropriate recommendations for its further implementation. Parity of representation was discarded as the Assembly packed the Special Committee with eight African and Asian members, three from Eastern Europe, two from Latin America, and one each from Australia, Italy, the United Kingdom, and the United States. For its terms of reference, the Committee was given a blank check. In the words of the Assembly, it was

> To carry out its task by employment of all means which it will have at its disposal within the framework of the procedures and facilities which it shall adopt for the proper discharge of its functions.[15]

If that meant anything, it meant that the Committee was free to do whatever it was able to do in implementing the 1960 Declaration. Under this broad grant of authority the Committee assumed the powers to hear peti-

[14] Official Records of the Security Council, 987th meeting, December 18, 1961, p. 9.
[15] General Assembly Resolution 1654 (XVI), November 27, 1961.

tions, send missions to the field, and make specific recommendations relating to individual territories—powers that the Trusteeship Council had exercised in regard to trust territories but that had been denied to the Committee on Information. This was a committee calculated to give the Assembly's anti-colonial majority the action it was looking for.

The Assembly was not disappointed, if action is equated with many meetings, much bold talk, and systematic harassment of the remaining colonial powers. Setting off at a feverish pace, the Committee of Seventeen held 117 meetings from February to September, including sessions in Morocco, Ethiopia, and Tanganyika. Concentrating on eleven African territories and British Guiana, the Committee rendered its first report to the Assembly (1962) with the smug self-appraisal that "its observations and recommendations on each of the territories," had

> provided the administering powers with specific lines of action, based on the Declaration itself and the basic objectives of the Charter of the United Nations, which will materially assist in hastening the end of colonial rule in the territories concerned.[16]

Obviously impressed, the Assembly commended the Committee, echoed its railing against noncooperative administering authorities, and commissioned it to render a full report the following year on all territories that had not yet achieved independence. The Committee was enlarged to twenty-four members but its political complexion remained the same with twelve Asian and African members, four from Eastern Europe, three Latin Americans and five others. By 1963 the Committee of Twenty-four had so plainly overshadowed and usurped the role of the Committee on Information that the latter was abolished and all its functions formally conferred on the Committee of Twenty-four. The all-out assault on colonialism by the Assembly was now well under way. The Declaration on the Granting of Independence to Colonial Countries and Peoples fixed the goal and rationale, and the Committee of Twenty-four was its chosen instrument.

Scraps of Empire and Hard-Core Holdouts

The United Nations was able to launch its massive assault upon colonialism only because colonialism was already in full retreat. The Committee of Twenty-four has in fact been engaged in a mopping-up operation. In its 1963 report to the Assembly, the Committee listed 64 colonies, mandates, and trust territories that had not yet achieved self-government.[17] Of this number, however, only ten boasted as many as a million inhabitants and

---

[16] Quoted in *Everyman's United Nations*, 7th ed. (New York: United Nations, 1964), p. 387.

[17] Forty of the sixty-four were British, consisting, as Emerson aptly puts it, mostly of "little islands scattered about the face of the globe, representing the days when Britain was an indefatigable collector of scraps of empire." Emerson, *op. cit.*, p. 498.

the total population of the entire group of sixty-four was estimated at less than 50,000,000. By the end of 1966, thirteen of the sixty-four with a combined population of about 25,000,000 had achieved self-government or independence.[18] Except for a few hard-core holdouts, most of the remaining territories are "scraps of empire" too small and too weak for independence to be sensible. If the anticolonialists can keep their zeal from outrunning their judgment, and settle for something less than independence, the smaller territories may complete a peaceful transition to a realistic form of self-government.

The real colonial problem now rests with a few hard-core holdouts consisting principally of the colonies of Portugal and South Africa. The United Kingdom has also been under pressure from the Committee of Twenty-four to grant immediate independence to Aden, but the delay is due to the special circumstances of the case rather than to any basically negative attitude on the part of Britain. Portugal and South Africa, however, have exhibited an intransigence that is quite equal to the zeal of the anticolonialists. The growth of the anticolonial consensus in the United Nations has left these two countries more and more isolated. Even their former colleagues on the colonial side of the aisle have become unwilling to pay the costs of opposing the anticolonial forces in support of so questionable a cause. Portugal, nevertheless, continues to combine systematic repression of native nationalism in Angola, Mozambique, and Portuguese Guinea with a steadfast refusal to admit that its African territories are not self-governing.

South Africa, already under intense fire in the United Nations for its apartheid policies at home, has shown its contempt for the anticolonial majority by proceeding toward the virtual annexation of its South West Africa mandate and the application of apartheid there. Although South Africa has not formally renounced its mandate, it has refused to recognize any right in the United Nations to exercise a supervisory function. For practical purposes the mandate has been a dead letter since the war. An attempt by Ethiopia and Liberia, as former members of the League of Nations, to enforce the mandate through legal action came to a dead end in 1966 when the International Court of Justice ruled that the two individual complainants had no legal right or interest in the subject matter of their claim. An exasperated anti-colonial majority in the General Assembly responded to the Court decision by declaring the mandate at an end and asserting UN political and administrative authority over South West Africa. Detailed

18 These include Barbados, Basutoland (Lesotho), Bechuanaland (Botswana), British Guiana (Guyana), Kenya, Malta, Northern Rhodesia (Zambia), Nyasaland (Malawi), Rhodesia, and Singapore as independent states; North Borneo and Sarawak as parts of Malaysia; and Zanzibar, joined with Tanganyika in the state of Tanzania. No Soviet-controlled territory and none of the remaining quasi-colonial attachments of France (such as French Somaliland) were included on the list, except for New Hebrides which is administered jointly by France and Britain.

plans for implementing the decision awaited the report of a special committee in 1967. South Africa opposed the Assembly action and is certain to resist UN efforts to take over the territory. The situation could lead to wider Security Council sanctions against South Africa and further deterioration of prospects for peace and stability in this troubled part of the world.

The status of Rhodesia also looms as one of the most difficult legacies of colonialism, although it is not a colonial problem in the traditional sense. The issue does not revolve around the unwillingness of the metropolis to let its colony go free. On the contrary—Britain has been severely criticized by the anticolonial bloc for failing to prevent a unilateral declaration of independence by the white-minority-dominated Rhodesian government. African states have threatened the use of force, and several of them severed diplomatic relations with Britain in protest of the latter's failure to take more strenuous measures to thwart Rhodesia's premature secession from the empire in 1965. The situation still contains the seeds of violence which are virtually certain to germinate unless the governing white minority of Rhodesia can become reconciled to political participation by the black majority.

The confrontation between the anticolonialists and the hard-core holdouts is presently a stalemate. The Committee of Twenty-four can count on the ready endorsement and moral support of the Assembly for the most intemperate and unenlightened criticism. On the other hand, the Assembly has no means to enforce its recommendations. Even Britain, which has a good colonial record and continues to participate in the work of the Committee, has persistently refused to accept a visiting mission to its Aden protectorate.

Britain's realistic susceptibility to winds of change and her basic commitment to self-government should make possible a long-run accommodation with the forces of anticolonialism in her remaining dependencies. But the behavior of Portugal, South Africa, and Rhodesia does not warrant the same optimistic appraisal. The Assembly has called for sanctions against Portugal's colonial policies, Rhodesia's unilateral declaration of independence, and the apartheid and South West African policies of the Republic of South Africa. The Security Council has also begun to move in that direction with a recommended arms embargo against South Africa in 1963 and broad economic and diplomatic sanctions against Rhodesia in 1965, including non-recognition, severance of economic relations, an arms embargo, and an embargo on petroleum products. In 1966 the Security Council took the unprecedented step of making the arms and oil embargo mandatory under Chapter VII of the Charter dealing with threats to the peace. A boycott of Rhodesian exports was also made mandatory.

If pressure through the United Nations is insufficient, as thus far it has been, the African countries themselves might resort to force. Already the Organization of African Unity has urged the use of violence against all three if necessary, and OAU funds are being channeled to "freedom fighters" in South Africa and the Portuguese territories. Unless some softening of attitudes occurs, the only reasonable prognosis is continued stalemate until a solution is sought by violence.

THE UNITED NATIONS AND COLONIALISM

Decolonization is one of the great revolutions of our century. It has not been accomplished without violence, and its emerging pattern is not wholly consonant with either rationality or the welfare of the peoples concerned. Nevertheless, it is remarkable that such a vast transformation of international life should occur with as little violence and as much concern for the welfare of people. The relative orderliness of change is attributable primarily to the liberal values of the major colonial powers in which, ultimately, native demands for self-determination and justice struck a responsive note. If other colonial countries had followed the course of Portugal and South Africa, the whole Asian and African world might now be a seething volcano preparing to erupt with all the pent-up fury of repressed nationalism and the recklessness of desperate men having literally little to lose but their chains.

Caught up in this revolution of self-determination, international organization has helped to promote a more rapid, peaceful, and orderly transition to independence and self-government. The League of Nations established the principle of international accountability in a limited area of colonialism, and helped eliminate the worst evils and abuses of the system. Since 1945 the United Nations has done much more. It has provided a forum in which the forces of anticolonialism could unitedly articulate their case, it has greatly expanded the principle of international accountability, and it has provided more effective instruments for international supervision of colonial administration. By holding aloft the standard of self-determination, it has served as a reminder to the majority of the colonial countries that the demands of the anticolonialists were basically consonant with enduring values in the Western political tradition. When violence has occurred, as in Indonesia or Palestine, the United Nations has sometimes intervened to curb hostilities. The bitterest and most protracted colonial wars of the post-war period have been those in Algeria and Viet Nam where the United Nations was not able effectively to intervene. In the end, the United Nations has hastened acceptance of the new order by legitimizing its tenets.

The UN record on colonial problems is not, however, entirely above reproach. In some instances UN action has hastened territories to premature independence. In other cases United Nations policy on colonial questions may have encouraged a resort to violence by native nationalists who felt that creating a threat to peace and security was the best way to gain the attention of the organization. There is reason to believe that violence was consciously used as a strategy of the Algerian rebels to gain a hearing in the United Nations.[19] More recently, the Assembly's 1960 Declaration on Colonialism has been used to justify India's armed action against Goa and African threats of forcible action against Rhodesia, South Africa, and Portuguese rule in Africa. If the United Nations has increased the militancy of anticolonialists, the conduct of Portugal and the Republic of South Africa gives some color to the allegation that perpetual harassment in the United Nations has hardened their attitudes and made them even more resistant to the winds of change.

On balance, the shortcomings of the organization seem far overshadowed by its contribution to the more peaceful and orderly evolution of the international system. The role of peacemaker has extended to relations among the emerging nations themselves as well as their relations with colonial powers. In retrospect, the organization may have made its most important contribution by hastening the acceptance of the new order before relations between colonial masters and subject peoples became impossibly embittered. As colonialism recedes into history, the tasks of the United Nations will change. Even now its energies are shifting to the problems of political and economic nation-building among the newer and less developed sovereignties. The challenge of the postcolonial era is to maintain a dialogue among new nations and old upon which fruitful cooperation in this task can be built.

Selected Readings

EMERSON, RUPERT. "Colonialism, Political Development, and the UN," *International Organization*, Vol. 19, Summer, 1965, pp. 484–503.

HAAS, ERNST B. "The Attempt to Terminate Colonialism: Acceptance of the United Nations Trusteeship System," *International Organization*, February, 1953, pp. 1–21.

————. "The Reconciliation of Conflicting Colonial Policy Aims: Acceptance of the League of Nations Mandate System," *International Organization*, November, 1952, pp. 521–36.

HALL, H. DUNCAN. *Mandates, Dependencies and Trusteeship.* Washington, D.C.: Carnegie Endowment for International Peace, 1948.

JACOBSON, HAROLD KARAN. "The United Nations and Colonialism: A Tentative Appraisal," *International Organization*, Winter, 1962, pp. 37–56.

MURRAY, JAMES N., JR. *The United Nations Trusteeship System.* Urbana: University of Illinois Press, 1957.

RIVLIN, BENJAMIN. *Italian Colonies.* New York: Carnegie Endowment for International Peace, 1950.

[19] See the comments of Harold Karan Jacobson, "The United Nations and Colonialism: A Tentative Appraisal," *International Organization*, Vol. 16 (Winter, 1962), p. 50.

SADY, EMIL J. *The United Nations and Dependent Peoples.* Washington, D.C.: The Brookings Institution, 1956.

THULLEN, GEORGE. *Problems of the Trusteeship System: A Study of Political Behavior in the United Nations.* Geneva: Librairie Droz, 1964.

WAINHOUSE, DAVID W. *Remnants of Empire: The United Nations and the End of Colonialism.* New York: Harper & Row, for the Council on Foreign Relations, 1964.

Part IV

The Dynamics of
International Cooperation

14 | *Organizing for Social Progress*

Security matters dominate the headlines issuing from international organizations, but welfare absorbs a considerably larger share of manpower and economic resources. The rapid growth of welfare-oriented intergovernmental organization in our century is a response to the expanding volume of public and private contacts across international boundaries, underpinned by faith that the road to world peace is paved with economic and social well-being. Organizations for international economic and social cooperation are now widely referred to as functional organizations, and advocates of such cooperation as an approach to peace are known as functionalists.[1]

Historically, the earliest functional organizations were created in response to needs generated by the growing flood of international transactions in an industrial age. River commissions were created to speed the flow of river traffic; postal and telegraphic unions were organized to provide faster, cheaper, and more reliable transmission of messages; sanitary councils were established to check the spread of communicable diseases along the arteries of international trade and travel. The articulation of a functionalist approach to peace came after—not before—pioneering organizations in these and other fields had set an impressive example of successful international cooperation. Once articulated, however, the basic premise that functional cooperation breeds peace found a ready audience in a world where the increasing destructiveness of war was placing an ever-higher premium upon the quest for peace. In recent decades, the tenets of functionalism have joined hands with specific economic and social needs to stimulate an unprecedented expansion of international organizations. Today it is a rare functional organization that does not espouse peace-building as one of its objects. And it is a rare statesman who does not justify his country's participation in such organizations on the ground of their contribution to peace.[2]

[1] This is obviously a different meaning from that conveyed by the terms *functionalism,* or *structural-functionalism,* as used in theories of social systems.

[2] The theory of functionalism will be examined in greater detail in Chapter 17.

EXPANDING FUNCTIONALISM AND ORGANIZATIONAL DECENTRALIZATION

The nineteenth-century system of international economic and social cooperation developed without any plan or means of central coordination. The natural result was a patchwork of international institutions tending toward common structural forms, but each juridically and politically separate from all the others. Such unplanned growth is a common affliction of national societies, including the United States and its fifty constituent parts. A national government, however, has an authoritative decision-making center that can undertake reorganization when its administrative structure grows too cumbersome. The international system has no central authority capable of rationalizing the random growth of its institutions. As a consequence, the pattern of decentralization has continued largely unabated to the present day.

The impact of the League of Nations upon nineteenth-century organizational patterns was to multiply institutions and activities without providing effective over-all coordination. The League Covenant (Article 24) extended its sheltering arms to existing "international bureaus established by general treaties" if the parties to such treaties consented, and provided that any international bureaus or commissions thereafter constituted should be "placed under the direction of the League." Only a half dozen or so of the existing agencies chose to accept League direction.

Even the organizations within the aegis of the League functioned without vigorous central direction. The Council was designated as the organ of supervision, but it was too busy and too concerned with political questions to give functional matters the attentive and expert treatment they deserved. The Assembly exerted influence through its control of the purse strings, and its second committee filled part of the directional void by offering guidance and encouragement. But this arrangement was not entirely satisfactory, and in the later years of the League there was a growing concern with the problem of coordination. At one time the Assembly considered a proposal to reconstitute economic and social activities in a separate organization wholly outside the League. Although absolute divorce won little favor, a special committee (the Bruce Committee) in 1939 recommended sweeping reorganization under a semi-autonomous "Central Committee for Economic and Social Questions." Coming just a few days before the German attack on Poland, the Bruce report was too late to affect the development of the League; but it was part of the legacy bequeathed to the framers of the UN Charter.

League functional programs were widely recognized as being vigorous, constructive, and worth preserving, and this opinion was reflected in the copious Charter prescriptions for economic and social cooperation. The impact of League experience was also evident in the establishment of the Economic and Social Council as a separate coordinating center.[3] The principle of decentralization was accepted, however, in the overall system of world economic and social collaboration. The Charter abandoned the Covenant's vain hope that all international bureaus and commissions would be placed under the direction of the general organization. Instead, the various "specialized agencies" were authorized to maintain cooperative relationships with the Economic and Social Council and accept such coordination as might flow from consultation and recommendation. The pattern of expanding functionalism and organizational decentralization was thus accorded the legitimacy of Charter endorsement.

THE SCOPE OF FUNCTIONAL COOPERATION

In the following pages, the substance of existing functional cooperation will be considered in three broad categories based upon the policy output of the organization—(1) standards for intra-state conduct, (2) regulation of inter-state contacts, and (3) international services. No attempt will be made to cover every functional organization, or every function of the organizations covered. The "output" basis of classification is deliberately chosen to place emphasis upon functional cooperation as a homogeneous process rather than a congeries of variously interrelated institutions performing relatively discrete functions. Either view offers a valid approach to reality, but our preference in this chapter is to stress the process.

The three output categories are not derived from anything immanent in the process; they simply correspond to the kinds of functions that international organizations perform. The first category—prescribing *standards* for the domestic conduct of states—appears at first to be an inappropriate function for international organization. Yet, a great amount of energy is devoted to setting and maintaining norms of state behavior in such matters as human rights and labor standards, which have only incidental relevance for inter-state affairs. This kind of policy output exists and must be recognized. The second category, *regulation* of inter-state contacts, is obviously an appropriate activity for international organization. In our study the term *regulation* will embrace any organizational action intended to promote the observance of specified norms of conduct in international affairs, from a simple statement of the norm to the application of sanctions for its non-observance. The third category, *services,* is interpreted broadly to include all forms of assistance to governments and peoples to meet their self-perceived needs. In this chapter, discussion of services is directed primarily to informational activities, relief and rehabilitation, and assistance to refugees.

[3] A brief outline of ECOSOC structure and function is given in Chapter 5.

STANDARDS FOR INTRA-STATE CONDUCT: HUMAN RIGHTS

The rights of persons are essentially matters of domestic jurisdiction. International protection for the rights of individuals has not been completely foreign to the law and practice of the modern state system, but until recently the concern has been limited to special groups—diplomatic representatives, consular personnel, and aliens—whose status involved the interests of a foreign sovereignty. From time to time states have also undertaken treaty obligations with respect to their own nationals, as evidenced by the various European treaties from the sixteenth century onward guaranteeing freedom of worship to religious minorities. More recently, the peace architects at Versailles required new states and defeated countries of eastern Europe to assume treaty guarantees of the linguistic, educational, and other rights of ethnic minority groups incorporated within their territories. Neither the religious guarantees nor the minorities treaties were very effective in securing the rights of persons, and their strictly limited nature underscored the general freedom of a state to deal as it wished with those living within its jurisdiction.

Against this background the UN Charter emphasis upon the promotion of human rights constitutes a sharp break with tradition.[4] The new approach did not take the form of specific legal obligations but it did assert an international interest in the rights of individuals everywhere. One reason for the framers' stress on human rights was the strong position taken by the American delegation, reacting to the importunings of private groups whose representatives had converged on San Francisco with a zeal to do something for humanity. In a larger sense, the atrocities of the Nazi era had awakened people throughout the world to the shortcomings of an international system in which a government could impose gross indignities upon its nationals and those of occupied countries without reference to any external standard of decency. In a still broader context, the concern voiced at San Francisco represented a fusion of the old and the new in liberal democratic thought— the traditional emphasis upon the worth and dignity of the individual, and the new liberal emphasis upon freedom *through*, rather than *from*, community action. At the same time, the absence of binding commitments in the Charter and its safeguarding of domestic jurisdiction paid tribute to the realities of an international political system still deeply rooted in national pluralism.

Since 1945, proponents of international action have waged a continuing

[4] No less than seven references to human rights are found in the Charter—the Preamble, and Articles 1 (purposes and principles), 13 (responsibilities of the Assembly), 55 (objectives of economic and social cooperation), 62 (functions and powers of ECOSOC), 68 (responsibility of one of ECOSOC's commissions), and 76 (objective of the trusteeship system).

battle with the conservative forces of national sovereignty, although few countries have been consistent in their support of either camp. Positions on humanitarian principles have often been tinged with ironic political expediency—the Soviet Union weeping for the lot of American Negroes and the United States bewailing the plight of Soviet Jews and the inmates of Siberian forced-labor camps. With all the sound and fury, attempts to coerce or to create binding guarantees of human rights have borne little fruit. The most concrete achievement for this approach has been at the regional level through the operation of the European Human Rights Convention. The enunciation of common standards of human rights, without legal force or sanctions, has proceeded much more rapidly; and the meager evidence now available suggests that the techniques of standard-setting, education, and persuasion may in the long run be better suited to the task of promoting human rights than the attempt to impose legally binding international obligations.

At the present time, the functions of international organization in the field of human rights include (1) setting voluntary norms, (2) creating legal rules and procedures, (3) supplying information and assistance, and (4) penalizing violations. The supplying of information and technical assistance could appropriately be studied in connection with the service function of organizations, but it has relevance for standard-setting and will be considered here in that context.

Voluntary Norms

Voluntary norms are commonly set by an international forum through the declaration of generally applicable rules of behavior. The enunciation of a rule produces no legal obligation; it simply expresses a goal, an aspiration, a guide to conduct, and perhaps a moral imperative. The most celebrated of such statements in the field of human rights is the Universal Declaration of Human Rights, approved by the General Assembly on December 10, 1948, by a vote of forty-eight to zero, with eight abstentions.[5] Anyone who has not read that memorable document should do so to savor the lofty sentiments it echoes and to appreciate what a hodge-podge of differing aspirations and values had to be mediated in order to secure such a high degree of agreement for its adoption. The political and civil rights of the old liberalism are joined with economic and social ideals of the new, while all are hedged with the right of the sovereign state to limit individual rights and freedoms as necessary to meet "the just requirements of morality, public order and the general welfare in a democratic society." Although the practical application of some of the enumerated economic and social rights might require more governmental control than is consistent with some of the

---

[5] Abstaining were the USSR, Ukraine, Byelorussia, Czechoslovakia, Poland, Saudi Arabia, South Africa, and Yugoslavia. See Appendix D for the text of the Declaration.

political rights, the net effect of the declaration is to set an admirable standard of conduct. Even the self-employed barber would be happy to have "the right to rest and leisure, including reasonable limitations of working hours and periodic holidays with pay" (Article 24), if it could be reconciled with his self-employed status.

Other declarations approved by the Assembly include the Declaration of the Rights of the Child (1959), the Declaration on the Granting of Independence to Colonial Countries and Peoples (1960), and the Declaration on the Elimination of All Forms of Racial Discrimination (1963).

Whether such declarations have brought increased observance of human rights may be debatable, but they have undoubtedly influenced the way governments talk about human rights. They are continually used as yardsticks for representatives of some states to measure and judge (and usually condemn) the conduct of others, and they serve as models for legal instruments or decisions having binding effect. The Universal Declaration, in particular, has widely served both of these functions. Scarcely a UN debate on human rights fails to produce some reference to the Declaration as a standard applicable to the particular question under discussion. It has been used to belabor the Soviet Union for its emigration policies, to condemn the Republic of South Africa for its racialism, and to prod colonial powers to eliminate discriminatory practices in their non-self-governing territories.

As a model for authoritative rule making, the Universal Declaration has inspired numerous multilateral treaties on various phases of human rights (to be discussed later on), and its principles have been incorporated into such diverse documents as the 1951 Treaty of Peace with Japan and the 1954 Special Statute for Trieste. The constitutions of at least seventeen new African states make a direct reference to the Universal Declaration, and others have bills of rights or other provisions modeled upon it. The constitution of the Republic of Rwanda, for example, makes the sweeping assertion that the "fundamental freedoms as defined by the Universal Declaration of Human Rights are guaranteed to all citizens." [6] References to the Universal Declaration have also appeared in the legislation and court decisions of various countries. All this does not, of course, prove that human rights are being better observed than before, but it does mean that the principles of the Declaration have begun to acquire legal status which may eventually enable them to influence the practice of human rights.

Lawmaking Treaties

Organs of the United Nations have not been content to let the Universal Declaration filter into national legal systems through the slow and uncertain process of unilateral action. When the Declaration was adopted in 1948 it was regarded as only a preliminary to the drafting of a multilateral treaty

[6] Quoted in Egon Schwelb, *Human Rights and the International Community* (Chicago: Quadrangle Books, 1964), p. 51.

that would translate the exhortations of the Declaration into legal obligations by the process of treaty ratification. Since that time the organization
has drafted multilateral instruments on a variety of special topics, as well as
preparing two omnibus draft covenants—one on civil and political rights
and another on economic, social, and cultural rights—roughly paralleling
the Universal Declaration. The process of preparing such treaties is lengthy,
involving initial consideration in the ECOSOC Commission on Human
Rights, reconsideration by the ECOSOC parent body, a third detailed
examination in the Third Committee of the General Assembly, and final
approval by the Assembly in plenary meeting. A number of the shorter,
special-purpose treaties have successfully run the gantlet and have entered
into force among ratifying states. These include, among others, treaties on
genocide, slavery, and the political rights of women.

The general covenant on human rights that was to follow the Universal
Declaration has encountered stormy waters in the United Nations. Much
of the initial difficulty sprang from an uneasy marriage of the civil and political rights of the traditional democratic state with the economic and social
rights of the modern welfare state. The traditional freedoms of speech, press,
worship, assembly, and procedural due process are prohibitions against unreasonable and arbitrary governmental action. Guarantees of a living wage,
education, social security, full employment, medical care, holidays with pay,
and a right to "leisure," on the other hand, are invitations to a vast expansion
of governmental functions. Many states which might be willing to accept
treaty obligations for the promotion of the former do not regard national
social welfare standards as an appropriate subject to be governed by mutual
contract with other states. This problem was "solved," although not to the
satisfaction of all, by preparing two covenants instead of one, so that either
might be ratified separately.

Heated dispute has also been raised by individual articles relating to
self-determination and the status of federal states. Colonial countries have
argued, unavailingly, that self-determination is not an individual right and
has no place in the covenants. Federal states have objected, with as little
success, to clauses making the covenants applicable throughout federal
states "without any limitations or exceptions." These no-limitation clauses,
if retained in the final drafts, may present insuperable difficulties to ratification by federal states whose constituent territorial units share constitutional
responsibility for the protection of individual rights.

Despite an obvious lack of consensus, the covenants have progressed to
the Assembly stage, and the Third Committee is pressing for completion of
the documents in time to open them for ratification by the twentieth
anniversary of the Universal Declaration in 1968. The only portions of the
covenants remaining to be approved by the Committee majority are the
controversial implementation and final clauses. For the draft Covenant on
Civil and Political Rights, the anticipated implementation measures include

national reporting on measures of compliance, a Human Rights Committee to hear complaints by states (not by aggrieved individuals or groups), and a right of appeal from the Committee to the International Court of Justice. Even without the right of individual petition such measures are unquestionably too advanced for many states to accept. In view of the very broad provisions of the draft Covenant on Economic, Social and Cultural Rights, and the expected difficulties of enforcement, implementation will probably be limited to periodic progress reports on observance.

There is no evidence to indicate that great behavioral changes have occurred in response to the spate of postwar human rights treaties. Since implementation is generally dependent upon the good faith of the parties to the various instruments, one may reasonably assume that progress, if it occurs at all, will come through a gradual accommodation to the norms rather than by sweeping transformation of legal systems and social practices. A commitment to gradualism and voluntarism is implicit in the absence of effective sanctions. Although more thoroughgoing enforcement schemes have been suggested, the time has not yet come when states are willing on a broad scale to submit their relations with their own citizens to effective international scrutiny and control.

THE EUROPEAN CONVENTION. By far the most impressive system for the international protection of human rights is the European Convention on Human Rights signed in 1950 and in force since 1953. Fifteen European states [7] have agreed to submit certain types of human rights controversies among themselves to the binding determination of an international body. Ten of the fifteen have gone even further, in a significant break with traditional international law, by granting individuals and private associations the right to complain.

To discourage frivolous complaints and ensure due deliberation, the process of petition is long and complicated. Petitions are first considered by the fifteen-member Human Rights Commission (one from each ratifying state, appointed by the Committee of Ministers of the Council of Europe, from a list of three nominees submitted by each member state). If found admissible the complaint is heard by a subcommission with the object of negotiating an amicable settlement. Of more than 2,600 complaints submitted through 1965, all but three were by private petitioners and less than two per cent were found admissible. Numerous complaints have been rejected because the state in question had not accepted the jurisdiction of the Commission to hear petitions by private persons. Other common reasons for inadmissibility are failure to exhaust domestic remedies, expiration of the

---

[7] Austria, Belgium, Cyprus, Denmark, Greece, Iceland, Ireland, Italy, Luxembourg, the Netherlands, Norway, Sweden, Turkey, the United Kingdom, and West Germany. The signatories are all members of the Council of Europe, which inspired the drafting of the Treaty. France, Malta, and Switzerland, also members of the Council of Europe, have not become parties to the Treaty.

time limit fixed for appeal from the decision of a domestic court, and insubstantiality of the complaint. If settlement is not reached through the subcommission, the case may go to the full commission for a finding of fact and an opinion on the merits, which are reported to the Committee of Ministers of the Council of Europe.

Up to this point the emphasis is upon the quiet negotiation of a "friendly solution" among the parties directly involved. The Committee of Ministers may also try its hand at persuasion, but if this fails, it is empowered to issue a binding decision by a two-thirds vote. For the states (presently nine) which have ratified an optional protocol conferring jurisdiction upon the European Court of Human Rights, a final decision is left to the Court.[8] The Court is composed of eighteen individuals elected by the Assembly of the Council of Europe, one from each state which is a member of the Council. By 1966 the Court had considered but three cases, and neither the Court nor the Committee of Ministers had yet found a state in violation of the Convention.

In the last analysis, the European system rests on good faith since no penalties other than bad publicity are provided for noncompliance. Compared with traditional concepts of international law, the idea behind the European Convention is revolutionary. But its workability may in fact be attributable to the cautious, conservative manner in which the idea has been applied. A number of particularly favorable circumstances should be noted. First, the Convention itself has been limited to traditional civil and political rights already widely guaranteed in Western European countries. Second, the legal systems of the parties have sufficient homogeneity to produce similarity in interpretation and application of the treaty guarantees. Third, the emphasis throughout is upon quiet negotiation of settlement, utilizing a judicial or quasi-judicial body as the final arbiter, and at no stage providing a public forum for political harassment of one state by another. Fourth, states have in fact rarely utilized the machinery in their dealings with one another. The fact that only three petitions have been filed by states is convincing testimony to the forbearance and mutual confidence that makes the system possible. Fifth, petitions by individuals are carefully screened to rule out frivolous or insubstantial complaints. Sixth, no state has yet been found to violate the Convention.[9] The special conditions that contribute to

[8] By specific provision of the Convention, an individual may not appeal either to the Committee of Ministers or to the Court. He must rely on the Human Rights Commission to lay his case before the Ministers or the Court in instances deemed appropriate by the Commission.

[9] In a case not decided by late 1966, 324 French-speaking citizens of Belgium have asked relief from Belgian laws compelling their children to attend Dutch-speaking schools. The outcome may be a stern test of the viability of the system for international adjudication of individual rights. An adverse decision, obligating Belgium to modify laws dividing the country into two language areas, could well convince Belgium not to renew its ratification of protocols accepting the Court's jurisdiction and agreeing to stand as a respondent to individual complaints.

the success of the European experiment do not encourage the hope that it can readily or soon be applied as a model elsewhere.[10]

Supplying Information and Assistance

Standard setting and treaty making are regularly supplemented by the wide circulation of information about human rights through UN meetings, studies, reports, publications, and technical assistance. UN discussions of human rights are all too frequently dominated by political polemics, but on some subjects they serve a useful informational function. It is quite probable, for example, that the ECOSOC Commission on the Status of Women has contributed to the extension of political rights to women through its efforts to gather information and exchange views and experience. Talk has been enlightened by special UN studies on such topics as forced labor, slavery, and discrimination in education, employment, religion, and political rights. In addition, national reports on human rights are regularly discussed in ECOSOC's Human Rights Commission. The informational character of the reporting is shielded from extremer aspects of political controversy by ground rules limiting the Commission to general recommendations that do not pass judgment on the performance of particular governments.

Since 1946 the United Nations has published an annual *Yearbook on Human Rights* compiled from national reports of legislation adopted and other measures taken to promote the observance of human rights. Reporting is voluntary and states are free to select what information they wish to submit. The *Yearbook* nevertheless provides a means of sharing information on the most favorable developments and practices throughout the world.

In the realm of technical assistance, the UN program now includes seminars, fellowships, and the advisory services of experts for countries requesting special help.

Penalizing Violations

The United Nations has frequently attempted to mobilize the pressures of world opinion in cases of the alleged violation of human rights. The record suggests that this exercise, in its short-run effects at least, is less promising than standard setting, treaty making, and information sharing as a means of promoting the observance of human rights. Domestic jurisdiction is the legal refuge of the violators, and their practical response has most often been a stony resistance to the pleas, commands, and denunciations of the United Nations. In a few instances, where only a marginal national interest has been involved and UN action has been conciliatory, states have reacted favorably

---

[10] The European Convention has served as a model for a draft convention prepared by the Inter-American Council of Jurists, a specialized body of the Organization of American States. The draft has not yet been submitted to an Inter-American Conference for approval, and its status appears uncertain.

to the pressure. In the early 1950's Greece rescinded death sentences previously imposed upon a number of political offenders after public expressions of concern were voiced in the Assembly. Spain rescinded a mass death sentence in 1952 under similar circumstances. No formal resolution of disapproval was adopted by the Assembly in either case but the circumstances suggest that Greece and Spain may have been influenced by the sentiment against the death penalties which crystallized at the United Nations.

Most other attempts by the organization to serve as the censor of international morals or the voice of a collective world conscience have not proved very efficacious. In 1949 and 1950 the General Assembly cajoled, exhorted, and ultimately condemned Bulgaria, Hungary, and Romania for the arrest and imprisonment of Catholic churchmen in violation of postwar peace treaties. Several resolutions were approved by huge majorities and all without noticeable effect upon the East European states. At various times the United Nations has also criticized the Soviet Union for violation of human rights in such matters as forced labor and the failure to repatriate World War II prisoners. Over a period of years the Soviet Union did in fact repatriate most of the prisoners still living, and evidence of forced labor declined. These developments appeared more closely related to changes within the Soviet Union and the international environment, however, rather than to UN action. If UN action had any effect, it was long-delayed and well mixed with other more basic causes.

The most obvious, continued, and still current case of intransigence in the face of UN pressure is that of the Republic of South Africa whose policies of racial discrimination have been before the United Nations every year since the establishment of the organization. UN action of gradually increasing stringency, ranging through requests, appeals, creation of special negotiating and investigative bodies, condemnation, and the imposition of a voluntary arms embargo and economic boycott have coincided with progressive entrenchment of the apartheid system of complete segregation. When the Assembly in 1962 recommended an arms embargo, an economic boycott, and the severance of diplomatic relations, UN pressure passed well beyond the mobilizing of world opinion. The Security Council subsequently endorsed the recommendation for an arms embargo (August, 1963) and most countries now respect it.

The important European and American trading partners of South Africa have not yet complied with the Assembly recommendation for diplomatic sanctions and general economic boycott. The militant Afro-Asian forces hope to persuade the Security Council that apartheid is a threat to world peace falling under Chapter VII of the Charter, which authorizes the Council to impose mandatory diplomatic and economic sanctions. Thus far the United States and Britain have resisted such sanctions as impractical and more damaging to the British economy than to South Africa. If South Africa and the United Nations continue on their present collision course, the outcome may very well be violent without necessarily being a net gain for the cause of human rights.

REGULATION OF LABOR STANDARDS

Closely akin to UN action in the field of human rights are the efforts of the International Labor Organization to upgrade labor standards around the world. The ILO has been an active force for higher labor standards since its creation in 1919, when Allied statesmen, responding to labor pressures and honoring their wartime commitments to trade union groups, drafted the constitution of the ILO as Part XIII of the Versailles Treaty. The organization has ever since been marked by a vigorous secretariat, known as the Labor Office, and a unique form of tripartite representation for employer, worker, and government interests in its policy-making bodies. Each member state sends two government delegates, one employers' delegate, and one workers' delegate to the annual meeting of the International Labor Conference, and the same tripartite distribution is found in its forty-eight-member Governing Body.[11]

Like the United Nations, the ILO functions by setting standards, giving advice, facilitating the exchange of information, and mobilizing world opinion in support of higher standards. Standards are set through legally binding conventions, subject to state ratification, and through recommendations voicing goals and aspirations that are yet beyond the reach of many states and hence not proper subjects for lawmaking treaties. Publications, conferences, seminars and fellowships, and technical experts have been the common means of giving advice and exchanging information. Following the trend of other international organizations, the ILO has in recent years expanded its technical assistance programs in the direction of general economic development as a means of providing the social and economic base for improved labor standards.

In the foregoing aspects of standard setting and promotion, the ILO differs little from the work of the United Nations in the field of human rights. The ILO, however, has unusually well-developed techniques for bringing the weight of criticism to bear in support of its conventions and recommendations. This is done by an annual review of member states' reports, a judicious use of its powers of investigation, and a procedure for hearing complaints in specific cases.

The annual review is made possible by the extensive reporting obligations imposed by the ILO Charter. Members are required to report annually on

---

[11] Although the purpose of the tripartite structure is to have each of the three categories of delegates represent the views of their respective groups, those from states such as the Soviet Union have generally expressed a single governmental position.

compliance with all conventions they have ratified. They must also report whether they have submitted recommendations and unratified conventions to the proper authorities for action, whether they intend to ratify the conventions, and what action has thus far been taken. Since 1949, states have had to report the extent to which national practice conforms to standards laid down in recommendations and unratified conventions. Fortunately for the sanity of national labor bureaus, the Governing Body of the ILO requires a report each year only on selected recommendations and unratified conventions, rather than an annual report on every instrument.

Unlike many reports solicited by the General Assembly of the United Nations, the annual reports to ILO are not simply compiled and recorded for information purposes. They are carefully read and analyzed by the secretariat staff and referred to a special committee of independent experts appointed by the ILO Governing Body. The Committee of Experts has developed such autonomy in its operations that the Governing Body now generally forwards Committee reports without comment to the Annual Conference, which invariably approves them. This is all the more remarkable because the report is a hard-hitting summary and evaluation of individual members and offers forthright criticism.

The substance of the report is a detailed analysis of member state compliance with conventions and recommendations, with pointed reference to cases of noncompliance or nonconformity, and specific recommendations—or even demands—for remedial action when states default in their reporting obligations or fail to implement conventions they have ratified. The Committee of Experts is not limited to the examination of information submitted by states. Working closely with the Secretariat, the Committee exploits many sources, including

> national official documentation, press reports, complaints from trade unions, information furnished by national ILO correspondents, conversations with visiting national officials, reports from returning technical assistance experts, and—last but by no means least—information picked up informally by secretariat members on home leave.[12]

In addition to reproof and admonition for special cases, the Committee of Experts annually draws up lists of states which have failed to submit conventions and recommendations to their respective domestic authorities, or which have not submitted reports as required. States that have "persistently disregarded" the observations of the Committee of Experts are placed on a special "blacklist." At one time or another about half of the members have appeared on the blacklist since 1948. Some states are relatively immune to this kind of pressure (Albania is perennially on the blacklist), but others respond to the adverse publicity by mending their ways.

[12] Ernst B. Haas, *Beyond the Nation State* (Stanford, California: Stanford University Press, 1964), pp. 254–55.

The reporting system is by far the most important enforcement tool available to the ILO, but investigations have sometimes been utilized. On several occasions the Governing Body has sent an ad hoc mission to investigate alleged violations of worker rights.[13] This practice is limited to instances where the state in question is willing to admit the investigative mission and negotiate with it. Other more generalized investigations of special subjects have been carried out by means of documentary reports of national legislation, newspaper and monograph sources, and governmental replies to questionnaires, without sending missions to survey conditions in the field. Two extensive investigations of freedom of association, in 1926 and 1955–56, were carried out by the Labor Office under the direction of a distinguished committee of specialists, to provide a factual basis for subsequent ILO programs.

The ILO complaint procedure is yet another technique for mobilizing world opinion against countries that violate treaty obligations. Any group of workers or employers may bring an alleged violation of a ratified Convention to the attention of the Governing Body of the ILO. The Governing Body invites a statement from the government concerned and, if the reply is not satisfactory, publishes both the text of the allegation and the government's statement, if any. If the complaint originates with a government, the Governing Body has the option of referring it to a tripartite Commission of Inquiry for fact-finding and recommendation. Should a government party to the dispute reject the Commission's recommendation, the complaint may be placed before the International Court of Justice whose decision is final. The original constitution of 1919 provided for voluntary economic sanctions against a defaulting government, but the sanctions were never used and provision for them was deleted by constitutional amendment in 1946. The Governing Body may now recommend to the Annual Conference whatever measures it deems helpful. As a practical matter, if the publicity and embarrassment of the complaint procedure does not secure compliance, more stringent action is likely to alienate the member from the organization without raising labor standards.

REGULATION OF INTERSTATE CONTACTS

Human rights and labor standards are matters of domestic concern which have traditionally been beyond the reach of international law. By contrast, most aspects of functional cooperation involve inter-state contacts that fall beyond the jurisdiction of any single state and must be regulated by international action, if they are to be regulated at all. In recognition of this fact,

[13] Such missions have been sent to Hungary (1920), Venezuela (1949), India and Pakistan (1949), Panama (1950), Iran (1950), and the Suez Canal Zone (1951–52). See Haas, *op. cit.*, p. 572n.

states have submitted a number of their functional relationships to the regulative processes of international organization. This is the kind of behavior that Woolf in 1916 aptly termed "international government." [14] It does not justify the functionalist premise that economic and social cooperation leads to peace, but it does demonstrate that states will subject themselves and their citizens to international regulation in limited functional areas when the exigencies of international intercourse seem to require it. Some of the more significant regulatory institutions will be briefly examined here as illustrative of the process.[15]

Postal Service

Probably the best observed international regulations are those of the Universal Postal Union, an organization dating from 1874. Under its auspices letters can be delivered anywhere in the world by the most expeditious route at a modest uniform cost and in accordance with general uniform procedures. The technical nature of UPU functions is conducive to consensus, and consensus on broad objectives provides the foundation for functioning majority rule within the organization, when the goal of complete unanimity cannot be attained. Revisions of the Postal Convention, when initiated at the quinquennial meetings of the Congress of the Postal Union, may be adopted by a two-thirds or simple majority, depending on the issue, and become effective upon ratification. During the interim between Congresses, proposals for amendments are circulated by the Bureau (secretariat) and take effect when a sufficient number of affirmative replies are received, varying from unanimity, to two-thirds, to a simple majority of the membership. Although no state is legally bound if it does not ratify, the penalty for noncompliance is to lose the privileges of membership. No state has yet chosen to suffer these consequences.[16]

Compliance with the rules of the system is attributable to a simple balance of benefits and burdens—the benefits of participation outweigh the burdens of compliance with regulations. This should not suggest, however, that the burdens are equally spread. A fundamental rule of the system allows each state to keep its own postal receipts, a practice making for ease of administration but not for equity. It bears harshly on transit countries

[14] L. S. Woolf, *International Government* (London: Allen and Unwin, 1916).

[15] Agencies for the regulation of international trade and payments, although of obvious significance in this context, will be discussed in a subsequent chapter on international economic relationships.

[16] Privileges within the Union may be maintained by provisional adherence and actual compliance. Formal ratification is not absolutely necessary to good standing as long as the state in fact observes the regulations.

Every member state must accept the Postal Convention and regulation of letter-mail service. Eight other postal services—insured letters and boxes, parcel post, money orders, COD, and four others—are established by special agreement and are binding only upon members that have acceded.

like France which must carry a great deal of mail for other people, receiving only a minimal "gratuity" of transit for the service. Underdeveloped countries with high delivery costs, which receive much more second and third class mail than they sell stamps for, are also placed at a disadvantage. Such countries have protested the unequal burden-sharing but have nevertheless remained in the system.

Telecommunications

The work of the International Telecommunications Union is in many respects analogous to that of the UPU, especially in its efforts to create a single homogeneous communication system by joint regulation of telegraph, telephone, and radio-telegraph services. Methods of legislation and enforcing compliance are also broadly similar. The ITU Conference meets at five-year intervals to make general policy and initiate amendments to the ITU Convention, by unanimous agreement if possible but through simple and qualified majorities if necessary. States are permitted to ratify amendmends with reservations and still remain in good standing, but the penalty for nonratification is deprivation of its vote in ITU organs.

Compliance with ITU rules, a product of necessity and convenience, has been very high except in the special problem area of radio broadcasting. There the ITU has sometimes been faced with defiance by countries refusing to be limited to the use of the frequencies allotted by the ITU's International Frequency Registration Board. If a recalcitrant member broadcasts on a frequency not assigned to it, the ITU may punish the offender by freeing other states to use its assigned frequencies. Interference with authorized radio signals, otherwise known as radio jamming, is another special problem. The practice is clearly in violation of ITU regulations but is so entwined with the vital interests of states that ITU sanctions are unable to curb it. Faced with the fact of radio jamming, the ITU has generally resigned itself to the fact that retaliation through the release of frequencies would only add to the confusion and further impair radio transmission.

Civil Aviation

In the field of air transportation, international efforts to promote safety, regularity of transport, uniformity, and nondiscrimination are centered in the International Civil Aviation Organization. The Communist countries and a few others have remained aloof from this specialized agency, a circumstance which detracts from universality but raises the level of consensus within the organization. The rule-making function is exercised principally by the organization's twenty-seven-member Council, rather than its triennial Assembly. Standards approved by a two-thirds vote of the Council become effective within three months (or some other period fixed by the Council) after submission to member states, unless a majority of states indicate their disapproval during the time period. The organization distinguishes between binding *standards,* which are necessary to the safety or regularity of international air navigation, and nonbinding *recommended practices* which represent desirable goals.

A state that cannot conform to a new standard may notify the Council within the time period fixed for raising objectives and be released from its legal obligation. Other states will be notified of the discrepancy, however, and the aircraft and personnel of the noncomplying state thereafter may not enjoy the benefits of air navigation in the territories of other members without their express authorization. The ICAO Convention commits all members to the principle of nondiscrimination against the aircraft of any country; but noncompliance with standards revives the discretionary rights of one state against another that would prevail under the rules of customary international law.[17] If a member is found by the Council to default on its obligations under the ICAO constitution, other members may close their air space to the aircraft of the offender and the Assembly may suspend its right to vote in the Assembly or Council. These sanctions have been sufficient to obtain widespread compliance with the technical standards prescribed by ICAO.

Health

Health problems have long been a subject of international regulation. The international health councils established during the nineteenth century in seaport cities of North Africa, the Middle East, and Southeast Europe—sometimes by imposition of the more powerful European states—represented an early form of international action to improve sanitary conditions and prevent the spread of epidemics along the channels of commerce. Later the councils were supplemented by multilateral conventions establishing rules for quarantine and other precautionary measures to be taken in ports, and prohibiting vessels from leaving port without a clean bill of health. Exchange of information through conferences was put on a more systematic basis in 1907 with the establishment of the International Office of Public Health in Paris, and League health machinery subsequently forged ahead with direct efforts to fight disease and improve world levels of health.

Today the World Health Organization as a specialized agency of the United Nations has combined and expanded international cooperation in all of these fields, although its regulatory function is the one which particularly concerns us here. The WHO Assembly has effective rule-making power in

---

[17] The ICAO regulation is primarily *technical,* relating to such matters as air traffic control, communication and navigational aids, safety standards for aircraft, rules of the air, and so forth. The organization has *not* been given the authority to regulate commerce, a right jealously guarded by states. Commercial privileges are still exchanged through bilateral agreement.

several limited but important areas, including (1) the establishment of standards of safety, purity, and potency of biological and pharmaceutical substances passing in international commerce; (2) the promulgation of sanitary and quarantine regulations applicable to ground, sea, and air travel; (3) setting standards for diagnostic procedure; and (4) standardization of medical nomenclature. When approved by the Assembly, health regulations come into force for all members after a specified period of notice, except for states that specifically object or enter reservations.

The WHO Assembly has the right to formulate conventions and make recommendations on virtually any health-related matter. Although the recommendations do not take effect until ratified or otherwise implemented by national action, noncomplying members must face the sanction of adverse publicity. The WHO constitution requires all states to accept or reject conventions within eighteen months of their adoption by the Assembly, and to notify the Director-General of the action taken. If the convention is rejected, the report must include reasons for nonacceptance. After the pattern of the ILO, each state must also submit an annual report on the implementation of WHO recommendations and of conventions it has ratified.

In addition to its general health function, WHO cooperates with the United Nations and related agencies for the control of the production, use, and traffic in narcotics.

SERVICE FUNCTIONS

Most of the services now rendered by international organizations consist of programs for economic and social development, relief and rehabilitation, and sharing information. International action for economic and social development, which is absorbing an ever larger share of the budgets of the United Nations and specialized agencies and some regional organizations, will be examined in a subsequent chapter. Here we will review some of the relief and informational services.

Information

Among international organizations, the United Nations Educational, Scientific and Cultural Organization (UNESCO) has a special responsibility for the dissemination of information. Although a growing portion of UNESCO's energy is being turned to technical assistance in education, because of grants from the UN Development Program and demands from developing countries within its own membership, UNESCO continues to engage in a staggering variety of information-sharing activities outside the realm of technical assistance. Titles in the catalog of UNESCO and UNESCO-sponsored publications now number in the thousands. Periodical publications range in scope from the UNESCO *Courier* (topical themes and events of popular interest) and the UNESCO *Bulletin* (a running review of the organization's activities) to the *International Social Science Journal, Diogenes* (humanities), *Impact* (science), and *Museum*. These titles are illustrative, not exhaustive. Other publications include bibliographies, reports, and special studies on all manner of subjects within UNESCO's fields of interest, and increasingly valuable statistical documentation in education, the social sciences, library services, mass communication, and other fields.

UNESCO publications have not always been a model of objectivity or even of scholarship. One problem is the concern to prepare studies that will not invite strong criticism from one member country or another. This can sometimes lead to the production of colorless surveys, devoid of all but the most anemic analysis and screened for unacceptable facts. Of a different nature is the UNESCO policy of not using information about a state which does not originate from sources within the state itself. An open society like the United States is at an obvious disadvantage to the Soviet Union, for example, in a UNESCO study of a subject like race relations. All sides of the question are discussed freely in the United States, but no indigenous Soviet source is likely to produce anything but fulsome praise of the Soviet system. These and other shortcomings of UNESCO publications should not be overstressed. Some individual pieces have been very good indeed, and, considered as a whole, the UNESCO publication program is both massive in quantity and highly informative in substance, if not constituting a really significant contribution to the store of humanistic and scientific knowledge.

Publications are only the beginning of UNESCO information services. Film strips are now available on subjects ranging from arid-zone research to practical education in building a stove. Conferences are called for every conceivable occasion. A former American representative on the UNESCO Executive Board has termed the number of UNESCO conferences "nothing short of awesome" and observed, with tongue only slightly in cheek, that any professor of education "who has not participated in some gathering under UNESCO auspices" must have "deliberately gone into hiding." [18] Another important UNESCO informational activity, often fostered by means of conferences, is the promotion of interchange among scientists, scholars, and artists. To further this interchange, UNESCO has encouraged the formation of international professional societies and often supported them through financial subventions. Educational exchange, elimination of barriers to the free flow of information, the improvement of mass communication techniques, and securing a Universal Copyright Convention are other aspects of the multiform UNESCO approach to the dissemination of information. If UNESCO fails in its task of spreading

[18] George N. Shuster, *UNESCO: Assessment and Promise* (New York: Harper and Row, 1963), p. 24.

education, science, and culture, it will not be from lack of variety in its method.

Other international organizations also render informational services on which governments, business, the professions and others throughout the world have come to rely. The Statistical Office of the United Nations, for example, publishes a number of annual basic reference works, including the *Statistical Yearbook,* the *Demographic Yearbook,* the *Yearbook of International Trade Statistics, World Energy Supplies,* and the *Yearbook of National Accounts Statistics.* Reference has already been made to the UN *Yearbook on Human Rights.* The United Nations also issues periodicals on special subjects, such as the *International Review of Criminal Policy* and the *International Social Service Review.* These titles, of course, are representative rather than exhaustive. These and other regular UN publications are supplemented by numerous special reports.[19] The specialized agencies likewise produce a flood of facts in their own special fields of competence and interest.[20] When publications are considered together with the many conferences, seminars, and other meetings whose primary function is the spreading of knowledge, the informational services of international organization assume a wide scope indeed.

Relief and Rehabilitation

Since World War II, international organization has been continuously involved in programs for the relief of people in distress. If one considers the League of Nations efforts to provide protection to refugees during the interwar years, the period of continuous involvement begins much earlier. Although the long-term problems of economic development now claim the focus of attention in the economic and social field, international organizations have compiled a substantial record of accomplishment in meeting the short-term needs of selected groups of people in distress.

[19] For example, *National and International Measures for Full Employment* (1950), *Measures for the Economic Development of Underdeveloped Countries* (1951), *The Determinants and Consequences of Population Trends* (1954), *Water for Industrial Use* (1958), *Capital Punishment* (1962), *New Sources of Energy and Energy Development* (1962), and *Training for Social Work—An International Survey* (1963), and *Report on the World Social Situation* (biennial).

[20] The International Labor Organization publishes a monthly *International Labor Review,* a quarterly *ILO News,* an annual *Year Book of Labor Statistics,* and a host of reports and special studies. The Food and Agriculture Organization has an impressive array of yearbooks, periodicals, and bulletins, regularly supplemented by topical reports on matters ranging from *Food Additive Control in Denmark* and *Land Reform in Italy* to *Timber Trends and Prospects in the Asia-Pacific Region.* The World Health Organization, in addition to its *Bulletin of the World Health Organization,* the *Epidemiological and Vital Statistics Report,* the *International Digest of Health Legislation,* and other regular periodicals, has published hundreds of special studies of such diverse matters as *Health Hazards of Ionizing Radiation, Accidents in Childhood,* and *Guide to Hygiene and Sanitation in Aviation.* These lists could be vastly expanded and similar ones compiled for other international organizations.

THE UNITED NATIONS RELIEF AND REHABILITATION ADMINISTRATION. In terms of manpower, extent of operations, and expenditures within a relatively short period of time, UNRRA stands as the most impressive intergovernmental relief agency ever established and, indeed, "the largest non-military intergovernmental organization in history," [21] regardless of function. At its peak of activity, UNRRA employed 27,800 persons, more than the entire system of the United Nations and specialized agencies in 1966. Expenditures for goods and services, from its inception in November, 1943, to its disbandment in 1947, totaled $3.9 billion. This compares with expenditures of $3.5 billion from 1946 through 1961 by the United Nations, all of its special programs, and all specialized agencies, excluding the international lending agencies.

UNRRA was created "in a time of brave and generous action" before the bloom of wartime cooperation had withered. It was a joint effort of mammoth proportions, standing in bold contrast to the relief operations of World War I when the most pressing needs had been met through private action, notably Herbert Hoover's Commission for Relief in Belgium and his American Relief Administration operating in Germany, Austria, Russia, and Eastern Europe. The initiative, the basic planning, and most of the financial support for UNRRA came from the United States government, which early recognized that the problems of relief and rehabilitation created by World War II could only be met by concerted governmental action.

The effort was made on a heroic scale. Food, clothing, and medicine supplied by UNRRA filled a critical need of millions in Europe and Asia. In China alone, direct food relief was provided to more than ten million persons. In Eastern Europe, UNRRA aid during the winter of 1945–46 meant the narrow margin between survival and starvation for a war-debilitated people still looking forward to their first postwar harvest. The process of rehabilitation also extended to the revival of agricultural and industrial production. Transportation systems were put in motion with UNRRA-supplied ships, trucks, locomotives, horses, and mules. Seed, fertilizer, farm machinery, and livestock were pumped into agricultural systems decimated by the war, while raw materials, tools and heavy equipment were applied to the revival of industry. On the social welfare front, UNRRA financed public health programs, supported public education, and assisted governments with social services.

UNRRA also assumed the responsibility of caring for millions of refugees and displaced persons [22] and assisted with their resettlement or return home. By the end of 1945, over 5,000 UNRRA specialists in Europe alone

---

[21] L. K. Hyde, Jr., *The United States and the United Nations: Promoting the Public Welfare* (New York: Manhattan Publishing Co., 1960), p. 53.

[22] A displaced person has a home state to which he may return. A refugee is a person who has fled from his home state and is unable or unwilling to return.

were aiding military authorities in the care and repatriation of uprooted populations. UNRRA supplied food, clothing, shelter, medical attention, and even civil government to communities of homeless refugees.

This far-flung operation was administered from Washington by an American Director-General, under the supervision of a four- (later nine-) member Central Committee of government representatives. This body in turn was responsible to a Plenary Council on which all participating Allied governments were represented. Most decisions could be made by a majority vote of the participating states. Financial contributions were supposed to represent a one per cent levy upon annual national income, which meant that the lion's share of the burden would necessarily fall to the United States. Private organizations contributed about $200 million to UNRRA operations and, of the remaining $3.7 billion, the United States donated seventy-three per cent or about $2.7 billion.

The dependence upon American funds and personnel gave the United States a predominant influence in the decisions of the organization. In 1942 an Office of Foreign Relief and Rehabilitation Operations had been created in the State Department, with former New York Governor Herbert Lehman as director. When UNRRA was established, Lehman and his staff were transferred to the new program, and expanded staffing needs were met largely by "officials, clerks and secretaries fresh from OPA, Agriculture, FEA, SPB, State, Commerce, Treasury" and other government agencies. Not too surprisingly, "the idea that UNRRA was an international body never quite got across" in Washington.[23]

In the field, however, recipient countries had the last word, and this proved the organization's financial undoing. UNRRA rules made governmental consent a prerequisite to operation in the territory of any nonenemy state, and supplies were generally to be distributed through governments.[24] UNRRA had considerable leverage, including the threat of withholding aid, and in China the agency violated its basic agreement for a time by resorting to direct distribution out of frustration with governmental bungling. But UNRRA (which had its own problems of administration) was never able to eliminate problems of government inefficiency, occasional venality, and the use of UNRRA aid for political purposes.

The problems inhering in an international operation of such size and scope, hastily put together in a period of great need and great shortages of supplies and competent manpower, conspired with an increasingly difficult

[23] John Perry, director of Food branch of OFFRO, quoted in Benjamin H. Higgins, *The United Nations and U.S. Foreign Economic Policies* (Homewood, Illinois: Richard D. Irwin, 1962), p. 83.

[24] UNRRA regulations prescribed that supplies should be distributed through governments and intermediaries. Governments, which received the goods without cost, were supposed to sell them on the commercial market through government stores or private outlets and utilize the proceeds for reconstruction or relief purposes.

political environment to bring about UNRRA's premature demise. The immediate cause of death was the refusal of the United States Congress to grant further financial support. Congressional support was undermined by persistent charges, not altogether justified, of UNRRA inefficiency and "political intrigue," and by a rather well-justified suspicion that the Soviet Union was using UNRRA aid to consolidate its hold upon occupied areas of Eastern Europe. Related sources of irritation and resentment were the Soviet refusal to let American reporters enter Soviet-occupied areas and report on the distribution of UNRRA supplies; Soviet insistence upon repatriation of all displaced persons to their homelands, involuntarily if necessary; and general Soviet obstructionism in a program paid for largely by United States money.

The United States decision to withdraw support from UNRRA was communicated to members of the Council meeting at Geneva in August, 1946. The American delegate's unceremonious announcement that "the gravy train has gone around for the last time" left his disconcerted fellow delegates no recourse but to seek alternative arrangements. In point of fact, the indelicate reference to the "gravy train" proved to be inaccurate. The train continued to make its appointed rounds but more selectively and more closely tied to American controls and political objectives. Massive infusions of economic aid to Europe under the Marshall Plan gave ample evidence of continuing American willingness to send help abroad when it appeared to serve United States interests.

The demise of UNRRA nevertheless created an alarming gap in the world's machinery for economic and social defense, and provision was made for UNRRA functions to be assumed by other organizations wherever possible. The handwriting on the wall had been apparent well before the August announcement, and plans for the continuation of certain UNRRA functions were already afoot. Upon the initiative of the UN General Assembly an International Refugee Organization was established to deal with the continuing refugee problem; a United Nations International Children's Emergency Fund (UNICEF), supported by private donations and voluntary government contributions, was created to administer relief programs for children in the war-devastated areas; and the United Nations itself assumed responsibility for the advisory social welfare services. Portions of the health program were picked up by the World Health Organization.

KOREAN RELIEF AND RECONSTRUCTION. War in Korea provided the setting for another UN relief operation of substantial proportions. Under a Security Council authorization, the UN Unified Command (United States) administered a $450 million program of civilian and refugee relief. The United States government contributed more than $400 million of the total sum, and American private agencies provided about half of the remainder. A longer-range program of reconstruction was authorized in December, 1950, by a General Assembly resolution which established the United Nations Korean Reconstruction Agency (UNKRA). By the time the UNKRA operations were phased out in 1960, nearly $150 million had been expended for the rehabilitation of Korean agriculture, manufacturing, transportation, mining, electric-power production, housing, education, health, sanitation, and welfare. The United States limited itself to sixty-five per cent of the total UNKRA budget.

The UNKRA program was smaller than had originally been anticipated, but the agency was beset by a number of unfortunate political complications which led ultimately to the withdrawal of support by all of its major contributors. American allies became disenchanted with a rehabilitation program that was largely dominated by the United States, and the United States lost interest in a multilateral program that was poorly supported by others. If American funds were to be the mainstay of the program, why should they be subjected to any degree of UN control? The Korean Government also had been irked with UNKRA regulations on the letting of contracts and the control of local currencies derived from the sale of UNKRA supplies, and it disagreed with the Agency's relative emphasis upon consumer supplies at the expense of capital investment. The Republic of Korea was inclined to sabotage the UNKRA operations if there were good prospect of receiving still larger sums directly from the United States under less onerous restrictions.[25]

Despite the political stumbling blocks that hampered its usefulness, UNKRA made solid if limited contributions to Korean economic recovery. It served as a useful agent for systematizing the efforts of private groups, who contributed $28 million in supplies to UN relief operations and expended an additional $8 million in behalf of their own programs in Korea. The Korean experience also demonstrated that specialized agencies could be mobilized in a common cause in a war-created emergency to provide specialized personnel and technical services.

UNICEF. The United Nations Children's Fund was established in 1946 as a temporary organization to administer residual funds left over from UNRRA's operations. Over the years, however, the approach which was so satisfactory in assisting children of war-devastated areas proved adaptable to the problems of underdeveloped countries as well. The General Assembly responded

[25] The prospect was very good. Congressman Walter H. Judd of Minnesota was obviously well informed when he told the House Committee on Foreign Affairs, "A further fact is that the President of the United States promised them if they would agree to the truce we would give them up to one billion dollars of assistance in rehabilitating the country. We didn't say we would give it to the United Nations. This was one of the prices we paid for getting our boys out of the war there." The Judd statement was confirmed by a State Department official. U.S. Congress, House Committee on Foreign Affairs, *Hearings on the Mutual Security Act of 1954*, 83rd Cong., 2d Sess. (1954), pp. 450, 455–56. Aid to Korea has since been far in excess of the promised $1 billion.

by placing the organization on a permanent basis.[26] It now has a budget running in the neighborhood of $35 million a year, raised through contributions of governments, private donations, and the sale of greeting cards. The Fund has its own thirty-nation executive board elected by ECOSOC.

The initial program emphasis upon emergency supplies of food, clothing, and medicines has shifted toward longer-range programs for the benefit of children. UNICEF is still a source of drugs, insecticides, vaccines, and field equipment for mass disease-control campaigns, as well as food and medical supplies in emergency situations. But it is no longer simply a supply program. UNICEF's grants-in-aid, usually matched by two or three times as much in local funds, are now available to governments for help in project planning and training national personnel. As a condition of the grant, a government must agree to conduct the program as part of its permanent services if the need persists.

UNICEF does not operate projects of its own, although it supervises the national programs it sponsors. UNICEF-aided projects are often conducted with the advice and cooperation of other UN agencies such as WHO, FAO, UNESCO, ILO, and the UN Department of Social Affairs. Such joint endeavors have included mass disease control, family education in better nutrition practices, teacher training and local production of teaching materials, and the establishment of child welfare services.

Refugees

The problem of the refugee is not unique to the twentieth century, but sustained intergovernmental cooperation in dealing with it is a hallmark of our era. Governments have tried to regard refugees as a series of temporary problems, each capable of a discrete solution, but from a world perspective the existence of refugees and displaced persons in substantial numbers has become a continuing fact of life.

REFUGEES AND THE LEAGUE. In 1921 the League of Nations established the office of High Commissioner for Refugees as a temporary agency to deal with the influx of nearly two million refugees from the Russian civil war into countries of eastern and central Europe. The hard shell of the problem had scarcely been dented when new streams of Greek, Armenian, and Assyrian refugees began to pour out of Turkey, beginning in 1922. The League High Commissioner was still attempting to cope with these problems when the Nazi persecutions of the 1930's produced a new flow of refugees from the Saar, Austria, and Czechoslovakia. The League agency was intended to be temporary, but the problem was continuous and recurrent.

[26] The organization was originally designated the United Nations International Children's Emergency Fund. The words International and Emergency were deleted when it was given permanent status, but the acronym UNICEF was retained in preference to a less pronounceable UNCF.

The homeless multitudes of the interwar period needed legal and political protection, as well as relief and assistance with resettlement. The League High Commissioner and his small staff, however, never had the resources to render direct assistance on any significant scale. On their meager budget of $50,000 to $75,000 a year they could do little more than serve as an advocate with governments, work for uniform standards of legal protection, give advice to national governments, and attempt to coordinate the efforts of public and private agencies engaged in refugee relief work.

Although the League High Commissioner obviously did not and could not solve the refugee problem, his office made modest contributions to improving the refugee's lot. In the field of legal protection, the most noted accomplishment was the introduction of the Nansen passport—a certificate issued to refugees by a national government on the recommendation of the High Commissioner—which served as the equivalent of the regular passport and greatly facilitated refugee travel throughout Europe. For purposes of general liaison, the High Commissioner maintained representatives in fifteen European capitals—the appointee usually being a governmental official of the state concerned whose primary duty was to serve his own government. The League also convoked a number of conferences in the hope of arriving at common policy. Except for the Nansen passport, these conferences were largely fruitless. In the long run, the High Commissioner found direct negotiation with individual states to be the most useful means of securing governmental cooperation in improving refugee conditions.

REFUGEES AND WORLD WAR II. World War II produced new millions of homeless persons in Europe, and the responsibility for massive relief and repatriation was undertaken by military authorities and UNRRA. Of some eight million refugees and displaced persons in Allied-occupied zones at the time of the German surrender, five to six million were repatriated within a year through the prodigious efforts of military authorities, and numerous others were assimilated or resettled. UNRRA repatriated an additional 750,-000 refugees during its lifetime.

A special problem was created by the increasingly large group of persons who refused to be repatriated, particularly those who feared to return to countries dominated by newly ascendant Communist regimes. The first major Soviet-Western split in the UNRRA Council occurred on the issue of repatriation. In the Soviet view, anyone refusing to return to his native land was assumed to be an enemy collaborator and hence subject to extradition. The Western majority decided in favor of voluntary repatriation, a position that was morally more satisfying but practically more difficult to implement. If refugees were not repatriated, other countries would have to be persuaded to offer them haven. The problem of resettlement grew still more formidable as new refugees began to flood into the Western Allied zones from Eastern Europe.

THE INTERNATIONAL REFUGEE ORGANIZATION. This was the legacy bequeathed to the International Refugee Organization, a nonpermanent specialized agency which began operations in July, 1947. Despite continued pressure from the Soviet Union for forcible repatriation if necessary, the IRO held out the further options of resettlement or integration in the asylum country, to the extent that the latter was feasible. During its term of existence, which expired in February, 1952, the IRO spent nearly $400 million in assisting more than 1,600,000 refugees who came under its mandate in Africa, the Americas, Asia, and Europe. Approximately 73,000 were repatriated, and more than a million were resettled abroad through the active advocacy and assistance of the IRO.

Robert E. Asher has concisely summarized the major elements of IRO's refugee aid program—a summary which still aptly describes national and international programs to provide refugee relief:

> The work of assisting refugees in returning to their former homes or going to new ones involved the identification, registration, and classification of persons; reuniting scattered families or what remained of them; the provision of food, clothing, housing; health services; vocational training, including special training for the handicapped; unearthing opportunities for resettlement and employment; arranging for the institutional care of persons who would require it for most or possibly all of their lives; the operation of a transport fleet for moving refugees under its mandate; and the provision of political protection for refugees.[27]

IRO's mandate included the refugees inherited from UNRRA in Europe, certain other refugee victims of Nazi persecution, refugees from the Franco regime in Spain, and refugee groups that had been under the protection of the League of Nations. At the termination of the IRO, most of the refugees remaining from the original mandate were of the "hard-core" group—the sick, the aged, and the infirm—for whom resettlement was especially difficult. A number of states had urged that IRO be continued in existence beyond 1952, but the United States, which underwrote more than half of the IRO budget, insisted on the early termination date. American spokesmen argued that the problem was now small enough in scope to be handled by the countries of asylum and by voluntary organizations.

THE UN HIGH COMMISSIONER. In anticipation of IRO's disbandment, the Fifth General Assembly created the Office of the United Nations High Commissioner for Refugees (UNHCR) to serve as a continuing focus for UN refugee activities. The High Commissioner was given the assignment of providing international protection for refugees and assisting governments and voluntary organizations to find "permanent solutions" through resettlement and assimilation.

[27] Robert E. Asher, et al., *The United Nations and the Promotion of the General Welfare* (Washington, D.C.: The Brookings Institution, 1957), p. 207.

During the debates on the establishment of the UNHCR, the United States urged that the High Commissioner be limited to giving legal and administrative protection. Consistent with its position on the termination of IRO, the United States maintained that any necessary material assistance could be supplied by the asylum countries and by voluntary organizations. Other countries such as France, which still played host to large numbers of refugees, were equally insistent that the right to give material aid be included in the High Commissioner's terms of reference. The authorization to assist governments and voluntary organizations in seeking "permanent solutions" was a compromise between these points of view.

The United States position did not reflect unwillingness to contribute to refugee relief, but rather an unwillingness to contribute through UN agencies. The refugee question, especially in Europe, had become so enmeshed in cold war politics that the United States (especially Congress) wanted to work through agencies more narrowly oriented toward a non-Communist viewpoint. The United States thus turned away from the United Nations to instrumentalities that would not have even nominal Communist participation. Upon American initiative, a twenty-four-nation Intergovernmental Committee for European Migration (ICEM) was formed to take over the IRO organization of land, sea, and air transport and utilize it for the movement of refugees and other migrants from Europe. In addition, a unilateral United States Escapee Program (USEP) was initiated in 1952 for the benefit of Iron Curtain refugees. This pattern of refugee aid has persisted to the present time. Today the bulk of material assistance to refugees is still rendered by the governments of asylum countries, voluntary organizations, and USEP and ICEM.

The UN High Commissioner, however, has enjoyed a gradual if modest expansion of function and financial resources. The rigid American opposition to UNHCR programs of material assistance abated with the passing of the McCarthy era, and UNHCR has been able to render limited supplementary assistance to refugees under its mandate. The High Commissioner now works in close cooperation with USEP and ICEM, utilizing the latter's transportation facilities for the resettlement of UNHCR refugees. The World Refugee Year (1959–60), proclaimed by the General Assembly, brought heightened status and some additional contributions to the work of the Office. UNHCR programs of material aid are dependent upon voluntary contributions, although administrative expenses of the Office are part of the regular UN budget.

The present UNHCR mandate excludes refugees receiving aid from other UN programs (such as the Palestine refugees) and those who have the rights of nationals in the country of asylum (for example, refugees from India to Pakistan, and vice versa; East Germans fleeing to West Germany). Otherwise the mandate extends to nearly all persons outside their country of origin whose "well-founded fear of persecution for reasons of race, religion, nationality, or political opinion" prevents them from seeking the protection of the home country. Technically, these number between one and two million persons in various parts of the globe, although the great majority are firmly reestablished in the communities where they reside and are "refugees" only in the sense that they have not yet acquired the nationality of their new homeland.

Nevertheless, demands are made upon the UNHCR to the full extent of its resources. The Office has assisted Hungarian refugees, refugees from the Algerian war, Chinese refugees in Hong Kong, Tibetan refugees in Nepal and India, Cuban refugees in Spain, and African refugees from Rwanda, Angola, Congo, Mozambique, and Portuguese Guinea. In 1965 the UNHCR program of assistance exceeded $3.5 million, over half going to Africa. "Newly recognized refugees" falling within the High Commissioner's mandate have recently numbered about 10,000 a year. Obviously, the UNHCR can make only a marginal contribution to the material needs of refugees, and its larger role is that of coordinator, initiator, and catalyst in programs supported largely by governments, voluntary agencies, and other international organizations.

The High Commissioner's primary responsibility of providing international protection for refugees is carried out by promoting the adoption and supervising the application of international conventions and by encouraging governments to take other measures for the benefit of refugees. Of special importance is the 1951 Convention Relating to the Status of Refugees, which codifies minimum rights in such matters as freedom of religion, access to courts, the right to work, education, social security, and travel documents. Many refugees fall outside the protection of the 1951 Convention, however, because it is limited to specified categories of persons who became refugees as the result of events occurring before 1951. The General Assembly has urged the ratifying states (forty-nine by early 1966) voluntarily to extend the protection to newer refugees, and consideration is being given to the adoption of a protocol removing this limitation. Other UNHCR-sponsored measures of protection have included measures to facilitate refugee travel and efforts to provide legal assistance, advice, representation in court, and assistance in approaching administrative authorities. Such activities have now come to be regarded as a normal and legitimate function of the United Nations. In an age of international organization it seems peculiarly appropriate that the man without a country should have an organ of the international community as his protector and advocate.

PALESTINE REFUGEES. Since 1949 a United Nations Relief and Works Agency for Palestine Refugees in the Near East (UNRWA) has cared for refugee victims of the Arab-Israeli war. Over the years it has absorbed far more money than any other UN refugee program (more than $600 million through 1966) and, thus far, has done very little to solve the refugee problem. UNRRA, the IRO, and the High Commissioner have had the satisfaction of seeing old refugee groups diminish through repatriation, resettlement, and assimilation, even though new needs have arisen from new refugee groups. But UNRWA, which started with approximately 900,000 Arabs who fled from their homes in 1948, had nearly 1,300,000 persons on its rolls in 1965—largely a matter of natural increase—and was supplying rations to approximately 875,000 of them. As it now operates, the program includes food, shelter, health services, education, and vocational training to Arab refugees in Jordan, Syria, Lebanon, and the Gaza Strip. The United States contributes about seventy per cent of an annual budget fluctuating around $35 million, and voluntary organizations are an important source of supplementary services and support.

The root of the continuing problem is political. Arab governments and the Arab refugees have continued to insist upon repatriation, a right affirmed in General Assembly resolutions, and Israel regards mass repatriation as absolutely inconsistent with its national security. Israel at one time offered to accept 100,000 Arab refugees as part of a general settlement, but the Arab states rejected this proposal. Resettling the majority of the refugees in Arab lands, with Israel obligated to accept a few and compensate the rest, would be a sensible long-range solution. But the relationship of Arab states with Israel is not characterized by much good will or good sense. When Tunisian President Habib Bourguiba suggested in 1965 that a negotiated settlement of Arab-Israeli differences might be possible, his proposals were roundly denounced by other Arab leaders and some even sought to expel Tunisia from the Arab League. Meanwhile, UNRWA carries on a thankless task, criticized by the Arab leaders and by the refugees for not doing more, while major financial contributors grow restive in support of a "temporary" relief operation in which neither the refugees nor the states concerned are willing to consider realistic permanent solutions. If the "great accomplishment" of the United Nations is that "it has at least kept the refugees alive," [28] it may also have become the palliative that postpones the need for the hard decisions which alone can remove the blight of the Palestinian refugee.

THE PATTERN OF FUNCTIONAL COOPERATION

The contribution of expanding functionalism to international peace and security is highly speculative but its contribution to welfare is subject to more concrete evaluation. Where inter-state transactions have been of a sufficiently technical and noncontroversial character, as in communication and transportation, international organizations have provided effective forms

[28] Asher, *op. cit.*, p. 212.

of cooperative regulation. The attempt to set international standards of behavior in such intranational fields as human rights and labor standards has not been eminently successful. One cannot be certain that international standard-setting will not upgrade national standards of behavior and produce a more homogeneous social universe in the long run; but thus far a trend toward uniformly good observance of human rights throughout the world is not apparent. The many services provided by the United Nations and other international agencies can stand on their own merits. While most human needs are being met by individual action organized within a national setting, international organizations have in many local situations provided a significant margin of difference for the war victim, the refugee, the socially underprivileged, and the economically deprived.

The tradition of decentralization bequeathed to the UN system has continued unabated, along with the steady proliferation of new agencies. This situation has given rise to criticisms of overlapping and duplication of effort, unhealthy competition among agencies, and nonrational overall allocation of resources. Overlapping is illustrated in the variety of UN approaches to water resource development. UNESCO has a program of research in the problems of "arid lands," FAO is concerned with the proper use of irrigation, and the UN Bureau of Technical Assistance Operations is in charge of river development and "ground water."

The unwholesome effects of interagency competition have been especially apparent in the apportionment of funds under the UN Development Program and its predecessors, where participating agencies have engaged in a competitive scramble to "sell" underdeveloped countries on projects which they administer and to make sure that the agency's share of the annual assistance is not less than last year's. Given the proper stimulus, autonomous international organizations can exhibit the same instincts for preservation of their "sovereign" prerogatives as do states.

The decentralized pattern of functional organization also creates an almost insuperable barrier to the unified, rational allocation of limited resources within the total system. There is no world budget for economic and social affairs. Each government decides how much it will contribute to each agency or function, the precise amount of the contribution being determined by the government's own interests and resources with some weight given to considerations emerging from the various bargaining processes of the several organizations in which the government participates. However rational each state's allocation of its own resources may be, the sum total does not necessarily add up to a rational allocation within the system of international cooperation as a whole.

All of these criticisms undoubtedly have merit. But the disadvantages of decentralization should not be exaggerated. Instances of unedifying competition and empire-building are more than matched by evidences of fruitful cooperation, both in planning and execution of programs. Although no agency has the authority to achieve coordination by fiat, a great deal of coordination has been introduced by cooperation across agency lines and between universal and regional organizations. An Administrative Committee on Coordination provides a forum in which representatives of UN and specialized agency secretariats at the highest level can attempt a substantive meshing of their programs, as well as achieving greater uniformity in administrative matters. Organizations engaged in related activities are regularly represented at one another's meetings. Inter-secretariat liaison, by means of committees and other devices, is a standard operating procedure.

The problem of rationality in the allocation of resources is yet another matter, but a fair amount of centralized allocation has been introduced in the realm of technical aid by means of the United Nations Development Program which currently distributes $150 million annually for approved technical assistance and preinvestment projects among participating intergovernmental agencies. One might well argue that the present pluralistic state of international society defies consensus upon any rational criteria for overall allocation as between regional and universal levels, and among individual programs on the same level. Greater centralization of resource allocation could result in different but not necessarily more rational matching of resources to needs.

The most formidable barriers to improved functional cooperation are in fact political, not organizational. Existing organizational forms have proved serviceable enough to hold all the international cooperation that states have been willing to pour into them. The cold war and the colonial struggle have impinged upon most functional activities often turning their forums into ideological battlegrounds and shaping their programs with reference to political criteria. A political problem of another type is the weighty position of the United States in most international welfare programs, which has subjected them to the vagaries of the American political scene. The decision of the Soviet Union to participate more extensively in economic and social programs has furnished more opposition to American policies during the past decade, but it has not erased the basic dependence upon United States economic resources. In the long run, functional cooperation may provide cement for the foundations of world peace; but in the short run, functional growth depends upon an expansion of the area of political agreement.

Selected Readings

ALEXANDROWICZ, CHARLES H. *World Economic Agencies: Law and Practice.* New York: Praeger, 1962.

ASHER, ROBERT E., et al. *The United Nations and Promotion of the General Welfare.* Washington, D.C.: The Brookings Institution, 1957.

BERKOV, ROBERT. *The World Health Organization: A Study in Decentralized International Administration.* Geneva: Librairie Droz, 1957.

CODDING, GEORGE A., JR. "Contributions of the World Health Organization and the International Civil Aviation Organization to the Development of International Law," *Proceedings of the American Society of International Law.* Washington, D.C.: April, 1965, pp. 147–53.

———. *The Universal Postal Union: Coordinator of the International Mails.* New York: New York University Press, 1964.

DAVIS, HARRIET E., ed. *Pioneers in World Order.* New York: Columbia University Press, 1944.

HAAS, ERNST B. *Beyond the Nation State.* Stanford, California: Stanford University Press, 1964.

HOLBORN, LOUISE W. *The International Refugee Organization.* New York: Oxford University Press, 1956.

HYDE, L. K., JR. *The United States and the United Nations: Promoting the Public Welfare.* New York: Manhattan Publishing Co., for the Carnegie Endowment for International Peace, 1960.

JACOBSON, HAROLD K. *The USSR and the UN's Economic and Social Activities.* Notre Dame, Indiana: University of Notre Dame Press, 1963.

LAVES, WALTER H. C., and THOMSON, CHARLES A., *UNESCO: Purpose, Progress, Prospects.* Bloomington: Indiana University Press, 1957.

McDOUGAL, MYRES S., and BEBR, GERHARD. "Human Rights in the United Nations," *American Journal of International Law.* July, 1964, pp. 603–41.

MENON, M. A. K. "Universal Postal Union," *International Conciliation,* No. 552, March, 1965.

READ, JAMES M. "The United Nations and Refugees—Changing Concepts," *International Conciliation,* No. 537, March, 1962.

SHARP, WALTER R. *Field Administration in the United Nations System.* New York: Praeger, for the Carnegie Endowment for International Peace, 1961.

SHUSTER, GEORGE N. *UNESCO: Assessment and Promise.* New York: Harper and Row, 1963.

STOESSINGER, JOHN G. *The Refugee and the World Community.* Minneapolis: University of Minnesota Press, 1956.

WALTERS, FRANK P. *A History of the League of Nations.* London: Oxford University Press, 1952, Chaps. 16, 36, 42, 60.

WOODBRIDGE, GEORGE, ed. *UNRRA,* 3 vols. New York: Columbia University Press, 1950.

15 | *Engineering Economic Development*

Economic development offers the crucial test and the great preoccupation of functional cooperation in our era. An awakening of aspirations for material betterment has fired the imagination of deprived millions throughout the world, in new nations and old. Two thirds of mankind are caught up in a revolution of rising expectations that has triggered profound and widespread social changes. The leaders of preindustrial societies are looking to the values and practices of the industrialized countries for the key that will unlock the door to status and material prosperity.

This revolution of rising hopes has opened a Pandora's box of problems. How can ancient societies be ushered quickly and peacefully into the twentieth century? What basic societal and governmental changes are necessary? What are the keys to economic growth and modernization? From whence will come the help that is so desperately needed? What impact will urbanism and industrialism have on peasant cultures? What role should international organization play in the revolution? Obviously, there are no ready answers to these and similar questions, but the challenge is real and will face the world for a long time to come.

To meet this global challenge, the United Nations, regional international organizations, and individual governments have launched a series of programs aimed at helping societies to help themselves. Institutional approaches combine technical assistance and capital grants with a broad range of educational, health, welfare, and internal improvement programs to build a base from which each society may launch itself into the stage of self-sustaining economic growth.

Despite these efforts, change is slow and seldom measures up to expectations. Societies steeped in tradition and guided by conservative values resist the onslaught of change. Societies in transition grope for new values to replace those rejected. Improved living conditions produce population explosions which cancel out gains in national income. But poverty-stricken societies no longer accept their lot as the will of the gods, and the disparity between hopes and realities has produced a dangerous "frustration gap." Next to the problem of global war, closing this gap is the major problem facing the United Nations and regional organizations today and for the remainder of the twentieth century.

PROBLEMS OF DEVELOPMENT

The undeveloped world covers vast areas of the planet stretching eastward from Latin America through Africa and the Middle East to South and Southeast Asia and the islands of Melanesia. In meeting the problems of development, states are in some respects like individuals. No two individuals are exactly alike, but those living in poverty have many common characteristics and environmental problems that help to explain their plight. Ending poverty for individuals depends not only on improving their economic lot, but also in changing their thinking, their attitudes, their environments—in effect, their whole ways of life.

Leaders of the developing countries are generally committed to making the transition to the world reflected in Western material values. Their centuries-old otherworldliness is giving way to modern demands. Whether such changes will solve their problems and enrich their lives is a moot question; they have caught a vision of plenty through the windows of the Western world and they want to have a share in it.

A Profile of an Undeveloped Nation

Understanding of the problem of economic development may be promoted if we put together a composite of the features that characterize most developing states. Such a picture of a typical state's base or starting point can highlight what needs to be done for economic development, and will point up the difficulties of doing it. A note of caution, however, is in order since great differences in size, population, resources, power supplies, native skills, and other natural and human variables exist in states as diverse as Brazil and Sierra Leone, Nigeria and Afghanistan.

First, and most basic, our profile state is *poor.* A comprehensive United Nations study in 1949 showed that about two thirds of the world's population produced less than one sixth of the world's income. Income distribution disparities become even more pronounced when compared in per capita terms. Average annual income per person in the developed states is about $1,830, a sum more than eleven times greater than the approximately $165 per capita annual income in the developing countries. Although statistics for the developing states are less accurate than those for advanced states, in some countries, such as India, the figure may be as low as $60 if the incomes of the few well-to-do are not included in the average. If present trends continue, the developing states will achieve an annual income of only $370 per capita by the end of the twentieth century.

Poverty in the developing states is chronic, not a result of misfortune or a downturn in the business cycle. Poverty is both the basic problem and the major obstacle to its own cure. In the poorest countries, for example, the average annual per capita income runs between $75 and $150. Savings and investment, the essential ingredients of economic growth, are obviously not possible on any significant scale in these subsistence-level economies.

Second, the profile state is located in the *southern hemisphere* and has a *tropical* climate. More precisely, the poorest of the developing countries with few exceptions are located south of 30 degrees north latitude, which runs along the southern boundary of the United States and along the northern reaches of the African continent. Tropical jungles, vast mountain ranges, arid deserts, and wild bush country make up great portions of the land masses of these countries, forcing the people to carry on a daily struggle with nature to eke out a bare existence. Once-rich soils leached by tropical rains and high temperatures and humidity make the job of wresting a living a precarious one. The profile state lacks the energy sources of coal and oil, although potential hydroelectric power sources in the form of great tropical rivers wind through the jungles and deltas.

Third, the profile state is experiencing a great *population surge* that is rapidly assuming the proportions of an "explosion." Birth rates continue high, as they have for centuries, but a new factor—death control—has been added to the equation. The first benefits of the Western way of life to reach many of the peoples of the developing nations have been drugs and medicines to save lives, chemicals to control mosquitoes and other disease carriers, and water-purifying agents. Technical assistance programs have likewise concentrated on teaching people good health and sanitation habits through public health programs. The result in the profile state has been a lengthening of the life span and a pronounced imbalance in the population favoring the under-eighteen youth groups stemming from decreased infant mortality and controls over epidemic diseases. Population growth has reduced or canceled increases in gross national income in all developing countries during the decade from 1955 to 1965. In the future, with great masses of young people coming of child-bearing age, a population explosion of hitherto unknown proportions threatens to destroy all chances for improvements in standards of living.

Fourth, the profile state rests on an economic base of *primitive agriculture.* Peasant families painfully tilling their small plots or working on large haciendas or plantations for absentee landlords are living symbols of the plight of agriculture in these lands. Most of the profile state's farming is geared to a subsistence level with little or no effort or capability to develop a cash crop for its almost nonexistent market economy. Farming is intensive, with peasants crowded onto the land in such numbers that the soil's fertility is low and unproductive. Unpredictable natural disasters in the forms of droughts, floods, hurricanes, and crop diseases, insects, wild animals, and rodents can ruin the efforts of months of toil. Primitive, handmade plows pulled by plodding buffalos or oxen, sometimes by human beings, and wooden hoes provide the only mechanical aids to productivity. Out of this syndrome of inefficiency must come the surpluses to provide "social capital" for community improvements, labor for the hoped-for factories, and the extra food to feed those who leave the land.

Fifth, the profile state has a *colonial background* that since independence has helped determine the direction of modernization and continues to affect the thought and action of its people. In many cases the rudimentary physical framework for development was laid out by the colonial power in the nineteenth and first half of the twentieth centuries. Surpassing the influence of physical developments is the lasting imprint colonialism left on the attitudes and emotions of the people. The humiliation and sense of frustration fostered by foreign rule has left scars of anti-Westernism and reservoirs of long submerged desires for prestige, equality, and dignity. Internal disunity exists as a hold-over of a carefully cultivated colonial policy of "divide and rule" or as a result of boundary lines drawn by imperial design that sundered established communities or tribes and mixed traditional enemies within the same political unit. In societies lacking almost all internal impulses for modernization, colonialism produced a ferment for change which independence brought to a crescendo.

Sixth, the profile state is built on the social fabric of a *traditional society.* Custom and tradition provide the social cement, religion and conservative values the guidelines for human action. Small elite groups dominate the society and oppose virtually all change because change would mean a loss of their status. Rigid class structures immobilize even the able and ambitious individual. Objective conditions of social stagnation are reinforced by group attitudes, requiring a revolution of perspectives as a prelude to modernity. No society completely abandons its traditional culture; transitional societies in a state of vigorous change reshape the old values, resulting in a social, political, and economic restlessness and rootlessness. Interaction between the old and the new may yield turmoil, revolution, or civil war as rival groups offer the people new ideologies imported from foreign sources, each seeking to capture the modernization process and direct it toward ideologically determined goals.

The Puritan concepts that work is a source of personal gratification and that personal success is the highest human goal are almost unknown in the traditional society. A caste system often places each individual at birth into his social position and determines his future occupation. The concept of the joint family or clan binds small groups together into the basic social unit and provides the individual with a social insurance antedating the modern welfare state. Women hold an inferior status in the society and are socially and economically restricted until the impact of change leads to their emancipation. Religious taboos, magic, and a prevailing mysteriousness about physical events reject the idea of scientific inquiry into the nature of things. Making headway in the process of modernization demands not only a change in societal values but a gross modification of those individual and family habits that are impediments to progress and development.

Seventh, the profile state is characterized by mass *illiteracy.* Contrasted with the United States and Europe, where illiteracy rates range from 1 to 8 per cent, the proportion of illiterates in South Asia in a population of 700 million averages 80 per cent. In some countries of the Middle East and in tropical Africa illiteracy reaches 95 per cent, and very few nations can claim 50 per cent literacy. Latin American illiteracy rates range from 40 to 80 per cent, with most countries crowding the higher figure and only a few, such as Argentina and Costa Rica with their predominantly European populations, ranking high in literacy.

But educational needs to achieve modernization go beyond basic literacy to include technical, secondary, and university training. A university-trained elite exists in most of the undeveloped countries, but it is extremely small in number and, for the most part, consists of specialists in law, the humanities, and the social sciences. This elite provided the leadership in the march to independence, but a new elite of scientists, engineers, and technicians is needed to exploit resources and organize the productive machinery. Technical and secondary school graduates are also in extremely short supply, with technical schools a new development in some of the advancing states and secondary opportunities limited in many areas to isolated missionary schools.

Eighth, the profile state rests on a *weak economic base.* The economies of most undeveloped countries are based on the production or extraction of one or a few primary commodities. Living standards beyond the subsistence level provided by local agriculture, therefore, depend on the export market for these commodities. Foreign exchange earnings desperately needed for buying capital goods from the advanced countries are limited by adverse world market conditions. These include (1) an oversupply of most primary commodities; (2) competition from advanced states with greater productive efficiency; (3) fluctuating prices resulting from speculation among buyers, changes in supply, and other conditions beyond the control of the developing states; (4) the introduction of synthetics and substitutes to replace natural commodities; (5) high shipping costs in getting commodities to distant markets; and (6) deteriorating terms of trade resulting in lower prices for primary commodity exports and higher prices for imports of manufactured consumer and capital goods.

Ninth, the profile state suffers from *political instability.* Most developing states are characterized by one-party, authoritarian regimes. Some are ruled by traditionalist royal autocrats; others, as in Latin America, are run by a strong man or dictator supported by the landed aristocracy, the church, and the military. In many of the new nations, early attempts to establish democratic systems failed when the promised bounty of independence could not be delivered. A strong man, usually exuding charisma and often a military officer, or a group of oligarchs, typically a military clique, then seized power. Opposition groups and parties either do not exist or exist in a highly innocuous form to provide the shadow but not the substance of a democratic system. Political activity is generally confined to the capital city and involves only in-fighting among the political elite jockeying for positions of strength or attempting a *coup.*

The peasantry and the urban proletariat tend to be equally apathetic toward the national political system and its leaders. Local and regional loyalties, however, often constitute strong bonds of a political nature, particularly when nurtured by ethnic loyalties. A national language and educational system, two vital ingredients in promoting political nationalism, do not exist in most of the new nations. Often, radical groups imbued with a new ideological faith carry on a sporadic guerrilla warfare against the central government from jungle and mountain havens. The essence of politics in the developing world, then, is one of autocracy on the top and the unsophisticated political parochialism of the masses, with the latter disintegrating slowly under the challenges of national unity and economic development.

In summary, a typical undeveloped state suffers from chronic mass poverty, its location, topography, and climate limit its potentials, its predominantly young population threatens to outstrip economic growth, its inefficient economy rests on an outmoded agricultural base, its customs and traditions thwart change, its colonial background induces contemporary conflicts, its illiteracy rate is high, its competitive position in world trade is poor, and its people are apolitical and its government is autocratic. These human and environmental conditions should reflect little but despair. They are, however, counterbalanced by the overriding urge to develop, by the help offered by advanced states and international organizations, and by the significant changes now under way in the developing world. Together, the new forces may yet produce dramatic results in economic development over the next twenty years.

A Blueprint for Economic Development

Economic growth and modernization do not just happen. A carefully planned, multiphased program based on strategies that match national needs and capabilities must first be formulated. This long-range national plan must be worked out in detail to move the economic and social sectors forward in tandem. Old prejudices against planning held by the Governing Board of the World Bank and some of the leading capitalist states have largely disappeared, and recipient countries are now required to have developmental blueprints to show how foreign assistance will fit into their master strategies.

Acceptance of government planning for economic development has been accompanied by a recognition that positive governmental action to promote development programs is an essential follow-up. Whether an economy is predicated on free-enterprise principles, Soviet-style total planning, or falls somewhere on the vast spectrum between these two extremes, it will in any case demand a significant role by government in budgeting, taxing, spending, regulating, promoting, programming, and determining foreign economic policies. Government planning and programs must vary, of course, according to the indigenous conditions of each country; no two cases will be exactly alike.

Governmental plans and programs cannot, however, provide a shortcut or easy route to modernization. Economic development has always been a slow and painful process. Despite unprecedented amounts of outside help from the United Nations and other regional organizational and national sources, the job remains largely one of local initiative and self-help. Today, a great race is developing, not between rival ideologies or approaches or between developing countries, but within each developing society. That race involves a desperate attempt to push development ahead of its two dangerous competitors—hunger and mass frustration.

PREPARING THE BASE. Except for certain natural factors not subject to human alteration, most of the characteristics of our profile state are susceptible to change and improvement. Governmental development plans aim at modifying these factors to support a virtual economic and social revolution. The proximate objective of every developing society is to reach the point from which the society will launch itself into an upward trend of steady, self-sustaining growth.

SOCIOLOGICAL AND POLITICAL CHANGES. An adequate "take-off" base requires a modernization of social and political institutions and practices. The following changes are fundamental to that objective.

1. Attitudinal Changes. In many countries a privileged elite will be challenged to adopt new attitudes favoring a modernization that may itself threaten their traditional status. The choice, however, is not between self-instituted change and maintaining the status quo. The alternative may be a violent left-wing revolt that would sweep away all elements of feudal privilege, carried out by those in the society whose attitudes changed more rapidly than those of their leaders. Other critical value changes may involve new orientations toward "worldliness" and "getting ahead," the psychic satisfactions of work, the profit incentive, and other sometimes crass but essential motivations to economic advances. Regardless of whether the society moves toward individualism or collectivism, individuals must shed their fatalism and resignation for a desire for self-improvement, and fair means of rewarding those who contribute to the society's forward movement must be created.

2. *Political Evolution.* Tangible societal changes must proceed apace of changing attitudes. First, a political socialization must occur, taking the form of support for a minimally effective national political system. Government, a distant power that extracts taxes and drafts village youth for military service, must take on a new image through directing and servicing functions. Political leadership must be selected on the basis of its abilities and policies rather than accepted as a right accruing to inherited status or wealth. Political leaders must perceive the necessity of popular education, fair tax programs, land reform, and scientific and technological advances and adopt policies aimed at achieving them. A corps of administrators recruited and trained in modern governmental techniques must provide a degree of unity for the entire country, reaching even remote villages. Whether modernization takes place at all, the forms it will take, and the successes it may enjoy will depend on whether officials vested with public responsibility make the "hard" decisions essential to preparing the base.

3. *Educational Development.* Education may be the keystone in building a modern society. Not only do technicians of varying degrees of skills need to be trained, but fundamental learning in the "Three R's" must be imparted to a large portion of the population. In many developing countries over 80 per cent of the people are dispersed in agricultural pursuits and fewer than 20 per cent of them have the barest claim to literacy. Schools can also serve an integrating function in selecting the best and most compatible traits of the old world to mesh with those of the new world of modernity. As in the advanced states, education must also provide a significant nationalizing force in developing a single language and in cultivating national myths, traditions, and popular heroes. Beyond producing a literate, informed citizenry and a trained labor force, secondary and college educated elites must be developed to direct the nation's changeover to a world of business, commerce, industry, and modern administration. The quality of human resources has increasingly come to be recognized in the emerging nations as a critical factor in the modernization process, with education seen in the new perspective of providing the key that unlocks the door to opportunity for the nation.

4. *Population Control.* Population control, like education, is crucial to developmental success, and may in fact be primarily a problem of education. The ubiquitous right of parents to produce unlimited numbers of off-

spring must be checked if per capita national income is to rise to the point where economic growth can be sustained through savings. Demographers speak of the self-limiting nature of the population explosion, noting that rising living standards in the advanced nations had the effect of reducing birthrates drastically. If preindustrialization birthrates had continued in Europe during the nineteenth and twentieth centuries, for example, some European countries would now have populations almost ten times larger. But in the developing world of today, the problem is that the population surge is of such a magnitude that living standards can scarcely be raised to the point where they constitute a self-limiting control on family size. Where will the savings come from if every additional increment of national income is used to maintain an ever-increasing population? How can rising labor productivity be achieved from an undernourished population whose individual diets are less than 2,000 calories daily and are deficient in proteins?

Birth control is, of course, a logical answer to the problem, but technical potentialities are widely thwarted by vast human barriers of religion, morality, economics, apathy, and ignorance. In India, one of the few developing states to attempt population control, governmental and private organizations have distributed birth-control information widely and provided the means of contraception, with little apparent result. Positive governmental programs must go beyond this approach to encourage smaller families. In the West, for example, such programs have included (1) prohibitions against child labor; (2) emancipation of women; (3) social mobility leading to economic independence of children from their parents; (4) mechanization of agriculture; and (5) social insurance freeing parents from dependence upon children in their old age. When large families become an economic burden rather than an asset, when children can no longer be exploited for economic and dowry purposes, when large families are no longer accepted as a status symbol, populations will be brought under a measure of control. Regardless of what gains may be made in terms of national income and development, if population growth exceeds or equals them, no improvement in standards of living can result, and frustration and revolutionary zeal may intensify.

5. *Community Development.* Finally, social change must stress the development of local communities. The potentials for modernization rest on a base of village life that has not changed in its social characteristics for many centuries. Villagers must discover, through outside help, that by working together their lives can be enriched, their living conditions improved, and social barriers erased. Through increasing self-reliance, awakened by programs of community development, villages can take the lead in implementing national programs, reducing thereby the shock-impact of urbanism and industrialism on the new society.

ECONOMIC CHANGES. The central objective of modernization in all developing societies is economic betterment. Social and political changes are aimed mainly at making these societies more receptive to and more efficient at promoting economic development. But, given changes in these areas, the economic problem remains of how to achieve a modern economy, of how to move an undeveloped state to the "take-off" point from which it can progress through self-sustaining growth.

What are the economic variables in the development equation? How can an undeveloped state marshal its forces in a collective economic offensive? A United Nations delegate recently observed apropos economic development that "it was easy enough to recognize what had to be done but difficult to decide how to go about it." Though no two states would proceed in exactly the same way, some common approaches can be delineated as "prescriptions for development."

1. Increasing Agricultural Output. The objectives of greater farm productivity are a healthier, better-fed, and harder-working population, increased foreign exchange earnings through exports, and a savings—extracted from an increased output—destined for investment. In the early stages of development, there may be no increase in the peasant's food consumption, but there must be a rise in his food production in order to produce a surplus. The most obviously useful means to expand productivity fall into the category of improved farming technology—modern implements, fertilizers, insect and disease spraying, good seed stocks, weed control, and scientific farming techniques. Agrarian reform, though highly controversial both between social groups within developing states and among experts who disagree over whether it would increase or decrease output, is a local approach that has proved successful in a few societies. Basic to agrarian reform is a land redistribution among the peasants achieved by splitting up large estates. Although such a redistribution would increase incentives, small holdings are generally uneconomic because they cannot take advantage of economies of scale, and mechanization is nigh impossible. Peasant cooperatives to encourage joint production may provide an answer to this dilemma, aided by a reform of inheritance laws which encourages continual fragmentation of plots.

2. Developing Simple Industries. Agricultural production must be supplemented by an increasing development of fishing, mining, and raw material potentials. Most of the new nations have access to the world's oceans and some have sizable inland lakes on or within their borders, both sources for food rich in proteins. Expansion in the production of primary commodities may help the nation to earn critically needed foreign exchange, although highly competitive conditions in the world commodity market may negate increased supplies with lower prices. Increased productivity, however, will enable such states to take advantage of periods of peak demand and high prices when the advanced countries are engaged in war or enjoy economic boom conditions.

3. *Investing in Social Overhead.* A modern economy can be built only on a broad economic base or infrastructure. This means that each undeveloped country professing modernization as a goal must be prepared to devote human and financial resources to building facilities for basic transport, communication, irrigation, and power supplies. The labor surplus engaged in inefficient agricultural pursuits must be taken off the land, mobilized into construction units, and its energies applied to simple "social capital" projects. Added incentives underlying this approach may include reduced unemployment, increased agricultural production as more efficient labor-saving techniques are introduced, and a conservation of foreign exchange so that it may be devoted to buying machinery from the advanced nations. Psychologically, the personal involvement of thousands of young men in social projects of this kind may help to unleash a national pride and surge of development spirit.

4. *Acquiring the Technical Skills.* Modern factories and transportation, communication, and power facilities can be operated only with skilled personnel. An industrializing society faces an enormous task in forging a new labor force of energetic and capable workers from a peasant society. Trainees must be supported out of the savings yielded from a surplus of production over consumption in the society. Exceptions to this rule may be found in apprentice-type training programs and in the technical assistance rendered by advanced states or international institutions. New workers must adjust to the strict discipline of industrial life—regular hours, machine-dictated work speeds, the rhythmic monotony of life on a production line. Managerial and administrative personnel will constitute a new elite, culled out of the indigenous population through ruthless competition for unprecedented rewards.

5. *Fostering Industrialization.* The capstone of the host of social, political, and economic changes predicated as useful or necessary to modernization can be summed up in the word *industrialization.* Many leaders in developing states equate development and industrialization, and stress the latter as the key to growth and prosperity. However, if given such a high priority that other changes have not occurred to prepare a proper base, industries will exist precariously in a modernizing enclave while the rest of the country and most of its people sink deeper into poverty. Sometimes overlooked by developing societies are those nonindustrialized states with high productivity and living standards, such as New Zealand and the Netherlands.

To industrialize, most of the machinery, tools, and skills must be imported. Unlike social capital improvements that need sheer muscle power, industrial capital can only be built locally *after* some measure of industrialization has occurred. If they had the time and patience, modernizing states could follow the lead of the West in moving from primitive handicraft to increasingly complex machines over a century or more, but time is of the essence in their societies. Quite naturally, most leaders of the new nations prefer to hurdle the successive steps of development and start with modern, sophisticated—even automated—factories. Since the more efficient factory uses less labor, the rise of a large, disgruntled, unemployed urban proletariat seems unavoidable and a dangerous accomplice to that kind of industrialization. Experts from advanced nations who urge leaders to build simple, labor-using industries may be suspected of having protectionist motives or, worse still, neocolonialist attitudes.

Industrialization, if it occurs, can produce many salutary results for the undeveloped society. For one thing, manufactured goods become more readily available and cheaper for the masses. Foreign exchange formerly expanded on imports of similar consumer items can be saved. Sales in the world market can improve a nation's export position appreciably. Savings for investment should increase substantially once industrialization has taken place since national income will be higher. Industrialized plants may also contribute much to a local fabrication of capital goods. Despite its pitfalls and the problems it may create, industrialization *is* a logical route for many developing countries to take in their "great leap forward" to modernization. The extent, however, to which their people may view it as a singularly facile solution to problems of mass poverty is more of an emotional than a rational reaction.

Acquiring the Means

Capital accumulation is the *sine qua non* of every development plan. Like a catalytic agent in a chemical process, capital can produce a desirable reaction between the human and mechanical elements in the economic equation by providing supplies, tools, plant facilities, power, and modern production machines. It can also attract foreign technicians and pay for training local personnel to fill skilled and semiskilled positions. Capital is most useful when applied to a carefully prepared social and economic base, when invested in sound economic ventures rather than projects aimed at feeding national egos, and when investments produce goods that have a ready market abroad.

Since capital accumulation will set the pace for industrialization, it has become the main objective of leaders of undeveloped states. This overriding fascination with capital as the central theme of developmental programs has not always been shared by foreign advisers and planners, or by international institutions and advanced nations in their aid programs. Their restraint is voiced in favor of a "balanced, over-all process," but it may also reflect a fear that developing states will be unable to compete effectively in world markets or that, from a narrower viewpoint, industrial development may cut into their own foreign trade. Regardless of these caveats, the hunt for capital to supply the voracious appetites of the new nations accelerates each year. Major sources of capital for the undeveloped states include (1) local savings, (2) foreign trade, (3) private investment, and (4) foreign aid.

LOCAL SAVINGS. Leadership elites within developing states must come to grips with two fundamental economic imperatives. First, domestic consumption must be restrained so that production yields a surplus; second, the surplus or savings must be invested creatively to increase production. A surplus can be provided (1) by raising output but not consumption, (2) by reducing consumption but not output, or (3) by raising output faster than consumption. The first two choices are clearly dangerous to the stability of the state since they could provoke a bitter reaction from workers who are either working harder for the same pay or receive pay cuts in the interest of development. In none of the three options will domestic consumption be likely to measure up to popular demand, reflecting the harshness of economic development and the widespread resort to authoritarian methods to force savings through work pressures and by controlled, subsistence-level standards of living.

Local savings can be accrued through taxation, private profit, profit from socialized industries, expropriation, rationing, or by inflation. All involve some ingredients of compulsion or exploitation, but the objective is to move as rapidly as possible to a stage of development where progress is reflected in the increasing consumption necessary to attract capital investments from abroad, as well as in expanded output. Local savings, however, have a limited applicability to this early forward movement since the germinal core of industrial capital must come from abroad and, consequently, must be paid for in foreign exchange. Local savings are best fitted for "social overhead" projects which contribute to the building of an infrastructure base for more sophisticated development to follow.

FOREIGN TRADE. Foreign markets, particularly those of the advanced countries of the West, are the major source of capital useful to economic development. In the early 1960's, foreign trade earnings accounted for about 80 per cent of the foreign exchange funds of the developing countries as a group, and over 90 per cent of their exports were primary commodities. Many advanced countries have followed this same route to industrialization and diversification. In the first half of the nineteenth century, for example, the United States depended largely upon cotton exports to feed the engine of economic growth. Foreign earnings financed a growing textile industry, which in turn increased exports and spurred the growth of related industries, such as iron foundries and machine tool and farm implement manufactures.

The leaders of undeveloped countries, however, whether they accept the theory or not, believe that the cards are stacked against them in the world of trade realities. First, they point out, seesawing demand for primary commodities brought about by war-peace and boom-recession fluctuations in the West has produced chaos in developing supply sources. Second, specialization in producing primary products tends to perpetuate existing trade patterns and to condemn the developing states to remain raw material suppliers.

Third, supplies of primary commodities have tended to exceed demand because of increasing development of primary production in advanced states, the substitution of a synthetics for natural products, and a change in consumer demand toward more sophisticated products having a smaller raw material content.[1] Protectionist trade policies, price-support programs for marginal domestic producers, and subsidies for exporters have helped accelerate this trend toward securing primary commodities from local producers in the advanced states.

Fourth, and probably the most significant factor for states with preindustrial economies, the terms of trade between the developed and the developing nations have increasingly favored the former. The terms of trade involve the prices undeveloped states receive for their exports in relationship to the prices they pay for goods and machinery imported from the advanced states. Over the past fifty years, the trend has favored higher prices for industrial goods and lower prices for primary commodities, with the exceptions of the periods encompassing World War I, World War II, and the Korean War.

Amid efforts to obtain capital for development in recent years, the long-range trend of the terms of trade has continued. From 1950 to 1962, for example, the average unit price for exports from undeveloped countries deteriorated 4 per cent while the prices of their imported goods rose approximately 8 per cent. During the same period, the total value of their exports increased by only 50 per cent, and that resulting from the vastly greater amounts exported, while exports from the advanced states increased 151 per cent and those of the Communist bloc nations increased 253 per cent. This growing problem can be illustrated by a simple example: In 1956, Morocco had to sell 200 tons of phosphate abroad to pay for one imported truck; in 1963, Morocco had to export 318 tons of phosphate to pay for the same truck.[2] Such marketing conditions have undermined development plans, arrested economic growth, and produced widespread despair in the developing world.

[1] See, for example, the treatment of this problem in Raul Prebisch, *Towards a New Trade Policy for Development*, United Nations Publication Sales No. 64, II.B.4, 1964. The magnitude of this problem is illustrated by the fact that, in 1963, of a $65 billion world trade in commodities, the developing nation's share amounted to only 40 per cent of the total. See "Commodity Survey, 1964," United Nations Document TD/B/C.1/3, 16 June 1965.

[2] United Nations Doc. E/CONF.46/C.1/SR.9, May 1, 1964, p. 8.

PRIVATE INVESTMENT. Historically, most funds for the development of emergent economies have come from capital transfers in the form of investments by individuals, corporations, and banks in capital-surplus countries. In the 1960's, the net flow of private investment has dwindled, amounting to only one fifth of the total flow of funds into the developing countries, with four fifths taking the form of governmental bilateral or multilateral assistance.[3] The significance of this decline was recognized by President George D. Woods of the International Bank when he stressed that "economic development in many countries will never really get into high gear until they find a way to tap the vast resources of capital and know-how that are available in the private sector of the industrialized nations."[4] The key to unlock the door to this vast storehouse of available but unused capital in the industrialized countries is still missing, but the search goes on.

The major obstacle, over which the developing countries have little or no control, is the vast source of lucrative investment opportunities available in the advanced countries themselves. Most private investment capital in the United States, for example, flows through the domestic stock exchanges or is invested directly in business expansions in the United States, Western Europe, Japan, Australia, and other relatively "safe" countries. Not only are these countries politically stable and economically viable, but investments are safe from governmental expropriation, skilled labor is available, mass consumer markets provide local outlets for manufactured goods, and conversions of profits into dollars and their transfer to investors in the United States is a simple matter. None of these conditions generally obtains in the developing countries.

Unlike the flow of governmental funds which is determined by political and military objectives, that of private capital is influenced mainly by commercial considerations. The United Nations Conference on Trade and Development (UNCTAD), attended by the representatives of 120 nations at Geneva in 1964, searched for answers to the problem of making emergent economies more attractive as investment opportunities. Proposals recommended by the Conference included (1) tax exemptions or reductions and

---

[3] See *World Economic Survey, 1963*, Part I, United Nations Publication Sales No. 64.II.C.1. The net flow of private investment capital averaged $1 billion annually in the late 1950's, then rose to $1.13 billion in 1960, and subsequently fell to $984 million in 1961 and $877 million in 1962. The downward trend has continued since 1962 (see, for example, "The Promotion of the International Flow of Private Capital," United Nations Document E/3905, May 26, 1964). Also, in the 1960's, Latin America has received about 60 per cent of the total flow of private capital into the undeveloped countries, and most of that has gone to several of the more developed countries of that region.

[4] George D. Woods, "World Bank and Affiliates Examine Pressing Problems of Economic Development," *United Nations Monthly Chronicle*, Vol. I (November, 1964), p. 60. The statement was made in relation to strengthening the International Finance Corporation so that it could encourage greater use of private resources for development purposes.

governmental investment guarantees by the developed countries; (2) informational, promotional, and technical assistance centers set up by developing countries and international institutions; (3) cooperation between private investors and local entrepreneurs aimed at encouraging a "reinvestment of profits"; and (4) studies by the International Bank leading to establishment of international investment insurance, machinery for arbitrating disputes between investors and governments of developing states, and guarantees for securities of developing states in world capital markets.[5]

Private borrowing is related to private investment but poses some additional problems. As with a young married couple, the attraction of consumer goods from the advanced countries may lead newly independent and undeveloped societies to try to live beyond their means. In the competition for overseas markets, many private firms may be far too willing to risk loans to facilitate the peddling of their wares. The result may be a growth in private debts that sacrifices future capital needs, raises false expectations of higher living standards, and causes a disastrous inflation within the country. Cuba during the 1940's and 1950's, for example, frittered away its sugar-market foreign exchange surpluses on fancy American automobiles and other luxury goods, with little devoted to building the Cuban economy.

FOREIGN AID. Capital inflows in the form of public grants or loans have become a significant source for development financing in the decades of the 1950's and the 1960's. Foreign economic assistance offers the advantage of reducing the harshness of life in an industrializing society which, without this alternative, must employ painful methods of economic "forced marches" and compulsorily reduced consumption to achieve a surplus. Regardless of the motivations underlying it—national self-interest, philanthropy, ideological rivalry, economic dependence, regional growth, or global stability—foreign aid has become an established institution of the contemporary state system. The sources, kinds, extent, and problems of public international grants and loans will be discussed in the subsequent sections of this chapter.

Promoting International Action

The major interest in and responsibility for formulating plans and undertaking action leading to economic development quite naturally falls to the lot of the undeveloped states themselves. It would be difficult, indeed, to discover a single "poor" state in today's world in which the people did not consider economic betterment the major objective and in which the government did not regard it as the most pressing problem. Yet, more than good

[5] "Issues Before the Nineteenth General Assembly," *International Conciliation*, No. 550 (November, 1964), p. 161. Following the recommendation embodied in point 4, the International Bank formulated a Convention on the Settlement of Investment Disputes between States and Nationals of Other States; the Convention, which will go into effect after ratification by twenty states, provides for international conciliation and arbitration facilities.

intentions and local efforts are needed, and it has become increasingly obvious that few if any of the undeveloped economies could achieve even minimal economic goals without outside help. In response to numerous appeals, diverse programs of assistance have been planned and executed over a period of almost two decades, starting with the Point IV Program of the United States in 1949. These international efforts, although based on converging interests of donors and recipients, for the most part have been shaped and directed by donor countries and have reflected their political, economic, military, moral, or community interests. This relationship has produced problems of coordinating aid programs to fit constructively with developmental plans of the recipients. Major issues have arisen which occasionally have embroiled relations between giver and receiver and have puzzled the architects of developmental schemes searching for the best approach.

SHOULD DONORS USE BILATERAL OR MULTILATERAL CHANNELS? One such issue involves the means by which aid is funneled into developing economies. Although most aid comes from about a dozen capital-surplus countries, each contributor may use a variety of approaches. A bilateral approach provides for the administration of aid programs by a governmental agency of the donor country working closely with each recipient government. Regional and global programs provide other options for aid-giving states, and each of the three channels offers certain advantages while suffering from specific defects.

Donor states favor bilateral aid because they can exercise a significant measure of control over programs by imposing conditions upon recipient states. In this way, industries competitive with those of the donor state can be discouraged, economic and social reforms can be encouraged, and counterpart funds can be required. Cold war ideological and political objectives have often been critical determinants of the direction, kinds, and amounts of bilateral aid. Propaganda advantages are also not overlooked by donor governments since local populations can easily be made aware of the source of their beneficence. Large amounts of foreign aid may permit the donor to significantly influence the receiving state's foreign policy, and directed trade patterns together with a need for spare parts may foster increasing economic dependence.

Most developing countries prefer receiving aid through multilateral channels because interference in their domestic and foreign affairs is likely to be minimal. Exceptions to this preference include states having a close and favorable relationship with major aid-givers, and those which for strategic reasons have been able to secure large amounts of aid from competitive East-West assistance programs. The United Nations probably offers the best hope for a fair and impartial program worked out through a partnership of all donor and recipient countries, and most undeveloped nations have accorded this approach their full support. Regional aid programs also associate donor and recipient countries together in a partnership arrangement, but in some cases a single donor country may dominate the arrangement.

Should the Emphasis Be on Long-Range or Short-Term Projects? Regardless of how funds are transmitted to needy countries, decisions must be made on how they can best be applied to realize economic goals. Short-term projects may be dramatic and provide good window dressing for a regime, but they may also raise hopes for a better life that cannot be fulfilled for many years. Projects that cannot be completed for five or ten years may lose popular support, may suffer from changes in governments or state policies, or may be curtailed by a cut-off of funds from donor countries or international institutions. Expert advice on economic, political, social, and psychological factors should be sought, and extensive joint consultations carried out between donor and recipient governments before embarking on projects. Some balance between long- and short-term projects is usually desirable, and in either case they should conform to the national plan.

Should Technical Assistance or Capital Goods Have Priority? A well-planned and rationally executed aid program should match up inputs of capital and technical assistance so that balanced growth can occur. This rarely happens even under the very best aid programs. Donor countries, while often generous to a fault in providing technical assistance, are reluctant to provide large amounts of capital through governmental channels. For them the first priority is to help undeveloped countries prepare the base and develop the skills that will support a modern economy. But the leaders of the developing countries, under great pressure from their peoples to produce tangible results, clamor for capital. These demands for many years have focused pressures on the advanced nations to agree to set up a Special United Nations Fund for Economic Development (SUNFED) incorporating a huge capital bank from which grants for developmental projects would be based on need and fair apportionment. Contributions to SUNFED, its many sponsors held, should come from all advanced states on the basis of 1 per cent of each nation's Gross National Product, an amount which continues to be far in excess of most national aid programs.[6]

The SUNFED project was rejected by the advanced nations, probably for a variety of reasons. The announced explanation was that no funds were available for additional aid projects, but that if the developing nations could prevail upon the "other" side in the East-West struggle to agree to extensive disarmament, the money saved could be routed into a SUNFED program.

[6] Under this guideline, for example, the United States would have contributed over $7 billion to SUNFED in 1966, as contrasted with actual bilateral and multilateral aid expenditures in 1966 of approximately $4 billion. Most American aid in 1966 was allocated for military, defense support, and technical assistance projects. If, however, programs related to foreign aid are included, such as the Food for Peace program, total American contributions approached $7 billion.

More likely reasons for the rejection of the project were the aversion of many advanced countries to provide grants of capital rather than loans through established institutions, their lack of control over funds granted through an *international* agency, and their continuing preference for technical assistance over capital grants.[7] Growing pressures for the SUNFED project forced the United States in 1958 to propose an alternative in the form of a Special Fund to help nations set up development programs and to encourage capital investments through preinvestment surveys. In 1965 the Special Fund was consolidated with the Expanded Program for Technical Assistance into a new United Nations Development Program, but emphasis continues on providing technical assistance, and no capital development funds are yet available through United Nations channels.

SHOULD AID FUNDS BE GRANTED OR LOANED? To give or to lend is a perennial problem facing aid-giving states and international institutions. In bilateral programs, the United States has moved from a predominantly grant basis to one of granting low-interest loans repayable in local currencies, while the Soviet Union gives its aid in the form of long-term, low-interest loans repayable in local commodities. International institutions generally extend short-term loans at moderate to high interest rates and expect repayment in hard currency.

Those who favor grants over loans argue that grants are more flexible than loans because they can be used to develop educational and other social overhead facilities, whereas loans must ordinarily be used to expand self-liquidating productive facilities so that interest payments can be made and the principal of the loan amortized. Grants, since they do not have to be repaid, have a minimal disturbing impact upon the recipient country's balance of payments, unlike hard currency loans which force the aid-receiving country to increase its exports or decrease its imports to obtain foreign exchange for installment payments. Grants, therefore, permit a better allocation of resources within a state and speed up economic growth by permitting a more rational application of aid funds.

The most compelling argument favoring loans over grants is that a loan, since it must be repaid with interest, encourages recipient countries to devote such funds to productive projects rather than to monuments or imported luxury goods. The discipline imposed upon a developing country

---

[7] The American position reflects the view that foreign aid is an effective weapon in fighting cold war battles, and should normally be guided by national interest considerations. For example, Richard N. Gardner, U.S. Deputy Assistant Secretary of State for International Organization Affairs, has explained American opposition to SUNFED and to new efforts to establish a capital development fund as violative of American national interest "precisely because large amounts of aid would be dispersed under circumstances that would not assure the promotion of U.S. foreign policy objectives. It is not merely that large amounts of aid might be given to Communist countries; it is also that the standards essential to the successful application of external aid would not be likely to be maintained." Richard N. Gardner, *In Pursuit of World Order* (New York: Praeger, 1964), pp. 120–21.

in paying off loans provides a good training ground for acquainting new leaders with the economic facts of life. To peoples newly removed from a status of colonial subservience, grants may create feelings of inferiority, of being forced to ask for and to receive charity, creating a natural resentment against donor nations. Loans can be negotiated with no loss of face, as a business transaction between equal sovereign states, without creating resentment or ill will. Loans, furthermore, are more acceptable politically within donor countries than grants, making it possible to offer far greater sums to developing countries. American Congressmen, for example, have been able to gain the support of their constituents for loan programs of foreign aid—bilateral, regional, and through United Nations agencies—at a time when the American public was reacting negatively to "give-away" programs.

Like most aid issues, that of loans versus grants poses somewhat of a false dichotomy. Both are needed in undeveloped societies, grants to help develop a substantial and suitable infrastructure, loans to provide the capital for industrial growth and diversification. To increase the capacities of developing states to pay off loans, however, expanding world trade and open markets in the advanced countries for primary commodities are necessary corollaries.

REGIONAL PROGRAMS

Most foreign aid granted to developing countries since 1945 has been through bilateral programs, particularly those of the United States and the Soviet Union, and sizable proportions of such aid have been in the forms of military aid and defense support projects.[8] Here we are concerned with international programs taking the form of regional and global multilateralism, two increasingly significant sources for development assistance reflecting the growing influence of the developing states in shaping the nature of such programs. Statements concerning the trend from bilateral to multilateral aid programs, however, should be made guardedly since much aid that is proclaimed to be multilateral may prove to be largely bilateral in fact.[9]

[8] For discussions of American and Soviet bilateral aid programs, see, for example, Gustav Ranis, ed., *The United States and the Developing Economies* (New York: W. W. Norton, 1964); Charles P. Fitzgerald, "The Sino-Soviet Balance Sheet in the Underdeveloped Areas," *Annals*, Vol. 351 (January, 1964), pp. 40–49; and Milton Kovner, "Soviet Aid Strategy in Developing Countries," *Orbis*, Vol. 8 (Fall, 1964), pp. 624–40.

[9] In the United States, for example, the Johnson Administration announced that 85 per cent of its development loans for Asia and Africa and most of its Latin American aid under the Alliance for Progress for the fiscal year 1967 would be committed under international arrangements. Much of this aid, however, would fall short of true multilateralism and would encompass only procedures of consultation and coordination with final decisions about kinds and amounts of aid and the execution of the program remaining bilateral.

The Colombo Plan

The first regional technical assistance and capital aid program emerged out of a Commonwealth Conference in 1950 at Colombo, Ceylon. The Colombo Plan initially provided for a $5.2 billion, six-year development program in which the advanced Commonwealth states—the United Kingdom, Canada, Australia, and New Zealand—furnished one half, with the other half supplied by the recipient Asian governments, representing together a quarter of the population of the world. The Plan has since been extended through 1966 and will probably be continued until its goal of Asian economic development has been achieved. The United States has joined as a contributor of aid, and recipients include not only Commonwealth states (India, Ceylon, Pakistan, Malaysia, and Singapore) but other Asian countries as well (Burma, Cambodia, Indonesia, Laos, Nepal, and South Viet Nam).

The Colombo Plan represents an ideal balance between a regional and bilateral approach to development. International machinery has been kept to a minimum. A Consultative Committee representing all participating states meets annually to review past activities, plan specific programs for the year ahead, and provide a forum for recipient nations to lobby for more aid and for donors to announce new projects. Contributions take the form of both grants and loans, and, although multilateral consultation is a significant factor in coordinating the program, all aid funds are provided through bilateral arrangements. An auxiliary program of technical assistance operates under the Plan through a permanent secretariat at Colombo known as the Council for Technical Cooperation in South and Southeast Asia. Every effort is made to balance imputs of capital with improved absorptive capacities so that balanced growth can occur. Technical cooperation has flourished, not only between donor and recipient countries, but among the Asian members themselves. Over $20 billion in loans and grants have been extended to Asian nations for agricultural and developmental purposes since 1950.

European Development Fund

A program similar to the Colombo Plan is carried on by the European Economic Community through a European Development Fund created in 1958 to offer aid to members' dependent territories in Africa. The program continued after Belgium and France granted independence to their colonies and today the Community's aid goes to eighteen African associated states, most of them former members of the French Community, and to several remaining dependent territories. Control over dispensing aid from the Fund is exercised by the Community's Council of Ministers casting weighted votes on projects recommended by the EEC Commission.[10] The latter body supervises negotiations and proposals for the former's official consideration, then oversees the administration of the approved programs.

The program started with an initial $581 million for the first five-year period and a second Fund created by the Yaoundé Convention of 1963 provides for Community contributions of $800 million for the period 1964–69. Most of the Fund credits are granted for improving economic infrastructure, such as railways, ports, roads, telecommunications, and urban development. Modernization of agriculture has the second highest priority. Since 1964 the Fund has also supplied the receiving countries with technical assistance in the form of advice from experts, technicians, economic surveys, and aid for vocational and professional training. The magnitude of the program can be measured by the Community's official disclosure that in 1965 the Six were contributing aid through the Fund equivalent to about $2.50 per capita.[11]

Organization for Economic Cooperation and Development

The Organization for Economic Cooperation and Development (OECD) is unique as a regional organization fostering technical and development assistance because its membership of twenty-one includes only donor nations. The OECD was created in 1961 as an outgrowth of the Organization for European Economic Cooperation (OEEC) which had been established in 1948 to coordinate Marshall Plan aid. Its membership includes eighteen former members of OEEC (Austria, Belgium, Denmark, France, Greece, Iceland, Ireland, Italy, Luxembourg, the Netherlands, Norway, Portugal, Spain, Sweden, Switzerland, Turkey, the United Kingdom, and West Germany), plus Canada, the United States, and Japan, with Yugoslavia and Finland as associate members. One of several major objectives of the new grouping was to expand Western aid to developing states, a goal which could more frankly be explained as an effort by the United States—the main force behind OECD's establishment—to encourage European states to carry a share of financing economic development.

The OECD pursues its aid-fostering role through a Development Assistance Committee (DAC) which establishes general policies, coordinates individual programs, and reviews annually the aid efforts of its members. No aid is offered through the organization's channels, however; in all cases

10 Council votes are weighted as follows: France, 4; Italy, 4; West Germany, 4; Belgium, 2; Netherlands, 2; and Luxembourg, 1. Any twelve votes constitutes a majority for a decision when voting on a proposal made by the Commission; questions not proposed by the Commission require twelve votes including affirmative votes by at least four member countries.

11 *European Community* (Washington, D.C.: European Community Information Service, October, 1965), No. 86, pp. 12–13.

aid is dispensed through bilateral or other multilateral programs.[12] Recommendations adopted at a recent annual meeting illustrate DAC's role as an advisory and coordinating body: [13] (1) Each member should reexamine the adequacy of the level and nature of its aid efforts. (2) The conditions of financial assistance offered by members (e.g., debt-servicing and repayment terms) should relate to the economic circumstances of recipient countries. (3) The problem of "untying" aid to permit a more efficient spending of aid monies by recipients should be studied further. (4) The needs of the less developed states for technical assistance, and the means of improving the supply and quality of technical personnel must be assessed and acted on. (5) Means of stimulating an increased flow of private capital and private managerial and technical skill to the developing states must be achieved.

Alliance for Progress

In the Western Hemisphere, the regional approach to economic development has been spurred by the Alliance for Progress program adopted at the Punta del Este Conference of 1961. The Punta del Este Charter provides for an economic alliance between the United States and nineteen governments of Latin America (Cuba's excepted) aimed at realizing a steady increase in living standards through joint action. Specifically, the program calls for (1) a minimum inflow of $20 billion in capital to Latin America over the decade 1962–72; (2) the implementation of various social and economic reforms within each of the recipient countries; (3) a strengthening of democratic institutions and the role of private enterprise in Latin America; and (4) a stabilization of markets and prices for Latin American primary commodities.

The huge $20 billion capital inflow was predicated on a sizable investment of private capital from North America, Western Europe, and Japan and annual transfers of public funds from the United States through low- or no-interest loans. Public funds have been directed to high priority "social overhead" projects, especially in agriculture, education, communications, and transportation, to build sturdy countrywide bases for private investments in industry. Priorities are determined multilaterally by a special panel of the Organization of American States, with specific commitments made by

[12] In 1963, for example, public assistance to developing states by DAC members totaled over $6 billion, of which $5.6 billion was bilateral and the remainder was channeled through other regional agencies or the United Nations. The United States provided the largest amount of total economic aid that year—$3.8 billion—with France contributing $858 million, West Germany $421 million, and the United Kingdom $413 million. The twelve members of the DAC that supply the bulk of economic assistance to the 133 countries and territories receiving aid are Canada, Belgium, Denmark, France, Italy, Japan, the Netherlands, Norway, Portugal, the United Kingdom, the United States, and West Germany.

[13] "Organization for Economic Cooperation and Development," *International Organization,* Vol. XIX, No. 1 (Winter, 1965), p. 151.

the Export-Import Bank, the Inter-American Bank for Development and the United States Agency for International Development. Although the United States has poured over $4 billion into Latin America during the first four years of the Alliance program, other results have been disappointing. Internal land and tax reforms have lagged in most countries, private investment has not measured up to expectations, and runaway population growth has cancelled out much of the gross development gains. However, steady improvement in primary commodity prices and markets, based largely on American prosperity and increasing war production, gives some hope that Alliance goals may yet be realized by 1972.

The Regional Banks

The regional approach to provide assistance for economic development is rounded out by three international area banks—the Inter-American Development Bank established in 1959, the African Development Bank established in 1964, and the Asian Development Bank established in 1966. Initial capital subscriptions for the three banks include: Inter-American, $1 billion; African, $250 million; and Asian, $1 billion. The United Nations Economic Commissions for Latin America (ECLA), for Africa (ECA), and for Asia and the Far East (ECAFE) laid the groundwork and fostered the development of each financial institution. As a rule, the banks extend hard loans (i.e., interest rates of 6 or 6½ per cent, repayable over 25 to 30 years in hard currencies) and give preference to loans that encourage further inflows of public and private capital into the region. Priorities in loans are also given to national, regional, and subregional projects that promote harmonious regional growth and which meet the needs of small or less-developed countries in the region. The relatively small capitalization of the African Development Bank results from a membership limited to the thirty-eight members of the Organization for African Unity, which are at the same time contributors and beneficiaries of the Fund.

In conclusion, the regional approach to economic development affords a viable compromise between outright bilateralism and a globalism which suffers from a dearth of donor countries and surfeit of those desperately in need. Most regional approaches, however, involve only consultation, coordination, and review, leaving the hard decisions on contributions, projects, and priorities to be made bilaterally (often unilaterally) by the major donor members. The regional banks, conversely, may more closely approximate models of true multilaterialism with their Councils of Governors determining basic policies and their Boards of Directors making loan decisions. But even here multilateralism may be modified by a voting system weighted by amounts of capital contributed, so that the form of multilateralism may mask a *de facto* national control. Most of the regional organizations, including two of the three development banks are also instruments of cold war policy as their memberships and loan clientele clearly indicate. Major contributors regard it as a *sine qua non* that most aid given must be justified by serving national interests. Recipients desperate in their need for help willingly accept bilateral and regional aid so directed, but little doubt remains that most of the developing states would prefer more or all assistance to be allotted, administered, and supervised through the truly *international* channels of the United Nations.

United Nations Programs

Economic development has become the major focus of debate in the General Assembly, the Economic and Social Council, and subsidiary organs. Most UN programs have economic development as their basic objective, and most UN personnel administer development programs. Even crucial questions like disarmament, collective security, and pacific settlement are smothered under an avalanche of words paying homage to the great god of economic development. How can this feverish, almost single-minded, activity be explained?

The United States and other major grantor nations indubitably prefer to give their aid through bilateral or carefully selected regional channels. Utilizing these means, they can exercise control over the nature of the program, the direction of the aid, the determination of how much aid shall go to which countries, the conditions attached to its dispensation, and related political and economic considerations. In United Nations programs they have less control over such matters. So great have been the pressures placed upon donor states by the almost one hundred members which fall into the category of "developing states" that the advanced states have contributed hundreds of millions of dollars to a variety of global programs. The Soviet Union, for example, looked askance in 1945 at the creation of an Economic and Social Council and disdainfully regarded economic aid programs as no more than neocapitalistic imperialism. The Soviets have since succumbed to the same pressures, however, and have contributed sizable amounts to many UN development programs. Soviet contributions have furthered economic progress in new states whose peoples, without UN help, might be prone to Communist-directed revolutions.

The early lack of concern by the Soviet Union for solving problems of economic development was in fact shared by other original members. This lack of concern was reflected in the Charter of the United Nations where only one broad, general provision can be found directly charging the United Nations with fostering economic development. Article 55 provides among other objectives that "the United Nations shall promote: (a) higher standards of living, full employment, and conditions of economic and social progress and development. . . ." No authority is provided in the Charter to require any governmental or organizational action in the economic field, and aid programs must rest on a foundation of cooperation and voluntary contributions. The organization has in no way been deterred by the reticence of the Charter, and a great variety of UN programs, resembling an "alphabet soup" in their short-hand acronymic symbolization, have been established in three broad categories—planning and research, technical assistance, and capital financing.[14]

Planning and Research Programs

The leaders of most developing countries recognize that the principal responsibility for promoting economic advancement is theirs, that foreign aid and international cooperation are not substitutes for national action. But nations newly launched on programs of modernization lack the experience and sophistication needed to avoid costly mistakes and dead-end objectives. One of the most significant approaches of the United Nations, consequently, has been that of creating opportunities for a meaningful dialogue between advanced nations and those seeking that status, and among the developing countries themselves. The dialogue has been carried on almost endlessly for over twenty years, constituting a novel "school" for imparting desire, knowledge, judgment, and common sense to national purveyors of development schemes. Principal forums for carrying on the dialogue have been the Economic and Social Council (ECOSOC), the General Assembly, the Second (Economic and Financial) Committee of the Assembly, the informal forum of UN Headquarters, and countless conferences, committees, commissions, and agencies of the UN system.

The United Nations dialogue has also been a learning experience for the advanced countries. From 1946 onward, the chambers of the United Nations have rung with the clamor of many voices setting forth the views of the world's less fortunate on the urgency of economic development, the causes and cures for poverty, and the responsibilities of the more fortunate to alleviate these conditions through direct and substantial aid. The main cleavage between the two groups has been over the approach to development, with Western nations advocating gradualist policies tested in their centuries-long

[14] For a summarized view of the broad range of United Nations activities in the field of economic development, see Roy Blough, "The Furtherance of Economic Development," *International Organization*, Vol. XIX, No. 3 (Summer, 1965), pp. 562–80. Blough's "abbreviated list" of areas of UN activities includes "economic and social theories of economic development, and theory and practice of development planning; science and technology; land tenure, taxation, and budgeting; improvement of public administration; economic 'infrastructure' of harbors, airports, transportation, and communication facilities, electric power and other public utilities; industrial development; health, housing, education, 'community development,' and other aspects of social development; population; vocational training of workers, labor organizations, cooperatives, improvements of labor, and social security laws; regional river development; and agriculture, fishing, forestry, mining, and manufacturing."

development struggles, and the developing states demanding rapid progress through short-cuts and massive technical and capital assistance programs. Communist bloc states have increasingly joined the fray, offering a socialist pattern as the best means for achieving progress.

Out of the debates has emerged not only a communication of existing ideas but new approaches, increased knowledge, and a better understanding of the problems of development. This interchange has been complemented by special studies, by information-gathering and analysis conducted by various secretariats, and widespread publication of the new knowledge. In fact, so extensive has been the research on problems of development that ECOSOC delegates have complained that they are being drowned in a spate of resolutions, reports, and discussions "beyond the analytical capacity and memory of the human brain." But the search for short-cuts, for new formulas, for sound plans continues, with the demands of the developing bloc appearing ever-more insatiable to the advanced states, placing them increasingly on the defensive.

THE REGIONAL COMMISSIONS. On urging from the General Assembly, the Economic and Social Council in 1947 established an Economic Commission for Europe (ECE) and an Economic Commission for Asia and the Far East (ECAFE) to give aid to countries devastated by the war. The following year demands by the Latin American bloc that economic development be recognized as a problem of equal significance resulted in the creation of the Economic Commission for Latin America (ECLA). In 1958 an Economic Commission for Africa (ECA) was established to help plan and organize economic development drives for the new nations of that continent. Plans for a Middle East regional commision were abandoned in the 1960's for lack of regional harmony.

Membership of the commissions includes the countries within each of the areas and certain others having special interests in the regions. Initially, their role was one of forging a regional outlook among diverse nations with different economic and social systems and, in some cases, with long histories of mutual hostilities. States not members of the United Nations are eligible for membership on the commissions, but they may choose a consultative or advisory status. Cooperation within each of the regions has been fostered by numerous conferences, regular exchanges of information, the development of personal and official contacts, and by an atmosphere of unity created and fostered mainly by the work of each commission's secretariat.[15] Each of the commissions makes annual and special reports to ECOSOC on progress within its area and recommendations to increase the pace of development. Each also makes recommendations to member gov-

---

[15] For an evaluation of the significance of the role of the Secretariat of the ECE, see Jean Siotis, "The Secretariat of the United Nations Economic Commission for Europe and European Economic Integration: The First Ten Years," *International Organization*, Vol. XIX, No. 2 (Spring, 1965), pp. 177–202.

ernments and to the specialized agencies on matters falling within their competencies.

The main objective of the commissions has been to provide research and planning which can stimulate a spirit of self-help in meeting regional problems. Annual economic surveys of the commissions have served as bases for developing "country plans," for the distribution of aid by donor countries as well as regional and UN agencies, and for the creation of new regional programs, such as the Inter-American, African, and Asian Development Banks. The commissions have also functioned as a catalyst in promoting movements within their respective regions towards economic integration, as reflected by the establishment of the European Economic Community, the Latin American Free Trade Association, and the Central American Common Market.[16] Annual sessions of the commissions have become major economic planning conferences with broad participation.[17]

THE DEVELOPMENT DECADE. In 1961, the sixteenth General Assembly proclaimed a "United Nations Development Decade" to dramatize the organization's efforts, to call attention to the need for long-range planning, and

> to mobilize and to sustain support for the measures required on the part of both developed and developing countries to accelerate progress towards self-sustaining growth of the economy of the individual nations and their social advancement.[18]

The target set by the Assembly was to raise the annual rate of growth in the developing countries from a 1960 average of about 3.5 per cent to a 1970 minimum annual rate of 5 per cent. All UN member states were urged to pursue policies and adopt measures aimed at achieving this goal. The Assembly's resolution also requested the Secretary-General to consult with UN economic organs and agencies to develop proposals to intensify UN development activity.[19]

---

[16] See Chapter 16 for an analysis of regional integration and its impact upon economic development.

[17] The eleventh session of the Economic Commission for Latin America held in Mexico City from May 6 to 17, 1965, provides an example of the support given the commissions regionally. Four hundred representatives from more than forty countries, specialized agencies, inter-American institutions, and nongovernmental organizations attended. Debates centered about the critical issues of expanding exports, attracting public and private investments, social overhead and infrastructure projects, industrial development, economic integration of the entire region, and the construction of a Latin American communications network.

[18] General Assembly Resolution 1710 (XVI), December 19, 1961.

[19] Secretary-General Dag Hammarskjold proposed on the basis of his consultations that the Development Decade be devoted to (1) more systematic surveys of conditions and needs; (2) development and use of physical and human resources; (3) formulation of "true" development plans free of exaggerated goals; (4) improved administration; (5) better production incentives; (6) redirection of science and technology to the problems of low-income countries; (7) increased export earnings; and (8) a larger and steadier flow of capital.

The Development Decade has succeeded in dramatizing UN development efforts and in stimulating new approaches and new programs. In the mid-point year of 1965, designated International Cooperation Year by the General Assembly, the organization evaluated its work and found that much progress had been achieved. Country economic planning for development was almost universally accepted and implemented, technical assistance programs were accelerated, and new research institutes and planning agencies were operational. At the mid-point, however, the flow of development capital remained on the 1960–61 plateau, wreaking havoc with development goals of most states and leading Secretary-General U Thant to comment that financial assistance programs appeared to have "lost the *élan* of a new venture before they had acquired the respectability of old usage." [20] Burgeoning population growth further atrophied the program's goals by diverting attention within the developing countries to the need for increasing food production to avert mass famine and by emasculating aggregate national gains when measured in terms of per capita standards of living.

The Development Decade's mid-point evaluation emphasizes once again that increased awareness, planning, research, technical assistance, and an abundance of good intentions cannot overcome the two knottiest problems—too much population growth and too little capital.

Technical Assistance Programs

Technical assistance involving the teaching of skills and new technologies is an indispensable instrument of any development program. Of the three main legs of the development stool—the infrastructure base, technical competence, and development capital—technical cooperation is the least controversial and has consumed a sizable portion of the energies and funds of the advanced countries and of UN development programs. The transference of any skill from ever so rudimentary to the most highly complex—from teaching a farmer how to wield a steel hoe most effectively to training technicians to run an atomic power plant—falls within the scope of technical assistance. The most significant categories include technological, managerial, administrative, educational, and medical, all fields in which there has been a sharing of skills but growing scarcity of technicians.

Fortunately, some modern skills were transmitted to societies in the developing states during the nineteenth and first half of the twentieth centuries by the colonialists, by missionaries, by the League of Nations programs, or by private business and philanthropic organizations.

The first government program of technical assistance on a substantial scale began during World War II when the United States sought to increase

[20] "The United Nations Development Decade at Mid-Point: An appraisal by the Secretary-General," United Nations Document E/4071, June 11, 1965, pp. 3–28.

production of primary commodities essential to the war effort through a major program of technical and cultural exchange with Latin American countries. American experts in agriculture, mining, and education accepted inservice posts in Latin America while large numbers of Latin Americans received training in the United States as medical doctors and technicians, engineers, agronomists, and public administrators. The program was phased out after the war, but in 1949 President Harry S. Truman urged Americans to adopt "a bold new program for making the benefits of our scientific advances and industrial progress available for the improvement and growth of under-developed areas." Set forth in his inaugural address as the last of four policies aimed at achieving peace and security in the world, "Point Four" was implemented by Congress in the Act for International Development. The Act provided for two programs: one, an expanded program of technical assistance carried out through the United Nations, and two, a bilateral program of technical cooperation. Both programs with some changes in titles and administrative procedures continue today as the world's leading multilateral and bilateral technical assistance programs.

UNITED NATIONS DEVELOPMENT PROGRAM. The American decision in 1949 to offer the undeveloped world a large-scale technical assistance program led the General Assembly in November of that year to adopt an Expanded Program of Technical Assistance (EPTA) going far beyond the existing meager program and financed by voluntary contributions rather than through the regular budget. Nine years later, in October, 1958, the Assembly complemented the EPTA program by establishing a Special Fund to lay the groundwork for encouraging capital flows into developing states. In November, 1965, the Assembly combined the EPTA and Special Fund programs into a new United Nations Development Program (UNDP) to secure a unified approach. Although administratively joined, each of the approaches of the dual-phased program needs some individual background treatment to place the new UNDP program in perspective.

Expanded Program of Technical Assistance (EPTA). The EPTA was hailed in the General Assembly as "the true expression of that spirit of international cooperation which was envisaged by the founders. . . ." and as "one of the most constructive acts of international statesmanship ever undertaken under the auspices of the United Nations." EPTA's program incorporated three main forms of assistance: (1) providing experts, including some from the undeveloped countries themselves, to train cadres of technicians; (2) awarding fellowships for technical training in advanced countries; and (3) supplying limited amounts of equipment needed for training and demonstration purposes. Funds for the EPTA program came from voluntary contributions offered at annual pledging conferences, a system continued by the Development Program. Contributions may be made in local as well as hard currencies, but donors may not attach any conditions to the use of their contributions.[21]

The Technical Assistance Committee (TAC), composed of representatives of the twenty-seven members of the Economic and Social Council, exercised general supervision over EPTA on behalf of the Council until replaced in 1965 by a thirty-seven-member Governing Council for the United Nations development Program. Day-to-day operations of EPTA were the responsibility of the Technical Assistance Board (TAB), composed of the specialized agencies participating in the program and headed by an Executive Chairman until replaced in 1966 by a new Inter-Agency Consultative Board.[22] The Consultative Board provides the machinery for joint consultations between UN administrators and governmental officials, for liaison and coordination, and for appraisal of country and regional programs.

Resident Representatives in the field assist governments in developing sound programs and advise the Consultative Board on their feasibility in relation to local conditions. The Resident Representative is rapidly becoming the central figure in UN field operations. More than seventy such offices around the globe, most organized on a single country basis, coordinate technical assistance programs, function as "country representatives" for some of the specialized agencies, lend assistance on preinvestment surveys, and serve as a link between the United Nations and the recipient government. Indications are that the Resident Representative's office will grow in significance

---

[21] The Soviet Union, although originally opposed to EPTA, backed the program under pressures from an overwhelmingly favorable majority in the General Assembly. The first year the Soviets tried to restrict the use of their funds by excluding the then five participating specialized agencies and by specifying particular aspects of the program. This attempt by a donor country to control the direction of the program was rejected as a violation of the principles of EPTA, and the Soviet Union again bowed to majority pressures. More recently, the United States took issue with the use of some of its contributions for an educational project in Cuba, a protest that was also rejected.

[22] Five specialized agencies, along with the United Nations Organization itself, constituted the founding "participating organizations" for the EPTA: (1) the International Labor Organization (ILO); (2) the Food and Agriculture Organization (FAO); (3) the United Nations Educational, Scientific and Cultural Organization (UNESCO); (4) the International Civil Aviation Organization (ICAO); and (5) the World Health Organization (WHO). Five additional organizations subsequently joined the program: (6) the International Telecommunication Union (ITU) and (7) the World Meteorological Organization (WMO), both joining in 1951; (8) the International Atomic Energy Agency (IAEA) in 1959; (9) the Universal Postal Union (UPU) in 1962; and (10) the Inter-Governmental Maritime Consultative Organization (IMCO) in 1964. In 1965 the International Bank (IBRD) joined in the new Development Program, bringing the number of participating organizations (including the UN Organization) to twelve. All are represented on the Inter-Agency Consultative Board for the Development Program which coordinates all UN technical assistance and related programs. The International Monetary Fund, while not participating directly in the program, works closely with the Consultative Board to aid in moderating balance of payments problems affecting development programs.

under the new United Nations Development Program as efforts are increased to achieve a greater measure of coordination and unity of purpose in UN assistance programs.

Evaluating the contribution of EPTA to economic development over a fifteen-year period is a hazardous undertaking considering its diverse activities and its far-flung programs.[23] In 1953, its third operational year, the expanded program provided technical assistance through 502 projects in eighty-six countries and territories utilizing a budget of $22.8 million.[24] By 1965, its fifteenth operational year, EPTA extended technical assistance to some 150 states and territories in expending a budget of $54 million contributed by 109 governments.[25] Over its first fifteen years, it offered training and new skills to an estimated 150,000 persons and included almost every developing society in its program. Services contributed by EPTA amounted to the equivalent of 32,000 man-years of experts, 31,000 fellowships, and $36 million worth of equipment, with a total cost for the period of $450 million. Although these figures sound impressive, the need for skilled persons is so great that the total program could have easily and profitably been absorbed by a single developing country if capital inflow and development projects had proceeded apace. Yet, no one can accurately calculate the "multiplier effect" by which the skills initially transmitted might spread within countries at a geometric rate. The fact that developing states have not been critical of the pace of the UN technical assistance program can only indicate that other crucial factors in the development equation—particularly capital transfers—have been seriously lagging over the more than twenty years of UN technical assistance activity, thereby reducing the need for skilled personnel. Leaders recognize that large-scale frustration and political unrest find fertile ground among people who have acquired modern skills but are unable to apply them for lack of parallel development in industrialization, land reform, or other sectors of the nation's economy.

The Special Fund. To correct this imbalance, a Special Fund was established by the General Assembly in 1958 to provide "systematic and sustained assistance in fields essential to the integrated technical, economic and social development of the less developed countries. . . ."[26] The Special Fund was a belated recognition by the advanced states that technical assistance is only meaningful as a development tool if matched by inputs of capital. At

[23] For an official evaluation of EPTA by the former Executive Chairman of the TAB and current Co-Administrator of the Development Program, see David Owen, "Fifteen Years and 150,000 Skills," *UN Monthly Chronicle,* United Nations Office of Public Information, Vol. II, No. 6 (June, 1965), pp. 105–09.

[24] "Issues Before the Ninth General Assembly," *International Conciliation,* No. 499 (September, 1954), pp. 60–67.

[25] "Issues Before the Twentieth General Assembly," *International Conciliation,* No. 554 (September, 1965), pp. 162–67.

[26] General Assembly Resolution 1219 (XII), December 14, 1957.

that, it was only a compromise falling far short of the perennial demands of the developing states for the creation of a massive capital development fund to provide capital grants and to be replenished annually at a contributory rate of 1 per cent of GNP from each advanced state. The advanced states, however, prefer that capital flows take the form of private investments, regarded by some of the developing states as a form of economic imperialism. The Special Fund compromise embodied the concept of paving the way for increased private, national, and international investment by conducting "preinvestment" surveys, by discovering wealth-producing potentials of unsurveyed natural resources, by training and research institutes, and by "feasibility reports on the practicability, requirements, and usefulness" of development projects.[27]

Over its seven-year period of independent operations, the Special Fund in its "broker role" encouraged a better working relationship between the governments of developing states and capital suppliers, but did little to satiate the immense demand for capital. By 1965 its Managing Director, Paul G. Hoffman, was able to report that 485 Special Fund-assisted projects had been undertaken since 1958. These included 154 in Africa concentrated on opening new land areas and strengthening educational facilities, 129 in Latin America centered mainly on developing industry, 133 in Asia and the Far East to improve agriculture and develop industry, forty in the Middle East to overcome water shortages and control land erosion, twenty-eight in Europe of diverse objectives, and one special inter-regional project.[28] Economic and Social Institutes have been established by the regional commissions through Special Fund financing at Santiago in 1962 and at Dakar and Bangkok in 1964. More than 80 per cent of the Special Fund's annual budget was expended by FAO, UNESCO, and by the United Nations special assistance programs. Although the EPTA and Special Fund programs were to be coordinated from the start, the Managing Director of the Fund functioned more independently than TAB in allocating funds and determining priorities. The amalgamation of the two in 1966 in the United Nations Development Program with Paul G. Hoffman as Administrator gave some assurance that both programs would operate thereafter from a single source of direction.

Miscellaneous Technical Assistance Programs. The diversity of needs in the developing world has helped spawn a variety of special UN projects, each devoted to an attack on some particular problem of economic development not covered or covered inadequately by the general technical assistance program. To fill a need for top-level administrators in developing societies, a new Operational, Executive and Administrative (OPEX) personnel service was established in 1958 by the General Assembly. Internationally

27 United Nations Document SF/L.6, January 26, 1958.
28 "Report on Special Fund," *UN Monthly Chronicle, op. cit.* (June, 1965), pp. 81–82.

recruited experts are assigned under OPEX to governments with the proviso that their duties include training nationals to replace them.[29] Another complementary personnel program emerged in 1963 when the General Assembly established the United Nations Institute for Training and Research (UNITAR).[30] Fully operational by 1966, the Institute specializes in training individuals for work in social and economic fields, particularly for technical assistance programs and as national counterpart personnel. A unique feature of UNITAR involves training young people for careers as foreign affairs officers and for international appointments. Institute faculty are recruited through fellowship programs and through the voluntary participation of eminent scholars and statesmen.

A number of programs, peripheral yet significant to economic development, complete the United Nations efforts to provide technical assistance. A United Nations Conference on the Application of Science and Technology for the Benefit of the Less Developed Areas (UNCSAT) was convened in Geneva in 1963 to foster development of technologies attuned to the needs of particular regions and countries, particularly labor-using industries to moderate the growing unemployment problem in the developing states. An Advisory Committee on the Application of Science and Technology to Development continues these efforts by encouraging research in diverse fields of inquiry.[31] In 1963 a new Industrial Development Center began functioning as a clearinghouse in the fields of economics and industrial technology, and an Economic Projections and Programming Center began developing long-term projections of world economic and industrial trends to facilitate national planning. Both centers are located at UN Headquarters, although the latter program also operates through regional subcenters.

In 1963 a World Food Program was undertaken jointly by the United

[29] For a description of the OPEX program, see "Issues Before the Fourteenth General Assembly," *International Conciliation*, No. 524, (September, 1959), pp. 124–26. A sampling of national personnel requests discloses the nature of the approximately one hundred positions filled by OPEX: General Manager, Jamaican Broadcasting Corporation; Director of Studies, National Center of Political, Administrative and Juridical Studies, Laos; Air Traffic Controller, Tunisia; and Manager of the Bank of Nepal.

[30] General Assembly Resolution 1934 (XVIII), December 11, 1963. An interesting project undertaken by UNITAR in 1965 involved the preparation of a glossary in five languages explaining the activities of such agencies as UNITAR itself, UNESCO, UNDP, WHO, IBRD, and other United Nations organizations and programs usually referred to by their acronyms. UNITAR also took steps in 1965 to hold resident seminars in developing countries to reach more students than it could by bringing them to its New York headquarters. Another reason behind resident seminars is the reluctance of many developing countries to permit their best students to go abroad because many secure jobs in advanced countries after receiving their training and do not return to their homeland.

[31] In 1965, the Committee established a list of research targets grouped under eight major headings: food supplies, health, population, natural resources, industrialization, housing and urban planning, transportation, and educational techniques. Under the food supplies rubric, for example, priorities included water resources, meteorology, edible protein, prevention of food losses, and control of the tsetse fly.

Nations and FAO to provide food for economic and social development projects and to supply food aid in emergencies. Under the program, food aid for workers has been provided in such fields as mining, industry, community development, and irrigation. In the field of demography, the United Nations Population Commission conducts extensive research on population problems affecting states' abilities to develop and, in 1965, sponsored a World Population Conference. Not surprisingly, virtually all the support for population control as a means of furthering economic development comes from the advanced states.[32] Other programs contribute indirectly to technical cooperation, such as UNICEF which fosters the development of future leaders and technicians through food and educational programs for children, and the United Nations itself which helps train political leaders in statesmanship, and Secretariat technicians in modern administrative techniques. Finally, the International Bank has become active in the field of technical assistance in recent years through project preparation, development programming, and in training senior development officials in its Economic Development Institute.

THE FUTURE OF TECHNICAL ASSISTANCE. Technical assistance programs enable one nation to help another, making both nations better off. There has been little criticism of the principle of technical cooperation, either from the advanced or the developing countries. Duplication and overlapping of jurisdictions have abounded in the UN programs, however, and between them and bilateral and regional programs; and they have sometimes aroused petty jealousies and conflicts. Efforts within the United Nations to coordinate programs have been only partially effective, and future consolidations and partnership arrangements, such as that carried out by EPTA and the Special Fund through the United Nations Development Program, are in order so that limited resources and personnel will be employed with maximum advantage. Finally, as already noted, no technical assistance program, no matter how well financed and administered, can possibly succeed unless capital accumulation and investment move forward in tandem with it. We now turn our attention to the UN role of fostering inflows of capital into developing economies to seek that balance so essential for economic development.

Development Financing Programs

United Nations efforts for *financing* economic development are limited to loan programs carried on by the World Bank Group—the International Bank for Reconstruction and Development (IBRD), the International Finance Corporation (IFC), and the International Development Association (IDA). Although developing states have not given up their attempts to establish a

[32] See "Population Conference," *UN Monthly Chronicle, op. cit.,* (June, 1965), pp. 77–78.

sizable SUNFED-type capital development fund from which grants could be made to all developing member states, most capital-surplus states, led by the United States, have refused to support the project.[33]

THE INTERNATIONAL BANK. The International Bank with its more than one hundred members is the central unit in UN lending operations. The Bank is a specialized agency established under the Articles of Agreement drawn up at the Bretton Woods Monetary Conference of 1944. Lending operations began in 1946. Since private international capital had virtually disappeared during the 1930's, the World Bank reflected the prevailing attitude on international finance that some form of public financing was essential as a supplement to private loans. From its inception to 1949, virtually all of the Bank's loans were directed to the urgent task of restoring Europe's war-torn economies, with only seven loans committed to developing countries by the end of 1949. The pace of development lending quickened, however, rising from an aggregate of almost $1 billion disbursed to developing states by 1953 to a cumulative total of almost $6 billion a decade later. A total of 461 loans have been made by the Bank to 79 countries or territories for reconstruction and development in the two decades since 1946, totaling over $9 billion by 1966 (*see* Table 15-1). Sizable as these figures are, they could well be doubled over the next decade.

Lending policies are developed by the Bank's Board of Governors within guidelines laid down by member states using a weighted voting system based on subscribed capital. The Bank makes "hard loans" repayable in convertible currency and most loans have run for thirty or thirty-five years at 5½ or 6 per cent interest. Emphasis has been placed on infrastructure financing of power, transport, and communication projects, with less than 20 per cent of its loans devoted to industry and mining. Loans are made either to member governments or to private firms if guaranteed by a member government. Loans to private companies have been minimal because firms have found it impossible to obtain their government's guarantee or have preferred not to get involved with governmental red tape. Moreover, the Bank has no facilities for investigating and administering loan applications from thousands of small businesses, and few large firms exist in the developing states.

The World Bank is run by bankers, giving it a conservative image which its Board of Governors regards as a proper one. The Bank operates on sound principles of international finance and its loan criteria are aimed at protecting the interests of the Bank and its creditors. This image of soundness and bankability of loans is a necessary one since most of the Bank's loan funds are obtained not from governments but from world capital markets. Loan applicants must use a "project" approach in which the borrower can

[33] The Soviet Union dropped its early opposition to a UN capital fund in 1955 and accepts the idea without commiting itself on the extent of its financial support.

demonstrate that the loan will finance a carefully planned undertaking that will contribute to the productive capacity of the country. Social project loans (for building hospitals and schools or for slum clearance), general purpose loans, and loans to meet rising debt or to resolve balance of payments problems are all frowned upon. For some years the Bank limited its use of funds to "self-liquidating projects" which would provide revenues large enough to service debt payments, but the Bank now measures the repayment capacity of the nation's entire economy in making its loans. On average, World Bank loans have financed only 25 per cent of the cost of projects with other investors providing the balance.

TABLE 15-1. World Bank Group (June 30, 1966)

	International Bank for Reconstruction and Development (IBRD)	International Development Association (IDA)	International Finance Corporation (IFC)
Date Operational	December, 1945	September, 1960	July, 1956
Members	103	96	81
Capital			
Subscribed	$22,426,400,000	$1,552,000,000	$99,400,000
Funds Available for Loans	$1,143,267,000		$31,500,000
Loans			
Cumulative Amount (net)	$9,583,630,294	$1,371,540,000	$161,161,225
Loans Granted	461	89	124
Countries and Territories	79	32	34
Terms			
Interest Rate	Variable, 6 to 7%	Interest free, but ¾ of 1% annual service charge	Variable, with 1% annual commitment fee
Payment Period	Variable, 10–35 years, with an average of 20 years	50 years, with 10-year period of grace	Variable, 7–12 years
Repayable Currency	Convertible foreign exchange	Convertible foreign exchange	Convertible foreign exchange

Source: International Bank for Reconstruction and Development, Information Department.

During the 1960's the Bank has undergone a change, both in its self-image and in its operations, from a strictly financial institution to that of a development agency concerned intimately with solving problems of economic development. Instead of remaining aloof and merely passing judgment on loan applications, the Bank now assists states in their development planning, helps prepare project proposals, and provides training for senior development officials through an Economic Development Institute. Its economic survey missions check resource and investment potentials in member countries and determine priorities for country and regional projects. The Bank has also participated increasingly in consortium arrangements for financing major projects, with funds provided jointly by global, regional, and local lending institutions. The development of the Indus river multipurpose project by India and Pakistan, using World Bank, regional, bilateral, and local funds in a consortium agreement, illustrates how joint financing can make projects of this magnitude possible. It also demonstrates that the World Bank can use its funds to secure the cooperation of political enemies on a mutually beneficial development plan. Diversification in the Bank's lending programs led to a doubling of its capital stock in 1959 from $10 billion to $20 billion to provide effective governmental guarantees for the stepped-up pace of its operations.[34] New funds available for loans and changing attitudes toward economic development have led the Bank to further liberalize its lending criteria by granting loans to countries not fully measuring up to the Bank's high standards of fiscal management.

Despite its increased pace of activity, the World Bank is severely limited in its capacity to meet the vast demands for capital in developing states. For one thing, repayment of loans in hard currencies imposes grave difficulties upon those borrowing states not ranking high as foreign exchange earners. Many developing states are already overstraining their long-run debt-servicing capacities and new loans under similar conditions jeopardize their financial stability. Moreover, since economic activity in many developing states is carried on predominantly by private companies, a practical means of making loans to relatively small firms without government guarantees is almost essential for the attainment of economic development. These weaknesses were at least partially overcome by the establishment of two new lending affiliates of the International Bank.

INTERNATIONAL FINANCE CORPORATION (IFC). From the start of the Bank's operations it was recognized that some kind of affiliate was necessary to help finance private investment. Such an affiliate, it was predicated, would permit the stimulation of private companies by injections of international capital

[34] More specifically, the purpose of doubling capital subscriptions from governments was to increase the uncalled reserves so that the Bank's securities could be sold to private investors in world capital markets. Guarantees backed by member government reserves make it possible for the Bank to borrow money from private investors at considerably less interest cost than that charged by the Bank on its own loans. The result, of course, is a significant profit for the Bank from its operations which is ploughed back into its lending operations. By 1966, the Bank's subscribed capital was over $22 billion, of which $2 billion was paid-in capital and $20 billion remained on call from members.

secured from private sources. This kind of circular financing was provided by the establishment of the International Finance Corporation (IFC) in 1956. With 81 members and a subscribed capital of almost $100 million, the IFC promotes the flow of capital from world money markets, stimulates the formation of investment capital within member countries, and encourages private enterprise and private investment opportunities. It makes loans and, since 1961, direct equity investments in private companies, including companies owned jointly by local and foreign interests. In the fiscal year 1965, for example, the IFC entered into mixed equity-loan commitments amounting to $26 million in such industries as steel, textiles, cement, jute, pulp, food processing, and pharmaceuticals. IFC's aggregate total of commitments by the end of Fiscal 1966 amounted to $161 million representing 124 transactions in 34 different countries.

Obviously, IFC is merely scratching the surface of world needs for public capital to stimulate private investment. Small and medium sized firms are not included in the IFC's scope of operations, although the IFC has encouraged members to establish local development banks to do this job and has offered to help finance them. IFC itself has recently been authorized to borrow large sums from the International Bank. The result is effective but again circular: the International Bank secures funds from private capital markets, it loans some of these to the IFC which in turn loans some to country development banks, from whence the funds finally return through direct loans to private businesses. Are these international and national institutional middlemen really necessary? Obviously they are because they were created in response to urgent needs. Most investors refuse to risk their capital in developing states without governmental guarantee programs. The stage of self-sustaining economic growth may finally be reached by a developing country when significant inflows of private funds occur without global, regional, or local institutional stimulation or direct protection.

INTERNATIONAL DEVELOPMENT ASSOCIATION (IDA). In response to a growing chorus of demands for a capital grant program and a continuing criticism of the conservative nature of the International Bank's operations, the International Development Association was established in 1960 as a "soft loan" affiliate. IDA was also a response by the United States (the idea was developed in Congress) to the stepped-up Soviet aid/trade offensive of the late 1950's. Although IDA is a separate legal entity and its funds and reserves are separate from those of the International Bank, the management and staff of the two institutions are the same.

The "soft loan" features of IDA pertain to the long period for repayment (50 years), the slow amortization rate (which begins after a ten-year period of grace, with 1 per cent of the loan's principal repayable annually during the second ten years and 3 per cent annually for the remaining thirty years), and the low cost of the loan (no interest but a ¾ of 1 per cent annual service charge). Loans are not "soft," however, in one highly significant respect to the borrowing countries—they must be paid off in "hard" (convertible) foreign exchange. This usually means American dollars or a currency freely convertible into dollars.

Developing states, recognizing the advantages of IDA's terms—especially the provision that no payments on a loan are due for ten years—quickly depleted initial and several subsequent subscriptions. By mid-1966, IDA had a subscribed capital of over $1.5 billion and had loaned an aggregate sum of more than $1.3 billion representing 89 transactions in 32 countries and territories. Like International Bank loans, recipients of IDA funds must finance a portion of all loan projects, usually with local currency. IDA's loans go mainly to government agencies for projects similar to those financed by the International Bank, although IDA makes funds more readily available for economic infrastructure development and "social overhead" projects. Whether IDA loans will be paid off regularly once the ten-year grace period ends for the first series in 1970 will depend, of course, on the progress in economic development made by each borrowing country. It will also depend on general world conditions—war or peace, boom or bust, population control or "explosion," the terms of trade, the development of synthetics, changes in consumer tastes, and numerous other unpredictable factors which may either ease repayment or turn current loans into, for all practical purposes, grants.

The World Bank Group operates on a professional, nonpolitical level. The activities of the Bank and its two affiliates have benefited almost every developing state, and indications are that the pace of its lending operations will accelerate over the next decade. Yet, the Group's operations are subject to extensive criticism. The fact that it is controlled by Western (former colonial) powers, through a voting system weighted on the basis of contributions, arouses widespread suspicion of its motives and its policies. Some Communist and Socialist states have consistently criticized the Group as exemplars of neo-imperialism and neo-colonialism. Critics point out that the International Bank's loan terms are no bargain, that they are no easier, and sometimes are harsher, than those of private banks. The International Finance Corporation, critics charge, has never gained acceptance in the advanced donor states or, for that matter, in the developing world, as evidenced by its inadequate funding and modest lending activity. Its objective of furthering private investment by meshing capital from both the public and private sectors is a novel approach but one that has failed to surmount the basic incompatibilities inherent in such a combination. The International Development Association has enjoyed a singular success in dispensing funds, probably because it comes closest to the capital grant system sought by developing states. Despite criticism, the record of the

World Bank Group indicates that most developed and developing countries support the system. Its loans have helped almost one hundred countries to finance useful development projects, and it has often successfully encouraged internal financial reforms within borrowing countries. This last role, sometimes referred to as "the art of development diplomacy," may go beyond domestic matters, as in the Indus River Agreement between India and Pakistan negotiated by the Bank.[35] Given the fantastic capital needs for economic development in the world today and the lack of an international capital development fund, one can only conclude that the role of the World Bank Group is predestined to grow in significance.

CONCLUSIONS ON ECONOMIC DEVELOPMENT

Where, on balance, do the developing states stand today? Where will they stand in terms of economic development when the Development Decade ends in 1970? What are the prospects for development in the decades beyond 1970? Although more has been done in promoting economic development in the world over the last two decades than in all past eons of history, more also has been needed and expected. Progress, if defined as an improvement in standards of living, has failed to measure up to even minimally optimistic hopes. Agricultural output, while increasing substantially in developing states, has barely kept pace with population growth, and over 400 million people of the world remain undernourished. The future portends even greater difficulties, with the danger that undernourishment may turn first to serious malnutrition and then to large-scale famine.[36] In the field of housing, millions of new dwellings must be built each year merely to stay abreast of population growth. Education, despite extensive UN and national programs fostered by UNESCO, remains a major problem at all points on the educational scale—too many illiterates, too few trained technicians, and a great paucity of university-trained professionals. For example, in Europe six or seven physicians graduate each year for each 100,000 people, whereas in Asia there are only 0.8 and in Africa 0.5 per 100,000 annually.[37] Unemployment and underemployment have increased drastically in many countries despite efforts to expand productive facilities.

Although some countries and subregions have failed to dent the problem

[35] For a discussion of the Bank's role in "development diplomacy," see Eugene R. Black, *The Diplomacy of Economic Development and Other Papers*, (New York: Atheneum, 1963), particularly Chap. 2.

[36] Based on projections of population growth and other factors relating to food consumption, the Food and Agriculture Organization has estimated that to maintain current inadequate levels of nourishment, food supplies will have to be increased by 70 per cent between 1960 and 1970. See *Agricultural Commodities—Projections for 1970*, FAO Commodity Review 1962, Special Supplement, Rome: FAO, Part I, p. 31.

[37] "Issues Before the Seventeenth General Assembly," *International Conciliation*, No. 539, (September, 1962), p. 96.

of economic stagnation, others—such as Yugoslavia, the United Arab Republic, and Mexico—are making determined efforts to join the world of developed states. Some societies have received huge infusions of aid resources but have failed to use the aid effectively to broaden the base of their economies or to integrate new productive enterprises with the demands of the world market. Efforts of the international community through bilateral, regional, and global programs are scattered and largely uncoordinated, often wasting efforts through duplication and overlap. Yet, a variety of programs encourages experimentation and is likely to extract greater support from capital-surplus states than a single program.

Clearly, developing states prefer to receive aid through UN programs that leave them unencumbered politically and militarily and avoid damage to national egos. As already noted, the United Nations offers a partnership arrangement with assisted countries cooperating in planning, developing, and administering aid programs free of power rivalries. No other organization can provide such a storehouse of development information and experience or possess so many useful contacts. The United Nations also provides a natural focus for coordinating development programs, an "agitation chamber" for stimulating action by member states, a forum for the exchange of information and ideas, and a repository of skills available to developing states. But the key objective of the great majority of members to set up a capital development fund *with the cooperation of the advanced states* has not been realized. The votes are readily available in the General Assembly, but without a willingness of capital-surplus states to volunteer large contributions, the fund would not serve its intended purpose. Without it, UN programs remain useful and desirable but not central to development in the eyes of the leaders of developing states. Given this impasse, the outlook for development then depends mainly on private investments and on capital surpluses secured through international trade. How trade and investment can be maximized, and the role of economic integration in encouraging both, are the subjects for the next chapter.

Selected Readings

BELL, DAVID E. "The Quality of Aid," *Foreign Affairs,* Vol. 44, No. 4, July, 1966, pp. 601–07.

BLACK, EUGENE R. *The Diplomacy of Economic Development and Other Papers.* New York: Atheneum, 1963.

BOURGEOIS-PICHAT, JEAN. "Population Growth and Development," *International Conciliation,* No. 556, January, 1966.

FEINSTEIN, OTTO, ed. *Two Worlds of Change,* Garden City, N.Y.: Doubleday, 1964.

FICKETT, LEWIS P., JR., ed. *Problems of the Developing Nations.* New York: Crowell, 1966.

MIKESELL, RAYMOND F. *Public International Lending for Development.* New York: Random House, 1966.

MILLIKAN, MAX F. and BLACKMER, DONALD L. M., eds. *The Emerging Nations.* Boston: Little, Brown, 1961.

PAPANEK, GUSTAV F. "Framing a Development Program," *International Conciliation,* No. 527, March, 1960.

RANIS, GUSTAV, ed. *The United States and the Developing Economies.* New York: W. W. Norton, 1964.

ROSTOW, W. W. *The Process of Economic Growth,* 2nd ed. New York: W. W. Norton, 1962.

TINBERGEN, JAN. "International Economic Planning," *Daedalus,* Vol. 95, No. 2, Spring, 1966, pp. 530–57

VON DER MEHDEN, FRED R., *Politics of the Developing Nations.* Englewood Cliffs, N.J.: Prentice-Hall, 1964.

WARD, BARBARA. *The Rich Nations and the Poor Nations.* New York: W. W. Norton, 1962.

ZIMMERMAN, L. J. *Poor Lands, Rich Lands: The Widening Gap.* New York: Random House, 1965.

16 | *Integrating Economic Policies*

$\mathbf{A}$ccess to raw materials, labor mobility and skill, rate of investment, sources of fuel and power, and organization of the domestic economy determine the *potential* level of economic development for each country. But no state's economic life evolves out of purely local conditions. Growing specialization and interdependence among states over a period of four centuries have related economic regionalism and the nature of the world economy to the material fortunes of each. The international system may foster or impede the exchange of goods, the flow of credits and investments, the exchange of currencies, and the balancing of accounts, making economic growth and improved living standards a function of both domestic and foreign considerations. In this chapter we are concerned with the effort to build an international milieu receptive to the fulfillment of the economic potential of individual states.

EARLY MODELS

From the sixteenth to the latter part of the eighteenth century a state-dominated system of mercantilism pervaded the economic scene in the western world. Economic activity, both domestic and foreign, was regulated and directed by government in support of state power. Each state sought to enhance its security by amassing treasures of precious metals useful to buy off opponents and to hire mercenary troops for military campaigns. The major objective of trade was to achieve a favorable balance that would enable states to enlarge their national treasuries through an international payment's system that settled accounts by transfers of gold and silver.

In the latter part of the mercantilist era a rising class of merchants and entrepreneurs began to use their political and economic influence to demand greater measures of economic freedom. The American Revolution, although justified by the new political doctrines of freedom and democracy, was fundamentally a reaction against the mother country's narrowly restrictive

457

trade and tax policies. These policies were aimed at keeping the colonies functioning within the mercantilist framework as suppliers of cheap raw materials and as a market restricted to high-priced British manufactures. It was not an accident of history that Adam Smith published his *Wealth of Nations* in the same year that the American colonists declared their independence. The new liberalism, grounded in the philosophy of laissez-faire, broke down internal restrictions in European states and, following the Napoleonic wars, fostered the development of an international trading system embracing the concept of free trade. International market forces replaced the dictates of government officials in shaping national specialization and the direction of trade. Under the new system, trade flourished and Europe became an industrial and commercial center for the entire world.

The rebirth of nationalism in the twentieth century signaled that the long period of relatively free trade and general economic multilateralism was coming to an end. World War I accelerated this movement, and the economic dislocation and rivalry fostered by five years of hostilities carried over to undermine the efforts of political and economic leaders to return to the relatively stable period of the nineteenth century. Attempts to regain stability centered on restoring the unity formerly provided by the gold standard and the British pound sterling. Neither effort was wholly successful; Britain failed during the 1920's to regain her economic strength wasted during the war, and the gold standard functioning out of the London money market reflected this weakness. Some semblance of free trade was regained by the latter part of the decade, however, and monetary stability appeared within grasp by 1928.

The American stock market crash in 1929 and the deepening world depression of the early 1930's dealt a death blow to hopes of restoring the stability of the prewar period. They ushered in a period of economic nationalism unprecedented even during the heyday of mercantilism. The traumatic shock to domestic and international economic institutions produced by the Great Depression was probably matched only by the mass psychological depression in its wake. The world of the 1930's was a world poised on the brink of revolution—economic, social, and political. Millions were unemployed, the economic plant of most countries was stagnated, and politicians and statesmen alike groped blindly for solutions to mounting problems. The natural reaction of most leaders was to protect the national economy from foreign competition and to open up bigger foreign markets to absorb the growing surpluses resulting from insufficient domestic demand. That these policies of economic nationalism were contradictory made little difference; popular demand for policies of short-range advantage or retaliation could not be resisted.

The multilateral, relatively low-tariff world of the nineteenth century virtually disappeared during the 1930's. Although some semblance of a world market economy continued to function, it was rigidly circumscribed by the neo-mercantilist practices of governments. High tariffs became endemic in all countries; quota restrictions permitting only small amounts of foreign goods to enter the domestic market buttressed high tariff walls in most. Widespread use of currency depreciation to achieve trade advantage was followed by equal or greater depreciations in scores of other states. Subsidies for domestic producers, state licensing of importers, barter agreements, preferential trade arrangements, and exchange control were freely used in desperate efforts to stimulate or protect economic activity. Often such devices provided only a brief stimulus and were bitterly resented by trading partners as "beggar thy neighbor" policies. Retaliation became the guiding principle for state economic policy, growing ever-stronger by feeding on itself. Feeble attempts to arrest the cycle of economic nationalism through world monetary and trade conferences and the American-sponsored reciprocal trade agreements system produced much verbal support but little action for a return of the trading system to its former multilateral basis. The division of labor and free trade postulated by Adam Smith as the basis for national productivity disappeared except as ideals for a future world economy.

REBUILDING THE WORLD ECONOMY—A NEW APPROACH

World War II arrested the trend toward the unilateral determination of economic policies. Under American leadership the allies implemented a system of economic cooperation to facilitate the war effort and laid plans for rebuilding a working multilateral trading system when peace was restored. Unlike the laissez-faire approach used in the nineteenth century, the new liberalized world economy was to be constructed by building regional and global institutions to facilitate reaching agreement on trade, monetary, and investment matters. The new approach offered a compromise between the requirements of a free-trading system and the growing role of government to provide economic stability.

But more was needed than optimism and plans for a bright new world of plenty. At war's end, the old problems created during the era of economic nationalism remained as major hurdles to the reestablishment of a multilateral trading system. Added to them were the newer ones growing out of the devastation and dislocation caused by the war itself. Ideological dangers, too, lurked amidst the chaos and despair of Europe, with the masses fearful of a capitalistic recovery that would return them to prewar days of mass unemployment and general depression. To meet these needs, four areas were identified by planners and programmers as fields for fruitful effort: (1) Economic recovery of Europe and other areas suffering economic deprivation from the war must be assigned the highest priority; (2) global trade must be returned to a rational basis freed of most of the restrictive encumbrances instituted since 1930; (3) regional economic cooperation should be fostered so that critical areas of the world could develop a viable economic unity; and (4) international monetary stability must be achieved through harmonization of exchange rates and expanding international liquidity. A review of twenty years of continuous efforts in the last three categories, and of a relatively brief but intensive postwar recovery effort, will permit an evaluation of how far economic integration has moved the world toward true multilateralism.

RECONSTRUCTION OF WESTERN EUROPE

In the spring of 1945, at the end of World War II, the economic plant of Europe was moribund. Heavy shelling and bombing had destroyed industrial and transport facilities, power supplies were low, food scarce, raw materials almost nonexistent, and whole populations were dispersed and homeless. The immediate task, the feeding and housing of millions, was directed by the temporary United Nations Relief and Rehabilitation Administration (UNRRA) which expended almost $4 billion, much of it in direct aid to needy and homeless refugees. Slowly and painfully, displaced persons were sorted out and returned to their homelands, trains started running again, and rebuilding campaigns got under way. But the major problem remained: Where would Europe obtain the fantastic amounts of capital needed to restore its economic vitality?

European capital needs in the form of outside help were estimated in the postwar period at $22 billion. Even this sizable figure was underestimated— by 1950 Europe's cumulative deficit with the rest of the world amounted to $24.4 billion, three fourths of it with the United States.[1] Europe's leaders realized already in 1945 the projected size of this "dollar gap" and its implications. Since fantastic amounts of imports were needed and foreign exchange earnings were insignificant, critical measures were obviously needed. Exchange control, licensing, bilateral arrangements, and other protective devices of the 1930's were refurbished to meet the new crisis. Fast action was needed if the world economy was to be kept from returning permanently to the restrictive economic nationalism of the prewar period.

The European Recovery Program

No commencement address ever kindled the spark of hope for millions quite like the one delivered by Secretary of State George C. Marshall at

---

[1] P. T. Ellsworth, *The International Economy* (New York: Macmillan, 1964), p. 429. The European deficits by year were: 1946: $5.8 (billion); 1947: $7.4; 1948: $4.9; 1949: $3.8; and 1950: $2.5. Ellsworth lays the blame for Europe's huge deficit on two factors: inflation and "structural changes" resulting from the war.

Harvard University in June, 1947. Marshall called for a massive injection of American aid into Europe, both Western and Eastern, but before the assistance would be granted Europe must reach agreement on the amount of aid required and what each participating state could contribute to the common effort. The Soviets rejected the offer to include Eastern Europe in the program [2] and attacked it as a policy of political interference and economic imperialism. American policy makers then began to push the concept of an integrated Western Europe which could not only restore economic viability to the region but build political stability and military defense capability on the new economic base. At a major conference called in the summer of 1947 in response to American initiatives, sixteen West European countries worked out a plan for joint recovery, formed a Committee of European Economic Cooperation (CEEC) to determine individual capital needs, and agreed to cooperate in the reduction of barriers to trade and the free movement of labor. From this impetus emerged a European integration movement which was to attain unprecedented objectives of economic and political unity in an area that for centuries had exuded mutual suspicion and hostility through a carefully nurtured nationalism.

The following year the cooperating sixteen nations [3] established the Organization for European Economic Cooperation (OEEC) to provide the means for implementing the Marshall Plan and to progress toward building a sound European economy. Stimulated by a growing intraregional trade and over $10 billion in direct American aid, the participating European states had by 1951 achieved a production level 35 per cent above their average output in 1938. To facilitate the expansion of intra-European trade, the OEEC established the European Payments Union (EPU) in 1950 to provide for a common system of payments among its members. The arrangement worked so well that by the late 1950's full convertibility of OEEC currencies was achieved.

The full extent of European recovery began to be realized after 1956 when the balance of payments took a favorable turn for Europe. The "dollar gap" changed suddenly but decisively to a "dollar surplus" for Europe, a trend which acquired a look of permanency in the 1960's and became the most pressing problem of American foreign economic policy. Increasing competition in the American market from revitalized European industry revived some of the old demands for greater tariff protection in the United

---

[2] Countries that were invited but refused to participate in the Marshall Plan included Albania, Bulgaria, Czechoslovakia, Finland, Hungary, Poland, Romania, the Soviet Union, and Yugoslavia.

[3] Initial membership in OEEC included Austria, Belgium, Denmark, France, Greece, Iceland, Ireland, Italy, Luxembourg, the Netherlands, Norway, Portugal, Sweden, Switzerland, Turkey, and the United Kingdom. Western Germany first participated unofficially and became a member when granted independence by the Allied occupation forces.

States Congress, confirming that the European Recovery Program had attained its basic objective. The successful application of the new institutional approach in lifting Europe from despair to prosperity augured well for its future potential. The question remained, however, whether the United States would continue to give its unstinting support to liberalizing the world economy once the immediate threat of Communism in Western Europe had receded and the recovered countries became sharp competitors for world markets.

THE ATTACK ON TRADE RESTRICTIONS

The early success of the common effort to secure the recovery of Western Europe raised hopes that the postwar period might be an appropriate time to launch a major offensive against tariffs and other barriers to trade. Tariffs have a depressing effect on world living standards because they violate basic economic principles. An international division of labor with its resulting specialization—the key to higher standards of living in all states —is negated by the artificial restrictions of tariffs which encourage the development of noncompetitive industries and distort the direction of trade. Tariffs are a tax on goods which is paid ultimately by the consumer, thereby giving him less for his money, restricting his freedom of choice, and forcing him to reduce his consumption of protected articles. Although the intellectual argument favoring free or freer trade is irrefutable, tariffs and other restrictive devices have been common trade practices for centuries. Tariffs are sometimes justified as a revenue measure, as an inducement for new industry, as an equalizer to safeguard infant industry, as a means of improving a nation's adverse terms of trade, as a measure to reduce unemployment, as a useful bargaining tool to obtain concessions, or as a device for sustaining industries essential to national defense. The most compelling purpose has always been the pragmatic one of protection of the home market for domestic producers.

Psychological factors have often been more decisive than economic considerations in state decisions to increase barriers to trade. It was this problem of changing popular attitudes about "protectionism" that presented the most difficult obstacle to proponents of freer trade in the postwar era. The architects of an orderly and relatively free trading system recalled how irresistible public pressures in the United States following the stock market crash in 1929 had forced the enactment by Congress of the Smoot-Hawley Tariff of 1930 with its viciously high protective rates. They remembered, too, how that American action had the effect of "exporting" the depression to other countries in the trading system when it touched off worldwide retaliation, resulting in a cycle of deepening restrictionism powered by fear, rising nationalism, and deteriorating domestic conditions. Once these powerful forces of economic nationalism had been unleashed, it was recognized, it would be difficult if not impossible to close the floodgates. To prevent a recurrence of the 1930 tragedy, two needs became obvious: one, to establish a world trading organization that would provide an orderly, systematic means by which states could carry on their trading activities and devise common policies; and two, to foster a cycle that would move the trading world toward freer commercial conditions.

ITO—An American Cul-de-sac

The United States took the initiative in promoting the first objective of a world trade organization by working out a preliminary blueprint for the organization and circulating these ideas in a pamphlet entitled, "Proposals for Expansion of World Trade and Employment." After preliminary conferences in London and Geneva, a final draft Charter for the International Trade Organization (ITO) was worked out at the United Nations Conference on Trade and Employment at Havana in 1948. The Havana Charter represented the most extensive attack ever attempted on barriers to trade. Like the Bank and the Fund, the new ITO was to function as a specialized agency within the overall framework of the United Nations. The major principles embodied in the complex 106-article Charter dealt with the four problem areas of

1. *Commercial policy*, by which members would agree to reduce their tariffs, to eliminate all preferences and other barriers to trade, to curtail discrimination in trade policies, and to refrain from using governmental subsidies as a means of gaining trade advantage;

2. *Commodity agreements*, which would permit member states under ITO rules to enter into agreements providing for an orderly production and marketing of those primary commodities subject to wide fluctuations in supply and prices, but allow for exceptions by underdeveloped states subject to ITO veto;

3. *Restrictive business practices*, by which member governments would agree to encourage domestic policies favorable to freer international trade, including the restraint of public and private cartels and monopolies and the development of fair labor standards; and

4. *Full employment policies*, by which each member would agree to take action to achieve and maintain full employment and to encourage an expanding demand by measures appropriate to its political, economic, and social institutions.

After the Charter was drafted, battle lines were drawn in the struggle over ratification between the forces of protectionism and liberal trade advocates. An American trade expert who had participated in the writing of the Havana Charter warned:

The ITO is recognized everywhere as an American project. Our country brought the rest of the world along on it, step by step, over a period of five years. If we were now to abandon it, as we abandoned the League of Nations a generation ago, there is small chance that the world could seriously consider another such program proposed by the United States for years to come.[4]

This warning and many others went unheeded. The State Department, after converting most world leaders to the ITO ideal, failed to get its message across to the Senate. The old fear that American producers might not be able to compete effectively in a free world market with low-wage producers abroad was exploited by lobbyists and pressure groups in a massive trek to Washington. Other groups attacked ITO as a Communist plot (despite the fact that Communist states had refused to participate in the ITO Conference) and as an organization that would weaken American sovereignty. These arguments carried the day in Congress. Other nations, cognizant that an ITO without the United States would be like an arch without a keystone, refused to ratify the Charter in numbers necessary to put it into effect. Some years later the Eisenhower administration sought to recapture the spirit of Havana by proposing an Organization for Trade Cooperation, but Congress recognized that a thorn by any other name would be just as prickly for local interests and let the OTC idea die aborning. The first major effort to establish an institutional basis for trade cooperation had fallen victim to America's fumbling efforts to provide leadership in the postwar world without encumbrances.

GATT—An Innovation Succeeds

While early negotiations for the anticipated ITO were going on, many nations urged an immediate attack on trade barriers through an *ad hoc* conference that would function as a stopgap arrangement until ITO came into operation. Meeting in Geneva in 1947, twenty-three nations worked out a vast number of bilateral tariff concessions which were written into a final act called the General Agreement on Tariffs and Trade (GATT).

The Conference was an adaptation of the reciprocal trade agreement system inaugurated by Secretary of State Cordell Hull in 1934 and subsequently implemented by most of the world's trading nations. That program provided for bilateral negotiations on a selective product-by-product basis, with all tariff reductions based on the principle of reciprocity. Agreements reached through bilateral bargaining sessions were embodied in trade agreements incorporating the most-favored-nation clause, thus making lower tariff rates applicable to all other nations participating in the program as

[4] Clair Wilcox, *A Charter for World Trade*, (New York: Macmillan, 1949), p. 214. This volume is the most thorough piece of analysis on the Havana Charter. It contains the Charter with Annexes and Interpretive Notes in the Appendix.

well as the two (most favored) nations that signed the agreement. This application of the nondiscriminatory, most-favored-nation approach made it an outward-looking program aimed at rebuilding a liberal trading system as a base for restoring depression-battered national economies. Although numerous trade agreements had been concluded before 1947, tariffs remained generally high and a speeded-up approach was clearly called for to overcome the hiatus of the war period. The GATT Conference was the means selected for accelerating the program by providing for multilateral participation in a series of simultaneous bilateral bargaining sessions.[5]

The failure of the ITO gave impetus to the GATT approach and led to the establishment of permanent international machinery. GATT's role has been progressively expanded after 1947 and it now serves four major purposes:

1. It is a forum for negotiations on tariff reduction and the progressive elimination of other barriers to trade.
2. It functions as a vehicle for developing and articulating new trade policy.
3. It provides a set of rules which govern the conduct of trade policy.
4. It offers the means for interpreting rules and procedures for the adjustment of trade disputes.

Since its initial effort in 1947, GATT has sponsored major rounds of negotiation in 1949, 1951, 1956, 1960–61, and 1964–65. Its membership by 1966 had reached sixty-six full contracting parties with thirteen additional countries associated with the organization on a limited basis. Together, the members carry on more than 80 per cent of total world trade, leading some non-members to refer to it as "the rich man's club." [6]

GATT's most successful innovation has been that of bringing third countries directly into the negotiating process to overcome the reluctance of nations to grant bilateral reductions under the most-favored-nation clause. Formerly, states which entered into an agreement bilaterally granted concessions automatically to others from whom they received nothing in return. This situation led GATT to foster *multilateral negotiations* in recent years as a step beyond its earlier conferences in which it had provided for *multilateral participation* but strictly *bilateral negotiations*. The new approach has encouraged concessions and substantial tariff cuts.

The rule against discrimination for imports and exports is proclaimed to

---

[5] At Geneva, 123 bilateral talks were held over a period of six months in which tariff reductions were considered on 50,000 items of commerce. The United States engaged in twenty-two bilateral sessions, one with each participating country. The results of all these negotiations were incorporated in a single document, the General Agreement on Tariffs and Trade, and all concessions became applicable to each of the twenty-three members of the group.

[6] The influx of Asian and African nations into the organization in recent years has resulted in a proportion of approximately two-thirds developing states to one-third advanced. Only three Communist countries—Cuba, Czechoslovakia, and Yugoslavia—are members of GATT.

be the hub of the GATT wheel. Tariffs, quantitative restrictions, and other barriers to trade must be administered under GATT rules without favor except for established systems of preference. New systems aimed at establishing complete preference—a customs union, common market, or free trade area—are permitted only if their basic purpose is "to facilitate trade between the constituent territories and not to raise barriers to the trade of other . . . parties." This leaves only new, partial systems of preferences absolutely outlawed under the GATT rules. The exceptions clearly weaken the principle of nondiscrimination, and GATT has fought endless rear guard actions to prevent their broad interpretations.

Originally concerned only with tariffs, GATT's rules today are also directed toward limiting the use of quantitative restrictions in imports. Import quotas are more rigid barriers to trade than tariffs; a tariff is a tax that increases the price for the consumer whereas a quota permits only a fixed number of imports regardless of consumer demand. Exceptions to the general rule against import quotas include (1) those states suffering from a serious deficit in their balance of payments, (2) developing countries fostering economic advancement, and (3) states which restrict domestic production and marketing of agricultural and fishery products. Because these exceptions include almost all GATT members (including the United States for the first and third exceptions), emphasis is placed on a requirement for consultation with GATT or the International Monetary Fund prior to the imposition of quotas by any state.

Probably the most useful function performed by GATT is that of helping to resolve disputes over alleged infractions of its trading rules. In reviewing the period of the 1930's, the lesson that is burned indelibly into the pages of economic history is that retaliation that touches off a spiral of increasing protectionism is the greatest danger to a liberal trading system. With the past as a guide, every complaint brought to GATT over a violation of rules is treated as a grave matter. Disputing parties are first urged to settle their disagreement bilaterally; failing this, the aggrieved party may take the matter to a special GATT panel which, in consultation with the parties, hears the issues and makes a recommendation. If the offending state fails to abide by the panel decision, then, and only then, the complaining state may retaliate by withdrawing a concession. The resolution of numerous disputes and the absence of major trade wars testify to the effectiveness of these settlement procedures.

THE "KENNEDY ROUND." The formation of an economic union by the Treaty of Rome in 1957 presented a formidable challenge to GATT and an ominous threat to many of its members. The European Economic Community (EEC) composed of six continental countries (Belgium, the Netherlands, Luxembourg, France, West Germany, and Italy) provides for the abolition of all internal tariffs among its members and the erection of a common outer tariff wall. A common market arrangement of this kind is discriminatory by its very nature. A British businessman selling his product in the French market, for example, may find that the price for his wares is uncompetitive with a similar product sold in France by a German businessman, since the British price to the consumer would include the duties paid on each article.

President John F. Kennedy recognized that, even though it was a logical capstone to American efforts to encourage European integration, the EEC nevertheless had become a serious threat to both American trade with the continent and to the building of a liberal trading system. He decided on a strategy of using the appeal of a wide-open American market as a bargaining weapon to tear down the tariff wall surrounding the EEC. To turn the Common Market from an "inward-looking" to an "outward-looking" policy, he needed lots of bargaining power. Congress obliged by enacting the most liberal tariff act in American history. The major provisions of the Trade Expansion Act of 1962 authorized the President

1. To reduce most U.S. tariffs by 50 per cent and to eliminate those of 5 per cent or less.

2. To negotiate on an across-the-board basis (i.e., a flat rate percentage reduction applying to all tariffs of a certain class) rather than on a product-by-product basis.

3. To negotiate reductions on tropical products exported by developing countries (aimed at wooing the support of the eighteen African countries associated with the EEC).

The President's power to terminate trade concessions was continued, but the Act permits him to invoke the "escape clause" only to avoid "genuine hardship." Armed with the new tariff-cutting power, American negotiators began their attack on the EEC redoubt in the GATT negotiating session of 1964, widely heralded as the Kennedy Round.

Although some tariff cuts were effected, performance failed to measure up to anticipations in 1964, and the Kennedy Round of that year turned into the Kennedy Round of 1965 GATT negotiations, followed by more of the same in 1966. The Trade Negotiations Committee of GATT, which carries on spadework negotiations betwen major conferences, has so far failed to find a formula to break the deadlock. The reasons for the failure of the Kennedy Round to achieve its objectives are mainly economic. For one thing, the American goal of a linear across-the-board cut of 50 per cent of all tariffs is regarded as too steep by some EEC members, especially France which prefers at best a 30 per cent reduction. Europeans also express concern about "tariff disparities," noting that although American and EEC tariffs on manufactured articles are about equal, many extremely high American tariffs are concealed by the average. The highest American tariffs, Europeans have noted, are those protecting key articles of commerce, and a reduction of these from, say, 60 per cent to 30 per cent would still leave the items well protected. The across-the-board "shortcut" to general tariff reductions of industrial items was thus in effect vetoed by the insistence of Common Market negotiators to bargain on the basis of "exception lists." Each exception under GATT rules must be justified as basic to national economic health, a proviso that has created much concern about chimerical threats to national economies and dubious contributions to freer trade in the past.

The major hurdle to tearing down the Common Market's high external tariff has been the failure to reach agreement on a common agricultural policy between the EEC and the rest of the world. Because farmers exercise political power far out of proportion to their numbers in EEC states, elaborate systems of governmental subsidies and protective devices had been built into their domestic policies. Since 1966, these discriminatory policies have been harmonized by setting up a common EEC agricultural fund to provide joint subsidies. EEC policy since 1962 has also provided that demand for agricultural products be met first by domestic production, then by imports from EEC countries, and, finally, by nonmember imports to meet the remaining unsatiated demand. The EEC has also offered a plan for GATT consideration that would freeze the margin of governmental support for domestic agriculture in every country in the world. Under this proposal, each country would relate its tariffs on farm products to its margin of support (*montant de soutien*) so that if the world price fell below this reference point, it could increase its tariff accordingly. Obviously, such a policy is incongruent with GATT's efforts to open up the continental market by freeing it of discriminatory trade practices.

Other factors have helped stiffen the resistance of continental negotiators to substantial tariff cutting despite voluminous lip service paid to the ideal of a multilateral trading world. The protection offered domestic producers by the Common Market has contributed to a wave of prosperity that has engulfed its membership. The EEC's external tariff has also led many foreign businessmen to establish subsidiaries in Common Market countries to assure continued access for their companies to the huge continental market. This vast inflow of private capital has helped prolong the boom, maintain full employment, and foster economic growth. Added to the congeries of economic factors is a political contest for leadership of continental Europe waged between France and the United States. The Franco-American split and growing European polycentrism make an economic rapprochement between the Common Market and the outside world an ever more fleeting possibility.

For two thirds of GATT's members, the most important facet of the Kennedy Round is not the effort to open the Common Market to freer trade but the campaign to secure a reduction of trade barriers for the exports of developing countries. In these negotiations the developing countries have requested that the usual GATT practice of *quid pro quo* or reciprocity in all tariff cuts be moderated so that infant industries unable to compete on equal terms could continue to be protected in developing economies. The developed countries have agreed only to require something less than "full" reciprocity from the developing states in return for their tariff reductions on primary commodity imports. Developing states, especially those of Africa, also seek the lifting of tariff barriers on all tropical products since they do not compete directly with those produced in most advanced states. Agricultural interests in the advanced states, however, have demanded that this question be considered as an integral part of agricultural trade policy. Like the efforts to tear down the Common Market tariff wall, the developing states' plan to destroy all barriers to their export markets through new GATT policies ran head on into powerful, vested agricultural interests. The educational experience probably proved more valuable than the minor policy changes obtained. Nevertheless, the effort continues.

THE FUTURE OF GATT. In the midst of stalemated negotiations during the Kennnedy Round, GATT met in special session in 1965 and adopted three amendments to the General Agreement. All three were enunciations of new principles aimed at changing its focus from "the rich man's club" to that of a "war on poverty." The influence of the growing number of developing states' members was reflected in the establishment of a new permanent Committee on Trade and Development which relates GATT's objectives more closely to fostering economic development (see Figure 16-1).

Despite the prolonged impasse in Kennedy Round negotiations, GATT's expanded membership and broadened scope of interests have helped it to remain a vigorous and useful tool for achieving freer trade. Tariffs have been cut significantly over its almost twenty-year period of operations and many other once-malignant barriers to trade have been excised from state policies. A degree of orderliness in tariff rate-setting and an acceptance of trading rules unprecedented for such a sizable portion of the world community overshadow its failures to eliminate trade discrimination and unfair business practices. GATT's objective has never been to eliminate all tariffs but only to encourage *freer* trade and the acceptance of rules to systematize trade practices and harmonize trade policies. Progress toward these limited objectives has been steady and sturdy since 1947. The ITO ideal, rejected at the front door, has been permitted to sneak in through the back door so that today the broad institutional framework anticipated by ITO's sponsors has come close to full realization.

A New Global Approach—UNCTAD

A new organization in the field of international trade, the United Nations Conference on Trade and Development (UNCTAD), owes its existence at least partially to GATT's pre-UNCTAD policies of relative exclusivity. The idea of a new world trade organization started with a developing nations' resolution adopted by the General Assembly at its Sixteenth Session in 1961

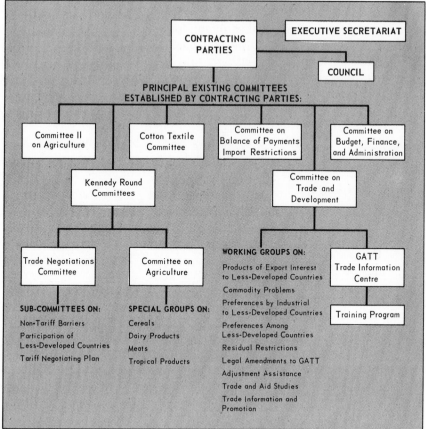

FIGURE 16-1. General Agreement on Tariffs and Trade (GATT). [*Source: "Issues Before the Twentieth General Assembly,"* International Conciliation, No. 544, September, 1965.]

calling upon the Secretary-General to make preliminary plans for an international trade and development conference. Debated extensively in the Economic and Social Council, the proposal grew out of the exasperation and frustration of the developing nations' failure to breach the defenses of the developed states' restrictions on commodity trade. With a battle cry of "export or die," the trade conference was pushed by the Assembly majority with such determination that the opposition of seventeen advanced nations that had objected to it because it duplicated GATT's work was finally overcome.[7]

[7] See "Issues Before the Eighteenth General Assembly," *International Conciliation,* No. 544 (September, 1963), pp. 147–53. The developing states argued in the Assembly for holding a trade conference at an early date because (1) primary commodity prices are declining; (2) high tariff barriers in the developed states need to be reduced; (3) GATT does not meet the needs of most developing states; (4) regional groups like EEC discriminate against states not associated with them; and (5) intensive study and debate of the problem would help eliminate trade barriers in all states.

In one of the largest international meetings ever held, the United Nations Conference on Trade and Development met in Geneva for three months in the spring of 1964. The fact that over two thirds of the 120 delegations represented developing states was reflected in the composition of agenda topics: [8]

1. Expansion of international trade and its significance for economic development.
2. International commodity problems.
3. Trade in manufactures and semi-manufactures.
4. Improvement of the invisible trade of developing countries.
5. Implications of regional economic groupings.
6. Financing for an expansion of international trade.
7. Institutional arrangements, methods and machinery to implement measures relating to the expansion of international trade.

In addition, the Conference's Preparatory Committee dusted off a sixteen-year-old idea and proposed that the Conference "set up a completely new specialized agency, a United Nations International Trade Organization, on the basis of universal membership." To many members, GATT was an instrument of cold war policy and unfitted to meet the needs of the developing states; ergo, a new forum and set of rules for removing trade barriers was needed. Conference objectives were brought into still sharper focus by a scholarly background paper prepared by Raul Prebisch, Secretary-General of UNCTAD.[9]

From a policy point of view, the Conference objectives of developing states can be summarized as an effort to pressure the developed states into accepting a liberal trade policy as the best means for promoting economic development. As noted in the preceding chapter, the industrialized states prefer programs of technical assistance and loans as the means for fostering development. They object to increased imports from developing states because of the impact on their domestic economies and because of the very low wages paid in the developing world. This viewpoint overlooks the basic comparative cost rationale for international trade. Imports and exports exist simply because countries have advantages in producing particular articles of commerce. If costs were equalized in all states, international trade would become an irrelevancy. If each state refused to trade with another because its labor was cheaper or its general costs were lower, obviously no trade would take place in the world. Moreover, the high productivity of labor in the advanced states tends to equalize costs with the low-wage countries. The developing states take the position that since the advanced states have professed a willingness to help them develop, why not give this help in the form of liberalized trade opportunities rather than aid?

[8] United Nations Document E/Conference 46/PC/12/Addendum 2, May 24, 1963.

[9] Raul Prebisch, *Towards a New Trade Policy for Development,* United Nations Publication Sales No. 64. II. B. 4, 1964.

The developing countries recognized that to secure economic concessions political muscle was needed. Consequently, most functioned within a voting bloc at the Conference that came to be known as the "Caucus of the Seventy-Five." Regional caucuses and informal contact groups supplemented the major caucus. Their political unity made some concessions from the advanced nations almost inevitable.

The Final Act of the Conference represented three months of committee sessions, speeches, negotiations, and what some of the disillusioned delegates from Asia and Africa referred to as the "deaf man's dialogue" between developing and developed states. Yet the final document also represented a signal victory for the developing states even though no major liberalization of trade was the immediate result.

First, the Final Act contained a set of principles setting forth the economic and social development of developing countries as the first concern of international economic relations. Realization of the principles is to be secured through (1) an increase in export earnings; (2) a stabilization of primary commodity prices; (3) the attainment of a new specialization based on an international division of labor; and (4) the extension of the most-favored-nation principle to developing states without reciprocity. These principles represent a political victory for the developing-state bloc; however, the problem remains: Can the developed states be persuaded to apply the principles in future negotiations? By 1966, the question remained unanswered.

Second, the Final Act recommended that UNCTAD be established as a permanent organ of the General Assembly, that it be convened at least once every three years, and that its purpose be "to promote international trade, especially with a view to accelerating economic development. . . ." The Nineteenth General Assembly in 1964 accorded UNCTAD permanent status to function as a center for harmonizing trade and development policies of countries and regional groupings, as a coordinator between the Assembly and ECOSOC, and as an initiator of multilateral trade policies.[10] Although neither the Final Act nor the Assembly resolution made mention of it, UNCTAD's main purpose will be to serve as a means for the developing states to exert pressures upon the advanced states to relent in their restrictionist policies.

Third, the Final Act urged and the Assembly acted to establish a fifty-five-member Trade and Development Board to function as a developer of policy between UNCTAD sessions. Like the Conference, the developing states have a voting majority on the Board, although the "principal trading states" are represented on it so that pressures can be applied continuously.

Fourth, the Final Act also called for the establishment of a permanent

---

[10] General Assembly Resolution 1995 (XIX) December 30, 1964.

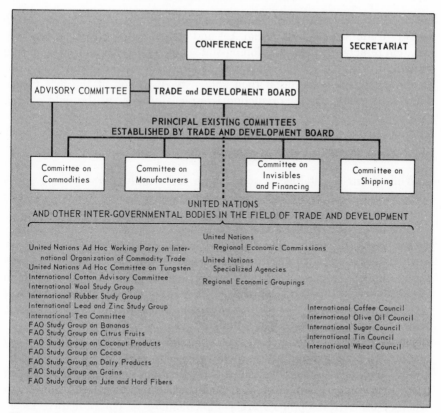

FIGURE 16-2. United Nations Conference on Trade and Development (UNCTAD). [*Source: "Issues Before the Twentieth General Assembly," International Conciliation, No. 554, September, 1965.*]

secretariat "within the United Nations Secretariat." The first Secretary-General of UNCTAD, Raul Prebisch, was appointed by Secretary-General U Thant and confirmed by the General Assembly. After lengthy debate over whether the headquarters of the secretariat should be located in Geneva or New York, the Trade and Development Board unanimously selected the European Office of the United Nations at Geneva. Those preferring New York had regarded the coordination of the UNCTAD Secretariat with the UN Secretariat of highest priority, but other members argued that the Geneva location would give it a proximity to the headquarters of other trade and economic organizations which would prove more useful.

UNCTAD clearly represents a *political* victory for the developing states. Neither the Western advanced states nor the Communist bloc ventured to bring their revised proposals for the Final Act to a vote, sensing that defeat was certain. Whether UNCTAD represents an *economic* triumph is less clear, since the advanced countries which carry on 70 per cent of the world's trade accepted the Final Act and the establishment of a new organization reluctantly. The developing-states bloc may reap some sizable trade concessions from their determination to press for better market conditions in the advanced countries if their solidarity displayed at the first Conference remains intact. But prediction is especially risky in the field of trade policy.

Promoting Regional Integration

While plans to establish a sound base for a multilateral trading system through ITO, GATT, and UNCTAD were unfolding, a coterminous regional movement to facilitate trade and economic progress was under way. This second movement has resulted in a spate of new regional organizations, first in Western Europe, then in Latin America and elsewhere. The former are composed of advanced countries seeking means to foster economic growth and broaden the base of their prosperity; the latter are developing countries trying through the fusion of their trade policies to gain a taste of the kind of prosperity accepted as a starting point for the European model. Although contemporary organizations represent different levels of cooperation and integration, they have the common objective of promoting economic well-being through regional unity.

The simultaneous development of organizations fostering the growth of a world trading system and of regional groupings raises the question of whether these developments are complementary or contradictory. Does a regional common market, for example, contribute to world multilateralism or is it frankly a new form of bloc nationalism that hampers world trade? Does the integration of national economies provide a unifying or disintegrating force for the goal of an orderly world economy? Does it foster political unity or rivalry? In sum, are the benefits of regional economic integration local or global, and what, if any, are its disadvantages? These questions will be analyzed and some answers will be suggested, first, by a survey of contemporary regional institutions, and then by an assessment of the objectives and the effectiveness of economic integration.

Economic Regionalism Defined

Regional cooperation on economic matters may range in *participation* from simple bilateralism to a multilateralism which includes most or all states in a geographical area or a group having a common bond of political unity or economic necessity. Each association, whether bilateral or multilateral, may also vary in its *level* of cooperation, that is, the degree to which economies are integrated, and the extent to which common policies are devised. In some associations, common economic policies emerge out of the traditional *quid pro quo* of diplomatic negotiations; in others, common political institutions have been created to formalize and speed up the process of economic decision-making. Using these criteria, economic cooperation on less than a global basis can be divided into five classifications: bilateralism, a preferential system, a free trade area, a customs union, and an economic union.

A *bilateral arrangement* is the simplest form of economic association. Bilateral agreements may involve a simple barter deal in which two states exchange goods, thus obviating the need for foreign exchange. They may also take the form of a clearing agreement in which payments for imports and exports are paid through a single central bank account, or of a payments agreement to include all categories of payments on current account and debt service between the two countries. In the postwar period, most bilateral arrangements were payments agreements, although facilities for multilateral clearances and the abolition of exchange control in many countries has now reduced the need for them. The most common use of bilateral arrangements today is by the Communist-bloc nations in their foreign aid programs. For example, under a bilateral agreement between the Soviet Union and the United Arab Republic, the construction of the Aswan High Dam by Soviet technicians will be paid for by shipments of Egyptian cotton over a period of many years.

Under a *preferential agreement,* members of the "club" offer each other favored trade treatment. Such arrangements usually take the form of a common tariff reduction for all members of the trading group, and the difference in the level of tariff rates for members and nonmembers is called the *margin of preference.* The best-known preferential system is that of the Commonwealth of Nations which through its system of Imperial preference provides for favored tariff treatment among its members on most trade items. Developing states of the Commonwealth are thus accorded a preferred position in selling primary commodities in the British market, and Britain's sale of manufactures in these developing states is likewise given partiality. Imperial preference, dating from 1931 when Britain introduced her comprehensive tariff system, is probably the most important single factor cementing today's multiracial Commonwealth together. Other preferential arrangements include France's trade relations with her former colonies and an American-Philippine agreement for favored treatment. Under GATT's rules for trade conduct, however, *new* preferential agreements are prohibited because of their discriminatory nature, and existing arrangements may not increase the margin of preference without GATT approval.

A *free trade area* goes a step beyond a preferential system by eliminating all tariffs and other impediments to trade among participants. Each member, however, retains its own tariff rates with the rest of the world. The European Free Trade Association (EFTA), for example, provides for the progressive elimination of all industrial tariffs and trade barriers among its eight participating members while permitting each to pursue whatever trade policies it wishes with nonmember states.

A *customs union* provides for a free trade area and for a common external tariff on imports from nonmember countries. Under this arrangement, import duties may be collected centrally and divided among members of the customs agreement. Ordinarily, the uniform external tariff rates are based on the average of pre-union individual rates, which means that the level of tariff protection for some members will be increased. Historically, customs unions were precursors to the political unification of such nations as Germany and Austria-Hungary. In the contemporary world, the Benelux customs union serves as an example of the application of the device to three small, adjacent countries.

Except for political federation, an *economic union* offers the highest level of integration. Besides establishing a customs union, an economic union provides for the free internal movement of labor and capital and for the consonance of certain fiscal and monetary policies. Members operate their economies and carry on their trade behind a common tariff wall which can be raised or lowered only through common consent. Some harmonization of general economic and social policies may also occur, especially in those areas affecting industry, agriculture, and trade. Political institutions which provide the means to reach agreement on internal matters and trade policy are almost a *sine qua non* for an economic union. Ultimately, such a union may adopt a common currency and establish a single central bank. The European Economic Community (EEC) has functioned as an economic union since it became a going concern in 1958.

A Survey of Regional Groups

All of the higher levels of economic integration—the free trade area, the customs union, and the economic union—provide for what may be called a free market. This survey will examine contemporary regional market arrangements in terms of their origins, their objectives, and the institutional machinery each uses to gain consensus.

Some organizations are well along in the process of establishing a free market. These, which will be examined in some detail, include the Benelux customs union, the European Coal and Steel Community (ECSC), the European Economic Community (EEC), the European Atomic Energy Community (Euratom), the European Free Trade Association (EFTA), the Council for Mutual Economic Assistance (COMECON), the Latin American Free Trade Area (LAFTA), and the Central American Common Market (CACM). Other incipient regional market arrangements can be found in Asia and in Africa. The Arab League agreed in 1962 to create an Arab Economic Community within a decade and instituted the first stage of a common market arrangement on January 1, 1965. In Africa, several important regional market groups have emerged. The contemporary East African Common Services Organization (EACSO) has its roots in the East African Common Market (EACM) established in 1922 under British rule in Kenya, Uganda, and Tanganyika. On January 1, 1966, a new Central African Customs and Economic Union (UDEAC) took effect. Its five members (Cameroon, Chad, Central African Republic, Congo-Brazza-ville, and Gabon) plan for an ultimate full integration of their economies. Finally, many political and military regional groups, such as the OAS, OAU, CENTO, NATO, and SEATO, provide for economic cooperation short of the goal of a common market or free trade area.

BENELUX—AN ECONOMIC EXPERIMENT. Three small countries—Belgium, Luxembourg, and the Netherlands—inaugurated the economic integration movement in Western Europe when their governments signed a customs union agreement in 1944. The agreement anticipated rapid progress to establish a common market followed by a slower evolution into full economic union with a single set of monetary, fiscal, wage, and price policies, and free internal movement of labor and capital.

Within three years after the agreement entered into effect on January 1, 1948, most internal tariffs were abolished and a common external tariff was set up. Despite its early successes, Benelux has been unable to achieve its ultimate goal of economic union. Progress toward that goal is stymied by powerful economic groups in the three countries which refuse to face up to the full implications of competition freed from government's protective mantle. The fear in the Netherlands and Luxembourg of a powerful and rich Belgium dominating the industrial sector of the market, and in Belgium of low-wage competition from the other two, has proved to be a serious stumbling block. Similarly, farmers in Belgium and Luxembourg have demanded that protection against the more efficient Dutch agriculture be continued. The major obstacle, however, is a difference in economic phi-losophy between a Belgian government espousing policies of a limited intervention in the economy, and a Dutch government which believes that managing the economy is its necessary and proper role.

A Benelux treaty for full economic union was signed in 1960. The treaty, however, was aimed more at maintaining some semblance of small-nation bargaining power in the EEC vis-à-vis the three economic giants—West Germany, France, and Italy—than at actual integration. The failure of Benelux to achieve its main objective of economic union over a twenty-year period raises the question of whether full economic integration is ever feasible without a parallel political development. Obviously, economic theories that postulate the advantages of integration cannot win out over the fears and public breastbeating of major economic groups who believe that it would endanger their economic interests. In politics, power is local, and can be exercised in a democratic system only so far as decisions are accepted as legitimate. In the final analysis, economic integration rests almost wholly on the ability of its proponents to conciliate hostile interests and ameliorate conflicts that have little relevance to the economic rationale for integration. Apparently, the keen competition of a common market may produce more irritation than solidarity, more defense of national interest than sense of community interest. The Benelux common market continues to encourage trade among the three, but the spark that kindled the original interest in complete economic union has been snuffed out by the lack of political consensus.

THE EUROPEAN COMMUNITY—AN ECONOMIC MODEL. The failure of the three Benelux countries to achieve economic union has been overshadowed by their integration into a larger economic community with France, Italy, and West Germany. This broader integration movement embraces the European Coal and Steel Community (ECSC), the European Economic Community (EEC), and the European Atomic Energy Community (Euratom). The three communities, although established by separate treaties, overlap in their origins and objectives and have been merged through common decision-making organs into the broader framework of the European Community.

The Emergence of the Community. The postwar movement toward European economic unity began with the creation of a Coal and Steel Community for essentially political reasons. As a policy matter, the initial objective of ECSC was not so much to obtain an increase in coal and steel production as it was to gain a rapprochement between France and Germany and to control the latter's war-making potentiality. But there was also a vision of a greater Europe, prosperous and stable, underlying the decision to experiment in unity. Robert Schuman, the architect of the ECSC Plan, saw in this limited integration scheme the opportunity to prepare the base for a future political union by a pragmatic demonstration of the advantages of economic solidarity. The Schuman Plan recognized that coal and steel represent the major ingredients of military power and industrial might; a fusion of production and trade capacities would have symbolic as well as practical consequences. After three years of planning and negotiating, the Schuman Plan came to fruition in 1952 with the signing of the Treaty of Paris creating the Coal and Steel Community.[11]

[11] For an analysis of the steps leading up to the creation of the Coal and Steel Community and its early objectives, see John Goormaghtigh, "European Community for Coal and Steel," *International Conciliation* (May, 1955). A broader survey of ECSC may be found in William Diebold, *The Schuman Plan* (New York: Praeger, 1959); and, Louis Lister, *Europe's Coal and Steel Community: An Experiment in Economic Union* (New York: Twentieth Century Fund, 1960). Current operations of ECSC and its changing institutional structure, and statistical information related to its operations, are reported in the monthly *European Community* and *European Community Bulletin*, both published by the European Community Information Service, Washington, D.C., and Brussels.

By 1955, the ECSC was pronounced a success—probably prematurely—by its members, and planning was started by an intergovernmental committee of the six nations to prepare the ground for a general common market. Governments and their people alike were goaded on by European leaders—men like Paul-Henri Spaak, Jean Monnet, and Walter Hallstein who viewed integration as a matter of politics more than a matter of business. In March, 1957, only two years after planning was initiated, the six governments signed the Treaty of Rome providing for a gradual elimination of all barriers to trade among themselves and the eventual establishment of a single outer tariff wall. Following ratification by the six parliaments, the EEC became a going concern on January 1, 1958.[12] In 1962, Greece joined the EEC as an associate member and will eventually become a full member. Eighteen African states, former French, Belgian, and Italian colonies, are also linked with the European Community as Associate States by the Yaoundé Convention of 1964.[13]

The motives underlying the creation of the Economic Community emerged from a mixture of economic and political forces and views. The attraction of a continental market free from centuries-old obstructions to commerce was regarded as the simplest rationale and the most obvious advantage and, therefore, the most likely to gain the support needed for ratification. By the late 1950's the advanced nations of the world were caught up in a competitive race to spur economic growth rates. Growth became more than an ideological contest with the Soviets; rapid economic expansion was recognized as a necessary corollary to expanding populations and the cybernetics-automation revolution if a return to the mass unemployment of the 1930's was to be fended off. A recognition that sophisticated economies expand largely in response to growing demands for products led to the development of economic theories and proposals for stimulating purchasing power by broadening markets. Thus, the Economic Community with a common market as its central focus was viewed as a logical means for creating a vastly increased demand which in turn would stimulate an upswing in the economic growth rates of member countries. The objectives of full employment and higher standards of living would be realized as a direct result of freer and broader markets and the increase in economic activity they would produce.

Other motives contributed to making economic integration a reality. All

[12] For a compendium of views on the origins of the EEC and its objectives, see Lawrence B. Krause, ed., *The Common Market* (Englewood Cliffs, N.J.: Prentice-Hall, 1964). For a scholarly analysis of the EEC's role in the broader European picture, see Michael Curtis, *Western European Integration* (New York: Harper and Row, 1965).

[13] The Yaoundé Treaty establishes a free trade area between the Six and the Associated States. The latter include Burundi, Cameroon, the Central African Republic, Chad, Congo (Brazzaville), Congo (Democratic Republic of), Dahomey, Gabon, Ivory Coast, Madagascar, Mali, Mauritania, Niger, Rwanda, Senegal, Somalia, Togo, and Upper Volta. In 1966, Nigeria became the first Commonwealth country to sign an association agreement with EEC.

six members had suffered defeat and occupation during World War II, a war regarded in part as an outgrowth of the economic malaise of the Great Depression. No surer way could be found to prevent a recurrence of that calamity than to harness the economies of the continent to a single economic cart. Together with the Coal and Steel Community, the new common market of the EEC would prevent a resurgence of German nationalism by substituting a new European nationalism for it. By turning German interests westward, the Economic Community might also temper premature demands for reunification and reduce the threat posed by German remilitarization. Others viewed the new association as a means of restoring Europe to its prewar position of power and influence in the world. Separately, none of the six could match the American and Soviet colossi, but jointly they would constitute an economic and political force of consequence. American policy makers lent encouragement to the development of EEC as consonant with the American postwar objective of European unity and self-defense. Finally, the concept of European political unity, though viewed from varying perspectives by the leaders of the continental countries, captured the imagination of the younger generation in all and proved to be a powerful force impelling leaders to overcome their differences and reach agreement.

At Rome, a second treaty was signed creating a third partnership, the European Atomic Energy Community. Although less publicized than EEC, its originators believed that it might in time exceed the other two Communities in its contribution to European well-being. During the negotiation of the Treaties of Rome, the goal of cheap atomic power rivaled the objective of a continental common market in the interest accorded it by the diplomats. Anxiety over future power sources—intensified by dwindling coal resources and an oil shortage in Europe which resulted from the blocking of the Suez Canal during the Middle East crisis of the preceding year—gave a dramatic impetus to the joint development of atomic power. The treaty provided for a coordination of atomic research and development, joint financing of power projects, and a pooling of scientific know-how.

Several significant issues were raised at Rome. A French proposal to give Euratom responsibility for military as well as peaceful atomic development was turned down mainly because of opposition raised by the United States and Britain through NATO channels. France also preferred that atomic development be carried on by the six governments and controlled through a common political organ, but the German demand for private development within a framework of Community promotion and regulation won out. Britain, invited to join Euratom, rejected the offer because it would jeopardize the Anglo-American policy of sharing atomic information and because the British had a significant lead in nuclear technology over the continental countries. On January 1, 1958, Euratom began its operations aimed at ushering the Community nations into the atomic age.

Community Political Organs. The Treaties of Paris and Rome, although unconcerned with general political matters, established three complex *political* organizations for making *economic* decisions for the three Communities. These institutions are in the process of being merged into a single political organization which will make all decisions for a unified Community combining the ECSC, the EEC, and Euratom. Although it may be premature to speak of the European Community as a single entity, the treaties providing for a complete merger are already under consideration, and the process of merging the institutions is well underway. Four major institutions provide the basic political structure for the European Community: The Council of Ministers, the Commission, the Assembly, and the Court of Justice.

The Community's Dual Executive. Three Councils of Ministers were established by the Paris and Rome treaties as high-level bodies to represent directly the views of the six governments. At the same time, three Community executives—the High Authority of the ECSC, and the separate Commissions for the EEC and Euratom—were established as supranational organs to make decisions within each Community, subject to review in most cases by the pertinent Council. This dual-executive system provided a compromise between those member states which wanted to make the Communities into self-contained federations and those which wanted them kept under the control of individual governments. Thus some decisions are made by the Council, some by the Community executives, and some by the Council upon the proposal of the executives. As unification progresses, the scope of decision-making within the latter two categories increases. In the Council some decisions require unanimity, some require a qualified majority through a weighted voting system, and others need only a simple majority of the Six.[14]

In the Treaty of Brussels of 1965, provisions were made for the merging of the executive bodies into a single Council of Ministers and a single Community executive.[15] The projected double executive consists of a six-member Council of Ministers and a nine-member (fourteen-member during the transition period) Commission functioning as executive bodies for the three-in-one European Community.

[14] The Treaty of Rome provides the following voting procedure for the Council of Ministers: "Article 148: 1. Except where otherwise provided for in this Treaty, the conclusions of the Council shall be reached by a majority vote of its members. 2. Where conclusions of the Council require a qualified majority, the votes of its members shall be weighted as follows: Belgium, 2; France, 4; Germany, 4; Italy, 4; Luxembourg, 1; Netherlands, 2."

[15] Although there has been some hesitation on the part of the Benelux countries to ratify the treaty, the new arrangement has generally received the support of the six parliaments. See *European Community*, No. 90, March, 1966 (Washington, D.C.: European Community Information Service), p. 3. The Community has also established a goal of 1967 for the complete merging of the Paris and Rome treaties.

Membership on the Council of Ministers consists of one representative of ministerial rank from each member government, with the actual composition of the Council varying with the issues considered. When, for example, decisions are concerned with farm policy, the Ministers of Agriculture of the six governments constitute the Council. On questions of research and development, Ministers of Science and Education assume the Council seats. In all cases, Council members, unlike Commission members, represent the views of their respective governments.

The Commission functions as a collegiate body and, through its individual members, as administrator of Community operations. Before merger, the Commissions had the following membership: High Authority, 9; EEC Commission, 9; Euratom Commission, 5. An executive secretariat serves the Commission in researching problems and in carrying out the decisions made by the Community. Numerous advisory bodies make studies on pertinent questions of Community policy, reporting their findings to the Commission which in turn makes recommendations to the Council of Ministers. The decision process through the double executive system aims at merging the interests of the Community with those of the member states. The integration of Community institutions and the progressive merging of Community objectives, however, have strengthened the role of the Commission in the decision process. Advocates of European union anticipate the day when a single executive, the European Commission, functions as the top policy organ of a fully integrated European Community.

The European Parliament. Although the original Schuman proposal made no provision for a parliamentary body, advocates of European union pressed for its establishment. As a result, the Coal and Steel Community treaty provided for a Common Assembly but assigned it only the powers to debate and recommend Community policies. The ECSC Assembly was accepted in 1958 by the new EEC and Euratom Communities, enlarged from 78 to 142 members, and given expanded powers and authorized to consider policy matters across the range of the three Communities.[16] In 1962 its name was changed to the European Parliament. The Parliament has no permanent seat, although it holds most of its sessions at Strasbourg so that it can use the facilities of the Consultative Assembly of the Council of Europe. Its Secretariat is located in Luxembourg and most of its committee work is carried on in Brussels.

Delegates to the Parliament are appointed by their national parliaments but the Rome Treaty provides for their future direct election from national constituencies. Most of the prominent members of the parliaments of the

[16] Seats in the Assembly were divided as follows (the ECSC figure is followed by the 1958 enlarged figure): France, 18, 36; Germany, 18, 36; Italy, 18, 36; Belgium, 10, 14; the Netherlands, 10, 14; Luxembourg, 4, 6. Four official languages are used in debates: French, German, Dutch, and Italian.

Six have served in the European Parliament at one time or another. Members are organized into three major transnational political groups—Christian Democrat, Socialist, and Liberal—and several smaller splinter groups which the Gaullists are trying to organize into a fourth force. All of the political groups have a greater degree of voting cohesion than do the national delegations, emphasizing the international character of the Parliament.

Parliamentary sessions include an annual debate reviewing the activities of the Community, special sessions called to deal with pressing issues, and an annual joint meeting with the Council of Europe's Consultative Assembly. Several special sessions have included delegations from the eighteen African states associated with the Community. Presidents of the European Parliament have included such distinguished Europeans as Robert Schuman, Paul-Henri Spaak, and Alcide de Gasperi.

Although the Parliament cannot pass laws or make decisions that bind the Community or its members, it plays a significant role as a consultative organ and as an overseer of Community actions. The Parliament in its regular annual session in January, 1966, for example, debated the issue of Commission powers and majority decision-making which had produced a six-month boycott by France of Community institutions. The near unanimity in the Parliament in condemnation of the French position may have contributed to the understanding reached by the Council of Ministers in the same month to end the boycott and to resume normal Community operations in March, 1966. Major proposals, such as that of merging the three Community executives, have originated in the Parliament. Finally, the Parliament can require written or oral answers to questions presented to the Commission or Council of Ministers and may force the resignation of the Community executive by a two-thirds majority vote of censure. Censure of the executive, however, has never yet been seriously contemplated. The Parliament has consistently been a force pressing for European integration and for a broadening of membership to encompass all of Western Europe or the entire Atlantic Community.

The Court of Justice. The Court of Justice, first established for the Coal and Steel Community in 1952, became the common court for the three Communities in 1958. The Court has seven judges appointed for six-year terms by agreement of the six governments but independent of national control. They sit *en banc* or may form Chambers of three or five judges for special cases noted in the Treaties of Rome. Two advocates-general assist the Court and are charged with presenting "reasoned conclusions" and recommendations on each case. The judges elect the President of the Court and determine its rules of procedure subject to approval by the Council of Ministers.

The Court applies law and equity in fulfilling its basic responsibility of "the interpretation and application" of the Treaty of Paris and the Treaties of Rome. It decides cases that involve disputes between member states and/or Community organs and it has the power to annul decisions made by the Council of Ministers or the Commission. The Court also functions as an administrative tribunal to resolve technical questions arising out of Community regulation of private enterprises. In each case the Court renders a single judgment with no dissenting opinions. Over two hundred decisions have been rendered by the Court, some of which have had a significant impact on the shaping of Community economic policies and the decision process through the interpretation of political and economic clauses in the applicable treaties. In its role of interpreting the constitutions of the Community it functions as a court of last resort, although member governments could reverse its decisions by amending the treaties.

The self-executing provisions of the three treaties have resulted in a complicated relationship between the role of the Court of Justice and that of domestic courts in applying Community law within member countries. National courts must apply the interpretations given to Community law by the Court and other organs of the Community, and, under an interpretation rendered by the Court in 1964, laws enacted by member governments which contravene Community obligations are invalid. The problem remains, however, of securing compliance with this international dictum by national officials and courts. Like the European Paliament, the Court of Justice has become a major force moving the Six toward union by building the foundations of a common European law. Its decisions interpreting treaty provisions represent the highest development of supranationalism because they are final and the consent of member states is not needed. In these operations, the Court of Justice bears a stronger resemblance to the United States Supreme Court than to most international courts.

Community Achievements. Many of the early objectives of the three Communities have been attained and progress continues to be made toward the achievement of long-range goals. Community steel production, a good indicator of general industrial activity, more than doubled over thirteen

TABLE 16-1.   Community Crude Steel Production 1952–65
(million metric tons)

	1952	1958	1961	1964	1965	1952–65 % 65/52
Germany	10.6	26.3	33.5	37.3	37.3	252
France	10.9	14.6	17.6	19.8	19.6	80
Italy	3.6	6.4	9.4	9.8	12.6	250
Netherlands	0.7	1.4	2.0	2.7	3.1	343
Belgium	5.2	6.0	7.0	8.7	9.2	77
Luxembourg	3.0	3.4	4.1	4.6	4.6	53
ECSC	42.0	58.0	73.5	82.9	85.9	105

Source: *European Community*, European Community Information Service, Washington, D.C. (Community statistics).

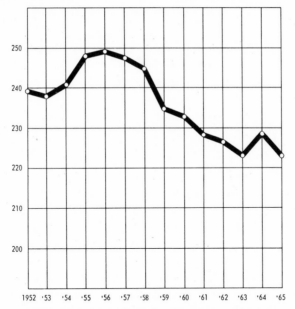

FIGURE 16-3. European Community coal production, 1952–1965 (million metric tons). [*Source:* European Community, *European Community Information Service, Washington, D. C.*]

years of ECSC operation from 1952 to 1965 (see Table 16-1). The retaliatory impact of the general common market arrangement established in 1958, however, has resulted in a 10 per cent decrease in Community steel sales to the rest of the world. Community policies have failed to halt the decline in coal production (see Figure 16-3). Transport costs militate against shipment to distant continental markets, other energy sources have steadily replaced coal,[17] and little modernization of coal-mining machinery has occurred. As coal production slumped in the 1960's, the ECSC inaugurated new programs for retraining superfluous miners and integrating them into the more prosperous sectors of the economy.

The major success of the European Community has been in promoting economic growth and general economic well-being in the countries of the Six. Economists can measure these substantial accomplishments but they may disagree in assigning cause-and-effect relationships. Some, for example, regard the unprecedented prosperity of the Six as a direct result of the

[17] In 1966, the Consultative Committee of the ECSC composed of representatives of Community producers, workers, and consumers recommended to the High Authority that oil, natural gas, and nuclear energy be brought under the same policies as those for coal. These policies deal mainly with the regulation of prices and antitrust action, and the Committee's recommendations were aimed at "saving a sick industry—coal." In 1957, for example, 416 coal mines were operated within the Community; by 1966, only 240 pits remained in operation.

TABLE 16-2. Growth of European Community Trade (1958–64)
(in billions of dollars)

	Exports			Imports		
	1958	1964	Per Cent Increase	1958	1964	Per Cent Increase
Inter-Member Trade	6.86	18.39	168	6.79	18.04	166
Other Trade	15.91	24.16	52	16.16	26.83	66
Total Trade Growth	22.77	42.55	87	22.95	44.87	96

Source: *European Community,* European Community Information Service, Washington, D.C. (Community statistics).

common market and other measures of economic integration; others believe that the success of the EEC stems from general prosperity and a substantial export trade, neither of which resulted from Community actions. While recognizing that other economic forces were working in favor of economic progress since 1958, the achievements of the Community must by any kind of measurement be judged no less than outstanding. Trade among Community states has risen over 150 per cent during the 1958–64 period, contrasted with an increase of only one third of that amount with the rest of the world (see Table 16-2). The total gross product of the Six rose from about $165 billion in 1958 to approximately $305 billion in 1965. Private per capita consumption in the Community was one third higher in 1965 than in 1958, an average annual increase of 4.2 per cent in living standards. These figures can only partially depict the vibrant activity that has characterized the European Community. New policies of joint action or restraint have emerged in almost every major sector of the economies of the Six. The free flow of capital has been encouraged, millions of workers have migrated to labor-scarce areas, a common transport policy has been established, Community multilane highways crossing national frontiers are under construction, common policies to accelerate economic growth have been developed, and trade with the eighteen African Associated States has increased. Atomic research and development have prospered under joint Euratom programs. Duties on industrial goods within the Community were lowered to 20 per cent of their 1957 levels by January 1, 1966, and indications are that they may be eliminated completely by mid-1967, the current objective.

Duties on agricultural products have been reduced by more than 50 per cent, but proposals for further reductions have met stiff resistance and created political crises. In 1966, however, agreement was finally reached on the knotty problem of subsidies for agricultural production and export. A common EEC agricultural fund, financed equally from import levies on farm products and from contributions by member countries, will be used to provide subsidies jointly and will replace former national arrangements.

The agreement, especially favorable for France and the Netherlands, overcame one of the most persistent sources of Community conflict.

But the European Community has also known failure. The French veto of Britain's petition for membership at least temporarily kept the Community limited to the original Six. The rival European Free Trade Association, created as a response to the Community's preferential system, has weakened the market for Community exports to the rest of Europe and has exacerbated the political schism within the European integration movement. The struggle within the Community to develop a common agricultural policy has left some nasty political scars and a residue of ill will among national interest groups. France continues to reject the concept of a supranational organ capable of making decisions by a majority vote binding upon all members. The Community is increasingly forced to bargain with the outside world in GATT and UNCTAD without first resolving some of its own contradictions and without developing a common external policy. Events may be moving too fast for the political machinery of the European Community to cope with them. The development of new common markets and free trade areas in other parts of the world may make the Community aware that it cannot have its cake and eat it—that it cannot, in other words, discriminate against the rest of the world through an internal preferential system while continuing its normal export trade as though nothing had changed.

Whether the European Community is headed toward full economic and political union or toward a hidden disaster and disintegration cannot be foretold. The test of experience is too brief and too mixed with success and failure. The Community and its common institutions do represent, however, the highest degree of integration achieved in the world of sovereign states. The old concept of a European man, of European problems, and of European solutions has been widely accepted ideologically by the man-in-the-street in the countries of the Six. Public opinion is pressing governments to move rapidly toward full economic union. The *functional* nature of the association may now be in the process of changing toward a broader, *political* arrangement.

THE EUROPEAN FREE TRADE ASSOCIATION. Very early in the planning for a European Community, the question of membership for the United Kingdom presented a special problem, both for Britain and for the Community. Britain's worldwide interests, her special arrangements with the Commonwealth, and her close relationship with the United States militated against her joining despite the economic threat posed by the potential loss of the continental market. Moreover, British policy traditionally has been based on maintaining a power balance by preventing continental hegemony. The proposal for a European economic community appeared to British policy makers to be a peaceful means for a revitalized Germany to accomplish what two world wars had prevented. Nor would a Franco-German domination of the continent hold better prospects for long-range British interests. A Western European free trade area would have been acceptable to Britain, but the fuller unity of economic integration embraced by the Treaty of Rome and the objective of eventual political unification proclaimed by the Europeans did not coincide with British national interests.[18]

In the European Community, France has consistently opposed British entry unless the special British relationship with the Commonwealth could be terminated. The main French fear has been that if Britain were accorded a special status, Germany might demand similar concessions and her key role in the continental association might be jeopardized. French aversion to the "Anglo-Americans" and the belief of de Gaulle and other French leaders that France can assume the leadership of a continental group without Britain led to rebuffs of British petitions for membership despite the support of the other five members of EEC for British inclusion.

It was against this background that the seven countries of Europe which favored a free trade area but not a common external tariff met in Stockholm in 1959 and signed a convention that established the European Free Trade Association (EFTA). EFTA members, at once known as the "Outer Seven" (Austria, Britain, Denmark, Norway, Portugal, Sweden, and Switzerland; subsequently, Finland was admitted as an associate member.), agreed in the Stockholm Convention to reduce tariffs and quotas on industrial products progressively until trade could flow freely among all. Although the treaty did not provide for reductions in barriers to trade in farm products and fish, future agreements in these areas were anticipated. Any private or governmental internal measure that would have the effect of vitiating concessions was banned by the Convention. The original target set for the complete elimination of trade barriers among EFTA members was 1970.

EFTA's political structure is much simpler than that of EEC in keeping with its narrower objectives. Decision-making is centered in a Council of Ministers which consists of one representative from each country. The Council serves as a focus for negotiations by the members and all decisions on policy questions must be unanimous. The Council may also review complaints, settle disputes referred to it, and publish reports and recommendations, all by a simple majority vote. Six permanent committees assist the Council in developing trade policies. In addition, a small secretariat of 80 persons headed by a secretary-general is headquartered at Geneva. Al-

---

[18] The eighteen members of the Organization for European Economic Cooperation (OEEC) had engaged in extensive planning for an all-European free trade area during the mid-1950's. These negotiations were broken off in 1958 when it became clear that British and continental interests could not be harmonized, and the six members of ECSC went their separate way.

TABLE 16-3. EFTA Intra-Area Trade 1959–65
(in millions of dollars, rounded figures)

	Imports			Exports		
	1959	1965	Per Cent Increase	1959	1965	Per Cent Increase
Austria	135	313	132	117	294	151
Denmark	531	1,020	92	568	1,059	86
Finland	239	561	135	250	470	88
Norway	484	925	91	328	646	97
Portugal	99	194	96	51	157	207
Sweden	608	1,424	134	816	1,692	107
Switzerland	247	549	122	277	591	113
United Kingdom	1,318	2,189	66	1,115	1,921	72
EFTA Totals	3,661	7,175	96	3,522	6,830	94

Source: *EFTA Reporter* (OECD and National Statistics).

though no assembly has been established, the representatives from EFTA countries to the Consultative Assembly of the Council of Europe meet informally in Strasbourg during annual sessions.

In the beginning, EFTA appears to have had a pronounced success in enlarging trade among its members. Intra-area trade in the six years before the formation of EFTA increased only $1 billion, but in the six years following the creation of the free trade area, trade jumped by over $3 billion, nearly doubling in value from 1959 to 1965 (see Table 16-3).[19] Yet, while these figures are impressive, others make conclusions on the efficacy of the Association uncertain. EFTA's increased trade with EEC countries during the five-year period 1959–64 almost equalled the increases within the bloc, and ironically, one member—the United Kingdom—actually increased its two-way trade with the EEC more rapidly than with its EFTA partners (see Table 16-4). In total, EFTA imports from the EEC increased by 62 per cent in the five years from 1959 to 1964, while EFTA exports to the EEC grew by 65 per cent. The balance of trade between the two groups, however, favors the EEC which in 1964, for example, gained an almost $3 billion surplus which Germany, France, and Italy used to finance their trade deficits with the rest of the world. Although the results of forming rival trading blocs is inconclusive, the evidence over the first six years of simultaneous operations does not indicate that such arrangements have yet had a significant impact upon trade one way or the other. When both reach their ultimate goals—now slated for 1967—of eliminating all internal restrictions on

[19] Recent statistics and discussions of current issues and operations of the Free Trade Association can be found in *EFTA Reporter* published by the EFTA Information Office, Washington, D. C. See also Michael Curtis, *op. cit.*, pp. 238–47; Sidney Dell, *Trade Blocs and Common Markets* (New York: Knopf, 1963), pp. 108–64.

TABLE 16-4.   Changes in Direction of EFTA Trade
(Percentage of total trade of each country)

Exports					Imports			
To EFTA		To Six			From EFTA		From Six	
1959	1964	1959	1964	Country	1959	1964	1959	1964
11.6	18.4	49.1	47.5	Austria	11.7	14.4	57.1	58.8
40.5	46.3	30.4	27.2	Denmark	37.8	38.3	37.8	36.5
38.9	43.1	26.0	26.2	Norway	36.3	40.5	35.1	28.9
17.4	25.1	22.7	20.6	Portugal	20.7	21.4	39.0	33.1
33.7	36.7	31.0	31.6	Sweden	24.4	30.0	41.2	37.4
15.3	18.2	39.9	40.5	Switzerland	12.7	14.7	60.2	62.0
10.2	12.9	14.7	20.6	United Kingdom	9.9	11.3	14.0	16.8
17.9	22.3	23.2	27.0	EFTA	16.2	18.8	28.0	30.3

Source: *European Community,* European Community Information Service, Washington, D.C. (OECD statistics).

trade, the effect on interbloc trade may be more decisive. Also, EEC's goal to establish a common external tariff may seriously curtail continental markets for EFTA countries after 1967.

EFTA's future role depends mainly on policies made at Whitehall. For example, in 1964, Britain imposed a 15 per cent surcharge on all imports as an emergency measure to manage her growing balance of payments deficit. The action was undertaken in cavalier fashion without consultation with EFTA partners and in blunt violation of the Stockholm Convention. The economies of most EFTA members are too closely tied in with Britain's for them to go their own ways. When Britain petitioned for membership in the EEC, other EFTA members did likewise, and when Britain's entry was rejected, the others withdrew their applications. The primary objectives of EFTA—to serve as a bargaining weapon to force concessions from the EEC on trade policies or to pressure it into adoption of an open membership policy—have been unsuccessful. Although both groups have prospered since 1959, the period has been one of unparalleled world trade and prosperity. The real test of the stability of the EEC and EFTA and the question of whether the high level of trade activity between them can continue may await a downturn in economic activity which, as we have already noted, brings out the worst in beggar-thy-neighbor trade policies.

THE COUNCIL OF MUTUAL ECONOMIC ASSISTANCE (COMECON). One of the first European economic groups—the Council of Mutual Economic Assistance composed of the Communist states of Eastern Europe—remained dormant during most of the first decade of its existence. Known by the acronym COMECON or CEMA, the organization was forged in 1949 by Joseph Stalin as an instrument of Soviet control over the Eastern European satellites. COMECON was also a response to what the Soviets regarded as the extension of American hegemony over Western Europe through the Marshall Plan. Politically, it was aimed at keeping the Communist states of Eastern Europe from following Tito's nationalist example in Yugoslavia; economically, it was directed at tying satellite economies to that of the Soviet model through a specialization planned to create economic dependence. COMECON's original members—Bulgaria, Czechoslovakia, Hungary, Poland, Romania, and the Soviet Union—have been joined by Albania (1949), East Germany (1950), and Mongolia (1962).

The institutional machinery of COMECON provided by its Charter is basically that of international organization rather than a supranationalism of the kind found in the European Community. Each member country retains its sovereignty and casts one equal vote. Decisions must be made unanimously, although a member not directly involved in a production or trade arrangement cannot veto the action of other members. The COMECON Council functions as the supreme organ for decision, although decisions are limited to questions of organization and procedure, and on matters of policy only recommendations to member governments can be made. An Executive Committee of permanent, high-level officials implements policies adopted by the Council. The Executive Committee also attempts to function as a coordinator of trade policies, national development plans, and investment programs. Over twenty standing commissions, each related to a specific field of economic activity—coal, agriculture, foreign trade, and so forth—and a secretariat headquartered in Moscow carry on the day-to-day planning and operations.

In practice, COMECON did not have a significant existence under Stalin who preferred the time-tested methods of bilateralism. In 1956, Nikita Khrushchev refurbished it as a hoped-for means of economic control to replace some of the harsher political and police controls of the Stalin era. Each country today still retains responsibility for its own economic plans, and COMECON with its unanimity rule has not been strikingly successful in getting countries to subordinate their national interests to the interest of the group.

Since 1962, however, COMECON has substantially stepped up the pace of its integration efforts. The new burst of activity may reflect an awareness of the success of the European Community and an effort to emulate it, or a growing sense of disillusionment with economic development within the Soviet bloc. At a Council session in 1962, the "Basic Principles of the International Socialist Division of Labor" were proclaimed as the fundamental objective of COMECON. The major problem raised by the integration plan—not unlike the basic hurdle facing capitalist states involved in similar integration schemes—is that of reconciling national economic objectives with the interests of the entire group. The slow growth of intra-COMECON trade and the emergence of economic nationalism in Eastern Europe *within* the bloc highlight the dimensions of the problem. Less-developed members increasingly have refused to accept a specialization that bestows a dominant industrial role upon the Soviet Union and East Germany. The fear of a new political domination by the Soviets—a return to "Stalinism"—and the rivalry of the Sino-Soviet split also limit progress toward economic integration in Eastern Europe. Although surface manifestations of a transformation in the economic life of the Communist countries are apparent, the natural tendency toward autarky of socialist states keeps progress toward economic unity lagging behind the Western European movements.[20]

THE LATIN AMERICAN FREE TRADE ASSOCIATION (LAFTA). A new objective for a regional economic group—to accelerate the rate of economic development in the area—was proclaimed by nine Latin American states in the Montevideo Treaty of 1960. The treaty, which became operational in 1961, established the new Latin American Free Trade Association (LAFTA). LAFTA's nine members—Argentina, Brazil, Chile, Colombia, Ecuador, Mexico, Paraguay, Peru, and Uruguay—account for over 80 per cent of that continent's population, gross product, and trade. The integration scheme was part of a movement fostered by the United Nations Economic Commission for Latin America (ECLA) to spur intra-regional trade as a key to economic growth.

The Montevideo Treaty provides for a gradual liberalization of trade among members through periodic negotiations. The list of items freed of duties and other import restrictions will be progressively expanded so that by the end of a twelve-year period substantially all intra-LAFTA trade will be free. Members also agree to facilitate an "increasing integration and complementarity" in their economic policies so that conditions will emerge to encourage a broader regional economic integration. LAFTA's founders wanted to move toward an arrangement that is less than full economic union but is decidedly more than a free trade area. This goal, however, is seriously jeopardized by the more pragmatic sections of the Treaty which provide for escape clauses, for the renegotiation of tariff cuts that cause injury, and for special treatment for agriculture.

A simplified framework for making decisions is provided by two organs, a Conference of the Contracting Parties and a Standing Executive Committee. The Conference meets annually and determines general policy for LAFTA by a two-thirds vote, although any member may veto a substantive

---

[20] For a discussion of COMECON's objectives and activities, see Andrzej Korbonski, "COMECON," *International Conciliation*, No. 549 (September, 1964). Trade, which is the best yardstick for measuring the degree of economic unity, has consistently reached higher levels in Western than in Eastern Europe. Even before the formation of EEC, countries in Western Europe far exceeded COMECON nations of equal population and per capita income in the amount of foreign trade carried on with countries within the area. This differential has been increased since the Treaty of Rome despite the increased vigor of COMECON in the 1960's.

proposal. The Executive Committee oversees the implementation of treaty provisions and trade policies. Each member is represented on the Committee and a small secretariat of technical and administrative personnel facilitates its supervisory role.

The operations of LAFTA over its first five years do not lend encouragement to the view that a free trade area quickens the pace of development.[21] The bulk of trade among members during the period 1961–66 consisted mainly of an exchange of foodstuffs and other primary commodities, with only negligible amounts of manufactured goods in the trade flow. Argentina has consistently maintained a huge balance-of-trade surplus with other members while Brazil has had an annual deficit of somewhat equal size. These payments disequilibria, however, are not a result of LAFTA because the relative trade position of members has not changed appreciably since 1961. The two least-developed members of LAFTA—Ecuador and Paraguay —and the one most highly developed—Argentina—have enjoyed the smallest percentage increase in intra-LAFTA trade. Although Mexico has increased her trade with LAFTA countries by the largest percentage, it remains of little consequence in terms of total value.

As restrictions are torn down over the next five or six years, a point may be reached in which trade among LAFTA members may suddenly flourish. The difficulty of reaching this point stems mainly from the procedures for reducing trade barriers through almost continuous negotiations. Unlike the EEC and EFTA, there is no schedule for automatic, across-the-board tariff cuts; each reduction is based on a specific agreement which requires an appropriate *quid pro quo*. The wholesale invocation of escape clauses during the first five-year period indicates, too, that a concession once gained may not prove durable.

Perhaps LAFTA's main drawback arises out of the fact that members' economies tend to be competitive rather than complementary. If economic development could proceed to the point where each member of LAFTA specialized in the manufacture of articles in demand in other LAFTA countries, freer trade might be more easily accomplished and longer-lasting. Heavy industry—steel, chemicals, consumer durables—needs the attraction of a large market with a potential for economies of scale and with adequate purchasing power. LAFTA, however, has thus far been singularly ineffective in realizing its major goal—the stimulation of economic development.

THE CENTRAL AMERICAN COMMON MARKET (CACM). A group of small nations in Central America have also accepted economic integration as a means to promote their economic development. In 1960, five countries— Costa Rica, El Salvador, Guatemala, Honduras, and Nicaragua—embarked

[21] For a review and analysis of LAFTA's first five years, see Miguel S. Wionczek, "Latin American Free Trade Association," *International Conciliation*, No. 551 (January, 1965), pp. 29–51.

on a program to establish a customs union in their area within five years and to encourage industrial specialization through an Integration Industries agreement. The 1960 treaty superseded two 1958 agreements that had produced more conflict than unity. The 1960 integration treaty was the capstone of a decade of efforts by the United Nations Economic Commission for Latin America (ECLA) to encourage an economic union in Central America.

Some practical difficulties attended ECLA's efforts to secure economic integration. The economies of the five small states are almost parallel: all depend mainly on the production of primary commodities. The few industries that exist depend almost completely on a local market. Political quarrels and armed conflicts have kept relations strained among the five from the time of their emergence as independent states. Yet, the urge to develop healthy, viable economies proved strong enough to overcome old nationalist animosities and new economic rivalries.

The strategy to promote development recognized first that income from primary commodity sales was limited and unlikely to produce the needed capital. The inelasticity of demand, the tendency toward wild price fluctuations, the inescapable glut and price collapse which result from unilateral attempts to increase production and secure a larger share of the market—all of these hard lessons of experience had shown that expanded income from primary commodity sales was an undeliverable will-of-the-wisp. An alternative approach to economic development, ECLA officials counseled, would be to diversify national economies by industrializing and to reorient their production toward regional consumption. The result forecast by ECLA would be a regional specialization, new employment opportunities, increased national and per capita income with savings invested in new capital, improvement in transport and communication facilities, expanded educational opportunities—in short, the achievement of self-sustaining economic growth and a general movement toward modernization.

The integrated-industries feature of the Central American program is a relatively novel approach to encourage industrialization and specialization. Each member may designate one "integration industry" which is given free access to the entire market. After each country has such an industry, all may designate a second and, subsequently, additional industries for favorable treatment. Although foreign businessmen are opposed to the preferential system, its obvious objective of stimulating locally owned industries is a proper one. Criticism that the system fosters cartel arrangements are answered by pointing to the comprehensive regulations imposed by the five governments to protect the consumer's interest.

Although experience since 1960 indicates that integration does not offer a quick or easy way to economic development, it has shown some promise for the future. New industries have been established and many new jobs created, but for the most part conditions in the five countries remain in their pre-1960 state. Until ECLA's hoped-for social revolution occurs, widespread economic stagnation will remain the order of the day. The danger of political revolution in all member states except Costa Rica provides a shaky political base for further economic integration. Lack of a common currency and inadequate transportation facilities have provided the main economic obstacles to success. Yet, despite its weaknesses, the Central American Economic Integration Program has contributed to regional development and marks the highest level of regional cooperation in that area since members achieved independence more than a century ago. The main question of whether economic integration can contribute to the solution of the problems of economic development remains unanswered, but continuing tests are being carried out in the Central American laboratory. The results, which may have a significant impact on many developing countries, should provide a fuller evaluation by 1970.

Why Regional Integration?

Governments representing several hundred millions of people in Western and Eastern Europe and in Latin America have applied theories of economic integration in their efforts to solve common economic problems through various levels of regional organization. Although each of these experiments in integration has indigenous characteristics, they are all aimed at promoting *national* welfare through *regional* cooperation. The common denominator among diverse approaches used in the integration movements is the creation of a free trade area. Each one of the five integration schemes examined has established "free trade among members" as its fundamental objective. Difficulties in moving beyond that point, however, tend to increase at a progressive rate and a parallel political understanding is usually necessary to pave the way to higher integration goals.

Whatever the level of unity, the economic integration movement is a well-established contemporary phenomenon. Despite its growing popularity, the question might be asked, Is it really a useful economic approach? This question is extremely difficult to answer with any degree of certainty because it is too early in many cases, and in others empirical evidence is confused by crosscurrents of social, political, and economic forces that make it difficult to draw definite conclusions. Nevertheless, some kind of analysis is in order. The most apparent advantages of regional economic integration include

1. *Increased trade*—trade among members will normally expand as the barriers that prohibit it, make it difficult, or make it too costly are reduced or eliminated.

2. *Lower costs*—the cost of production may decrease if free internal movement of labor and capital is encouraged.

3. *Greater specialization*—a freer market will encourage a division of labor and a consequent specialization.

4. *Increased investment*—investment may be spurred by the mobility of capital and labor and by the expanded demand of a larger market.

5. *Expanded production*—a freer and larger market with close economic ties among members will tend to stimulate production to fill a larger demand.

6. *Monetary stability*—balance of payments disequilibria with outside nations may be ameliorated by increased trade within the market. Ultimately, a common currency could resolve most monetary and exchange problems among members.

7. *Greater efficiency*—more highly competitive conditions within the free trade area may result in greater efficiency and higher productivity. Economies of scale from larger production units may result from the expanded market.

8. *Improved terms of trade*—the elimination of artificial barriers to trade within the market area may have the effect of evening out the price exchange ratio among members. In the trade relations of members with nonmembers, domestic competition may result in lower consumer prices for imports and, hence, improved terms of trade.

9. *A better bargaining position*—members as a bloc may substantially increase their bargaining power in tariff negotiations.

To this list, functionalists might add that regional economic arrangements may serve as a base for building political integration. A regional market's institutional machinery, its harmonization of economic policies, and the spillover effect of its successes may help to create an awareness within the region of the advantages of the integrative process. COMECON, for example, is an obvious effort by Soviet leaders to promote political solidarity and gain ideological advantage by advancing the economy of each member and by giving Communism a good image. The EEC serves the political as well as economic interests of France by strengthening her competitive position with the United States in the struggle to provide leadership in other programs that involve the continental countries.

A regional economic group composed of developing states may offer special advantages to its members. It may serve as a key to unlock the door to economic development by encouraging diversification and a system of production geared to regional rather than national consumption. The Central American Common Market, as already noted, may provide a market substantial enough to encourage local industrialization by eliminating competition for each specialized industry within the entire market area. This kind of "specialization through agreement" may prove to be the best way to create a "developmental force." Acting alone, the five might duplicate each other's efforts, fail to industrialize for lack of a sufficient demand for goods in any single state, or put their efforts into increasing the production of primary commodities with a resulting glut.

Some of the highly vocal proponents of a regional approach to solve economic problems bear some resemblance to the old-time huckster peddling snakeoil as a cure for all ills. Although its advantages are real and its potentiality great (and it should not be equated with snakeoil), it does have some significant drawbacks. Foremost among these is the basic *discriminatory* nature of a free trade area or common market. Each member agrees to give preferential trade treatment to its fellow members. Since other trading nations do not share in this *internal* reduction or elimination of trade barriers, they are, *ipso facto*, the objects of its discrimination. This is true even when the single external tariff of a common market remains at an average level no greater than that of its members' individual rates prior to the formation of the market. Trade discrimination, no matter whether direct or indirect or how good its intentions, is inimical to the development of true multilateralism.

Within a free trade area or common market, partially dormant forces of the market place are awakened. As governments remove their protective mantles, competition becomes keen. If economic growth falters or the business cycle takes an adverse swing, keen competition could quickly turn to cuthroat competition in a battle for survival. No regional group has yet had to face this kind of challenge. Even during prosperity, free trade is most advantageous for the strongest trading partners. If new economic freedom within a regional group permits one or several members to attract a major portion of available investment funds and to dominate the market place, economic integration will merely serve to accelerate the process of enriching the rich and impoverishing the poor. In the EEC, for example, free trade over the long run may encourage the domination of continental markets by West Germany. France, though hardly impoverished, has resented her growing balance-of-payments deficit with the Federal Republic and the latter's large gains in selling industrial products in France.[22] Trade wars among free market states may be encouraged by the dismemberment of governmental mechanisms which had helped to equalize competition.

Although a common market may stimulate efficiency and productivity—driving marginal producers out of business—this process could well redound to the disadvantage of market consumers. The natural forces of a free economy encourage the concentration of business into larger units. This concentration and the specialization promoted by common policies increase the potentiality for businessmen to reach an understanding with each other, divide up the market, and raise prices. In the EEC, for example, leading industrialists in all member countries have supported the common market idea partly because of the opportunities it provides for dividing up the continental market.[23] A high and growing incidence of mergers and cartel

[22] Sidney Dell, *op. cit.*, p. 154.
[23] See, for example, Piero Malvestiti, "Enterprise and the Common Market," *Bulletin of the European Economic Community*, Brussels: European Community Information Service, (September, 1959), p. 5.

arrangements in EEC countries raises the threat of monopoly pricing once outside competition has been reduced by the cost differential between members and nonmembers. Although cartels could be brought under governmental regulation—and the EEC's Treaty of Rome contains provisions that authorize such action—the continental tradition for restrictive marketing practices and the political power of the giants of industry militate against it.

A free trade area or common market represents a *substantial* movement toward laissez-faire. Governmental restrictive and promotional systems are dismantled by common agreement to eliminate artificial cost differentials and restraints on trade within the market. The impact of such policies may be a collapse in the delicately engineered internal equilibrium of power among business, labor, and agriculture. Within West Germany and France, for example, a new struggle for ascendancy may be shaping up among the three major economic forces. Whether a natural equilibrium will emerge or whether, as it now appears, business will increasingly dominate the internal economy and political mechanisms of the state remains an unanswered question. What is clear is that internal instability could wipe out the gains secured by other advantageous features of a common market.

In a regional group composed of developing states, many of these same infirmities may exist. Extremes in levels of development and economic potentials may bestow even greater favors upon the more advanced members of the market than in a group composed wholly of developed states. Although classical economists argued that free trade would tend to equalize incomes in all states, the evidence negates this theory. Within a free market, the state which develops most rapidly will attract additional shares of investment capital and a high proportion of skilled labor from neighboring states. Competitive advantages in a free market will tend to increase the rate of industrial development in more advanced states and will serve to frustrate weaker states in their attempts to industrialize. This propensity for unequal development was recognized by the noted Swedish economist, Gunnar Myrdal:

> That there is a tendency inherent in the free play of market forces to create regional inequalities, and that this tendency becomes the more dominant the poorer a country is, are two of the most important laws of economic underdevelopment and development under *laissez-faire*.[24]

Finally, the development of common market arrangements, whether in developed or developing states, may have an unhealthy impact on the building of a world multilateral system. The very factors that lend strength to a common market system may also foster restrictions on world trade. Preferential treatment for members' trade, for example, may encourage retaliation by outsiders. The movement to reduce world trade barriers may

---

[24] Gunnar Myrdal, *Economic Theory and Underdeveloped Regions*, (London: Duckworth, 1957), p. 13.

be stymied by the realization that freer trade with the rest of the world will weaken the rationale for a regional preferential system. In a common market, the "invasion" of external capital to surmount the common external tariff by investing "inside" the market causes balance-of-payments disequilibria and reactions within member countries against foreign domination of their economies. Moreover, the discriminatory features of a free trade area or a common market encourage the development of rival trading blocs. If common markets multiply—and evidence of planning for market arrangements in Asia and Africa lend credence to this assumption—a world of regional blocs may restore much of the rivalry that characterized the economic nationalism of the 1930's.

On balance, the development of regional free market arrangements has proved thus far to be a healthy one. In Europe, rivalry between EEC and EFTA may yet prove to be more than mildly troublesome in the future. The political and military consensus underlying the Atlantic Community may itself be at stake if the gap between the two widens. The objective of using a regional market to promote economic development remains largely untested. And as an element related to the problem of political unity, no one has as yet been able to unravel the tangled skein of economic factors to produce a definitive explanation of which produce closer ties and which invite disunity. Perhaps the main reason why free trade areas and common markets will continue to find favor is the *psychological* satisfactions which major interest groups derive from them. One observer's evaluation of the European Common Market, for example, concludes that

it is not surprising that everyone sees something for himself in the Rome Treaty—it is all things to all men. The free trader sees a cutting down of the internal barriers to trade. The protectionist sees the building of a new tariff wall around Western Europe. The right wing sees the strengthening of business interests and the possibility of stiffer resistance to wage demands on the grounds of competitive requirements. The left wing looks to the international unity of workers and sees the approach of the ideal of world brotherhood. The federalists see the creation of new supranational powers and the gradual emergence of a federal government. The confederalists look forward to *l'Europe des patries*—the Europe of nation states. The "Europeans" see the growth of a new European spirit and self-consciousness. The supporters of an Atlantic Community see the development of much broader loyalties. The one thing that is clear is that not all of these views can be right.[25]

THE PURSUIT OF INTERNATIONAL LIQUIDITY

The removal of barriers to trade may spur the exchange of goods, but another factor—the means of payment for goods received—may also deter-

[25] Sidney Dell, *op. cit.*, pp. 360–61.

mine the volume of the exchange. When a businessman in India buys German Volkswagens for example, he must pay for them not in Indian rupees but in German marks, or in an "international" currency, such as the American dollar or British pound. Foreign currencies needed for carrying on trade are known as foreign exchange. They may be obtained from a free foreign exchange market or, in the case of a state using some form of exchange control, a governmental agency determines if the projected transaction warrants the use of scarce foreign exchange. In a free exchange market, the rate of exchange between domestic and foreign currency is determined by supply and demand forces similar to those operating in a stock market or a commodity market place. In the controlled market, the price of foreign currencies is pegged at an official rate favorable to the exchange-control state.

One of the main objectives of states in the area of international finance is to accumulate sufficient reserves of foreign currencies to carry the state over a lean period. Two types of currencies, distinguished from each other by the role each plays in relation to international trade and finance, are useful in providing that kind of security for the state. First, an international "trading" currency is used by businessmen to carry on their day-to-day transactions in foreign markets. Bankers use trading currency to make loans and investments in most countries of the world. The trading currency, in other words, is the working currency accepted as an international monetary unit in a world of diverse national currencies. For some years, the dollar has functioned as the major trading currency, with over $11 billion currently in the hands of foreign bankers and businessmen. A second category, "reserve" currency, provides governments with the means for protecting the value of their national currencies in foreign exchange markets. When the value of a national currency threatens to drop below its parity or stability level, the government purchases quantities of its own currency in the free market using its international reserves. If its national currency becomes overvalued in the free market, the government then reverses the process, accumulating reserves in exchange for its national currency. Countries, therefore, need sizable amounts of reserves to keep the value of their national currency stable and within agreed limits.

International reserves held by countries for this purpose are in the form of gold or foreign exchange. The latter consists mainly of American dollars and, to a much lesser extent, the pound sterling. The dollar has become the kingpin of the international monetary system for several reasons. For one, the United States is committed to buy or to sell gold to foreign monetary authorities at the fixed price of $35 an ounce. Because gold is in short supply, the American dollar supplements gold in national reserves with the understanding that dollars could be converted into gold at any time. All other currencies consequently are tied to the dollar in terms of their exchange ratios and to the extent that they hold dollars as a reserve currency. This preeminent role as a reserve currency was not planned for the dollar; it occurred because of the willingness of private businessmen and bankers as well as public officials in various countries to hold dollars as a safe, universal currency. Since the American government stands ready to redeem dollar reserves for gold, there has been a general acceptance of dollars in lieu of gold in what might be described as a gold-exchange-standard system. The unrivaled prosperity of the United States and the ubiquitous immersion of its businessmen in business operations around the globe have also helped place the dollar in the center of the world monetary stage.

Finally, the American dollar has become the world's reserve currency because unprecedented numbers of dollars have been available to foreign traders and monetary agencies. This bonanza of dollars has resulted from a series of annual deficits in the American balance of payments, averaging an almost $3 billion annual deficit since 1957. These deficits have put $26 billion dollars into foreign hands—about $14 billion in the form of official reserves—and provided the liquidity for the high level of prosperity in the advanced nations in the decade 1957–67. In addition, billions of dollars have been exchanged for gold, reducing American gold reserves from $23 billion in 1957 to under $14 billion of a world total of almost $45 billion in 1966. American policies for several years have sought to reduce or eliminate the balance-of-payments deficit and to halt the outflow of gold. The inevitable result of these policies, if successful, would be to halt the increasing of reserves abroad at the very time when greater international liquidity is needed to support expanding trade and general prosperity. As a result, the world faces a serious monetary crisis in the collective efforts of the advanced countries to reach agreement on a solution to the problem of increasing international liquidity. Before examining that crisis and the proposals that have been offered for its solution, a survey of the United Nations system to create and to safeguard monetary stability is in order.

The International Monetary Fund (IMF)

The world's monetary system, weakened during the period of economic nationalism of the 1930's, emerged from World War II in almost complete disarray. In planning for the postwar world, the need for an orderly international payments system was given concern equal to that of building a new trading system free of restrictionism and of establishing a lending agency to aid in recovery from war and development of poor societies. The three legs of the stool to support international economic well-being were the International Trade Organization, the International Bank, and the International Monetary Fund. The Articles of Agreement for the Fund and the Bank were fitted together into the broad framework of a world economic policy at the Bretton Woods Conference of 1944. Although the IMF is a specialized agency of the United Nations, its membership is open to any nation that subscribes to its Articles of Agreement.[26] The main purposes of the IMF, as set forth in its Articles of Agreement, are

1. to promote *international monetary cooperation;*
2. to facilitate the *expansion of international trade;*
3. to promote *exchange stability;*
4. to assist in the establishment of a *multilateral system of payments;*
5. to give *confidence* to members by making the Fund's resources available;
6. to *shorten the duration and lessen the degree of disequilibrium* in member's balances of payments.

These objectives reflect the founders' concern lest the world slip back into the financial anarchy of the 1930's or retain strangling wartime controls. As in the proposals for a world trade system, the Fund's originators foresaw a new, orderly world of international finance based on a common code to guide member-state actions and governed by an international institution which could determine exchange and payments policies.

The Fund's primary role takes it along this pathway. It is first and foremost an institution through which governments can consult on major monetary questions. Beyond this, it seeks to provide exchange stability by two means: (1) by regulating currency values; and (2) by permitting members to draw foreign exchange from the Fund to tide them over periods of serious financial hardship.

Each member, when it joins the IMF, establishes in consultation with the governing board a par value for its currency in relation to gold or the dollar. Members must thereafter maintain these rates, permitting them to vary no more than 1 per cent in exchange transactions. Under the rules, a member may not devalue its currency unless it suffers from a "fundamental disequilibrium" and devaluation is a likely prescription for its ills. If the devaluation is no more than 10 per cent, the IMF governing board need not concur with the proposal. If a state's changes in its currency's value depart from its par value by more than 10 per cent, the organization must be consulted. Generally, currency values of members have remained relatively stable over the twenty-year period of the Fund's operations. Only one major devaluation has occurred, that of the sterling bloc in 1949. One of the major disintegrative forces of the earlier period appears to have been tamed, for the time being at least.

The plan underlying the use of the Fund as a pooling arrangement is fairly simple. All members contribute to a common bank of monetary reserves which they can draw upon to overcome short-term disequilibria in their balances of payments. The contributions are based on a quota system

[26] Membership in 1947 when the Fund commenced operations was 39; by 1957 it had reached 68, and by 1966 it was 102. Only one Communist nation (Yugoslavia) had joined the Fund by 1966.

that reflects national income, gold reserves, and other factors related to ability to contribute. The Fund's voting system is weighted according to each member's contribution, and the United States casts over one fourth of all votes. Each member must contribute 25 per cent of its quota in gold— the so-called gold tranche—but the remainder may be in its own currency. Each may annually purchase from the Fund amounts of foreign exchange up to the value of its gold tranche; the maximum ordinarily permitted, however, is five annual purchases amounting to 125 per cent of its quota. By 1965, members' subscriptions provided a pool of $16 billion available for drawing purposes, although as a practical matter the portion of the Fund made up of soft currencies is of little use. When a state withdraws an amount from the Fund for an emergency, it actually purchases the foreign exchange with its own domestic currency; when it repays the amount, it returns foreign exchange to the Fund for its own currency. In this way the reserve pool as a revolving fund remains fairly constant in the total value of its holdings, but the amounts of different currencies tend to fluctuate, depending on demand for them.

The objective underlying the currency pool is to maintain fairly stable exchange values for members' currencies. When a member suffers a short-term disequilibrium in its balance of payments, purchases of foreign exchange from the Fund should carry it through the crisis. Without the Fund, a state might be forced to devalue its currency or undertake some protectionist policies to combat its deficit.

The Liquidity Crisis

The crisis in the world monetary system results from a fear that monetary reserves are in short supply. The need for reserves became particularly acute during monetary battles in the 1960's to preserve the par value of the pound sterling, the Canadian dollar, and the Italian lira. But the crisis goes beyond the currencies immediately threatened; it involves the dollar and a continental fear, fanned by the French, that dependence upon the dollar as a reserve threatens a calamity. The French position is that if the American balance-of-payments deficit is corrected, there subsequently will be a shortage of reserves abroad because the outflow of dollars has itself been the major source of reserves. But if the deficit is not corrected, the dollar will then inescapably have to be devalued with a consequent depreciation in the value of dollars held as reserves by the European countries. Neither prospect appeals to de Gaulle or other continental leaders. Moreover, the growing tendency for continental countries to convert their dollar reserves into gold results in an equivalent reduction in international reserves since the dollars in American hands do not constitute a foreign exchange reserve. If a crisis of confidence in the dollar should occur, the small remaining cushion of disposable gold reserves held by the United States could disappear quickly. World monetary reserves—approximately $68 billion in 1965 and $66 billion in early 1966—have been falling at the very time when the need for liquidity has soared because of an annual 10 per cent rise in trade during the mid-1960's. (See Table 16-5)

TABLE 16-5.   Reserves and Levels of Foreign Trade
of Principal Countries March 31, 1966
(in millions of dollars)

| Country | National Reserves | | Foreign Trade | |
	Gold	Convertible Currency	Imports	Exports
Australia	223	1,182	3,658	2,937
Belgium	1,556	400	6,721	6,600
Canada	1,086	1,434	8,859	8,672
France	4,806	765	11,721	10,686
Germany	4,402	1,719	17,986	18,950
Italy	2,369	1,271	8,438	7,544
Japan	328	1,515	9,621	8,389
Netherlands	1,756	241	8,040	6,166
Portugal	595	387	735	502
Spain	785	314	3,822	990
Switzerland	2,652	181	3,791	3,044
United Kingdom	2,036	1,537	17,310	14,759
United States	13,738	559	25,606	29,077
Totals	36,332	11,505	126,308	118,316
World Totals	43,340	22,775	183,300	171,100

Source: *International Financial Statistics,* Vol. XIX, No. 8, (August, 1966), published by the International Monetary Fund.

Several approaches to increase the amount or availability of international reserves have been offered to meet the liquidity crisis. The French have suggested that the dollar and other national currencies be disestablished as reserve currencies. In their place, the French have called for accepting gold as the sole reserve unit or the creation of truly *international* reserves —Composite Reserve Units, or CRU's—which would have "the character of real money" because they would be related at an agreed proportion to the gold reserves of the leading nations. Gold, though preferable as a reserve, is in short supply and additions of new gold to official monetary stocks— currently at the rate of 1 per cent annually—is insufficient to provide the needed liquidity. Insufficient, that is, unless the price of gold were increased; French financial expert, Jacques Rueff, has recommended that national currencies be banned as exchange reserves and the price of gold doubled to assure adequate liquidity. In a related gesture, President de Gaulle called for the liquidation of the gold-exchange-standard system and the reinstitution of the gold standard system, praising gold as an international reserve which does not change in nature, which can be made either into bars, ingots, or coins, which has no nationality, which is considered in all places and at all times, the immutable fiduciary value par excellence.[27]

Increasing the value of gold would mean the devaluation of the dollar. If gold were doubled in value, those nations holding large amounts of dollars would suddenly find the value of their reserves cut in half. The fear that this may some day happen has led some nations, especially France, to increase the rate of conversion of dollars into gold. Ironically, if the fear became widespread enough to touch off a run on the conversion of dollars to gold, the United States would be forced to devalue the dollar or stop its free conversion into gold.

To counter the French proposal a plan has been advanced by E. M. Bernstein to create a similar set of Composite Reserve Units by which the ten major trading nations would hold an agreed proportion of each others' currencies to settle accounts between themselves. Although the Bernstein plan is similar to the French proposal in linking the CRU's to gold, it differs in the significant aspect that dollars and sterling could continue in their present role as major reserve currencies. A third plan, sponsored by Robert V. Roosa, would set up reserve units unrelated to gold and consequently more flexible in their creation and use.

Another approach seeks to increase international liquidity through a more effective use of the IMF. To enlarge the Fund's resources for meeting financial crises of members, for example, quotas could be increased or special arrangements worked out for transfers of reserves among the major members of the organization. The latter approach was instituted in 1962 when a "Group of Ten" of the industrialized nations agreed to lend the Fund up to $6 billion in their currencies to expand the drawing rights of members during a crisis. Other proposals for strengthening IMF's role would have it purchase government securities in the capital markets of different countries to give it some of the flexibility of a central bank (the Robert Triffin proposal), or have it add to international liquidity by investing directly in developing countries by granting them IMF certificates spendable in advanced countries (the Maxwell Stamp proposal). Others have recommended an expansion of liquidity arrangements outside of IMF to bolster the Fund's efforts during a crisis. Some bilateral agreements between central banks involving currency swaps and ad hoc lending arrangements have been instituted.

The problem of providing international liquidity will probably not be resolved through a revolutionary approach. Conservative financiers are wary of innovation. Yet, it has become increasingly apparent that the United

[27] *Ambassade de France,* "Speeches and Press Conferences," No. 216, (February 4, 1965), p. 6.

States' role as the world's banker and the heavy dependence upon the dollar as the world's reserve currency is changing. Strengthening and expanding the present system is clearly in order, but more is needed. The real problem in adapting the monetary system to new conditions is political, and much remains to be done in reconciling divergent views to build a new consensus. Among the issues that must be resolved are the nature of the new reserves, the control over their creation and distribution, their link with gold, and the reconciliation of international with national policies so that domestic monetary stability does not become a victim of external policies. And, then, there is still the largest political question wrapped up in the Franco-American struggle for leadership in the West. Much of the controversy over the dollar's role as a reserve currency relates to this political contest.

The International Monetary Fund as an institution provides the setting for working out a common solution to these and related problems. Not only must the select group of industrialized nations reach an accord to ensure their future liquidity needs, all member countries in the IMF must increasingly share in the development and benefits of the reserve system. Thus far the Fund has functioned almost exclusively as a tool for the richer nations. Continued progress toward world economic unity depends upon the coterminous evolution of a truly multilateral payments system with the movement toward freer trade.

Selected Readings

BALASSA, BELA. *The Theory of Economic Integration.* Homewood, Ill.: Richard D. Irwin, 1961.

CURTIS, MICHAEL. *Western European Integration.* New York: Harper and Row, 1965.

ELLSWORTH, P. T. *The International Economy,* 3rd ed. New York: Macmillan, 1964.

GARDNER, RICHARD N. "GATT and the United Nations Conference on Trade and Development," *International Organization,* Vol. XVIII, No. 4, Autumn, 1964, pp. 685–704.

HURTIG, SERGE. "The European Common Market," *International Conciliation,* No. 517, March, 1958.

KORBONSKI, ANDRZEJ. "COMECON," *International Conciliation,* No. 549, September, 1964.

KRAUSE, LAWRENCE B., ed. *The Common Market.* Englewood Cliffs, N.J.: Prentice-Hall, 1964.

LINDBERG, LEON N. *The Political Dynamics of European Economic Integration.* Stanford, California: Stanford University Press, 1963.

MAYNE, RICHARD. *The Community of Europe.* New York: W. W. Norton, 1962.

STERN, ROBERT M. "Policies for Trade and Development," *International Conciliation,* No. 548, May, 1964.

Wightman, David. *Toward Economic Cooperation in Asia.* New Haven: Yale University Press, 1963.

Wilcox, Clair. *A Charter for World Trade.* New York: Macmillan, 1949.

Wionczek, Miguel S. "Latin American Free Trade Association," *International Conciliation*, No. 551, January, 1965.

17 | *Building Political Community*

The study of international organization is necessarily the study of particular institutions, processes, and functions. No subject of such breadth and complexity can be digested unless it is examined piece by piece. At some point, however, the student must come to grips with questions of ultimate objectives and overall impact. In this study some of these questions will be explored in the context of the evolution of political community at the international level through the process of political integration.

The choice of such a context is not entirely arbitrary. The literature on the integration of political communities has burgeoned in recent years, and some of the most hopeful beginnings of an empirical theory to explain the interaction of international organization with its political environment have come out of that literature.[1] Our intention in this concluding chapter is not so much to examine systematically the theories which have been propounded as to use some of the concepts to enlighten and order our own appraisal of international organization in the twentieth century.

POLITICAL COMMUNITY DEFINED

The concept of "political community" does not have an entirely settled or agreed content. In general, the notion of community implies the existence of "mutual ties of one kind or another" which give a social group "a feeling of identity and self-awareness."[2] Although such a definition lacks the operational qualities that would enable the investigator to distinguish communities from noncommunities with perfect ease and precision, it has a common-sense flavor which at least suggests operational criteria.

[1] See, in particular, the writings of Karl Deutsch, Ernst B. Haas, and Amitai Etzioni cited in the chapter bibliography. The works cited are exhaustive neither of the output of these writers nor of other valuable and stimulating studies of political integration.

[2] Philip E. Jacob and Henry Teune, "The Integrative Process: Guidelines for Analysis of the Bases of Political Community," in Philip E. Jacob and James V. Toscano, eds., *The Integration of Political Communities* (Philadelphia: J. B. Lippincott, 1964), p. 4.

In practice, students of political integration have generally assumed the existence of communities from a volume of social transactions sufficiently large to create a continuing consciousness of common interest, and have directed their attention to the means of identifying and the process of creating communities which are "political." The varying approaches to the subject can be illustrated by the writings of Karl Deutsch, Amitai Etzioni, and Ernst B. Haas, three scholars who have made significant contributions to the literature of political integration.

In Etzioni's terms, a political community is a social unit which has "effective control" over the use of force, embraces a decision-making center able to "affect significantly the allocation of resources and rewards throughout the community," and serves as the "dominant focus of political identification for the large majority of politically aware citizens." [3] For all practical purposes, political community is another name for state. Nothing short of a voluntary amalgamation of two or more existing states within a unified governmental framework, involving dissolution of the former constituent states as independent entities, could constitute an enlarged community at the international level. World government, apparently, is the only basis for a political community that is worldwide in scope, as Etzioni uses the term.

Somewhat more flexible is the definition of Ernst Haas, who conceives of political community as a social unit in which "there is likelihood of internal peaceful change in a setting of contending groups with mutually antagonistic claims." [4] This condition is achieved when "political actors in several distinct national settings are persuaded to shift their loyalties, expectations, and political activities toward a new and larger center, whose institutions possess or demand jurisdiction over the pre-existing national states." [5] The reference to a "jurisdiction over pre-existing national states" makes the new community sound very statelike, but the definition still allows for a political community which stops short of a monopoly of the legitimate use of force, which is the hallmark of the modern state.

Deutsch offers still greater breadth in defining a political community as a social group "with a process of political communication, some machinery for enforcement, and some popular habits of compliance." [6] Within the community, "common or coordinated facilities for the making of decisions and enforcement of commands are supplemented by habits of compliance"

[3] Amitai Etzioni, *Political Unification* (New York: Holt, Rinehart and Winston, 1965), p. 4. See also Etzioni, "A Paradigm for the Study of Political Unification," *World Politics* (October, 1962), pp. 44–74.

[4] Ernst B. Haas, "International Integration: The European and the Universal Process," *International Organization* (Summer, 1961), p. 366.

[5] *Ibid.*, pp. 366–67. See also Haas, *The Uniting of Europe* (London: Stevens and Sons, 1958), pp. 5, 7–8.

[6] Karl Deutsch, et al., *Political Community and the North Atlantic Area*, (Princeton, N.J.: Princeton University Press, 1957), p. 5.

sufficient to make enforcement feasible.[7] Of special concern to Deutsch and his associates, at least in their study of *Political Community and the North Atlantic Area,* is the analytical concept of "security-community," a term used to distinguish a type of political community which has attained a "sense of community" and "institutions and practices strong enough and widespread enough to assure, for a 'long' time, dependable expectations of 'peaceful change.'"[8] Security-communities, as well as other political communities, are further classified into "amalgamated" and "pluralistic" types, depending on whether or not the constituent members retain their legal independence and their separate governmental decision-making centers. In the terminology of the Deutsch study, the United States would be an amalgamated security-community, while the United States and Canada, considered as a unit, would be a pluralistic security-community. Presumably, the cooperative relationships obtaining between the United States and Canada provide adequate channels of political communication, machinery for enforcement of agreed decisions, well established habits of compliance, a requisite "sense of community," and dependable expectations of peaceful change.

Each of these definitions has special merit within a particular analytical context; however, a definition like that of Deutsch, which includes "amalgamated" communities but which also leaves room for less integrated political systems, may be more useful in studying international organizations.[9] In this chapter, therefore, a political community will be defined as any political system in which relationships are characterized by (1) a fairly wide range of shared interests, (2) some kind of machinery to make and implement decisions, (3) some habits of compliance with the community's rules, and (4) dependable expectations that conflict will be resolved by nonviolent means. At the international level these requirements might be minimally satisfied by any two or more friendly countries having a significant range of public and private contacts, including the ordinary institutions of diplomatic intercourse. By requiring dependable expectations that conflict will be resolved by nonviolent means, *political community* as thus defined becomes roughly synonymous with Deutsch's security-community. Modification of the Deutsch terminology, although clinging to the essential concepts, produces a definition more compatible with other definitions of political

---

[7] Karl Deutsch, *Political Community at the International Level,* (New York: Doubleday, 1954), p. 40.

[8] Deutsch, *Political Community and the North Atlantic Area, op. cit.,* p. 5. For an earlier discussion of the security-community concept, see Richard W. Van Wagenen, *Research in the International Organization Field: Some Notes on a Possible Focus,* (Princeton, N.J.: Center for Research on World Political Institutions, 1952).

[9] In Dahl's terms, a political system is "any persistent pattern of human relationships that involves, to a significant extent, power, rule, or authority." Robert A. Dahl, *Modern Political Analysis* (Englewood Cliffs, N.J.: Prentice-Hall, 1963), p. 6.

community commonly used. It also obviates the possibility of applying the term *community* to a group so lacking in perception of shared or compatible interests that its members anticipate resort to violence as an ultimate means of settling differences.

Forms of Political Community at the International Level

Thus conceived, political community may exist at the international level in a variety of institutional forms, although in general one may distinguish three broad types: intergovernmental, supranational, and supergovernmental institutions. Each type has numerous variations, and mixed forms are both theoretically and practically possible. For analytical purposes, however, these categories are theoretically distinguishable and sufficiently congruent with the real world to be useful. The existence of political community is not, of course, to be implied from the existence of institutions for decision-making at the international level. In practice such institutions are essential to political community, but they may also exist in the absence of the wide range of shared interests and expectations of peaceful settlement that political community requires.

With *intergovernmental* institutions the final decision-making authority rests with each of the constituent states, and each must consent to be bound by a decision. Agreements are reached through bargaining and negotiation, and they may be enforced or implemented either by the individual states or by agreed instrumentalities acting for the collectivity. In this category are the traditional and continuing machinery of bilateral cooperation, and the paraphernalia of most international organizations. In the intergovernmental community, decision-making systems are coordinated for some purposes but not merged in any significant way.

Supranational institutions possess authority, within prescribed areas of activity, to make decisions that are binding upon individual members of the system or their peoples, even though one or more members may not have concurred in the decision. Supranationalism thus represents a partial transfer of authoritative decision-making functions from the constituent parts to the central institutions, the members nevertheless retaining their separate identities as sovereign, independent states.[10] Supranationalism, in its minimal form, emerges when governments agree to be bound by future decisions with which they may not concur. Any voting arrangement that calls for less than unanimity may give rise to supranationalism if the de-

---

[10] There obviously is a point when transfer of decision-making authority to central institutions becomes so substantial as to result in the abandonment of independence by the individual participants in the system. Historically, such mergers have been marked by a frank recognition by one or all of the states concerned that sovereignty was in fact being merged. History has yet to record a case of states moving gradually from independence to complete merger through the medium of expanding supranational institutions.

cisions are legally binding upon those who dissent or abstain. The General Assembly, despite its majoritarian voting regulations, is not a supranational body because the decisions it addresses to governments are merely recommendations. The Security Council, on the other hand, has supranational powers (very sparingly exercised) to order enforcement action. This minimal supranationalism, which consists of an agreement to be bound by the decisions of other governments, may be called *governmental* supranationalism. A second, and perhaps more common usage of the term supranationalism, sometimes designated as the *community* type, refers to the bestowal of decision-making authority upon officials representing the collectivity rather than individual national governments.[11] Community supranationalism is typified by the Commission of the European Community of Six which not only plays a crucial role as executive and policy-initiator within the Community but possesses, in limited areas, the authority to make decisions that are binding upon governmental and private entities within its jurisdiction.

Supergovernmental communities are created by the merger of heretofore separate governmental jurisdictions to form a single, amalgamated entity with a common decision-making center. At the international level, this would typically mean the establishment of a new state through the merger of two or more previously independent states. If a supergovernmental community were to become universal, we would call it world government. Recent examples of supergovernmental association are the temporary merger of Syria and Egypt to form the United Arab Republic (1958–61), and the union of Tanganyika and Zanzibar to form Tanzania. The tensions leading to the secession of Syria from the United Arab Republic in 1961 raise the question of whether this association, while supergovernmental during the short period of its existence, ever had sufficient expectations of peaceful conflict resolution to qualify as a political community.

POLITICAL INTEGRATION

Political integration, for our purposes, will refer to a process of unification within a political system, characterized by a growing volume and range of social transactions affected by the system, increasing centralization or coordination of authoritative decision-making, and a rising probability that conflict will be resolved by nonviolent means.[12] The process has no pre-

[11] The terms *governmental* and *community* supranationalism are borrowed from Uwe Kitzinger, *The Politics and Economics of European Integration* (New York: Praeger, 1963), pp. 61–62.

[12] Political integration is sometimes regarded as a process (Haas), a condition or state of affairs (Etzioni), or both (Deutsch). We see no inherent grammatical or logical reason why the term *integration* cannot appropriately be used to designate a process, while *level* of integration may refer to a condition or state of affairs obtaining at a particular stage in the process. Karl Deutsch treats integration as the basic condition of a security-community (i.e., "a group of people that has become integrated"), and also as the

ordained terminal stage, and political systems may be distinguished from one another by their *level* of integration as measured along three dimensions —(1) social transactions affected by the system, (2) centralization of decision-making, and (3) nonviolent resolution of conflict.

Given this definition, the relationship between political integration and political community is obvious. If political integration goes far enough it will eventually lead to political community; and political community is the level of integration within a system at which the flow of social transactions is broad enough to support a fairly wide range of shared interests, the decision-making apparatus is highly enough centralized or coordinated to handle the transactions adequately, and the expectations of peaceful settlement of disputes are dependable. It should be equally obvious that in any given political system the integrative process may stop short of the level requisite for political community, or that the process may continue after political community has been achieved. The range and volume of shared interests may continue to increase beyond the minimum requisite for community, and an intergovernmental community may subsequently become a more highly integrated supranational or supergovernmental community. One might even assume that "dependable" expectations of peaceful change could become still more dependable. On the other hand, the process may go into reverse. A given system may recede to a lower level of integration and perhaps cross and recross the threshold of political community.

Political integration is a complex process which may move unevenly along each of the three dimensions although progress on any one of them should ordinarily reinforce the others. An increase in transactions should stimulate more joint decision-making and raise the predisposition to settle differences peacefully through an augmenting of shared interests. More centralized or better coordinated regulative institutions ought to stimulate the rate of transaction and ease strains within the system through more efficient allocation. Expectations of peaceful adjustment of differences should be conducive both to social interchange and to the establishment of cooperative institutions for their regulation.

---

transactional process by which security-community is achieved. See Deutsch, *Political Community and the North Atlantic Area, op. cit.*, pp. 5, 70; and, Deutsch, *Political Community at the International Level, op. cit.*, pp. 33–40, 51–63. Haas says that this is "confusing," and asserts: "All transactional modes of analysis fuse and confuse the aspects of process and condition. . . . I conceive of integration as referring *exclusively* to a process that links a given concrete international system with a dimly discernible future concrete system. If the present international scene is conceived of as a series of interacting and mingling national environments, and in terms of their participation in international organizations, then integration would describe the process of *increasing* the interaction and the mingling so as to obscure the boundaries between the system of international organizations and the environment provided by their nation-state members." Haas, *Beyond the Nation State* (Stanford: Stanford University Press, 1964), pp. 28, 29.

However, as Deutsch suggests, it is possible that a sudden increase in the volume of transactions, without an increase in the effectiveness of "institutions, processes and habits of peaceful change and adjustment" may lead to disintegration and conflict.[13] Presumably, too, the premature centralization of political decision-making, accompanied by rapid reallocation of resources within the community, may elicit strong opposition from disadvantaged groups.

Students of political unification have been particularly concerned with the dynamics of the process—what it is that fuels a unification process or, in other instances, sets disintegrative forces in motion. Unique factors have been found in every case, but also enough similarities to raise some tentative generalizations. It is to an analysis of the conditions and forces that feed the integrative process that we now turn.

The Functionalist Theory of Integration

One explanation of the integrative process lies in the functionalist theory of international organization. Functionalism is a prescription for action as well as an explanation of processes, and its postulates are grounded as much in *a priori* assumptions as in empirical investigation. Indeed, functionalism is not a consistent, coherent, carefully articulated body of propositions. In this respect it is like realism or idealism; it has no single prophet and no absolutely fixed content. Functionalist theory has had a profound impact upon the theory and practice of international organization, however, and thus cannot be ignored. Our discussion is consistent with what appears to be the general trend of functionalist thought, if not wholly consistent with any particular version of it.

The basic premise of functionalism is that problems of international peace and security can best be alleviated by cooperation in the sphere of economic and social welfare. Implicit in this premise is the Marxian concept that conflict among states is the result of social inequality, arising primarily from the maldistribution of economic benefits. An assault upon economic and social ills will thus be directed at the basic causes of inter-state conflict, and not merely at its symptoms. The functionalist premise is also sustained by the conviction that most problems involving the power and prestige of states are too intractable to be solved by a direct approach through political international organization. Emotion-laden concepts of state sovereignty and narrow national interests are resistant to compromise and conciliation.

[13] "What is of concern," Deutsch says, "is the race between the growing rate of transaction among populations in particular areas and the growth of integrative institutions and practices among them." Deutsch, *Political Community at the International Level, op. cit.*, p. 40. On the other hand, he observes in a later work, "The one thing which is unlikely to accompany a high level of transaction is continued high tension and conflict." See "Communication Theory and Political Integration," in Jacob and Toscano, *op. cit.*, p. 67.

Simply as a matter of strategy, priority of emphasis should be given to welfare matters where cooperation is feasible in a joint endeavor to subdue the common enemies of disease, poverty, human degradation, and misery.

Such concentration upon economic and social problems presumes that welfare is sufficiently divorced from politics to permit governments and private groups to pursue their common welfare interests without the troublesome conflicts of power politics. And yet the separation is only temporary, since the treatment of social ills is supposed to effect a simultaneous cure of political ailments.

It is not anticipated that governments will suddenly launch an all-out effort to solve functional problems generally, but rather that particular functions—health, mail service, telecommunications, and the like—can become the subject of international cooperation as the interest is recognized. Functionalists would proceed pragmatically, searching out areas of mutuality and "binding together those interests which are common, where they are common, and to the extent to which they are common." [14] The result, hopefully, will be a piecemeal transfer of governmental functions and thus the substance of sovereignty from the national level to the international. In the words of one exponent of functionalism.

> Sovereignty cannot in fact be transferred effectively through a formula, only through a function. By entrusting an authority with a certain task, carrying with it command over the requisite powers and means, a slice of sovereignty is transferred from the old authority to the new; and the accumulation of such partial transfers in time brings about a translation of the true seat of authority. [15]

Functionalists thus are committed to the efficacy of gradualism, moving from one functional context to another, building the edifice of world community piece by piece. This outcome emphasizes the temporary and partial separation of welfare from politics, since the final result of dealing with welfare problems in a "working" rather than a "political" context is to extirpate the roots of political conflict and infuse the whole area of international relations with learned habits of cooperation.

Functionalism also makes rather specific assumptions about the capacity of institutions to structure social action. In particular, the nation-state system is held to be incompatible with a coherent attack upon the world's economic and social problems. The problems are worldwide in scope, while national boundaries and sovereign jurisdictions force men to act within limited geographical areas, with obviously unsatisfactory results. Transferring authority to an international agency will eliminate these artificial

[14] David Mitrany, *A Working Peace System*, 4th ed. (London: National Peace Council, by arrangement with the Royal Institute of International Affairs, 1946), p. 40.

[15] *Ibid.*, p. 9. Mitrany's functionalism obviously contemplates supranational, and ultimately supergovernmental, institutions rather than mere intergovernmental cooperation.

national barriers and permit a concerted attack upon the problem as a whole. Institutions thus determine how effectively men can act to root out the economic and social basis of war.

Functionalist faith in the efficacy of international institutions goes yet further. Quite apart from the approach to political community through the elimination of sources of conflict, the very act of promoting common interests through international cooperation has integrative effects in at least two contexts. First, the habits of cooperation learned in one sphere of activity are presumed to be readily transferable to others. As Haas puts it,

> An important corollary of the separation of functional spheres is the notion of transferability of lessons. Integrative lessons learned in one functional context will later be applied by the actor in new contexts until the dichotomy between functional contexts is overcome. Unlimited learning and transferability are apparently assumed.[16]

Second, a transfer of functions from national to international institutions is supposed to be accompanied by a corresponding transfer of loyalty and support. As functional organizations rather than national governments become the agents of human welfare, they also become a focus of human loyalties, with resulting accretions of support to the international institutions.

The assumptions of functionalist theory, as they have been restated here, are subject to criticism on several counts.[17] First, and perhaps foremost, the functionalist analysis of the causes of war is inadequate. At best it is simplistic and, if taken to mean that international wars are usually started by the economically deprived and exploited, it is not consonant with historical facts. Although economic and social inequality cannot be discarded as an explanation of war, the existing state of knowledge suggests that the picture is much more complex. Certainly, a clear and necessary connection between the outbreak of war and economic and social inequity has yet to be demonstrated empirically.

Second, the separability of power from welfare, of politics from functional activities, seems to be an obvious overstatement of reality. The history of recent adventures in functional cooperation is replete with instances of political wrangling and obstructionism. If modern studies of politics have demonstrated anything, they have surely shown that the process of authoritatively allocating values is inherently political, whether the values are economic, social, or strictly "political" in their content.

Third, experience also raises doubt that cooperative habits learned in one functional context will necessarily be transferred to another, or that a widening sphere of functional cooperation will finally lead to a substitution

---

[16] Haas, *Beyond the Nation State, op. cit.*, p. 21.

[17] For further evaluation of functionalism, see *ibid.*, pp. 3–50; and, Inis L. Claude, Jr., *Swords into Plowshares*, 3rd ed. (New York: Random House, 1964), pp. 344–55.

of cooperation for conflict in the so-called political sphere. Functional co-operation has increased, but conflict or the threat of it does not appear to have undergone any corresponding decrease.

Fourth, the assumption that loyalties are created by functions, and hence transferred rationally as functions are shifted from one institutional setting to another, is also subject to question. If loyalty to a community is defined as self-identification with the community, perceived interest in its main-tenance, and support for its institutions, the proposition is at best partially valid. It depends upon the individual's psychological readiness to identify, the adequacy of his perceptions, and the exercise of rationality. These con-ditions are all essential but do not always exist. The European Community appears to have become the focus of a limited amount of loyalty, as so defined, without overriding national loyalties and attachments. The phe-nomenon is much less in evidence with respect to most international organizations, however. Typically their activities are perceived by few and their good works are quite as likely to reflect credit upon national govern-ments as upon the international community.

Despite its weaknesses, functionalism remains an intellectually respec-table theory of political integration. A recent reformulation of the theory by Ernst Haas has gone far toward meeting many of the obvious objections by tying functionalism more closely to observed experience and suggesting that many of its postulates are only relatively true, or true with certain qualifications.[18] Haas in fact provides some empirical basis for the func-tionalist faith in the capacity of institutions to affect social action. His find-ings indicate that participation in international organizations does promote the learning of cooperative habits (at least occasionally) and provide opportunities for states to discover common or converging interests. More-over, if the experts and managers in the international bureaucracy are given enough scope, they may be able to seize upon moments of limited consensus to suggest programs that result in an expansion of the "organizational task" and an "upgrading" of the common interests. Thus the creation of inter-national institutions may have integrative consequences which originally were unforeseen and unintended.

In answer to our central question of what provides the thrust for move-ment from one level of integration to another, functionalism gives a fairly coherent answer. Initially, governments enter into cooperative arrangements because of converging technical interests in dealing with common problems. Once the system is established, however, the convergence of technical in-terests is supplemented by systemic forces unleashed by the act of coopera-

[18] See Haas, *Beyond the Nation State, op. cit.*, esp. pp. 3–53, and *passim*. Besides pro-viding his own model and application for functionalism, Haas refurbishes the theory by substituting qualifications, probabilities, and possibilities for the absolutes that tend to exude from the writings of many functionalists.

tion. Cooperative habits prove applicable to other functional areas as attitudinal reorientations take place through a learning process inherent in the system. At the same time, loyalties are rationally transferred to the new institutions. Thus, progress to a higher (and higher) level of integration occurs as a by-product of functional cooperation until, presumably, a world government of interlocking functional units comes into existence.

Conditions of Integration

Functionalism gives insight into the processes of political integration, even though its usefulness as an analytical tool is often limited by the tendency of its exponents to a wholesale intermingling of fact and value in their enthusiasm for building a better world. Additional insight is being provided by a growing body of empirical research into the conditions under which the integrative process is likely to occur.[19] No one has yet produced a list of conditions claimed to be both necessary and sufficient, but good arguments have been adduced that certain conditions are either necessary or helpful to the process of integration. Without attempting an exhaustive catalog of all conditions that have been said to have special relevance for integration, we will briefly examine some that appear well considered and illustrative of the thinking in the field.

There is substantial agreement that *compatibility of the main values* held by politically relevant strata of the populations is essential to a high level of integration. What constitutes "main values" and "politically relevant strata" remains to be identified in particular cases, as determined by their capacity to affect the processes of authoritative decision-making within the units concerned. Values relevant in one political context may not be in another. Religion, for example, has been depoliticized in relations between Britain and France, but is still highly relevant to relations between India and Pakistan. Moreover, values compatible at one level of integration may not be compatible at another. Vast differences in government control of national economies might be compatible within an intergovernmental political community, but prove incompatible if integration toward the supranational or supergovernmental level were attempted.

A second essential factor is *mutual responsiveness*—the capacity of the integrating units to respond to each other's needs, messages, and actions

---

[19] See, for example, Karl Deutsch, et al., *Political Community and the North Atlantic Area, op. cit.;* Amitai Etzioni, *Political Unification, op. cit.;* Jacob and Toscano, *op. cit.;* Ernst B. Haas, *Beyond the Nation State, op. cit.;* Haas, "International Integration: The European and the Universal Process," *op. cit.;* Haas and Philippe C. Schmitter, "Economics and Differential Patterns of Political Integration: Projections About Unity in Latin-America," *International Organization* (Autumn, 1964), pp. 705–37; and J. S. Nye, Jr., "Patterns and Catalysts in Regional Integration," *International Organization* (Autumn, 1965), pp. 870–84.

quickly and adequately, and a mutual predictability of behavior.[20] Responsiveness is a function of communication, attitudes, and governmental capabilities. Without effective communication the partners may be slow to perceive one another's needs. Without appropriate attitudes and frames of reference, they may fail to grasp the significance of the messages received or lack the mutual sympathy, trust, and identification of common interests that creates the will to respond. Without adequate capabilities the partners may be unable to make an appropriate response, regardless of their will to do so. Responsiveness spans the whole gamut of needs for economic well-being, military security, diplomatic support, and psychological gratification. The inability or unwillingess of the United States to respond adequately to the psychological needs of France under de Gaulle is undoubtedly one factor contributing to the current rift.

Power is a third essential condition. While integrative processes may be fed by the unintended consequences of specific acts of cooperation, every significant institutional advance can be examined in terms of what countries (or groups) were in favor of the step and what kind of power they exerted to accomplish it.[21] A large portion of the impetus for Western European integration, especially in its earlier stages, may be attributed to United States' economic and military support and diplomatic pressure. Part of the fuel for the process also came from the mutual exchanges among the European countries themselves. Integration within SEATO and CENTO, to the extent that it has occurred, was purchased by American economic and military power. Integration within the Soviet bloc has been largely a response to Soviet pressures. These are illustrative of the proposition that integration exacts costs which must be paid by someone as a tariff on anticipated benefits.

Another condition, not essential but sometimes said to facilitate the integrative process, is *pluralism*—the existence in each of the units of a multitude of articulate, voluntary groups having congruent or complementary interests.[22] Complementary pluralisms facilitate the formation of "cross-cutting cleavages," that is, the development of interests that cut across national lines and create new solidarities that temper the former national exclusiveness. Without a vigorous pluralism, the consequences of governmental participation in an integrative process are not readily felt in other parts of the social structure, and integration is unable to feed on the

[20] Deutsch, et al., *Political Community and the North Atlantic Area, op. cit.*, identify value compatibility and mutual responsiveness as essential to the establishment of both pluralistic and amalgamated security-communities.

[21] An explicit and detailed treatment of power as a condition of integration is found in Etzioni, *Political Unification, op. cit.*

[22] This concept is borrowed from Ernst B. Haas, "International Integration: The European and the Universal Process," *op. cit.*, pp. 374–75; see also Haas, *Beyond the Nation State, op. cit.*, especially pp. 447–58.

dynamics of interaction among groups whose interests are engaged in the functioning of the larger system.

Another helpful condition is *complementarity of political elites*—the political leaders of the integrating units have values and interests that are common or complementary. This may be just another way of saying that integration is unlikely to take place unless the political leaders favor it—a commonplace, if not wholly redundant, assertion. But attitudes of governmental leaders are important enough to be regarded as a separate variable for examination. The relations among political elites may in fact be the most important variable in underdeveloped countries where the group structure is amorphous and inarticulate.[23] The union of Zanzibar with Tanganyika to form the new state of Tanzania was accomplished by a deal between the rulers of the two states, motivated by a threat to the Zanzibar regime by Peking-backed dissidents. Undoubtedly the level of social transactions within Tanzania would be greater, and the interest of more people would be directly engaged in the union, if the two merged African societies were more highly pluralistic; but a very high level of integration along the institutional dimension was accomplished simply by action of the political elites.

The five conditions just examined are but illustrative of those which have been suggested as indicative of integrative potential. One might also mention such factors as geographical proximity, political structure, degree of political autonomy, governmental effectiveness, previous integrative experience, and many others. Implicit in this line of investigation is the hypothesis that integration will occur, or is more likely to occur, in the presence of an appropriate configuration of objective conditions. This does not really explain why integration occurs, however, and students of political integration have been wary of stating that they have found just the right set of conditions that will trigger and sustain the process of integration under any and all circumstances. Too many unique, accidental or as yet unidentified factors appear to be at work. Perhaps, as one writer has suggested, the unique or accidental factors ought to be classified under the general heading of "catalyst." [24] Once the conditions are right, the process may be triggered by some catalytic factor which cannot necessarily be identified in advance.

Although our knowledge of the dynamics of political integration is far from complete, a tentative model of the integrative process at the international level might be constructed in something like the following manner. A group of countries, perhaps as a result of their previous integrative ex-

---

[23] So suggests J. S. Nye, Jr., from a study of the East African Common Services Organization. See his "Patterns and Catalysts in Regional Integration," *International Organization* (Autumn, 1965), pp. 870–84 and *Pan Africanism and East African Integration* (Cambridge, Mass.: Harvard University Press, 1965).

[24] See Nye, "Patterns and Catalysts in Regional Integration," *op. cit.*

perience, possess the minimal conditions for integration. Their "main values" are compatible, they are capable of mutual responsiveness, and sufficient resources are available to support a higher level of integration. Perhaps other helpful conditions, such as rising elite complementarity are also present. Given these conditions, the process is initiated by a catalytic agent. This may be a technological change or the discovery of new resources that stimulates a rising flow of social transactions. It may be mutual concern with the devastation and dislocation of war, the need for economic development, defense against a common enemy, pressure from outside states, a desire to increase the power and prestige of the group in international affairs, or any of a thousand motives that might impel governments toward unity. Once the integrative drive has led to the creation of common institutions, an international bureaucracy lends its support to the process. Cooperative habits are learned, and the effects of rising integration in one sector may create problems which invite cooperation in other sectors, thus inducing a systemic spillover. As perceptions of interest are modified, a gradual shift toward the collectivity as the focus of interest and loyalties may occur. By this time the process feeds on itself. A kind of political "take-off" has occurred.

The logical outcome of such a process is complete political union. In fact, however, integrative processes are much more likely to stop short of the ultimate. The catalytic agent becomes less compelling, the costs of increasing integration rise, value compatibility and elite complementarity may be sufficient to support only a certain level of integration and no more. In effect, the process runs out of gas. Disintegrative forces may even be unleashed if the transaction load begins to exceed capabilities, or opposition groups gain the upper hand. This generalized model of the integrative process is necessarily tentative and incomplete, but it suggests some of the more significant variables to look for in the life cycle of integration movements.

INTERNATIONAL ORGANIZATION AND GLOBAL COMMUNITY

The preceding survey of the broad field of political integration has suggested some of the vast possibilities for theorizing and empirical study of the process by which people forge bonds of union among themselves. Given the focus of this book upon international organization, however, our emphasis must come to rest upon the role of international organizations in the integrative process. In broad terms, the relationship between organization and the three dimensions of integration is obvious—international organizations are created for the specific purpose of facilitating international transactions, they constitute machinery for coordinated or centralized decision-making, and to the extent that they function smoothly they heighten expectations that differences will be settled without violence within the area of the organization's competence. The contribution of regional and global organization to the growth of political community can be appraised more meaningfully, however, if some of the concepts discussed above are applied with somewhat greater particularity.

For this purpose we have selected seven categories that seem especially relevant to the appraisal of international organization and political community: (1) transactions and shared interests; (2) value compatibility; (3) mutual responsiveness; (4) transference of loyalties; (5) the dynamics of institutional bureaucracies; (6) the learning of integrative habits; and (7) spillover—the phenomenon by which cooperation in one sector creates a need for cooperation in another. Global organization will be discussed in terms of each of these categories. Their application to the various regional organizations will be discussed on a more selective basis. We turn first to an examination of global organization and political community.

Patently, the world does not constitute a political community. The task of raising international relations everywhere to a level of cooperation and mutual compatibility sufficient to support a wide range of shared interests and dependable expectations of peaceful change is staggering in its immensity. There are, of course, segments of genuine political community among nations scattered about the globe. Nearly all countries have a generalized commitment to peaceful settlement, and most differences between most countries are settled peacefully. But there is no settled expectation that all differences will be so resolved. Quite the contrary, there exists a fairly dependable expectation among governmental officials and informed citizens alike that many disputes among nations—if they are resolved at all—will be resolved by the threat or use of violence.

Given the proposition that the international political system has a long way to go before it reaches a level of integration capable of supporting a general political community, what contribution is world organization making to the achievement of community as an ultimate goal?

Social Transactions and Shared Interests

The United Nations touches upon a multitude of international transactions, involving both shared and conflicting interests. UN operations may be "spread very thinly among the myriad contacts already flourishing outside that system," [25] but they are also spread very widely. An Assistant Secretary of State for International Organization Affairs once observed that "there is a United Nations angle, presently or prospectively, to every major subject of

[25] Richard W. Van Wagenen, "The Concept of Community and the Future of the United Nations," *International Organization* (Summer, 1965), p. 820. Our discussion of global community is substantially indebted to Van Wagenen's analysis.

foreign policy." [26] In their "service" functions—primarily in the fields of information, relief and rehabilitation, technical assistance, and economic development—UN agencies have themselves generated increased international contacts. In their regulative activities, world organizations have been mainly used to systematize existing contacts in trade, transportation, and communication. One can presume, however, that the establishment of uniform rules and regulations under the auspices of the UPU, the ITU, and the ICAO has in fact stimulated the flow of mail, telecommunications, and air transportation. In both areas of activity—service and regulation—the UN agencies have provided an effective institutional framework for finding and acting upon shared interests.

Compatibility of Values

The search for institutional impact upon the compatibility of main values raises some interesting, difficult, and largely unexplored questions. What, indeed, are the "main" values that must be compatible and how compatible must they be for world political community to exist? Does this in practice mean that authoritarian and democratic systems cannot coexist within a single political community? Authoritarian Portugal's generally peaceful relations with its more democratic European neighbors would suggest that the two are not necessarily incompatible, at least for purposes of maintaining a pluralistic or intergovernmental political community. Desire to settle disputes peacefully, distaste for the sacrifices entailed by war, and fear of a nuclear holocaust are values which, if held strongly enough, might be sufficient to support a political community. Nearly all countries share these values in some degree, however, and violent conflict continues to arise because other values are dominant, such as strong imperialist drives, aggressive ideologies, concern for national prestige and influence, and perhaps economic motivations.

What, then, does the United Nations do to relieve the incompatibility in national values that might lead to conflict? One informed analyst has concluded that

> The most that can be said about this indicator at present is close to simple assertion: Most students and observers of the UN system would probably judge that major national values are rendered slightly more compatible by constant exposure to each other in the UN system.[27]

At least in a marginal way, UN discussions tend to strengthen the commitment to peaceful settlement, and dramatize the common concern to avoid a nuclear conflagration. One cannot be sure that this kind of exposure does

[26] Harlan Cleveland, in Francis O. Wilcox and H. Field Haviland, Jr., eds., *The United States and the United Nations* (Baltimore: Johns Hopkins, 1961), p. 147.
[27] Van Wagenen, *op. cit.*, p. 819.

much to temper incompatible imperialistic urges, but nearly all members of the United Nations pretend in their public utterances not to have such urges. John Foster Dulles in his book *War or Peace* (1950) suggested that this tribute that vice pays to virtue is in itself a restraining influence upon conduct—at least upon the more overt forms which make public professions of peaceful intent appear as sheer hypocrisy.[28] Charles Osgood has speculated that role acting in international forums may lead to a basic psychological transformation in accordance with the Festinger principle of "cognitive dissonance." As Osgood states it

> When people are made to keep on behaving in ways that are inconsistent with their actual attitudes (e.g. as if they really trusted each other), their attitudes tend to shift into line with their behaviors. . . .[29]

This kind of reasoning, however inconclusive, provides some slight basis for the assertion that participation in UN processes may have a positive if marginal effect on the compatibility of the main values of its members.

Mutual Responsiveness

If the contribution of the UN system to value compatability is highly speculative, its enhancement of mutual responsiveness and predictability is much less open to doubt. Constant multilateral communication is one of the most celebrated functions of the United Nations and related agencies. Countries cannot respond to one another's needs unless they know what the needs are, and the United Nations is one important channel through which they can "get the message." International organization also provides institutions through which an appropriate response may be made in the form of a return communication, the rendering of economic and other assistance, and participation in other cooperative activities.

There is some evidence that participation in multilateral processes also enhances the will to respond, through a better appreciation of needs, the recognition of shared interests, and the identification that comes from working together in a common enterprise. The camaraderie among individuals who are members of the "club" has been frequently noted, and some observers have regarded "the personal relationships established at the UN" as having "as much, if not greater, importance than the formal decisions which are reached." [30] One careful scholar has ventured the judgment that even "a skeptical trust" may be fostered "among those who are ideologically permitted such an adventure." [31]

[28] John Foster Dulles, *War or Peace* (New York: Macmillan, 1950), pp. 66–69.

[29] "Suggestions for Winning the Real War with Communism," *The Journal of Conflict Resolution* (December, 1959), p. 321.

[30] John G. Hadwen and Johan Kaufmann, *How United Nations Decisions Are Made*, 2nd ed. (New York: Oceana, 1962), p. 58.

[31] Van Wagenen, *op. cit.*, p. 820.

How far this personal interaction goes toward affecting national policy undoubtedly differs widely from case to case and from state to state. The links between the UN process and national policy have only been hinted at and remain a fruitful subject for future investigation. Nevertheless there are some indications that policy is affected. One participant in the process, writing in 1950, gave his opinion that the United Nations

> has caused American policy to be formulated with greater consciousness of wider interests which may profoundly affect American interests. . . . The United Nations has broadened the scope of American foreign policy and made it more quickly conscious of and responsive to political, economic and social problems which sooner or later must affect the interests of the United States as a world power. The United Nations has also made the United States more quickly conscious of and responsive to the effects of its own foreign policy on world public opinion.[32]

In 1955, members of the United States delegation to the General Assembly reacted to their experience in that forum by publishing a statement at the end of the session urging the United States government to channel more economic aid through multilateral agencies. Indeed the entire history of the economic development issue in the United Nations reveals the usefulness of multilateral diplomacy in stimulating responsiveness to the demands of the developing countries. Likewise, it can be said of the self-determination issue that international organization encouraged the colonial powers to make a more appropriate and peaceful response to demands for independence and self-government.

Another aspect of multilateral diplomacy that has relevance for mutual responsiveness is the phenomenon of shifting majorities and coalitions which permits a member to be aligned with numerous groupings of states in a variety of causes. A country like Panama, conceivably, might vote with the United States on a cold war issue, with the Soviet Union on a colonial question, and with neither great power on a question of economic development. Nearly every resolution adopted during a session of the General Assembly, except for the numerous instances of unanimity, will have the support of a different majority. Such shifting patterns of interest enable countries to keep open their channels of communication with other members, and, on one occasion or another, to make common cause with virtually all of them. Just as domestic societies are often stabilized and knit together by their overlapping group memberships, the cross-cutting cleavages in the forums of international organizations can play a role in mitigating conflict and enhancing responsiveness. Certainly, the links between the multilateral political process and the processes of national policy formulation still remain

---

[32] Benjamin V. Cohen, "The Impact of the United Nations on United States Foreign Policy," *International Organization* (May, 1951), p. 280.

to be clarified and carefully mapped out; but apparently the impact is one of heightened responsiveness.[33]

The United Nations also contributes to political community through its role in the pacific settlement of particular disputes. What has been said in an earlier chapter need not be repeated here. We would simply restate the obvious, that in the performance of its pacific settlement function the United Nations has sometimes increased mutual responsiveness and has raised at least slightly the level of expectations that disputes among members will in fact be settled with a minimum of violence.

Transference of Loyalties

Admittedly there has been no mass transfer of loyalties and attachments to the United Nations and its specialized agencies.[34] These organizations are simply not an issue in the lives of most people. They have low budgets and little coercive power; and their capacity to grant rewards or administer penalties extends to the regular experience of relatively few. The European Community has become a growing hub of interest-group activity because the Community institutions have acquired the power to affect significantly the economic interests of many Europeans. No institution or set of institutions at the global level has been able to touch the interests of so many people in such an obvious, vital, and continuing way.

Nevertheless, global international organizations have created vested interests in their maintenance. Not the least interested are the international civil servants, now exceeding 20,000 in the system of the United Nations and specialized agencies. The career bureaucrat's loyalty is of course founded on his job-holding interest. "Whose bread I eat, his song I sing," is a fact of life in most areas of economic endeavor. There is also the proprietary interest of international officials who identify their fortunes with the organiza-

---

[33] For interesting and suggestive, though admittedly tentative, generalizations about the significance of interpersonal relations in the United Nations, see the work of Chadwick F. Alger, especially his "Non-Resolution Consequences of the United Nations and Their Effect on International Conflict," *Journal of Conflict Resolution* (June, 1961), pp. 128–45; "Hypotheses on Relationships Between the Organization of International Society and International Order," *Proc. Am. Soc. Int. Law* (1963), pp. 35–46; "United Nations Participation As a Learning Experience," *Public Opinion Quarterly* (Fall, 1963), pp. 411–26; and "Personal Contact in Intergovernmental Organizations," in Herbert C. Kelman, ed., *International Behavior* (New York: Holt, Rinehart and Winston, 1965), pp. 523–47.

[34] "Loyalty" to a community has been earlier defined as "self-identification with the community, perceived interest in its maintenance, and support for its institutions." See p. 517, *supra*. Transference of loyalties to the international level does not necessarily imply that national loyalties are thereby supplanted. Loyalties and attachments in the political realm can be divided among various objects, just as in other areas of social behavior. For a thoughtful analysis of this phenomenon see Harold Guetzkow, *Multiple Loyalties: A Theoretical Approach to a Problem in International Organization* (Princeton, N.J.: Princeton University Center for Research on World Political Institutions, 1955).

tion and consciously or unconsciously seek to magnify their own importance by magnifying the work of the organization. Not to be dismissed, as well, is the intellectual and emotional commitment of many a world civil servant to the objectives of the organization—a commitment which inspires loyalty in every sense of the word.

Governments also have vested interests in the continuance of international organizations. The expectation of concrete benefits is the principal cement that binds governments to the support of international organizations. The small, the weak, the poor look for aid in dealing with their economic and social problems and for leverage in conducting their political relations with the great powers. The overwhelming support of Dag Hammarskjold in the face of the blistering Soviet attack during the Congo crisis bespoke the concern of the small powers that the executive arm of an organization that had served them well should not be weakened. The larger powers, while often less enthusiastic about multilateral processes in which they are confronted with the greater numbers and manifestly greater material needs of most of the smaller nations, still value the institutions as channels of regulation, communication, and negotiation. Aside from calculations of interest, one suspects that even governmental officials participating in the UN processes occasionally have moments of psychological identification with the organization and its interests; [35] and, at the verbal level, national officials are often prone to identify their interests and objectives with the noble purposes and principles of the UN Charter. This is far, indeed very far, from seriously supplanting national loyalty with international attachments; but governmental interest has in the past decades been strong enough to maintain and support a gradually growing institutional structure at the global level, with attendant integrative effects.

In a limited way, the UN family of agencies has also been able to build support among private groups and individuals. Our earlier discussion of non-governmental organization clientele which secretariats cultivate as a source of political support (Chapter 8) is relevant in the present context. Members of UN Associations, national UNICEF committees, UNESCO national commissions, women's groups, church agencies and others with an ideological commitment to world cooperation often exhibit deep emotional attachment to their cause. Some build loyalty to international organization upon intellectual commitment, while others are bound by ties of special interest. The international professional associations subsidized by UNESCO unquestionably have a vested interest in the benefactor organization. The

[35] Chadwick F. Alger concludes that the interaction of national delegates and other participants in the political process of international organization such as the United Nations "permits the development of an international 'interest group' that coalesces around a common desire to develop and strengthen the organization." "Hypotheses on Relationships Between the Organization of International Society and International Order," *op. cit.*, p. 45.

national medical groups and experts with whom WHO is affiliated in a consultative or advisory capacity often develop an identification with the organization and an interest in the perpetuation of its work. To some extent, this can also be said of FAO's impact upon the world community of professional agriculturists. The world is not yet interlaced with unbreakable bands of functional interest. We are a very long way from the "world government of interlocking functional units" contemplated by the functionalist theorists. But the existing international organizations with their interest group clientele and their incipient communities of functional specialists have made at least a start in that direction.

The Dynamics of Institutional Bureaucracies

International bureaucracies themselves have proved to be a dynamic, integrative force at the global as well as the regional level. As mediators and informal participants in multilateral negotiations they have characteristically worked to compromise conflicting governmental positions at the highest possible level of cooperation rather than settling for the lowest common denominator. Through expertise, prestige, judicious counsel, and persuasion they have sometimes developed a capacity, in Haas' terminology, to upgrade common interests and expand the organizational task. The establishment of UNEF and ONUC represented creative innovations and significant upgrading of interests—accomplishments due in large measure to the stature and ability of Hammarskjold and his staff. Other secretariats have exhibited dynamic creativity on a less spectacular scale. The common mode of decision-making in international organizations still hovers around the lowest common denominator, but dedicated secretariats have been able to work with national delegations to achieve outcomes with a higher integrative effect.

Learning and Spillover

Functionalist assumptions about the learning of integrative habits have been partially vindicated in the experience of world organizations. The learning has not been sufficient to bring general cooperation in the political sphere, or even to keep political controversies out of functional forums. But it has been evidenced by continuing expansion of the institutions of cooperation and in government propensities to act through them. Reasonably satisfactory performance of organizations in one sector has made more organization an acceptable means of dealing with problems in other sectors. Governments have gradually become adjusted to participation in this kind of community activity and have oriented their own diplomatic and policy machinery to cope with it.

There has been little apparent spillover, in the sense that international cooperation in one sector has raised problems of adjustment in other related sectors, thus giving rise to demand for new institutions—or the expansion of the old ones—to deal with the new problems. This kind of spillover was early evident in the European Coal and Steel Community where a common market raised problems of national subsidies, transport discrimination, and so on. But thus far, the various forms of cooperation in global dimensions have been within fairly self-contained, or autonomous, contexts. The establishment of a General Postal Union (1874) came only a few years after the International Telegraphic Union (1865), but the connection, if any, could more appropriately be labeled learning rather than spillover. The same can be said of most of the recent developments in global organization.

REGIONAL COMMUNITY AND INTERNATIONAL ORGANIZATION

Western Europe and the Atlantic Community

In contrast to the global scene, a political community exists today among most members of the Western European and Atlantic region (defined to include the United States, Canada, Turkey, and all non-Communist European states). Relations among them are characterized by a large measure of cooperation in promoting shared interests, and expectations that differences will be settled peaceably are generally high. The one sub-area in which doubt exists as to the viability of political community is the southeast portion of Europe where the Cyprus dispute may yet lead to international violence. Spain, while still diplomatically and institutionally somewhat isolated from the rest, is well enough integrated to be classified as part of the political community. Germany (West Germany), for years the symbol of aggressiveness in Europe, has been integrated into the European community since World War II with a speed and thoroughness that is almost unbelievable in historical perspective.

The Atlantic–West European political community has been achieved without any regionwide institutions for decision-making and policy coordination. There are world organizations, such as the United Nations, in which all participate; but no regional organization claims a membership coterminous with the entire region. The Council of Europe, and the Organization for Economic Cooperation and Development, come the closest to being regional in scope (see Table 17-1).

Organized subsystems within the region have increased in number, however, and their total effect upon regional integration has been positive, despite the divisive effects of creating subregional economic blocs. No supergovernmental unions have been formed in the postwar period—the trend has been in the opposite directions, with Cyprus and Malta achieving full independence from the United Kingdom. The European Community of Six, however, has proved to be a model and an inspiration for attempts at economic union and supranational association elsewhere.

TABLE 17-1. Membership of Western European and Atlantic Organizations   June 1966

Country	Council of Europe	Organization for Economic Cooperation and Development (OECD)	North Atlantic Treaty Organization (NATO)	Western European Union (WEU)	European Free Trade Area (EFTA)	European Coal and Steel Community (ECSC)	European Economic Community (EEC)	Euratom
Austria	M	M			M			
Belgium	M	M	M	M		M	M	M
Canada		M	M					
Cyprus	M							
Denmark	M	C	M		M			
Finland		C			A			
France	M	M	M*	M		M	M	M
W. Germany	M	M	M	M		M	M	M
Greece	M	M	M				A	
Iceland	M	M	M					
Ireland	M	M						
Italy	M	M	M	M		M	M	M
Japan		M						
Luxembourg	M	M	M	M		M	M	M
Malta	M							
Netherlands	M	M	M	M	M	M	M	M
Norway		M	M		M			
Portugal		M	M		M			
Spain		M						
Sweden	M	M			M			
Switzerland	M	M			M			
United Kingdom	M	M	M	M	M			
Turkey	M	M	M				A	
United States	M	M	M					
Yugoslavia		C						

Key
M—Member
A—Associate member
C—Cooperates in some activities

* France has withdrawn from the military organization but remains a party to the North Atlantic Treaty and participates in meetings of the NATO Council.

THE COUNCIL OF EUROPE. The dynamism of the Six contrasts with the disappointed hopes for the Council of Europe. Created in 1949, the Council of Europe was the miscegenous offspring of an enthusiastic European federalism united with a cautious, selective, functional approach to the unity of Europe. The drive for a widely empowered federal or supranational organization was pushed by a congeries of private organizations, loosely joined in a European movement and boasting supporters in key political positions throughout Europe. The more conservative approach, epitomized by the position of the United Kingdom and designated by the term "functionalist," [36] was to favor intergovernmental cooperation in specific areas of economic and social concern. The outcome of this misalliance was a two-chamber body—a Consultative Assembly composed of members of national parliaments, appointed by their respective parliaments but free to speak as individuals, and a Committee of Ministers representing member governments. The distribution of powers between the two organs left governments with the final word. Although the Assembly might talk on virtually any subject it wished, other than defense (even there, it has occasionally overstepped its bounds), its power to act was nil, except to make recommendations to the Committee of Ministers. On the Committee of Ministers each government was given a veto on all important matters, including recommendations to governments.

Despite the controlling hand of sovereign states, the Council in its earlier years was the paladin of federalist hopes and a germinal source for ideas of European unity. Its most ambitious project was the drafting of a statute for a European Political Community, complete with executive, court, and parliament elected by and responsible to the people of Europe. In the perspective of the early 1950's the EPC was to be the third pillar of a united Europe, joining ECSC in the economic field and the European Defense Community in the military. The failure of EDC at the hands of the French parliament also sounded the death knell of the Political Community. With these events, and the growing success of the Community of Six, much of the initiative for European unity shifted from the Council of Europe to the Six. As a result the Council has not lived up to the promise, or at least the federalist hopes, of its earlier years. It remains a sounding board for European ideas and contributes modestly to European integration through the formulation of conventions and recommendations for uniform laws and common policies.[37]

REGIONAL INTEGRATION. The contribution of international organization to regional integration is especially striking in the European Communities

[36] In this context, European "functionalists" are similar to the functionalists discussed previously in their preference for biting off limited pieces of economic and social cooperation, but differ in their basic attachment to national sovereignty.

[37] The most celebrated achievement of the Council of Europe is the European Convention on Human Rights, discussed in Chapter 14.

where all reliable economic indices show a marked expansion of intra-community transactions representing an enlarged area of shared interests. NATO also, on a lesser scale and in a different field, has expanded the area of shared interests through its elaborate provisions for consultation, joint military commands, infrastructure, and its various civilian and military operating agencies.

Institutions have also contributed to integration by encouraging the learning of cooperative habits, the evocation of loyalties to the system represented by the central institutions, and the processes of functional spillover. There is at least an element of learning in the development of military organization in Europe, running from the Franco-British Dunkirk Treaty of 1947 to the Brussels Treaty Organization of 1948, the establishment of NATO in 1949, and the Western European Union in 1954. One could also make a case that learning from the experience of the Benelux Union and the OEEC increased receptiveness to the idea of the European Coal and Steel Community, while the lessons of the latter were unquestionably influential in the establishment of the Common Market and Euratom.

The partial transference of loyalties to the collectivity (defined in terms of identification, interest, and support) has of course taken place among the staff of the various organizations. Governments, too, have evinced strong attachments to the various institutions, although generally in instrumental terms as a means of promotion of national interest rather than treating the organization as having a useful existence for its own sake. The concept of an Atlantic Community has fired the imagination of small but articulate private groups in Europe and the United States who are now engaged in the active propagation of ideas favorable to the building of stronger Atlantic institutions. The European Common Market, in spite of French resistance to further progress along the supranationalist path, has given the most striking example of transferred loyalties. Brussels is now becoming the focus of international pressure group activity on behalf of private associations—representing a wide range of business, farm, and labor groups—whose members have a stake in the continuance and even the expansion of community institutions. This stake in the functioning of the community also extends to ministers and lesser bureaucrats in national administrations (particularly ministries of agriculture) who, as part of the EEC "community of functional specialists," participate in the technical planning for EEC programs and subsequently administer community rules that they have helped to formulate.[38] The European Parliament, as well as the deliberative bodies of the Council of Europe and the Western European Union, have been especially active in espousing a United Europe as a new focus of loyalties. Chosen by fellow members of their national parliaments, and devoid of any

[38] See Leon Lindberg, "Decision Making and Integration in the European Community," *International Organization* (Winter, 1965), pp. 56–80.

real policy-making authority within their respective organizations, members of these international parliaments have not hesitated to express attachment to the ideal of European unity and to press for closer ties.[39]

The European Community institutions also provide the world's best example of spillover in a context of international cooperation among sovereign states. Some tasks, apparently, are inherently more expansive than others. International cooperation in the transmission of mail is so functionally autonomous or self-contained that it can take place regardless of cooperation or lack of cooperation in other functional areas. Creation of a common market, however, is inherently more expansive. A common market in goods creates pressures for the free movement of labor and capital, the harmonization of transportation policies, the coordination of price levels and many other related activities. The mutual removal of tariff barriers, which have served to equalize differences in costs, may result in an unfair advantage to the producers in a country that retains discriminatory freight rates, subsidies to producers, or meager social insurance benefits. In the Europe of the Six, the control of coal by the ECSC created a need to arrive at common policies for other forms of energy, a need that was one factor in the formation of Euratom. The common market in coal and steel also raised problems to which a solution seemed to be offered in a broader common market embracing all kinds of products, services, and capital. Within the Six, the limits of Community expansiveness through the spillover effect have apparently not yet been reached.

The whole process of integration within the Communities has been pressed by an activist bureaucracy headed by a Commission (formerly, also, a High Authority for the ECSC and a separate Commission for Euratom) with constitutionally defined prerogatives in the decision-making process which give weight to its views and actions. The Commission has continually worked for solutions involving an upgrading of the common interests. The effect has been to expand the task of the Community organs, and raise the level of integration by extending supranationalism to functions previously handled through intergovernmental negotiation or unilateral national action.

The institutions of the Western European–Atlantic region have likewise contributed in obvious ways to the development of dependable expectations of peaceful settlement. Germany did not form a political community with the rest of Western Europe when the process of institution-building began in the early postwar years. The rise of a common threat from the Communist bloc tended to drive former enemies in the West together. The institutions of Western European Union and NATO provided the basis for a controlled German rearmament, and economic integration through ECSC and EEC gave some assurance that German economic strength could not readily be

[39] Their independence of national views is suggested by the practice of organizing and often voting along international party lines rather than as national delegations.

turned against the West. The maturing economic and military ties created common interests which further reinforced expectations that future disputes among them would not be settled by violence.

NATO ties have also exercised a restraining influence upon the parties to the Cyprus dispute, and NATO institutions have been utilized at various stages in the dispute, even though a final settlement of the quarrel has not yet been achieved. The fact that other disputes within the region have not led to the use of violence testifies to its viability as a political community.

In general terms, regional institutions have undoubtedly contributed to mutual responsiveness and compatibility of values. The arguments used with respect to global organizations should be applicable here.

The movement has not been all one way, in complete vindication of the functionalist faith. The attitude of France, and certain other problems, have set in motion counter-integrative currents within NATO, and the progress toward supranationalism within the Six has at least temporarily been slowed. The very success of the EEC has raised some divisions within the larger regional system, as evidenced by the formation of the competitive European Free Trade Association and by American pressure for the creation of OECD in which the Six could be confronted by the United States and others of the Atlantic community in regular multilateral economic consultations. Nevertheless, international organizations have reinforced the rather considerable bonds of community that existed at the close of the war, forged new ones in an enlarged area of political community, and enabled the region to move piecemeal to higher levels of political integration.

Eastern Europe

The status of the East European regional system is somewhat more difficult to assess. In the 1950's the Soviet bloc unquestionably was not a political community. Revolts in Germany and Hungary were suppressed by the use of Soviet military force, and in Poland violence lurked very near the surface. During the past decade, however, the controls emanating from the Soviet Union have been relaxed, national regimes in the satellite countries have become more popularly based, and elements of genuine regional cooperation are developing. The Eastern European countries may well be on the threshold of political community. Their similarly patterned social and economic systems and political ideologies provide built-in compatibility of many important values, although this does not preclude serious divergences within the Communist orbit—as Yugoslavia and Albania have shown. Mutual responsiveness has been enhanced through frequent inter-state contacts of governmental and party agencies. The dominant power of the Soviet Union still looms behind the unity, but the days of Stalinist coercion within the Soviet system are past. The bloc is not nearly as monolithic as formerly, and some of the ties based upon coercion and political necessity have been replaced with ties of mutual interest.

Formal regional organizations have probably had a minimal effect upon whatever degree of integration exists. During the Stalin era the bonds all ran to Moscow and back, with no real attempt to put relationships on a multilateral basis. COMECON was formed in 1949 as a formal response to the Marshall Plan and the OEEC, but during the life of Stalin it was scarcely more than window dressing. In 1955, the Warsaw Treaty Organization was established with organs for multilateral consultation, but they have in fact met infrequently.

COMECON was revitalized in 1956, possibly as a hoped-for means of Soviet control to replace some of the dissolving political links of the Stalin era. COMECON organs have put multilateral consultation on a much more frequent basis, including interchange between permanent representatives to the COMECON Executive Committee located in Moscow. Thus far, COMECON has functioned for consultation only, despite an abortive Soviet effort in 1962 and 1963 to convert it into a Soviet-dominated instrument of economic planning with supranational powers. The evidence indicates that the vital plans are still national economic plans, and most trade and clearance of payments continue through bilateral rather than multilateral arrangements. On the other hand, some significant integration has taken place through the operation of joint companies and a limited amount of agreement upon "socialist specialization" in the production of goods within the bloc. International organization, particularly in the economic field, has promoted the flow of intrabloc transactions and provided some coordination of decision-making, but the effects thus far have been marginal.

The Americas

The American regional system presents a noticeable contrast to Europe and the Atlantic area. Although substantial pockets of political community exist among the states of the Western Hemisphere, the region as a whole is far from a political community. In view of the frequent forcible changes of regime in many Latin American countries and other evidences of violent conflict so endemic to the hemisphere, many of the individual states lack sufficient assurance of peaceful conflict resolution to be classified as political communities.[40] In inter-state contacts, bonds of political community do not extend to Castro's Cuba, and the record of threats and outbreaks of violence among countries of Central America, the Caribbean, and elsewhere in the Americas does little to create settled expectations that conflicts will be resolved peaceably.

[40] In the European-Atlantic region, Cyprus is obviously not a political community either.

In further contrast to the Atlantic-European region, the Americas boast a comprehensive organization of general jurisdiction, although membership does not extend to every state within the region. Canada has never been a member of the OAS. The Castro regime of Cuba was expelled in 1962, and the new states of Jamaica, Guyana, and Trinidad and Tobago, have not yet been admitted. The Organization of American States, including affiliated conferences and specialized agencies, is well endowed with formal organs of international cooperation and consultation. The hemisphere also has sub-regional groupings—the Latin American Free Trade Association (LAFTA), the Organization of Central American States (ODECA), and the Central American Common Market.[41] These purely American systems are supplemented by the UN regional Economic Commission for Latin America (ECLA), which includes not only every state in the hemisphere but also three non-American powers retaining territorial interests in the Americas—Britain, France, and the Netherlands. In many ways, ECLA has proved to be the most dynamic and creative of international organizations within the hemisphere. The pattern of these organizations is essentially intergovernmental, although the formal authority of the OAS to commit members to economic or diplomatic sanctions by a two-thirds vote adds an element of supranationalism.

All this organization has not yet produced a high level of integration. Economic and other contacts across national boundaries are low, intergovernmental institutions have not achieved effective coordination of national decision-making in areas of common interest, and resort to violence in international relations is all too frequent. Despite certain cultural affinities, the compatibility of main values is inhibited by vastly differing stages of economic development, differing social structures, and an uneven commitment to democratic values. Unstable political structure, lack of social capital, and the absence of vigorous group associations restrict mutual responsiveness and serve to depress the general level of international transactions. Vast disparities in wealth, power, interest, and outlook between the United States and the other American republics impede the kind of interchange on which voluntary forms of integration seem to thrive. Much more work, apparently, needs to be done at the bottom before institutional tinkering at the top can have a substantial impact upon regional integration. Subregional associations, such as LAFTA and the Central American Common Market, are probably in a better position to promote integration through concentration upon functionally more specific activities among relatively more homogeneous partners.

[41] Members of ODECA and the Common Market are Costa Rica, El Salvador, Guatemala, Honduras, and Nicaragua. Members of LAFTA are the original signatories—Argentina, Brazil, Chile, Mexico, Paraguay, Peru, and Uruguay—since joined by Colombia and Ecuador.

The region does, of course, show marks of the learning process that results from participation in international organizations. The proliferation of regional agencies dealing with the problems of women, children, Indians, human rights, nuclear energy, and a host of others is all of one piece. The functioning of machinery for consultation, study, and action in one area encourages the belief that such machinery can and ought to be established in another.

Any transference of loyalties to a new, integrated center of activities has been minimal. Secretariats obviously have their attachments to their jobs and the normal yen to build their own influence through building the organization. But the OAS Secretariat, in particular, has been kept weak and limited largely to administrative activities. The first Secretary-General of the OAS, Alberto Lleras Camargo, came to the office with a political background in Colombian politics, including a short period as President of Colombia, and attempted to assume political functions in a style suggestive of the UN Secretary-General. He was quickly pulled into line by member states and resigned before his term expired. While governments have proclaimed their attachment to the organization, their conduct indicates that the attachment is selective indeed as well as changeable. There is no hemispheric equivalent of the community-oriented parliamentary assembly that exists in Europe and no community-oriented interest groups functioning across national lines.

The one really active center for the promotion of Latin American integration has been the Secretariat of ECLA, under the dynamic leadership of Raul Prebisch, who resigned in 1963 to become Secretary-General of UNCTAD. ECLA's vigorous and persistent efforts over the years to promote Latin American economic development and unity have resulted in the creation of LAFTA, the Central American Common Market, and the gradual development of a community of interest among national economists, financial experts, and government administrators in related fields. Where other regional organizations in the Americas have had to settle for the lowest common denominator, or occasionally splitting the difference, ECLA has sometimes been able to bring about a significant upgrading of the common interests.

Despite important contributions in the area of pacific settlement, regional organization has not yet been able to create political community in the Americas. In some respects, the community has disintegrated during the past decade. Economic and diplomatic sanctions have been used against the Castro regime in Cuba and the former Trujillo regime in the Dominican Republic. Cuba, with its Communist system and avowed revolutionary objectives, has passed completely outside the pale of the community. United States military intervention in the Caribbean, a practice renounced in the early 1930's, has raised fears that the United States may once again be contemplating the use of direct military force in its relations with neighbors to the south. These disintegrative tendencies are spawned by forces over which the institutions of regional cooperation have little control. However, the level of political integration would undoubtedly be still lower without the complex programs carried on by international organizations.

Political Community in Asia

Nearly every daily newspaper bears witness that there is no political community of Asia. In Viet Nam, the latent antagonisms of many powers have been released in a continuing ordeal of violence. The two halves of Korea keep armed watch against each other; India and Pakistan are barely restrained from flying at one another's throats; Israel and the Arab states maintain an implacably hostile confrontation across a no-man's-land watched over by UN observers who at most points are too few in number to prevent periodic forays of destruction and bloodshed. China keeps hostile pressure upon Taiwan and India and maintains an uneasy peace with most of her other neighbors, including the Soviet Union. Asia has its UN regional economic commission, its Colombo Plan, SEATO, CENTO, the Arab League, and various other organizational subsystems that perform limited integrative functions among limited groups of states. But the overall picture is one of an extremely low level of integration in the region as a whole.

THE ARAB LEAGUE. Of the various regional groupings in Asia, the Arab League is probably the most ambitious and the one in which the prospects for a high level of integration are the best. But even the League has not yet achieved political community. The United Arab Republic and Saudi Arabia have been arrayed against one another through their support of opposing armed factions in Yemen. Rivalries of ancient vintage keep Iraq, Saudi Arabia, and the United Arab Republic on mutually suspicious terms. A border controversy between Algeria and Morocco erupted into a major armed clash in 1963, and full-scale war was headed off only by the active intervention of the Organization of African Unity. In 1958 Lebanon and Jordan claimed that their security was threatened by massive armed infiltration from the UAR, and invited protective intervention by the United States and Britain. In 1961 Kuwait called for British protection against an alleged threat of attack from Iraq, and armed assistance was provided, first by the United Kingdom and later by an Arab League force consisting mostly of Egyptian and Saudi Arabian troops. Mercifully, armed clashes between Arab League members have been few, but tensions and political rivalries have been frequent and persisting.

Despite these divisive influences, the Arab states are united by their hostility to Israel, their common Islamic culture, a tradition of Arab unity that has considerable emotional impact in the Arab world, and a desire to gain strength through unity in facing the rest of the world. These and other common values have been sufficient to support a growing organizational superstructure, including the Arab League Council and a vigorous secretariat located in Cairo. Machinery for consultation in political, economic, and military affairs has been supplemented by such cooperative endeavors as an Arab Development Bank, a Postal and Telecommunications Union, a Health Organization, a Higher Center of Arab Studies, an Institute of Arabic Manuscripts, an Anti-Narcotics Bureau, an Arab League Petroleum Bureau, and an Arab Press. In 1965 the first stage of an Arab Economic Union went into effect, with the goal of creating a common market within ten years.

In dealing with outsiders, particularly Israel, the League has had a significant unifying influence. Policies at the United Nations also are generally coordinated, and a League office in New York furnishes secretarial services for the Arab caucus. Joint military forces, the subject of much talk and some planning, have heretofore failed to materialize except in the case of the peace force created in 1961 to protect Kuwait against Iraq and secure the withdrawal of British troops. A commander-in-chief of Arab forces was appointed in 1964, but no troops have yet been assigned to him.

These organizational developments suggest a rising level of transactions and shared interests within the Arab world, and represent the learning of certain integrative habits. The machinery of cooperation probably increases mutual responsiveness and value compatibility as well. The institutions have not cracked the hard core of political separatisms and rivalries, or succeeded in laying a broad transactional base for political community, but the trend is toward wider cooperation and institutional growth. One might venture to predict that these developments may yet conspire with the elements of compatibility in the common Arab background to produce the mutual responsiveness and shared interests essential to an integrated political community.

African Regionalism

Africa, as a totality, falls far short of the requisites for political community. Indigenous regimes are implacably aligned against the white-minority-dominated territories of South Africa, Rhodesia, and Portugal; and the new African governments have not been above bitter wrangling among themselves. In Africa, as in parts of Latin America and Asia, many of the sovereign states are not sufficiently integrated to constitute national political communities.

Most international organizations in Africa are of too recent origin for their integrative effects to be meaningfully appraised. The Organization of African Unity (OAU), the most comprehensive regional organization in

Africa, dates only from 1963. It appears to be providing new channels of communication and to that extent an opportunity for value sharing and development of greater responsiveness to one another's needs, at least among the elites. Attempts by the OAU to encourage pacific settlement of disputes is also obviously integrative in its effects. The Common Organization of Africa and Malagasy (OCAM), the Conseil de l'Entente, and the Central African Customs and Economic Union are subsystems aimed at providing varying measures of political and economic cooperation, but they too have not yet stood the test of time.

One regional economic organization of much older vintage is the East African Common Services Organization (EACSO), formerly the East African Common Market, initiated by the British in Kenya, Tanganyika (now Tanzania), and Uganda in the 1920's during the period of British colonial rule. In the first flush of statehood for these new countries, there was talk of building on the existing common institutions toward the goal of political unity. Separatist impulses have now halted the trend toward union and raised a question whether even the time-tested Common Services Organization will endure. A system that seemed mutually advantageous when buttressed by British support appears to have lost cohesiveness under the impact of national particularisms.

TOWARD WORLD ORDER

During the past half century the world has witnessed the gradual disintegration of colonial empires, two world wars, an almost unbroken series of local conflicts, and a variety of hostile rivalries among nations large and small. Amid these signs of political disintegration, a technological revolution in transportation, communication, and industry has drastically increased the points of social contact across national boundaries and thus the opportunities for both cooperation and hostile collision. At the same time, military technology has drastically increased the penalties of resort to organized violence, and consequently, brought added incentive to avoid at least the more destructive forms of warfare. Faced with the social consequences of technological progress, as they affect international relations, governments have increasingly turned to international organization as a means of eliminating frictions and resolving differences through nonviolent means.

Some people, disappointed with the slow progress toward political community, have concluded that salvation lies in the creation of world government. This conclusion is reached by analogy to the nation-state, in which order is presumed to result from common governmental institutions. This doctrine is attractive because of the common-sense appeal of the analogy and the existence of some evidence, however inconclusive, that governmentally enforced order can foster the growth of community over a period of time.[42] One would be hard pressed, however, to find instances of political unification under a common government in which the union was not forced upon weaker units by stronger ones—a precedent hardly to be emulated— or else the combining units already shared substantial ties of community. Moreover, the case for world government overlooks the numerous instances of violence in the form of revolution or civil war that have marked the history of nation-states, and discounts the experience of numerous existing entities which are called sovereign states but can scarcely be regarded as political communities.[43]

More than a hundred years of experience with functional international organizations, vastly augmented during the past half century by general international organization, has not yet produced a global political community. It has, however, produced a practical approach to political integration. The processes of international organization are geared to a world in which common problems must be attacked by multilateral means, while making full allowance for local particularisms and national freedom of action. As vessels for common action, they have proved adaptable and adequate to bear all of the international cooperation that existing bonds of community will generate. Welfare and political community, in freedom, still lie at the top of distant peaks. But at this stage in history, international organization is an indispensable way station on the road to global community.

Selected Readings

CLAUDE, INIS L., Jr. *Swords into Plowshares,* 3rd ed. New York: Random House, 1964, Chap. 17.

DEUTSCH, KARL. *Political Community at the International Level.* New York: Doubleday, 1954.

DEUTSCH, KARL, *et al. Political Community and the North Atlantic Area.* Princeton, N.J.: Princeton University Press, 1957.

[42] For instance, Joseph R. Strayer, writing about the unification of France in its early stages, concluded that "the ringwall of the state" cut off the various regions of France from the rest of the world, forcing them "to work together and adapt to each other. They had time to gain a clear sense of identity, to smooth out some of their regional differences, and to become attached to their ruler and the institutions through which he ruled. Where the framework of the state was strong enough and persistent enough, it even created a common nationalism out of very different linguistic and cultural groups." "The Historical Experience in Europe," in Karl W. Deutsch and William J. Foltz, eds., *Nation-Building* (New York: Atherton Press, 1963), p. 23.

[43] Disarmament is a related but separate problem, discussed in Chapter 12. It could occur with or without world government. Obviously the destructiveness of violent conflict would be diminished—whether the conflict was called revolution, civil war, or international war—by the unavailability of nuclear weapons and a low level of conventional armaments.

ETZIONI, AMITAI. *Political Unification: A Comparative Study of Leaders and Forces.* New York: Holt, Rinehart and Winston, 1965.

HAAS, ERNST B. *Beyond the Nation State.* Stanford: Stanford University Press, 1964.

JACOB, PHILIP E. and TOSCANO, JAMES V., eds. *The Integration of Political Communities.* Philadelphia: J. B. Lippincott, 1964.

MITRANY, DAVID. *A Working Peace System.* 4th ed. London: National Peace Council, by arrangement with the Royal Institute of International Affairs, 1946.

SEWELL, JAMES P. *Functionalism and World Politics: United Nations Programs Financing Economic Development.* Princeton, N.J.: Princeton University Press, 1966.

Appendixes

A | *The Covenant of the League of Nations* [1]

The High Contracting Parties,

In order to promote international cooperation and to achieve international peace and security

by the acceptance of obligations not to resort to war,

by the prescription of open, just and honorable relations between nations,

by the firm establishment of the understandings of international law as the actual rule of conduct among Governments, and

by the maintenance of justice and a scrupulous respect for all treaty obligations in the dealings of organized peoples with one another,

Agree to this Covenant of the League of Nations.

ARTICLE 1. Membership and Withdrawal

1. The original Members of the League of Nations shall be those of the Signatories which are named in the Annex to this Covenant and also such of those other States named in the Annex as shall accede without reservation to this Covenant. Such accessions shall be effected by a declaration deposited with the Secretariat within two months of the coming into force of the Covenant. Notice thereof shall be sent to all other Members of the League.

2. Any fully self-governing State, Dominion or Colony not named in the Annex may become a Member of the League if its admission is agreed to by two-thirds of the Assembly, provided that it shall give effective guaranties of its sincere intention to observe its international obligations, and shall accept such regulations as may be prescribed by the League in regard to its military, naval and air forces and armaments.

3. Any Member of the League may, after two years' notice of its intention so to do, withdraw from the League, provided that all its international obligations and all its obligations under this Covenant shall have been fulfilled at the time of its withdrawal.

ARTICLE 2. Major Organs

The action of the League under this Covenant shall be effected through the instrumentality of an Assembly and of a Council, with a permanent Secretariat.

[1] Amendments in italics.

ARTICLE 3. Assembly

1. The Assembly shall consist of representatives of the Members of the League.

2. The Assembly shall meet at stated intervals and from time to time, as occasion may require, at the Seat of the League or at such other place as may be decided upon.

3. The Assembly may deal at its meetings with any matter within the sphere of action of the League or affecting the peace of the world.

4. At meetings of the Assembly each Member of the League shall have one vote and may have not more than three Representatives.

ARTICLE 4. Council

1. The Council shall consist of representatives of the Principal Allied and Associated Powers, together with Representatives of four other Members of the League. These four Members of the League shall be selected by the Assembly from time to time in its discretion. Until the appointment of the Representatives of the four Members of the League first selected by the Assembly, Representatives of Belgium, Brazil, Greece and Spain shall be Members of the Council.

2. With the approval of the majority of the Assembly, the Council may name additional Members of the League, whose Representatives shall always be Members of the Council; the Council with like approval may increase the number of Members of the League to be selected by the Assembly for representation on the Council.

2. *bis. The Assembly shall fix by a two-thirds' majority the rules dealing with the election of the non-permanent Members of the Council, and particularly such regulations as relate to their term of office and the conditions of re-eligibility.*

3. The Council shall meet from time to time as occasion may require, and at least once a year, at the Seat of the League, or at such other place as may be decided upon.

4. The Council may deal at its meetings with any matter within the sphere of action of the League or affecting the peace of the world.

5. Any Member of the League not represented on the Council shall be invited to send a Representative to sit as a member at any meeting of the Council during the consideration of matters specially affecting the interests of that Member of the League.

6. At meetings of the Council, each Member of the League represented on the Council shall have one vote, and may have not more than one Representative.

ARTICLE 5. Voting and Meeting Procedures

1. Except where otherwise expressly provided in this Covenant or by the terms of the present Treaty, decisions at any meeting of the Assembly or of the Council shall require the agreement of all the Members of the League represented at the meeting.

2. All matters of procedure at meetings of the Assembly or of the Council, including the appointment of Committees to investigate particular matters, shall be regulated by the Assembly or by the Council and may be decided by a majority of the Members of the League represented at the meeting.

3. The first meeting of the Assembly and the first meeting of the Council shall be summoned by the President of the United States of America.

ARTICLE 6. Secretariat, Secretary-General and Expenses

1. The permanent Secretariat shall be established at the Seat of the League. The Secretariat shall comprise a Secretary-General and such secretaries and staff as may be required.

2. The first Secretary-General shall be the person named in the Annex; thereafter the Secretary-General shall be appointed by the Council with the approval of the majority of the Assembly.

3. The secretaries and the staff of the Secretariat shall be appointed by the Secretary-General with the approval of the Council.

4. The Secretary-General shall act in that capacity at all meetings of the Assembly and of the Council.

5. *The expenses of the League shall be borne by the Members of the League in the proportion decided by the Assembly.*

ARTICLE 7. Seat, Qualifications and Immunities

1. The Seat of the League is established at Geneva.

2. The Council may at any time decide that the Seat of the League shall be established elsewhere.

3. All positions under or in connection with the League, including the Secretariat, shall be open equally to men and women.

4. Representatives of the Members of the League and officials of the League when engaged on the business of the League shall enjoy diplomatic privileges and immunities.

5. The buildings and other property occupied by the League or its officials or by Representatives attending its meetings shall be inviolable.

ARTICLE 8. Reduction of Armaments

1. The Members of the League recognize that the maintenance of peace requires the reduction of national armaments to the lowest point consistent with national safety and the enforcement by common action of international obligations.

2. The Council, taking account of the geographical situation and circumstances of each State, shall formulate plans for such reduction for the consideration and action of the several Governments.

3. Such plans shall be subject to reconsideration and revision at least every ten years.

4. After these plans shall have been adopted by the several Governments, the limits of armaments therein fixed shall not be exceeded without the concurrence of the Council.

5. The Members of the League agree that the manufacture by private enterprise of munitions and implements of war is open to grave objections. The Council shall advise how the evil effects attendant upon such manufacture can be prevented, due regard being had to the necessities of those Members of the League which are not able to manufacture the munitions and implements of war necessary for their safety.

6. The Members of the League undertake to interchange full and frank information as to the scale of their armaments, their military, naval and air programs and the condition of such of their industries as are adaptable to warlike purposes.

ARTICLE 9. Permanent Military, Naval and Air Commission

A permanent Commission shall be constituted to advise the Council on the execution of the provisions of Articles 1 and 8 and on military, naval and air questions generally.

ARTICLE 10. Guaranties Against Aggression

The Members of the League undertake to respect and preserve as against external aggression the territorial integrity and existing political independence of all Members of the League. In case of any such aggression or in case of any threat or danger of such aggression the Council shall advise upon the means by which this obligation shall be fulfilled.

ARTICLE 11. Collective Action

1. Any war or threat of war, whether immediately affecting any of the Members of the League or not, is hereby declared a matter of concern to the whole League, and the League shall take any action that may be deemed wise and effectual to safeguard the peace of nations. In case any such emergency should arise the Secretary-General shall on the request of any Member of the League forthwith summon a meeting of the Council.

2. It is also declared to be the friendly right of each Member of the League to bring to the attention of the Assembly or the Council any circumstance whatever affecting international relations which threatens to disturb international peace or the good understanding between nations upon which peace depends.

ARTICLE 12. Disputes

1. The Members of the League agree that, if there should arise between them any dispute likely to lead to a rupture, they will submit the matter either to arbitration *or judicial settlement* or to inquiry by the Council, and they agree in no case to resort to war until three months after the award by the arbitrators *or the judicial decision,* or the report by the Council.

2. In any case under this Article the award of the arbitrators *or the judicial decision* shall be made within a reasonable time, and the report of the Council shall be made within six months after the submission of the dispute.

ARTICLE 13. Arbitration or Judicial Settlement

1. The Members of the League agree that, whenever any dispute shall arise between them which they recognize to be suitable for submission to arbitration *or judicial settlement,* and which can not be satisfactorily settled by diplomacy, they will submit the whole subject-matter to arbitration *or judicial settlement.*

2. Disputes as to the interpretation of a treaty, as to any question of international law, as to the existence of any fact which, if established, would constitute a breach of any international obligation, or as to the extent and nature of the reparation to be made for any such breach, are declared to be among those which are generally suitable for submission to arbitration *or judicial settlement.*

3. *For the consideration of any such dispute, the court to which the case is referred shall be the Permanent Court of International Justice, established in*

accordance with Article 14, or any tribunal agreed on by the parties to the dispute or stipulated in any convention existing between them.

4. The Members of the League agree that they will carry out in full good faith any award *or decision* that may be rendered, and that they will not resort to war against a Member of the League which complies therewith. In the event of any failure to carry out such an award *or decision*, the Council shall propose what steps should be taken to give effect thereto.

ARTICLE 14. Permanent Court of International Justice

The Council shall formulate and submit to the Members of the League for adoption plans for the establishment of a Permanent Court of International Justice. The Court shall be competent to hear and determine any dispute of an international character which the parties thereto submit to it. The Court may also give an advisory opinion upon any dispute or question referred to it by the Council or by the Assembly.

ARTICLE 15. Disputes not Submitted to Arbitration or Judicial Settlement

1. If there should arise between Members of the League any dispute likely to lead to a rupture, which is not submitted to arbitration *or judicial settlement* in accordance with Article 13, the Members of the League agree that they will submit the matter to the Council. Any party to the dispute may effect such submission by giving notice of the existence of the dispute to the Secretary-General, who will make all necessary arrangements for a full investigation and consideration thereof.

2. For this purpose, the parties to the dispute will communicate to the Secretary-General, as promptly as possible, statements of their case with all the relevant facts and papers, and the Council may forthwith direct the publication thereof.

3. The Council shall endeavor to effect a settlement of the dispute, and, if such efforts are successful, a statement shall be made public giving such facts and explanations regarding the dispute and the terms of settlement thereof as the Council may deem appropriate.

4. If the dispute is not thus settled, the Council either unanimously or by a majority vote shall make and publish a report containing a statement of the facts of the dispute and the recommendations which are deemed just and proper in regard thereto.

5. Any member of the League represented on the Council may make public a statement of the facts of the dispute and of its conclusions regarding the same.

6. If a report by the Council is unanimously agreed to by the Members thereof other than the Representatives of one or more of the parties to the dispute, the Members of the League agree that they will not go to war with any party to the dispute which complies with the recommendations of the report.

7. If the Council fails to reach a report which is unanimously agreed to by the members thereof, other than the Representatives of one or more of the parties to the dispute, the Members of the League reserve to themselves the right to take such action as they shall consider necessary for the maintenance of right and justice.

8. If the dispute between the parties is claimed by one of them, and is found by the Council, to arise out of a matter which by international law is solely within the domestic jurisdiction of that party, the Council shall so report, and shall make no recommendation as to its settlement.

9. The Council may in any case under this Article refer the dispute to the Assembly. The dispute shall be so referred at the request of either party to the dispute, provided that such request be made within 14 days after the submission of the dispute to the Council.

10. In any case referred to the Assembly, all the provisions of this Article and of Article 12 relating to the action and powers of the Council shall apply to the action and powers of the Assembly, provided that a report made by the Assembly, if concurred in by the Representatives of those Members of the League represented on the Council and of a majority of the other Members of the League, exclusive in each case of the Representatives of the parties to the dispute, shall have the same force as a report by the Council concurred in by all the members thereof other than the Representatives of one or more of the parties to the dispute.

ARTICLE 16. Sanctions and Expulsion

1. Should any Member of the League resort to war in disregard of its covenants under Articles 12, 13, or 15, it shall *ipso facto* be deemed to have committed an act of war against all other Members of the League, which hereby undertake immediately to subject it to the severance of all trade or financial relations, the prohibition of all intercourse between their nationals and the nationals of the covenant-breaking State, and the prevention of all financial, commercial or personal intercourse between the nationals of the covenant-breaking State and the nationals of any other State, whether a Member of the League or not.

2. It shall be the duty of the Council in such case to recommend to the several Governments concerned what effective military, naval or air force the Members of the League shall severally contribute to the armed forces to be used to protect the covenants of the League.

3. The Members of the League agree, further, that they will mutually support one another in the financial and economic measures which are taken under this Article, in order to minimize the loss and inconvenience resulting from the above measures, and that they will mutually support one another in resisting any special measures aimed at one of their number by the covenant-breaking State, and that they will take the necessary steps to afford passage through their territory to the forces of any of the Members of the League which are cooperating to protect the covenants of the League.

4. Any Member of the League which has violated any covenant of the League may be declared to be no longer a Member of the League by a vote of the Council concurred in by the Representatives of all the other Members of the League represented thereon.

ARTICLE 17. Disputes Involving Non-Members

1. In the event of a dispute between a Member of the League and a State which is not a Member of the League, or between States not Members of the League, the State or States not Members of the League shall be invited to accept

the obligations of membership in the League for the purposes of such dispute, upon such conditions as the Council may deem just. If such invitation is accepted, the provisions of Articles 12 to 16 inclusive shall be applied with such modifications as may be deemed necessary by the Council.

2. Upon such invitation being given, the Council shall immediately institute an inquiry into the circumstances of the dispute and recommend such action as may seem best and most effectual in the circumstances.

3. If a State so invited shall refuse to accept the obligations of membership in the League for the purposes of such dispute, and shall resort to war against a Member of the League, the provisions of Article 16 shall be applicable as against the State taking such action.

4. If both parties to the dispute when so invited refuse to accept the obligations of membership in the League for the purposes of such dispute, the Council may take such measures and make such recommendations as will prevent hostilities and will result in the settlement of the dispute.

ARTICLE 18. Registration and Publication of Treaties

Every treaty or international engagement entered into hereafter by any Member of the League shall be forthwith registered with the Secretariat and shall as soon as possible be published by it. No such treaty or international engagement shall be binding until so registered.

ARTICLE 19. Review of Treaties

The Assembly may from time to time advise the reconsideration by Members of the League of treaties which have become inapplicable, and the consideration of international conditions whose continuance might endanger the peace of the world.

ARTICLE 20. Abrogation of Inconsistent Obligations

1. The Members of the League severally agree that this Covenant is accepted as abrogating all obligations or understandings *inter se* which are inconsistent with the terms thereof, and solemnly undertake that they will not hereafter enter into any engagements inconsistent with the terms thereof.

2. In case any Member of the League shall, before becoming a Member of the League, have undertaken any obligations inconsistent with the terms of this Covenant, it shall be the duty of such Member to take immediate steps to procure its release from such obligations.

ARTICLE 21. Engagements that Remain Valid

Nothing in this Covenant shall be deemed to affect the validity of international engagements, such as treaties of arbitration or regional understandings like the Monroe doctrine, for securing the maintenance of peace.

ARTICLE 22. Mandates System

1. To those colonies and territories which as a consequence of the late war have ceased to be under the sovereignty of the States which formerly governed them and which are inhabited by peoples not yet able to stand by themselves under

the strenuous conditions of the modern world, there should be applied the principle that the well-being and development of such peoples form a sacred trust of civilization and that securities for the performance of this trust should be embodied in this Covenant.

2. The best method of giving practical effect to this principle is that the tutelage of such peoples should be intrusted to advanced nations who by reason of their resources, their experience or their geographical position can best undertake this responsibility, and who are willing to accept it, and that this tutelage should be exercised by them as Mandatories on behalf of the League.

3. The character of the mandate must differ according to the stage of the development of the people, the geographical situation of the territory, its economic conditions and other similar circumstances.

4. Certain communities formerly belonging to the Turkish Empire have reached a stage of development where their existence as independent nations can be provisionally recognized subject to the rendering of administrative advice and assistance by a Mandatory until such time as they are able to stand alone. The wishes of these communities must be a principal consideration in the selection of the Mandatory.

5. Other peoples, especially those of Central Africa, are at such a stage that the Mandatory must be responsible for the administration of the territory under conditions which will guarantee freedom of conscience and religion, subject only to the maintenance of public order and morals, the prohibition of abuses such as the slave trade, the arms traffic and the liquor traffic, and the prevention of the establishment of fortifications or military and naval bases and of military training of the natives for other than police purposes and the defense of territory, and will also secure equal opportunities for the trade and commerce of other Members of the League.

6. There are territories, such as South West Africa and certain of the South Pacific islands, which, owing to the sparseness of their population, or their small size, or their remoteness from the centers of civilization, or their geographical contiguity to the territory of the Mandatory, and other circumstances, can be best administered under the laws of the Mandatory as integral portions of its territory, subject to the safeguards above mentioned in the interests of the indigenous population.

7. In every case of mandate, the Mandatory shall render to the Council an annual report in reference to the territory committed to its charge.

8. The degree of authority, control or administration to be exercised by the Mandatory shall, if not previously agreed upon by the Members of the League, be explicitly defined in each case by the Council.

9. A permanent Commission shall be constituted to receive and examine the annual reports of the Mandatories and to advise the Council on all matters relating to the observance of the mandates.

ARTICLE 23. Social Responsibilities

Subject to and in accordance with the provisions of international conventions existing or hereafter to be agreed upon, the Members of the League;

(a) will endeavor to secure and maintain fair and humane conditions of labor for men, women and children, both in their own countries and in all countries to which their commercial and industrial relations extend, and for that purpose will establish and maintain the necessary international organizations;

(b) undertake to secure just treatment of the native inhabitants of territories under their control;

(c) will intrust the League with the general supervision over the execution of agreements with regard to the traffic in women and children, and the traffic in opium and other dangerous drugs;

(d) will intrust the League with the general supervision of the trade in arms and ammunition with the countries in which the control of this traffic is necessary in the common interest;

(e) will make provision to secure and maintain freedom of communications and of transit and equitable treatment for the commerce of all Members of the League. In this connection, the special necessities of the regions devastated during the war of 1914–1918 shall be borne in mind;

(f) will endeavor to take steps in matters of international concern for the prevention and control of disease.

ARTICLE 24. International Bureaus

1. There shall be placed under the direction of the League all international bureaus already established by general treaties if the parties to such treaties consent. All such international bureaus and all commissions for the regulation of matters of international interest hereafter constituted shall be placed under the direction of the League.

2. In all matters of international interest which are regulated by general conventions but which are not placed under the control of international bureaus or commissions, the Secretariat of the League shall, subject to the consent of the Council and if desired by the parties, collect and distribute all relevant information and shall render any other assistance which may be necessary or desirable.

3. The Council may include as part of the expenses of the Secretariat the expenses of any bureau or commission which is placed under the direction of the League.

ARTICLE 25. Promotion of Red Cross

The Members of the League agree to encourage and promote the establishment and cooperation of duly authorized voluntary national Red Cross organizations having as purposes the improvement of health, the prevention of disease and the mitigation of suffering throughout the world.

ARTICLE 26. Amendments

1. Amendments to this Covenant will take effect when ratified by the Members of the League whose Representatives compose the Council and by a majority of the Members of the League whose Representatives compose the Assembly.

2. No such amendment shall bind any Member of the League which signifies its dissent therefrom, but in that case it shall cease to be a Member of the League.

ANNEX I. Original Members of the League of Nations, Signatories of the Treaty of Peace

United States of America *	Guatemala
Belgium	Haiti
Bolivia	Hedjaz *
Brazil	Honduras
British Empire	Italy
Canada	Japan
Australia	Liberia
South Africa	Nicaragua
New Zealand	Panama
India	Peru
China	Poland
Cuba	Portugal
Czechoslovakia	Romania
Ecuador **	Serb-Croat-Slovene State [Yugoslavia]
France	Siam
Greece	Uruguay

  * Did not ratify.
  ** Did not ratify peace treaty but was admitted to membership in 1934.

States Invited to Accede to the Covenant

Argentine Republic	Persia
Chile	Salvador
Colombia	Spain
Denmark	Sweden
Netherlands	Switzerland
Norway	Venezuela
Paraguay	

ANNEX II. First Secretary-General of the League of Nations The Honorable Sir James Eric Drummond, K.C.M.G., C.B.

B | *The Charter of the United Nations*

We the Peoples of the United Nations Determined

to save succeeding generations from the scourge of war, which twice in our lifetime has brought untold sorrow to mankind, and

to reaffirm faith in fundamental human rights, in the dignity and worth of the human person, in the equal rights of men and women and of nations large and small, and

to establish conditions under which justice and respect for the obligations arising from treaties and other sources of international law can be maintained, and

to promote social progress and better standards of life in larger freedom,

And for These Ends

to practice tolerance and live together in peace with one another as good neighbors, and

to unite our strength to maintain international peace and security, and

to ensure, by the acceptance of principles and the institution of methods, that armed force shall not be used, save in the common interest, and

to employ international machinery for the promotion of the economic and social advancement of all peoples,

Have Resolved to Combine Our Efforts to Accomplish These Aims.

Accordingly, our respective Governments, through representatives assembled in the city of San Francisco, who have exhibited their full powers found to be in good and due form, have agreed to the present Charter of the United Nations and do hereby establish an international organization to be known as the United Nations.

Chapter I
Purposes and Principles

ARTICLE 1. The Purposes of the United Nations are:

1. To maintain international peace and security, and to that end: to take effective collective measures for the prevention and removal of threats to the peace, and for the suppression of acts of aggression or other breaches of the peace, and to bring about by peaceful means, and in conformity with the principles of justice and international law, adjustment or settlement of international disputes or situations which might lead to a breach of the peace;

2. To develop friendly relations among nations based on respect for the principle of equal rights and self-determination of peoples, and to take other appropriate measures to strengthen universal peace;

3. To achieve international cooperation in solving international problems of an economic, social, cultural, or humanitarian character, and in promoting and encouraging respect for human rights and for fundamental freedoms for all without distinction as to race, sex, language, or religion; and

4. To be a center for harmonizing the actions of nations in the attainment of these common ends.

ARTICLE 2. The Organization and its Members, in pursuit of the Purposes stated in Article 1, shall act in accordance with the following Principles.

1. The Organization is based on the principle of the sovereign equality of all its Members.

2. All Members, in order to ensure to all of them the rights and benefits resulting from membership, shall fulfil in good faith the obligations assumed by them in accordance with the present Charter.

3. All Members shall settle their international disputes by peaceful means in such a manner that international peace and security, and justice, are not endangered.

4. All Members shall refrain in their international relations from the threat or use of force against the territorial integrity or political independence of any state, or in any other manner inconsistent with the Purposes of the United Nations.

5. All Members shall give the United Nations every assistance in any action it takes in accordance with the present Charter, and shall refrain from giving assistance to any state against which the United Nations is taking preventive or enforcement action.

6. The Organization shall ensure that states which are not Members of the United Nations act in accordance with these Principles so far as may be necessary for the maintenance of international peace and security.

7. Nothing contained in the present Charter shall authorize the United Nations to intervene in matters which are essentially within the domestic jurisdiction of any state or shall require the Members to submit such matters to settlement under the present Charter; but this principle shall not prejudice the application of enforcement measures under Chapter VII.

Chapter II
Membership

ARTICLE 3. The original Members of the United Nations shall be the states which, having participated in the United Nations Conference on International Organization at San Francisco, or having previously signed the Declaration by United Nations of January 1, 1942, sign the present Charter and ratify it in accordance with Article 110.

ARTICLE 4. 1. Membership in the United Nations is open to all other peace-loving states which accept the obligations contained in the present Charter and, in the judgment of the Organization, are able and willing to carry out these obligations.

2. The admission of any such state to membership in the United Nations will be effected by a decision of the General Assembly upon the recommendation of the Security Council.

ARTICLE 5. A Member of the United Nations against which preventive or enforcement action has been taken by the Security Council may be suspended from the exercise of the rights and privileges of membership by the General Assembly upon the recommendation of the Security Council. The exercise of these rights and privileges may be restored by the Security Council.

ARTICLE 6. A Member of the United Nations which has persistently violated the Principles contained in the present Charter may be expelled from the Organization by the General Assembly upon the recommendation of the Security Council.

Chapter III
Organs

ARTICLE 7. 1. There are established as the principal organs of the United Nations: a General Assembly, a Security Council, an Economic and Social Council, a Trusteeship Council, an International Court of Justice, and a Secretariat.

2. Such subsidiary organs as may be found necessary may be established in accordance with the present Charter.

ARTICLE 8. The United Nations shall place no restrictions on the eligibility of men and women to participate in any capacity and under conditions of equality in its principal and subsidiary organs.

Chapter IV
The General Assembly

COMPOSITION

ARTICLE 9. 1. The General Assembly shall consist of all the Members of the United Nations.

2. Each Member shall have not more than five representatives in the General Assembly.

FUNCTIONS AND POWERS

ARTICLE 10. The General Assembly may discuss any questions or any matters within the scope of the present Charter or relating to the powers and functions of any organs provided for in the present Charter, and, except as provided in Article 12, may make recommendations to the Members of the United Nations or to the Security Council or to both on any such questions or matters.

ARTICLE 11. 1. The General Assembly may consider the general principles of cooperation in the maintenance of international peace and security, including the principles governing disarmament and the regulation of armaments, and may make recommendations with regard to such principles to the Members or to the Security Council or to both.

2. The General Assembly may discuss any questions relating to the maintenance of international peace and security brought before it by any Member of the United Nations, or by the Security Council, or by a state which is not a Member of the United Nations in accordance with Article 35, paragraph 2, and, except as provided in Article 12, may make recommendations with regard to any such questions to the state or states concerned or to the Security Council or to both. Any such question on which action is necessary shall be referred to the Security Council by the General Assembly either before or after discussion.

3. The General Assembly may call the attention of the Security Council to situations which are likely to endanger international peace and security.

4. The powers of the General Assembly set forth in this Article shall not limit the general scope of Article 10.

ARTICLE 12. 1. While the Security Council is exercising in respect of any dispute or situation the functions assigned to it in the present Charter, the General Assembly shall not make any recommendation with regard to that dispute or situation unless the Security Council so requests.

2. The Secretary-General, with the consent of the Security Council, shall notify the General Assembly at each session of any matters relative to the maintenance of international peace and security which are being dealt with by the Security Council and shall similarly notify the General Assembly, or the Members of the United Nations if the General Assembly is not in session, immediately the Security Council ceases to deal with such matters.

ARTICLE 13. 1. The General Assembly shall initiate studies and make recommendations for the purpose of:

a. promoting international cooperation in the political field and encouraging the progressive development of international law and its codification;

b. promoting international cooperation in the economic, social, cultural, educational, and health fields, and assisting in the realization of human rights and fundamental freedoms for all without distinction as to race, sex, language, or religion.

2. The further responsibilities, functions and powers of the General Assembly with respect to matters mentioned in paragraph 1(b) above are set forth in Chapters IX and X.

ARTICLE 14. Subject to the provisions of Article 12, the General Assembly may recommend measures for the peaceful adjustment of any situation, regardless of origin, which it deems likely to impair the general welfare or friendly relations among nations, including situations resulting from a violation of the provisions of the present Charter setting forth the Purposes and Principles of the United Nations.

ARTICLE 15. 1. The General Assembly shall receive and consider annual and special reports from the Security Council; these reports shall include an account of the measures that the Security Council has decided upon or taken to maintain international peace and security.

2. The General Assembly shall receive and consider reports from the other organs of the United Nations.

ARTICLE 16. The General Assembly shall perform such functions with respect to the international trusteeship system as are assigned to it under Chapters XII and XIII, including the approval of the trusteeship agreements for areas not designated as strategic.

ARTICLE 17. 1. The General Assembly shall consider and approve the budget of the Organization.

2. The expenses of the Organization shall be borne by the Members as apportioned by the General Assembly.

3. The General Assembly shall consider and approve any financial and budgetary arrangements with specialized agencies referred to in Article 57 and shall examine the administrative budgets of such specialized agencies with a view to making recommendations to the agencies concerned.

VOTING

ARTICLE 18. 1. Each member of the General Assembly shall have one vote.

2. Decisions of the General Assembly on important questions shall be made by a two-thirds majority of the members present and voting. These questions shall include: recommendations with respect to the maintenance of international peace and security, the election of the non-permanent members of the Security Council, the election of the members of the Economic and Social Council, the election of members of the Trusteeship Council in accordance with paragraph 1(c) of Article 86, the admission of new Members to the United Nations, the suspension of the rights and privileges of membership, the expulsion of Members, questions relating to the operation of the trusteeship system, and budgetary questions.

3. Decisions on other questions, including the determination of additional categories of questions to be decided by a two-thirds majority, shall be made by a majority of the members present and voting.

ARTICLE 19. A Member of the United Nations which is in arrears in the payment of its financial contributions to the Organization shall have no vote in the General Assembly if the amount of its arrears equals or exceeds the amount of the contributions due from it for the preceding two full years. The General Assembly may, nevertheless, permit such a Member to vote if it is satisfied that the failure to pay is due to conditions beyond the control of the Member.

PROCEDURE

ARTICLE 20. The General Assembly shall meet in regular annual sessions and in such special sessions as occasion may require. Special sessions shall be convoked by the Secretary-General at the request of the Security Council or of a majority of the Members of the United Nations.

Article 21. The General Assembly shall adopt its own rules of procedure. It shall elect its President for each session.

Article 22. The General Assembly may establish such subsidiary organs as it deems necessary for the performance of its functions.

Chapter V
The Security Council

Composition

Article 23. 1. The Security Council shall consist of eleven [1] Members of the United Nations. The Republic of China, France, the Union of Soviet Socialist Republics, the United Kingdom of Great Britain and Northern Ireland, and the United States of America shall be permanent members of the Security Council. The General Assembly shall elect six [2] other Members of the United Nations to be non-permanent members of the Security Council, due regard being specially paid, in the first instance to the contribution of Members of the United Nations to the maintenance of international peace and security and to the other purposes of the Organization, and also to equitable geographical distribution.

2. The non-permanent members of the Security Council shall be elected for a term of two years. In the first election of the non-permanent members, however, three shall be chosen for a term of one year. A retiring member shall not be eligible for immediate re-election.

3. Each member of the Security Council shall have one representative.

Functions and Powers

Article 24. 1. In order to ensure prompt and effective action by the United Nations, its Members confer on the Security Council primary responsibility for the maintenance of international peace and security, and agree that in carrying out its duties under this responsibility the Security Council acts on their behalf.

2. In discharging these duties the Security Council shall act in accordance with the Purposes and Principles of the United Nations. The specific powers granted to the Security Council for the discharge of these duties are laid down in Chapters VI, VII, VIII, and XII.

3. The Security Council shall submit annual and, when necessary, special reports to the General Assembly for its consideration.

Article 25. The Members of the United Nations agree to accept and carry out the decisions of the Security Council in accordance with the present Charter.

Article 26. In order to promote the establishment and maintenance of international peace and security with the least diversion for armaments of the world's human and economic resources, the Security Council shall be responsible for formulating, with the assistance of the Military Staff Committee referred to in

[1] Expanded to fifteen members by Charter amendment in 1965.

[2] Ten elective members, five chosen each year, provided for by Charter amendment in 1965.

Article 47, plans to be submitted to the Members of the United Nations for the establishment of a system for the regulation of armaments.

VOTING

ARTICLE 27. 1. Each member of the Security Council shall have one vote.

2. Decisions of the Security Council on procedural matters shall be made by an affirmative vote of seven [3] members.

3. Decisions of the Security Council on all other matters shall be made by an affirmative vote of seven [4] members including the concurring votes of the permanent members; provided that, in decisions under Chapter VI, and under paragraph 3 of Article 52, a party to a dispute shall abstain from voting.

PROCEDURE

ARTICLE 28. 1. The Security Council shall be so organized as to be able to function continuously. Each member of the Security Council shall for this purpose be represented at all times at the seat of the Organization.

2. The Security Council shall hold periodic meetings at which each of its members may, if it so desires, be represented by a member of the government or by some other specially designated representative.

3. The Security Council may hold meetings at such places other than the seat of the Organization as in its judgment will best facilitate its work.

ARTICLE 29. The Security Council may establish such subsidiary organs as it deems necessary for the performance of its functions.

ARTICLE 30. The Security Council shall adopt its own rules of procedure, including the method of selecting its President.

ARTICLE 31. Any Member of the United Nations which is not a member of the Security Council may participate, without vote, in the discussion of any question brought before the Security Council whenever the latter considers that the interests of that Member are specially affected.

ARTICLE 32. Any Member of the United Nations which is not a member of the Security Council or any state which is not a Member of the United Nations, if it is a party to a dispute under consideration by the Security Council, shall be invited to participate, without vote, in the discussion relating to the dispute. The Security Council shall lay down such conditions as it deems just for the participation of a state which is not a Member of the United Nations.

Chapter VI
Pacific Settlement of Disputes

ARTICLE 33. 1. The parties to any dispute, the continuance of which is likely to endanger the maintenance of international peace and security, shall, first of all, seek a solution by negotiation, enquiry, mediation, conciliation, arbitration, judi-

[3] Changed to nine members by Charter amendment in 1965.
[4] Changed to nine members by Charter amendment in 1965.

cial settlement, resort to regional agencies or arrangements, or other peaceful means of their own choice.

2. The Security Council shall, when it deems necessary, call upon the parties to settle their dispute by such means.

ARTICLE 34. The Security Council may investigate any dispute, or any situation which might lead to international friction or give rise to a dispute, in order to determine whether the continuance of the dispute or situation is likely to endanger the maintenance of international peace and security.

ARTICLE 35. 1. Any Member of the United Nations may bring any dispute, or any situation of the nature referred to in Article 34, to the attention of the Security Council or of the General Assembly.

2. A state which is not a Member of the United Nations may bring to the attention of the Security Council or of the General Assembly any dispute to which it is a party if it accepts in advance, for the purposes of the dispute, the obligations of pacific settlement provided in the present Charter.

3. The proceedings of the General Assembly in respect of matters brought to its attention under this Article will be subject to the provisions of Articles 11 and 12.

ARTICLE 36. 1. The Security Council may, at any stage of a dispute of the nature referred to in Article 33 or of a situation of like nature, recommend appropriate procedures or methods of adjustment.

2. The Security Council should take into consideration any procedures for the settlement of the dispute which have already been adopted by the parties.

3. In making recommendations under this Article the Security Council should also take into consideration that legal disputes should as a general rule be referred by the parties to the International Court of Justice in accordance with the provisions of the Statute of the Court.

ARTICLE 37. 1. Should the parties to a dispute of the nature referred to in Article 33 fail to settle it by the means indicated in that Article, they shall refer it to the Security Council.

2. If the Security Council deems that the continuance of the dispute is in fact likely to endanger the maintenance of international peace and security, it shall decide whether to take action under Article 36 or to recommend such terms of settlement as it may consider appropriate.

ARTICLE 38. Without prejudice to the provisions of Articles 33 to 37, the Security Council may, if all the parties to any dispute so request, make recommendations to the parties with a view to a pacific settlement of the dispute.

Chapter VII
Action with Respect to Threats to the Peace, Breaches of the Peace, and Acts of Aggression

ARTICLE 39. The Security Council shall determine the existence of any threat to the peace, breach of the peace, or act of aggression and shall make recommendations, or decide what measures shall be taken in accordance with Articles 41 and 42, to maintain or restore international peace and security.

ARTICLE 40. In order to prevent an aggravation of the situation, the Security Council may, before making the recommendations or deciding upon the measures provided for in Article 39, call upon the parties concerned to comply with such provisional measures as it deems necessary or desirable. Such provisional measures shall be without prejudice to the rights, claims, or position of the parties concerned. The Security Council shall duly take account of failure to comply with such provisional measures.

ARTICLE 41. The Security Council may decide what measures not involving the use of armed force are to be employed to give effect to its decisions, and it may call upon the Members of the United Nations to apply such measures. These may include complete or partial interruption of economic relations and of rail, sea, air, postal, telegraphic, radio, and other means of communication, and the severance of diplomatic relations.

ARTICLE 42. Should the Security Council consider that measures provided for in Article 41 would be inadequate or have proved to be inadequate, it may take such action by air, sea, or land forces as may be necessary to maintain or restore international peace and security. Such action may include demonstrations, blockade, and other operations by air, sea, or land forces of Members of the United Nations.

ARTICLE 43. 1. All Members of the United Nations, in order to contribute to the maintenance of international peace and security, undertake to make available to the Security Council, on its call and in accordance with a special agreement or agreements, armed forces, assistance, and facilities, including rights of passage, necessary for the purpose of maintaining international peace and security.

2. Such agreement or agreements shall govern the numbers and types of forces, their degree of readiness and general location, and the nature of the facilities and assistance to be provided.

3. The agreement or agreements shall be negotiated as soon as possible on the initiative of the Security Council. They shall be concluded between the Security Council and Members or between the Security Council and groups of Members and shall be subject to ratification by the signatory states in accordance with their respective constitutional processes.

ARTICLE 44. When the Security Council has decided to use force it shall, before calling upon a Member not represented on it to provide armed forces in fulfilment of the obligations assumed under Article 43, invite that Member, if the Member so desires, to participate in the decisions of the Security Council concerning the employment of contingents of that Member's armed forces.

ARTICLE 45. In order to enable the United Nations to take urgent military measures, Members shall hold immediately available national air-force contingents for combined international enforcement action. The strength and degree of readiness of these contingents and plans for their combined action shall be determined, within the limits laid down in the special agreement or agreements referred to in Article 43, by the Security Council with the assistance of the Military Staff Committee.

Article 46. Plans for the application of armed force shall be made by the Security Council with the assistance of the Military Staff Committee.

Article 47. 1. There shall be established a Military Staff Committee to advise and assist the Security Council on all questions relating to the Security Council's military requirements for the maintenance of international peace and security, the employment and command of forces placed at its disposal, the regulation of armaments, and possible disarmament.

2. The Military Staff Committee shall consist of the Chiefs of Staff of the permanent Members of the Security Council or their representatives. Any Member of the United Nations not permanently represented on the Committee shall be invited by the Committee to be associated with it when the efficient discharge of the Committee's responsibilities requires the participation of that Member in its work.

3. The Military Staff Committee shall be responsible under the Security Council for the strategic direction of any armed forces placed at the disposal of the Security Council. Questions relating to the command of such forces shall be worked out subsequently.

4. The Military Staff Committee, with the authorization of the Security Council and after consultation with appropriate regional agencies, may establish regional subcommittees.

Article 48. 1. The action required to carry out the decisions of the Security Council for the maintenance of international peace and security shall be taken by all the Members of the United Nations or by some of them, as the Security Council may determine.

2. Such decisions shall be carried out by the Members of the United Nations directly and through their action in the appropriate international agencies of which they are members.

Article 49. The Members of the United Nations shall join in affording mutual assistance in carrying out the measures decided upon by the Security Council.

Article 50. If preventive or enforcement measures against any state are taken by the Security Council, any other state, whether a Member of the United Nations or not, which finds itself confronted with special economic problems arising from the carrying out of those measures shall have the right to consult the Security Council with regard to a solution of those problems.

Article 51. Nothing in the present Charter shall impair the inherent right of individual or collective self-defense if an armed attack occurs against a Member of the United Nations, until the Security Council has taken measures necessary to maintain international peace and security. Measures taken by Members in the exercise of this right of self-defense shall be immediately reported to the Security Council and shall not in any way affect the authority and responsibility of the Security Council under the present Charter to take at any time such action as it deems necessary in order to maintain or restore international peace and security.

Chapter VIII
Regional Arrangements

ARTICLE 52. 1. Nothing in the present Charter precludes the existence of regional arrangements or agencies for dealing with such matters relating to the maintenance of international peace and security as are appropriate for regional action, provided that such arrangements or agencies and their activities are consistent with the Purposes and Principles of the United Nations.

2. The Members of the United Nations entering into such arrangements or constituting such agencies shall make every effort to achieve pacific settlement of local disputes through such regional arrangements or by such regional agencies before referring them to the Security Council.

3. The Security Council shall encourage the development of pacific settlement of local disputes through such regional arrangements or by such regional agencies either on the initiative of the states concerned or by reference from the Security Council.

4. This Article in no way impairs the application of Articles 34 and 35.

ARTICLE 53. 1. The Security Council shall, where appropriate, utilize such regional arrangements or agencies for enforcement action under its authority. But no enforcement action shall be taken under regional arrangements or by regional agencies without the authorization of the Security Council, with the exception of measures against any enemy state, as defined in paragraph 2 of this Article, provided for pursuant to Article 107 or in regional arrangements directed against renewal of aggressive policy on the part of any such state, until such time as the Organization may, on request of the Governments concerned, be charged with the responsibility for preventing further aggression by such a state.

2. The term enemy state as used in paragraph 1 of this Article applies to any state which during the Second World War has been an enemy of any signatory of the present Charter.

ARTICLE 54. The Security Council shall at all times be kept fully informed of activities undertaken or in contemplation under regional arrangements or by regional agencies for the maintenance of international peace and security.

Chapter IX
International Economic and Social Cooperation

ARTICLE 55. With a view to the creation of conditions of stability and well-being which are necessary for peaceful and friendly relations among nations based on respect for the principle of equal rights and self-determination of peoples, the United Nations shall promote:

a. higher standards of living, full employment, and conditions of economic and social progress and development;

b. solutions of international economic, social, health, and related problems; and international cultural and educational cooperation; and

c. universal respect for, and observance of, human rights and fundamental freedoms for all without distinction as to race, sex, language, or religion.

ARTICLE 56. All Members pledge themselves to take joint and separate action in cooperation with the Organization for the achievement of the purposes set forth in Article 55.

ARTICLE 57. 1. The various specialized agencies, established by inter-governmental agreement and having wide international responsibilities, as defined in their basic instruments, in economic, social, cultural, educational, health and related fields, shall be brought into relationship with the United Nations in accordance with the provisions of Article 63.

2. Such agencies thus brought into relationship with the United Nations are hereinafter referred to as specialized agencies.

ARTICLE 58. The Organization shall make recommendations for the coordination of the policies and activities of the specialized agencies.

ARTICLE 59. The Organization shall, where appropriate, initiate negotiations among the states concerned for the creation of any new specialized agencies required for the accomplishment of the purposes set forth in Article 55.

ARTICLE 60. Responsibility for the discharge of the functions of the Organization set forth in this Chapter shall be vested in the General Assembly and, under the authority of the General Assembly, in the Economic and Social Council, which shall have for this purpose the powers set forth in Chapter X.

Chapter X
The Economic and Social Council

COMPOSITION

ARTICLE 61. 1. The Economic and Social Council shall consist of eighteen [5] Members of the United Nations elected by the General Assembly.

2. Subject to the provisions of paragraph 3, six [6] members of the Economic and Social Council shall be elected each year for a term of three years. A retiring member shall be eligible for immediate reelection.

3. At the first election, eighteen members of the Economic and Social Council shall be chosen. The term of office of six members so chosen shall expire at the end of one year, and of six other members at the end of two years, in accordance with arrangements made by the General Assembly.

[5] Expanded to twenty-seven members by Charter amendment in 1965.

[6] Changed to provide for the election of nine members each year by Charter amendment in 1965.

4. Each member of the Economic and Social Council shall have one representative.

FUNCTIONS AND POWERS

ARTICLE 62. 1. The Economic and Social Council may make or initiate studies and reports with respect to international economic, social, cultural, educational, health, and related matters and may make recommendations with respect to any such matters to the General Assembly, to the Members of the United Nations, and to the specialized agencies concerned.

2. It may make recommendations for the purpose of promoting respect for, and observance of, human rights and fundamental freedoms for all.

3. It may prepare draft conventions for submission to the General Assembly, with respect to matters falling within its competence.

4. It may call, in accordance with the rules prescribed by the United Nations, international conferences on matters falling within its competence.

ARTICLE 63. 1. The Economic and Social Council may enter into agreements with any of the agencies referred to in Article 57, defining the terms on which the agency concerned shall be brought into relationship with the United Nations. Such agreements shall be subject to approval by the General Assembly.

2. It may coordinate the activities of the specialized agencies through consultation with and recommendations to such agencies and through recommendations to the General Assembly and to the Members of the United Nations.

ARTICLE 64. 1. The Economic and Social Council may take appropriate steps to obtain regular reports from the specialized agencies. It may make arrangements with the Members of the United Nations and with the specialized agencies to obtain reports on the steps taken to give effect to its own recommendations and to recommendations on matters falling within its competence made by the General Assembly.

2. It may communicate its observations on these reports to the General Assembly.

ARTICLE 65. The Economic and Social Council may furnish information to the Security Council and shall assist the Security Council upon its request.

ARTICLE 66. 1. The Economic and Social Council shall perform such functions as fall within its competence in connection with the carrying out of the recommendations of the General Assembly.

2. It may, with the approval of the General Assembly, perform services at the request of Members of the United Nations and at the request of specialized agencies.

3. It shall perform such other functions as are specified elsewhere in the present Charter or as may be assigned to it by the General Assembly.

VOTING

ARTICLE 67. 1. Each member of the Economic and Social Council shall have one vote.

2. Decisions of the Economic and Social Council shall be made by a majority of the members present and voting.

PROCEDURE

ARTICLE 68. The Economic and Social Council shall set up commissions in economic and social fields and for the promotion of human rights, and such other commissions as may be required for the performance of its functions.

ARTICLE 69. The Economic and Social Council shall invite any Member of the United Nations to participate, without vote, in its deliberations on any matter of particular concern to that Member.

ARTICLE 70. The Economic and Social Council may make arrangements for representatives of the specialized agencies to participate, without vote, in its deliberations and in those of the commissions established by it, and for its representatives to participate in the deliberations of the specialized agencies.

ARTICLE 71. The Economic and Social Council may make suitable arrangements for consultation with non-governmental organizations which are concerned with matters within its competence. Such arrangements may be made with international organizations and, where appropriate, with national organizations after consultation with the Member of the United Nations concerned.

ARTICLE 72. 1. The Economic and Social Council shall adopt its own rules of procedure, including the method of selecting its President.

2. The Economic and Social Council shall meet as required in accordance with its rules, which shall include provision for the convening of meetings on the request of a majority of its members.

Chapter XI
Declaration Regarding Non-Self-Governing Territories

ARTICLE 73. Members of the United Nations which have or assume responsibilities for the administration of territories whose peoples have not yet attained a full measure of self-government recognize the principle that the interests of the inhabitants of these territories are paramount, and accept as a sacred trust the obligation to promote to the utmost, within the system of international peace and security established by the present Charter, the well-being of the inhabitants of these territories, and, to this end:

a. to ensure, with due respect for the culture of the peoples concerned, their political, economic, social, and educational advancement, their just treatment, and their protection against abuses;

b. to develop self-government, to take due account of the political aspirations of the peoples, and to assist them in the progressive development of their free political institutions, according to the particular circumstances of each territory and its peoples and their varying stages of advancement;

c. to further international peace and security;

d. to promote constructive measures of development, to encourage research, and to cooperate with one another and, when and where appropriate, with specialized international bodies with a view to the practical achievement of the social, economic, and scientific purposes set forth in this Article; and

e. to transmit regularly to the Secretary-General for information purposes, subject to such limitation as security and constitutional considerations may require, statistical and other information of a technical nature relating to economic, social, and educational conditions in the territories for which they are respectively responsible other than those territories to which Chapters XII and XIII apply.

ARTICLE 74. Members of the United Nations also agree that their policy in respect of the territories to which this Chapter applies, no less than in respect of their metropolitan areas, must be based on the general principle of good-neighborliness, due account being taken of the interests and well-being of the rest of the world, in social, economic, and commercial matters.

Chapter XII
International Trusteeship System

ARTICLE 75. The United Nations shall establish under its authority an international trusteeship system for the administration and supervision of such territories as may be placed thereunder by subsequent individual agreements. These territories are hereinafter referred to as trust territories.

ARTICLE 76. The basic objectives of the trusteeship system, in accordance with the Purposes of the United Nations laid down in Article 1 of the present Charter, shall be:

a. to further international peace and security;

b. to promote the political, economic, social, and educational advancement of the inhabitants of the trust territories, and their progressive development towards self-government or independence as may be appropriate to the particular circumstances of each territory and its peoples and the freely expressed wishes of the peoples concerned, and as may be provided by the terms of each trusteeship agreement;

c. to encourage respect for human rights and for fundamental freedoms for all without distinction as to race, sex, language, or religion, and to encourage recognition of the interdependence of the peoples of the world; and

d. to ensure equal treatment in social, economic, and commercial matters for all Members of the United Nations and their nationals, and also equal treatment for the latter in the administration of justice, without prejudice to the attainment of the foregoing objectives and subject to the provisions of Article 80.

ARTICLE 77. 1. The trusteeship system shall apply to such territories in the following categories as may be placed thereunder by means of trusteeship agreements:

a. territories now held under mandate;

b. territories which may be detached from enemy states as a result of the Second World War; and

c. territories voluntarily placed under the system by states responsible for their administration.

2. It will be a matter for subsequent agreement as to which territories in the foregoing categories will be brought under the trusteeship system and upon what terms.

ARTICLE 78. The trusteeship system shall not apply to territories which have become Members of the United Nations, relationship among which shall be based on respect for the principle of sovereign equality.

ARTICLE 79. The terms of trusteeship for each territory to be placed under the trusteeship system, including any alteration or amendment, shall be agreed upon by the states directly concerned, including the mandatory power in the case of territories held under mandate by a Member of the United Nations, and shall be approved as provided for in Articles 83 and 85.

ARTICLE 80. 1. Except as may be agreed upon in individual trusteeship agreements, made under Articles 77, 79, and 81, placing each territory under the trusteeship system, and until such agreements have been concluded, nothing in this Chapter shall be construed in or of itself to alter in any manner the rights whatsoever of any states or any peoples or the terms of existing international instruments to which Members of the United Nations may respectively be parties.

2. Paragraph 1 of this Article shall not be interpreted as giving grounds for delay or postponement of the negotiation and conclusion of agreements for placing mandated and other territories under the trusteeship system as provided for in Article 77.

ARTICLE 81. The trusteeship agreement shall in each case include the terms under which the trust territory will be administered and designate the authority which will exercise the administration of the trust territory. Such authority, hereinafter called the administering authority, may be one or more states or the Organization itself.

ARTICLE 82. There may be designated, in any trusteeship agreement, a strategic area or areas which may include part or all of the trust territory to which the agreement applies, without prejudice to any special agreement or agreements made under Article 43.

ARTICLE 83. 1. All functions of the United Nations relating to strategic areas, including the approval of the terms of the trusteeship agreements and of their alteration or amendment, shall be exercised by the Security Council.

2. The basic objectives set forth in Article 76 shall be applicable to the people of each strategic area.

3. The Security Council shall, subject to the provisions of the trusteeship agreements and without prejudice to security considerations, avail itself of the assistance of the Trusteeship Council to perform those functions of the United Nations under the trusteeship system relating to political, economic, social, and educational matters in the strategic areas.

ARTICLE 84. It shall be the duty of the administering authority to ensure that the trust territory shall play its part in the maintenance of international peace and security. To this end the administering authority may make use of volunteer forces, facilities, and assistance from the trust territory in carrying out the obligations towards the Security Council undertaken in this regard by the administering authority, as well as for local defense and the maintenance of law and order within the trust territory.

ARTICLE 85. 1. The functions of the United Nations with regard to trusteeship agreements for all areas not designated as strategic, including the approval of the terms of the trusteeship agreements and of their alteration or amendment, shall be exercised by the General Assembly.

2. The Trusteeship Council, operating under the authority of the General Assembly, shall assist the General Assembly in carrying out these functions.

Chapter XIII
The Trusteeship Council

COMPOSITION

ARTICLE 86. 1. The Trusteeship Council shall consist of the following Members of the United Nations:

a. those Members administering trust territories;

b. such of those Members mentioned by name in Article 23 as are not administering trust territories; and

c. as many other Members elected for three-year terms by the General Assembly as may be necessary to ensure that the total number of members of the Trusteeship Council is equally divided between those Members of the United Nations which administer trust territories and those which do not.

2. Each member of the Trusteeship Council shall designate one specially qualified person to represent it therein.

FUNCTIONS AND POWERS

ARTICLE 87. The General Assembly and, under its authority, the Trusteeship Council, in carrying out their functions, may:

a. consider reports submitted by the administering authority;

b. accept petitions and examine them in consultation with the administering authority;

c. provide for periodic visits to the respective trust territories at times agreed upon with the administering authority; and

d. take these and other actions in conformity with the terms of the trusteeship agreements.

ARTICLE 88. The Trusteeship Council shall formulate a questionnaire on the political, economic, social, and educational advancement of the inhabitants of each trust territory, and the administering authority for each trust territory within the competence of the General Assembly shall make an annual report to the General Assembly upon the basis of such questionnaire.

VOTING

ARTICLE 89. 1. Each member of the Trusteeship Council shall have one vote.

2. Decisions of the Trusteeship Council shall be made by a majority of the members present and voting.

PROCEDURE

ARTICLE 90. 1. The Trusteeship Council shall adopt its own rules of procedure, including the method of selecting its President.

2. The Trusteeship Council shall meet as required in accordance with its rules, which shall include provision for the convening of meetings on the request of a majority of its members.

ARTICLE 91. The Trusteeship Council shall, when appropriate, avail itself of the assistance of the Economic and Social Council and of the specialized agencies in regard to matters with which they are respectively concerned.

Chapter XIV
The International Court of Justice

ARTICLE 92. The International Court of Justice shall be the principal judicial organ of the United Nations. It shall function in accordance with the annexed Statute, which is based upon the Statute of the Permanent Court of International Justice and forms an integral part of the present Charter.

ARTICLE 93. 1. All Members of the United Nations are *ipso facto* parties to to the Statute of the International Court of Justice.

2. A state which is not a Member of the United Nations may become a party to the Statute of the International Court of Justice on conditions to be determined in each case by the General Assembly upon the recommendation of the Security Council.

ARTICLE 94. 1. Each Member of the United Nations undertakes to comply with the decision of the International Court of Justice in any case to which it is a party.

2. If any party to a case fails to perform the obligations incumbent upon it under a judgment rendered by the Court, the other party may have recourse to the Security Council, which may, if it deems necessary, make recommendations or decide upon measures to be taken to give effect to the judgment.

ARTICLE 95. Nothing in the present Charter shall prevent Members of the United Nations from entrusting the solution of their differences to other tribunals by virtue of agreements already in existence or which may be concluded in the future.

ARTICLE 96. 1. The General Assembly or the Security Council may request the International Court of Justice to give an advisory opinion on any legal question.

2. Other organs of the United Nations and specialized agencies, which may at any time be so authorized by the General Assembly, may also request advisory opinions of the Court on legal questions arising within the scope of their activities.

Chapter XV
The Secretariat

ARTICLE 97. The Secretariat shall comprise a Secretary-General and such staff as the Organization may require. The Secretary-General shall be appointed by the General Assembly upon the recommendation of the Security Council. He shall be the chief administrative officer of the Organization.

ARTICLE 98. The Secretary-General shall act in that capacity in all meetings of the General Assembly, of the Security Council, of the Economic and Social Council, and of the Trusteeship Council, and shall perform such other functions as are entrusted to him by these organs. The Secretary-General shall make an annual report to the General Assembly on the work of the Organization.

ARTICLE 99. The Secretary-General may bring to the attention of the Security Council any matter which in his opinion may threaten the maintenance of international peace and security.

ARTICLE 100. 1. In the performance of their duties the Secretary-General and the staff shall not seek or receive instructions from any government or from any other authority external to the Organization. They shall refrain from any action which might reflect on their position as international officials responsible only to the Organization.

2. Each Member of the United Nations undertakes to respect the exclusively international character of the responsibilities of the Secretary-General and the staff and not to seek to influence them in the discharge of their responsibilities.

ARTICLE 101. 1. The staff shall be appointed by the Secretary-General under regulations established by the General Assembly.

2. Appropriate staffs shall be permanently assigned to the Economic and Social Council, the Trusteeship Council, and, as required, to other organs of the United Nations. These staffs shall form a part of the Secretariat.

3. The paramount consideration in the employment of the staff and in the determination of the conditions of service shall be the necessity of securing the highest standards of efficiency, competence, and integrity. Due regard shall be paid to the importance of recruiting the staff on as wide a geographical basis as possible.

Chapter XVI
Miscellaneous Provisions

ARTICLE 102. 1. Every treaty and every international agreement entered into by any Member of the United Nations after the present Charter comes into force shall as soon as possible be registered with the Secretariat and published by it.

2. No party to any such treaty or international agreement which has not been registered in accordance with the provisions of paragraph 1 of this Article may invoke that treaty or agreement before any organ of the United Nations.

ARTICLE 103. In the event of a conflict between the obligations of the Members of the United Nations under the present Charter and their obligations under any other international agreement, their obligations under the present Charter shall prevail.

ARTICLE 104. The Organization shall enjoy in the territory of each of its Members such legal capacity as may be necessary for the exercise of its functions and the fulfilment of its purposes.

ARTICLE 105. 1. The Organization shall enjoy in the territory of each of its Members such privileges and immunities as are necessary for the fulfilment of its purposes.

2. Representatives of the Members of the United Nations and officials of the Organization shall similarly enjoy such privileges and immunities as are necessary for the independent exercise of their functions in connection with the Organization.

3. The General Assembly may make recommendations with a view to determining the details of the application of paragraphs 1 and 2 of this Article or may propose conventions to the Members of the United Nations for this purpose.

Chapter XVII
Transitional Security Arrangements

ARTICLE 106. Pending the coming into force of such special agreements referred to in Article 43 as in the opinion of the Security Council enable it to begin the exercise of its responsibilities under Article 42, the parties to the Four-Nation Declaration, signed at Moscow, October 30, 1943, and France, shall, in accordance with the provisions of paragraph 5 of that Declaration, consult with one another and as occasion requires with other Members of the United Nations with a view to such joint action on behalf of the Organization as may be necessary for the purpose of maintaining international peace and security.

ARTICLE 107. Nothing in the present Charter shall invalidate or preclude action, in relation to any state which during the Second World War has been an enemy of any signatory to the present Charter, taken or authorized as a result of that war by the Governments having responsibility for such action.

Chapter XVIII
Amendments

ARTICLE 108. Amendments to the present Charter shall come into force for all Members of the United Nations when they have been adopted by a vote of two thirds of the members of the General Assembly and ratified in accordance with their respective constitutional processes by two thirds of the Members of the United Nations, including all the permanent members of the Security Council.

ARTICLE 109. 1. A General Conference of the Members of the United Nations for the purpose of reviewing the present Charter may be held at a date and place to be fixed by a two-thirds vote of the members of the General Assembly and by a vote of any seven members of the Security Council. Each Member of the United Nations shall have one vote in the conference.

2. Any alteration of the present Charter recommended by a two-thirds vote of the conference shall take effect when ratified in accordance with their respective constitutional processes by two thirds of the Members of the United Nations including all the permanent members of the Security Council.

3. If such a conference has not been held before the tenth annual session of the General Assembly following the coming into force of the present Charter, the proposal to call such a conference shall be placed on the agenda of that session of the General Assembly, and the conference shall be held if so decided by a majority vote of the members of the General Assembly and by a vote of any seven members of the Security Council.

Chapter XIX
Ratification and Signature

ARTICLE 110. 1. The present Charter shall be ratified by the signatory states in accordance with their respective constitutional processes.

2. The ratifications shall be deposited with the Government of the United States of America, which shall notify all the signatory states of each deposit as well as the Secretary-General of the Organization when he has been appointed.

3. The present Charter shall come into force upon the deposit of ratifications by the Republic of China, France, the Union of Soviet Socialist Republics, the United Kingdom of Great Britain and Northern Ireland, and the United States of America, and by a majority of the other signatory states. A protocol of the ratifications deposited shall thereupon be drawn up by the Government of the United States of America which shall communicate copies thereof to all the signatory states.

4. The states signatory to the present Charter which ratify it after it has come into force will become original members of the United Nations on the date of the deposit of their respective ratifications.

ARTICLE 111. The present Charter, of which the Chinese, French, Russian, English, and Spanish texts are equally authentic, shall remain deposited in the archives of the Government of the United States of America. Duly certified copies thereof shall be transmitted by that Government to the Governments of the other signatory states.

IN FAITH WHEREOF the representatives of the Governments of the United Nations have signed the present Charter.

DONE at the city of San Francisco the twenty-sixth day of June, one thousand nine hundred and forty-five.

C | Members of the United Nations

(January 1967)

Date of Admission	Member
Original members	Argentina
	Australia
	Belgium
	Bolivia
	Brazil
	Byelorussian Soviet Socialist Republic
	Canada
	Chile
	China
	Colombia
	Costa Rica
	Cuba
	Czechoslovakia
	Denmark
	Dominican Republic
	Ecuador
	Egypt (United Arab Republic)
	El Salvador
	Ethiopia
	France
	Greece
	Guatemala
	Haiti
	Honduras
	India
	Iran
	Iraq
	Lebanon
	Liberia

Date of Admission	Member
Original members	Luxembourg
	Mexico
	Netherlands
	New Zealand
	Nicaragua
	Norway
	Panama
	Paraguay
	Peru
	Philippines
	Poland
	Saudi Arabia
	South Africa
	Syria
	Turkey
	Ukrainian Soviet Socialist Republic
	Union of Soviet Socialist Republics
	United Kingdom of Great Britain and Northern Ireland
	United States of America
	Uruguay
	Venezuela
	Yugoslavia
1946	Afghanistan
	Iceland
	Sweden
	Thailand

Date of Admission	Member	Date of Admission	Member
1947	Pakistan	1960	Dahomey
	Yemen		Gabon
			Ivory Coast
1948	Burma		Madagascar
			Mali
1949	Israel		Niger
			Nigeria
1950	Indonesia		Senegal
			Somalia
1955	Albania		Togo
	Austria		Upper Volta
	Bulgaria		
	Cambodia	1961	Mauritania
	Ceylon		Mongolia
	Finland		Sierra Leone
	Hungary		Tanganyika *
	Ireland		
	Italy	1962	Algeria
	Jordan		Burundi
	Laos		Jamaica
	Libya		Rwanda
	Nepal		Trinidad and Tobago
	Portugal		Uganda
	Romania		
	Spain	1963	Kenya
			Kuwait
1956	Japan		Zanzibar *
	Morocco		
	Sudan	1964	Malawi
	Tunisia		Malta
			Zambia
1957	Ghana		
	Malaysia	1965	Gambia
			Maldive Islands
1958	Guinea		Singapore
1960	Cameroon	1966	Barbados
	Central African Republic		Botswana
	Chad		Guyana
	Congo (Brazzaville)		Lesotho
	Congo (Dem. Republic)		
	Cyprus		

* Tanganyika and Zanzibar merged in 1964 to form the Republic of Tanzania, with a single UN membership.

D | *The Universal Declaration of Human Rights*

(Adopted December 10, 1948)

Preamble

Whereas recognition of the inherent dignity and of the equal and inalienable rights of all members of the human family is the foundation of freedom, justice and peace in the world,

Whereas disregard and contempt for human rights have resulted in barbarous acts which have outraged the conscience of mankind, and the advent of a world in which human beings shall enjoy freedom of speech and belief and freedom from fear and want has been proclaimed as the highest aspiration of the common people,

Whereas it is essential, if man is not to be compelled to have recourse, as a last resort, to rebellion against tyranny and oppression, that human rights should be protected by the rule of law,

Whereas it is essential to promote the development of friendly relations between nations,

Whereas the peoples of the United Nations have in the Charter reaffirmed their faith in fundamental human rights, in the dignity and worth of the human person and in the equal rights of men and women and have determined to promote social progress and better standards of life in larger freedom,

Whereas Member States have pledged themselves to achieve, in co-operation with the United Nations, the promotion of universal respect for and observance of human rights and fundamental freedoms,

Whereas a common understanding of these rights and freedoms is of the greatest importance for the full realization of this pledge,

Now, therefore,

The General Assembly

Proclaims this Universal Declaration of Human Rights as a common standard of achievement for all peoples and all nations, to the end that every individual and every organ of society, keeping this Declaration constantly in mind, shall strive by teaching and education to promote respect for these rights and freedoms and by progressive measures, national and international, to secure their universal and effective recognition and observance, both among the peoples of Member States themselves and among the peoples of territories under their jurisdiction.

Article 1

All human beings are born free and equal in dignity and rights. They are endowed with reason and conscience and should act towards one another in a spirit of brotherhood.

Article 2

Everyone is entitled to all the rights and freedoms set forth in this Declaration, without distinction of any kind, such as race, colour, sex, language, religion, political or other opinion, national or social origin, property, birth or other status.

Furthermore, no distinction shall be made on the basis of the political, jurisdictional or international status of the country or territory to which a person belongs, whether it be independent, trust, non-self-governing or under any other limitation of sovereignty.

Article 3

Everyone has the right to life, liberty and the security of person.

Article 4

No one shall be held in slavery or servitude; slavery and the slave trade shall be prohibited in all their forms.

Article 5

No one shall be subjected to torture or to cruel, inhuman or degrading treatment or punishment.

Article 6

Everyone has the right to recognition everywhere as a person before the law.

Article 7

All are equal before the law and are entitled without any discrimination to equal protection of the law. All are entitled to equal protection against any discrimination in violation of this Declaration and against any incitement to such discrimination.

Article 8

Everyone has the right to an effective remedy by the competent national tribunals for acts violating the fundamental rights granted him by the constitution or by law.

Article 9

No one shall be subjected to arbitrary arrest, detention or exile.

Article 10

Everyone is entitled in full equality to a fair and public hearing by an independent and impartial tribunal, in the determination of his rights and obligations and of any criminal charge against him.

Article 11

1. Everyone charged with a penal offence has the right to be presumed innocent until proved guilty according to law in a public trial at which he has had all the guarantees necessary for his defence.

2. No one shall be held guilty of any penal offence on account of any act or omission which did not constitute a penal offence, under national or international law, at the time when it was committed. Nor shall a heavier penalty be imposed than the one that was applicable at the time the penal offence was committed.

Article 12

No one shall be subjected to arbitrary interference with his privacy, family, home or correspondence, nor to attacks upon his honour and reputation. Everyone has the right to the protection of the law against such interference or attacks.

Article 13

1. Everyone has the right to freedom of movement and residence within the borders of each State.

2. Everyone has the right to leave any country, including his own, and to return to his country.

Article 14

1. Everyone has the right to seek and to enjoy in other countries asylum from persecution.

2. This right may not be invoked in the case of prosecutions genuinely arising from non-political crimes or from acts contrary to the purposes and principles of the United Nations.

Article 15

1. Everyone has the right to a nationality.

2. No one shall be arbitrarily deprived of his nationality nor denied the right to change his nationality.

Article 16

1. Men and women of full age, without any limitation due to race, nationality or religion, have the right to marry and to found a family. They are entitled to equal rights as to marriage, during marriage and at its dissolution.

2. Marriage shall be entered into only with the free and full consent of the intending spouses.

3. The family is the natural and fundamental group unit of society and is entitled to protection by society and the State.

Article 17

1. Everyone has the right to own property alone as well as in association with others.

2. No one shall be arbitrarily deprived of his property.

Article 18

Everyone has the right to freedom of thought, conscience and religion; this right includes freedom to change his religion or belief, and freedom, either alone or in community with others and in public or private, to manifest his religion or belief in teaching, practice, worship and observance.

Article 19

Everyone has the right to freedom of opinion and expression; this right includes freedom to hold opinions without interference and to seek, receive and impart information and ideas through any media and regardless of frontiers.

Article 20

1. Everyone has the right to freedom of peaceful assembly and association.

2. No one may be compelled to belong to an association.

Article 21

1. Everyone has the right to take part in the government of his country, directly or through freely chosen representatives.

2. Everyone has the right of equal access to public service in his country.

3. The will of the people shall be the basis of the authority of government; this will shall be expressed in periodic and genuine elections which shall be by universal and equal suffrage and shall be held by secret vote or by equivalent free voting procedures.

Article 22

Everyone, as a member of society, has the right to social security and is entitled to realization, through national effort and international co-operation and in accordance with the organization and resources of each State, of the economic, social and cultural rights indispensable for his dignity and the free development of his personality.

Article 23

1. Everyone has the right to work, to free choice of employment, to just and favourable conditions of work and to protection against unemployment.

2. Everyone, without any discrimination, has the right to equal pay for equal work.

3. Everyone who works has the right to just and favourable remuneration ensuring for himself and his family an existence worthy of human dignity, and supplemented, if necessary, by other means of social protection.

4. Everyone has the right to form and to join trade unions for the protection of his interests.

Article 24

Everyone has the right to rest and leisure, including reasonable limitation of working hours and periodic holidays with pay.

Article 25

1. Everyone has the right to a standard of living adequate for the health and well-being of himself and of his family, including food, clothing, housing and medical care and necessary social services, and the right to security in the event of unemployment, sickness, disability, widowhood, old age or other lack of livelihood in circumstances beyond his control.

2. Motherhood and childhood are entitled to special care and assistance. All children, whether born in or out of wedlock, shall enjoy the same social protection.

Article 26

1. Everyone has the right to education. Education shall be free, at least in the elementary and fundamental stages. Elementary education shall be compulsory. Technical and professional education shall be made generally available and higher education shall be equally accessible to all on the basis of merit.

2. Education shall be directed to the full development of the human personality and to the strengthening of respect for human rights and fundamental freedoms. It shall promote understanding, tolerance and friendship among all nations, racial or religious groups, and shall further the activities of the United Nations for the maintenance of peace.

3. Parents have a prior right to choose the kind of education that shall be given to their children.

Article 27

1. Everyone has the right freely to participate in the cultural life of the community, to enjoy the arts and to share in scientific advancement and its benefits.

2. Everyone has the right to the protection of the moral and material interests resulting from any scientific, literary or artistic production of which he is the author.

Article 28

Everyone is entitled to a social and international order in which the rights and freedoms set forth in this Declaration can be fully realized.

Article 29

1. Everyone has duties to the community in which alone the free and full development of his personality is possible.

2. In the exercise of his rights and freedoms, everyone shall be subject only to such limitations as are determined by law solely for the purpose of securing due recognition and respect for the rights and freedoms of others and of meeting the just requirements of morality, public order and the general welfare in a democratic society.

3. These rights and freedom may in no case be exercised contrary to the purposes and principles of the United Nations.

Article 30

Nothing in this Declaration may be interpreted as implying for any State, group or person any right to engage in any activity or to perform any act aimed at the destruction of any of the rights and freedoms set forth herein.

Index

584